THE CHINESE LEXICON
A Comprehensive Survey

'An outstanding piece of work.'

Feixia Yu, University of Central Lancashire

The Chinese Lexicon is a detailed study of the words and word combinations used in modern Chinese.

The author defines the general properties of a language's lexicon, or vocabulary, prior to a thorough discussion of the organisational features of the Chinese lexicon. Comparisons are made between Chinese and English, highlighting the similarities and differences between the two lexicons.

This fascinating work examines the relationships between words and meanings, and demonstrates the ability of language to combine continuity and change.

Features include:

- a wealth of language examples;
- clear comparisons between Chinese and English;
- Chinese characters and *pinyin* romanisation throughout;
- a comprehensive index.

The Chinese Lexicon surpasses the scope of a dictionary and reveals the systematic nature of vocabulary. It will prove an invaluable resource for students and teachers of Chinese, as well as an easy reference for all those with an interest in the Chinese language.

Yip Po-Ching is Lecturer in Chinese Studies at the University of Leeds. He is the author (with Don Rimmington) of *Chinese: An Essential Grammar, Basic Chinese: A Grammar and Workbook* and *Intermediate Chinese: A Grammar and Workbook*.

THE CHINESE LEXICON

A Comprehensive Survey

Yip Po-Ching

Routledge
Taylor & Francis Group

LONDON AND NEW YORK

First published 2000
by Routledge
2 Park Square, Milton Park, Abingdon, Oxon OX14 4RN

Simultaneously published in the USA and Canada
by Routledge
270 Madison Ave, New York, NY 10016

This edition published in paperback 2007

Routledge is an imprint of the Taylor & Francis Group, an informa business

Typeset in Times by Graphicraft Limited, Hong Kong
Printed and bound in Great Britain by TJ International Ltd, Padstow, Cornwall

British Library Cataloguing in Publication Data
A catalogue record for this book is available from the British Library

Library of Congress Cataloging in Publication Data
Yip, Po-Ching, 1935–
    The Chinese lexicon; a comprehensive survey / Yip Po-Ching.
        p. cm.
    Includes bibliographical references and index.
    1. Chinese language—Lexicology.   I. Title.
    PL1280.Y56 2000
    495.1'3'028—dc21

                                                        99–048886

ISBN10: 0–415–15174–0 (hbk)
ISBN10: 0–415–42954–4 (pbk)

ISBN13: 978–0–415–15174–0 (hbk)
ISBN13: 978–0–415–42954–2 (pbk)

CONTENTS

PREFACE

Since I embarked on the study of my own native language when I came to Britain in 1981, I have always dreamed of writing a book on the Chinese lexicon: not a purely lexicological study or a work of practical lexicography, but a *sensible* combination of the two. This work is to be read as *thesis* and used for reference, by specialists, students and interested lay readers alike. A hybrid, yes, but an exploratory journey into the constitution of the Chinese verbal repertory. Thanks to the enthusiasm of my previous editor Mr Simon Bell and my present editor Miss Sophie Oliver at Routledge, my dream has finally come true. I hope I have lived up to their expectations.

The present book is in fact based on my original doctoral thesis for the Department of Linguistics and Phonetics at the University of Leeds. But, as so many years have passed in the meantime, the book and the thesis are now very different. However, throughout the whole period of writing the book, whenever I referred back to what I had written for my dissertation, I could still vividly recall the many fruitful hours I spent with my two remarkable supervisors, Dr A. T. C. Fox and Mr D. Barber, and the many invaluable pieces of advice they gave me.

The book in its present form has an organisational advantage. Each chapter stands on its own and approaches the lexicon from a particular perspective: each can therefore be read as a separate topic. The appendix entitled 'Intra- and Inter-lexical Strategies of the Chinese and English Lexicons' zooms in on the vagaries as well as the regularities of Chinese lexemes alongside their English counterparts and may be browsed through as an independent summary recapitulation of the Chinese lexicon.

To conclude, I must not forget to mention how deeply indebted I am to Mr David Arrandale of the Brotherton Library, the University of Leeds, who read my entire manuscript and made valuable suggestions. I am equally grateful to Mr Kaiying Yang of Praetorius, who helped me in every way he could to solve my computer and software problems. Last but not least, my gratitude goes to my wife Quzhen Li, who, using much of her spare time and annual leave, helped to key the whole book into the computer and painstakingly proofread every single entry whilst facing with me the enormous pressure of meeting the publisher's deadlines. Without her dedication and wholehearted support, it would have been impossible to complete this book at all.

The errors which remain are, of course, the author's sole responsibility.

YIP Po-Ching
April 1999

ABBREVIATIONS

adj.	adjective/adjectival
adv.	adverb/adverbial
AE	American English
BE	British English
biol.	biological
bot.	botanical
colloq.	colloquial
contem.	contemporary
conj.	conjunction
def.	definite
dial.	dialectal
derog.	derogatory
fig.	figurative
honor.	honorific
humor.	humorous
incompl.	incomplete
indef.	indefinite
med.	medical
meta.	metaphorical
mil.	military
mw	measure word
n	noun
offens.	offensive
onom.	onomatopoeic
palaeontol.	palaeontological
pl.	plural
pop.	popular
pred.	predicative
sb	somebody
sing.	singular
sth	something
tech.	technical/technological
v	verb
vs	versus
zool.	zoological

INTRODUCTION

The purpose of this introduction is threefold: first, to define the general properties of a language's lexicon as we see it, which will serve as the backdrop to our description of the Chinese lexicon in particular; second, to provide a holistic view of the organisational features of the Chinese lexicon, which will be discussed in detail in the body of the book; and third, to relate, where possible, these lexicalisation strategies of Chinese to those of English so that our readers, who are speakers of English, may identify for themselves the similarities and differences which exist between the two lexicons.

LEXICON IN GENERAL

The lexicon of a natural language may be understood as all its words and their set combinations in synchronic use (and open to diachronic change when unique situations in future provide the catalyst). Lexicon, in linguistic parlance, is synonymous with the more usual term vocabulary.

From the viewpoint of linguistic studies, lexicon is the analytic target of lexicology (i.e. the combined study of word structure, word-formation and semantics), which constitutes part of the tripartite schema of the language proper, being complementary to syntax and phonology. It can therefore be seen as part of a system, a sub-structure in itself, an indispensable cogwheel built into the language's coordinated whole. It is the best testimony to a language's intrinsic property of simultaneous continuity and change, stability and flux. The traditional misconception that it is but 'an unrelated aggregate of words'[1] is perhaps due to the imperceptible influence of the conventional practice of a dictionary's organising its entries in an alphabetical way, which only highlights the seemingly unsystematic nature of the lexicon. In fact, ordinary dictionaries, which depend very much on the arbitrary decision or intuition of the lexicographer concerned and do not usually base themselves on systematic analysis or differentiation of a language's lexical units and their meaningful relationships, are but practical aids to language learning; they are certainly not intended as a systematic representation of the inherent organisation of a language's lexicon.

Viewed in its totality, a language's lexicon should have at least the following properties:

[1] Kempson 1977: 83.

(1) being open-ended, i.e. containing an ever-increasing set of words to keep pace with the ever-changing environment – this is particularly true of such major classes as nouns, verbs, adjectives and adverbs;

(2) taking words (or their archetypical representations – lexemes) as its basic constituents, which can be further broken down into morphemes, sub-morphemes or symbolic phonaesthemes (but the differentiation must stop short of phonemes, which belong to the realm of phonology) or amalgamated into compounds, set expressions, idioms or formulaic patterns or sentences (though the amalgamation must stop short of free grammatical constructions, phrasal or sentential, which belong to the realm of syntax);

(3) representing only the semantic content of the above-mentioned lexical units in themselves or, in other words, only the semantic (and perhaps cultural) content of these items in their paradigmatic contrasts with one another in the light of their syntagmatic co-selectional potentiality and no more, i.e. not representing the semantic content which naturally accrues in the process of free syntactic configuration of these units or the semantic content which is derived pragmatically from paralinguistic or extralinguistic contexts in which these items are used in keeping with the speaker-hearer's intention, past experience, knowledge of the world or power of logical inference;

(4) revealing the organisation of the whole lexicon in such a way that crucial information on the systematic and significant relationships within and between different units of the lexicon can be disclosed by reference to their structural characteristics, formal properties, collocational potentialities, meaning relations, usage conventions, registral differences, stylistic nuances, affective overtones, and possibly even semantic components;

(5) being able to relate the lexicon's own properties systematically to those of phonology and syntax so that a coherent, coordinating picture of the whole linguistic system can be established. The indication of pronunciation and word class of lexical units in a dictionary is merely a rudimentary step.

It must, however, be pointed out that though the lexicons of all languages share similar properties, they do not necessarily contain similar lexical items: the lexicalization of the objective world with its multifarious phenomena and relations and that of the imaginary products of the more capricious subjective (and collective) consciousness of different speech communities is always an arbitrary language- and culture-specific process. Any lexicon is therefore a unique realization of those shared properties outlined above.

Open-Endedness of a Lexicon

That the lexicon of a language is open-ended can perhaps be accounted for in terms of the language's lexical development, its semantic change, and the individualistically creative and transient nature of a speaker-hearer's verbal repertoire.

A language's lexical development can be regarded as a never-ending process. Compared with the near-closedness and almost glacial nature of its phonological and syntactic systems in a given synchronic stage, a language's lexicon is indeed a fast-flowing river, whose fountainhead seems to be perpetually fed by the human need to cope with the unceasing change and development in the physical and social environment and the human race's ever-deepening understanding of it.

Semantic change in a language's lexicon is inevitable owing to the ever-expanding experience of a speech community. A semantic change in any individual item of a lexicon may take the form of minor deviations, i.e. progressive minimal meaning contaminations resulting from use in ever-varying linguistic co-texts or that of major departures, i.e. figurative breakaways from normal literal usage either as metaphor (i.e. paradigmatic association of similarity) or as metonymy (i.e. syntagmatic association of contiguity).

The individualistic and transient nature of a speaker-hearer's verbal repertoire can be understood as, first, that no two speaker-hearers of a given language ever share precisely the same verbal repertoire; as, second, that no one speaker-hearer ever retains precisely the same verbal repertoire throughout his life; and as, third, that every speaker-hearer in his lifetime will invariably stumble upon occasions where he needs to make himself understood by perhaps unwittingly resorting to impromptu, makeshift coinages to supplement the verbal repertoire at his command. Linguistic phenomena like these are too obvious to need any substantiation or proof.

To review our view of this open-ended nature of a language's lexicon, we may fairly conclude that lexical development and semantic change in the lexicon are the main characteristics of the objective lexicon alive in the public consciousness or cultural heritage of a given speech community, while difference in size, transience in nature, and originality in propensity characterise an individual speaker-hearer's subjective lexicon.

While the subjective lexicon, by its very nature, is smaller in size and less stable in denotative precision than the objective lexicon, it is nevertheless richer in connotation and perhaps more imaginative in its expressiveness. It forms only part of the objective lexicon, yet by necessity the most essential part; otherwise, any communication between one speaker-hearer and another within the same community, if not totally impossible, will be extremely difficult. However, the relationship between the two lexicons is far more dynamic than one of inclusion. The objective lexicon in a way channels the flow of the subjective lexicon whereas the latter (as an 'inbuilt dictionary'[2]) modifies and enriches the former in the most diverse and inventive ways.

[2] Leech 1981: 204.

The open-endedness of the lexicon can therefore be taken as the ultimate cause of productivity on the part of the speaker and miscomprehension on the part of the hearer; and as a speaker-hearer of a given language, a person will often find himself, in any normal instance of communication, playing the dual yet alternating role of a speaker and a hearer: on him is equally bestowed the proclivity to create and to misinterpret.

The main task of the lexicologist is, of course, to describe the existing structure of the objective lexicon; but he must not lose sight of the rule-governed creativity inherent in the subjective lexicon, which to some extent reveals the rule-governed fluidity of the objective lexicon itself.

Though it seems unnecessary to make too fine a distinction between the two lexicons, it might be true to say that the objective lexicon seems more amenable to a static analysis – in terms of structural features – whereas the subjective lexicon is more amenable to a dynamic approach – in terms of generative rules.[3] It must nevertheless be borne in mind that any positive notion of structure must necessarily stem from the notion of generation. In other words, only patterns which can only be generated in terms of rules can be recognized as systematic structures, despite the fact that some of the rules might operate only at certain synchronic stages in the life of a lexicon.[4]

A lexicon's open-endedness certainly does not invalidate its overall systematic nature, for the continual mapping or remapping taking place in the lexicalization and semantic redistribution process is but a homomorphic replication of our orderly yet imperfectly understood world.

Constituent Units of a Lexicon

Words are usually taken as the basic constituents of the lexicon. But 'word' is too loose a word. Is it supposed to mean only the conventional unmodified entry form in a dictionary (e.g. 'speak' – but of course different dictionaries decide on different entry forms) or does it include all inflected forms (e.g. 'speak', 'spoke', 'spoken', etc.) or even derivatives (e.g. 'speaker', 'bespeak', etc.)? In present-day lexicographical practice, it is generally accepted that all grammatical declensions or inflected forms are taken as word-tokens belonging to the same word or lexeme; and all derivations are taken as belonging to separate words or lexemes. Therefore, 'speak' and 'spoke' are of the same lexeme; and 'speak' and 'speaker' are two separate lexemes. Theoretically, the demarcation is clear but in practice lexicographers are often more flexible and less consistent. For example, 'spoke' and 'spoken' may sometimes be listed as separate entries to refer back to 'speak' (perhaps for the convenience

---

[3] Cf. Aronoff 1979.
[4] For example, before disyllabification became the main driving force of word-formation, the Chinese lexicon used to increase its word stock by incessantly coining new characters.

of language beginners), while 'slowly', 'slowness' and even 'slowish' may well be listed in the same entry under 'slow'.

But 'words' alone do not tell the whole lexical story. In any natural language, there are discernible sub-word-level lexemes and hyper-word-level lexemes, i.e. units of meaning which are smaller or bigger in size than words.

There can be such sub-lexemic units as (a) bound morphemes (e.g. in the lexeme 'speaker' 'speak' is a free morpheme whilst '-er' is a bound morpheme); (b) sub-morphemes (e.g. '-ceive' in 'receive', 'conceive' or '-tain' in 'retain', 'detain', etc.), which are obviously word-building primes but have no generalisable meaning as ordinary morphemes do; and (c) phonaesthemes, which are only faintly suggestive of certain meaning associations (e.g. 'sl-' in 'slow', 'slack', 'slur', etc. suggests a kind of 'sluggishness'), perhaps more manifest in poetry.

Hyper-lexemic units are units larger in size than ordinary words. They can be such lexical composites as (a) compounds, consisting of at least two free morphemes (e.g. 'bookmark', 'happy-go-lucky', 'loudspeaker', etc.); (b) collocations, i.e. phrases consisting of words which are strictly co-selectional but transparent in meaning (e.g. 'blond hair', 'addled mind', 'take the risk', 'have a go', etc.); (c) set expressions, i.e. phrases in which words are in a fixed order signifying meanings unpredictable from the constituent elements (e.g. 'white elephant', 'in view of', 'set up', 'spill the beans', etc.), usually called 'idioms', with different degrees of idiomaticity; (d) formulaic sentences, which include proverbs, quotations, as well as everyday sentences conventionalised for certain situations (e.g. 'actions speak louder than words', 'to be or not to be – that is the question', 'How are you?', etc.); and (e) phrase or sentence schemata, i.e. set constructions of a phrasal or sentential nature which are readily reformulatable with different elements of a certain grammatical class (e.g. 'for __'s sake', 'what's the use of __ ing . . . ?', etc.).[5]

Such a scheme of lexical differentiation, as we can see, fits in with the multi-layered or stratal properties of a natural language, ranging from the most arbitrary to the most free. At the phonemic level, every phoneme is learned and used by the speaker of the language with conscious or unconscious effort and no intentional innovation or violation is usually allowed; at the lexemic level, however, arbitrariness is often tempered with creation, which, if not often encouraged or always accepted, is never forbidden; while at the sentential level, free construction tends to be the general rule.

The birth of a lexical unit, however, is always motivated by the need for a concise and untrammelled communication of meaningful information and experience. We will therefore turn our attention first to the formulation of meaning.

[5] Lyons 1968: 178.

Semantic Categories in Communication

To start with, one important distinction must be made in defining the semantic content of a lexicon, that is, the semantic content of a language's lexicon is in no way the same as that of the language itself. In other words, the semantic dimension which the lexicon of a given language is capable of is different from and, in a sense, smaller than the semantic dimension which the language itself is capable of.

The word 'knowledge' in the English lexicon, for example, despite its polysemic capacity, does not seem to be able to mean 'ignorance'. Yet in actual communication, it is not uncommon that when said with a sarcastic intonation, it can be made to stretch its meaning to this very semantic opposite.[6] Such a potential twist in the meaning of the word does not arise totally from the word itself but also partly from the systematic workings of the language's phonological properties and, therefore, cannot be readily explained by analysing the word or looking into the lexicon alone; it is to be accounted for by looking into the very complex linguistic mechanism of a language as a whole.

In a like manner, syntactic structure also adds vastly and systematically to the total meaning of the elements which constitute a concatenation. The semantic value of a syntactic structure is therefore always greater than the sum value of its constituent parts. This extra semantic input, again, cannot be very well accounted for by just analysing the words in question or looking into the lexicon alone; it can only be accounted for by taking into consideration the grammatical devices involved or the syntactic relationships present between the constituent elements.

Similarly, a word in actual use constantly undergoes a semantic growth, nourished by the underlying intention, knowledge, experience and inferential capability of its users. Any additional contribution to the original meaning comes not from the word itself but from the linguistic maturity, life experience, cultural background and encyclopaedic knowledge of the user concerned. An account of semantic underpinnings of this kind must therefore have recourse to sources outside the word proper or the lexicon to which it belongs.

To duly represent the semantic properties of a lexicalized unit in the lexicon, one important decision must therefore be taken; that is, should the uncontaminated semantic value of the unit be accounted for alone or should it also include all or part of the semantic value obtained from phonological, syntactic and pragmatic sources? If part, which part?

The inclusion of semantic contributions from all or part of the sources mentioned above involves a process of integration. And all integration, as we know, begins with differentiation, like the 'dispersing' of light waves in a secondary colour by means of a prism.

[6] Cf. Palmer 1981: 39–41.

To recapitulate the points already made, we should perhaps see how different sources come together to signify the value of a semantic unit in use. As we know, any semantic unit can be said to divide its value between its meaning proper – called *denotation* (not to be equated with *reference*, which is to be taken as only part of denotation in some lexemes) and its additional overtones – called *connotation*. The denotation of a semantic unit seems to be generally a shared property, more stable and less vulnerable to dramatic changes within a short period of time; its connotation, however, varies from case to case and from individual to individual. There might be parts of the connotative meaning of the semantic unit in question which are more or less uniform in the public consciousness of a given speech community at a given period of time;[7] yet situational and idiosyncratic associations may be quite often present.

In deciding the meaning of a semantic unit, denotation, as a less wayward property, is therefore more essential than connotation. However, when the latter is emphasised, it invariably overrides the former and pushes it to the background (cf. the example of 'knowledge' vs 'ignorance' quoted earlier).

Denotation is encoded in the semantic unit itself when it stands in potential paradigmatic contrasts with other units in the lexicon. It can perhaps be referred to as *semantic constant*; whereas connotation is more often conditioned by the phonological variations, paralinguistic features and any pragmatic and cultural underpinnings which are brought into association with the unit concerned. It can therefore be called the *semantic variable*.

Standing aloof from a linguistic *co-text* or extralinguistic *context*, a semantic unit is usually more manifest in its 'denotative meaning', which can be aptly described in paradigmatic or syntagmatic terms. Paradigmatic relations with other semantic units not only differentiate its meaning from that of others but also reveal its *registral contrasts* (i.e. neutral vs technical, etc.), *stylistic differences* (i.e. formal vs informal, etc.), *affective implications* (i.e. commendatory vs derogatory) and *figurative nuances* (i.e. literal vs metaphorical, etc.); whereas potential syntagmatic relations with other semantic units reveal its *collocational restrictions*, reflecting the unit's conventional co-usage with other units (e.g. have a go vs *take a go; a tattered shirt vs *a broken shirt) or its *collocational areas*, which bring to light the unit's systematic semantic association with other units (e.g. sweet/sugar vs sour/vinegar), or even its *collocational violations*, producing, either intentionally or unintentionally, an out-of-the-ordinary, jokey, or nonsensical effect (e.g. green ideas). But such unusual structures are anormal in nature and may always be counted as an unpredictable variable. Under normal circumstances, syntactic relations add systematically to the lexical meaning of a semantic unit in free and regular combinations with other units. This is called *grammatical meaning* by some linguists;[8] it forms a constant part of the meaning of all

---

[7] Cf. Osgood and Tannenbaum 1957.
[8] Lyons 1968: 435–8.

lexical items and even the whole of that of some. Grammatical meaning is also commonly expressed in inflexions, inside derivations and compounds, or in sequences (i.e. word order). But difference in syntactic sequence does not always encode difference in grammatical meaning: it may sometimes only indicate different emphasis of the same grammatical meaning. This difference in emphasis actually overlaps with *focal meaning*, which as part of connotation, can be similarly encoded in phonological terms.

Phonologically speaking, the semantic unit usually picks up extra connotation in keeping with extra stress or prominence, which we have referred to as 'focal meaning', or with specific intonation, which we might call *tonal meaning*. Focal meaning serves to call the hearer's attention to a particular paradigmatic contrast implied by the semantic unit in use in the utterance (e.g. for *your* good, i.e. not for mine) whereas tonal meaning is particularly versatile as a means of 'irony' and 'satire' or any unspoken 'implication' deducible from the context.

Phonaesthetic meaning is the potential meaning carried by sound clusters in comparison or syllabic patterns in alternation, which are usually foregrounded when certain regular associations of meaning are discovered and fully exploited through immediate contrasts in the utterance. *Rhythmic meaning*, for example, gives pace and tempo to speech patterns while *harmonic* shows up rhyme, consonance and alliteration; *onomatopoeic* is imitative of real life acoustics, however crude and language-specific the imitation, while *symbolistic* is only partially suggestive.

Paralinguistically, facial and gestural expressions often strengthen or offset the actual words used in communication, which we might call *paralinguistic hints*.

Pragmatically, *referential meaning* builds a bridge for the speaker-hearer to cross from the linguistic world to the actual world of life. While *presuppositional meaning* helps to refer to previous experience or events, true or untrue, *inferential* points to the future. *Intentional meaning* reveals the underlying *motive* of the speaker, which may sometimes be different from the superficial *motif* expressed in verbal terms. Linguistic manoeuvres of such a kind sometimes coincide with *functional meaning*, which tacitly suggests what speech-acts the speaker commits himself to and how he wishes the hearer to respond to their illocutionary force rather than propositional content (e.g. It's hot in here → Open the window, please).[9] *Attitudinal meaning*, through the choice of words or intonation, betrays or conveys the attitude of the speaker towards the hearer or the topic of his conversation. *Phatic meaning*, in particular, signals the speaker's desire to keep open future communication channels with the hearer.[10] *Cultural meaning* reflects the speaker-hearer's awareness of the traditions and customs of his speech community at a given period, e.g. the word 富 **fù**

---

[9] Austin 1962; Grice 1975; Zgusta 1967: 578: identity of function versus divergence of form.
[10] Malinowski 1923.

'rich' bears drastically different cultural meaning in present-day China from, say, that of twenty years ago;[11] whereas *encyclopaedic* displays the speaker-hearer's degree of specialised knowledge concerning the topics dealt with by the semantic unit, whether in terms of extension or intension.[12] *Idiosyncratic* is the most wilful (even ungrounded) association on the part of the individual speaker-hearer regarding the semantic unit in use. Language, in fact, provokes not only sound-waves for the ear but also the contemplation of the pragmatic world it describes. Hand in hand, they coordinate to enrich the meaning for the hearer of what is being said. Generally, one over-understands what is said rather than under-understands it, which happens only when one is too ignorant of a situation or too immature about life.

Diagrammatically, the above-mentioned units of meaning may be classified as follows, based on the four-dimensional perspective of the average communicative act, i.e. the speaker, the audience, the verbal message and its environs, where meaning is being issued, construed and transacted:

verbal message (meaning per se)	verbal/non-verbal environs (genre-related and extralinguistic)	speaker (pragmatic and paralinguistic)	audience (interpretation)
denotation	registral contrasts	+ stylistic differences	connotation
referential	+ stylistic differences	affective implications	+ presuppositional
functional	figurative nuances	focal	+ inferential
phatic	collocational restrictions	tonal	cultural
	collocational areas	paralinguistic hints	encyclopaedic
	grammatical	+ presuppositional	+ idiosyncratic
	phonaesthetic	+ inferential	
	rhythmic	intentional	
	harmonic	attitudinal	
	onomatopoeic	+ idiosyncratic	
	symbolistic		

+ indicates the type of meaning that recurs in more than one domain

We can well imagine that lexemes or similar categories of lexical units in the lexicon will be able to denote only part of these meanings, especially when the items each stand by themselves. When linked together in linguistic co-texts (which are what we call verbal environs) or extralinguistic contexts (which will naturally include the non-verbal environs, the speaker and the audience), these items not only increase but also become more sophisticated and refined in their communicative power: they invariably take on additional meaning, which is expressed through phonological, paralinguistic or pragmatic means.

In an actual act of communication, certain meanings will no doubt stand out more prominently than others depending on the occasion. The resynthesis

[11] Cf. Lyons 1968: 432; Makkai 1972: hypersememic.
[12] Evans et al. 1980: 4.

or integration of meanings relevant to the situation instinctively happens with every speaker-hearer involved in any particular verbal exchange. It is certainly an undeniable responsibility on the part of the lexicologist to reveal in a more or less systematic way every strand of the 'semantic variable' as well as that of the 'semantic constant' built into the lexemes of a language. This is not, of course, to say that a lexicon is capable of codifying every category of meaning we have so far identified.

Nevertheless, every lexicon, in its formulation of meaning, makes full use of the semantic potentialities inherent in every aspect of the language of which it is a part. In the following section we shall be able to see how a lexicon taps, with or without conscious design,[13] a language's linguistic resources to their very limits.

Formal Categories of a Lexicon

The formally definable units of a lexicon do not occur at will or at random: they are inventions of necessity, dictated by the need for effective communication (e.g. basic terms for prototypes) or for linguistic flexibility or aesthetic diversity (e.g. peripheral terms for subtypes). Metaphorically speaking, linguistic brainchildren as such are all traceable to their line of descent or their diverse kindred relationships with one another, differentiable by virtue of their intra- and inter-lexical connections in terms of paradigms or syntagms.

To explain this systematic nature of intra- and inter-lexical relations in a lexicon, we will have to begin with a detailed examination of the lexical formation process itself. In other words, we will need to find out if there is any correlation between meaning and sound, between meaning and script, between basic forms and their derivations or combinations, and so on. In what follows, we will focus on exploring the motivation behind the linguistic artefacts[14] specific to a given lexicon and attempting to arrive at an explanatory understanding of their relationships whilst leaving the exhaustive cataloguing of a lexicon's formal categories to the appendix.[15]

It is true to say that there is a universal consensus among linguists that the sound-and-meaning relationship is generally arbitrary. That is the conventional side of a language. But language is at the same time systematic. It will therefore also be unreasonable to ignore obvious sound-and-meaning correlation in words like: flip and flop, drip and drop, hustle and bustle, burst and bust, splash and splotch, stalactite and stalagmite, and slow, slur, slack and sluggish, etc. in the English lexicon and 叽哩咕噜 **jīligūlū** 'talking indistinctly' and 叽哩呱啦 **jīliguālā** 'talking loudly', and 细 **xì** 'slender', 小 **xiǎo** 'small', 稀 **xī** 'scarce', 鲜 **xiǎn** 'rare', 狭 **xiá** 'narrow', etc. in Chinese.

---

[13] The occurrence of homophones, for example, is certainly not a conscious design of a language.
[14] Leech 1981: 41.
[15] A complete inventory of lexical categories in Chinese and English can be found in the Appendix on p. 348.

Onomatopoeia goes still further. It is not only employed for the imitation of natural sounds (e.g. 咪咪 **mīmī** 'mew', 怦怦 **pēngpēng** 'pit-a-pat', 喔喔喔 **wōwōwō** 'cock-a-doodle-doo', 嘻嘻哈哈 **xīxīhāhā** 'laughing merrily', etc.) but also for the coinage of names for sound-related entities: e.g. 知了 **zhīliǎo** 'cicada' is supposed to be a sound representation of the insect, and 布谷 **bùgǔ** 'cuckoo' that of the bird. 娃娃鱼 **wáwayú** 'giant salamander' (lit. 'baby fish') is so called in Chinese for the noise it makes: to the ear of the Chinese, the noise resembles that made by a 'baby' 娃娃 **wáwa**, which is itself derived from the way it cries.

Semantic affinity through sound resemblance becomes even more evident when a change of word class or a shift of meaning takes place within a lexical item, when, for example, 钉 **dīng** 'nail' changes to its related verb 钉 **dìng** 'drive in a nail'; 'to nail', 凉 **liáng** 'cool'; 'cold' changes to its related verb 凉 **liàng** 'to let something cool', 量 **liàng** 'quantity' changes to its related verb 量 **liáng** 'to measure', 吐 **tǔ** 'spit (voluntarily)' changes to a meaning-related verb 吐 **tù** 'vomit (involuntarily)', and so on.

Once it is clear that phonic motivation behind and between lexical items does exist, it is not totally implausible to find even more subtle sound-and-meaning correlations between, for example, the following pairs of words in Chinese:

牙 **yá** 'front tooth'/咬 **yǎo** 'bite'
齿 **chǐ** 'tooth'/吃 **chī** 'eat'
咽 **yān** 'pharynx'/咽 **yàn** 'to swallow'
喉 **hóu** 'throat'/喝 **hē** 'drink'
唇 **chún** 'lip'/吮 **shǔn** 'suck'

We are not saying that such sound-and-meaning correlation may be found everywhere, but there is little doubt that such a correlation is a sub-system built into a lexicon's integrated whole.

We will now turn to our second question on the correlation between meaning and script. It is, of course, too far-fetched to say that meaning and script have an inherent correlation. Written forms, particularly in European languages, are direct replicas of sounds. In their relation to meaning, they are just as arbitrary as the sounds they represent. However, when we examine the lexicon of a language like Chinese, we will be surprised to find that quite a number of script forms were originally created with reference to the meaning intended: e.g. 山 **shān** 'mountain'; 'hill' is a pictorial representation of three towering peaks while 川 **chuān** 'river' is a picturesque depiction of flowing waters. If 大 **dà** 'big' draws its inspiration from a person standing with his arms stretched out to their full length and 小 **xiǎo** 'small' from grains of sand, then 尖 **jiān** 'sharp'; 'pointed', formed with the concept of 'small' at the top and 'big' at the bottom, will certainly call up the image of a pointed object. When 上 **shàng** 'above' and 下 **xià** 'below' are joined together in 卡 **qiǎ** 'get stuck', the script amusingly calls forth the notion of 'neither up nor down'.

It would, of course, be misleading to conclude that all Chinese script bases its formation on these principles alone,[16] but they are undoubtedly the very foundation on which the whole of Chinese script is built.

If we go a step further, we will see that in Chinese script, sound and form representations sometimes work hand in hand to relate themselves to the prescribed meaning: e.g. 浅 **qiǎn** 'shallow', 钱 **qián** 'copper coin (originally of little value)', 贱 **jiàn** 'cheap', 笺 **jiān** 'commentary (usually quite short)', and so on, all sharing a diminutive connotation; and 蒙 **méng** 'to cover', 朦 **méng** '(of moonlight) hazy', 曚 **méng** '(of sunlight) dim', 濛 **méng** 'drizzly'; 'misty', 矇 **méng** 'drowsy', 懵 **měng** 'muddled', 梦 **mèng** 'dream', etc., all associated with the notion of non-clarity.

Finally, if we probe into the relationship between various forms and their derivations and combinations, we shall find even more regular and systematic correlations in terms of meaning and form.

Semantically speaking, words often contract a varying yet consistent sense or field[17] relationship with one another: e.g.

synonym:
　　界说 **jièshuō** (classic, obsolete)/定义 **dìngyì** (contemporary) 'definition'
　　南瓜 **nánguā** (neutral lit. 'south gourd')/北瓜 **běigua** (dialectal lit. 'north gourd') 'pumpkin'
　　搬家 **bānjiā** (neutral)/挪窝儿 **nuówōr** (dialectal) 'move (house)'
　　拨冗 **bōrǒng** (polite)/抽时间 **chōu shíjiān** (colloquial) 'find time'
　　贻贝 **yíbèi** (zoological)/淡菜 **dàncài** (food) 'mussel'
　　沥青 **lìqīng** (technical)/柏油 **bǎiyóu** (popular) 'asphalt'; 'bitumen'
　　有了 **yǒu le** (euphemistic lit. 'have got it')/怀孕 **huáiyùn** 'pregnant'
　　诸位 **zhūwèi** 'ladies and gentlemen' (very formal)/各位 **gè wèi** 'everybody' (formal)/大家 **dàjiā** 'everyone' (informal)

periphrasis: the same idea expressed in different derivatives or clusters of words
　　不禁 **bùjīn**/禁不住 **jīnbuzhù** 'can't help (doing)'
　　不得了 **bùdéliǎo**/了不得 **liǎobude** (as a complement) 'extremely'; 'exceedingly'
　　好容易 **hǎo róngyi**/好不容易 **hǎo bù róngyi** 'not at all easy'; 'with great difficulty'

antonym:
　　大 **dà** 'big'/小 **xiǎo** 'small'
　　买 **mǎi** 'buy'/卖 **mài** 'sell'
　　旺季 **wàngjì** 'busy season'/淡季 **dànjì** 'slack season'
　　微观 **wēiguān** 'microcosmic'/宏观 **hóngguān** 'macroscopic'
　　男女老少 **nán nǚ lǎo shào** 'men and women, old and young'

[16] Cf. Chapter 2 on the graphetic composition of the Chinese lexicon.
[17] The word 'field' is used here to mean 'lexical field', groups of words that belong together.

hyponym:

花儿 **huār** 'flowers'/玫瑰 **méigui** 'rose'; 郁金香 **yùjīnxiāng** 'tulip'; etc.

车 **chē** 'vehicle'/汽车 **qìchē** 'motor-car'; 火车 **huǒchē** 'train'; 电车 **diànchē** 'tram'; 自行车 **zìxíngchē** 'bicycle', etc.

meronym:[18] words with a part–whole meaning relationship

树 **shù** 'tree'/树干 **shùgàn** 'tree trunk'; 树枝 **shùzhī** 'branch', 'twig'; 树根 **shùgēn** 'root'; 树叶 **shùyè** 'leaf'; 树皮 **shùpí** 'bark', etc.

consecutives: words belonging to a hierarchy or series

星期一 **xīngqī yī** 'Monday', 星期二 **xīngqī èr** 'Tuesday', etc.

一月 **yīyuè** 'January', 二月 **èryuè** 'February', etc.

班 **bān** 'squad', 排 **pái** 'platoon', 连 **lián** 'company', 营 **yíng** 'battalion', etc.

polyseme:

脚 **jiǎo** 'foot'/墙脚 **qiángjiǎo** 'foot of a wall'

杜鹃 **dùjuān** (zoology) 'cuckoo'; (botany) 'azalea'

Morphologically speaking, words related in meaning seem to be often mutually derivable. In one way or another they bear some kind of formal resemblance to each other: e.g.

morphemic derivation:

speak/speaker; dine/dinner; love/lovely; top/atop

学 **xué** 'study'; 'learn'/学者 **xuézhě** 'scholar'; 爱 **ài** 'love'/可爱 **kě'ài** 'lovely'

submorphemic derivation:

retain/detain/contain

领子 **lǐngzi** 'collar'/袖子 **xiùzi** 'sleeve'/里子 **lǐzi** 'lining'

凉丝丝 **liángsīsī** 'coolish'/甜丝丝 **tiánsīsī** 'pleasantly sweet'

兴冲冲 **xìngchōngchōng** 'animatedly'/怒冲冲 **nùchōngchōng** 'furiously'

morphological analogy:

路透社 **lùtòushè** 'Reuter's News Agency'; 'Reuters'/路边社消息 **lùbiānshè xiāoxi** 'grapevine news' (路边 **lùbiān** 'wayside'; 社 **shè** 'news agency'; 消息 **xiāoxi** 'news')

促进 **cùjìn** 'promote'; 'advance'/促退 **cùtuì** 'help to retrogress'

气力 **qìlì** 'effort'; 'energy'/力气 **lìqi** 'physical strength'

直率 **zhíshuài** 'frank'; 'candid'/率直 **shuàizhí** 'straightforward'; 'blunt'

空闲 **kòngxián** 'idle'; 'free'/闲空 **xiánkòng** 'spare time'; 'leisure'

morphological oddity: where words are interrupted by other elements for the sake of emphasis

absolutely/abso-posi-lutely; fantastic/fan-damn-tastic

滚蛋 **gǔndàn** 'beat it'; 'scram'; 'piss off'/滚你妈的蛋 **gǔn nǐ māde dàn** 'get lost'

喝醉 **hē zuì** 'get drunk'/喝他一个醉 **hē tā yī gè zuì** 'have a drinking spree'

---

[18] Carter 1987: 21.

Syntactically speaking, words are not always born of derivation or root creation: compounding, for example, particularly in the lexicon of a morphologically deficient language like Chinese, is a common word-formation device where the language's syntax is exploited to the full to tailor-make not only words but also concatenations longer than words: e.g.

compound: words of various syntactic relationships between the components, usually disyllabic in Chinese
killjoy; user-friendly
扫兴 **sǎoxìng** 'dampen one's spirits' (lit. 'sweep off one's interest')
有钱 **yǒu qián** 'rich' (lit. 'have money')
足球 **zúqiú** 'football'; 'soccer'
地震 **dìzhèn** 'earthquake'

situational formula:
你好 **nǐ hǎo** 'how are you'; 'how do you do'
再见 **zàijiàn** 'goodbye'
一路平安 **yī lù píng'ān** 'a safe journey (home)'

set expression:
依我看 **yī wǒ kàn** 'in my opinion'
换句话说 **huàn jù huà shuō** 'in other words'
总而言之 **zǒng ér yán zhī** 'all in all'

vernacular idiom: trisyllabic expression, especially with a verb + object structure
开绿灯 **kāi lǜdēng** 'give the go-ahead' (lit. 'switch on the greenlight')
吃豆腐 **chī dòufu** (dialectal) 'flirt with a woman' (lit. 'eat beancurd')
磨洋工 **mó yánggōng** 'dawdle over one's work' (lit. 'waste time on a foreign job')

classical idiom: fixed quadrisyllabic expression
两面三刀 **liǎngmiàn sāndāo** 'double-dealing' (lit. 'two faces and three knives')
一箭双雕 **yī jiàn shuāng diāo** 'kill two birds with one stone' (lit. 'one arrow two vultures')
趁热打铁 **chèn rè dǎ tiě** 'strike the iron while it is hot'

proverbial saying: a single or parallel saying of any length
a friend in need is a friend indeed; no pains, no gains
礼多人不怪 **lǐ duō rén bù guài** 'nobody will blame you for being too polite'
人要脸, 树要皮 **rén yào liǎn | shù yào pí** 'face is as important to man as the bark is to the tree'
千里之行, 始于足下 **qiān lǐ zhī xíng | shǐ yú zú xià** 'a thousand-mile journey begins with the first step'

So we see that all items in a lexicon (here taking English and Chinese as examples) are in fact intra- or inter-related in diverse ways, their well-formedness somewhat dictated by their paradigmatic and syntagmatic association with other items in synchronic use. For example, even in the making of the term, 'funfair' becomes more acceptable than 'pleasure-fair' just as 'pleasure park' than 'fun park', following the syntagmatic awareness of alliteration; and one can hardly say there is no paradigmatic influence between 'shrink', 'shrank', 'shrunk' on the one hand and 'drink', 'drank', 'drunk' on the other. However, such etymological reflections, like metanalysis or the reshaping of words (e.g. an eke-name → a nickname or an ewt → a newt) seem to be more relevant for diachronic studies.[19]

In a different lexicon from that of English or Chinese, we might discern a different set of comparable items, but the point is that if any valuable differentiations are to be made, we must first of all know where and how to look. The present book will only survey part of the comparable set from the list relevant to the Chinese lexicon.

THE CHINESE LEXICON IN BRIEF

Viewed in the light of these organizational features of a lexicon in general, the Chinese lexicon has properties which it shares with and in which it differs from those of other languages.

The distinctive semantic significance of tones associated with a syllable and the determinedly logographic nature of its written symbols contribute to the unique system of its lexicon, which differs vastly from the spelling and non-tonal system of most European languages. Taking into account these specific features will enable us to make a more penetrating study of the lexicon and reveal its peculiar aspects.

(a) Monipnymic Nature

As we shall see, a lexicon of this nature constitutes a set of monosyllabic word-building primes, which we would like to call *monyms*. With the introduction of the concept of monym, we can in most cases therefore dispense with that of morpheme in our analysis and that will greatly facilitate our description of the lexical structure of Chinese. A monym will then differ from a morpheme in the sense that (i) it can be not only a meaningful morpheme, free or bound, but also a meaningless sub-morpheme; (ii) it is exclusively monosyllabic; and (iii) it is always potentially separable from other monyms and formally deployable in its own right.

[19] Ullmann 1962: 41.

Being deficient in consonant clusters in its syllabic structure, Chinese abounds in homophonic monosyllables. But to maintain maximal possible differentiation between them, these homophonic monosyllables are usually made heterotonic; and homophonic, homotonic monosyllables, fully or partially heterographic. But it must be clearly understood that not every heterographic monosyllable will necessarily be a different mononym. Quite often, more than one heterographic monosyllable (particularly so with the introduction of simplified characters) can represent the same mononym in particular contexts if they are semantically indifferentiable, e.g. 押韵 = 压韵 **yāyùn** 'to rhyme'; 踉跄 = 踉蹡 **liàngqiàng** 'stagger'; 烂漫 = 烂熳 **lànmàn** 'bright-coloured'; 轶事 = 逸事 **yìshì** 'anecdote'; 仿佛 = 彷彿 **fǎngfú** 'seem'; 'as if'; etc. This can be compared to the relationship between morphemes and their contextual allomorphs. On the other hand, homographic symbols are not necessarily the same mononyms. They can in fact represent quite different, and sometimes quite unrelated, meanings and must therefore be counted as totally different mononyms. For example, 降 **jiàng** in 降落 **jiàngluò** 'descend'; 'land' is phonetically and semantically different from 降 **xiáng** in 投降 **tóuxiáng** 'surrender'; 'capitulate'; and so is 乐 **lè** in 快乐 **kuàilè** 'happy' from 乐 **yuè** in 音乐 **yīnyuè** 'music'. This can be compared to a situation where the same surface morph represents different underlying morphemes like the English '-s' for either 'plural' or 'third-person singular, present'. The fact that there are more characters than mononyms, apart from time-honoured written variants, may also stem from the simplification process, so that the simplified and the original unsimplified characters coexist: e.g. (i) with a different positioning of the radical, e.g. 峰 and 峯 **fēng** 'peak' and 够 and 夠 **gòu** 'enough'; (ii) using different but equally logical radicals for the same purpose, e.g. 愿 and 願 **yuàn** 'willing' (the former incorporating 心 the 'heart' radical, the latter, 頁 the 'head' radical, as 'willingness', can associate itself equally with 'heart' or with 'head'), and 捆 and 綑 **kǔn** 'bind'; 'tie' (the former incorporating 扌 the 'hand' radical, the latter 糸 the 'silk' radical for 'rope', as 'binding' may be made to associate with either 'hand' or 'rope')); and (iii) owing to folk simplification, e.g. 歺 for 餐 **cān** 'meal', 祘 for 算 **suàn** 'calculate', etc.[20]

(b) Disyllabic Tendencies

We know that since the Yuan Dynasty (1206 AD), Mandarin has gradually lost its consonantal endings like **-t, -k, -p, -m**, retaining only **-n** and **-ng**. This has greatly reduced the usable number of monosyllables in the language whilst, on the other hand, new mononyms had to be created to cope with the more and more sophisticated requirements of verbal communication. This state of affairs invariably brought about an increase in homophonic clashes.

---

[20] Cf. Zhou, Zumo (周祖谟) 1983: 290.

For the language to find a way out of this dilemma, disyllabification naturally becomes the device to resolve these homophonic clashes. Once this tendency sets in, it cuts across the lexicon in both directions – it goes on to disyllabify not only monosyllables but also polysyllabic constructions. For example, a quadrisyllabic verbal phrase like 互相帮助 **hùxiāng bāngzhù** (in which 互相 **hùxiāng** means 'mutual'; 'each other' and 帮助 **bāngzhù** means 'help'; 'assist') is shortened to a disyllabic lexeme 互助 **hùzhù** (meaning: 'help each other'), taking the first and the last mononym of the original structure; and similarly, a quadrisyllabic nominal phrase like 化学工业 **huàxué gōngyè** (in which 化学 **huàxué** means 'chemistry' and 工业 **gōngyè** means 'industry') is abbreviated into a disyllabic noun 化工 **huàgōng** (meaning: 'chemical industry'), retaining only the first and the third mononyms for the new structure.

Thus condensation works hand in hand with expansion to disyllabify every possible lexical structure that comes its way.[21]

According to one set of statistics,[22] in the polysyllabic component of the sampled texts, the proportion of different polysyllabic structures is as follows:

disyllabic:	49,938	86%	– on its own
trisyllabic:	6,786	14%	– all other multisyllabic words
quadrisyllabic:	1,401		taken together
pentasyllabic:	69		
hexasyllabic:	19		
heptasyllabic:	12		
octosyllabic:	5		
nonasyllabic:	0		
decasyllabic:	1		

According to other sample statistics we have taken from the MSC Dictionary (1983), where in Section B 500 mononyms are registered, which become the first syllable of approximately 2,500 polysyllabic items, the proportion of different polysyllabic structures is:

disyllabic:	1,791	72%	– on its own
trisyllabic:	396	27%	– all other multisyllabic words
quadrisyllabic:	288		taken together
pentasyllabic:	15		
hexasyllabic:	6		
heptasyllabic:	1		
octosyllabic:	3		

These statistics should give some idea of disyllabic predominance either in actual usage or in the lexicon proper.

---

[21] Lü, Shuxiang (吕叔湘) 1963: 13.
[22] Yi, Xiwu (易熙吾) 1954: 10–11.

In Eric Shen Liu's *Frequency Dictionary of Chinese* (1973), which lists 3,000 lexemes, we find 2,076 polysyllabic lexemes, amongst which only 29 items are non-disyllabic while the other 2,047 are all disyllabic. So we see that disyllabic lexemes account for 98 per cent of the 3,000-lexicon's polysyllabic component and 68 per cent of the whole of the 3,000-lexicon.[23]

We have also noted that an increase of disyllabic lexemes can be detected as the vocabulary moves further away from the more common and basic everyday words. The following table shows the number of disyllabic lexemes in every 300 units:

1st 300 units:	126 disyllables
2nd 300 units:	188
3rd 300 units:	218
4th 300 units:	210
5th 300 units:	216
6th 300 units:	242
7th 300 units:	203
8th 300 units:	206
9th 300 units:	223
10th 300 units:	244

From the table, we find that from the second 300 units upwards (i.e. after the first 600 items) disyllabic lexemes remains well above 200, accounting for more than two-thirds of the vocabulary quoted in each instance.

Disyllabification has not only the passive role of fighting homophonic clashes but also the dynamic role of creating new lexemes in Modern Standard Chinese. Some sinologists[24] attribute the situation mainly to the influence of other languages on Chinese. What we can clearly see is that in the monosyllabically oriented classical lexicon, the increase in words is reflected in the increase in written symbols, whereas in the modern lexicon, the increase in words corresponds directly with the increase of disyllabic combinations, whilst the number of individual characters employed for the purpose has not only been vastly reduced but has subsequently remained constant. The following statistics will indicate the gradual increase of the lexicon's mononyms in the period from 206 BC up to AD 1915. After that the main concern of the lexicon is reflected in the use of a more or less fixed set of mononyms with a drastic increase in their disyllabic combinations in the form of words:[25]

---

[23] Cf. Beijing Yuyan Xueyuan (北京语言学院) 1985.
[24] Kratochvil 1968: 141.
[25] The statistics were collected from the following three sources: Lin, Yushan (林玉山) 1992; Liu, Yeqiu (刘叶秋) 1992; Chen, Bingtiao (陈炳迢) 1985.

dictionary	author(s)	year	characters
Erya (尔雅)	Qin-Han Scholars (秦汉学者)	206 BC[a]	2,091
Fangyan (方言)	Yang Xiong (扬雄)	53 BC–18 AD	9,000
Shuowen Jiezi (说文解字)	Xu Shen (许慎)	100 AD	10,516
Zi Lin (字林)	Lü Chen (吕忱)	265 AD[b]	12,824
Guang Ya (广雅)	Zhang Yi (张揖)	227–32 AD	18,150
Yu Pian (玉篇)	Gu Yewang (顾野王)	519–81 AD	16,917
Jinben Yu Pian (今本玉篇)	Chen Pengnian et al. (陈彭年)	1013 AD	22,561
Guang Yun (广韵)	Chen Pengnian (陈彭年)	961–1017 AD	26,194
Lei Pian (类篇)	Wang Zhu et al. (王洙)	1039–66 AD	31,319
Zi Hui (字汇)	Mei Yingzuo (梅膺祚)	1615 AD	33,179
Kangxi Zidian (康熙字典)	Chen Yushu et al. (陈玉书)	1710–16 AD	47,035
Zhonghua Da Zidain (中华大字典)	Lu Feikui et al. (陆费逵)	1909–14 AD	48,000
Ciyuan (辞源)	Lu Erkui et al. (陆尔奎)	1908–15 AD	87,790
			words
Xinhua Zidian (新华字典)	Wei Jiangong et al. (魏建功)	1901–80 AD	3,500
Xiandai Hanyu Cidian (现代汉语词典)	Ding Shusheng et al. (丁树声)	1961 AD	60,000
Xinban Cihai (新版辞海)	Xia Zhengnong et al. (夏征农)	1989 AD	120,000
Hanyu Da Cidian (汉语大词典)	Luo Zhufeng et al. (罗竹风)	1993 AD	300,000

[a] The year is actually made up to indicate approximately the time when the dictionary was compiled. It is no exact indication of the year.
[b] The year is actually made up to indicate approximately the time when the dictionary was compiled. It is no exact indication of the year.

A thorough analysis of disyllabic structures in the Chinese lexicon will therefore be a representative account of the lexicon as a whole.

1 THE PHONOLOGICAL MAKE-UP OF THE CHINESE LEXICON

Items in the Chinese lexicon, compared with their counterparts in European languages, have vastly different representations in speech as well as in writing. Here we shall first look at the phonological make-up of these lexical entities before delving into their graphetic compositions in chapter 2.

THE SYLLABIC STRUCTURE

The foundation of a Chinese word is the set of monosyllables available to the language. All words in the vocabulary are built on these monosyllables. That is to say, a word in Modern Standard Chinese is represented by one, or by a combination, of these monosyllables.

The phonological structure of such a monosyllable is extremely simple. There are only four possibilities:

(1) V
(2) CV
(3) VC
(4) CVC[1]

where C signifies a consonant and V signifies a full vowel, which may, of course, be either a simple vowel or a diphthong or a triphthong.

There are, however, three additional points to note regarding these rudimentary syllabic constructions:

(1) The initial consonant does not allow a cluster, that is, CCV, etc. does not occur in the language;
(2) The final consonant is limited to either *n* or *ng*;[2]
(3) A tone (i.e. one out of four tones[3]) must be assigned to a syllable unless it is unstressed.

---

[1] There are 5 'nasalised' syllables in the language, namely *hm*, *hng*, *m*, *n* and *ng*, which can be said to be mere C enjoying a syllabic property. They are, however, only exceptions to the general rule.

[2] The present book is concerned with the description of Modern Standard Chinese or Mandarin in common parlance. Other dialects of Chinese (e.g. Cantonese) do have consonantal endings other than *n* and *ng*, such as *p*, *t*, *k*, *m*, etc.

[3] Again, Modern Standard Chinese or Mandarin is limited to four tones plus an unstressed tone. Other dialects (e.g. Cantonese) may have more than four tones.

We shall now look at the total entry of C, i.e. consonants which form the initials of such a syllable, and then that of V, i.e. vowels which form the finals of such a syllable.

THE CONSONANTS

The consonants used in the language are listed in the Table below in terms of the relevant parts of the oral or nasal cavity involved and also the manner in which these consonants are pronounced. The grid which each of the consonants falls into should, therefore, be able to encapsulate the essential phonological characteristics of the particular consonant in question by reference to the parameters provided by their place and manner of articulation:

	plosive unaspirated/ aspirated	affricate unaspirated/ aspirated	fricative	nasal	lateral	voiced continuant
bilabial	b [p] /p [p'] ㄅ / ㄆ			m [m] ㄇ		
labio-dental			f [f] ㄈ			
alveolar	d [t] /t [t'] ㄉ / ㄊ			n [n] ㄋ	l [l] ㄌ	
alveo-dental		z [ts] /c [ts'] ㄗ / ㄘ	s [s] ㄙ			
retroflex		zh [tʂ] /ch [tʂ'] ㄓ / ㄔ	sh [ʂ] ㄕ			r [ɹ] ㄖ
palatal		j [tɕ] /q [tɕ'] ㄐ / ㄑ	x [ɕ] ㄒ			
velar	g [k] /k [k'] ㄍ / ㄎ		h [χ] ㄏ	ng* [ŋ] ㄫ		

* *ng* is included to make the set of consonants used in the language complete. *ng*, however, is not used as the initial consonant of a syllable in Mandarin though it is in some dialects.

As we can see from the table above, what have been given as direct phonemic representations are actually *pinyin* (拼音) romanisations,[4] which, in the author's view, with the help of a few mappings and rules, may just as well be used to outline the phonological system of the language and in a most neat and illuminating way at that. The corresponding IPA[5] equivalents of these *pinyin*

[4] The Chinese Language Phonetic Spelling (i.e. *pinyin*) Plan was adopted and promulgated by the National People's Congress in 1958.
[5] Phonetic symbols known as the International Phonetic Alphabet.

symbols, however, are given next to each of them within square brackets to help determine their phonological values. *Zhuyin fuhao* (注音符号), a set of notations still in use in Taiwan for the purpose of standardising pronunciation (which was first published in 1918, amended in 1920 and later authorised by the Nationalist government in 1930) is also included alongside the *pinyin* romanisations for cross references. However, only *pinyin* will be used to indicate the pronunciation of the illustrative words throughout the book.

The slash / used in the table indicates 'unaspirated/aspirated' distinctions and the expression 'alveo-dental' was coined particularly for the description of a set of sibilants articulated somewhere behind the gums and the front teeth. All the consonants are invariably employed as initials, except for *ng*, which may only occur at the end of a syllable.

THE VOWELS

The simple vowels or monophthongs used in the language are given below by reference to the position of the highest point of the tongue in relation to the oral cavity and also to the shape of the lips in the process of enunci-ation. Again, *pinyin* romanisations will be taken as direct indications of the phonemes. Corresponding international phonetic symbols are given next to the romanisations within square brackets and *zhuyin fuhao* is also provided:

	front *spread/rounded*	central *neutral*	back *spread/rounded* *otherwise rounded*
high	i [i] /ü [y] ㄧ / ㄩ		u [u] ㄨ
mid–high			e [ɣ] /o [o] ㄜ / ㄛ
mid			
mid–low			
low		a [A] ㄚ	

The slash / in the table indicates the 'spread/rounded' distinctions of the lips. The values ascribed to each vowel are to be taken as of an archi-phonemic nature since most of them (i, e, o, a) have regular allophonic variants in designated phonetic contexts. The variations on *i* are caused by the nature of the consonant that precedes it, e.g. [ɿ] when preceded by the alveo-dental consonants z, c, s, [ʅ] by the retroflex consonants zh, ch, sh, r, and [i] by the others. The variations on *e*, *o* and *a* occur in their nasal or diphthongic combinations, e.g. *e* is pronounced as [ɣ] on its own, as [e] in *-ei*, as [ə] in *-en*, *-eng*, as [ɤ] in *er*, as [ɛ] in *-ie*, *è* and as [ʌ] in *-eng* and *-ueng*; *a* is pronounced as [A] on its own, as [a] in *-an*, *-uan*, as [ɛ] in *-ian*, as [ʌ] in *-uang*, and as [ɑ] in *-ang*, *-iang*; *o* is pronounced as [ɔ] in *-uo*, as [u] in *-ao*, and as [o] on its own and in *-ong*.

The positions of the simple vowels and their contextual variants relative to the highest point of the tongue in the oral cavity are summarised in the following diagram in terms of IPA. Where a pair of vowels is given side by side, the first of the two is pronounced with spread lips and the second with rounded lips:

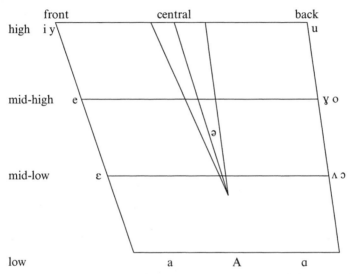

(cf. 钟棨: 关于汉语语音的若干问题 in 语言教学与研究 No. 3, 1978, 北京语言学院)

The simple vowels as summarised in the Table on page 22 may combine in various ways to form *diphthongs*:

	a	e	i	o	u
a-			ai [ai] 历	ao [ɑu] 幺	
e-			ei [ei] ㄟ		
i-	ia [iA] ㅣㄚ	ie [iɛ] ㅣㄝ			
o-					ou [ou] ㄡ
u-	ua [uA] ㄨㄚ			uo [uɔ] ㄨㄛ	
ü-		üe [yɛ] ㄩㄝ			

Four of the diphthongs as seen in the above table may be preceded by either *i* or *u*, which serves as a *medial*, to form the four *triphthongs* of the language:

	ao	ou	ai	ei
i-	iao [iɑu] ㊉ ㄠ	i(o)u [iou] ㊉ ㄡ		
u-			uai [uai] ㄨ ㄞ	u(e)i [uei] ㄨ ㄟ

* Note the orthographic convention of the triphthongs *iu* and *ui*. See section on *pinyin* orthography.

The consonants *n* and *ng* are suffixable to most simple vowels and also some vowel combinations (not necessarily diphthongs) begun with *i*, *u*, and *ü*, forming an independent set of *nasal finals* in the language:

	a	e	i	o	ü	ia	io	ua	ue	üa
-n	an	en	in		ün	ian		uan	u(e)n	üan
	[an]	[ən]	[in]		[yn]	[iɛn]		[uan]	[uən]	[yan]
	ㄢ	ㄣ	ㄧ ㄣ		ㄩ ㄣ	ㄧ ㄢ		ㄨ ㄢ	ㄨ ㄣ	ㄩ ㄢ
-ng	ang	eng	ing	ong		iang	iong	uang	ueng	
	[aŋ]	[ʌŋ]	[iŋ]	[oŋ]		[iaŋ]	[ioŋ]	[uaŋ]	[uʌŋ]	
	ㄤ	ㄥ	ㄧ ㄥ	ㄨ ㄥ		ㄧ ㄤ	ㄧ ㄥ	ㄨ ㄤ	ㄨ ㄥ	

INITIALS AND FINALS

Owing to the peculiar behaviour of the nasal endings *n* and *ng*, as we have seen from above, syllabic structures in Chinese may perhaps be more aptly redefined as sequences of *initials* and *finals*. All the consonants in the language (except *ng*) may constitute the initial of a syllable and if the syllable begins without a consonant, it is counted as having a *zero initial*. This gives a total of 22 (including the zero initial). The finals of a syllable, on the other hand, will comprise all the simple vowels, diphthongs, triphthongs and nasal endings, totalling 35 (not including variants of *i*, which only occur after the retroflex and alveo-dental fricatives, and *e* and the *er*ised vowel *er*). At this point one may probably assume that the 22 initials and the 35 finals will then combine variously to form a syllable in the Chinese language. This is, however, far from being the case. The general picture, in fact, is:

The palatal fricatives *j*, *q*, *x* are always in *complementary distribution* with their retroflex and alveo-dental counterparts *zh*, *ch*, *sh*, *r* and *z*, *c*, *s*. As a result, *j*, *q*, *x* may only precede finals beginning with *i* and *ü*, whereas the other fricatives may only precede the other finals. The velar set *g*, *k*, *h* behaves similarly to those non-palatal fricatives and shuns finals beginning with *i* and *ü*; whereas the retroflex and alveo-dental fricatives are always in complementary distribution with all the other consonants when preceding the simple vowel *i*: in the former case, the retroflex fricatives may only be followed by the variant [ɻ] and the alveo-dental by the variant [ɹ], whereas all the other consonants may be followed by the normal *i*.

The labial and labio-dental set *b, p, m, f* seems to stay idiosyncratically away from finals begun with *u* and *ü*, except for *u* on its own.

Apart from these *systematic gaps* in the syllabic structure of the language, there are *accidental gaps*. For example, only the labial and labio-dental set *b, p, m, f* comes into combination with the single-vowel final *o* while all the other consonants keep themselves away from it, and both the labial and the alveolar set *b, p, m, f* and *d, t, n, l* (with the exception of a few instances) seem to avoid the finals *ia, iang,* and *iong*. The alveolar set *d, t, n, l* feels generally uncomfortable with finals begun with *u* and *ü* (with the exception of *u* itself) and there are more gaps than realisations. The alveo-dental fricatives *z, c, s* are choosy customers, they miss out such finals as *ei, ua, uai, uang,* and *ueng* besides all those beginning with *i* and *ü* as mentioned earlier. The final *ueng* (like the *e* variant and the erised vowel *er*) may only be used on its own.

All the finals may be preceded by a zero initial except *ong*.

PINYIN ORTHOGRAPHY

As *pinyin* symbols are used in the present book as notational representations of the language's phonological system, we are in this section concerned with their orthographical conventions.

In actual phonetic reproduction, whether spoken or written, of all finals beginning with *i* when preceded by a zero initial, the *semi-vowel* symbol *y* is introduced in *pinyin* to replace this *i* (e.g. *ia* → *ya, iong* → *yong*) except in the case of a single-vowel *i* or *ü* or finals begun with *i* or *ü* where the semi-vowel *y* is added to the syllable and the umlaut above *u* is no longer necessary (e.g. *i* → *yi, ü* → *yu, ün* → *yun*). Similarly, in all finals beginning with *u* when preceded by a zero initial, the semi-vowel symbol *w* is introduced to replace this *u* (e.g. *ua* → *wa, ueng* → *weng*) except in the case of a single-vowel *u* itself where the semi-vowel *w* is added to the syllable (e.g. *u* → *wu*).

As we have already mentioned briefly in a footnote, *pinyin* orthography also requires that the triphthongs *iou* and *uei* become respectively *iu* and *ui* when initialised (e.g. 'diou' → *diu*, 'kuei' → *kui*) and respectively *you* and *wei* when zero-initialised. Apart from these two triphthongs, the nasal final *uen* also needs to change orthographically into *un* when initialised (e.g. 'kuen' → *kun*) and to *wen* when zero-initialised.

In line with general *pinyin* orthographical tradition the umlaut over *ü* naturally disappears (as in the case of *yu*) when *ü* comes after *j, q,* and *x* (e.g. *ju, que, xuan*). In fact, the umlaut is only retained in the following four syllables: *nü, nüe, lü, lüe* in the entire lexicon.

To recapitulate the syllabic structure table in terms of *pinyin*, we will quote here a few examples of actual monosyllabic words containing simple vowels:[6]

---

[6] The examples given are unspecified for tones. The English annotations are given only to indicate the first (or level) tone realisations of these syllables.

(1) V   **a** 'an interjection'
(2) CV   **ta** 'he'; 'she'; 'it'
(3) VC   **an** 'peaceful'
(4) CVC   **tang** 'soup'

In the case of a disyllabic word, an *apostrophe* is introduced between the two syllables if the second syllable begins with a vowel rather than a consonant: e.g.

(5) CV + V   **bei'ai** 'sorrowful'
             ping'an 'safe and sound'[7]

If no apostrophe is present in a disyllabic word, then it is taken for granted that the second syllable begins with a consonant rather than a vowel, e.g.

fangan is **fangan** 'disgust'   rather than   **fang'an** 'programme'

In *pinyin* orthography, capital letters are also adopted to indicate proper names, e.g. *Beijing* 'Beijing'. However, as we use *pinyin* only for phonetic notation purposes in this book, we will not use capitals.

TONES AND TONE SANDHI

Chinese has always been a tone language. Modern Standard Chinese has four word tones. Being differentiators of meaning, their association with individual monosyllables is determined by convention. In *pinyin*, these tones are specified by a tone mark (or diacritic) over the *main vowel* of the syllable.[8] If no tone mark appears over a syllable, it means that the syllable is unstressed. For example, the same syllable *ma* may occur in any of the four tones or have no tone at all. The four tones always appear in the following order and can, therefore, be labelled respectively as the first, the second, the third and the fourth tone:

1st tone (**yīnpíng** 阴平)   **mā** 'mother'
2nd tone (**yángpíng** 阳平)   **má** 'hemp'
3rd tone (**shǎngshēng** 上声)   **mǎ** 'horse'
4th tone (**qùshēng** 去声)   **mà** 'scold'
unstressed (**qīngshēng** 轻声)   **ma** end-of-sentence particle for the
  (non-tone)   formulation of a general question

If we adopt Chao Yuen-ren's five-level differentiation (which does not specify absolute values and is relative to individual speakers), the contour of each of the four tones in Chinese may be represented thus:

---

[7] The English phrasal annotation 'safe and sound' does not alter the fact that *ping'an* is a disyllabic word (rather than an expression) in Chinese.
[8] In diphthongs and triphthongs, the main vowels are always *a, e, o*, while *i, u, ü* are usually medials. The tone diacritics therefore invariably fall on *a, e, o* except in the cases of *ao*, where the tone mark is to be placed over *a*, and *iu*, where the tone mark is to go over *u*, and *ui*, where the tone mark is to go on *i*, since the latter two are actually standard *pinyin* orthographical abbreviations of *iou* and *uei*.

	1st tone *level*	2nd tone *rise*	3rd tone *fall-rise*	4th tone *fall*
5 high				
4 mid-high				
3 mid				
2 mid-low				
1 low				
numerical tonotation:[9]	5–5	3–5	2–1–4	5–1

Despite the fact that tones are word-specific, *tone sandhi* may still occur between two consecutive tones in a disyllabic word or expression. It usually takes place in a third tone followed by another tone or non-tone (i.e. an unstressed syllable) or between two consecutive third tones. In the former case, the preceding third tone loses its rising inflection and becomes a low tone (i.e. 2–1–4 → 2–1), e.g. **lǎoshī** 'teacher', **yǔyán** 'language', **bǐjiào** 'compare', **lǐbian** 'inside'; and in the latter case, the preceding third tone becomes a second (i.e. 2–1–4 → 3–5), e.g. **shuǐguǒ** 'fruit' becomes **shuíguǒ**, and **yǒuhǎo** 'friendly' becomes **yóuhǎo**. When there are three successive third tones in a word, the first two third tones must both be rendered as second tones while the tone of the last syllable remains unchanged, e.g. **zhǎnlǎnguǎn** 'exhibition hall' → **zhánlánguǎn**, **xiǎozǔzhǎng** 'group leader' → **xiáozúzhǎng**, etc.

Tone sandhi also occurs between two consecutive fourth tones. Under such circumstances, the fall in the preceding fourth tone is truncated (i.e. 5–1 → 5–3), e.g. **diànhuà** 'telephone', **zhàoxiàng** 'take a photograph', **mìmì** 'secret', **lìyì** 'benefit', **shìjiè** 'world', etc.

Apart from these systematic tone changes, tone sandhi may also happen by convention in a specific set of words in the lexicon when they are followed by words of different tones. This set includes numericals: **yī** 'one', **qī** 'seven', **bā** 'eight', and the negator **bù** 'not'. For example,

yī	on its own or not followed by other tones	**dì yī** 'first'
yī → **yí**	when followed by a fourth tone	**yí yàng** 'the same'
yī → **yì**	when followed by other tones	**yì tiān** 'one day' **yì nián** 'a year' **yì běn** 'a copy'
qī/bā	on their own or followed by tones other than a fourth	**qī/bā tiān** '7/8 days' **qī/bā nián** '7/8 years' **qī/bā běn** '7/8 copies'
qī/bā → **qí/bá**	when followed by a fourth tone	**qí/bá cì** '7/8 times'
bù	on its own or followed by tones other than a fourth	**bù duō** 'not much' **bù xíng** 'won't do' **bù hǎo** 'not good'
bù → **bú**	when followed by a fourth tone	**bú duì** 'incorrect'

[9] Tonotation is a coined abbreviation of 'tone notation'.

Tone sandhi may also occur by choice in adverbial or adjectival reduplications: e.g.

màn 'slow'	→ mànmàn 'slowly'	→ mànmān(r)
gānjìng 'clean'	→ gāngānjìngjìng 'neat and tidy'	→ gānganjīngjīng
jímáng 'hurriedly'	→ jíjímángmáng 'in a hurry'	→ jíjimāngmāng

where we can see that in a disyllabic reduplication, the second syllable may choose to become a first tone (usually with some kind of erisation[10] at the speaker's discretion), and in a quadrisyllabic reduplication, the second syllable often becomes unstressed and the last two syllables may become first tones no matter what tones they were originally in.

All these tone sandhi applications are actually more or less rule-governed and will not generally be reflected in the *pinyin* or phonetic notations of the disyllabic words or expressions in question.

WORD STRESS

Word stress in Chinese coincides with tones. An unstressed syllable naturally loses its tones. Generally speaking, all monosyllabic words which have lexical meanings are tonal and therefore stressed (e.g. **dà** 'big', **xiǎo** 'small', etc.) and only those monosyllabic words which are grammatical or functional in nature are toneless and therefore unstressed (e.g. **de** 'a particle introducing an attributive', **ne** 'an indicator for special questions', etc.). In any disyllabic word, if there is an unstressed syllable present, it is always the second and never the first. In other words, the two syllables of a disyllabic word are either evenly stressed or tied in with a trochaic rather than iambic rhythm. For example,

xiūxi to rest	**shétou** tongue
dǎsuan to plan	**lìhai** terrible

Unstressed syllables do not have a tone yet they acquire a *pitch* with reference to the preceding tone in accordance with the five tone-level scheme. When an unstressed syllable follows a first (level) or second (rising) tone, it is pitched at mid (i.e. 3) level; when it follows a third (falling-rising) tone, it is pitched at mid-high (i.e. 4) level; when it follows a fourth (falling) tone, it is pitched at low (i.e. 1) level.[11]

Loss of stress in a word is more often not only the loss of tone but also the abbreviation or *schwarisation*[12] of originally fuller vowels in the unstressed syllable.[13] For example,

---

[10] See section on *erisation* and sound assimilation.
[11] Hu, Yushu (胡裕树) 1981: 131.
[12] 'Schwarisation' was coined to mean that a full vowel is reduced phonetically to [ə].
[13] Hu, Yushu (胡裕树) 1981: 132.

zuǐba 'mouth'	→	zuǐbə
ěrduo 'ear'	→	ěrdo
xǐhuan 'to like'	→	xǐhuə
chūqu 'go out'	→	chūqə

Schwarisation is, in fact, often accompanied by the *vocalisation* of the consonant in the unaccented syllable.

Unstressed syllables with nasal or fricative initials (involving simple vowel finals like *i, u, e*) tend to lose their vowel quality altogether and retain only the nasal and fricative elements, particularly in quick delivery:

bízi 'nose'	→	bíz
yìsi 'meaning'	→	yìs
dōngxi 'thing'	→	dōngx
dòufu 'beancurd'	→	dòuf
wǒmen 'we'; 'us'	→	wǒm

Unstressing usually occurs with functional words or mononyms like the following:

(1) grammatical particles:
   ba an imperative marker
   le a sentence particle
   guo experiential aspect indicator
   ge a common measure word for nouns

(2) suffixes:
   nǎr 'where'
   háizi 'child'
   shítou 'stone'
   shénme 'what'

(3) some location or direction indicators:
   jiā li 'at home'
   tiān shang 'in the sky'
   lǐbian 'inside'
   zǒu jìnqu 'walk in'

(4) second syllable of a reduplication:
   māma 'mother'
   bàba 'father'
   kànkan 'have a look'
   xiǎngxiang 'consider it for a moment'

Stress or non-stress in the second syllable of a disyllabic word may sometimes differentiate meaning:

duìtóu 'on the right track'	duìtou 'adversary'
lìhài 'advantages and disadvantages'	lìhai 'devastating'
dàyì 'gist'	dàyi 'careless'

Otherwise, unstressing is just a question of convention or non-emphasis derived from the context, e.g.:

pútao 'grape'	**yǎnjing** 'eye'	**shìqing** 'affair'
dìfang 'place'	**yuèliang** 'moon'	**nuǎnhuo** 'nice and warm'

yī:	**kàn yi kàn** 'have a look'	**xiǎng yi xiǎng** 'think about it'
bù:	**chībukāi** 'unpopular'	**qù bu qù** 'would like to go or not'

*ER*ISATION AND SOUND ASSIMILATION

By '*erisation*' is meant the potential addition of an unstressed 'r' at the end of all finals (except the variant *e* and the simple vowel *er*, where *r* has already been built in), e.g.

huà	→	**huàr**	'picture'
gē	→	**gēr**	'song'
niǎo	→	**niǎor**	'bird'
yīdiǎn	→	**yīdiǎnr**	'a little'

In the case of *n* or *ng* finals, *n* and *ng* are sometimes dropped to give way to *r*: e.g.

huāyuán	→	**huāyuár**	'garden'
bāngmáng	→	**bāngmar**	'to help'

Apart from being a distinctive habit of speakers from the Beijing area, erisation generally serves to encode syntactic, semantic and stylistic differences, e.g.:

xìn 'letter'	vs	**xìr** 'oral message'	semantic
tóu 'head'	vs	**tóur** 'ringleader'	semantic
gài 'to cover'	vs	**gàir** 'a cover'	syntactic
huà 'to draw'	vs	**huàr** 'a drawing'	syntactic
xiǎohái 'child'	vs	**xiǎoháir** (endearing) 'little child'	stylistic
gùnzi 'a stick'	vs	**gùnr** (diminutive) 'small stick'	stylistic

In rapid speech, *sound assimilation* is more likely to occur. For example, when spoken quickly, **guǎngbō** 'broadcast' may become **guǎmbō**, and **shénme** 'what' may become **shém**.

A most prevailing phenomenon of such assimilation in Chinese is the phonological adaptation (with accompanying graphetic changes[14]) of the exclamatory

---

[14] The graphetic changes of **ā** 啊 are: **yā** 呀, **wā** 哇, **lā** 啦, **nā** 哪.

particle ā at the end of a sentence in keeping with the nature of the sound that precedes it. For example,

-ng, [ŋ], [ɻ]	+	ā	=	ā
-a, -o, -e, -i, -ü	+	ā	=	yā
-u	+	ā	=	wā
-le	+	ā	=	lā
-n	+	ā	=	nā

DIALECTAL INTERFERENCE

In Modern Standard Chinese, the retroflex consonants *zh*, *ch* and *sh* are clearly differentiated from the alveo-dental set *z*, *c*, and *s*. However, whilst the distinction is important for the learner-speaker of the language, he or she must also be prepared to accept the fact that native speakers, particularly those from the south of the country or Taiwan and who are originally other dialect speakers, might not, through carelessness or ignorance, make any difference in pronunciation between words beginning with *zh*, *ch* and *sh* and their non-retroflex counterparts *z*, *c*, *s*.

South of Yangtse dialect speakers may also mix up *n* and *ng* endings, pronouncing all *n* finals as *ng* finals, and Cantonese speakers do not usually distinguish between *n* and *l* and will, like other dialect speakers, more often than not, literally replace *r* initial with the semi-vowel *y*, and replace *h* with *f*.

Tones present even greater problems for native speakers from different regions, whether they are educated or not. The non-native-speaking learner will soon have to learn to deduce meaning from the context rather than from the actual pronunciation or tonalisation of the words dropped from a native speaker's lips.

SYLLABLES VERSUS WORDS

Phonological habits of the language make use of only 413 actual syllables through the combination of the language's existing initials and finals. If a few exceptional syllables like *hm*, *hng*, *m*, *n*, *ng* are added, the actual number of monosyllables used by the language is (413 + 5 =) 418 in total.[15]

In theory, the potential number of tonal syllables available for the language should come up to at least (418 × 4 =) 1,672 and with the addition of unaccented syllables, the total usable syllables should be (1,672 + 418 =) 2,090.

[15] Cf. Zhong, Qin (钟棪) 1978; Hu, Bingzhong (胡炳忠) 1978.

However, language is not codified with strict logic: not all the 418 mono-syllables are used with all the four tones or found to be equally unstressed. For example, *sēn* is only found in the first tone, *fó* in the second, *nuǎn* in the third, *cè* in the fourth, and *me* as an unaccented syllable. The actual number of heterotonic monosyllables used in the language therefore only adds up to around 1,273.[16]

It is these 1,273 monosyllables and their combinations, particularly their disyllabic combinations, that form the bulk of the Chinese lexicon, which is inevitably replete with *homophones*, whether *homotonic* or *heterotonic*, e.g.

homotonically:	**tián** 'field'	**tián** 'sweet'	**tián** 'fill in'
	tiánjìng '(sport) track and field'	**tiánjìng** 'tranquil'	
heterotonically:	**tiān** 'sky'	**tiǎn** 'lick'	**tiàn** 'dip (brush) in ink'
	tiānjǐng 'courtyard'		

Of course, homophonic clashes happen more often in monosyllabic words rather than disyllabic words[17] or multisyllabic expressions or idioms. In the former case, the clarification of the ambiguity in question may only come from the context.

Now we can give an overall view of the phonological representation of the lexical items in the Chinese language.

As we have already seen, a word or expression in Chinese may consist of one such monosyllable as analysed above, e.g.:

V:	**è**	'hungry'	**ài**	'to love'
CV:	**pá**	'climb'	**wǒ**	'I'; 'me'
VC:	**àn**	'dark'	**èn**	'to press'
CVC:	**dàn**	'egg'	**dēng**	'lamp'; 'light'

or a combination of two or more such syllables. Theoretically, there are six-teen possible disyllabic combinations and sixty-two trisyllabic ones. Here are some examples,

---

[16] The number of syllables using any particular tones:

1st tone:	330
2nd tone:	247
3rd tone:	312
4th tone:	353
the unaccented tone:	31
	1,273

[17] Some scholars believe that the disyllabification tendency of the language is a design feature to counteract the prevailing homophonic clashes latent in monosyllables.

V + CV:	**àihù** 'cherish'	**àohuǐ** 'to regret', 'to repent'
CV + V:	**kě'ài** 'lovely'	**jiāo'ào** 'proud'
CVC + V:	**tiān'é** 'swan'	**chǒng'ài** 'dote on'
CV + CV:	**gōngzuò** 'work'; 'to work'	**xiūxi** 'to rest'
CV + CVC:	**xǐhuan** 'to like'	**shíjiān** 'time'
CVC + CV:	**jǐngchá** 'policeman'	**tóngyì** 'agree'
CVC + CVC:	**shēngyīn** 'sound, voice'	**gēnběn** 'fundamental, essential'
CV + CV + CV:	**zìláishuǐ** 'tap water'	
CV + CV + CVC:	**yóudìyuán** 'postman'	
CVC + CV + CVC:	**chuàngshǐrén** 'founder'	
CVC + CVC + CVC:	**yùndòngchǎng** 'playground'[18]	

Trisyllabic combinations may in fact be either words (as quoted above) or set expressions (particularly vernacular phrasal verbs) while all combinations of more than three syllables are usually idioms or established phrases:

kāi yèchē[19]	'work late into the night', 'burn the midnight oil'
dá jiāodao	'come into contact with', 'have dealings with'
huǎnchōng dìdài	'buffer zone'
qí hǔ nán xià	'he who rides a tiger finds it difficult to dismount' – 'irrevocably but unwillingly committed'
yī wèn sān bù zhī	'know nothing', 'be entirely ignorant' (lit. 'three don't-knows even when asked once')
léishēng dà, yǔdiǎn xiǎo	'much talk, little action' (lit. 'the thunderclap is loud, the raindrops are small')
dǎpò shāguō wèn dào dǐ	'insist on getting to the bottom of the matter' (lit. 'break the clay pot in such a way that the crack goes right to the bottom')

[18] The combinations given in the list are not meant to be exhaustive.

[19] Please note that the writing conventions of *pinyin* with reference to particular words or idioms do not necessarily coincide with the speech rhythm of the linguistic items in question, e.g. *kāi yèchē* is usually said in the rhythm of **kāiyè** | **chē** and *dǎ pò shāguō wèn dào dǐ*, in the rhythm of **dǎ pò** | **shāguō** | **wèn dào** | **dǐ**. In other words, everything is usually said in a disyllabic trochaic rhythm.

As a general rule, quadrisyllabic expressions are classical idioms, e.g.:

jīngshén dǒusǒu	'in high spirits', 'in excellent form'
duìniú tánqín	'cast pearls before swine' (lit. 'play lute to a cow')
lǐ suǒ dāngrán	'as a matter of course'
kān jiā běnlǐng	'one's stock-in-trade' (lit. 'the skill to look after one's home')
tóutóu shì dào	'clear and logical'
yī sī bù gǒu	'conscientious and meticulous'

There are only a very small number of quadrisyllables which may probably be regarded as words, e.g.:

shèhuìzhǔyì	'socialism'
xíng'érshàngxué	'metaphysics'

2 THE GRAPHETIC COMPOSITION OF THE CHINESE LEXICON

The written equivalent of a monosyllable in Chinese is a graphic form composed of a varying number of *strokes* and confined to a square-shaped area. In linguistic parlance, it may be called a *grapheme*. However, in everyday language, such a grapheme is usually known as a *character*. The number of strokes in such a character ranges from 1 in the simplest to 36 in the most complicated[1] (averaging around 10 strokes per character – based on the 7,000 characters normally used – or 9 strokes – based on the most commonly used 3,500 characters).[2] Here are some examples:

一 **yī** 'one'	(1 stroke)
人 **rén** 'person'	(2 strokes)
小 **xiǎo** 'small'	(3 strokes)
风 **fēng** 'wind'	(4 strokes)
他 **tā** 'he'; 'him'	(5 strokes)
我 **wǒ** 'I'; 'me'	(7 strokes)
国 **guó** 'country'	(8 strokes)
说 **shuō** 'speak'	(9 strokes)
矗 **chù** (formal) 'stand tall and upright'	(24 strokes)

A monosyllabic word in the language will therefore be represented by one such grapheme, a disyllabic word by two such graphemes, and a multisyllabic word or expression by as many such graphemes as there are syllables.

THE BASIC MONOSTROKES

The above-quoted characters, simple or complicated, are formed by using a set of 8 basic monostrokes.[3] All monostrokes are supposed to be executed with one continuous movement of the writing brush:

---

[1] In Modern Standard Chinese, the simplest character is 一 **yī** 'one' and the most complicated is 齉 **nàng** 'snuffle'; 'speak with a twang'. In classical Chinese, the most complicated word had as many as sixty-eight strokes with four complex forms of 龍 **lóng** 'dragon' written in two rows one on top of the other like this: 䨻, to mean 'garrulous'.

[2] Cf. Zhang, Jingxian (张静贤) 1992: 12–13.

[3] Zhang Jingxian (张静贤) (See above note p. 33), on the basis of the 6,196 characters given in 印刷通用汉字字形表 (1965), concludes that horizontal stroke 一 (including 𠃊) accounts for 27.68%, vertical stroke 丨, 17.60%, left-falling stroke 丿, 15.95%, dot stroke 丶, 13.62%, and right-falling stroke 乀, 2.97%.

(1) 一 horizontal stroke (called 横 **héng**)
(2) 丨 vertical stroke (called 竖 **shù**)
(3) 丶 dot stroke (called 点 **diǎn**)
(4) 丿 rising stroke (called 提 **tí**)
(5) 丿 left-falling stroke (called 撇 **piě**)
(6) 乀 right-falling stroke (called 捺 **nà**)
(7) 乛 horizontal bend stroke (called 横折 **héngzhé**)
(8) 乚 vertical bend stroke (called 竖折 **shùzhé**)

With rising and falling strokes, the angle of rising or falling may change aesthetically to accommodate a position relative to other strokes in the character for balance or contrast. Compare the following pairs of characters where a rising or falling stroke in particular is found to be executed at a different angle either owing to the overall arrangement or when there is a similar stroke immediately present at the top or by the side: e.g.

rising:	冰 **bīng** 'ice'	vs	刁 **diāo** 'sly'
left-falling:	手 **shǒu** 'hand'	vs	川 **chuān** 'river'
right-falling:	天 **tiān** 'sky'; 'heaven'	vs	奏 **zòu** 'perform (a musical composition)'
	火 **huǒ** 'fire'	vs	炎 **yán** 'inflammation'; 'hot'
	人 **rén** 'person'	vs	从 **cóng** 'from'; 'follow'
	木 **mù** 'wood'	vs	林 **lín** 'woods'

We might have already noticed from the examples quoted above that four of these basic monostrokes may have a number of '*bend* or *hook*' extensions:[4] e.g.:

(1) The horizontal stroke 一 may have the following common extensions:
　　乛 with a hook　　　　　　as in 买 **mǎi** 'buy' and 你 **nǐ** 'you'
　　乛 with a leftward bend　　as in 又 **yòu** 'again'

(2) The vertical stroke 丨 may have the following common extensions:
　　亅 with a hook　　　　　　as in 到 **dào** 'arrive'
　　ㄥ with a reverse hook　　as in 切 **qiē** 'cut (downwards)'

(3) The horizontal bend stroke 乛 may have common extensions like:
　　乛 with a hook　　　　　　　　　　as in the first character of
　　　　　　　　　　　　　　　　　　　　司机 **sījī** 'driver';
　　　　　　　　　　　　　　　　　　　　'chauffeur'
　　乚 with a reverse hook　　　　　　as in 认 **rèn** 'recognise'
　　乁 with the bend slanting rightward　as in 飞 **fēi** 'to fly'
　　　and ending with a reverse hook
　　ㄅ with the bend begun with another　as in the second character
　　　bend, slanting leftward and　　　　of 吃亏 **chīkuī**
　　　ending with a hook　　　　　　　　'suffer losses'

---

[4] Cf. Fei, Jinchang (费锦昌) 1996.2: 107–13.

(4) The vertical bend stroke └ may have common extensions like:
     乚 with a reverse hook   as in 扎 **zā** 'to tie'; 'to bind'
     乙 with the bend begun with   as in the first character of
          another bend, slanting leftward   艺术 **yìshù** 'art'
          and ending with a reverse hook

All these graphetic extensions, as we can see, are based on the principle of incorporating bends at the beginning or hooks at the end. It is important to understand that being extensions of the original monostrokes, they must also be executed with a continuous and uninterrupted movement of the writing instrument so that they remain monostrokes. Such variations may be mnemonically remembered as modifications 'by hook or by crook'.

THE STYLISED PATTERNS

These monostrokes (or their extensions) may first combine into rudimentary patterns, which may either become a character itself or further combine to form a more complicated character. A character may itself represent a monosyllabic word in the language or it may come together with one or two other characters to form a disyllabic or trisyllabic word. This build-up from monostrokes to a stylised pattern, then to a character and finally to a word may be profitably viewed as a four-*tier* system, which can be clearly defined in a chart like the following. However, it must be remembered that in such a system there is theoretically no limit to the number of combinations which can be gone into at each tier, particularly at the third tier, and a character or a word may be formed at any tier:

	monostrokes →	*stylised patterns* →	*characters* →	*words*
1st tier	一 + 丿 →	厂		
2nd tier		厂 + 又 →	友	
3rd tier			朋 + 友	
4th tier			→	朋友 'friend'

Here is another example, in which one finds a word at every stage:

	monostrokes →	*stylised patterns* →	*characters*	→	*words*
1st tier	十 + 一 →	土			
	'ten' + 'one' →	'soil'			
2nd tier		土 + 也 →	地		
		'soil' + 'also'	'land'		
3rd tier			地 + 方		
			'land' + 'square'		
4th tier				→	地方
					'place'

Fei Jinchang (费锦昌), basing his investigation on the 3,500 commonly used characters in the language, identifies around (384 – 8 basic monostrokes =) 376 meaningful or less meaningful stylised patterns, while China's Language Reform Commission in collaboration with the Wuhan University identifies 648 such stylised patterns, based on the 16,296 characters listed in the 1979 edition of *Cihai* (辞海) and a few dozen others.[5] Some of these patterns (plus some others built on these patterns) have been identified as *radicals* in contemporary Chinese dictionaries,[6] e.g.

宀 'roof'
疒 'illness'
皿 **mǐn** 'utensil'
口 **kǒu** 'mouth'
虫 **chóng** 'insect'
舟 **zhōu** 'boat'

Other less semantically homogeneous patterns include, e.g.

彡 which has different associations in different characters:

colour:	彩色 **cǎisè** 'multicolour'
shade:	影子 **yǐngzi** 'shadow'
light:	彪炳 **biāobǐng** 'shining'; 'splendid'
sound:	澎 **pēng** 'splash'; 'spatter'
beard:	胡须 **húxū** 'beard'; 'moustache'; 'whiskers'

厶 which has contrastive semantic functions in different characters:

宏伟 **hóngwěi** 'magnificent'; 'grand'	vs	幺麽 **yāomó** (formal) 'petty'; 'insignificant'
公 **gōng** 'public'	vs	私 **sī** 'private'

When these patterns or radicals, whether meaningful or not, are not used on their own as words, but placed alongside other meaningful or less meaningful patterns to form individual characters (particularly when they form the left-hand or top/bottom component of a written character), they are generally modified, sometimes quite drastically, to fit into the reduced space allowed them in the square:

(1) the whole pattern being modified:

人 **rén** 'person'	→	亻	as in	住 **zhù** 'live'
衣 **yī** 'clothes'	→	衤		衬衫 **chènshān** 'shirt'
食 **shí** 'food'	→	饣		饭 **fàn** 'cooked rice'; 饿 **è** 'hungry'

[5] Zhang, Jingxian (张静贤) 1992: 50–1. The difference in the number of stylised patterns between the Commission and Fei Jinchang is perhaps due to the fact that the latter bases his differentiation on 3,500 commonly used characters and fails to include composites like ⺕, etc.
[6] The discernible number of radicals in the language is generally accepted to range from 189 to 214.

手 **shǒu** 'hand'	→	扌	打 **dǎ** 'hit'; 'beat'; 拉 **lā** 'pull'
水 **shuǐ** 'water'	→	氵	河流 **héliú** 'rivers'
心 **xīn** 'heart'	→	忄	怕 **pà** 'afraid'; 懒 **lǎn** 'lazy'
言 **yán** 'words'	→	讠	说话 **shuōhuà** 'say something'
金 **jīn** 'gold'; 'metal'	→	钅	钉 **dīng** 'nail'; 钱 **qián** 'money'
竹 **zhú** 'bamboo'	→	⺮	篱笆 **líba** 'bamboo or twig fence'
卉 **huì** 'grass'	→	艹	花 **huā** 'flower'; 草 **cǎo** 'grass'
火 **huǒ** 'fire'	→	灬	煮 **zhǔ** 'boil'; 'cook'

(2) the last stroke modified (e.g. a horizontal stroke becoming a rising one, a right-falling stoke turning into a dot, etc.):

车 **chē** 'car'	→	车	as in	车辆 **chēliàng** 'cars'; 'vehicles'
土 **tǔ** 'earth'; 'soil'	→	圡		土地 **tǔdì** 'land'
足 **zú** 'foot'	→	𧾷		跑 **pǎo** 'run'; 跳 **tiào** 'jump'
木 **mù** 'wood'; 'tree'	→	朩		树林 **shùlín** 'woods'
火 **huǒ** 'fire'	→	火		燃烧 **ránshāo** 'burn'

TRADITIONAL WAYS OF CHARACTER FORMATION

The kind of patterns we have just illustratively differentiated, whether meaningful or not, may nonetheless be seen as formalised graphetic prefabs on which the Chinese lexical script is built. Indeed there are four basic ways in which these prefabs may be utilised or assembled to form individual characters. Besides, two more underlying linguistic motivations may also be clearly discerned to have prompted the formation of new characters following these basic principles. In this section, we will first concentrate on the four basic character formation principles and then discuss the two linguistically motivated processes which have also contributed immensely to setting the character-formulating operation in motion.

The four basic ways in which characters are formed are:

(1) *pictographic*: an original drawing later stylised into a squarish pictograph (象形 **xiàngxíng** lit. 'resembling shape'): e.g.

日 **rì** 'sun' (originally the drawing of a circular sun with a dot inside)
月 **yuè** 'moon' (originally the drawing of a crescent moon with a stroke inside)
女 **nǚ** 'female' (originally the drawing of a woman in a kneeling posture)
母 **mǔ** 'mother' (originally the drawing of a woman whose breasts have been highlighted)

(2) *picto-synthetic*: two or more pictographs combined in a meaningful fashion (会意 **huìyì** lit. 'assembling meaning'): e.g.

明 **míng** 'bright' (日 **rì** 'sun' and 月 **yuè** 'moon' combined)

尘 **chén** 'dust'; 'dirt' (小 **xiǎo** 'small' and 土 **tǔ** 'earth' to indicate 'small particles of earth' combined)

休 **xiū** 'to rest' (亻 'person' and 木 **mù** 'tree' combined to mean that the person is resting in the shade of the tree)

卧 **wò** 'lie down' (臣 'the shape of a mat' and 卜 'a person in a lying position' combined to mean that the person is lying on a mat)

寶 **bǎo** 'treasure' (now simplified as 宝). The original complex form constitutes four meaningful pictographic elements, namely:

宀 'roof'

玉 **yù** 'jade'

缶 **fǒu** (formal) 'earthen jar'

贝 **bèi** 'shell (for money in ancient times)'

to mean that there is jade, pottery, and shells under the roof, that is, in the house).

A particular subset of this type is that one of the meaningful elements in the character is also used as its phonetic: e.g.

抓 **zhuā** 'grab'; 'clutch' – 扌 'hand' juxtaposed with 爪 **zhuǎ** 'claw'; 'paw', which also serves as the phonetic

忘 **wàng** 'forget'; 'let slip from one's mind' – 心 **xīn** 'heart' juxtaposed with 亡 **wáng** 'flee'; 'perish', which also serves as the phonetic

湾 **wān** 'gulf'; 'bay' – 氵 'water' juxtaposed with 弯 **wān** 'curved'; 'bend', which also serves as the phonetic

艉 **wěi** 'stern'; 'rear end of a ship or boat' – 舟 **zhōu** '(formal) boat' juxtaposed with 尾 **wěi** 'tail', which also serves as the phonetic

(3) *picto-logic*: a stroke added to a meaningful pictograph posing as a logical reference point for the matter under discussion (指事 **zhǐshì** lit. 'providing the logical reference'): e.g.

刃 **rèn** 'blade'; 'the edge of a knife' – 刀 **dāo** signifies 'knife' while the dot indicates where the 'blade' is

本 **běn** 'fundamental' – 木 **mù** signifies 'tree' while the horizontal stroke below indicates where the 'root' is

甘 **gān** 'sweet' – a dot is seen inside the mouth to suggest a sweet taste

天 **tiān** 'sky'; 'heaven' – a horizontal stroke 一 written above the head of a person 大 standing with his arms stretched and legs apart indicates where the 'heaven' is

A subset of this picto-logic type consists of characters whose component strokes are purely indicators of an abstract nature: e.g.

一 **yī** 'one'	二 **èr** 'two'	三 **sān** 'three'
上 **shàng** 'up'; 'above'; 'over'		下 **xià** 'down'; 'below'; 'under'
凹 **āo** 'concave'; 'sunken'		凸 **tū** 'convex'; 'protruding'

(4) *picto-phonetic*: a meaning category (known as 'radical') combined with a pronunciation guide (known as 'phonetic') (形声 **xíngshēng** lit. 'integrating shape and sound'): e.g.

妈 **mā** 'mother'; 'mum' – 女 **nǚ** 'female' signifies the meaning, and 马 **mǎ**,[7] the pronunciation

爸 **bà** 'father'; 'dad' – 父 **fù** 'father' signifies the meaning and 巴 **bā**, the pronunciation

护 **hù** 'to protect' – 扌 'hand' is the radical and 户 **hù**, the phonetic

溶 **róng** 'dissolve' – 氵 'water' is the radical and 容 **róng**, the phonetic

As we may see from the character-formation devices described above, the Chinese script, from the start, has never ever totally deviated from a pictographic stance. Even when the script has advanced to a stage where its main concern is to represent the sound of the word[8] in question, traces of this pictographic orientation may still be found in the presence of radicals. However, there are cases, particularly in the area of abstractions, where pictographic devices simply would not work. It is here that purely sound representation truly begins. What happened was a kind of internal borrowing entirely on phonetic grounds – the borrowing of a homophone in the language itself – a process now generally known as *jiǎjiè* (假借) *'borrowing a form for its sound'*. For example, to lexicalise the meaning of 'want', a notion which can hardly be pictorialised, it seems extremely handy that a character which originally depicts a human 'waist' 要 and happens to be pronounced similarly is borrowed for the purpose, despite the fact that there is no linkage of meaning between the two. So the script is suddenly loaded (and, in a way, encumbered) with a new pair of homonyms: one 要 *yào* meaning 'want' and another 要 *yāo* meaning 'waist', and this borrowing process may be endlessly reduplicated. As a safety device against the proliferation of such homonyms, the mechanism of the language finds it easier for the borrower to keep the borrowed form 要 *yào* with the meaning of 'want' and the lender, which usually depicts something more tangible like 'waist' in this case, to undergo reincarnation following the picto-phonetic principle. So a meaning category is added to the original form: the radical 月 *ròu* indicating 'human flesh'[9] is attached to the original 要 to form the new picto-phonetic character of 腰 *yāo* 'waist'. Similarly, to encode the meaning of 'also'; 'too', the original picto-synthetic form 亦 *yì* 'armpit', where the two dots indicate where the armpit is, is borrowed for its resemblance to the intended word in sound. This actually entails the lender's

---

[7] Some of the phonetics built into the characters may be characters or words themselves and therefore meaningful, but their meanings are immaterial to the character in question (e.g. 马 **mǎ** 'horse' in this case has nothing to do with 妈 **mā** 'mother' except for indicating the pronunciation of the latter character).

[8] Chinese characters, in their formative years, are identical with words, i.e. one character, one word.

[9] The radical **ròu** 'human flesh' and the radical **yuè** 'moon' have now become identical in form, both written as 月.

seeking a new coinage in a picto-phonetic form: 腋 *yè*, where 月 indicates 'human flesh' and 夜 *yè* represents the pronunciation.[10] Sometimes, where the lender finds that what it possesses is of no more use on its own, the borrower may completely inherit the borrowed form, keeping its pronunciation while altering its meaning, as, for example, in the case of 笨 *bèn* 'stupid' (with an integrated 𥫗 'bamboo' radical, whose original meaning must be a bamboo utensil of some kind which has fallen into disuse) or 骗 *piàn* 'deceive'; 'cheat' (with an integrated 马 'horse' radical, whose original meaning must be something like 'mounting a horse', which is now obsolete). In these cases, the lenders are completely forgotten.

This borrowing procedure, where necessary, may actually be reversed. This time the borrower may not be thinking in terms of the similarity of sound but that of meaning. If a meaning may draw inspiration from a near synonym or meaning-related item in the existing repertoire, there is no point in inventing a completely new form out of the blue. It seems convenient again for the borrower to borrow, if only partially, from existing forms to save whatever effort can be saved. For example, it so happened that the meaning of 'deceased father' finds a semantic overlap in the character 老 *lǎo* 'old (man)' and, deciding to borrow part of its form and pronunciation, comes up with 考 *kǎo*, retaining the top written element and vowel quality of the borrowed form. Now another meaning 'filial' also finds a meaning association with 老 *lǎo*, and following the picto-synthetic principle described earlier, it replaces the lower element of the borrowed form by 子 *zǐ* 'son' and coins a new character 孝 *xiào*, again retaining the top element and the vowel quality of the borrowed form. This process, which has been variously understood and interpreted by linguists and philologists over the years, is generally known as *zhuǎnzhù* (转注), that is, '*modelling on a form for its meaning*'.[11] Similar examples may be found in pairs like 没 *mò* 'submerge, disappear' and 殁 *mò* '(formal) die' (a change from 氵 'water' to 歹 'bones') and 在 *zài* 'exist' and 存 *cún* 'survive' (a change from 土 'land' to 子 'person'), where the script and the pronunciation in either case are partially retained or modelled upon.

NEW FORMATIVE DEVICES IN SIMPLIFIED CHARACTERS

The basic ways and processes of character formation described above have been time-honoured practices of the language since the very early stages.

---

[10] Note that there is a change of pronunciation from **yì** to **yè** as the original character rejuvenates itself in a different form.

[11] Cf. different interpretations of this type of character formation put forward by Liang, Donghan (梁东汉) 1959: 149–51; Fu, Donghua (傅东华) 1957: 27–8. Fu's interpretation is closer to what is presented here by us.

However, from *The Simplification Table* (汉字简化方案) promulgated by the Chinese government in January 1956, it may also be seen that new character-forming devices were adopted to cope with the simplification task in hand and four such new approaches can be identified:[12]

(1) retaining only the *contour* of the original form:

    e.g. 夺 **duó** 'seize'; 'take by force' instead of 奪

            伞 **sǎn** 'umbrella' instead of 傘

(2) reserving a *characteristic element* of the original form:[13]

    e.g. 电 **diàn** 'electricity' instead of 電

            声 **shēng** 'sound' instead of 聲

            从 **cóng** 'from'; 'follow' instead of 從

(3) regularising a popular *cursive form* of the original character:

    e.g. 书 **shū** 'book' instead of 書

            为 **wéi** 'do'; 'act' instead of 為

(4) replacing a complex or repetitive part in the original with *symbolic strokes*:

    e.g. 区 **qū** 'district'; 'region' instead of 區

            搀 **chān** 'support sb by the arm'; 'mix' instead of 攙

Whatever the ways of formulation and reformulation, it is the category of picto-phonetic characters which dominates the whole lexicon, comprising around 90 per cent of the characters in present-day use. It is therefore important for us to examine in greater detail the composition of this type of characters, first the radicals and then the phonetics.

THE RADICALS

Radicals in picto-phonetic characters may be regarded as meaning categories. They suggest broadly the area of meaning to which, for example, a particular character of this type belongs. Apart from a few radicals which are employed purely for the sake of their form (e.g. 丶, 丿, 一, 乙, etc.) and a few others whose meaning has been lost in the words that share them (e.g. 己, 艮, 辰, 臣, etc.), most of the 189 radicals commonly adopted by dictionaries may be divided into the following semantic domains:[14]

[12] Zhang, Jingxian (张静贤) 1992: 25–26.
[13] In some cases, this is a return to the primitive forms of the characters concerned, whose more elaborate forms in use before simplification are in fact brought about by the sound-borrowing process (**jiǎjiè** 假借) discussed earlier.
[14] Cf. Pan, Ziyou (潘自由) 1987.

(1) *Human beings themselves*

    (a) human beings in varying forms:

人	as in	众 **zhòng** 'crowd'
亻		代 **dài** 'replace'; 'represent'
儿		见 **jiàn** 'see'
卩 (kneeling)		叩 **kòu** 'kowtow'
巳 (kneeling)		跪 **guì** 'kneel'
大 (with outstretched arms)		天 **tiān** 'heaven'
尢 (crippled)		尤 **yóu** 'particularly'
尸 (corpse)		尾 **wěi** 'tail'
子 (child)		籽 **zǐ** 'seed'
女 (woman kneeling)		奴婢 **núbì** 'slave and maid'
比 (two people side by side)		皆 **jiē** 'both'; 'all'

    (b) body parts:

body:	身	躯 **qū** 'body'
chest:	文	纹 **wén** 'lines'; 'wrinkle'; 'tattoo'
breast:	母	母 **mǔ** (formal) 'mother'
	毋	毋 **wú** (formal) 'do not'
hand:	又	受 **shòu** 'accept'
	攵	收 **shōu** 'receive'
	攴	敲 **qiāo** 'knock'; 'tap'
	扌	打 **dǎ** 'hit'; 'beat'
	廾 (two hands)	弄 **nòng** 'handle'; 'play with'
	手	拿 **ná** 'hold (in hand)'
	爫	采 **cǎi** 'pick (fruit)'
wrist:	寸	付 **fù** 'pay (money)'
foot:	夕	舞 **wǔ** 'dance'
	舛	舛错 **chuǎncuò** 'mishap'
	𧾷	踢 **tī** 'kick'
mouth:	口	吃 **chī** 'eat'
tongue:	舌	舔 **tiǎn** 'lick'
tooth:	齿	啮 **niè** 'gnaw'
eye:	目	瞪 **dèng** 'stare at'
nose:	自	鼻 **bí** 'nose'
	鼻	打鼾 **dǎhān** 'snore'
ear:	耳	聋 **lóng** 'deaf'
head:	页	颈 **jǐng** 'neck'
hair:	毛 (on body)	毫毛 **háomáo** 'soft hair on body'
	髟 (on head)	髻 **jì** (of hair) 'bun'
skin:	皮	皱 **zhòu** 'wrinkled'; 'creased'
flesh:	月	皮肤 **pífū** 'skin'
bone:	骨	骷髅 **kūlóu** 'skeleton'
	歹 (broken bones)	死 **sǐ** 'die'

blood:	血	鼻衄 **bínǜ** 'nosebleed'
heart:	忄	情 **qíng** 'feeling'
	心	想 **xiǎng** 'think'
	小	恭敬 **gōngjìng** 'respectful'

(d) actions, activities or states:

speech:	言	信 **xìn** 'letter'; 'message'
	讠	说 **shuō** 'speak'
embrace:	勹	包 **bāo** 'wrap' and
		抱 **bào** 'embrace'
eat:	饣	饭 **fàn** 'cooked rice'
yawn:	欠	吹 **chuī** 'to blow'
see:	见	观 **guān** 'observe'
walk:	走	赶 **gǎn** 'to hurry (to a place)'
stand:	立	站 **zhàn** 'stand'
separate:	八	分 **fēn** 'divide'
ill:	疒	病 **bìng** 'illness'
old:	老	耄耋 **màodié** 'aged 70 to 90'

(e) senses:

colour:	白	白皑皑 **bái'ái'ái** 'pure white'
	黑	黑黝黝 **hēiyōuyōu** 'shiny black'
sound:	音	韵 **yùn** 'rhyme'
taste:	辛	辣 **là** 'spicy'; 'peppery'; 'hot'
	卤	卤 **lǔ** 'stew in soy sauce'

(2) *Nature*

(a) natural surroundings:

cliff:	厂	厅 **tīng** 'hall'; 'lounge'
mountain:	山	山岭 **shānlǐng** 'a chain of
		mountains'
cave:	穴	空 **kōng** 'empty'; 'hollow'
stone:	石	岩石 **yánshí** 'rock'
field:	田	田 **tián** '(paddy) field' and
		界 **jiè** 'boundary'

(b) natural phenomena:

vapour:	气	氧气 **yǎngqì** 'oxygen'
rain:	雨	雾 **wù** 'fog'
ice:	冫	冷 **lěng** 'cold'
sun:	日	晴 **qíng** '(of weather) fine'
moon:	月	明朗 **mínglǎng** 'bright'
night:	夕	夜 **yè** 'night' and
		汐 **xī** 'evening tide'

(c) five elements:[15]

| water: | 水 | 尿 **niào** 'urine' |
| | 氵 | 清 **qīng** 'clear' |

[15] Cf. Chapter 8.

earth:	土	尘 **chén** 'dust'
	圡	坟 **fén** 'tomb'; 'grave'
fire:	火	炙 **jiǔ** 'moxibustion'
	灬	热 **rè** 'hot'
wood:	木	柴 **chái** 'firewood'
	朩	树 **shù** 'tree'
metal:	金	金 **jīn** 'gold'
	钅	银 **yín** 'silver'

(d) plants and animals:

grass:	艹	草 **cǎo** 'grass'
bamboo:	⺮	笋 **sǔn** (veg.) 'bamboo shoots'
grain:	禾	稻 **dào** 'paddy'
rice:	米	糯米 **nuòmǐ** 'glutinous rice'
wheat:	麦	麸子 **fūzi** '(wheat) bran'
melon:	瓜	瓜瓤 **guāráng** 'melon pulp'
hemp:	麻	麻 **má** 'hemp'
dog:	犭	狗 **gǒu** 'dog' and 猫 **māo** 'cat'
horse:	马	骑 **qí** 'ride'
ox:	牛	牧 **mù** 'to herd'; 'tend'
sheep:	羊	羊羔 **yánggāo** 'lamb'
insect:	虫	蝴蝶 **húdié** 'butterfly'
	豸	豹 **bào** 'leopard'
bird:	鸟 (long-tailed)	鸡 **jī** 'chicken' and 鸭 **yā** 'duck'
	隹 (short-tailed)	麻雀 **máquè** 'sparrow'
fish:	鱼	鲤鱼 **lǐyú** 'carp'
deer:	鹿	麒麟 **qílín** 'Chinese unicorn'
pig:	豕	逐 **zhú** 'chase'
rat:	鼠	鼠 **shǔ** 'mouse'; 'rat' and
		鼬 **yòu** 'weasel'
dragon:	龙	龙 **lóng** 'dragon'
tiger:	虍	虎 **hǔ** 'tiger' and
		虐待 **nuèdài** 'maltreat'
frog:	黾	苍蝇 **cāngying** 'a fly'
claw/paw:	爪	爬 **pá** 'climb'
horn:	角	触 **chù** 'touch'; 'contact'
feather:	羽	翅 **chì** 'wing'

(3) *Artefacts*

(a) tools and instruments:

knife:	刀	切 **qiē** 'cut'
	刂	刻 **kè** 'engrave'
table:	几	凭 **píng** 'rely on'; 'base on'
tool:	工	巧 **qiǎo** 'skilful'
rope:	己	自己 **zìjǐ** 'oneself'
net:	罒	罗 **luó** 'to net birds'
farm tool:	耒	耕 **gēng** 'to plough'

(b) weapons:

weapon:	干		干 **gàn** 'to work'
	戈		战 **zhàn** 'fight'
bow:	弓		引 **yǐn** 'pull'; 'draw'
arrow:	矢		矮 **ǎi** 'short (i.e. not tall)'
spear:	矛		柔 **róu** 'soft'; 'tender'

(c) clothing:

cloth:	巾		布 **bù** 'cloth' and
	一		帘 **lián** 'curtain'
silk:	纟		绣 **xiù** 'embroider'
clothes:	衣		裹 **guǒ** 'wrap up'
	衤		衬衫 **chènshān** 'shirt'
leather:	革		鞋 **xié** 'shoe'

(d) residence:

roof:	宀		宫 **gōng** 'palace'
house:	广		廊 **láng** 'corridor'
door:	门 (two sides)		闩 **shuān** 'bolt'; 'latch'
	户 (one side)		房 **fáng** 'house'; 'room'

(e) transport:

crossroad:	彳 (one side)		行 **xíng** 'amble'
	辶 (plus one foot)		运 **yùn** 'to transport' and
			远 **yuǎn** 'far'
chariot:	车		库 **kù** 'garage'
boat:	舟		船 **chuán** 'boat'; 'ship'

(f) utensils:

trunk:	匚		匣子 **xiázi** 'casket'; 'small box'
pottery:	瓦		瓶 **píng** 'bottle'
container:	酉 (for wine)		酒 **jiǔ** 'wine'; 'spirit'; 'liquor'
utensil:	皿		盘 **pán** 'plate'
pottery:	缶		缸 **gāng** 'vat'; 'urn'
mortar:	臼		舂 **chōng** 'to pound'; 'dehusk'

(g) valuables:

jade:	王		玩 **wán** 'to play'; 'have fun'
shell:	贝		赌 **dǔ** 'gamble' and
(for money)			购 **gòu** 'to purchase'

(4) *Superstition*

altar:	示		祭 **jì** 'offer sacrifice'
	礻		祝 **zhù** 'to wish'
ghost:	鬼		魂 **hún** 'soul'
divinition:	卜		占卜 **zhānbǔ**
			'practise divination'

All the words in the Chinese lexicon may be organised around this set of radicals. however far-fetched it might seem at times. What actually facilitates this organisation is that radicals, like words, have also developed polysemy and multiple functions through use. Take the radical 食 shí (or 饣) for instance. It embraces around fifty characters[16] which cover the following areas of meaning and function:

(1) actions or activities associated with eating:
　　食 shí '(formal) eat'
　　饮 yǐn '(formal) drink'
　　烹饪 pēngrèn 'cooking'
　　饲养 sìyǎng 'feed'

(2) location associated with eating:
　　饭馆 fànguǎn 'restaurant'

(3) physiological attributes associated with eating:
　　饥饿 jī'è 'hunger'
　　饱 bǎo 'to have eaten one's fill'; 'surfeited'
　　饕餮 tāotiè 'gluttonous'

(4) meals:
　　餐 cān 'meal'
　　饔飧 yōngsūn '(formal) breakfast and supper'
　　盛馔 shèngzhuàn '(formal) a sumptuous dinner'

(5) various types of food:
　　饭 fàn 'cooked rice'
　　饼 bǐng 'cakes'; 'biscuits'; 'pastry'
　　馄饨 húntún 'stuffed dumplings'
　　饺子 jiǎozi 'Chinese ravioli'
　　饽饽 bōbo '(dialect) pies'; 'tarts'
　　馒头 mántou 'steamed buns'
　　馅儿 xiànr 'stuffing'
　　珍馐 zhēnxiū '(formal) delicacies'; 'dainties'

(6) attributes associated with food:
　　馊 sōu 'turn sour'; 'become spoiled'
　　饧 xíng '(of dough, sweets, etc.) get soft and sticky'

(7) metaphorical:
　　反馈 fǎnkuì 'feedback'

---

[16] The number of characters specified here does not include variants. Due to change of radical (through the simplification process) some of the characters originally having 食 shí as their radical have now adopted other radicals: e.g. 养 yǎng 'foster'; 'keep' originally had 食 underneath instead of the two vertical strokes, 喂 wèi 'feed (a baby, etc.)' originally had 食 instead of 口 kǒu 'mouth' as its radical (i.e. 餵), and the first part of 膳宿 shànsù 'board and lodging' originally had 食 instead of 月 ròu 'meat' as its radical.

(8) phonetic:

装饰 **zhuāngshì** 'decorations'; 'ornaments'
腐蚀 **fǔshí** 'corrode'; 'corrupt'
整饬 **zhěngchì** 'strengthen discipline'

In some cases, the meaning of a character cannot be traced back to any logical association with the radical it has, nor has the radical changed into a role of indicating any kind of pronunciation of the character. Under such circumstances, the radical, as far as the said character is concerned, is purely a salient, regularly shared form. For example,

立 **lì** 'stand' in 亲 **qīn** 'blood relations'
  章 **zhāng** 'seal (for stamping)'
凵 in 凶 **xiōng** 'fierce'
  凿 **záo** 'to chisel'

THE PHONETICS

The phonetic in a picto-phonetic character is originally meant to provide guidance to its pronunciation. Knowledge of the system is therefore important to the overall understanding of the sound-coding practice in the majority of Chinese characters.

According to Zhou Youguang (周有光),[17] 1,348 phonetics may be discerned, of which 1,175 can be independent words themselves and 173 are merely phonetic elements. For example,

(1) independent words serving as phonetics:
安 **ān** 'peace'; 'safe', which now functions as a sound element in
桉树 **ānshù** 'eucalyptus'
马鞍 **mǎ'ān** 'saddle'
氨气 **ānqì** 'amonia'
方 **fāng** 'square', which is now only a sound element in
防止 **fángzhǐ** 'prevent'
房子 **fángzi** 'house'
放 **fàng** 'put'

(2) phonetic elements only:
坴 as in
和睦 **hémù** 'harmony'; 'amity'
陆地 (originally: 陸地) **lùdì** 'land'
辰 as in
派 **pài** 'send'; 'dispatch'
脉搏 (originally: 脈搏) **màibó** 'pulse'

[17] Zhou, Youguang (周有光) 1980. However, 现代汉字形声字字汇 compiled by Zhonghua Publisher (中华书局) (Hong Kong 1979) lists 1,525 phonetics based on the 1971 edition of 新华字典.

It must be understood, however, that as time goes by and habits of pronunciation change, not all phonetics in a picto-phonetic character can now offer an accurate and foolproof guide to its pronunciation. On the contrary, they are only rough and sometimes even misleading clues to the sound of the character in question. Zhou Youguang indicates that on average the accuracy of these phonetics in indicating the actual pronunciation of the characters (disregarding discrepancy in tones) works out at only 39 per cent,[18] that is, only slightly more than one third. In other words, only one in every three characters that incorporate these phonetics can really represent its pronunciation. So we see that if the radicals can be said to be *polysemous*, then the phonetics used in the characters are *polyphonous*. If tone discrepancy is taken into account, the percentage of accuracy should become still less. Let us look at some examples:

票 **piào** is itself an independent word meaning 'ticket' and is pronounced in the fourth tone. When it is used as a phonetic in another character, its original meaning becomes immaterial. It has, however, acquired the capability of indicating four different tones in different characters:

飘 **piāo** 'float (in the air)'; 'flutter'
嫖 **piáo** 'visit prostitutes'; 'go whoring'
瞟 **piǎo** 'look sidelong (or askance) at'; 'glance sideways at'
骠 **piào** '(formal) (of horses) galloping'; 'fast' or '(of people) brave'; 'valiant'

It may even modify the initial consonant of its original pronunciation:

膘 **biāo** 'fat (of a domestic animal)' (from aspirated p to unaspirated b)

Here is another example:

山 **shān** 'mountain', pronounced in the first tone as an independent word.

As a phonetic, it retains its vowel quality throughout but changes the phonetic value of its initial consonant:

舢 **shān**   as in 舢板 **shānbǎn** 'sampan'
讪 **shàn**   as in 讪笑 **shànxiào** 'ridicule'; 'deride'
灿 **càn**   as in 灿烂 **cànlàn** 'magnificent'; 'resplendent' (originally: 燦)
仙 **xiān**   as in 仙人 **xiānrén** 'celestial being'; 'immortal'

In some cases, the pronunciation can deviate so far from the original that it becomes totally unrecognisable. For example, 册 'volume'; 'book' is pronounced as *cè*, but it becomes:

shān   as in 珊瑚 **shānhú** 'coral'
zhà   as in 栅栏 **zhàlan** 'railings'; 'paling'

---

[18] Zhou's percentage, as he indicates, disregards the discrepancy in tones. Ni, Haishu (倪海曙) (ed.) 1975 indicates that the accuracy of these phonetics in sound specification (including precise tone specification) is only 26.3% (quoted from Zhang, Jingxian (张静贤) 1992: 81–2).

Similarly, 享 is pronounced as *xiǎng* as in 享受 **xiǎngshòu** 'enjoy', but it becomes:

dūn	as in 伦敦 **lúndūn** 'London'
chún	as in 醇厚 **chúnhòu** 'mellow'; 'rich'; 'pure and honest'
zhūn	as in 谆谆 **zhūnzhūn** 'earnest and tireless'
guō	as in 城郭 **chéngguō** 'inner and outer city walls'

And 昔 **xī** 'former times'; 'the past', when used as a phonetic, it retains its pronunciation in 惜 **xī**, as in 可惜 **kěxī** 'it's a pity'; 'it's too bad', but it changes to:

jiè	in 借 **jiè** 'borrow'
què	in 喜鹊 **xǐquè** 'magpie'
cù	in 醋 **cù** 'vinegar'
cuò	in 错 **cuò** 'wrong'

And this kind of deviation is further complicated by simplification:

蜡 **là** 'wax' (originally: 蠟)
猎 **liè** as in 打猎 **dǎliè** 'hunt'; 'hunting' (originally: 獵)

In an extreme case like 台 **tái** 'stage'; 'platform', when it functions as a phonetic, it may indicate as many as nine different pronunciations:

(1)	**tāi**	as in	胎 **tāi** 'foetus'; 'embryo'
(2)	**tái**		抬 **tái** '(of two or more persons) carry'
(3)	**dài**		怠工 **dàigōng** 'slow down (work)'
(4)	**zhì**		统治 **tǒngzhì** 'govern'; 'rule'
(5)	**chī**		鞭笞 **biānchī** '(formal) flog'; 'lash'
(6)	**shǐ**		开始 **kāishǐ** 'begin'; 'commence'
(7)	**yí**		怡乐 **yílè** 'cheerful'
(8)	**xǐ**		枲麻 **xǐmá** 'male stem of hemp'
(9)	**yě**		冶炼 **yěliàn** 'to smelt'

In some cases, there can be as many as eleven (e.g. 且 **qiě**) or thirteen (e.g. 隹 **zhuī**) possibilities. This situation may even worsen owing to the simplification process, for the original phonetic in a character might have been abbreviated or curtailed and therefore no longer serves as a pronunciation clue to the character: e.g. in

盘 **pán** 'plate'; 'dish' (where 皿 **mǐn** 'utensil' is the radical; 舟 **zhōu**, the phonetic), this supposedly new phonetic becomes misleading as the original phonetic 般 **bān** in the unsimplified form 盤 has been curtailed. Again, in

凤 **fèng** 'phoenix', neither the new phonetic 几 nor the new radical 又 makes any sense as against the original long form 鳳, which has 凡 **fán** as its phonetic and 鳥 **niǎo** 'bird' as its radical.

So we see that the so-called 'phonetics' are no foolproof guide to the actual pronunciation of the characters concerned and the best strategy to follow is to look up the character or the word in a dictionary and relate knowledge-ably the changed pronunciation to the one that was originally intended. Native speakers of the language often mispronounce even the most commonly used characters like the following precisely because they are complacent and think that they know how to read them by relying on the built-in phonetics without consulting a standard dictionary. There are innumerable examples:

裸 **luǒ** in 裸体 **luǒtǐ** 'naked'; 'nude' can be easily mispronounced as 果 **guǒ**.

逊 **xùn** in 谦逊 **qiānxùn** 'modest' can be easily mispronounced as 孙 **sūn**.

瀑 **pù** in 瀑布 **pùbù** 'waterfall' can be easily mispronounced as 暴 **bào**.

萌 **méng** in 萌芽 **méngyá** 'to sprout'; 'bud' can be easily mispronounced as 明 **míng**.

讴 **ōu** in 讴歌 **ōugē** '(formal) to eulogize' can be easily mispronounced as 区 **qū**.

黠 **xiá** in 狡黠 **jiǎoxiá** '(formal) cunning' can be easily mispronounced as 吉 **jí**.

PICTO-PHONETIC ARRANGEMENT

Picto-phonetic characters, as defined earlier, are combinations of radicals (for meaning) and phonetics (for pronunciation). In a picto-phonetic character the pictographic element (i.e. the radical) is, in the majority of cases, featured on the left-hand side or (in fewer instances) at the top, while the phonetic element is on the right-hand side or at the bottom: e.g.

唱 **chàng** 'sing' (口 **kǒu** 'mouth', the radical; 昌 **chāng**, the phonetic)
烤 **kǎo** 'bake'; 'roast' (火 **huǒ** 'fire', the radical; 考 **kǎo**, the phonetic)
抱 **bào** 'hug'; 'embrace' (扌 'hand', the radical; 包 **bāo**, the phonetic)
到 **dào** 'arrive' (至 **zhì** 'arrive', the meaning element; 刂 **dāo**, the phonetic)
花 **huā** 'flower'; 'blossom' (艹 'grass', the radical; 化 **huà**, the phonetic)
客 **kè** 'guest' (宀 'roof', the radical; 各 **gè**, the phonetic)

However, their positions in a character might be reversed in some cases: e.g.

歌 **gē** 'song' (哥 **gē**, the phonetic; 欠 **qiàn** 'yawn' as in 哈欠 **hāqian**, the radical)
鹅 **é** 'goose' (我 **wǒ**, the phonetic; 鸟 **niǎo** 'bird', the radical)
斧 **fǔ** as in 斧头 **fǔtou** 'axe'; 'hatchet' (父 **fù**, the phonetic; 斤 **jīn** 'axe', the radical)
贷 **dài** as in 贷款 **dàikuǎn** 'loan' (代 **dài**, the phonetic; 贝 **bèi** 'shell (for money)', the radical)

On other occasions, the radical or the phonetic may be found anywhere: outside or inside the surrounding elements, or in a most unexpected corner. In the following list of examples, the radical or meaning element is indicated by R and the phonetic by P: e.g.

The phonetic surrounded by the radical:

赶 **gǎn** 'to hurry'   (R:走 **zǒu** 'walk'; P:干 **gān**)
疯 **fēng** 'mad'; 'insane'   (R:疒, 'illness'; P:风 **fēng**)
围 **wéi** 'surround'; 'encircle'   (R:囗 'surround'; P:韦 **wéi**)
衷 **zhōng** as in 衷心 **zhōngxīn** 'heartfelt'   (P:中 **zhōng**; R:衣 **yī** 'clothes')
懋 **mào** '(formal) diligent'; 'luxuriant'   (P:矛 **máo**; R: the rest)

The radical surrounded by the phonetic:

赢 **yíng** 'gain'; 'win'   (R:贝 **bèi** 'shell (for money)'; P: the rest)
问 **wèn** 'ask'   (P:门 **mén**; R:口 **kǒu** 'mouth')

The phonetic tucked away in a corner:

望 **wàng** 'gaze'   (P:亡 **wáng**; R: the rest)
在 **zài** 'exist in'; 'at'   (P:才 **cái** in the form of 才; R:土 **tǔ** 'land')
莅 **lì** '(formal) arrive'   (P:立 **lì**; R: the rest)

The radical tucked away in a corner:

疆 **jiāng** 'boundary'; 'border'   (R:土 **tǔ** 'land'; P: variant of 强 **qiáng**)
载 **zài** 'carry (in a vehicle)'   (R:车 **chē** 'car'; P:𢦏 **zāi**)
夜 **yè** 'night'   (R:夕 **xī** 'evening'; P:衣 **yī**)

Not only the position between the radical and the phonetic may change, but a number of radicals may change their role and function becoming phonetics in individual characters. For example,

示 **shì** 'altar'   as a sound element in   视 **shì** (formal) 'look'
耳 **ěr** 'ear'   饵 **ěr** as in 诱饵 **yòu'ěr** 'bait'
门 **mén** 'door'   闷 **mèn** 'bored'; 'depressed'
口 **kǒu** 'mouth'   扣 **kòu** 'button up'; 'deduct'
食 **shí** (formal) 'eat'; 'food'   饰 **shì** 'decorate'; 'adorn'
尸 **shī** 'corpse'   屎 **shǐ** 'excrement'
禾 **hé** 'standing grain (esp. rice)'   和 **hé** 'and'

土 **tǔ** 'earth'   吐 **tǔ** 'expectorate'; 'spit out'
鹿 **lù** 'deer'   麓 **lù** as in 山麓 **shānlù** 'foot of a mountain'

PICTO-PHONETIC VARIANTS

With picto-phonetic characters, there are often graphic variants owing to:

   (1) repositioning the radical and the phonetic in the character:

      够 = 夠 **gòu** 'enough'; 'sufficient'; 'adequate'

      阔 = 濶 **kuò** 'wide'

      勃谿 = 勃豀 **bóxī** '(formal) family quarrel'; 'tiff'; 'squabble'

   (2) adopting radicals with related meanings:

      欷歔 = 唏嘘 **xīxū** '(formal) sob or sigh' (the radicals: 欠 **qiàn** (formal) 'yawn'; 口 **kǒu** 'mouth')

      腼腆 = 靦觍 **miǎntiǎn** 'shy'; 'bashful' (the radicals: 月 **ròu** 'flesh'; 见 **jiàn** 'see'; 'meet')

      襁褓 = 繦緥 **qiǎngbǎo** 'swaddling clothes' (the radicals: 衤 'clothes'; 纟 'silk')

      髫年 = 齠年 **tiáonián** '(formal) childhood' (the radicals: 髟 and 齿 respectively in 髫 **tiáo** '(archaic) a child's hanging hair'; 齠 **tiáo** '(formal) (of a child) shed baby (or milk) teeth'; 'grow permanent teeth')

      耿直 = 梗直 = 鲠直 **gěngzhí** '(formal) upright'; 'honest and frank' (the radicals: 耳 **ěr** 'ear'; 木 **mù** 'wood'; 鱼 **yú** 'fish')

      疙瘩 = 纥繨 = 圪塔 = 咯嗒 **gēda** 'lump'; 'knot' (the radicals: 疒 'illness'; 纟 'silk'; 土 **tǔ** 'earth'; 口 **kǒu** 'mouth')

   (3) using homophonic alternatives:

      划拳 = 豁拳 = 搳拳 **huáquán** 'play the finger-guessing game'

      逶迤 = 委蛇 **wēiyí** 'winding'; 'meandering'

      其它 = 其他 **qítā** 'other'; 'else' (the former refers exclusively to 'objects' whereas the latter refers to 'people' as well)

   (4) integrating different phonetics:

      踉跄 = 踉蹡 **liàngqiàng** 'stagger' (the phonetics: 仓 **cāng** and 将 **jiàng**)

      偎依 **wēiyī** = 偎倚 **wēiyǐ** 'snuggle up to'; 'lean close to' (the phonetics: 衣 **yī** and 奇 **qí**)

      唆使 **suōshǐ** 'instigate'; 'abet (not yet achieved its purpose)' = 嗾使 **sǒushǐ** 'instigate'; 'abet (already achieved its purpose)' (where *uo* changes to *ou* or vice versa)

      踌躇 **chóuchú** 'hesitate'; 'dilly-dally' = 踟蹰 **chíchú** 'irresolute'; 'uncertain' = 踯躅 **zhízhú** 'vacillate'; 'loiter around'

   (5) unifying the radicals:

      剽悍 = 慓悍 **piāohàn** 'agile and brave'; 'quick and fierce' (忄 'heart' is used for both characters)

      飘渺 = 缥缈 **piāomiǎo** 'dimly discernible'; 'misty' (纟 'silk' is used for both characters)

CHARACTERS OLD AND NEW

At this point, it is perhaps useful to know that whatever they are, character-formation devices, traditional or new, are no longer used regularly to create new characters. The discussion of these devices and processes only serves to achieve a better and more enlightened understanding of the internal structure and mechanism of all existing characters in use. As Modern Standard Chinese increases its vocabulary basically through multisyllabification, particularly disyllabification (i.e. meaning- or sound-oriented combination of existing mono-syllabic characters), it no longer seeks to make full use of all the known devices to produce new characters, except, occasionally, in the field of *chemistry* or *onomatopoeia*:

(1) In *chemistry*, when a new element is found or synthesized. The radicals for gas, liquid, metal, etc. will be used in conjunction with a phonetic indic-ating the character's pronunciation, generally (but not always) based on the initial (or a prominent) sound of the chemical term's English counterpart. For example,

氕 **piē** 'protium'   镭 **léi** 'radium'   碘 **diǎn** 'iodine'
苯 **běn** 'benzene'   溴 **xiù** 'bromium'

(2) In *onomatopoeia*, when authors find it necessary to imitate a sound on an *ad hoc* basis. The radical used is generally 口 **kǒu** 'mouth' or a repres-entation of the object in customary association with the sound, whereas the phonetic can vary enormously in line with individual authors' original dialectal habits.[19] For example,

呵呵 **hēhē** 'hah-hah'   嘟嘟 **dūdū** 'toot toot'
哐啷 **kuānglāng** 'sound of crushing'   喀嚓 **kāchā** 'noise of snapping'
辘辘 **lùlù** 'rumbling'   淙淙 **cóngcóng** 'gurgling'[20]

STROKE SEQUENCE IN HANDWRITTEN CHARACTERS

Chinese characters (as well as their monostroke components themselves), when handwritten, invariably follow the graphic convention of starting from left to right and top to bottom, the only exceptions being when a character has a single dot but does not begin with it (then the dot comes last) or when a character has a vertical stroke in the middle with dot or falling strokes coming on both sides (then the vertical stroke is written first). For example,

---

[19] Cf. Chapter 5 on the phonaesthetic features of the Chinese lexicon.
[20] Onomatopoeic words with 口 **kǒu** 'mouth' radical are onomatopoeia *par excellence*. They can usually be coined more freely and are always represented in the first tone while those with other meaning-associated radicals can adopt any of the other tones.

川 **chuān** 'river', to be written from left to right in the sequence of 丿, 丨, 丨 whilst the left-falling and vertical monostrokes themselves start from the top and finish at the bottom.

三 **sān** 'three', to be written from top to bottom in the sequence of 一, 一, 一 whilst the horizontal strokes themselves are to be written from left to right.

Two exceptional examples incorporating a dot and a vertical stroke with dots on either side:

尤 **yóu** 'especially', to be written in the sequence of 一, 丿, 乚, 丶, where the dot comes last.

小 **xiǎo** 'small'; 'little', to be written in the sequence of 亅, 丿, 丶, where the vertical comes before the strokes on the sides.

Here are some slightly more complicated examples:

友 **yǒu** 'friend', to be written in the sequence of 一, 丿, 乛, 乀.

好 **hǎo** 'good', first 丿, 乀, 丿, 一 into 女 on the left and then 乛, 丨, 一, into 子 on the right.

头 **tóu** 'head', to be written in the sequence of 丶, 丶, 一, 丿, 乀.

京 **jīng** as in 北京 **běijīng** 'Beijing', to be written in the sequence of 丶, 一, 丨, 乛, 一, 丨, 丿, 丶.

就 **jiù** 'at once'; 'right away', to be written in the sequence of 京 and 尤.

日 **rì** 'sun', to be written in the sequence of 丨, 乛, 一 in the middle, and then 一 at the bottom.

景 **jǐng** 'scenery', to be written in the sequence of 日 and 京.

THE QUESTION OF HOMOPHONY

As there are far more written characters than usable monosyllables in the language, the relationship between the two is bound to be 'many to one'. In other words, one monosyllable will have to be matched to many written characters. This invariably results in homophony. In the worse case of *yi*, for instance, there can be as many as 107 heterotonic homophones as entered in a contemporary dictionary. Even if only the homotonic homophones are taken into account, the situation is no better. For example, **yī** has the following thirteen homotonic, homophonic characters which are in common use: 一,衣,伊,医,依,咿,铱,壹,猗,漪,噫,黟,揖.

There are in fact only twenty-three syllables[21] in the lexicon which happen to have no homophonic characters. To resolve such a drastic homophonic situation, the language's lexicon gradually metamorphosed from classical monosyllabic dominance into contemporary disyllabic dominance.

---

[21] These syllables are: **cèi** 瓰, **děi** 得, **dèn** 扽 **diǎ** 嗲, **fó** 佛, **gěi** 给, **hm** 噷, **hng** 哼, **kēi** 剋, **liǎ** 俩, **lo** 咯, **me** 么, **néng** 能, **nín** 您, **nòu** 耨, **nuǎn** 暖, **rì** 日, **ruá** 挼, **sēn** 森, **sēng** 僧, **shéi** 谁, **tēi** 忒, **zhèi** 这.

3 MORPHOLOGICAL FEATURES OF THE CHINESE LEXICON

Morphology is generally known to be concerned with all intra-lexemic relations, that is, relations between the constituent morphemes, free or bound, explicit or implied, of established or coined lexemes in the light of similar relations in other comparable lexemes. Traditionally, morphemes are taken as meaningful segments,[1] that is, form-and-meaning correlations, whether their meaning is more stable and distinctive as in compounds or less so as in derivations (e.g. cook vs cooker, draw vs drawer, etc.). In contemporary linguistics, however, morphemes may not necessarily be defined as segmentable units of meaning but as comparable units of grammatical analysis. A lexeme's *distributional proportion* is supposed to tell the story of its morphemic status in lexical compositions, e.g. bad : worse : worst = tall : taller : tallest.[2] In the Chinese context, for example, 羊 **yáng** 'sheep' may enter into a similar distributionally proportionate equation like this: (in narration) pre-verbal 羊 **yáng** : post-verbal 羊 **yáng** = the sheep (sing. or pl.) : a sheep or sheep (pl.).

With the introduction of this concept of distributional proportion, there arises the correlated concept of *morphological (* or *supramorphological) process* rather than morphological segmentation, e.g. boy : boys = woman : women. In the latter case, the notion of plurality is not derived from a discernable segment like *s* as in the former, but from a process of vowel change from /u/ to /i/. Furthermore, in cases like cow : cows = sheep : sheep, there also arises the concept of zero derivation, that is, sheep (singular) + context = sheep (plural), with no change in form at all. All Chinese countable nouns, in fact, may be said to be able to derive their notion of plurality from their linguistic or pragmatic contexts and always formally follow the principle of zero-derivation, e.g. 牛 **niú** 'ox' + context = 牛 **niú** 'oxen'.[3]

Even where segmental analysis is possible, meaning is no longer considered a prerequisite for a morpheme, which does not have to be a carrier of meaning as long as it is a regularly recognisable phonetic string in the language. What matters here is indeed not its meaning but its peculiar, arbitrary form.[4] In other words, morphemes may include what may be called *canonical forms* in a language (e.g. *-ceive* is one of such forms in English whereas *-cieve* is

---

[1] Black 1972: 41.
[2] Lyons 1968: 181–2.
[3] It is a common misunderstanding that 们 *men* is the plural suffix to human nouns. In fact, a human noun like 朋友 *péngyou* 'friend(s)', when suffixed with 们 *men*, i.e. 朋友们 *péngyoumen*, will mean 'the friends' or '(in a direct address) my friends'.
[4] Aronoff 1979: 15.

not) or even such contra-etymological fragments as *-burger* in *hamburger* (which reasserts itself in *beefburger*, *cheeseburger*, etc.) as long as they are recognisable forms of the language.[5] In Chinese, a number of similar forms have been discerned on grounds of their being 'devoid of meaning' (虚化 **xūhuà**). For example, 子 *zi* in 妻子 **qīzi** 'wife', 鸭子 **yāzi** 'duck' and 桌子 **zhuōzi** 'table' cannot be pinned down to any precise meaning apart from its being an inbuilt nominal indicator of all these items.

In the analysis of European languages, one condition, however, is imposed on such a differentiation, that is, a lexeme when thus differentiated, shall not leave behind any unrecognizable element as a residue. 'Rabbit', for example, is therefore only a mono-morphemic lexeme; it cannot be further differentiated into minor morphemes though we have perhaps recognized the segment '-bit' in it, because that will leave the remainder part 'rab-' unidentified. That is also why we can differentiate 'duckling' as 'duck-' and '-ling' (analogous to 'inkling') but not 'telling' as 'tel-' and '-ling' because that will leave 'tel-' unidentifiable. The latter should therefore be differentiated as 'tell-' and '-ing' (analogous to 'walking').

This problem will never actually arise in Chinese, for every mononym, meaningful or not, which enters into combination with another is at the same time potentially separable from it in form. If any segmentation is to take place, it may only occur between any two such mononyms and not elsewhere. For example, 蝴蝶 **húdié** 'butterfly', 蜘蛛 **zhīzhū** 'spider' and 葡萄 **pútáo** 'grape' are three disyllabic words. The two mononyms which make up each of the words are inseparable in meaning and linguists generally agree that these disyllabic words are mono-morphemic.

However, in the following words 蝶泳 **diéyǒng** (swimming) 'butterfly stroke' (analogous to 蛙泳 **wāyǒng** 'breaststroke'), 蛛网 **zhūwǎng** 'cobweb' (analogous to 鱼网 **yúwǎng** 'fishnet') and 葡糖 **pútáng** 'glucose' (analogous to 果糖 **guǒtáng** 'fructose'), we can see that the seemingly semantically inseparable elements 蝶 **dié**, 蛛 **zhū** and 葡 **pú** are now all separated from their source words and used on their own in the new combinations. Does this seem counter-intuitive? Here is another interesting example. In a word like 蚰蜒 **yóuyán** 'common house centipede', the two mononyms are again supposedly semantically inseparable. However, we find in the lexicon a dialect term 蜒蚰 **yányóu** meaning 'slug', which literally reverses the two mononyms in its new composition. All this goes to show that any mononym in the Chinese lexicon, whether or not it is independent in meaning, is nevertheless independent in form, and is therefore capable of entering into meaningful lexemic combinations.

The question we have to ask here is whether we should look at these newly formulated lexemes as *compounds* or *derivatives*. The lexemes we have just quoted are in our view best analysed as compounds rather than derivatives,

---

[5] Bolinger and Sears 1981: 42, 71.

for the simple reason that though the component elements 蝶 **dié**, 蛛 **zhū** and 葡 **pú** by themselves seem to be lame and incomplete in form, their meanings can be unmistakably retrieved from their source words.

Regarding these new forms as compounds, as we shall see, facilitates their analysis in syntactic terms.[6] On the other hand, in those semantically lopsided fusions we find in 妻子 **qīzi** 'wife' etc., some mononyms are clearly true mainstays in the semantic value of the lexemes concerned while others are but regular, categorial props or mere word class indicators, which either do not affect the consequent meanings (e.g. 老师 **lǎoshī** 'teacher', in which **lǎo** 'old' is not necessarily a meaning component of 'teacher'), or affect them in a most general way (e.g. 记者 **jìzhě** 'journalist' in which *zhě* suggests 'doer'). It is perhaps more appropriate to regard these lexemes as derivatives and such meaning-opaque or partially or totally *'desemanticised'* mononyms: 子 **zi**, 老 **lǎo**, 者 **zhě**, etc. as *sub-morphemes* or canonical forms. In morphological studies, they may be grouped under the general category of affixes.

This view does not, of course, imply that present theories and models in linguistics can already claim to be able to draw absolute and unmistakable distinctions between derivation and compounding. In some cases and to some extent, they are still fuzzy analytic categories, where demarcation often rests with the intuition of individual analysts (e.g. postman, cupboard – derivation or compounding?). Unfortunately, this is particularly the case in Chinese.

In this chapter, however, we shall first try to discern a number of affixes in the Chinese lexicon by adopting the two helpful criteria of *desemanticisation* and *versatility*.[7] Then, in view of the peculiar nature of the Chinese language, we will go beyond the discussion of segmental affixes and include a brief survey of the suprasegmental[8] (or supramorphological) processes we have seen at work in the semantic codification of Chinese lexemes in use, an indisputable fact which has so far escaped the scrutiny of purely form-oriented linguists.

AFFIXES FOR HUMAN NOUNS

Human nouns in Chinese appear to be particularly receptive to various types of affixes.[9] Two human *prefixes* commonly found in the lexicon are 老 **lǎo** and 阿 **ā**. Meaningless though they are, they express an attitudinal cline from 'respect and/or intimacy' to 'contempt'.

---

[6] The whole of the next chapter will be devoted to the discussion of compounds.

[7] Cf. Chao, Yuen-ren 1968: 'versatile first morpheme'.

[8] The word 'suprasegmental' is used in a different sense from its normal usage in linguistic literature. It is used here to indicate a unit of meaning which is retrievable through analytic processes not involving palpable linguistic segments.

[9] Ren, Xueliang (任学良) 1981. In the book, he has distinguished 7 human prefixes and 23 human suffixes (of which 1 is a disyllabic suffix). Ren justifies his inclusion of individual affixes with separate statements, mostly diachronically oriented and mainly centred around the semantic theme of what he calls the '**xūhuà**' (虚化 'being devoid') of meaning.

	lǎ 老	ā 阿
established words	老师 **lǎoshī** 'teacher' (respect)	阿姨 **āyí** 'auntie' (respect and intimacy)
	老板 **lǎobǎn** 'boss' (intimacy)	阿公 **āgōng** 'father of one's husband' (respect and intimacy)
	老乡 **lǎoxiāng** 'fellow villager or townsman' (intimacy)	阿斗 **ādǒu** 'doltish weakling' (contempt)
	老婆 **lǎopo** 'wife' (familiarity)	阿飞 **āfēi** 'hooligan' (contempt)
+ surname[10]	老王 **lǎo wáng** 'Mr Wang' (respect and intimacy)	阿王 **ā wáng** 'Mr Wang' (familiarity)

On the other hand, human nouns are teeming with *suffixes*, amongst which 人 **rén** 'person' is by far the most versatile in the language. It is neutral in meaning. It answers the first sociological question asked by children: 好人 **hǎorén** 'goodie' vs 坏人 **huàirén** 'baddie'. It finds itself in many similar dichotomies:

主人 **zhǔrén** 'host'	vs	客人 **kèrén** 'guest'
熟人 **shúrén** 'acquaintance'	vs	生人 **shēngrén** 'stranger'
圣人 **shèngrén** 'saint'	vs	常人 **chángrén** 'the man in the street'
敌人 **dírén** 'enemy'	vs	自己人 **zìjǐrén** 'people on one's side'

It includes, for example, the following most commonly used words:

亲人 **qīnrén** 'relative'	大人 **dàrén** 'adult'
诗人 **shīrén** 'poet'	病人 **bìngrén** 'patient'
商人 **shāngrén** 'businessman'	工人 **gōngrén** 'worker'
名人 **míngrén** 'celebrity'	军人 **jūnrén** 'serviceman'
佣人 **yōngrén** 'servant'	

Additional notes:

(1) 人 **rén** is a suffix equally attachable to nouns, adjectives or verbs.

noun:	友人 **yǒurén** 'friend'	媒人 **méirén** 'matchmaker'
	路人 **lùrén** 'passer-by'	仇人 **chóurén** 'personal enemy'
adjective:	外人 **wàirén** 'outsider'	前人 **qiánrén** 'predecessors'
	巨人 **jùrén** 'giant'	伟人 **wěirén** 'great man'
verb:	游人 **yóurén** 'tourist'	当事人 **dāngshìrén** 'person concerned'
	猎人 **lièrén** 'hunter'	牧人 **mùrén** 'herdsman'

(2) 人 **rén** is also used with different races and nationalities, e.g.

黑人 **hēirén** 'Black people'	白人 **báirén** 'white people'
汉人 **hànrén** 'the Hans'	洋人 **yángrén** 'foreigners'

(3) Being a most versatile suffix, 人 **rén** is used to form quasi-human nouns: e.g.

机器人 **jīqìrén** 'robot'	外星人 **wàixīngrén** 'exterrestrial being'

---

[10] Comparable to 老 **lǎo**, prefix 小 **xiǎo** is also often heard with surnames as a form of intimate address to people younger than oneself.

Other human suffixes may be seen to form the following sets:

(*a*) professionals:

-jiā 家 *dedicated to* *a profession*	-zhě 者 *committed to a* *particular task*	-shī 师 *master in a* *specific area*	-shēng/sheng 生 *educated personnel*	-shì/shi 士 *of various learning* *or beliefs*[11]
专家 **zhuānjiā** 'expert'	记者 **jìzhě** 'journalist'	教师 **jiàoshī** 'teacher'	医生 **yīshēng** 'doctor'	博士 **bóshì** 'PhD'
画家 **huàjiā** 'painter'	学者 **xuézhě** 'scholar'	导师 **dǎoshī** 'supervisor'	学生 **xuésheng** 'student'	硕士 **shuòshì** 'MA'; 'Msc'
作家 **zuòjiā** 'writer'	读者 **dúzhě** 'reader'	厨师 **chúshī** 'chef'	考生 **kǎoshēng** 'exam candidate'	学士 **xuéshì** 'BA'; 'BSc'
行家 **hángjiā** 'connoisseur'	作者 **zuòzhě** 'author'	骑师 **qíshī** 'jockey'	先生 **xiānsheng** 'gentleman'; 'Mr'	院士 **yuànshì** 'academician'
艺术家 **yìshùjiā** 'artist'	编者 **biānzhě** 'editor'; 'compiler'	律师 **lǜshī** 'lawyer'	书生 **shūshēng** 'scholar'	女士 **nǚshì** 'lady'; 'Mrs/Miss'
科学家 **kēxuéjiā** 'scientist'	患者 **huànzhě** 'sufferer'; 'patient'	牧师 **mùshi** 'priest'	研究生 **yánjiūshēng** 'research student'	绅士 **shēnshì** 'gentry'
哲学家 **zhéxuéjiā** 'philosopher'	爱好者 **àihàozhě** 'enthusiast'	工程师 **gōngchéngshī** 'engineer'	高材生 **gāocáishēng** 'outstanding student'	爵士 **juéshì** 'knight'; 'Sir'
政治家 **zhèngzhìjiā** 'statesman'	素食者 **sùshízhě** 'vegetarian'	摄影师 **shèyǐngshī** 'photographer'	门生 **ménshēng** 'disciple'; 'follower'	护士 **hùshi** 'nurse'
思想家 **sīxiǎngjiā** 'thinker'	侵略者 **qīnlüèzhě** 'aggressor'	魔术师 **móshùshī** 'magician'	儒生 **rúshēng** 'Confucian scholar'	骑士 **qíshì** 'cavalier'
美食家 **měishíjiā** 'gourmet'	旁观者 **pángguānzhě** 'onlooker'	理发师 **lǐfàshī** 'hairdresser'	见习生 **jiànxíshēng** 'probationer'	隐士 **yǐnshì** 'hermit'

Additional notes:

(1) 家 **jiā** originally means 'family'. As a suffix, it refers to an individual, yet it somewhat suggests the 'professional circle' or the 'school of thought' to which the individual belongs. Other examples include: 音乐家 **yīnyuèjiā** 'musician', 银行家 **yínhángjiā** 'banker', etc.

(2) 者 **zhě** (always stressed) is usually suffixed to verbs as we can see from the examples. It may also be suffixed to adjectives (e.g. 长者 **zhǎngzhě** 'the elderly', 能者 **néngzhě** 'the able', 死者 **sǐzhě** 'the dead', 前者 **qiánzhě** 'the former', 后者 **hòuzhě** 'the latter').

---

[11] It is difficult to generalise the meaning of these sub-morphemes or canonical forms as one will often find numerous exceptions. On the whole it is more a question of linguistic convention than otherwise.

It is still a fairly productive suffix due to its compatibility with any verb or adjective. This tendency can be seen from such an established classical idiom as:

来者不善, 善者不来   **láizhě bù shàn | shànzhě bù lái**
                   'whoever comes cannot be kind'; 'whoever is kind will
                   not come'

where 者 **zhě** is seen to be suffixed readily to the adjective 善 **shàn** 'kind'; 'friendly' to form a specific human category (i.e. the kind, friendly or virtuous).

(3) As 生 **shēng** means 'birth', it is used in 先生 **xiānsheng** 'teacher'; 'sir' to refer respect-fully to somebody as being born earlier than the speaker himself and in 晚生 **wǎnshēng** to refer modestly to oneself (particularly in the old days when addressing one's elders) as being born later and naturally less experienced and learned, and also in 畜生 **chùsheng** '(a term of abuse) son of a bitch'; 'dirty swine' to refer to somebody as if he were brought forth by an animal. 生 **shēng** (or sheng) is therefore also associated with studentship, e.g. 男生 **nánshēng** 'boy student', 女生 **nǚshēng** 'girl student', 新生 **xīnshēng** 'new student', etc. It is also used in connection with the male roles in Peking opera: 小生 **xiǎoshēng** 'one who plays a young man', 武生 **wǔshēng** 'one who plays a man of martial arts', 老生 **lǎoshēng** 'one who plays an old man', etc.

(4) Besides 'academicians', 士 **shì** is also used to denote a particular military rank: e.g. 上士 **shàngshì** (Br Infantry) 'staff sergeant'; (Br Navy) 'chief petty officer', 中士 **zhōngshì** '(Br Air Force) flight sergeant'; (Br Navy) 'petty officer first class', 下士 **xiàshì** '(Br Infantry or Air Force) corporal; (Br Navy) petty officer second class', etc. Hence people who are known either for their courage or for their religious devotion:

卫士 **wèishì** 'bodyguard'	战士 **zhànshì** 'fighter'
武士 **wǔshì** 'warrior'	勇士 **yǒngshì** 'brave man'
烈士 **lièshì** 'martyr'	修士 **xiūshì** 'friar'
居士 **jūshì** 'lay Buddhist'	道士 **dàoshì** 'Taoist priest'
志士 **zhìshì** 'person of ideals'	大力士 **dàlìshì** 'man of unusual strength'

(b) workmen:

-yuán 员 *member of a group/follower of a trade*	**-gōng** 工 *skilled or manual worker*	**-jiàng/ jiang** 匠 *craftsman*	**-fū** 夫/**-chāi** 差/ **dīng** 丁 *(obsolete) on a designated job*	**-mín** 民 *citizen*
会员 **huìyuán** 'member of a club'	车工 **chēgōng** 'lathe operator'	木匠 **mùjiang** 'joiner'	农夫 **nóngfū** (old use) 'farmer'	公民 **gōngmín** 'citizen'
委员 **wěiyuán** 'committee member'	旋工 **xuángōng** 'turner'	花匠 **huājiàng** 'gardener'	脚夫 **jiǎofū** (old use) 'porter'	居民 **jūmín** 'resident'
雇员 **gùyuán** 'employee'	钳工 **qiángōng** 'fitter'	铁匠 **tiějiang** 'blacksmith'	邮差 **yóuchāi** (old use) 'postman'	移民 **yímín** 'immigrant'
招待员 **zhāodàiyuán** 'receiptionist'	刨工 **páogōng** 'planer'	皮匠 **píjiang** 'cobbler'	听差 **tīngchāi** 'office attendant'	市民 **shìmín** 'city residents'

-yuán 员 member of a group/follower of a trade	-gōng 工 skilled or manual worker	-jiàng 匠 craftsman	-fū 夫/-chāi 差/ dīng 丁 (obsolete) on a designated job	-mín 民 citizen
炊事员 **chuīshìyuán** 'cook' 售货员 **shòuhuòyuán** 'shop-assistant'	管子工 **guǎnzigōng** 'plumber' 清洁工 **qīngjiégōng** 'cleaner'	石匠 **shíjiang** 'stonemason' 泥瓦匠 **níwǎjiàng** 'bricklayer'	园丁 **yuándīng** (poetic) 'gardener' 壮丁 **zhuàngdīng** 'conscript'	贫民 **pínmín** 'poor people' 难民 **nànmín** 'refugee'

Additional notes:

(1) 员 **yuán** 'member' is clearly a suffix indicating membership of a particular trade or group:

职员 **zhíyuán** 'office worker' 伤员 **shāngyuán** 'the wounded'
邮递员 **yóudìyuán** 'postman' 随员 **suíyuán** 'entourage'
议员 **yìyuán** 'MP' 售票员 **shòupiàoyuán** 'box-office clerk'

(2) 工 **gōng** is associated with 'workers' not only of different trades but also of different status:

女工 **nǚgōng** 'woman worker' 童工 **tónggōng** 'child labourer'
帮工 **bānggōng** 'helper' 替工 **tìgōng** 'temporary substitute'

The difference between 工 **gōng** and 匠 **jiàng** is that the former is a more recent development connoting due respect for the workmen of a particular trade whereas the latter is somewhat dated and no longer productive.

(3) 夫 **fū** is used with people who belong to less learned or respected trades and is therefore becoming increasingly obsolete in present-day Chinese. It may sometimes still be found in the following words:

屠夫 **túfū** 'butcher' 脚夫 **jiǎofū** '(old use) porter'
船夫 **chuánfū** '(old use) boatman' 渔夫 **yúfū** 'fisherman'
清道夫 **qīngdàofū** '(old use) scavenger'; 'street cleaner'

However, because of its strong association with the sense of 'a male adult', it still survives in:

丈夫 **zhàngfu** 'husband' 鳏夫 **guānfu** 'widower'

(4) 差 **chāi** has also become an obsolete suffix as it connotes someone who 'runs errands' and is usually 'ordered about' by his superiors. 邮差 **yóuchāi** 'postman'; 'mailman', for example, has long been replaced by 邮递员 **yóudìyuán** in present-day Chinese.

(5) 丁 **dīng**, too, has become obsolete except in one term: 园丁 **yuándīng** 'gardener', which is nowadays used often in a metaphorical sense. One popular collocation: 人丁兴旺 **rén dīng xīngwàng** meaning: 'having a growing family or flourishing population', which used to form part of Chinese New Year couplets, particularly in the rural areas not long ago, will, however, soon become a dated expression of hackneyed morality in view of the present-day governmental policy of strict family planning to curb the ever-increasing population.

(6) 民 **mín** 'common folks' is often used in a plural sense. Like 工 **gōng**, it replaces 夫 **fū** or 匠 **jiàng** in referring to many working people of ordinary trades, e.g. 农民 **nóngmín** 'peasant', 渔民 **yúmín** 'fisherman' instead of the once popular 农夫 **nóngfū** and 渔夫 **yúfū**.

(*c*) heads of departments, owners of properties, etc.:

-zhǎng 长 *head of a department*	-zhǔ 主 *owner of a property*	-háo 豪 *influential figure*	-fá 阀 *domineering person*
部长 **bùzhǎng** 'minister'	地主 **dìzhǔ** 'landowner'	土豪 **tǔháo** 'local tyrant'	军阀 **jūnfá** 'warlord'
市长 **shìzhǎng** 'mayor'	店主 **diànzhǔ** 'shop owner'	富豪 **fùháo** 'rich, powerful people'	财阀 **cáifá** 'magnate'; 'tycoon'
校长 **xiàozhǎng** 'headmaster'	雇主 **gùzhǔ** 'employer'	文豪 **wénháo** 'literary giant'	学阀 **xuéfá** 'scholar-tyrant'
船长 **chuánzhǎng** 'captain'	顾主 **gùzhǔ** 'client'	英豪 **yīngháo** 'outstanding figures'	党阀 **dǎngfá** 'party tyrant'

Additional notes:

(1) 长 **zhǎng** 'head' is very consistently used with the military leaders or civil leading personnel of any unit or division, e.g.

军长 **jūnzhǎng** 'army commander'　　师长 **shīzhǎng** 'division commander'
旅长 **lǚzhǎng** 'brigade commander'　　团长 **tuánzhang** 'regimental commander'
营长 **yíngzhǎng** 'battalion commander'　连长 **liánzhǎng** 'company commander'
排长 **páizhǎng** 'platoon leader'　　班长 **bānzhǎng** 'squad leader'; 'monitor'
厂长 **chǎngzhǎng** 'factory director'　科长 **kēzhǎng** 'section chief'
局长 **júzhǎng** 'director of a bureau'　县长 **xiànzhǎng** 'the head of a county'
省长 **shěngzhǎng** 'the provincial head'　队长 **duìzhǎng** 'team leader'

(2) 主 **zhǔ** 'host'; 'owner' seems to be used in connection with people to whom something originally belongs, e.g.

财主 **cáizhǔ** 'moneybags'　　施主 **shīzhǔ** 'almsgiver'
失主 **shīzhǔ** 'owner of lost property'　买主 **mǎizhǔ** 'customer'
债主 **zhàizhǔ** 'creditor'　　房主 **fángzhǔ** 'house-owner'

(3) 将 **jiàng**, which has not been listed above, is used exclusively with military personnel and ranks, sometimes metaphorically:

主将 **zhǔjiàng** 'chief commander'　　干将 **gànjiàng** 'capable person'
悍将 **hànjiàng** 'brave warrior'　　大将 **dàjiàng** 'senior general'
上将 **shàngjiàng** '(Br Air Force) air chief marshal'; '(Navy) admiral'　中将 **zhōngjiàng** '(Br Infantry) lieutenant general';
少将 **shàojiàng** '(Infantry) major general'; '(Navy) rear admiral'; '(Br Air Force) air vice marshal'　'(Br Air Force) air marshal'; '(Br Navy) vice admiral'
准将 **zhǔnjiàng** '(Br Infantry) brigadier'; '(Br Air Force) air commodore'; '(Navy) commodore'

(d) fans, ruffians and criminals:

-mí 迷 *fan or freak*	-guǐ 鬼 *addict or weakling*	-tú 徒 *disciple or evildoer*	-gùn 棍 *despot*	-fàn 犯 *criminal*
球迷 qiúmí 'football fan'	酒鬼 jiǔguǐ 'alcoholic'	学徒 xuétú 'apprentice'	赌棍 dǔgùn 'gambler'	罪犯 zuìfàn 'criminal'
戏迷 xìmí 'theatre fan'	烟鬼 yānguǐ 'heavy smoker'	教徒 jiàotú 'disciple'	恶棍 ègùn 'rogue'	监犯 jiānfàn 'prison convict'
影迷 yǐngmí 'movie fan'	醉鬼 zuìguǐ 'drunkard'	暴徒 bàotú 'ruffian'; 'thug'	土棍 tǔgùn 'local bully'	逃犯 táofàn 'escaped prisoner'
棋迷 qímí 'chess enthusiast'	魔鬼 móguǐ 'demon'; 'monster'	歹徒 dǎitú 'scoundrel'	讼棍 sònggùn 'legal pettifogger'	战犯 zhànfàn 'war prisoner'
财迷 **cáimí** 'moneygrubber'	胆小鬼 **dǎnxiǎoguǐ** 'coward'	叛徒 **pàntú** 'traitor'	学棍 **xuégùn** 'educator-despot'	政治犯 **zhèngzhìfàn** 'political prisoner'

Additional notes:

(1) It is interesting to know that 迷 **mí** 'someone who is obssessed by sth' (or sometimes its more exaggerated counterpart 狂 **kuáng** 'someone who is mad about sth') may be regarded as a universal equivalent to all the following different terms in English: a football fan, a photography bug, a cleanliness freak, a film buff, a fresh air fiend, a vegetarian nut, a bicycling enthusiast, a cinema aficionado, a car maniac, a lover of art, a devotee of Bach, a follower of Socrates, a fanatic for healthy food, a zealot against the use of narcotics, etc.

(2) 鬼 **guǐ** 'ghost' is generally used with people who are addicted to a particular hobby to the detriment of their health, livelihood and morality. It can also be associated with people whose behaviour one does not approve of. Here are more examples,

饿鬼 **èguǐ** 'glutton'　　　　　　　色鬼 **sèguǐ** 'sex maniac'
冒失鬼 **màoshiguǐ** 'harum-scarum'　　胆小鬼 **dǎnxiǎoguǐ** 'timid person'

迷 **mí** is often associated with more decent hobbies than 鬼. There are exceptions, however, like 财迷 **cáimí** 'miser'.

(3) 徒 **tú** 'disciple', like 鬼 **guǐ** 'ghost', generally implies dishonesty and villainy, with the exception of 门徒 **méntú** 'disciple'; 'follower' and 教徒 **jiàotú** 'follower of a religion', where 徒 **tú** seems to be more neutral in meaning. Here are a few more examples:

匪徒 **fěitú** 'bandit'　　　囚徒 **qiú** 'convict'

(4) 棍 **gùn** 'stick' normally means a 'bully' in a particular profession. 光棍儿 **guānggùnr** 'unmarried man' is an exception.

(5) 犯 **fàn** is used exclusively for 'criminals'. Here are some more examples,

首犯 **shǒufàn** 'principal culprit'　　从犯 **cóngfàn** 'accessory criminal'
惯犯 **guànfàn** 'habitual offender'　　疑犯 **yífàn** 'a suspect'
杀人犯 **shārénfàn** 'murderer'　　　盗窃犯 **dàoqièfàn** 'thief'
贪污犯 **tānwūfàn** 'grafter'　　　　强奸犯 **qiángjiānfàn** 'rapist'

(e) designated groups:

-zhòng 众 crowd	-shǔ 属 dependant	-pài 派 faction	-zú 族 peculiar group
观众 **guānzhòng** 'spectators'	亲属 **qīnshǔ** 'relatives'	左派 **zuǒpài** 'leftists'	民族 **mínzú** 'race'
听众 **tīngzhòng** 'audience'	家属 **jiāshǔ** 'family members'	右派 **yòupài** 'rightists'	家族 **jiāzú** 'family clan'
群众 **qúnzhòng** 'broad masses'	下属 **xiàshǔ** 'subordinates'	风派 **fēngpài** 'timeserver'	贵族 **guìzú** 'aristocrat'
大众 **dàzhòng** 'ordinary folks'	军属 **jūnshǔ** 'soldier's dependants'	保守派 **bǎoshǒupài** 'conservatives'	上班族 **shàngbānzú** 'goers-to-work'
民众 **mínzhòng** 'people'	部属 **bùshǔ** 'subordinates'	印象派 **yìnxiàngpài** 'impressionists'	皇族 **huángzú** 'imperial kinsmen'

(f) miscellaneous categories:

-hàn 汉	-shǒu 手	-kè 客	-cái 才/材
好汉 **hǎohàn** 'brave man'	选手 **xuǎnshǒu** 'athlete'	旅客 **lǚkè** 'tourist'	天才 **tiāncái** 'talent'; 'genius'
懒汉 **lǎnhàn** 'lazybones'	助手 **zhùshǒu** 'assistant'	乘客 **chéngkè** 'passenger'	蠢材 **chǔncái** 'idiot'; 'fool'
门外汉 **ménwàihàn** 'layman'	凶手 **xiōngshǒu** 'assassin'	顾客 **gùkè** 'customer'	奴才 **núcái** 'flunkey'; 'lackey'

Additional notes:

(1) 汉 **hàn** is chiefly used in connection with male persons. There are exceptions, of course, e.g. 门外汉 **ménwàihàn** 'man in the street', which applies to both sexes. A few more examples are listed below:

硬汉 **yìnghàn** 'unyielding man' 　老汉 **lǎohàn** 'old man'
大汉 **dàhàn** 'big fellow' 　　　　单身汉 **dānshēnhàn** 'bachelor (unmarried man)'
庄稼汉 **zhuāngjiahàn** 'peasant' 　男子汉 **nánzǐhàn** 'real man'

(2) 手 **shǒu** 'hand' is an obvious case of metonymy as a human suffix. A skilful person in a particular area of endeavour may often have this suffix: e.g.

水手 **shuǐshǒu** 'sailor' 　　　　猎手 **lièshǒu** 'hunter'
鼓手 **gǔshǒu** 'drummer' 　　　歌手 **gēshǒu** 'singer'
国手 **guóshǒu** 'national champion
　(in chess, etc.)'

More often 手 **shǒu** is used in terms of praise:

能手 **néngshǒu** 'skilled hand' 　　好手 **hǎoshǒu** 'good hand'
高手 **gāoshǒu** 'past master' 　　　熟手 **shúshǒu** 'practised hand'
舵手 **duòshǒu** 'helmsman' 　　　旗手 **qíshǒu** 'standard-bearer'
神枪手 **shénqiāngshǒu** 'crack shot' 多面手 **duōmiànshǒu** 'versatile person'

Of course, 手 **shǒu** can be more neutral in meaning in such combinations as:

老手 **lǎoshǒu** 'veteran' 　　新手 **xīnshǒu** 'raw recruit'
对手 **duìshǒu** 'opponent' 　敌手 **díshǒu** 'adversary'

It is also used in connection with some kind of immoral employment, where the 'hand' is put to an illegitimate use:

扒手 **páshǒu** 'pickpocket'   打手 **dǎshǒu** 'hired thug'

(3) 客 **kè** 'guest' generally refers to either a visitor or a client. Sometimes it means someone who is employed for some unapplaudable purpose:

房客 **fángkè** 'tenant (of a room)'   香客 **xiāngkè** 'pilgrim'
刺客 **cìkè** 'assassin'   政客 **zhèngkè** 'politician'

(4) 才 **cái** 'talent' is double-faced, with bias towards the better human category. For example,

人才/人材 **réncái** 'person of ability'   英才 **yīngcái** 'person of
通才 **tōngcái** 'all-round (or versatile) person'   outstanding ability'

(*g*) 子 **-zi**, used either colloquially for family relatives or for physically or mentally handicapped persons, or morally undesirable beings:

孩子 **háizi** 'child'; 'children'   妻子 **qīzi** 'wife'
老子 **lǎozi** '(colloq.) father'   老妈子 **lǎomāzi** '(colloq.) mother'
儿子 **érzi** 'son'   孙子 **sūnzi** 'grandson'
舅子 **jiùzi** '(colloq.) brother-in-law'   侄子 **zhízi** 'nephew'
婶子 **shěnzi** '(colloq.) aunt'   老头子 **lǎotóuzi** '(colloq.) husband'
嫂子 **sǎozi** '(colloq.) elder
    brother's wife'

瞎子 **xiāzi** 'blind person'   聋子 **lóngzi** 'deaf person'
哑子 **yǎzi** 'dumb person'   驼子 **tuózi** 'hunchback'
秃子 **tūzi** 'baldhead'   瘸子 **quézi** 'cripple'
麻子 **mázi** 'pock-marked person'   矮子 **ǎizi** 'dwarf'
胖子 **pàngzi** 'fat person'   呆子 **dāizi** 'idiot'
傻子 **shǎzi** 'fool'   疯子 **fēngzi** 'madman'

骗子 **piànzi** 'imposter'   拐子 **guǎizi** 'abductor'
婊子 **biǎozi** 'prostitute'

Additional note:

In fact, 子 *zi* is also used to indicate quite a number of human body parts: e.g.

身子 **shēnzi** (colloq.) 'body'   样子 **yàngzi** 'appearance'; 'manner'
脑子 **nǎozi** (colloq.) 'brain'   鼻子 **bízi** 'nose'
嗓子 **sǎngzi** 'throat'   胡子 **húzi** 'beard, moustache or whiskers'
脖子 **bózi** 'neck'   肚子 **dùzi** 'belly'
肠子 **chángzi** 'intestines'

(*h*) 头 **-tou/tóu**, used in a few human nouns with an inbuilt sense of contempt or disrespect:

孱头 **càntou** 'weakling'; 'coward'   姘头 **pīntou** 'paramour'
丫头 **yātou** 'maid'; 'servant girl'   滑头 **huátóu** 'slippery fellow'
对头 **duìtou** 'opponent'   冤头 **yuāntou** '(dial.) enemy'

(*i*) 儿 **ér**, found to denote love, sympathy or respect in a small number of human nouns:

婴儿 **yīng'ér** 'baby'　　幼儿 **yòu'ér** 'infant'　　孤儿 **gū'ér** 'orphan'
宠儿 **chǒng'ér** 'favourite'　女儿 **nǚ'ér** 'daughter'　健儿 **jiàn'ér** 'athlete'

(*j*) 分子 **fènzǐ** 'element', a disyllabic suffix attachable to adjectives, nouns, verbs or phrases:

坏分子 **huàifènzǐ** 'bad person'　　　积极分子 **jījí fènzǐ** 'activist'
落后分子 **luòhòu fènzǐ**　　　　　　知识分子 **zhīshi fènzǐ** 'intellectual'
　'backward person'　　　　　　　　投机分子 **tóujī fènzi** 'opportunist'

The following is a summary chart of human noun affixes:

Prefixes:
　老 **lǎo**-, 阿 **ā**-
Suffixes:
　人-**rén**
　家-**jia**, 者-**zhě**, 师 **shī**, 生-**sheng**, 士-**shì**
　员-**yuán**, 工-**gōng**, 匠-**jiàng**, 夫 **fū**, 差-**chāi**, 丁-**dīng**, 民-**mín**
　长-**zhǎng**, 主-**zhǔ**, 豪-**háo**, 阀-**fá**, 将-**jiàng**
　迷-**mí**, 鬼-**guǐ**, 徒-**tú**, 棍-**gùn**, 犯-**fàn**
　众-**zhòng**, 属-**shǔ**, 派-**pài**, 族-**zú**
　汉-**hàn**, 手-**shǒu**, 客 **kè**, 才 **cái**, 材 **cái**
　子-**zi**, 头-**tou**, 儿 **ér**
　分子 **fènzǐ**

AFFIXES FOR NON-HUMAN NOUNS

For non-human entities, the prefix 老 **lǎo**[12] is only found with a few animal nouns, e.g.

老虎 **lǎohǔ** 'tiger'　　老鹰 **lǎoyīng** 'eagle'　　老鼠 **lǎoshǔ** 'mouse'; 'rat'

Another prefix: 所 **suǒ**, whose grammatical meaning is to indicate an object, is found to be extremely prolific with verbs. It combines mostly with transitive verbs in the language to form nouns equivalent to 'what one does' in English. For example,

所见 **suǒjiàn** 'what one sees'　　所闻 **suǒwén** 'what one hears'
所知 **suǒzhī** 'what one knows'　　所有 **suǒyǒu** 'possession'
所在 **suǒzài** 'location'　　　　　所得 **suǒdé** 'income'

---

[12] The prefix 老 **lǎo** must be distinguished from the fully-fledged morpheme 老 **lǎo** 'old' in word formation: e.g. 老家 'native place', 老路 'beaten track', etc.

The most versatile non-human nominal suffix is 子 **zi**, which is affixable mostly to inanimate nouns. It is also used with a small number of non-human animate nouns. The following examples are arranged in semantic categories:

(1) animals, birds, and insects:

狮子 **shīzi** 'lion'		猴子 **hóuzi** 'monkey'	
豹子 **bàozi** 'leopard'		兔子 **tùzi** 'hare'; 'rabbit'	
骡子 **luózi** 'mule'		驴子 **lǘzi** '(dial.) donkey'; 'ass'	

燕子 **yànzi** 'swallow' 鸽子 **gēzi** 'pigeon'; 'dove'
鸭子 **yāzi** '(colloq.) duck'

虫子 **chóngzi** 'insect'; 'worm' 蚊子 **wénzi** 'mosquito'
蝎子 **xiēzi** 'scorpion' 虱子 **shīzi** 'louse'

(2) plants:[13]

种子 **zhǒngzǐ** 'seed' 麦子 **màizi** 'wheat'
稻子 **dàozi** '(colloq.) rice' 谷子 **gǔzi** 'millet'; (dialectal)
豆子 **dòuzi** 'beans or peas' 'unhusked rice'
柿子 **shìzi** 'persimmon' 橘子 **júzi** 'tangerine'
栗子 **lìzi** 'chestnut' 枣子 **zǎozi** 'jujube'; 'date'
桃子 **táozi** 'peach' 李子 **lǐzi** 'plum'
竹子 **zhúzi** 'bamboo' 藤子 **téngzi** '(colloq.) vine'
叶子 **yèzi** 'leaf'

(3) food:

包子 **bāozi** 'steamed stuffed bun'
饺子 **jiǎozi** 'dumpling (with meat and vegetable stuffing)'
粽子 **zòngzi** 'pyramid-shaped dumpling of glutinous rice wrapped in reed leaves'

(4) fabrics and articles of clothing or parts of clothing:

裤子 **kùzi** 'trousers'	裙子 **qúnzi** 'skirt'	帽子 **màozi** 'hat'; 'cap'
鞋子 **xiézi** '(dialectal) shoes'	靴子 **xuēzi** 'boots'	袜子 **wàzi** 'socks'; 'stockings'
	袖子 **xiùzi** 'sleeve'	
领子 **lǐngzi** 'collar'	扣子 **kòuzi** 'button'	袋子 **dàizi** 'pocket'
带子 **dàizi** 'belt'		里子 **lǐzi** 'lining'
绸子 **chóuzi** 'silk fabric'	缎子 **duànzi** 'satin'	呢子 **nízi** 'woollen cloth'

---

[13] It is particularly important in this context to distinguish between the suffix 子 **zi** and the fully-fledged 子 **zǐ** 'seed': e.g. 瓜子 **guāzǐ** 'melon seeds', 莲子 **liánzǐ** 'lotus seeds', etc. 子 **zǐ** is also used to mean 'particle' in the following lexical combinations:

原子 **yuánzǐ** 'atom' 分子 **fēnzǐ** (chemistry) 'molecule'
粒子 **lìzǐ** (physics) 'particle' 光子 **guāngzǐ** (physics) 'photon'
电子 **diànzǐ** 'electron' 中子 **zhōngzǐ** (physics) 'neutron'
质子 **zhìzǐ** 'proton' 介子 **jièzǐ** (physics) 'meson'; 'mesotron'
离子 **lízǐ** (physics) 'ion' 量子 **liàngzǐ** 'quantum'

It might have already been noted that only articles of clothing which are worn below the 'belt' seem to have the suffix -zi. Clothes worn on the upper part of the body are mostly organized around the 'generic' term 衣 **yī** 'clothes'; 'garment', e.g.

衬衣 **chènyī** 'shirt' 上衣 **shàngyī** 'jacket'
毛衣 **máoyī** 'woollen sweater' 大衣 **dàyī** 'overcoat'
雨衣 **yǔyī** 'raincoat' 浴衣 **yùyī** 'bathrobe'

(5) houses and parts of houses:

房子 **fángzi** 'house' 屋子 **wūzi** 'room'
院子 **yuànzi** 'courtyard' 窗子 **chuāngzi** 'window'
柱子 **zhùzi** 'post'; 'pillar' 椽子 **chuánzi** 'rafter'

(6) furniture:

桌子 **zhuōzi** 'table'; 'desk'   椅子 **yǐzi** 'chair'
箱子 **xiāngzi** 'chest'; 'case'; 'trunk' 凳子 **dèngzi** 'stool'
盒子 **hézi** 'box'; 'casket'   柜子 **guìzi** 'cupboard'; 'cabinet'

(7) bedroom or toilet things:

被子 **bèizi** 'quilt'   垫子 **diànzi** 'cushion'
褥子 **rùzi** 'cotton-padded mattress' 毯子 **tǎnzi** 'blanket'
席子 **xízi** 'mat'   镜子 **jìngzi** 'mirror'
梳子 **shūzi** 'comb'   刷子 **shuāzi** 'brush'
扇子 **shànzi** 'fan'   链子 **liànzi** 'chain'
掸子 **dǎnzi** 'duster (usually 帘子 **liánzi** '(colloq.)
made of chicken feathers or (hanging) screen';
strips of cloth)'   'curtain'

(8) kitchen utensils:

盘子 **pánzi** 'plate'   碟子 **diézi** 'small dish'
筷子 **kuàizi** 'chopsticks' 匙子 **chízi** 'spoon'
瓶子 **píngzi** 'bottle' 炉子 **lúzi** 'stove'; 'oven'
管子 **guǎnzi** 'tube'; 'pipe' 篮子 **lánzi** 'basket'
筛子 **shāizi** 'sieve' 勺子 **sháozi** 'ladle'; 'scoop'
刀子 **dāozi** 'pocket-knife' 罐子 **guànzi** 'tin or can'

So we see that the most common part of the furniture and all the things which are handy for daily use take the suffix -zi. Table, chairs, quilts, blankets, combs, brushes, spoons and chopsticks all fall into this category.

(9) tools and implements:

斧子 **fǔzi** 'axe' 锤子 **chuízi** 'hammer' 钳子 **qiánzi**
凿子 **zuòzi** 'chisel' 锯子 **jùzi** 'saw'   'pliers'; 'pincers'
铲子 **chǎnzi** 'shovel' 钩子 **gōuzi** 'hook' 刨子 **páozi** 'plane'
锥子 **zhuīzi** 'awl' 镊子 **nièzi** 'tweezers' 钉子 **dīngzi** 'nail'
梯子 **tīzi** 'ladder' 架子 **jiàzi**   轮子 **lúnzi** 'wheel'
滚子 **gǔnzi**   'frame, rack' 碾子 **niǎnzi** 'roller'
'stone roller' 剪子 **jiǎnzi** 'scissors' 绳子 **shéngzi** 'rope'

We can see that these '-zi' tools are mainly carpenter's tools, whereas their monosyllabic counterparts in the lexicon are mostly codes for farming implements: e.g.

犁 **lí** 'plough'	耙 **pá** 'harrow'	镐 **gǎo** 'pick'; 'pickaxe'
桶 **tǒng** 'bucket'	秤 **chèng** 'steelyard'	斗 **dǒu** 'a dou measure'
网 **wǎng** 'net'	磨 **mò** 'millstone'	箩 **luó** 'hamper'

(10) miscellaneous and more abstract concepts:

疹子 **zhěnzi** '(colloq.) measles'	辫子 **biànzi** 'pigtails'
单子 **dānzi** 'list'	方子 **fāngzi** 'prescription'
法子 **fǎzi** 'method'	例子 **lìzi** 'example'
胆子 **dǎnzi** 'courage'	性子 **xìngzi** 'temperament'
日子 **rìzi** 'days'	路子 **lùzi** 'way'; 'approach'

The suffix 头 **tóu** or **tou** may be found in most of the lexemes representing entities, the whole or parts of which are attached to one end or are reminiscent of the shape of 'head'. This, of course, is confined to concrete nouns only. There is no way of telling precisely why some abstract nouns also have 头 **tóu/tou**, just as they have 子 **zǐ/zi**, suffixes. However, the transferred meanings of 'head', i.e. 'end', 'target', etc. might be subconsciously at work in most cases.

锄头 **chútou** 'hoe'	榔头 **lángtou** 'hammer'
木头 **mùtou** 'wood'	砖头 **zhuāntou** '(dialectal) brick'
芋头 **yùtou** 'taro'	馒头 **mántou** 'steamed bun'
舌头 **shétou** 'tongue'	指头 **zhítou** 'finger'; 'toe'
骨头 **gútou** 'bone'	浪头 **làngtou** '(crest of) wave'
年头 **niántóu** 'year'	钟头 **zhōngtóu** (colloq.) 'hour'
苦头 **kǔtóu** 'suffering'	甜头 **tiántou** 'benefit (as an
奔头儿 **bèntour** 'prospect'	inducement)'
念头 **niàntou** 'thought'; 'idea'	想头 **xiǎngtou** (colloq.) 'hope'
噱头 **xuétóu** (dialectal)	看头 **kàntou** (colloq.) 'something
'works of art meant to	worth seeing or reading'
amuse or to excite laughter'	

The suffix 儿 **(e)r** is optional. It is a natural suffix to many nouns in Beijing dialect: e.g.

鸟(儿) **niǎo(r)** 'bird'	根(儿) **gēn(r)** 'root (of a plant)'
味(儿) **wèi(r)** 'flavour'	歌(儿) **gē(r)** 'song'
花(儿) **huā(r)** 'flower'	画(儿) **huà(r)** 'drawing'; 'painting'

In some cases, 儿 **(e)r** is an alternative suffix for -zi: e.g.

面(儿) **miàn(r)**	vs	面子 **miànzi** 'outside'; 'face'
里(儿) **lǐ(r)**		里子 **lǐzi** 'lining'
底(儿) **dǐ(r)**		底子 **dǐzi** 'bottom'; 'base'
盖(儿) **gài(r)**		盖子 **gàizi** 'lid'; 'cover'; 'cap'
牌(儿) **pái(r)**		牌子 **páizi** 'plate'; 'sign'

巴 **bā/ba** is also a suffix found in a small number of words: e.g.

尾巴 **wěiba** 'tail'　　　　　嘴巴 **zuǐba** '(dialectal) mouth'
下巴 **xiàba** 'chin'　　　　　哑吧 **yǎba** 'a dumb person'
泥巴 **níbā** '(dialectal) mud'　锅巴 **guōbā** 'crust of cooked rice'; 'rice crust'

Many non-human *pseudo-suffixes* may be found in the lexicon. They are monomyms that signify very general categories: e.g.

机 **jī** *'machine'; 'apparatus'*	器 **qì** *'instrument'*	具 **jù** *'tool'; 'utensil'*
飞机 **fēijī** 'aircraft'; 'aeroplane'	武器 **wǔqì** 'weapon'; 'arms'	工具 **gōngjù** 'tool'; 'instrument'
发动机 **fādòngjī** 'engine'; 'motor'	仪器 **yíqì** 'instrument'; 'apparatus'	文具 **wénjù** 'stationery'
打字机 **dǎzìjī** 'typewriter'	瓷器 **cíqì** 'porcelain'; 'chinaware'	炊具 **chuījù** 'cooking utensils'
计算机 **jìsuànjī** 'computer'	乐器 **yuèqì** 'musical instrument'	家具 **jiājù** 'furniture'
收音机 **shōuyīnjī** 'radio (set)'	喷雾器 **pēnwùqì** 'sprayer'	道具 **dàojù** 'stage property'; 'prop'
打火机 **dǎhuǒjī** 'lighter'	助听器 **zhùtīngqì** 'hearing aid'	玩具 **wánjù** 'toy'; 'plaything'
摄影机 **shèyǐngjī** 'camera'	变压器 **biànyāqì** 'transformer'	农具 **nóngjù** 'farm tools'

物 **wù** *'entity'; 'thing'*	品 **pǐn** *'item'; 'article'*	事 **shì** *'event'; 'affair'*
动物 **dòngwù** 'animal'	商品 **shāngpǐn** 'commodity'	公事 **gōngshì** 'public affairs'
植物 **zhíwù** 'plant'; 'flora'	产品 **chǎnpǐn** 'product'; 'produce'	私事 **sīshì** 'private affairs'
生物 **shēngwù** 'living things'	食品 **shípǐn** 'food'; 'foodstuff'	急事 **jíshì** 'a matter of urgency'
文物 **wénwù** 'cultural relic'	用品 **yòngpǐn** 'articles for use'	婚事 **hūnshì** 'marriage'
饰物 **shìwù** 'jewellery'	样品 **yàngpǐn** 'specimen'	逸事 **yìshì** 'anecdote'
货物 **huòwù** 'goods'	奖品 **jiǎngpǐn** 'prize'; 'trophy'	房事 **fángshì** 'sexual intercourse'
礼物 **lǐwù** 'gift'; 'present'	毒品 **dúpǐn** 'narcotics'; 'drugs'	心事 **xīnshì** 'a load on one's mind'
刊物 **kānwù** 'publication'	作品 **zuòpǐn** 'works of literature/art'	闲事 **xiánshì** 'other people's affairs'

Unlike concrete nouns which usually adopt native affixes, abstract nouns are very much influenced by translating from foreign languages. Regular quasi-suffixes indicating nounness may include: e.g.

体 **tǐ** *'entity'*	界 **jiè** *'circles (of people)'*	节 **jié** *'festival'*
固体 **gùtǐ** 'solid'	外界 **wàijiè** 'the outside world'	春节 **chūnjié** 'the Spring Festival'
液体 **yètǐ** 'liquid'	政界 **zhèngjiè** 'political circles'	灯节 **dēngjié** 'the Lantern Festival'
气体 **qìtǐ** 'gas'	学术界 **xuéshùjiè** 'academic circles.'	圣诞节 **shèngdànjié** 'Christmas'
半导体 **bàndǎotǐ** 'semiconductor'	戏剧界 **xìjùjiè** 'theatrical circles'	复活节 **fùhuójié** 'Easter'
园柱体 **yuánzhùtǐ** 'cylinder'	艺术界 **yìshùjiè** 'art circles'	国庆节 **guóqìngjié** 'National Day'

Additional notes: 体 **tǐ** is a suffix which presumes a shape or some kind of shared property: e.g. 球体 **qiútǐ** 'spheroid', 晶体 **jīngtǐ** 'crystal', etc.; 界 **jiè** is suffixable to most nouns to indicate a related circle of people: e.g. 电影界 **diànyǐngjiè** 'film circles', etc.; 节 **jié** is suffixable to most nouns to indicate a particular festival: e.g. 泼水节 **pōshuǐjié** 'Water-Splashing Festival of the Dais (傣族)', etc.

性 **xìng** *'spirit'*	度 **dù** *'degree'*	式 **shì** *'style'*
惰性 **duòxìng** 'inertia'	深度 **shēndù** 'depth'	老式 **lǎoshì** 'old style'
耐性 **nàixìng** 'patience'	广度 **guǎngdù** 'scope'; 'range'	新式 **xīnshì** 'new style'
弹性 **tánxìng** 'resilience'	高度 **gāodù** 'altitude'; 'height'	正式 **zhèngshì** 'formal'; 'official'
酸性 **suānxìng** 'acidity'	温度 **wēndù** 'temperature'	中式 **zhōngshì** 'Chinese style'
碱性 **jiǎnxìng** 'alkalinity'	强度 **qiángdù** 'intensity'; 'strength'	蛙式 **wāshì** 'breaststroke'
两重性 **liǎngchóngxìng** 'duality'	灵敏度 **língmǐndù** 'sensitivity'	蝶式 **diéshì** 'butterfly stroke'

Additional notes: 性 **xìng** and 度 **dù** are equally versatile: they are suffixable to most adjectival monyms. Here are some more examples of each: 本性 **běnxìng** 'nature', 个性 **gèxìng** 'individuality', 共性 **gòngxìng** 'generality', 特性 **tèxìng** 'specific property', 劣根性 **lièngēnxìng**, 'inherent weakness'; 密度 **mìdù** 'density'; 'thickness', 浓度 **nóngdù** 'concentration'; 'density', 湿度 **shīdù** 'humidity', 难度 **nándù** 'degree of difficulty', 限度 **xiàndù** 'limit'.

学 xué '-ology'	论 lùn 'theory'	处 chu 'locus'
科学 kēxué 'science'	理论 lǐlùn 'theory'	好处 hǎochu 'advantage'
文学 wénxué 'literature'	唯心论 wéixīnlùn 'idealism'	坏处 huàichu 'disadvantage'
化学 huàxué 'chemistry'	唯物论 wéiwùlùn 'materialism'	长处 chángchu strong point'
力学 lìxué 'mechanics'	认识论 rènshilùn 'epistemology'	短处 duǎnchu 'shortcoming'
数学 shùxué 'mathematics'	谬论 miùlùn 'fallacy'	益处 yìchu 'benefit'
心理学 xīnlǐxué 'psychology'	言论 yánlùn 'speech'	害处 hàichu 'harm'

Additional notes: 学 **xué**, as we can see, is essentially associated with academic disciplines, whereas 论 **lùn**, with different theories. 处 **chu** (or **chù**), more often unstressed than not, is suffixable to an adjectival or verbal monomym to refer to the area or locus where the specific feature indicated by the adjective or the verb is to be found. Here are some more examples: 难处 **nánchu** 'difficulty', 深处 **shēnchu** 'depths'; 'recesses', 用处 **yòngchu** 'use', 患处 **huànchù** 'the affected area (of a patient's body)', etc.

The following is a summary of non-human noun affixes.

> Prefixes:
> 老 **lǎo-**, 所 **suǒ-**
> Suffixes:
> 子 **-zi**, 头 **-tou**, 儿 **-(e)r**, 巴 **bā/ba**
> Quasi-suffixes:
> 机-**jī**, 器-**qì**, 具-**jù**, 物-**wù**, 品-**pǐn**, 事-**shì**
> 体-**tǐ**, 界-**jiè**, 节-**jié**, 性-**xìng**, 度-**dù**, 式-**shì**, 学-**xué**, 论-**lùn**, 处-**chù**

VERBAL AFFIXES

Except for the set of 'aspectual markers' which can be regarded as similar to inflectional suffixes and which we would like to exclude from our discussion purely because they are better dealt with from a syntactic point of view, verbs (and sometimes adjectives, i.e. stative verbs) are particularly receptive to a set of *suffixes* beginning with y-:

于 yú	以 yǐ	予 yǔ
濒于 bīnyú 'on the brink of'	借以 jièyǐ 'so as to'; 'by way of'	赐予 cìyǔ 'grant'; 'bestow'
等于 děngyú 'equal to'	得以 déyǐ 'so that . . . can . . .'	赋予 fùyǔ 'entrust'
属于 shǔyú 'belong to'	用以 yòngyǐ 'in order to'	给予 jǐyǔ '(formal) give'

于 yú	以 yǐ	予 yǔ
在于 zàiyú 'lie in'; 'rest with'	加以 jiāyǐ '(action) to be taken'	授予 shòuyǔ 'confer'; 'award'
出于 chūyú 'stem from'	可以 kěyǐ 'can'; 'may'	准予 zhǔnyǔ 'permit'
限于 xiànyú 'confined to'	予以 yǔyǐ 'bestow'	寄予 jìyǔ 'place (hope) on'
敢于 gǎnyú 'dare to'	足以 zúyǐ 'sufficient to'	
急于 jíyú 'eager'; 'anxious'	难以 nányǐ 'difficult to'	
便于 biànyú 'convenient for'		
善于 shànyú 'be good at'		
富于 fùyú 'imbued with'		
忠于 zhōngyú 'loyal to'		

Additional notes: 于 yú is the most versatile of the three as it is more readily suffixable to adjectival monosyms whereas the other two are generally confined to verbal monosyms. Semantically, 于 yú indicates the area, geographical or metaphorical, where a particular situation is to be expected; 以 yǐ highlights the purpose of an action, whether it is realisable or not; 予 yǔ refers to what is being granted to a target or patient in an act of giving or bestowing.

Other suffixes are more meaning-oriented:

化 -huà -en; -ise; -fy; -ate	得 de achieve or avoid	有 yǒu possess
变化 biànhuà 'change'	懂得 dǒngde 'understand'	占有 zhànyǒu 'to own'; 'occupy'
进化 jìnhuà 'evolve'	认得 rènde 'know'; 'recognise'	具有 jùyǒu 'possess'
老化 lǎohuà 'to age'	记得 jìde 'remember'	罕有 hǎnyǒu 'very rare'
硬化 yìnhuà 'harden'	觉得 juéde 'feel'	富有 fùyǒu 'be rich in'; 'be full of'
丑化 chǒuhuà 'defame'; 'uglify'	值得 zhíde 'be worth'; 'deserve'	附有 fùyǒu 'attach'
简化 jiǎnhuà 'simplify'	免得 miǎnde 'so as not'	赋有 fùyǒu 'be endowed with'
欧化 ōuhuà 'westernise'	懒得 lǎnde 'not feel like doing sth'	拥有 yōngyǒu 'possess'; 'have'
归化 guīhuà 'naturalise'	省得 shěngde 'so as to avoid'	含有 hányǒu 'contain'
大众化 dàzhònghuà 'popularise'	显得 xiǎnde 'look'; 'appear'	享有 xiǎngyǒu 'enjoy (rights, etc.)'
现代化 xiàndàihuà 'modernise'	晓得 xiǎode 'know'	持有 chíyǒu 'hold (e.g. passport)'

There is only one verbal prefix in the lexicon 相 **xiāng** 'mutual' which is extremely versatile:

相比 **xiāngbǐ** 'compare'
相差 **xiāngchā** 'differ'
相处 **xiāngchû** 'get along (with one another)'
相信 **xiāngxìn** 'be convinced of'
相等 **xiāngděng** 'be equal'
相符 **xiāngfú** 'conform to'; 'tally with'
相关 **xiāngguān** 'be interrelated'

相似 **xiāngsì** 'be similar'; 'be alike'
相同 **xiāngtóng** 'be identical'
相反 **xiāngfǎn** 'be opposite'; 'be contrary to'
相仿 **xiāngfǎng** 'be more or less the same'
相近 **xiāngjìn** 'be similar (or close) to'
相宜 **xiāngyí** 'be suitable for'
相应 **xiāngyìng** 'be corresponding to'

One could coin freely without offending native speakers, e.g.

相爱 **xiāng'ài** 'fall in love with each other'
相托 **xiāngtuō** 'entrust'

相敬 **xiāngjìng** 'respect each other'
相商 **xiāngshāng** 'consult each other'

ADJECTIVAL AFFIXES

Adjectives are extremely prolific with the following three prefixes:[14]

可 **kě** '-able/-ible'	好 **hǎo** (positive)	难 **nán** (negative)
可爱 **kě'ài** 'lovable'; 'lovely'	好吃 **hǎochī** 'tasty'; 'delicious'	难吃 **nánchī** 'taste bad'
可靠 **kěkào** 'reliable'	好听 **hǎotīng** 'pleasant to hear'	难听 **nántīng** 'unpleasant to hear'
可耻 **kěchǐ** 'disgraceful'	好闻 **hǎowén** 'smell pleasant'	难闻 **nánwén** 'smell unpleasant'
可恨 **kěhèn** 'detestable'	好看 **hǎokàn** 'good-looking'	难看 **nánkàn** 'ugly'; 'unsightly'
可观 **kěguān** 'considerable'	好办 **hǎobàn** 'easy to handle'	难得 **nándé** 'hard to come by'
可贵 **kěguì** 'praiseworthy'	好笑 **hǎoxiào** 'funny'; 'ridiculous'	难过 **nánguò** 'feel sorry'

Additional notes:

(1) 可 **kě** is almost as versatile as the English suffix *-able*. It combines profusely with verbal or adjectival monyms to form new adjectives. Here are some more examples:

[14] There are other adjectival prefixes arising out of translation, e.g. 亲 **qīn** in 亲美 **qīnměi** 'pro-American', etc., and 泛 **fàn** in 泛美 **fànměi** 'pan-American', etc., which have not been included in the discussion.

可怜 **kělián** 'pitiful'; 'pitiable', 可能 **kěnéng** 'possible'; 'probable', 可怕 **kěpà** 'terrifying', 可取 **kěqǔ** 'desirable', 可恶 **kěwù** 'abominable'; 'detestable', 可喜 **kěxǐ** 'gratifying'; 'heartening', 可笑 **kěxiào** 'ridiculous'; 'ludicrous', 可行 **kěxíng** 'feasible', 可疑 **kěyí** 'suspicious', etc. Sometimes it also combines with nouns, but then the resultant lexeme becomes a syntactically motivated 'verb + object' type of verb.[15] For example, 可口 **kěkǒu** 'good to eat' (口 **kǒu** means 'mouth'), 可身 **kěshēn** '(dialectal) fit nicely' (身 **shēn** means 'body'), 可意 **kěyì** 'gratifying' (意 **yì** means 'wish'), etc.

(2) 好 **hǎo** is very productive. It can combine with any verb if the occasion warrants it. For example, when talking about a bicycle or a very regular telephone number, one can form such *ad hoc* ones as: 好骑 **hǎoqí** 'easy to ride', 好记 **hǎojì** 'easy to remember', etc.

(3) 难- **nán-**, like 好- **hǎo-**, is also productive. It combines readily with verbs if occasion arises. For example, 难说 **nánshuō** 'hard to say', 难懂 **nándǒng** 'difficult to understand', 难做 **nánzuò** 'difficult to do', etc.

切 **qiè** indicates a condition or situation that suggests imminence or precision, which is probably the only monosyllabic adjectival suffix found in the lexicon, e.g.

迫切 **pòqiè** 'urgent'; 'imperative'   急切 **jíqiè** 'impatient'
确切 **quèqiè** 'exact'; 'precise'   贴切 **tiēqiè** '(of words) apt'; 'proper'
密切 **mìqiè** 'close'; 'intimate'   亲切 **qīnqiè** 'cordial'; 'kind'
恳切 **kěnqiè** 'earnest'; 'sincere'   凄切 **qīqiè** 'plaintive'; 'mournful'

Reiterated or associative phonaesthemes of adjectives may also be regarded as disyllabic or trisyllabic suffixes, e.g. 绿茸茸 **lǜróngróng** 'green', 黑咕隆咚 **hēigulōngdōng** 'pitch-dark', etc.[16]

ADVERBIAL AFFIXES

The most prolific prefix found with adverbs is 一 **yī** which combines with a great variety of mononyms to form words indicating either time or attitude: e.g.

time	*attitude*
一边 **yībiān** 'simultaneously'	一定 **yīdìng** 'certainly'
一次 **yīcì** 'once'	一概 **yīgài** 'one and all'
一道 **yīdào** 'together'	一律 **yīlǜ** 'without exception'

[15] See Chapter 4 on governmental type of verbs.
[16] Cf. Chapter 5 for details of this type of phonaesthetic suffixes.

time	attitude
一齐 **yīqí** 'at the same time'; 'unison'	一味 **yīwèi** 'blindly'
一起 **yīqǐ** 'together'; 'in company'	一心 **yīxīn** 'wholeheartedly'
一同 **yītóng** 'together'	一样 **yīyàng** 'the same'; 'alike'
一向 **yīxiàng** 'consistently'	一致 **yīzhì** 'unanimously'
一直 **yīzhí** 'always'; 'all along'	一准 **yīzhǔn** 'surely'
一生 **yīshēng** 'all one's life'	一贯 **yīguàn** 'persistently'
一下 **yīxià** 'in a short while'; 'all at once'	一会儿 **yīhuìr** 'in a moment'
一气 **yīqì** 'at one go'; 'without a break'; 'at a stretch'	一手 **yīshǒu** 'skill'; 'trick'; 'all by oneself'
一举 **yījǔ** 'one action'; 'one stroke'	一发 **yīfā** 'all the more'; 'even more'; 'together'

There is a set of suffixes in which attitude is built into the notion of time: e.g.

且 **qiě**	来 **lái**	地 **dì**	然 **rán**	而 **ér**
暂且 **zànqiě** 'for the moment'	原来 **yuánlái** 'at first'	蓦地 **mòdì** 'unexpectedly'	突然 **tūrán** 'abruptly'	时而 **shí'ér** 'from time to time'
聊且 **liáoqiě** 'tentatively'	本来 **běnlái** 'originally'	霍地 **huòdì** 'suddenly'	忽然 **hūrán** 'all of a sudden'	忽而 **hū'ér** 'now . . . now . . .'
姑且 **gūqiě** 'tentatively'	从来 **cónglái** 'all times'	忽地 **hūdì** 'all of a sudden'	骤然 **zhòurán** 'abruptly'	俄而 **é'ér** 'presently'
权且 **quánqiě** 'for the time being'	素来 **sùlái** 'always'	倏地 **shūdì** 'swiftly'	霍然 **huòrán** 'quickly'	进而 **jìn'ér** 'proceed'
而且 **érqiě** 'and also'	向来 **xiànglái** 'all along'	特地 **tèdì** 'specially'	仍然 **réngrán** 'still'; 'yet'	既而 **jì'ér** 'subsequently'
并且 **bìngqiě** 'moreover'	历来 **lìlái** 'constantly'	恁地 **nèndì** '(dial.) like that'	偶然 **ǒurán** 'accidentally'	率而 **shuài'ér** '(written) hastily'

Additional notes:

(1) 地 **dì**, though it is homographic with the structural particle 地 **de** (usually unstressed), is a derivational rather than inflectional suffix. The latter is used to form extemporaneous adverbs whereas the former is only suffixable to more classical and dependent monosyllabic monosyms to form disyllabic adverbs.

(2) Adverbs have a classical suffix 然 **rán** whose combinations are here classified into major semantic categories to show the full scope of the combinatory power of the suffix: e.g.

certainty and determination	majesty and solemnity	sadness and disappointment	quietude and calmness
当然 **dāngrán** 'of course'	赫然 **hèrán** 'impressively'	惘然 **wǎngrán** 'frustrated'	寂然 **jìrán** 'silent'; 'still'
自然 **zìrán** 'naturally'	昂然 **ángrán** 'upright'	凄然 **qīrán** 'mournful'	安然 **ānrán** 'peacefully'
断然 **duànrán** 'categorically'	凛然 **lǐnrán** 'awe-inspiring'	怅然 **chàngrán** 'disappointed'	泰然 **tàirán** 'composed'
毅然 **yìrán** 'resolutely'	俨然 **yǎnrán** 'solemn'	悄然 **qiāorán** 'sadly'	坦然 **tǎnrán** 'unperturbed'

indifference	surprise and excitement	happiness	clarity
漠然 **mòrán** 'indifferently'	哗然 **huārán** 'in an uproar'	欣然 **xīnrán** 'joyfully'	了然 **liǎorán** 'clearly'
孑然 **jiérán** 'lonely'; 'alone'	勃然 **bórán** 'agitatedly'	怡然 **yírán** 'contented'	显然 **xiǎnrán** 'obvious'
超然 **chāorán** 'aloof'	愕然 **èrán** 'stunned'	翩然 **piānrán** 'trippingly'	斐然 **fěirán** 'striking'
淡然 **dànrán** 'unenthusiastic'	竟然 **jìngrán** 'go so far as to'	飘然 **piāorán** 'smugly'	昭然 **zhāorán** 'manifestly'

completeness	futility	concession	others
全然 **quánrán** 'entirely'	枉然 **wǎngrán** 'of no avail'	固然 **gùrán** 'admittedly'	悠然 **yōurán** 'carefree'
截然 **jiérán** 'sharply'	徒然 **túrán** 'in vain'	诚然 **chéngrán** 'true'; 'indeed'	贸然 **màorán** 'rashly'
荡然 **dàngrán** 'all gone'	茫然 **mángrán** 'at a loss'	既然 **jìrán** 'since'; 'now that'	木然 **mùrán** 'stupefied'
浑然 **húnrán** 'wholly'	依然 **yīrán** 'as before'	纵然 **zòngrán** 'even though'	释然 **shìrán** 'relieved'

The most interesting thing to know about these 然 **rán** adverbs is that they are usually used to modify disyllabic verbs. If the verbs were originally monosyllabic, structural mononyms have to be introduced to make the verbs disyllabic in the first place.

(3) As the adverbial suffix 尔 **ěr** only occurs in one word 偶尔 **ǒu'ěr** 'occasionally', we have not included it in our discussion.

NUMERICAL PREFIXES

第一 **dìyī** 'first'   第二 **dì'èr** 'second'   第十 **dìshí** 'tenth'
初一 **chū yī** 'the first   初二 **chū èr** 'the second   初十 **chū shí** 'the tenth'
  (of a month)'   (of a month)'

There are some others which draw inspiration from foreign words: e.g.

半 **bàn** *'half; semi-'*	多 **duō** *'multi-'*	超 **chāo** *'over-; super-; ultra-'*
半价 **bànjià** 'half price'	多边 **duōbiān** 'multilateral'	超速 **chāosù** 'exceed the speed limit'
半票 **bànpiào** 'half fare'	多数 **duōshù** 'the majority'	超重 **chāozhòng** 'overload'; 'overweight'
半成品 **bànchéngpǐn** 'semi-manufactured products'	多样化 **duōyànghuà** 'diversify'	超声波 **chāoshēngbō** 'ultrasonic (wave)'; 'supersonic (wave)'

PRONOMINAL SUFFIX 们 **MEN** FOR PLURAL

我们 **wǒmen** 'we'; 'us'
咱们 **zánmen** we (including both the speaker and the person or persons spoken to)

你们 **nǐmen** 'you'
他们 **tāmen** 'they'; 'them'

PREPOSITIONAL SUFFIXES

于 **yú**	着 **zhe**	了 **le**
至于 **zhìyú** 'as for'	沿着 **yánzhe** 'along'	为了 **wèile** 'in order to'
由于 **yóuyú** 'due to'	接着 **jiēzhe** 'after that'	除了 **chúle** 'except'; 'besides'
对于 **duìyú** 'as to'	本着 **běnzhe** 'in the light of'	
关于 **guānyú** 'about'; 'concerning'	随着 **suízhe** 'along with'	

Additional notes:

(1) The prepositional suffix 着 **zhe** introduces a kind of dynamic into the co-textual verb whereas the original preposition without the suffix tends to indicate a static situation: e.g. 沿路 **yán lù** 'alongside the road' vs 沿着路走 **yánzhe lù zǒu** 'go along the road'.

(2) The prepositional suffix 了 **le** introduces a verbal notion whereas the original preposition introduces a (pro)nominal one: e.g. 为你 **wèi nǐ** 'for you' vs 为了保护 . . . **wèile bǎohù** . . . 'in order to protect . . .'.

CONJUNCTIONAL SUFFIXES

且 qiě	而 ér	然 rán	是 shì/shi	如 rú
并且 **bìngqiě** 'furthermore'	然而 **rán'ér** 'yet'	既然 **jìrán** 'now that'; 'since'	要是 **yàoshi** 'in case'	假如 **jiǎrú** 'if'
况且 **kuàngqiě** 'moreover'	从而 **cóng'ér** 'thus'; 'thereby'	纵然 **zòngrán** 'even though'	但是 **dànshì** 'but'	譬如 **pìrú** 'such as'
尚且 **shàngqiě** 'even'	反而 **fǎn'ér** 'on the contrary'	虽然 **suīrán** 'though';	可是 **kěshì** 'however'	比如 **bǐrú** 'for instance'
而且 **érqiě** 'and also'; 'but also'	因而 **yīn'ér** 'thus'; 'as a result'	'although'	就是 **jiùshì** 'even if'	例如 **lìrú** 'for example'
		不然 **bùrán** 'otherwise'		

All disyllabic conjunctions seem to be used to introduce clauses of different kinds, e.g. clauses of coordination, condition, concession, etc.

NEGATIVE PREFIXES

Six negative prefixes are found to produce nouns, verbs, adjectives, adverbs, and conjunctions.

verbs:

不 bù	非 fēi	无 wú	反 fǎn	未 wèi	否 fǒu
不得 **bùde** 'must not'	非难 **fēinàn** 'blame'	无视 **wúshì** 'disregard'	反对 **fǎnduì** 'oppose'		否决 **fǒujué** 'veto'
不用 **bùyòng** 'need not'	非议 **fēiyì** 'reproach'	无须 **wúxū** 'need not'	反问 **fǎnwèn** 'ask in reply'		否定 **fǒudìng** 'negate'
不禁 **bùjīn** 'can't help'	非礼 **fēilǐ** 'take liberties with'	无补 **wúbǔ** 'of no avail'	反驳 **fǎnbó** 'refute'; 'rebut'		否认 **fǒurèn** 'deny'
不可 **bùkě** 'should not'		无怪 **wúguài** 'no wonder'	反映 **fǎnyìng** 'reflect'		

adjectives:

不 bù	非 fēi	无 wú	反 fǎn	未 wèi
不便 **bùbiàn** 'incovenient'	非常 **fēicháng** 'unusual'	无比 **wúbǐ** 'unparalled'	反常 **fǎncháng** 'abnormal'	未详 **wèixiáng** 'unknown'
不错 **bùcuò** '(colloq.) not bad'	非法 **fēifǎ** 'illegal'	无耻 **wúchǐ** 'shameless'	反动 **fǎndòng** 'reactionary'	未婚 **wèihūn** 'unmarried'; 'single'

不 **bù**	非 **fēi**	无 **wú**	反 **fǎn**	未 **wèi**
不断 **bùduàn** 'unceasing'	非凡 **fēifán** 'extraordinary'	无辜 **wúgū** 'innocent'		未竟 **wèijìng** 'unfulfilled'
不利 **bùlì** 'unfavourable'	非人 **fēirén** 'inhuman'	无稽 **wújī** 'unfounded';		未遂 **wèisuì** 'abortive'
不同 **bùtóng** 'different'	非分 **fēifèn** 'presumptuous'	'absurd'		未定 **wèidìng** 'undefined'
不妥 **bùtuǒ** 'inappropriate'		无度 **wúdù** 'immoderate'		
不满 **bùmǎn** 'discontented'		无理 **wúlǐ** 'unreasonable'		
不良 **bùliáng** 'unhealthy'		无机 **wújī** 'inorganic'		
		无知 **wúzhī** 'ignorant'		

adverbs:

不 **bù**	非 **fēi**	无 **wú**	反 **fǎn**	未 **wèi**
不料 **bùliào** 'to one's surprise'		无非 **wúfēi** 'nothing but'	反之 **fǎnzhī** 'on the other hand'	未尝 **wèicháng** 'have not';
不巧 **bùqiáo** 'as luck would have it'		无从 **wúcóng** 'have no way'	反而 **fǎn'ér** 'on the contrary'	'did not'
		无不 **wúbù** 'invariably'	反倒 **fǎndào** '(inf.) instead'	未免 **wèimiǎn** 'a bit too'
不幸 **bùxìng** 'unfortunately'		无端 **wúduān** 'for no reason'		未必 **wèibì** 'not necessarily'
不意 **bùyì** 'unexpectedly'		无故 **wúgù** 'without rhyme or reason'		
不久 **bùjiǔ** 'before long'				

conjunctions:

不 **bù**	非 **fēi**	无 **wú**	反 **fǎn**	未 **wèi**	否 **fǒu**
不管 **bùguǎn** 'no matter'	非但 **fēidàn** 'not only'	无论 **wúlùn** 'regardless of'			否则 **fǒuzé** 'otherwise'
不过 **bùguò** 'but'	非特 **fēitè** 'not only'				
不但 **bùdàn** 'not only'	非独 **fēidú** 'not merely'				

nouns:

不 **bù**	非 **fēi**	无 **wú**	反 **fǎn**	未 **wèi**
不是 **bùshì** 'fault'	非命 **fēimìng** 'a violent death'	无常 **wúcháng** 'Death Messenger'	反面 **fǎnmiàn** 'reverse side'	未来 **wèilái** 'future'
			反馈 **fǎnkuì** 'feedback'	未然 **wèirán** 'non-existence'
			反应 **fǎnyìng** 'response'	

Additional notes:

(1) 不 **bù-**, as a prefix, differs from the negative adverbial particle 不 **bù** 'not' in the fact that it forms an inseparable bond with the following verbs or adjectives (or sometimes even nouns, as in 不法 **bùfǎ** '(adj.) criminal'. Its importance as a prefix cannot be overestimated as it readily combines to form a noun like 不是 **bùshì** 'fault', an adjective like 不错 **bùcuò** 'correct', a verb like 不容 **bùróng** 'not tolerate'; 'not brook', an adverb like 不时 **bùshí** 'frequently', a conjunction like 不论 **bùlùn** 'no matter (what, who, how), etc.' and a formulaic sentence like 不行 **bùxíng** 'won't do' or 不忙 **bùmáng** 'there's no hurry'.

(2) 不 **bù**, 非 **fēi**, 无 **wú**, 反 **fǎn** and 否 **fǒu** are found almost universally in all word classes. As a general rule, 不 **bù** and 反 **fǎn** mostly integrate with verbal and adjectival monyms, 非 **fēi** and 无 **wú** with nominal monyms, and 否 **fǒu** only with verbal monyms. When 不 **bù**, 非 **fēi** and 无 **wú** come into combination with a homographic monym, 法 **fǎ**, which could be part of 法律 **fǎlǜ** 'law'; 'statute' or 办法 **bànfǎ** 'way'; 'means'; 'measure', a distinction of meaning will then be made in the resultant lexeme:

不法 **bùfǎ** 'criminal' (adjective)　　非法 **fēifǎ** 'illegal'　　无法 **wúfǎ** 'unable'

The suffix 么 **me** 'mode'; 'manner' produces a closed set of words which are pronouns, adverbs, and conjunctions:

这么 **zhème** 'so'; 'like this' (adv.)	那么 **nàme** 'in that way' (adv.)
什么 **shénme** 'what' (pron.)	怎么 **zěnme** 'how' (adv.)
多么 **duōme** 'so' (adv.)	要么 **yàome** 'or' (conj.)

Here is a summary chart of affixes of word categories other than nouns:

Verbal affixes:
    Prefixes: 相 **xiāng-**
    Suffixes: 于 **-yú**, 以 **-yǐ**, 予 **-yǔ**, 化 **-huà**, 得 **-de**, 有 **-yǒu**
Adjectival affixes:
    Prefixes: 可 **kě-**, 好 **hǎo-**, 难 **nán-**
    Suffixes: 切 **-qiè**
Adverbial affixes:
    Prefixes: 一 **yī-**
    Suffixes: 且 **-qiě**, 来 **-lái**, 地 **-dì**, 然 **-rán**, 而 **-ér**
Numerical affixes:
    Prefixes: 第 **dì-**, 半 **bàn-**, 多 **duō-**, 超 **chāo-**
Pronominal affixes:
    Suffixes: 们 **-men**
Propositional affixes:
    Suffixes: 于 **-yú**, 着 **-zhe**, 了 **-le**
Conjunctional affixes:
    Suffixes: 且 **-qiě**, 而 **-ér**, 然 **-rán**, 是 **-shì/shi**, 如 **-rú**
Negative affixes:
    Prefixes: 不 **bù-**, 非 **fēi-**, 无 **wú-**, 反 **fǎn-**, 未 **wèi-**, 否 **fǒu-**
Miscellaneous affixes:
    Suffixes: 么 **-me**

INFIXES

Temporary infixes introduced into a lexeme as a syntactic device are not un-common in Chinese, e.g. 看见 **kànjiàn** 'see' → 看不见 **kànbujiàn** 'cannot see' or → 看得见 **kàndejiàn** 'can see'. Most verb compounds of the complemental type[17] are susceptible to this dichotomous pair of infixes.

But if the removal of the infix in a lexeme does not restore it to the status of an established disyllabic lexeme, the infix can be said to be frozen, a perman-ent part of the trisyllabic lexeme with no retrievable disyllabic counterpart, and therefore must be regarded as of lexical nature. In other words, only the 'marked form' occurs in the lexicon with no 'unmarked' counterpart. For example,

(a) 不 **bu**
  巴不得 **bābude** '(colloq.) eagerly look forward to'
  了不起 **liǎobuqǐ** 'amazing'
  犯不着 **fànbuzháo** '(colloq.) not worthwhile'
  吃不消 **chībuxiāo** 'unable to stand'
  择不开 **zháibukāi** 'unable to disentangle'; 'cannot get away from'
  保不住 **bǎobuzhù** 'most likely'; 'more likely than not'

(b) 得 **de**
  合得来 **hédelái** 'get along well'
  吃得开 **chīdekāi** 'much sought after'
  靠得住 **kàodezhù** 'reliable'
  买得起 **mǎideqǐ** 'can afford'
  信得过 **xìndeguò** 'trust'; 'trustworthy'
  谈得上 **tándeshàng** 'take into consideration'

The first mononym in such a combination is invariably a verbal mononym. The resultant lexeme may be a verb or an adjective or in some cases an adject-ive as well as a verb. In the majority of cases, if there is a positive form, there is usually a negative form to match it: e.g.

靠得住 **kàodezhù** 'reliable'	vs	靠不住 **kàobuzhù** 'unreliable'
犯得着 **fàndezháo**	vs	犯不着 **fànbuzháo**
'(colloq.) worthwhile'		'(colloq.) not worthwhile'

This does not mean that every negative form has a positive alternative: e.g.

了不起 **liǎobuqǐ** 'amazing'	but not:	*了得起 ***liǎodeqǐ**
巴不得 **bābude** '(colloq.) eagerly look forward to'		*巴得得 ***bādede**
备不住 **bèibuzhù** '(dial.) perhaps; possibly'		*备得住 ***bèidezhù**

---

[17] See Chapter 4 on the complemental type of verbs.

As we said earlier, there are no retrievable forms like *巴得 or *合来 for the words with a frozen infix; it seems therefore also plausible to consider these lexemes as having disyllabic suffixes. For example, the following pairs of established trisyllabic terms may be analysed thus: (1) 瞧不起 **qiáobuqǐ** '(colloq.) look down upon' and 瞧得起 **qiáodeqǐ** '(colloq.) think highly of', where 得起 **deqǐ** is the positive and 不起 **buqǐ** the negative suffix; or (2) 见得 **jiànde** '(used in the neqative or in questions) seem'; 'appear' and 见不得 **jiànbude** 'not fit to be seen', where one contains the monosyllabic positive suffix 得 **de** while the other contains the disyllabic negative suffix 不得 **bude**. But such an analysis will be far less economical and certainly does not correlate with non-frozen syntactic realisations.

The usually unstressed pseudo-infix 里 **li** is found with a limited number of disyllabic (rhymed) adjectives with a negative meaning or with an integrated mononym 气 **qì** 'air'; 'demeanour', where the adjective is partially reiterated, i.e. AB → A li AB:[18] e.g.

糊涂 **hútu**	→	糊里糊涂 **húlihútu**	'muddle-headed'; 'mixed up'
慌张 **huāngzhāng**	→	慌里慌张 **huānglihuāngzhāng**	'flurried'; 'flustered'
傻气 **shǎqì**	→	傻里傻气 **shǎlishǎqì**	'foolish-looking'
怪气 **guàiqì**	→	怪里怪气 **guàiliguàiqì**	'eccentric'; 'queer'
妖气 **yāoqì**	→	妖里妖气 **yāoliyāoqì**	'sexy'; 'seductively dressed'
土气 **tǔqì**	→	土里土气 **tǔlitǔqì**	'rustic'; 'uncouth'

Various infixes are employed to expand an originally disyllabic lexeme into its quadrisyllabic 'emphatic' form, i.e. the infix or parafix XX, often meaningless mononyms or numerals not intended for their literal meanings, expand the disyllabic lexeme AB into the form of AXXB, e.g.

滑溜 **huáliū**	→	滑不唧溜 **huábujiliū**	(dial.) 'slippery'
花哨 **huāshao**	→	花里胡哨 **huālihúshào**	'gaudy'; 'garish'
乱糟 **luànzāo**	→	乱七八糟 **luànqībāzāo**	'at sixes and sevens'; 'in an awful mess'

PARAFIXES

Parafixes are used to expand disyllabic adjectives into stylistically more vivid and emphatic quadrisyllabic expressions, e.g. AB → AXBX or XAXB, where XX is the parafix. Parafixes may be idiosyncratic with individual expression, e.g.

酸溜 **suānliū**	→	酸不溜丢 **suānbuliūdiū**	(AXBX)

---

[18] Cf. Liu, Shuxin (刘叔新) 1995: 87–88.

Generally speaking, number terms are common parafixes: e.g.

颠倒 **diāndǎo** → 颠三倒四 **diān sān dǎo sì** (AXBX)
零落 **língluò** → 七零八落 **qī líng bā luò** (XAXB)

The point to note is that such parafixing is not possible with every disyllabic adjective and is therefore to be regarded as a morphological means rather than a syntactic device. A number of quadrisyllabic idioms are actually formed by two disyllabic words mutually staggered: e.g.

手脚 **shǒujiǎo** 'hands and feet' + → 手忙脚乱 **shǒu máng jiǎo luàn**
忙乱 **mángluàn** 'in a hasty 'in a rush'; 'in a flurry'
and disorderly manner'
心神 **xīnshén** 'state of mind' + → 心领神会 **xīn lǐng shén huì**
领会 **lǐnghuì** 'understand' 'readily take a hint'
寻觅 **xúnmì** 'seek' + → 寻死觅活 **xún sǐ mì huó**
死活 **sǐhuó** 'life or death' 'attempt suicide (usu. as a threat)'
失落 **shīluò** 'drop'; 'lose' + → 失魂落魄 **shī hún luò pò**
魂魄 **húnpò** 'soul' 'scared out of one's wits'
和悦 **héyuè** 'affable'; 'amiable' + → 和颜悦色 **hé yán yuè sè**
颜色 **yánsè** 'facial expression' 'have a genial expression'

This can perhaps also be seen as a specific kind of 'parafixing', which, in fact, is fairly productive in literary coinage.

SUPRAMORPHOLOGICAL PROCESSES

There has been little systematic study or explanation of the way in which Chinese words undergo morphological (or more aptly perhaps, supramorphological) processes while in use. The added meaning to the word in question will certainly be lost if this functional aspect of a Chinese word in use is not precisely understood.

(a) Definiteness and Indefiniteness

We have already quoted in the first section that a noun, for example, will gain a notion of definiteness in a pre-verbal position or lose it in a post-verbal position in a narrative sentence. Formulaically,

pre-V N : post-V N = def. N : indef. N (in a narrative sentence)

For example,

我请了很多客人。 **wǒ qǐng le hěn duo kèren** 'I have invited a lot of
  guests.'
客人都到了。 **kènren dōu dào le** 'All *the guests* have arrived.'

(b) Completeness and Incompleteness

A post-verbal noun, if following a complete-aspect marked V without being preceded by a numeral and a classifier, turns definite yet incomplete. The formula is as follows:

post-V + 了 **le** + N : post-V + 了 **le** + Num. + Clas. + N = def. N (incompl.) : indef. N (compl.)

For example,

我写了信...	**wǒ xiě le *xìn*...**	'(When) I finished writing *the letter*,...'
我写了一封信。	**wǒ xiě le *yī fēng xìn***	'I finished writing *a letter*.'

(c) Contrast and Non-Contrast

Adjectives in Chinese, when used predicatively, will gain the added notion of 'contrast' if they are not modified at the same time. This looks like the following in a distribution equation:

pred. A (modified) : pred. A (unmodified) = without contrast : with contrast

这本书很好。	**zhèi/zhè běn shū *hěn hǎo***	'This is a (very) good book.'
这本书好。	**zhèi/zhè běn shū *hǎo***	'This book is good, but...'

The contrast implied in the second can be '... but that book isn't' or '... but it's too expensive', etc. depending on the stress pattern of the sentence.

(d) Dynamic and Static

Every verb in Chinese is semantically programmed in a dynamic or static dichotomy. A syntactic litmus test is the verb's position in relation to a location co-verbal phrase beginning with 在 **zài** 'at'. This dichotomy has to be part of the lexico-syntactic specification of Chinese verbs before they can be used in syntactic constructions. Formulaically,

V + 在 **zài**-phrase (allowed) : V + 在 **zài**-phrase (disallowed) = static V : dynamic V

For example,

坐在草地上	**zuò zài cǎodì shang**	'to sit on the grass'	(static)
躺在草地上	**tǎng zài cǎodì shang**	'to lie on the grass'	(static)
*走在草地上	***zǒu zài cǎodì shang**	'to walk on the grass'	(dynamic)
*跑在草地上	***pǎo zài cǎodì shang**	'to run on the grass'	(dynamic)

The dynamic verbs may only follow the 在 **zài**-phrase:

在草地上走(着)	**zài cǎodì shang zǒu (zhe)**	'walking on the grass'
在草地上跑(着)	**zài cǎodì shang pǎo (zhe)**	'running on the grass'

(e) Implicit and Explicit

When static verbs precede the 在 zài-phrase, they remain implicit and unmarked for aspect. However, either static or dynamic verbs, when they follow the 在 zài-phrase, need to be explicitly marked one way or another: by means of progression or experience aspect markers (not by a completion aspect marker on its own), by a complement of duration or frequency, by an additional syllable for rhythm, etc. in a narration. The equation is:

(in a narration) static V + 在 zài-phrase : 在 zài-phrase + static/dynamic V
= static V (unmarked) : static/dynamic V (marked)

For example,

在桌子上放着	**zài zhuōzi shang *fàng zhe***	'be left on the table' (aspect marker)
在那儿呆了一个月	**zài nàr *dāi le yī ge yuè***	'to stay there for a month' (duration complement)
在图书馆学习	**zài túshūguǎn *xuéxí***	'to study at the library' (an extra syllable for rhythm)

(f) Formal and Notional Passives

Transitive verbs need to be encoded in formal passive where necessary in a narrative sentence but only notional passive in a commentative sentence. A distributional proportion formula will be like this:

(Narrative) Subj + V : (Commentative) Topic + V = formal passive V : notional passive V

For example,

电脑被弄坏了。	**diànnǎo *bèi nòng huài* le**	'The computer was broken by someone' (narration) (where **bèi** is a formal passive marker)
电脑弄坏了。	**diànnǎo *nòng huài* le**	'The computer is broken' (comment) (where no formal passive marker is needed)

(g) Archi-Morphemic **de** for Manner Description

The archi-morpheme *de* can be respectively represented by 地 **de** or 得 **de** when manner is described by means of an adverbial or a complement. The adverbial 地 **de** indicates the 'manner intended' whereas the complemental 得 **de** indicates the 'manner observed'. The former therefore usually occurs in a narrative while the latter occurs in a comment. Formulaically:

manner adverb + 地 **de** + V : V + 得 **de** + manner adverb = manner intended : manner observed

他很快地跑着。　**tā hěn kuài de pǎo zhe**　'He ran very fast' (a narrative)

And it will naturally be wrong to say: *他真快地跑着 **tā zhēn kuài de pǎo zhe**, as that will be building an incompatible comment into the narrative. One may, of course, say as an observation:

他跑得真快。　**tā pǎo de zhēn kuài**　'He runs really fast' (a comment)

So far there has never been thorough research into the supramorphological processes inherent in Chinese lexemes while in use. We have, however, demonstrated here in some detail, using the distributional proportion formula device, some of these phenomenal processes. Having done this, we feel obliged to stop short of a comprehensive extrapolation. In fact, an extensive investigation of such supramorphological processes in Chinese will embark more and more on syntactic rather than lexical studies and is therefore beyond the scope of the present book.

4 SYNTACTIC FEATURES OF THE CHINESE LEXICON

Chinese is not a language totally deprived of morphological derivations, as we have already seen in the last chapter. However, it is perhaps far less morphologically prone than a language such as English. Generally speaking, instead of being composed of 'base + affix', a Chinese di- (or poly-) syllabic lexeme will, in the majority of cases, assume the look of a compound, that is, with the two (or more) constituent mononyms contracting a kind of quasi-syntactic relationship with each other, which makes it possible to analyse the internal composition of a Chinese word in syntactic terms.[1] Such analytic procedures, coupled with enlightening semantic perspectives, will indeed have the advantage of accounting for the essential structural features of the greater part of the Chinese lexicon. This is not, of course, saying that we may therefore equate such a syntactically oriented di- (or poly-) syllabic lexeme in the lexicon with a free syntactic construction of similar arrangement or motivation. In fact, the differences between them are manifold.[2]

First, an established lexeme, unlike a tailored expression, is semantically non-additive of its constituent elements. For example, a word like 刺眼 **cìyǎn** 'offensive to the eye' (刺 **cì** 'pierce'; 眼 **yǎn** 'eye') does not have the literal meaning of 'piercing the eye', and an idiom like 吹牛皮 **chuī niúpí** 'brag'; 'boast' (吹 **chuī** 'to blow'; 牛皮 **niúpí** 'oxhide') is synchronically non-relatable to any semantic connection with 'blowing' and 'oxhide'. Perhaps equally baffling is why a similar everyday idiom like 拍马屁 **pāi mǎpì** should have anything to do with (inf.) 'flatter'; 'fawn on', when the components of the word put together will only suggest the superficial meaning of 拍 **pāi** 'to pat' and 马屁 **mǎpì** 'wind from the bowels of a horse'. Only when the idiom's fuller original (拍马屁股 **pāi mǎ pìgu** (lit.) 'pat a horse's backside'), from which the existing rhythmically abbreviated version comes from, is understood may one establish a semantic link between 'patting the backside of a horse someone is riding' and 'showing excessive deference to the rider'.

This brings us to words with seemingly more literal orientations: a superficial addition of the semantic content of their components is, again, often insufficient. For instance, 狼烟 **lángyān** (狼 **láng** 'wolf'; 烟 **yān** 'smoke') does

---

[1] Cf. Selkirk 1982: 2: 'I will argue that word structure has the same general formal properties as syntactic structure and, moreover, that it is generated by the same sort of rule system. . . . In order to underline this fundamental similarity, I will often employ the terms W-syntax and W-syntactic rather than the terms morphology and morphological in speaking of the structure of words.'

[2] Cf. Baxter and Sagart 1998.

not just mean 'wolf smoke' but 'smoke from burning wolves' dung at northern border posts in ancient China to signal alarm of foreign attack' and 祈年 **qínián** (祈 **qí** 'pray'; 年 **nián** 'year') does not mean 'pray for a year' but 'pray for a year of bumper harvest'. In both cases, we see meaning retrieved from implicit cultural underpinnings added on to the explicit literal meanings in the lexemes' surface realisations.

In other cases, the intended meanings of the components of a lexeme may deviate dramatically (and even misleadingly) from their literal meanings yet become equally accepted by their speakers: e.g. 娃娃鱼 **wáwayú** (娃娃 **wáwa**: baby; 鱼 **yú**: fish) 'salamander' is certainly not a fish, and neither is 土豹 **tǔbào** (土 **tǔ**: earth; 豹 **bào**: leopard) 'buzzard' nor 海豹 **hǎibào** (海 **hǎi**: sea; 豹 **bào**: leopard) 'seal' a leopard. Despite the explicit and irrelevant literal meanings of the component headwords, native speakers of the language rightly register the intended meanings of these established words in their minds as holistic units.

Second, a lexeme is permanently fixed to cater for theoretically endless cases of a similar nature whereas a free construction is only used to specify a one-off case under discussion. 吃饭 **chīfàn** 'eat', for instance, when it functions as a word, refers to the eating of all meals alike regardless of what one eats, despite the fact that its internal syntactic structure is clearly a verb 吃 **chī** which means 'eat' plus an object 饭 **fàn** which means 'cooked rice'; whereas 吃饭 **chī fàn**, as a free syntactic construction, is used to refer particularly to an act of eating 'cooked rice', as opposed to other possibilities, e.g. 吃面 **chī miàn** 'eat noodles'. Similarly, 买菜 **mǎicài**, as a set expression, means 'buy all kinds of non-staple food (particularly food which is usually eaten to go with rice)' whereas 买菜 **mǎi cài**, as a free expression, means 'buy vegetables' as opposed to buying meat, chicken, etc.

Third, a lexeme may readily move away from the original syntactic characteristics of its components and change into a unit of an entirely different word class. For example, the two words 合理 **hélǐ** 'reasonable' and 苗条 **miáotiao** (of a woman) 'slender'; 'slim' are always used as adjectives although the underlying syntactic structure of the former is verbal: 合 **hé** 'tally with' followed by 理 **lǐ** 'reason' and that of the latter, nominal: 苗 **miáo** 'seedling'; 'sapling' and 条 **tiáo** 'strip'; 'twig'. Similarly, the word 行为 **xíngwéi** 'conduct'; 'behaviour' is always used as a noun, yet its two constituent mononyms are obviously of verbal nature: 行 **xíng** 'walk'; 'perform' and 为 **wéi** 'do'; 'act'. Conversely, a verb like 物色 **wùsè** 'seek out (qualified people)', synchronically speaking, consists of two nominal elements: 物 **wù** 'thing'; 'substance' and 色 **sè** 'colour'.

Fourth, a lexeme of a particular syntactic make-up does not necessarily have to follow the same grammatical rules as a comparable free syntactic construction. For example, while verbs like 动员 **dòngyuán** 'mobilize' (lit. 'move members'), 负责 **fùzé** 'be responsible for' (lit. 'shoulder responsibility'), 拨款 **bōkuǎn** 'appropriate money', etc. are intra-lexically already of a 'verb + object' structure, they are, nevertheless, commonly used as transitive verbs to form collocations like 动员群众 **dòngyuán qúnzhòng** 'mobilize the masses', 负责这件事 **fùzé zhè jiàn shì** 'be responsible for this matter', 拨款一百万元 **bōkuǎn yī bǎi wàn yuán** 'allocate a million dollars', where further objects are introduced.

Finally, an established lexeme is capable of moving between different or even contradictory semantic and syntactic planes or levels. For instance, 沽 **gū** may mean either 'buy' or 'sell' (e.g. 沽酒 **gū jiǔ** 'buy wine' vs 待价而沽 **dài jià ér gū** 'wait to sell at a good price'), 纳 **nà** may mean either 'accept' or 'offer' (e.g. 采纳 **cǎinà** 'accept' vs 纳税 **nà shuì** 'pay tax'), and 前 **qián** may refer either to 'past' or to 'future' (e.g. 前人 **qiánrén** 'predecessor' vs 前程 **qiánchéng** 'prospect'), purely in line with the established lexical context; and a word like 头痛 **tóutòng** 'headache' can mean either a physical experience or a psychological one. In the latter case, it means something that causes you difficulty and worry (这件事真头痛 **zhèi jiàn shì zhēn tóutòng** 'this business is a headache'). Moreover, words like, for example, 打针 **dǎzhēn** (打 **dǎ** 'to hit'; 针 **zhēn** 'needle'), 开刀 **kāidāo** (开 **kāi** 'open'; 刀 **dāo** 'knife'), 看病 **kànbìng** (看 **kàn** 'look'; 病 **bìng** 'illness'), etc. may indicate syntactically an active or passive role depending on whether the agent is a doctor or patient, to mean respectively 'give an injection' or 'receive an injection', 'operate on' or 'be operated on', 'see the patient' or 'consult the doctor'.

This also explains the seeming irrationality built into such fixed yet contradictory pairs of words and set expressions: e.g. 救火车 **jiùhuǒchē** 'fire engine' (lit. 'rescue fire car') vs 灭火筒 **mièhuǒtǒng** 'fire extinguisher' (lit. 'distinguish fire cylinder'), and 日以继夜 **rì yǐ jì yè** (lit. 'day follows night') vs 夜以继日 **yè yǐ jì rì** (lit. 'night follows day'), both of which are used to express the same idea of 'round the clock'.

Nevertheless, despite these differences between an established word and a free construction, a syntactic analysis of the internal composition of Chinese lexemes will provide many useful insights into the workings of the Chinese lexical structure at large. These insights will in turn help to generate words which are more readily acceptable to the ever-expanding lexicon.

Since disyllabic lexemes are lexemes *par excellence* in the Chinese lexicon, we will therefore base our analysis on them. The syntactic structures commonly found in disyllabic lexemes are:

(1) **juxtapositional**:   juxtaposer + juxtaposed/juxtaposed + juxtaposer
(2) **modificational**:   modifier + modified
(3) **governmental**:   verb/preposition + object
(4) **predicational**:   subject + predicator[3]
(5) **complemental**:   verb + complement

In polysyllabic lexemes or fixed idiomatic expressions or sayings, these specific structures are either repeated, extended or conflated.

---

[3] We use a coined word 'predicator' instead of 'predicate' to indicate that the predicational relationship specified here is only lexically true.

The terms that we have employed to label these syntactico-lexical categories will become clear as we go along. But what should be pointed out here is that in keeping with the usual convention, the slash used in the formulae means 'either-or' and that the plus sign is to indicate that, apart from the juxtapositional structure, the sequence of the monotyms in the lexemic structure is fixed and irreversible. For example, the 'modifier' must necessarily precede the 'modified', the 'verb/preposition', the 'object', and so on. As for the juxtapositional structure, the relative positions of the juxtaposer and the juxtaposed, as we shall see, are determined by the morphemic status and semantic orientation of the word or the particular set in which the word is a member. In other words, the internal arrangement of a juxtapositional lexeme is either *word bound* or *set bound*.

We shall now discuss each of these types in turn.

JUXTAPOSITIONAL TYPE

By juxtaposition, we mean the combination of two monotyms of similar semantic orientation and syntactic category to form a disyllabic word. As far as a particular lexeme is concerned, the primary motivation behind adopting a juxtapositional structure is perhaps to conform to the overall disyllabification tendency of the modern lexicon whilst other syntactic combinations are not immediately relevant.

In such a 'juxtaposer + juxtaposed' construction, the reason for calling one of the component monotyms the juxtaposer and the other the juxtaposed is because they are different on two counts.

First, the two constituent monotyms may differ in their syntactic independence or freedom. One of them may be a free morpheme and the other a bound one. In the following examples, F signifies a free morpheme and B signifies a bound morpheme:

墙壁 **qiángbì** 'wall'　　　　　　(墙 **qiáng**: wall F; 壁 **bì**: wall B)
道路 **dàolù** 'road'　　　　　　(道 **dào**: way, path B; 路 **lù**: road F)
遴选 **línxuǎn** (formal)　　　　(遴 **lín**: choose carefully B;
　'select'; 'choose'　　　　　　　 选 **xuǎn**: select F)
赏赉 **shǎnglài** (formal)　　　　(赏 **shǎng**: reward F;
　'give a reward'　　　　　　　　 赉 **lài**: grant, bestow B)
寒冷 **hánlěng** 'cold'; 'frigid'　(寒 **hán**: cold B; 冷 **lěng**: cold F)
富饶 **fùráo** 'abundant'　　　　(富 **fù**: rich, abundant F;
　　　　　　　　　　　　　　　 饶 **ráo**: plentiful B)

As a free morpheme is syntactically self-sufficient and can generally be used on its own, it therefore follows that such a morpheme is also semantically self-sufficient. In this regard, the free morpheme in a juxtapositional construction operates as the syntactic and semantic core of the lexeme whose meaning has been further enhanced and whose rhythm has been further extended: it may thus be regarded as the mononym which has now been juxtaposed whereas the function of the bound morpheme in such a juxtapositional construction is only peripheral: it serves as no more than a convenient filler in the disyllabification process, a juxtaposer that comes in to regulate the rhythm and reiterate the meaning.

In some cases, the two constituent mononyms of a juxtapositional lexeme are both free morphemes: e.g.

潮湿 **cháoshī** 'moist'; 'damp' (潮 **cháo**: damp F; 湿 **shī**: wet F)
搂抱 **lǒubào** 'hug'; 'cuddle' (搂 **lǒu**: embrace F; 抱 **bào**: hug F)

In the first instance, since the semantic orientation of the juxtapositional lexeme is 'moist or damp', it is only natural to regard 潮 **cháo** as the semantic core and therefore the juxtaposed mononym and 湿 **shī**, whose original meaning is 'wet', as a convenient supplement in this particular concatenation, and therefore the juxtaposer.

In the second instance, since the meaning of the resultant juxtaposition relates equally well to either of the component mononyms, we can only resort to characteristic features of other possible words in the same set. Though 搂 **lǒu** forms no other juxtapositional lexeme in the lexicon, it so happens that 抱 **bào** is part of another juxtapositional lexeme:

拥抱 **yōngbào** 'embrace' (拥 **yōng**: hold in one's arms F; 抱 **bào**: hug F)

The comparatively greater versatility of 抱 **bào** (despite the fact that it is a free morpheme) makes it more of a juxtaposer in these lexemes, a convenient supplement to 搂 **lǒu** and 拥 **yōng**.

In other cases, the two constituent components of a juxtaposition are both bound forms: e.g.

恬谧 **tiánmì** (formal) (恬 **tián**: tranquil, calm B;
'peaceful'; 'tranquil' 谧 **mì**: quiet, still, tranquil B)

We find 恬 **tián** in another similar juxtaposition: 恬静 **tiánjìng** 'quiet'; 'peaceful'; 'tranquil' (静 **jìng**: quiet F), where 恬 **tián** is obviously a juxtaposer; on the other hand, we also find 谧 **mì** in another similar juxtaposition: 静谧 **jìngmì** (formal) 'quiet'; 'tranquil', where again 谧 **mì** is a juxtaposer. Under such circumstances, it becomes immaterial to differentiate between the juxtaposer and the juxtaposed.

This leads us to the question of the internal structure of a juxtapositional lexeme being set bound.

In a set, the distinctive feature of a juxtaposer is actually its *juxtapositional capacity*. It is the mononym that finds a wider distribution and occurs more frequently in a group of similar juxtapositions. This is particularly true for adjectives. In a semantically related set of disyllabic adjectives, the juxtaposer is usually the one which occurs more frequently or enjoys greater combinatory power and therefore defines and charts the general semantic orientation of the set, whereas the juxtaposed is the one which tends to make more minute differentiations of meaning within the same general semantic orientation set down by the juxtaposer or determine the syntagmatic potentiality of the resultant combination. For example, in

悲哀 **bēi'āi** 'sorrowful'	(悲 **bēi**: sad B; 哀 **āi**: sorrowful B)
悲伤 **bēishāng** 'sad'	(悲 **bēi**: sad B; 伤 **shāng**: hurt, wounded B)
悲痛 **bēitòng** 'grieved'	(悲 **bēi**: sad B; 痛 **tòng**: painful F)
悲切 **bēiqiè** (written) 'mournful'	(悲 **bēi**: sad B; 切 **qiè**: anxious B)
悲惨 **bēicǎn** 'tragic'	(悲 **bēi**: sad B; 惨 **cǎn**: miserable F)

悲 **bēi** 'sad' is obviously the juxtaposer, which sets the tone for the whole set, otherwise, for example, 伤 **shāng** 'wounded' in 悲伤 **bēishāng** 'sad' and 痛 **tòng** 'painful' in 悲痛 **bēitòng** 'grieved' will be more physical than psychological and 切 **qiè** 'anxious' in 悲切 **bēiqiè** 'mournful' will mean a quite different psychological state. While the overall tone is set down by the juxtaposer, the juxtaposed monosyllable fine-tunes the meaning of the said lexeme: for example, within the general atmosphere of 悲 **bēi** 'sadness', 哀 **āi** 'grievous' redefines 悲哀 **bēi'āi** as 'sorrowful' and 惨 **cǎn** 'miserable' redefines 悲惨 **bēicǎn** as 'tragic', etc. In addition to its redefining capacity, the juxtaposed monosyllable also determines the syntagmatic potentiality of the resultant lexeme. For example, 悲哀 **bēi'āi** 'sorrowful' mainly collocates with human feelings and 悲惨 **bēicǎn** 'tragic' with situations or events.

The status of being the juxtaposer or the juxtaposed is, however, confined within the immediate set. In a wider semantic field, for example, a juxtaposed in one set can be a juxtaposer in another, or vice versa. Though 哀 **āi** 'grievous' is a juxtaposed monosyllable in the above set as we have seen, it can very well be a juxtaposer in the following set:

哀愁 **āichóu** 'melancholy'	(哀 **āi**: sorrowful; 愁 **chóu**: worried)
哀伤 **āishāng** 'grieved'	(哀 **āi**: sorrowful; 伤 **shāng**: hurt, wounded)
哀怨 **āiyuàn** 'plaintive'	(哀 **āi**: sorrowful; 怨 **yuàn**: resentful)

We have imposed two conditions in distinguishing the juxtaposer from the juxtaposed. Free and bound morpheme differentiation is generally found to be a valid rule. However, when such a differentiation cannot be made for a variety of reasons, a monosyllable's juxtapositional capacity is to be taken into account. In all cases, the semantic orientation of a juxtapositional lexeme should remain the key factor to be considered in determining the status of the constituent monosyllables.

Juxtaposition itself is a syntactic manoeuvre with phonological implications, but in the classification of different juxtapositional subtypes, semantic concepts prove to be more conducive to a better understanding of their intra-lexemic (or inter-monosyllemic) relationships.

Detailed analysis of juxtapositional structures yields six different subtypes: (a) *synonymous*; (b) *hyponymous*; (c) *antonymous*; (d) *sequential*; (e) *quantifying*; (f) *phonaesthetic*. Within synonymous juxtaposition, two further minor types may be discerned: *abbreviated* and *agglutinated*; and amongst hyponymous and antonymous juxtapositions, one may find a certain number of *telescoped* ones.

(a) Synonymous Juxtaposition

In a disyllabic synonymous juxtaposition, the two component mononyms A and B are synonymous or near-synonymous with each other. In fact synonymous juxtaposition may be found in lexemes of all word classes. Here are some examples.

noun:	朋友 **péngyou** 'friend'	(朋 **péng**: friend B; 友 **yǒu**: friend B)
adjective:	艰难 **jiānnán** 'difficult'	(艰 **jiān**: hard B; 难 **nán**: difficult F)
modal verb:	应该 **yīnggāi** 'should'	(应 **yīng**: should F; 该 **gāi**: ought to F)
verb:	跟随 **gēnsuí** 'follow'	(跟 **gēn**: follow F; 随 **suí**: follow B)
adverb:	刚才 **gāngcái** 'just now'	(刚 **gāng**: a while ago F; 才 **cái**: just now F)
conjunction:	假如 **jiǎrú** 'supposing'	(假 **jiǎ**: suppose B; 如 **rú**: if F)
preposition:	自从 **zìcóng** 'since'	(自 **zì**: since F; 从 **cóng**: from F)
interjection:	哎呀 **āiyā** 'Damn'	(哎 **āi** and 呀 **yā** are both interjections, both are F)

Naturally, the largest number of synonymous juxtaposition is to be found in nouns, adjectives and verbs.

noun:

房屋 **fángwū** 'houses'; 'buildings'	(房 **fáng**: house B; 屋 **wū**: room B)
田地 **tiándì** 'farmland'; 'cropland'	(田 **tián**: field F; 地 **dì**: land F)
沟渠 **gōuqú** 'irrigation canals'	(沟 **gōu**: ditch F; 渠 **qú**: channel, canal B)
仓廪 **cānglǐn** '(formal) granary'	(仓 **cāng**: warehouse B; 廪 **lǐn**: granary B)
机器 **jīqì** 'machine'; 'apparatus'	(机 **jī**: machine, engine B; 器 **qì**: utensil B)
岛屿 **dǎoyǔ** 'island'	(岛 **dǎo**: island F; 屿 **yǔ**: islet B)
海洋 **hǎiyáng** 'ocean'	(海 **hǎi**: sea F; 洋 **yáng**: ocean B)
声音 **shēngyīn** 'sound'; 'voice'	(声 **shēng**: voice F; 音 **yīn**: sound B)

疾病 **jíbìng** 'disease'; 'illness' (疾 **jí**: disease B; 病 **bìng**: illness F)
感觉 **gǎnjué** 'sense perception' (感 **gǎn**: to sense B; 觉 **jué**: feel B)
利益 **lìyì** 'benefit' (利 **lì**: interest, profit B;
  益 **yì**: benefit B)

差别 **chābié** 'disparity'; (差 **chā**: dissimilarity B;
  'discrepancy' 别 **bié**: difference B)
价值 **jiàzhí** 'value'; 'worth' (价 **jià**: price B; 值 **zhí**: value B)
愿望 **yuànwàng** 'aspiration' (愿 **yuàn**: willing F;
  望 **wàng**: hope F)
规则 **guīzé** 'rule'; 'regulation' (规 **guī**: regulation B;
  则 **zé**: norm, criterion B)
中央 **zhōngyāng** 'centre'; 'middle' (中 **zhōng**: middle F;
  央 **yāng**: centre B)

adjective:
巨大 **jùdà** 'enormous'; 'immense' (巨 **jù**: huge, gigantic B;
  大 **dà**: big, large, great F)
微小 **wēixiǎo** 'small'; 'little' (微 **wēi**: minute, tiny B;
  小 **xiǎo**: small, little F)
狭窄 **xiázhǎi** 'narrow'; 'cramped' (狭 **xiá**: narrow B;
  窄 **zhǎi**: narrow F)
宽阔 **kuānkuò** 'broad'; 'wide' (宽 **kuān**: wide F; 阔 **kuò**: broad B)
贫穷 **pínqióng** 'poor'; (贫 **pín**: poverty-stricken B;
  'impoverished' 穷 **qióng**: poor F)
勇敢 **yǒnggǎn** 'brave'; (勇 **yǒng**: brave B; 敢 **gǎn**:
  'courageous' daring, courageous B)
怯懦 **qiènuò** 'timid' (怯 **qiè**: timid B; 懦 **nuò**:
  cowardly B)
尖锐 **jiānruì** 'sharp'; 'incisive' (尖 **jiān**: pointed F; 锐 **ruì**: sharp B)
黑暗 **hēi'àn** 'dark' (黑 **hēi**: black F; 暗 **àn**: gloomy F)
凶恶 **xiōng'è** (of temper) 'fierce'; (凶 **xiōng**: ferocious F;
  'fiendish' 恶 **è**: evil, wicked B)
真诚 **zhēnchéng** 'sincere'; 'genuine' (真 **zhēn**: true, genuine F;
  诚 **chéng**: sincere B)
愚蠢 **yúchǔn** 'stupid'; 'foolish' (愚 **yú**: foolish B;
  蠢 **chǔn**: silly, stupid F)
腐败 **fǔbài** 'corrupt'; 'rotten' (腐 **fǔ**: rotten B; 败 **bài**: decayed B)
愤怒 **fènnù** 'indignant'; 'angry' (愤 **fèn**: indignant B;
  怒 **nù**: angry B)

verb:
跳跃 **tiàoyuè** 'jump'; 'leap'; (跳 **tiào**: jump, leap F;
  'bound' 跃 **yuè**: bounce B)
观看 **guānkàn** 'watch'; 'view' (观 **guān**: watch, observe B;
  看 **kàn**: see, look at F)

惧怕 **jùpà** 'fear'; 'dread' (惧 **jù**: fear, dread B; 怕 **pà**: be afraid of F)

迷惑 **míhuo** 'perplex'; 'baffle' (迷 **mí**: be confused F; 惑 **huò**: be bewildered B)

猜测 **cāicè** 'guess'; 'conjecture' (猜 **cāi**: guess F; 测 **cè**: survey, fathom B)

尊敬 **zūnjìng** 'respect'; 'esteem' (尊 **zūn**: venerate B; 敬 **jìng**: respect, honour F)

怜悯 **liánmǐn** 'take pity on' (怜 **lián**: pity B; 悯 **mǐn**: commiserate B)

派遣 **pàiqiǎn** 'send'; 'dispatch' (派 **pài**: send, assign F; 遣 **qiǎn**: dispatch B)

聘请 **pìnqǐng** 'employ' (聘 **pìn**: engage F; 请 **qǐng**: invite, employ F)

防守 **fángshǒu** 'defend'; 'guard' (防 **fáng**: guard against B; 守 **shǒu**: defend F)

掠夺 **lüèduó** 'plunder'; 'rob' (掠 **lüè**: plunder B; 夺 **duó**: seize F)

拯救 **zhěngjiù** 'save'; 'rescue'; 'deliver' (拯 **zhěng**: rescue B; 救 **jiù**: save F)

储存 **chǔcún** 'lay up'; 'deposit'; 'stockpile' (储 **chǔ**: store up B; 存 **cún**: deposit F)

品尝 **pǐncháng** 'taste'; 'sample'; 'savour' (品 **pǐn**: sample, savour B; 尝 **cháng**: taste F)

忍耐 **rěnnài** 'exercise patience' (忍 **rěn**: endure, tolerate F; 耐 **nài**: be able to bear F)

miscellaneous:

抑或 **yìhuò** 'or' (抑 **yì**: or B; 或 **huò**: or F)

因为 **yīnwèi** 'because' (因 **yīn**: because F; 为 **wèi**: for the purpose of B)

另外 **lìngwài** 'in addition'; 'besides' (另 **lìng**: other F; 外 **wài**: outside B)

罢了 **bàliǎo** 'be done with it' (罢 **bà**: cease B; 了 **liǎo**: finish, conclude B)

按照 **ànzhào** 'according to' (按 **àn**: on the basis of F; 照 **zhào**: in the light of F)

通过 **tōngguò** 'through' (通 **tōng**: go through F; 过 **guò**: go past F)

共同 **gòngtóng** 'jointly' (共 **gòng**: in company B; 同 **tóng**: together F)

单独 **dāndú** 'on one's own' (单 **dān**: one, single B; 独 **dú**: alone B)

宁愿 **nìngyuàn** 'would rather' (宁 **nìng**: would rather B;
愿 **yuàn**: wish F)

毕竟 **bìjìng** 'after all' (毕 **bì**: accomplish B;
竟 **jìng**: complete B)

However, it must be remembered that the component mononyms of the lexeme do not necessarily have to be in the same word class as the resultant lexeme. For example, synchronically speaking, 包 **bāo** is either a measure word or a verb meaning 'wrap' and 裹 **guǒ** can only be a verb meaning 'wrap', but their combination results in a noun 包裹 **bāoguǒ** 'parcel'; whereas 贿赂 **huìlù** 'to bribe', either component of which is in fact originally a noun 贿 **huì** meaning 'money' and 赂 **lù** 'costly presents', is generally used as a verb. This is particularly the case with abstract nouns whose components may often be of a verbal nature:

思想 **sīxiǎng** 'thoughts' (思 **sī**: ponder B; 想 **xiǎng**: think F)
知识 **zhīshi** 'knowledge' (知 **zhī**: know B; 识 **shí**: recognise B)
行为 **xíngwéi** 'behaviour'; (行 **xíng**: do, perform B; 为 **wéi**: act B)
  'conduct'
嗜好 **shìhào** 'hobby'; (嗜 **shì**: be addicted to B;
  'addiction' 好 **hào**: have a liking for F)

In many cases, nominal and verbal notions may, of course, coexist in one and the same lexeme:

赞扬 **zànyáng** 'praise'; 'to praise' (赞 **zàn**: praise B;
  扬 **yáng**: propagate B)

批评 **pīpíng** 'criticism'; 'to criticise' (批 **pī**: criticise B;
  评 **píng**: comment on F)

希望 **xīwàng** 'hopes'; 'to hope' (希 **xī**: wish B; 望 **wàng**:
  look forward to B)

行动 **xíngdòng** 'deeds'; 'to act' (行 **xíng**: walk, act B;
  动 **dòng**: move B)

命令 **mìnglìng** 'an order'; (命 **mìng**: command B;
  'to command' 令 **lìng**: order B)

The other thing to note is that there is a small number of synonymous or near-synonymous juxtapositions in which the position of the two constituent mononyms may be reversed. In other words, a juxtaposition AB may have a cousin form BA. The two forms may be similar or different in meaning or usage, e.g.

(1) 代替 **dàitì** 'substitute for' (代 **dài**: take the place of F; 替 **tì**: replace F)
    替代 **tìdài** 'replace'; 'supersede'
(2) 粮食 **liángshi** 'cereals' (粮 **liáng**: grain, provisions B; **shí**: food B)
    食粮 **shíliáng** 'food' (e.g. food for thought)

(3) 要紧 **yàojǐn** 'important' (要 **yào**: important B; 紧 **jǐn**: urgent F)
　　紧要 **jǐnyào** 'critical'; 'crucial'
(4) 裁剪 **cáijiǎn** 'cut out (garments)' (裁 **cái**: cut (cloth, etc.) F; 剪 **jiǎn**: cut
　　with scissors F)
　　剪裁 **jiǎncái** 'cut out unwanted material (from a piece of writing)'
(5) 爱恋 **àiliàn** 'feel deeply attached to' (爱 **ài**: love F; 恋 **liàn**: be attached
　　to B)
　　恋爱 **liàn'ài** 'love'
(6) 语言 **yǔyán** 'language' (语 **yǔ**: words B; 言 **yán**: words B)
　　言语 **yányǔ** 'speech'

AB and BA can be interchangeable as in (1); different in usage as in (2),
where the AB form is more specific and literal while the BA form is more
abstract and metaphorical; different in register as in (3), where AB is more
colloquial whereas BA is more formal; different in collocation as in (4), where
AB is used with 'garments' whereas BA, with 'compositions'; different in word
class as in (5), where AB is a verb while BA is a noun; or as in (6) a differentiation purposely made to distinguish between two related concepts.[4]
　　Other examples include:

(1) interchangeables:
　　士兵 **shìbīng**/兵士 **bīngshì** 'soldier'
　　源泉 **yuánquán**/泉源 **quányuán** 'source'; 'fountain-head'
　　痛苦 **tòngkǔ**/苦痛 **kǔtòng** 'pain'; 'agony'
　　争论 **zhēnglùn**/论争 **lùnzhēng** 'controversy'; 'debate'
　　并吞 **bìngtūn**/吞并 **tūnbìng** 'to annex'
　　寻找 **xúnzhǎo**/找寻 **zhǎoxún** 'look for'; 'seek'
　　式样 **shìyàng**/样式 **yàngshì** 'type'; 'pattern'; 'style'
　　商洽 **shāngqià**/洽商 **qiàshāng** 'talk over with'
　　依偎 **yīwēi**/偎依 **wēiyī** 'lean close to'
　　缩减 **suōjiǎn**/减缩 **jiǎnsuō** 'reduce'; 'cut'
　　察觉 **chájué**/觉察 **juéchá** 'be aware of'; 'detect'
　　仿效 **fǎngxiào**/效仿 **xiàofǎng** 'imitate'; 'follow the example of'
　　躲藏 **duǒcáng**/藏躲 **cángduǒ** 'hide oneself'
　　直爽 **zhíshuǎng**/爽直 **shuǎngzhí** 'frank'; 'candid'
　　真率 **zhēnshuài**/率真 **shuàizhēn** 'sincere'; 'unaffected'
　　笨拙 **bènzhuō**/拙笨 **zhuōbèn** 'clumsy'
　　穷困 **qióngkùn**/困穷 **kùnqióng** 'poverty-stricken'; 'destitute'
　　静谧 **jìngmì**/谧静 **mìjìng** 'quiet'; 'still'; 'tranquil'

(2) and (3) stylistical or registral differences:
　　熊猫 **xióngmāo** 'panda' (popular name for 猫熊 **māoxióng**)
　　监牢 **jiānláo** 'prison'; 'jail' (informal term for 牢监 **láojiān**)
　　省俭 **shěngjiǎn** 'econominal'; 'frugal' (dialectal term for 俭省 **jiǎnshěng**)

[4] Cf. Cao, Xianzhuo (曹先擢) 1979.

笆篱 **bālí** 'bamboo or twig fence' (dialectal term for 篱笆 **líba**)

闹热 **nàorè** 'bustling with noise and excitement' (dialectal term for 热闹 **rènào**)

斗争 **dòuzhēng** 'combat' (abstract) whilst 争斗 **zhēngdòu** 'fight' (concrete)

悔改 **huǐgǎi** 'repent and mend one's ways' (emphasis on mending one's ways) 改悔 **gǎihuǐ** 'repent' (emphasis on repentance)

激愤 **jīfèn** 'indignant' (emphasis on indignation) 愤激 **fènjī** 'roused and indignant' (emphasis on being roused)

(4) collocational differences:

玩赏 **wánshǎng** 'enjoy'; 'admire' vs 赏玩 **shǎngwán** 'fondle'
e.g. paintings   e.g. curios

计算 **jìsuàn** 'calculate'   算计 **suànjì** 'scheme against'
e.g. numbers   e.g. somebody

明显 **míngxiǎn** 'clear'; 'obvious'   显明 **xiǎnmíng** 'distinct';
e.g. improvement   'sharp' e.g. contrast

(5) word class differences:

报酬 **bàochou** 'reward'   vs   酬报 **chóubào** 'to reward'; 'to repay'

合适 **héshì** 'suitable'; 'appropriate'   vs   适合 **shìhé** 'suit'; 'fit'

互相 **hùxiāng** 'mutually'   vs   相互 **xiānghù** 'reciprocal'

负担 **fùdān** 'to bear'; 'a burden' (verb or noun)   担负 **dānfù** 'to bear'; 'to shoulder' (verb only)

和缓 **héhuǎn** 'gentle'; 'alleviate' (adjective or verb)   缓和 **huǎnhé** 'alleviate'; 'detente' (verb or noun)

积累 **jīlěi** 'accumulate'; 'accumulation' (transitive verb or noun)   累积 **lěijī** 'accumulate' (intransitive verb)

喷嚏 **pēntì** 'sneeze' (noun)   嚏喷 **tìpen** 'sneeze' (verb)

(6) conceptual or semantic differences:

力气 **lìqi** 'physical strength' vs 气力 **qìlì** 'effort'
搭配 **dāpèi** 'arrange in pairs'   配搭 **pèidā** 'to supplement'
整齐 **zhěngqí** 'neat and tidy'   齐整 **qízhěng** 'neat and uniform'
和平 **hépíng** 'peaceful'   平和 **pínghé** 'mild'
感情 **gǎnqíng** 'affection'   情感 **qínggǎn** 'emotion'; 'feeling'

In the item which is more frequently used, one may find in some cases the second syllable of the term unstressed: e.g.

报酬 **bàochou** 'reward'/酬报 **chóubào** 'to reward'; 'to repay'
力气 **lìqi** 'physical strength'/气力 **qìlì** 'effort'
篱笆 **líba**/笆篱 **bālí** 'bamboo or twig fence'
来往 **láiwang**/往来 **wǎnglái** 'contact'; 'dealings'
忌妒 **jìdu**/妒忌 **dùjì** 'envy'; 'be jealous of'

Abbreviated juxtaposition

Abbreviated juxtaposition is a special form of synonymous juxtaposition. In an abbreviated juxtaposition, the two monomyms are of equal semantic status and may be readily retrievable from respective disyllabic combinations. For example,

爱惜 **àixī** 'to treasure' = 喜爱珍惜 **xǐ'ài zhēnxī**
   (爱 **ài** ← 喜爱 **xǐ'ài**: be fond of; 惜 **xī** ← 珍惜 **zhēnxī**: cherish)
卑劣 **bēiliè** 'base'; 'mean' = 卑鄙恶劣 **bēibǐ èliè**
   (卑 **bēi** ← 卑鄙 **bēibǐ**: contemptible; 劣 **liè** ← 恶劣 **èliè**: abominable)
简要 **jiǎnyào** 'concise and to the point' = 简单扼要 **jiǎndān èyào**
   (简 **jiǎn** ← 简单 **jiǎndān**: simple; 要 **yào** ← 扼要 **èyào**: to the point)
骄纵 **jiāozòng** 'arrogant and willful' = 骄傲放纵 **jiāo'ào fàngzòng**
   (骄 **jiāo** ← 骄傲 **jiāo'ào**: proud; 纵 **zòng** ← 放纵 **fàngzòng**: self-indulgent)

If we put abbreviated juxtapositions side by side with average synonymous juxtapositions, we shall be able to see their difference a little more clearly.

In the following juxtapositions, the two component monomyms might be regarded as being synonyms or near synonyms:

爱好 **àihào** 'be keen on'   (爱 **ài**: love; 好 **hào**: be fond of)
爱恋 **àiliàn** 'feel deeply attached to'   (爱 **ài**: love; 恋 **liàn**: be attached to)

But in:

爱戴 **àidài** 'love and esteem'   (爱 **ài**: love; 戴 **dài**: respect)
爱护 **àihù** 'take good care of'   (爱 **ài**: love; 护 **hù**: protect)
爱怜 **àilián** 'show tender affection'   (爱 **ài**: love; 怜 **lián**: pity)
爱抚 **àifǔ** 'caress'   (爱 **ài**: love; 抚 **fǔ**: caress)
爱慕 **àimù** 'adore'   (爱 **ài**: love; 慕 **mù**: admire)

the two component monomyms are only broadly associable in meaning and all the juxtaposed monomyms have fully-fledged disyllabic originals retrievable from their own separate semantic paradigms:[5]

戴 **dài**   ←   感戴 **gǎndài** 'be sincerely grateful'
护 **hù**   ←   保护 **bǎohù** 'protect'
怜 **lián**   ←   怜悯 **liánmǐn** 'take pity on'
抚 **fǔ**   ←   抚摸 **fǔmō** 'stroke'; 'fondle'
慕 **mù**   ←   羡慕 **xiànmù** 'admire'

---

[5] The disyllabic original for any particular monomym in an abbreviated juxtaposition is not necessarily a fixed one. Where appropriate, it may be chosen from a number of synonymous counterparts. It must also be pointed out here that, apart from some clear-cut cases, it is sometimes difficult, and certainly unnecessary, to differentiate between average synonymous juxtapositions and abbreviated juxtapositions. Whilst abbreviated juxtapositions generally have for their constituent monomyms disyllabic lexemes retrievable from a separate semantic paradigm, synonymous juxtapositions may only have disyllabic lexemes retrievable from their own semantic paradigm.

Again, if we compare the word 骄傲 **jiāo'ào** 'proud'; 'arrogant' (骄 **jiāo**: proud; 傲 **ào**: haughty), which is obviously a synonymous juxtaposition, with its related set listed below:

骄纵 **jiāozòng**   (纵 **zòng** ← 放纵 **fàngzòng**: indulge)
　'arrogant and wilful'
骄横 **jiāohèng** 'overbearing'   (横 **hèng** ← 蛮横 **mánhèng**: peremptory)
骄矜 **jiāojīn** 'self-important'   (矜 **jīn** ← 矜夸 **jīnkuā**: conceited and
                                                                  boastful)
骄慢 **jiāomàn** 'conceited'   (慢 **màn** ← 轻慢 **qīngmàn**: to slight)

and even an *ad hoc* one like the following, which we have specifically coined for the purpose:

骄妄 **jiāowàng** 'presumptuous'   (妄 **wàng** ← 狂妄 **kuángwàng**: wildly
                                                                  arrogant)

we can see that abbreviated juxtaposition is an extremely loose type of synonymous juxtaposition which has a great potential in bringing together from existing lexemes in the lexicon any two semantically associable monomys in a disyllabic form.

Abbreviated juxtaposition is certainly the most prolific subtype amongst all juxtapositional constructions in the lexicon. It may potentially produce a large number of near-synonymous adjectives and verbs, which constitute various semantically and stylistically related paradigms within their respective semantic fields. As these abbreviated juxtapositions are too numerous to list, only a few examples are given below for illustration:

贫瘠 **pínjí** 'barren'; 'infertile';   (贫 **pín**: poor, impoverished;
　'poor'   瘠 **jí**: lean, barren)
富裕 **fùyù** 'well-to-do'; 'well-off'   (富 **fù**: rich; 裕 **yù**: abundant, plentiful)
宏大 **hóngdà** 'grand'   (宏 **hóng**: magnificent; 大 **dà**: big, great)
细小 **xìxiǎo** 'tiny'; 'trivial'   (细 **xì**: thin, slender; 小 **xiǎo**: small)
馁怯 **něiqiè** 'lose courage'   (馁 **něi**: disheartened; 怯 **qiè**: timid,
                                                                  cowardly)

泞滑 **nìnghuá**   (泞 **nìng**: muddy, miry;
　'muddy and slippery'   滑 **huá**: slippery)
干净 **gānjìng** 'clean'   (干 **gān**: dry; 净 **jìng**: clean)
辛酸 **xīnsuān** 'sad'   (辛 **xīn**: spicy; 酸 **suān**: sour)
积累 **jīlěi** 'accumulate'   (积 **jī**: amass, store up; 累 **lěi**: pile up)
庆祝 **qìngzhù** 'celebrate'   (庆 **qìng**: celebrate; 祝 **zhù**: congratulate)
救济 **jiùjì** 'relieve the distress of' (救 **jiù**: rescue, save; 济 **jì**: aid, relieve)
奖赏 **jiǎngshǎng**   (奖 **jiǎng**: award a prize;
　'award'; 'reward'   赏 **shǎng**: grant a reward)
荒废 **huāngfèi** 'lie waste'   (荒 **huāng**: disused; 废 **fèi**: wasted)
评判 **píngpàn** 'pass judgment on'   (评 **píng**: comment on; 判 **pàn**: to judge)

In some extreme cases, for example, a bound adjectival mononym like 凄 **qī** 'sad'; 'wretched' may establish as many as 20 abbreviated juxtapositions in the lexicon (e.g. 凄惨 **qīcǎn** 'miserable', 凄切 **qīqiè** 'mournful', 凄婉 **qīwǎn** '(of sound) plaintive', etc.) and a bound verbal mononym like 欺 **qī** 'deceive', as many as 12 (e.g. 欺骗 **qīpiàn** 'cheat'; 'dupe', 欺瞒 **qīmán** 'hoodwink', 欺诈 **qīzhà** 'swindle', etc.).

In such abbreviated juxtapositions, the mononym with the greater juxtapositional capacity usually seems to be the juxtaposer.

Finally, abbreviated juxtaposition is to be distinguished from an *ordinary disyllabic abbreviation*, which selects for combination two relevant mononyms from an originally longer syntagmatic construction. Some examples of ordinary disyllabic abbreviation are quoted below, the number indicating the position of the selected mononym in the original syntagm:

商务 **shāngwù** 'The Commercial Press'	1 and 2	←	商务印书馆 **shāngwù yìnshūguǎn**
土改 **tǔgǎi** 'land reform'	1 and 3	←	土地改革 **tǔdì gǎigé**
临了 **línliǎo** (inf.) 'finally'	1 and 3	←	临末了儿 **lín mòliǎor**
扫盲 **sǎománg** 'eliminate illiteracy'	1 and 4	←	扫除文盲 **sǎochú wénmáng**
流感 **liúgǎn** 'influenza'	1 and 4	←	流行性感冒 **liúxíngxìng gǎnmào**
花生 **huāshēng** 'groundnut'; 'peanut'	2 and 3	←	落花生 **luòhuāshēng**
人大 **réndà** 'The People's University'	3 and 5	←	中国人民大学 **Zhōngguó Rénmín dàxué**

In fact, quite a few of these abbreviations are truncated forms of originally quadrisyllabic expressions or idioms: e.g.

体检 **tǐjiǎn** 'health check-up'	1 and 3	←	体格检查 **tǐgé jiǎnchá** 'physical examination'
地铁 **dìtiě** 'subway'; 'the underground'	1 and 3	←	地下铁道 **dìxià tiědào** 'lit. underground railway'
沧桑 **cāngsāng** 'time brings great changes'	1 and 3	←	沧海桑田 **cānghǎi sāngtián** 'seas into mulberry fields and vice versa'

Agglutinated juxtaposition

Agglutinated juxtaposition is another special form of synonymous juxtaposition, but at the other extreme. An agglutinated juxtaposition is generally known as *lianmianci* (连绵词 **liánmiáncí**) amongst the Chinese linguists. In an agglutinated juxtaposition, the two mononyms may never be separated from each other and they generally share an identical element (which is usually the radical) in their written form. Strictly speaking, the partially homo-graphetic motivation behind the word plays just as important a role as the word's characteristic disyllabicity that knits it into an inseparable whole. For example,

word	shared radical
玻璃 **bōli** 'glass'	(玉 **yù**: jade, abbreviated as 王)
鹭鸶 **lùsī** 'egret'	(鸟 **niǎo**: bird)

in which neither 玻 **bō** nor 璃 **li** or 鹭 **lù** nor 鸶 **sī** has a separate meaningful existence of its own apart from its recognizable form as a mononym. On the other hand, both mononyms possess an identical element, e.g. 王, which is an abbreviation of 玉 **yù** 'jade' in the case of 玻璃 **bōli** as a radical or meaning category referring to or hinting at the meaning of the word. Other examples may include,

word	shared radical
nouns	
蟋蟀 **xīshuài** 'cricket (an insect)'	(虫: insect)
蝴蝶 **húdié** 'butterfly'	(虫: insect)
蝌蚪 **kēdǒu** 'tadpole'	(虫: insect)
鹦鹉 **yīngwǔ** 'parrot'	(鸟: bird)
麒麟 **qílín** '(Chinese) unicorn'	(鹿: deer)
骐骥 **qíjì** 'a fine horse'; 'steed'	(马: horse)
骷髅 **kūlóu** 'human skeleton'; 'human skull'	(骨: bone)
傀儡 **kuǐlěi** 'puppet'	(人: human)
狐狸 **húli** 'fox'	(犭: dog)
玫瑰 **méigui** 'rose'	(王: jade)
蘑菇 **mógu** 'mushroom'	(艹: grass)
葡萄 **pútáo** 'grape'	(艹: grass)
蓓蕾 **bèilěi** 'bud'[6]	(艹: grass)
桠杈 **yāchà** 'crotch'; 'fork (of a tree)'	(木: wood)
饕餮 **tāotiè** 'voracious eater'; 'glutton'	(食: eat)
verbs and adjectives	
嗫嚅 **nièrú** '(formal) speak haltingly'	(口: mouth)
蹂躏 **róulìn** 'trample on'; 'make havoc of'	(足: foot)
翱翔 **áoxiáng** 'hover'; 'soar'	(羽: feather)
扑打 **pūda** 'pat'	(扌: hand)
剥削 **bōxuē** 'exploit'	(刂: knife)
徘徊 **páihuái** 'pace up and down'	(彳: part of a crossroad)
逶迤 **wēiyí** 'winding'; 'meandering'	(辶: walk)
浪漫 **làngmàn** 'romantic'	(氵: water)

---

[6] Agglutinated juxtapositions are quite often phonaesthetically motivated as well. For example, they may often be rhymed, as in this case, or alliterated.

憔悴 **qiáocuì** 'wan and sallow';   (忄: heart)
  'thin and pallid'
崔嵬 **cuīwéi** (formal) 'lofty'; 'towering'   (山: mountain)
葳蕤 **wēiruí** (literary) 'luxuriant (foliage)'   (艹: grass)
肮脏 **āngzāng** 'dirty'; 'filthy'   (月: flesh)

As with a synonymous juxtaposition with two bound forms, it seems also immaterial to differentiate between the two component mononyms as the juxtaposer and the juxtaposed in an agglutinated juxtaposition. However, in some cases, particularly true of nouns, we might want to regard a semantically more self-sufficient form as the juxtaposed, which often proves to be more versatile in word-formation: e.g.

蝶 **dié**   as in   蝶泳 **diéyǒng** 'butterfly stroke in swimming'
狐 **hú**   狐臭 **húchòu** 'body odour'; 'bromhidrosis'
篱 **lí**   绿篱 **lùlí** 'hedgerow'
蕾 **lěi**   味蕾 **wèilěi** 'taste bud'

In quadrisyllabic classical idioms, near-synonymous juxtaposition is realised by two parallel disyllabic components, e.g.

  (a) 繁荣昌盛 **fánróng chāngshèng** 'thriving and prosperous'
      (繁荣 **fánróng**: flourishing; 昌盛 **chāngshèng**: prosperous)
  (b) 痴心妄想 **chīxīn wàngxiǎng** 'fond dream'
      (痴心 **chīxīn**: infatuation; 妄想 **wàngxiǎng**: vain hope)
  (c) 甜言蜜语 **tiányán mìyǔ** 'fine-sounding words'
      (甜言 **tiányán**: sweet words; 蜜语 **mìyǔ**: honeyed phrases)
  (d) 是非曲直 **shìfēi qūzhí** 'rights and wrongs'
      (是非 **shìfēi**: rights and wrongs; 曲直 **qūzhí**: crooked or straight)
  (e) 狂风暴雨 **kuángfēng bàoyǔ** 'a violent storm'
      (狂风 **kuángfēng**: fierce gale; 暴雨 **bàoyǔ**: torrential rain)

It is not important if the two parallel disyllabic components themselves are of a quite different nature from the resultant juxtaposition. For example, in (b) and (c), the juxtaposed disyllables are both of a 'modifier + modified' type; in (d), each of the disyllabic components 是非 **shìfēi** 'right and wrong' and 曲直 **qūzhí** 'crooked or straight' is itself an antonymous juxtaposition; and in (e) 风 **fēng** and 雨 **yǔ** are certainly co-hyponyms. Nonetheless, their overall meaning determines that they are synonymous juxtapositions in the form of quadrisyllabic idioms.

  The most frequent structure in quadrisyllabic juxtapositions is the double 'modifier + modified' type:

愁眉苦脸 **chóuméi kǔliǎn** 'have a worried look'; 'pull a long face'
  (愁眉 **chóuméi**: knitted brows; 苦脸 **kǔliǎn**: troubled face)
街头巷尾 **jiētóu xiàngwěi** 'in streets and lanes – everywhere'
  (街头 **jiētóu**: top end of street; 巷尾 **xiàngwěi**: bottom end of a lane)

Sometimes to achieve perfect symmetry, the modifiers in a quadrisyllabic construction can be the same mononym. For instance,

人山人海 **rénshān rénhǎi** 'oceans of people'　　（人 **rén**: people; 山 **shān**: mountain; 海 **hǎi**: sea)

大手大脚 **dàshǒu dàjiǎo** 'wasteful'; 'extravagant'　　（大 **dà**: large; 手 **shǒu**: hand; 脚 **jiǎo**: foot)

同心同德 **tóngxīn tóngdé** 'of one heart and one mind'　　（同 **tóng**: same; 心 **xīn**: heart; 德 **dé**: morals)

呆头呆脑 **dāitóu dāinǎo** 'stupid-looking'　　（呆 **dāi**: stupid; 头 **tóu**: head; 脑 **nǎo**: brain)

Numerals not indicating exact numbers but emphasising 'scarcity or numerousness' in a metaphorical way are often used to achieve this synonymous symmetry in a quadrisyllabic juxtaposition.[7] For instance,

仨瓜俩枣 **sā guā liǎ zǎo** 'only a few'; 'not many'
（仨 **sā**: three; 瓜 **guā**: melon; 俩 **liǎ**: two; 枣 **zǎo**: (bot.) dates)
三头六臂 **sān tóu liù bì** 'superhuman'
（三 **sān**: three; 头 **tóu**: head; 六 **liù**: six; 臂 **bì**: arm)
四分五裂 **sì fēn wǔ liè** 'disintegrate'
（四 **sì**: four; 分 **fēn**: divide; 五 **wǔ**: five; 裂 **liè**: split)
七嘴八舌 **qī zuǐ bā shé** 'all talking at once'
（七 **qī**: seven; 嘴 **zuǐ**: mouth; 八 **bā**: eight; 舌 **shé**: tongue)
十全十美 **shí quán shí měi** 'perfect in every way'
（十 **shí**: ten; 全 **quán**: complete; 美 **měi**: beautiful）

With quadrisyllabic synonymous juxtapositions whose two disyllabic components are reversible, the two variant forms are usually used interchangeably in consideration of the rhyming cadence in question rather than any real difference in meaning, e.g.

扬清激浊 **yángqīng jīzhuó** = 激浊扬清 **jīzhuó yángqīng** 'criticise the bad and praise the good' (扬 **yáng**: propagate; 清 **qīng**: the clear; 激 **jī**: wash away; 浊 **zhuó**: the dirty)
翻天覆地 **fāntiān fùdì** = 天翻地覆 **tiānfān dìfù** = 地覆天翻 **dìfù tiānfān** 'earthshaking'; 'tremendous' (天 **tiān**: heaven; 翻 **fān**: overturn; 地 **dì**: earth; 覆 **fù**: upset)

(b) Hyponymous Juxtaposition

Hyponymous juxtaposition is a juxtaposition in which the two (or more) component mononyms are co-hyponyms instead of synonyms. Generally speaking, the juxtaposition of co-hyponyms will denote the meaning of

---

[7] Cf. Chapter 3 on parafix.

their *superordinate term* or *hypernym*. Hyponymous juxtaposition seems to encode only lexemes in nouns, verbs and a few adverbs. With adjectives (of which there is such a vast number), hyponymous juxtaposition seems to coincide with what we have differentiated as abbreviated (synonymous) juxtaposition. Examples of nouns, verbs and adverbs are listed below:

noun

刀枪 **dāoqiāng** 'weapons'　　　　　(刀 **dāo**: sword; 枪 **qiāng**: spear)
岁月 **suìyuè** 'time'; 'years'　　　　(岁 **suì**: year; 月 **yuè**: month)
阡陌 **qiānmò** 'footpaths　　　　　(阡 **qiān**: vertical footpaths;
　between fields'　　　　　　　　　陌 **mò**: horizontal footpaths)
领袖 **lǐngxiù** 'leader'　　　　　　(领 **lǐng**: collar; 袖 **xiù**: sleeve)
铺盖 **pūgài** 'bedding'　　　　　　(铺 **pū**: spread; 盖 **gài**: cover)

Just as happens in a synonymous juxtaposition, the word class of the component monomys of a hyponymous juxtaposition does not necessarily match the word class of the resultant lexeme. In the last example, 铺 **pū** 'spread' and 盖 **gài** 'cover' are both verbs, but their combination results in a noun 铺盖 **pūgài** 'bedding'.

Sometimes the superodinate notion is a metaphorical extension of the co-hyponyms. For example, in 领袖 **lǐngxiù** 'leader', the co-hyponyms used are 领 **lǐng** 'collar' and 袖 **xiù** 'sleeve', but because 领 **lǐng** and 袖 **xiù** are supposed to be the most important part of a shirt or a jacket, their combination metaphorically suggests 'leader', the most important part of an organisation or movement. Other examples include:

骨肉 **gǔròu** 'kindred'　　　　　　(骨 **gǔ**: bone; 肉 **ròu**: flesh)
手足 **shǒuzú** 'brothers'　　　　　(手 **shǒu**: hand; 足 **zú**: foot)
眉目 **méimù** 'prospect of a solution'　(眉 **méi**: eyebrow; 目 **mù**: eye)
血汗 **xuèhàn** 'sweat and toil'　　　(血 **xuè**: blood; 汗 **hàn**: sweat)
拳棒 **quánbàng** 'martial arts'　　　(拳 **quán**: fist; 棒 **bàng**: stick, club)
子女 **zǐnǚ** 'children'　　　　　　(子 **zǐ**: son; 女 **nǚ**: daughter)
父母 **fùmǔ** 'parents'　　　　　　(父 **fù**: father; 母 **mǔ**: mother)
鱼虾 **yúxiā** 'fish and prawns';　　(鱼 **yú**: fish; 虾 **xiā**: shrimp, prawn)
　'seafood'
花卉 **huāhuì** 'flowers and plants'　(花 **huā**: flower, blossom;
　　　　　　　　　　　　　　　　卉 **huì**: various kinds of grass)
瓜果 **guāguǒ** 'various kinds of fruit'　(瓜 **guā**: melon, gourd; 果 **guǒ**: fruit)
茶饭 **cháfàn** 'food and drink'　　(茶 **chá**: tea; 饭 **fàn**: cooked rice)
门窗 **ménchuāng**　　　　　　　(门 **mén**: door; 窗 **chuāng**: window)
　'doors and windows'
瀛寰 **yínghuán** '(formal) the world'　(瀛 **yíng**: ocean; 寰 **huán**: extensive
　　　　　　　　　　　　　　　　region)
书报 **shūbào** 'books, newspapers,　(书 **shū**: book; 报 **bào**: newspaper)
　and periodicals'

被褥 **bèirù** 'bedding' (被 **bèi**: quilt; 褥 **rù**: cotton-padded mattress)

脏腑 **zàngfǔ** 'internal organs' (脏 **zàng**: heart, liver, etc.; 腑 **fǔ**: stomach, gallbladder, etc.)

The other point to note about nominal hyponymous juxtaposition is that one co-hyponym may choose to combine with different co-hyponyms to denote different meanings, literal or metaphorical. Take 口舌 **kǒushé** 'dispute' (口 **kǒu**: mouth; 舌 **shé**: tongue) for an example. We have:

口齿 **kǒuchǐ** 'enunciation' (口 **kǒu**: mouth; 齿 **chǐ**: tooth)

口吻 **kǒuwěn** 'tone; note' (口 **kǒu**: mouth; 吻 **wěn**: lips)

唇舌 **chúnshé** 'words'; 'argument' (唇 **chún**: lip; 舌 **shé**: tongue)

喉舌 **hóushé** 'mouthpiece' (喉 **hóu**: throat; 舌 **shé**: tongue)

adjective:

高深 **gāoshēn** 'advanced'; 'profound' (高 **gāo**: high; 深 **shēn**: deep)

浅近 **qiǎnjìn** 'simple'; 'easy to understand' (浅 **qiǎn**: shallow; 近 **jìn**: near)

辛酸 **xīnsuān** 'sad'; 'bitter' (辛 **xīn**: pungent; 酸 **suān**: sour)

名贵 **míngguì** 'rare' (名 **míng**: famous; 贵 **guì**: expensive, precious)

冻馁 **dòngněi** 'cold and hungry' (冻 **dòng**: cold; 馁 **něi**: hungry)

verb:

跋涉 **báshè** 'trek' (跋 **bá**: cross mountains; 涉 **shè**: wade, ford)

招呼 **zhāohu** 'greet' (招 **zhāo**: beckon; 呼 **hū**: call)

呼吸 **hūxī** 'breathe'; 'respire' (呼 **hū**: breathe out; 吸 **xī**: breathe in)

质对 **zhìduì** 'confront (in court)' (质 **zhì**: to question; 对 **duì**: to anwer)

网罗 **wǎngluó** 'enlist the services of' (网 **wǎng**: net for catching fish; 罗 **luó**: net for catching birds)

衡量 **héngliáng** 'judge' (衡 **héng**: weigh; 量 **liáng**: measure)

梳洗 **shūxǐ** 'wash and dress' (梳 **shū**: to comb; 洗 **xǐ**: wash)

牺牲 **xīshēng** 'to sacrifice'; 'give up' (牺 **xī**: a beast of a pure colour for sacrifice; 牲 **shēng**: a strong domestic animal for sacrifice)

裱褙 **biǎobèi** 'mount (a picture)' (裱 **biǎo**: mount (a picture); 褙 **bèi**: stick one piece of paper on top of another)

As is seen in nouns, the component monomyms do not have to be of the same word class as the resultant verb. 网 **wǎng** 'net for catching fish' and 罗 **luó** 'net for catching birds' are both, synchronically speaking, nominals, but their combination 网罗 **wǎngluó** 'enlist the services of' is undoubtedly a verb. The hypernymous notion can also be metaphorical: 衡量 **héngliáng** 'judge' is psychological whilst its constituent monomyms 衡 **héng** 'weigh' and 量 **liáng** 'to measure' are both physical actions.

adverb:

丝毫 **sīháo** 'not at all'   (丝 **sī**: a trace; 毫 **háo**: an iota)

再三 **zàisān** 'time and again'   (再 **zài**: a second time; 三 **sān**: a third time)

Trisyllabic or quadrisyllabic hyponymous juxtapositions, generally speaking, are often more literal and additive in meaning. In other words, the meaning of a trisyllabic or quadrisyllabic hyponymous juxtaposition is often that of the sum total of the component monomyms. For example, in trisyllables:

传帮带 **chuán bāng dài**
'pass on experience'; 'give help and set an example (in training new hands)'
   (传 **chuán**: pass on; 帮 **bāng**: help; 带 **dài**: set an example for)
稳准狠 **wěn zhǔn hěn** 'sure, accurate and relentless'
   (稳 **wěn**: sure; 准 **zhǔn**: accurate; 狠 **hěn**: relentless)
度量衡 **dùliànghéng** 'length, capacity and weight – weights and measures'
   (度 **dù**: degree; 量 **liàng**: quantity; 衡 **héng**: weight)
老大难 **lǎo dà nán** 'a long-standing, big and difficult problem'
   (老 **lǎo**: old; 大 **dà**: big; 难 **nán**: difficult)

In quadrisyllables, however, the resultant nominal expressions can have their constituent monomyms not only as nouns but also as verbs or adjectives:

with noun components:
喜怒哀乐 **xǐ nù āi lè** 'the gamut of human feeling'
   (喜 **xǐ**: delight; 怒 **nù**: anger; 哀 **āi**: sorrow; 乐 **lè**: joy)
之乎者也 **zhī hū zhě yě** 'pedantic terms'
   (之 **zhī**, 乎 **hū**, 者 **zhě**, 也 **yě** are four 'empty' or grammatical words in classical Chinese)

with verb components:
吃喝玩乐 **chī hē wán lè** 'idle away one's time in pleasure-seeking'
   (吃 **chī**: eat; 喝 **hē**: drink; 玩 **wán**: to play: 乐 **lè**: have fun)
坑蒙拐骗 **kēng mēng guǎi piàn** 'swindle'
   (坑 **kēng**: entrap; 蒙 **mēng**: deceive, dupe; 拐 **guǎi**: abduct, kidnap; 骗 **piàn**: cheat)

with adjectival components:
轻重缓急 **qīng zhòng huǎn jí** '(do things) in order of importance and urgency'
   (轻 **qīng**: light; 重 **zhòng**: heavy; 缓 **huǎn**: unhurried; 急 **jí**: urgent)
男女老少 **nán nǚ lǎo shào** 'men and women, old and young'
   (男 **nán**: male; 女 **nǚ**: female; 老 **lǎo**: old; 少 **shào**: young)

Sometimes a fourth item cannot be found to fill in the fourth syllable of the idiom, so the third item chosen is made into a disyllabic word, either an established or a coined one, e.g.

桌椅板凳 **zhuō yǐ bǎndèng** 'ordinary household furniture'
    (桌 **zhuō**: table; 椅 **yǐ**: chair; 板凳 **bǎndèng**: wooden bench or stool)
日月星辰 **rì yuè xīngchén** 'the heavenly bodies'
    (日 **rì**: the sun; 月 **yuè**: the moon; 星辰 **xīngchén**: stars)
金银财宝 **jīn yín cáibǎo** 'treasures'
    (金 **jīn**: gold; 银 **yín**: silver; 财宝 **cáibǎo**: valuables)

Of course, metaphorical transference, though rare, is not impossible in quadrisyllables as is shown by:

麟凤龟龙 **lín fèng guī lóng** 'honest, talented people'
    (麟 **lín**: unicorn; 凤 **fèng**: phoenix; 龟 **guī**: tortoise; 龙 **lóng**: dragon)
切磋琢磨 **qiē cuō zhuó mó** 'learn from each other by exchanging views'
    (切 **qiē**: carve and polish a bone into an object; 磋 **cuō**: carve and polish a section of ivory into an object; 琢 **zhuó**: carve and polish a piece of jade into an object; 磨 **mó**: carve and polish a stone into an object)

Quadrisyllabic hyponymous juxtapositions, like synonymous ones, may also take the form of two parallel structures, e.g.

noun:
    才子佳人 **cáizǐ jiārén**
    'gifted scholars and beautiful ladies' (in Chinese romances)
        (才子 **cáizǐ**: a talented scholar; 佳人 **jiārén**: a beautiful woman, beauty)
    名山大川 **míng shān dà chuān** 'famous mountains and great rivers'
        (名山 **míngshān**: famous mountains; 大川 **dàchuān**: great rivers)
    天罗地网 **tiānluó dìwǎng** 'tight encirclement'
        (天罗 **tiānluó**: nets above; 地网 **dìwǎng**: snares/nets below)

verb:
    争权夺利 **zhēng quán duó lì** 'fight for power and profit'
        (争权 **zhēngquán**: scramble for power; 夺利 **duólì**: fight for profit)
    品头论足 **pǐn tóu lùn zú** 'find fault with'
        (品头 **pǐn tóu**: comment on a person's head; 论足 **lùn zú**: comment on his/her feet)
    装聋作哑 **zhuāng lóng zuò yǎ** 'pretend to be ignorant of something'
        (装聋 **zhuāng lóng**: feign deafness; 作哑 **zuò yǎ**: affect dumbness)

subject and predicator:
    名正言顺 **míng zhèng yán shùn** 'perfectly justifiable'
        (名正 **míng zhèng**: justified in name; 言顺 **yán shùn**: justified in words)
    灯红酒绿 **dēng hóng jiǔ lù** 'scene of debauchery'
        (灯红 **dēng hóng**: lanterns are red; 酒绿 **jiǔ lù**: wine is green)
    龙飞凤舞 **lóng fēi fèng wǔ** 'a flamboyant style of Chinese calligraphy'
        (龙飞 **lóng fēi**: dragons fly; 凤舞 **fèng wǔ**: phoenixes dance)

(c) Antonymous Juxtaposition

By antonymous juxtaposition we mean that the two juxtaposed mononyms A and B are antonymous with or opposed to each other. For example,

(1) 老少 **lǎoshào** 'old and young' (老 **lǎo**: old; 少 **shào**: young)
宾主 **bīnzhǔ** 'hosts and guests' (宾 **bīn**: guest; 主 **zhǔ**: host)

(2) 迟早 **chízǎo** 'sooner or later' (迟 **chí**: late; 早 **zǎo**: early)
成败 **chéngbài** 'success or failure' (成 **chéng**: success; 败 **bài**: failure)

(3) 开关 **kāiguān** 'a switch' (开 **kāi**: switch on;
　　　　　　　　　　　　　　　　　　关 **guān**: switch off)

出入 **chūrù** 'discrepancy' (出 **chū**: exit, go out;
　　　　　　　　　　　　　　　　　　入 **rù**: enter, come in)

(4) 大小 **dàxiǎo** 'size'[8] (大 **dà**: big; 小 **xiǎo**: small)
始终 **shǐzhōng** 'all along' (始 **shǐ**: start; 终 **zhōng**: finish)

The juxtaposed antonyms, as we can see, can be related in different ways, e.g. indicating notions of *summation*, as in (1); or *choice*, as in (2); or *part-whole association* (usually with a metaphorical transference of meaning) as in (3), where the notion of open/shut or on/off stands for 'switch', enter/exit or in/out stands for 'discrepancy', etc.; or *coverage*, as in (4), in which the whole range of different sizes is covered by the two extremes of big and small, and the whole period is contained within the beginning and the end, etc.

It is conceivable that almost every adjective or any noun or verb in the lexicon which has an antonym may be thus juxtaposed to form disyllabic lexemes of every description. As we have seen, it is usually the positive or unmarked term of the antonymous pair that comes first. There are some exceptions for various reasons (e.g. for emphasis, more usual tonal sequence, etc.). The following are further examples of each category specified above:

(1) summation:

利弊 **lìbì** 'pros and cons' (利 **lì**: advantages;
　　　　　　　　　　　　　　　　　　弊 **bì**: disadvantages)

收支 **shōuzhī** 'income and expenses' (收 **shōu**: receive; 支 **zhī**: pay)
今昔 **jīnxī** 'the present and the past' (今 **jīn**: the present, today;
　　　　　　　　　　　　　　　　　　昔 **xī**: the past)

遐迩 **xiá'ěr** 'far and near' (遐 **xiá**: far; 迩 **ěr**: near)
盈亏 **yíngkuī** 'profit and loss' (盈 **yíng**: profit; 亏 **kuī**: loss)
朝野 **cháoyě** 'the governing party and the opposition' (朝 **cháo**: court; 野 **yě**: field)
师生 **shīshēng** 'teacher and student' (师 **shī**: teacher; 生 **shēng**: student)

---

[8] 大小 **dàxiǎo** may also mean 'adults and children of a family'. That will then have the 'summation' function.

前后 **qiánhòu**
'around (a certain time)'

(前 **qián**: front;
后 **hòu**: behind)

彼此 **bǐcǐ** 'each other; one another'

(彼 **bǐ**: that; 此 **cǐ**: this)

因果 **yīnguǒ** 'cause and effect'

(因 **yīn**: cause; 果 **guǒ**:
effect)

(2) choice:

去留 **qùliú** 'go or stay'

(去 **qù**: go; 留 **liú**:
stay behind, remain)

存亡 **cúnwáng** 'live or die'

(存 **cún**: survive;
亡 **wáng**: perish)

胜负 **shèngfù** 'victory or defeat'

(胜 **shèng**: win; 负 **fù**:
lose a battle, game, etc.)

缓急 **huǎnjí**
'greater or lesser urgency'

(缓 **huǎn**: slow, unhurried;
急 **jí**: anxious, fast)

荣辱 **róngrǔ** 'honour or disgrace'

(荣 **róng**: glory;
辱 **rǔ**: disgrace)

吉凶 **jíxiōng** 'good or ill luck'

(吉 **jí**: propitious;
凶 **xiōng**: ominous)

向背 **xiàngbèi** 'support or oppose'

(向 **xiàng**: side with; 背 **bèi**:
with the back towards)

隐现 **yǐnxiàn**
'now visible, now invisible'

(隐 **yǐn**: hidden from view;
现 **xiàn**: appear)

任免 **rènmiǎn**
'appoint and dismiss'

(任 **rèn**: appoint;
免 **miǎn**: dismiss)

游憩 **yóuqì** 'relax and play'

(游 **yóu**: stroll about;
憩 **qì**: take a rest)

朔望 **shuòwàng** 'the first and the
fifteenth day of the lunar month'

(朔 **shuò**: new moon;
望 **wàng**: full moon)

The notion of 'give and take' is related to that of 'choice':

左右 **zuǒyòu** 'approximately'
上下 **shàngxià** 'or thereabouts'

(左 **zuǒ**: left; 右 **yòu**: right)
(上 **shàng**: above; 下 **xià**: below)

(3) part-of association (metonymic or metaphorical):

行止 **xíngzhǐ** 'whereabouts'

(行 **xíng**: on the move;
止 **zhǐ**: stop)

虚实 **xūshí** 'the actual situation'

(虚 **xū**: false, hollow;
实 **shí**: true, solid)

冷暖 **lěngnuǎn** 'daily life';
'well-being'

(冷 **lěng**: cold; 暖 **nuǎn**: warm)

浓淡 **nóngdàn** 'shade of colour'

(浓 **nóng**: deep, dark;
淡 **dàn**: light, thin)

来往 **láiwang** 'dealings'; 'contact'
出纳 **chūnà** 'cashier'

(来 **lái**: come; 往 **wǎng**: go)
(出 **chū**: pay; 纳 **nà**: receive)

呼吸 **hūxī** 'breathe'   (呼 **hū**: breathe out;
     吸 **xī**: breathe in)

褒贬 **bāobiǎn** 'appraise'   (褒 **bāo**: praise; 贬 **biǎn**: cry down)

悠扬 **yōuyáng** 'melodious'   (悠 **yōu**: (of music) falling;
     扬 **yáng**: rising)

嫁娶 **jiàqǔ** 'marriage'   (嫁 **jià**: a woman marries a man;
     娶 **qǔ**: a man marries a woman)

(4) coverage:

多少 **duōshǎo** 'quantity'; 'amount'   (多 **duō**: much, many;
     少 **shǎo**: little, few)

轻重 **qīngzhòng** 'weight'   (轻 **qīng**: light in weight;
     重 **zhòng**: heavy)

长短 **chángduǎn** 'length'   (长 **cháng**: long; 短 **duǎn**: short)

高矮 **gāo'ǎi** 'height'   (高 **gāo**: tall, high; 矮 **ǎi**: short)

宽窄 **kuānzhǎi** 'width'; 'breadth'   (宽 **kuān**: wide, broad;
     窄 **zhǎi**: narrow)

深浅 **shēnqiǎn** 'depth'   (深 **shēn**: deep; 浅 **qiǎn**: shallow)

快慢 **kuàimàn** 'speed'   (快 **kuài**: fast; 慢 **màn**: slow)

好歹 **hǎodǎi** 'anyhow'; 'in any case'   (好 **hǎo**: good; 歹 **dǎi**: bad)

东西 **dōngxi** 'thing'   (东 **dōng**: east; 西 **xī**: west)

Actually the notion of 'coverage' is superordinate to notions of summation, choice and part-of and is therefore the primary tendency of an antonymous juxtaposition. In the last example 东西 **dōngxi** 'thing', even the tone on the second syllable 西 **xī** has been lost.

One peculiar semantic outcome of these antonymous juxtapositions is that in actual use quite often only one of the concepts (more often the negative one) in the juxtaposition seems to be the focus of emphasis in the meaning of the resultant construction. For example, 好歹 **hǎodǎi** (in which 好 **hǎo** means 'good' and 歹 **dǎi** means 'bad') does not just mean 'good or bad' but also in one context only 'mishap'; 'disaster' and in another only 'what is good for one'. Other examples include:

死活 **sǐhuó** 'life or death'; 'fate' or simply 'death'   (死 **sǐ**: dead; 活 **huó**: alive)

甘苦 **gānkǔ** 'weal and woe' or simply 'hardships'   (甘 **gān**: sweet, pleasant; 苦 **kǔ**: bitter)

是非 **shìfēi** 'right and wrong' or simply 'quarrel'   (是 **shì**: right; 非 **fēi**: wrong)

安危 **ānwēi** 'safety and danger' or simply 'safety'   (安 **ān**: safe; 危 **wēi**: dangerous)

动静 **dòngjing** 'the sound of sth astir'; 'movement'   (动 **dòng**: move; 静 **jìng**: keep still, quiet)

Only in these peculiar antonymous juxtapositions is it feasible (and perhaps useful) to distinguish between juxtaposer and juxtaposed mononyms: the mononym which is the focus of the meaning will naturally be the juxtaposed mononym and the other, the juxtaposer.

Antonymous juxtaposition may form the initial part of a trisyllabic lexeme: e.g.

来回票 **láihuípiào** 'return ticket'	(来 **lái**: come; 回 **huí**: return; 票 **piào**: ticket)
离合器 **líhéqì** (mech.) 'clutch'	(离 **lí**: separation; 合 **hé**: reunion; 器 **qì**: apparatus)
松紧带 **sōngjǐndài** 'elastic cord'	(松 **sōng**: loose; 紧 **jǐn**: tight; 带 **dài**: belt, ribbon)
升降机 **shēngjiàngjī** 'lift'; 'elevator'	(升 **shēng**: ascend; 降 **jiàng**: descend; 机 **jī**: machine)
吞吐量 **tūntǔliàng** 'handling capacity (of a harbour)'	(吞 **tūn**: swallow; 吐 **tǔ**: spit; 量 **liàng**: amount)
寒暑表 **hánshǔbiǎo** 'thermometer'	(寒 **hán**: cold; 暑 **shǔ**: summer; 表 **biǎo**: meter, gauge)
左右手 **zuǒyòushǒu** 'right-hand man'	(左 **zuǒ**: left; 右 **yòu**: right; 手 **shǒu**: hand)
姊妹篇 **zǐmèipiān** 'companion volume'	(姊妹 **zǐmèi**: sisters; 篇 **piān**: piece of writing)

A number of similarly structured trisyllabic words are actually *telescoped* forms of two antonymous disyllabic words which share the same headword:[9] e.g.

进出口 **jìnchūkǒu** 'imports and exports'	(进口 **jìnkǒu**: import; 出口 **chūkǒu**: export)
加减法 **jiājiǎnfǎ** 'addition and subtraction'	(加法 **jiāfǎ**: addition; 减法 **jiǎnfǎ**: subtraction)
上下文 **shàngxiàwén** 'context'	(上文 **shàngwén**: context above; 下文 **xiàwén**: context below)
中小学 **zhōngxiǎoxué** 'primary and secondary schools'	(中学 **zhōngxué**: secondary school; 小学 **xiǎoxué**: primary school)
寒暑假 **hánshǔjià** 'summer and winter holidays'	(寒假 **hánjià**: winter vacation; 暑假 **shǔjià**: summer holidays)

Antonymous juxtaposition may, of course, also form the initial or second part of many a quadrisyllabic idiom, or a pentasyllabic expression: e.g.

进退两难 **jìn tuì liǎng nán** 'in a dilemma'
(进 **jìn**: advance; 退 **tuì**: retreat; 两 **liǎng**: both; 难 **nán**: difficult)
本末倒置 **běnmò dàozhì** 'put the cart before the horse'
(本 **běn**: foundation; 末 **mò**: nonessentials; 倒 **dào**: upside down; 置 **zhì**: put)

---

[9] Cf. Guo, Liangfu (郭良夫) 1990: 6.

表里不一 **biǎo lǐ bù yī** 'think one way and act another'
(表 **biǎo**: surface, external; 里 **lǐ**: inside, internal; 不 **bù**: not; 一 **yī**: one, same)

哭笑不得 **kū xiào bude** 'not know whether to laugh or to cry'
(哭 **kū**: cry, weep; 笑 **xiào**: laugh; 不得 **bude**: must not, cannot)

黑白分明 **hēi bái fēnmíng** 'in sharp contrast'
(黑 **hēi**: black; 白 **bái**: white; 分明 **fēnmíng**: clear, distinct)

瑕瑜互见 **xiáyú hù jiàn** 'have defects as well as merits'
(瑕瑜 **xiáyú**: defects and merits; 互见 **hù jiàn**: (of two contrasting things) exist side by side)

休戚相关 **xiūqī xiāngguān** 'share joys and sorrows'
(休戚 **xiūqī**: weal and woe, joys and sorrows; 相关 **xiāngguān**: be mutually related)

毁誉参半 **huǐyù cānbàn** 'find a mixed reception'
(毁誉 **huǐyù**: praise or condemnation; 参半 **cānbàn**: half-and-half)

遐迩闻名 **xiá'ěr wénmíng** 'be known far and wide'
(遐迩 **xiá'ěr**: far and near; 闻名 **wénmíng**: well-known, famous)

吉凶未卜 **jíxiōng wèibǔ** 'one's fate is in the balance'
(吉凶 **jíxiōng**: good or ill luck; 未卜 **wèibǔ**: unpredictable)

霄壤之别 **xiāorǎng zhī bié** 'a world of difference'
(霄壤 **xiāorǎng**: heaven and earth; 之 **zhī**: a grammatical particle; 别 **bié**: difference)

老少咸宜 **lǎoshào xiányí** 'suitable for old and young alike'
(老少 **lǎoshào**: old and young; 咸 **xián**: all; 宜 **yí**: suitable, appropriate)

内外交困 **nèiwài jiāokùn**
'beset with difficulties both at home and abroad'
(内外 **nèiwài**: inside and outside, domestic and foreign; 交困 **jiāokùn**: beset by troubles)

良莠不齐 **liáng yǒu bù qí** 'the good and the bad are intermingled'
(良 **liáng**: the good; 莠 **yǒu**: the bad; 不 **bù**: not; 齐 **qí**: uniform)

不辨妍媸 **bù biàn yánchī**
'be unable to distinguish the beautiful from the ugly'
(不 **bù**: not; 辨 **biàn**: distinguish; 妍媸 **yánchī**: beautiful or ugly)

无足轻重 **wú zú qīngzhòng** 'of little consequence; insignificant'
(无 **wú**: not; 足 **zú**: worth; 轻重 **qīngzhòng**: light or heavy, degree of seriousness)

无关痛痒 **wúguān tòngyǎng** 'immaterial'
(无关 **wúguān**: have nothing to do with; 痛痒 **tòngyǎng**: ache or itch, relative importance)

世态炎凉 **shìtài yánliáng** 'warmth or coldness is the way of the world'
(世态 **shìtài**: the ways of the world; 炎凉 **yánliáng**: warm or cold)

人心向背 **rénxīn xiàngbèi** 'the feelings of the people'
(人心 **rénxīn**: popular feeling; 向背 **xiàngbèi**: support or oppose)

薰莸不同器 **xūn yóu bù tóng qì** 'good people must stay away from bad'
(薰 **xūn**: a fragrant grass; 莸 **yóu**: a stinking grass; 不 **bù**: not; 同 **tóng**: share; 器 **qì**: utensil)

水火不相容 **shuǐ huǒ bù xiāng róng** 'be incompatible as fire and water'
(水 **shuǐ**: water; 火 **huǒ**: fire; 不 **bù**: not; 相 **xiāng**: mutually; 容 **róng**: tolerate)

In some cases, gradable antonyms may be juxtaposed in threes:

敌我友 **dí wǒ yǒu** 'enemy, friends, and oneself'
(敌 **dí**: enemy, foe; 我 **wǒ**: I, we; 友 **yǒu**: friend)

上中下 **shàng zhōng xià** 'the upper, the middle and the lower'
(上 **shàng**: above; 中 **zhōng**: centre, middle; 下 **xià**: below)

早午晚 **zǎo wǔ wǎn**
'three times a day – in the morning, afternoon and evening'
(早 **zǎo**: morning; 午 **wǔ**: afternoon; 晚 **wǎn**: evening)

左中右 **zuǒ zhōng yòu** 'the leftists, the average people, and the rightists'
(左 **zuǒ**: the left; 中 **zhōng**: the middle; 右 **yòu**: the right)

In some quadrisyllabic idoms, two pairs of disyllabic antonymous juxtaposition are themselves juxtaposed: e.g.

悲欢离合 **bēi huān lí hé**
'joys and sorrows and partings and reunions – vicissitudes of life'
(悲 **bēi**: sad; 欢 **huān**: joyous; 离 **lí**: leave, part from; 合 **hé**: join, unite)

生死存亡 **shēng sǐ cún wáng** 'life or death'; 'survival or extinction'
(生 **shēng**: life; 死 **sǐ**: death; 存 **cún**: exist, survive; 亡 **wáng**: die, perish)

Many quadrisyllabic antonymous juxtapositions actually appear in staggered forms:

口是心非 **kǒushì xīnfēi** 'say yes and mean no'
(口 **kǒu**: mouth; 是 **shì**: yes; 心 **xīn**: heart; 非 **fēi**: no)

你死我活 **nǐ sǐ wǒ huó** 'life-and-death'; 'mortal'
(你 **nǐ**: you; 死 **sǐ**: dead; 我 **wǒ**: I; 活 **huó**: alive)

弄巧成拙 **nòng qiǎo chéng zhuō**
'try to be clever only to end up with a blunder'
(弄 **nòng**: handle; 巧 **qiǎo**: skilful; 成 **chéng**: turn into; 拙 **zhuō**: clumsy)

逆来顺受 **nì lái shùn shòu** 'meekly submit to maltreatment'
(逆 **nì**: adversity; 来 **lái**: come, arrive; 顺 **shùn**: without a struggle; 受 **shòu**: accept)

苦尽甘来 **kǔ jìn gān lái** 'the bitterness ends and the sweetness begins'
(苦 **kǔ**: bitterness; 尽 **jìn**: finished, exhausted; 甘 **gān**: sweetness; 来 **lái**: come)

上行下效 **shàng xíng xià xiào**
'subordinates follow the example of their superiors'
(上 **shàng**: above; 行 **xíng**: do, practise; 下 **xià**: below; 效 **xiào**: follow suit)

Polysyllabic antonymous juxtapositions usually comprise two parallel parts, each incorporating an antonymous item in corresponding positions:

高不成, 低不就 **gāo bù chéng | dī bù jiù**
'unfit for a high post but unwilling to take a lower one'
(高 **gāo**: high; 不 **bù**: not; 成 **chéng**: succeed; 低 **dī**: low; 不 **bù**: not; 就 **jiù**: willing)

雷声大, 雨点小 **léishēng dà | yǔdiǎn xiǎo** 'much ado about nothing'
(雷声 **léishēng**: noise of thunder; 大 **dà**: big, loud; 雨点 **yǔdiǎn**: raindrop; 小 **xiǎo**: small)

张家长, 李家短 **zhāng jiā cháng | lǐ jiā duǎn** 'gossip'
(张家: the Zhang family; 长 **cháng**: long, good; 李家: the Li family; 短 **duǎn**: short, bad)

前言不搭后语 **qiányán bù dā hòuyǔ** 'talk incoherently'
(前言 **qiányán**: what had been said before; 不 **bù**: not; 搭 **dā**: hang together with; 后语 **hòuyǔ**: what was said later)

前门拒虎, 后门进狼 **qiánmén jù hǔ | hòumén jìn láng**
'fend off one danger only to court another'
(前门 **qiánmén**: front door; 拒 **jù**: refuse entry to; 虎 **hǔ**: tiger; 后门 **hòumén**: back door; 进 **jìn**: enter; 狼 **láng**: wolf)

(d) Sequential Juxtaposition

If time and space are part of the built-in notions of human cognitive schemata, 'sequence' inevitably becomes an inseparable part of these notions. The concept of sequence, temporal or spatial, is therefore amply reflected in the meaning or composition of a language's lexical items. As we shall see, sequential juxtaposition in disyllabic structure is exclusively for verbs.

In many of these disyllabic verbs, the order of the two mononyms may indicate two consecutive actions from the same agent, e.g.

剪贴 **jiǎntiē** 'clip and paste (something out of a newspaper, etc.)' (剪 **jiǎn**: clip; 贴 **tiē**: paste)

提问 **tíwèn** 'put questions to' (提 **tí**: raise the question; 问 **wèn**: ask the question)

贩卖 **fànmài** 'buy and resell' (贩 **fàn**: buy; 卖 **mài**: sell)

查收 **cháshōu** (in letters) 'please find' (查 **chá**: check; 收 **shōu**: acknowledge receipt)

择伐 **zéfá** (forestry) 'selective felling' (择 **zé**: select; 伐 **fá**: to fell)

侵占 **qīnzhàn** 'invade and occupy' (侵 **qīn**: invade; 占 **zhàn**: occupy)

猎杀 **lièshā** 'hunt and kill' (猎 **liè**: hunt; 杀 **shā**: kill, slaughter, butcher)

签发 **qiānfā** 'sign and issue (a document, etc.)' (签 **qiān**: sign; 发 **fā**: send out, issue)

点交 **diǎnjiāo**
  'hand over item by item'

(点 **diǎn**: check one by one;
  交 **jiāo**: hand over)

厘定 **lídìng** 'collate and stipulate'

(厘 **lí**: rectify; 定 **dìng**: decide)

诊疗 **zhěnliáo** 'make a diagnosis
  and give treatment'

(诊 **zhěn**: make a diagnosis;
  疗 **liáo**: give treatment'

选送 **xuǎnsòng**
  'select and recommend sb
  (for admission to a school, etc.)'

(选 **xuǎn**: select, pick;
  送 **sòng**: send)

临眺 **líntiào** 'ascend a height and
  enjoy a distant view'

(临 **lín**: arrive, ascend; 眺 **tiào**:
  look into the distance from a
  high place)

The notion of *purpose* inherent in the second verbal mononym of these sequential juxtapositions is apparent in most cases. We can clearly see from the following examples that sometimes one and the same action is intended to entail various foreseeable results:

诬告 **wūgào** 'lodge a false accusation
against'

(诬 **wū**: accuse falsely;
  告 **gào**: take to court)

诬害 **wūhài** 'calumniate'; 'malign'

(害 **hài**: to harm, injure)

诬赖 **wūlài** 'falsely incriminate'

(赖 **lài**: blame wrongly)

诬蔑 **wūmiè** 'villify'; 'smear'

(蔑 **miè**: disdain, despise)

诬枉 **wūwǎng** 'slander'

(枉 **wǎng**: treat unjustly)

诬陷 **wūxiàn** 'frame a case against'

(陷 **xiàn**: to frame somebody)

诬栽 **wūzāi** 'fabricate a charge against'

(栽 **zāi**: impose)

If from different agents, i.e. when one person's action sets off that of another, these juxtapositions might be termed *causative* as in a formula (S) V (O) V, where the two juxtaposed V's have their respective agents understood, e.g.

召集 **zhāojí** 'call together'; 'summon'

(召 **zhāo**: summon; 集 **jí**: gather)

逼供 **bīgòng** 'extort a confession'

(逼 **bī**: extort; 供 **gòng**: confess)

催眠 **cuīmián** 'lull (to sleep)';
  'hypnotize'

(催 **cuī**: urge, hasten;
  眠 **mián**: sleep)

推动 **tuīdòng** 'give impetus to'

(推 **tuī**: push; 动 **dòng**: move)

派驻 **pàizhù** 'to post'; 'to station'

(派 **pài**: send, assign;
  驻 **zhù**: to post)

搦战 **nuòzhàn** '(obsolete)
  challenge to a fight'

(搦 **nuò**: provoke; 战 **zhàn**: to fight)

提升 **tíshēng** 'promote'

(提 **tí**: raise, lift; 升 **shēng**: rise)

勒交 **lèjiāo** 'force sb to hand over'

(勒 **lè**: coerce; 交 **jiāo**: hand over)

In quadrisyllabic juxtapositions, sequential actions are seen to be expressed in two parallel disyllabic parts. In some cases, the sequence is clear-cut, e.g.

过河拆桥 **guò hé chāi qiáo** 'kick down the ladder'
  (过 **guò**: cross; 河 **hé**: river; 拆 **chāi**: dismantle; 桥 **qiáo**: bridge)
得寸进尺 **dé cùn jìn chǐ** 'give him an inch and he'll take an ell'
  (得 **dé**: obtain; 寸 **cùn**: inch; 进 **jìn**: advance; 尺 **chǐ**: (measure) foot)

But this is not necessarily so in other cases; particularly if the verbal nature in the first disyllabic part is less obvious than the one in the second, the two consecutive actions might almost be seen as being 'simultaneous': e.g.

顾名思义 **gù míng sī yì**
'seeing the name of a thing one thinks of its function'; 'by definition'
  (顾 **gù**: look at; 名 **míng**: name; 思 **sī**: think of; 义 **yì**: meaning)
随风转舵 **suí fēng zhuǎn duò** 'take one's cue from changing conditions'
  (随 **suí**: adapt to; 风 **fēng**: wind; 转 **zhuǎn**: turn; 舵 **duò**: rudder)
趁热打铁 **chèn rè dǎtiě** 'strike while the iron is hot'
  (趁 **chèn**: take advantage of; 热 **rè**: heat, hot; 打铁 **dǎtiě**: forge the iron)

In fact, more often the sequence types are of the action-purpose or action-result type, e.g.

action-purpose:
剜肉补疮 **wān ròu bǔ chuāng** 'resort to a stopgap measure'
  (剜 **wān**: gouge out; 肉 **ròu**: flesh; 补 **bǔ**: mend; 疮 **chuāng**: wound)
削足适履 **xuē zú shì lǚ** 'act in a Procrustean manner'
  (削 **xuē**: whittle; 足 **zú**: foot; 适 **shì**: to fit; 履 **lǚ**: shoe)
杀鸡取卵 **shā jī qǔ luǎn** 'kill the goose that lays the golden eggs'
  (杀 **shā**: kill; 鸡 **jī**: chicken; 取 **qǔ**: get; 卵 **luǎn**: egg)

action-result:[10]
贪小失大 **tān xiǎo shī dà** 'seek small gains but incur big losses'
  (贪 **tān**: covet; 小 **xiǎo**: small; 失 **shī**: lose; 大 **dà**: big)
积羽沉舟 **jī yǔ chén zhōu** 'minor offences unchecked may bring disaster'
  (积 **jī**: accumulate; 羽 **yǔ**: feather; 沉 **chén**: sink; 舟 **zhōu**: boat)
过目成诵 **guò mù chéng sòng** 'having a photographic memory'
  (过目 **guò mù**: glance over; 成 **chéng**: turn into; 诵 **sòng**: recitation)

The sequence of action-result type is particularly apparent in two-part allegorical sayings (歇后语 **xièhòuyǔ**) and it is in the second part of such a saying where the logical conclusion or the 'pun' resides that the result is made explicit,[11] e.g.

瞎子点灯 – 白费蜡 **xiāzi diǎn dēng | bái fèi là** 'a sheer waste'
  (瞎子 **xiāzi**: the blind; 点 **diǎn**: to light; 灯 **dēng**: lamp; 白费 **báifèi**: waste; 蜡 **là**: wax)

---

[10] Action-result sequences encoded in disyllabic lexemes will be discussed in detail in 'verb + complement' type.
[11] Two-part allegorical sayings will be dealt with more thoroughly in Chapter 6.

外甥打灯笼－照舅 **wàisheng dǎ dēnglóng | zhào jiù** 'as of old'
(外甥 **wàisheng**: nephew; 打 **dǎ**: hold up; 灯笼 **dēnglóng**: lantern; 照舅 **zhào jiù**: light the way for one's maternal uncle, which finds a pun in the set expression 照旧 **zhàojiù**: as of old)

(e) Quantifying Juxtaposition

By quantifying juxtaposition we mean the juxtaposition of a noun and a word specifying its number or unit. In free syntactic constructions, for example, 俩 **liǎ** 'both' and 仨 **sā** 'three' may be seen juxtaposed to nouns or pronouns like the following:

哥弟俩 **gēdì liǎ** 'both of the brothers' (哥 **gē**: elder brother; 弟 **dì**: younger brother; 俩 **liǎ**: both)
姐妹仨 **jiěmèi sā** 'three sisters' (姐 **jiě**: elder sister; 妹 **mèi**: younger sister; 仨 **sā**: three of them)
咱俩 **zánliǎ** 'we two' (咱 **zán**: we; 俩 **liǎ**: both)

More important in lexical terms, however, is the interesting behaviour of some 'measure words' (or 'classifiers') which are permanently juxtaposed with their corresponding nouns with the intention to 'pluralise', e.g.

马匹 **mǎpǐ** 'horses'   布匹 **bùpǐ** 'cloth'; 'piece goods'
船只 **chuánzhī** 'vessels'   枪枝 **qiāngzhī** 'firearms'
车辆 **chēliàng** 'vehicles'; 'cars'   纸张 **zhǐzhāng** 'paper'
人口 **rénkǒu** 'population'   花朵 **huāduǒ** 'flowers'
米粒 **mǐlì** 'grains of rice'   书本 **shūběn** 'books'

项 **xiàng** and 件 **jiàn** are particularly prolific 'measure word' juxtaposers in forming such quantifying juxtapositions:

事项 **shìxiàng** 'items'; 'matter'   用项 **yòngxiàng** 'items of expenditure'
事件 **shìjiàn** 'incident'; 'event'   案件 **ànjiàn** 'law case'
稿件 **gǎojiàn** 'manuscript'   信件 **xìnjiàn** 'letters'; 'mail'
邮件 **yóujiàn** 'postal matter'   物件 **wùjiàn** (dial.) 'things'; 'articles'

In these juxtapositions, the measure word or classifier is the juxtaposer.

(f) Phonaesthetic Juxtaposition

By phonaesthetic juxtaposition we mean the structure of hundreds of phonaesthetically motivated disyllabic lexemes in the lexicon, traditionally known in Chinese linguistic theories as 双声 **shuāngshēng** 'alliterated' or 叠韵 **diéyùn** 'rhymed'. It is extremely rare for a word to be alliterated and rhymed at the same time. Words like 秘密 **mìmì** 'secret', 仇雠 **chóuchóu** (formal) 'enemy'; 'foe', 鞑靼 **dádá** 'Tartar', etc. are exceptions. Such a word is usually a reduplication, e.g. 靡靡 **mǐmǐ** 'decadent'.

In a phonaesthetic juxtaposition, the two alliterated or rhymed mononyms are formally and semantically dependent on each other (e.g. 踌躇 **chóuchú** 'hesitate'; 'shilly-shally' – alliterated; 彷徨 **pánghuáng** 'walk back and forth, not knowing which way to go' – rhymed). Each monomym in the disyllabic combination is a bound morpheme. These juxtapositions will receive special discussion in Chapter 5.

MODIFICATIONAL TYPE

Modification, seemingly a surface 'chain', actually implies an underlying 'choice' associated with the lexeme. For instance, 轻视 **qīngshì** 'look down upon' is not only a surface syntagmatic structure of 轻 **qīng** 'lightly' preceding 视 **shì** 'regard' but also implies its contrast with other paradigmatic possibilities such as those listed below. From the sheer number of differentiations that can be made, eyes must have always been the most expressive organ which a human being possesses. The list is compartmentalised in terms of

attitude:

重视 **zhòngshì** 'attach importance to' (重 **zhòng**: heavy, weighty)

珍视 **zhēnshì** 'value'; 'prize'; 'cherish' (珍 **zhēn**: treasure)

正视 **zhèngshì** 'face squarely'; 'face up to' (正 **zhèng**: straight, upright)

藐视 **miǎoshì** 'belittle'; 'look down upon' (藐 **miǎo**: tiny, insignificant)

小视 **xiǎoshì** 'slight'; 'look down upon' (小 **xiǎo**: small)

忽视 **hūshì** 'overlook'; 'neglect' (忽 **hū**: not paying attention)

漠视 **mòshì** 'ignore' (漠 **mò**: indifferent)

无视 **wúshì** 'disregard' (无 **wú**: nothing, nil)

歧视 **qíshì** 'discriminate against' (歧 **qí**: divergent, different)

蔑视 **mièshì** 'despise'; 'scorn' (蔑 **miè**: slight, disdain)

鄙视 **bǐshì** 'disdain'; 'show contempt for' (鄙 **bǐ**: low, mean, vulgar)

怒视 **nùshì** 'glower at'; 'scowl at' (怒 **nù**: angry)

狞视 **níngshì** 'stare fiercely at' (狞 **níng**: (of facial expression) ferocious)

敌视 **díshì** 'be hostile (or antagonistic) to' (敌 **dí**: enemy, foe)

仇视 **chóushì** 'look upon with hatred' (仇 **chóu**: hatred, enmity)

manner:

瞥视 **piēshì** 'cast a quick glance at' (瞥 **piē**: dart a look at, a glimpse)

睃视 **suōshì** 'look askance at' (睃 **suō**: look askance)

睇视 **dìshì** (formal)
  'cast a sidelong glance'

(睇 **dì**: look askance)

斜视 **xiéshì** 'give a sidelong glance'

(斜 **xié**: oblique, slanting)

眄视 **miànshì** (formal) 'look askance'

(眄 **miàn**: look askance)

睨视 **nìshì** 'look sideways'

(睨 **nì**: look askance)

凝视 **níngshì** 'gaze fixedly at'

(凝 **níng**: with fixed attention)

端视 **duānshì** 'look closely'

(端 **duān**: up and down)

注视 **zhùshì** 'look attentively at'

(注 **zhù**: concentrate, fix)

谛视 **dìshì** 'scrutinise'

(谛 **dì**: carefully, attentively)

逼视 **bīshì** 'watch intently'

(逼 **bī**: compel, press)

环视 **huánshì** 'look around'

(环 **huán**: ring, hoop, surround)

扫视 **sǎoshì** (of one's eyes or glance)
  'sweep'

(扫 **sǎo**: sweep, pass quickly
  along or over)

仰视 **yǎngshì** 'look up'

(仰 **yǎng**: face upward)

俯视 **fǔshì** 'look down at'; 'overlook'

(俯 **fǔ**: bow one's head)

purpose:

探视 **tànshì** 'visit'

(探 **tàn**: visit, pay a call on)

省视 **xǐngshì** 'call upon';
  'pay a visit to'

(省 **xǐng**: visit one's parents or
  elders)

监视 **jiānshì** 'keep watch on'

(监 **jiān**: supervise, inspect)

检视 **jiǎnshì** 'inspect'

(检 **jiǎn**: check up, inspect,
  examine)

审视 **shěnshì** 'examine closely'

(审 **shěn**: examine, go over)

巡视 **xúnshì**
  'make an inspection tour'

(巡 **xún**: patrol, make one's
  rounds)

窥视 **kuīshì** 'peep at'; 'spy on'

(窥 **kuī**: peep, spy)

侦视 **zhēnshì** 'detect'

(侦 **zhēn**: detect, scout)

诊视 **zhěnshì** 'examine (a patient)'

(诊 **zhěn**: examine a patient)

Equally impressive is the set describing different kinds of movement,[12] where 'manner' seems to be the sole category of modifiers.

摆动 **bǎidòng** 'swing'; 'sway'

(摆 **bǎi**: sway; 动 **dòng**: move)

晃动 **huàngdòng** 'rock'; 'sway'

(晃 **huàng**: sway)

摇动 **yáodòng** 'wave'

(摇 **yáo**: shake, wave)

振动 **zhèndòng** 'vibrate'

(振 **zhèn**: shake, flap)

跳动 **tiàodòng** 'pulsate'

(跳 **tiào**: jump, bounce)

搏动 **bódòng** 'throb'

(搏 **bó**: beat, throb)

颤动 **chàndòng** 'vibrate'; 'quiver'

(颤 **chàn**: quiver, tremble)

抽动 **chōudòng** 'twitch';
  'jerk spasmodically'

(抽 **chōu**: twitch)

[12] Theoretically, it is not impossible, though slightly far-fetched, to regard this set of lexemes as of juxtapositional structure with the mononym 动 **dòng** 'move' posed as the juxtaposer whose general meaning of movement is being further refined by juxtaposed verbal mononyms indicating more specific movements.

搐动 **chùdòng** '(of muscles) twitch'	(搐 **chù**: jerk, twitch)
抖动 **dǒudòng** 'shake'; 'tremble'	(抖 **dǒu**: tremble, shiver)
脉动 **màidòng** 'pulsate'	(脉 **mài**: pulse)
滚动 **gǔndòng** 'roll'; 'trundle'	(滚 **gǔn**: roll, trundle)
流动 **liúdòng** 'flow'; 'circulate'	(流 **liú**: flow, move from place to place)
蠕动 **rúdòng** 'wriggle'; 'squirm'	(蠕 **rú**: wriggle, squirm)
移动 **yídòng** 'move'; 'shift'	(移 **yí**: move, shift)
转动 **zhuàndòng** 'revolve'; 'rotate'	(转 **zhuàn**: revolve, rotate)
浮动 **fúdòng** 'drift'; 'fluctuate'	(浮 **fú**: float)
波动 **bōdòng** 'undulate'; 'fluctuate'	(波 **bō**: wave)
滑动 **huádòng** 'slide'	(滑 **huá**: slippery, slide)

Modification is therefore a process of making overt or transparent the potential features in the modified by means of the modifier. The purpose is solely to imply 'choice', a choice in any respect which is inherently possible in the modified or the headword. The headwords we have chosen for illustration in the above cases happen to be verbs. In fact, the headword is in most cases a noun or sometimes an adjective. As choices can be 'taxonomically' organised, they can therefore be classified into semantic categories. For example, a choice can be made in terms of:

function:	车库 **chēkù** 'garage'	(车 **chē**: vehicle; 库 **kù**: depot)
instrument:	笔记 **bǐjì** 'take notes'; 'notes'	(笔 **bǐ**: pen; 记 **jì**: record)
manner:	稳步 **wěnbù** 'steadily'	(稳 **wěn**: steady; 步 **bù**: steps)
time:	冬眠 **dōngmián** 'hibernation'	(冬 **dōng**: winter; 眠 **mián**: sleep)
location:	天堂 **tiāntáng** 'paradise'	(天 **tiān**: heaven; 堂 **táng**: hall)
degree:	深情 **shēnqíng** 'deep love'	(深 **shēn**: deep; 情 **qíng**: sentiment)
quantity:	四季 **sìjì** 'four seasons'	(四 **sì**: four; 季 **jì**: season)
colour:	红茶 **hóngchá** 'black tea'	(红 **hóng**: red; 茶 **chá**: tea)
shape:	圆顶 **yuándǐng** 'dome'	(圆 **yuán**: round; 顶 **dǐng**: top)
sound:	乒乓球 **pīngpāngqiú** 'table tennis'	(乒乓 **pīngpāng**: ping-pong; 球 **qiú**: ball)
taste:	甜味 **tiánwèi** 'sweet taste'	(甜 **tián**: sweet; 味 **wèi**: taste)
material:	皮鞋 **píxié** 'leather shoes'	(皮 **pí**: leather; 鞋 **xié**: shoe)
power:	电脑 **diànnǎo** 'computer'	(电 **diàn**: electricity; 脑 **nǎo**: brain)
owner:	象牙 **xiàngyá** 'ivory'	(象 **xiàng**: elephant; 牙 **yá**: tusk)

origin:	英语 **yīngyǔ** 'English'	(英 **yīng**: England; 语 **yǔ**: language)
resemblance:	冰糖 **bīngtáng** 'crystal sugar'	(冰 **bīng**: ice; 糖 **táng**: sugar)
style:	蛙泳 **wāyǒng** 'breaststroke'	(蛙 **wā**: frog; 泳 **yǒng**: swim)
sex:	女孩 **nǚhái** 'girl'	(女 **nǚ**: female; 孩 **hái**: child)
cause:	病逝 **bìngshì** 'die of illness'	(病 **bìng**: ill; 逝 **shì**: pass away)
method:	威慑 **wēishè** 'deter'	(威 **wēi**: military force; 慑 **shè**: terrorize)
subcategory:	樟木 **zhāngmù** 'camphor wood'	(樟 **zhāng**: camphor; 木 **mù**: wood)

We have listed some of the major possible choices; but in fact, the choices are open. There is no area in which a choice cannot be made and therefore it would be futile trying to be exhaustive. Chao Yuen Ren[13] has discerned 21 choices,[14] but the list still remains open. The result is perhaps not worth the effort since all possible semantic relationships can be recaptured in a 'modifier + modified' construction. For instance, in the following lexemes, one and the same modifier have different semantic relations with the modified, e.g.

水池 **shuǐchí** 'cistern'	(水 **shuǐ**: water; 池 **chí**: pool)	function
水解 **shuǐjiě** 'hydrolysis'	(解 **jiě**: resolve)	instrument
水牛 **shuǐniú** 'buffalo'	(牛 **niú**: ox)	association
水平 **shuǐpíng** 'horizontal'	(平 **píng**: level)	characteristic
水锈 **shuǐxiù** 'watermark' (in water vessels)	(锈 **xiù**: rusty)	cause
水银 **shuǐyín** 'mercury'	(银 **yín**: silver)	resemblance

Another way of looking at the internal characteristic of a modificational type of lexeme in Chinese is perhaps in terms of subcategorisation. In other words, a general, superordinate notion or category (the genus) is further differentiated into subcategories (the species) in terms of function, degree, manner, resemblance, and so on. And precisely because of this differentiating (apart from descriptive) nature in the relationship between the modifier and the modified, the modificational type mainly occurs with nouns, verbs and adjectives, notions that can be more easily assigned a place in a taxonomy.

So far we have been more concerned with the semantic relationship between the two constituent monomyms in a modificational lexeme. If we compare the word class of the resultant lexeme with that of its components, we shall find that a broad range of intra-lexemic syntactic combinations are possible:

[13] Cf. Chao 1968.
[14] Cf. Ren, Xueliang (任学良) 1981 – 17 choices.

+	noun	adjective	verb	
noun	台灯 **táidēng** 'desk-lamp' (台: desk; 灯: lamp)		电视 **diànshì** 'television' (电: electricity; 视: look)	= noun
		冰冷 **bīnglěng** 'icy-cold' (冰: ice; 冷: cold)	火烫 **huǒtàng** 'scalding' (火: fire; 烫: scald)	= adj.
			粉饰 **fěnshì** 'whitewash' (粉: powder; 饰: decorate)	= verb
adjective	真理 **zhēnlǐ** 'truth' (真: true; 理: reason)		速写 **sùxiě** 'sketch' (速: speedy; 写: write)	= noun
	高级 **gāojí** 'high quality' (高: high; 级: grade)	浅蓝 **qiǎnlán** 'light blue' (浅: shallow; 蓝: blue)	平行 **píngxíng** 'parallel' (平: level; 行: travel)	= adj.
			复活 **fùhuó** 'revive' (复: again; 活: be alive)	= verb
verb	交情 **jiāoqíng** 'friendship' (交: communicate; 情: feeling)			= noun
		飞快 **fēikuài** 'very fast' (飞: fly; 快: fast)		= adj.
			补考 **bǔkǎo** 'resit (exam)' (补: mend; 考: be examined)	= verb

Here are examples from the major word classes.
   Nouns:

   noun as the modifier:
   门票 **ménpiào** 'admission ticket'   (门 **mén**: door; 票 **piào**: ticket)
   路牌 **lùpái** 'signpost'   (路 **lù**: road; 牌 **pái**: sign, placard)
   地图 **dìtú** 'map'   (地 **dì**: land; 图 **tú**: picture, drawing)
   教堂 **jiàotáng** 'church'   (教 **jiào**: religion; 堂 **táng**: hall)
   风景 **fēngjǐng** 'landscape'   (风 **fēng**: wind; 景 **jǐng**: scenery)
   汽车 **qìchē** 'automobile'   (汽 **qì**: steam, vapour; 车 **chē**: car)

球场 **qiúchǎng** 'sports-field' (球 **qiú**: ball; 场 **chǎng**: area, place)
饭碗 **fànwǎn** 'bowl' (饭 **fàn**: rice; 碗 **wǎn**: bowl)
碗柜 **wǎnguì** 'cupboard' (碗 **wǎn**: bowl; 柜 **guì**: cabinet)
戏台 **xìtái** 'stage' (戏 **xì**: drama, opera; 台 **tái**: platform)
雨伞 **yǔsǎn** 'umbrella' (雨 **yǔ**: rain; 伞 **sǎn**: parasol, umbrella)
字典 **zìdiǎn** 'dictionary' (字 **zì**: Chinese script;
典 **diǎn**: standard book)
桌布 **zhuōbù** 'tablecloth' (桌 **zhuō**: table; 布 **bù**: cloth)
窗帘 **chuānglián** 'curtain' (窗 **chuāng**: window;
帘 **lián**: hanging screen)
罪证 **zuìzhèng** 'proof of crime' (罪 **zuì**: crime; 证 **zhèng**: evidence)

adjective as the modifier:
暖房 **nuǎnfáng** 'greenhouse' (暖 **nuǎn**: warm; 房 **fáng**: room)
凉亭 **liángtíng** 'summer house' (凉 **liáng**: cool; 亭 **tíng**: pavilion)
前途 **qiántú** 'prospect' (前 **qián**: ahead; 途 **tú**: journey)
喜事 **xǐshì** 'a happy event' (喜 **xǐ**: happy; 事 **shì**: affair, event)
小费 **xiǎofèi** 'tips' (小 **xiǎo**: small; 费 **fèi**: fee)
真理 **zhēnlǐ** 'truth' (真 **zhēn**: true; 理 **lǐ**: reason)

Most surprising is perhaps that quite a number of nouns actually have verbs either as the modifier or the modified in their make-up. This is possibly related to the prime importance of the notion of 'function' or 'purpose' we assign to everything we see or do. For example:

where the modifier is a verb:
请帖 **qǐngtiě** 'written invitation' (请 **qǐng**: invite; 帖 **tiě**: a note, card)
证书 **zhèngshū** 'certificate' (证 **zhèng**: certify, prove;
书 **shū**: document)
招牌 **zhāopái** 'signboard' (招 **zhāo**: greet, attract;
牌 **pái**: placard)
赠券 **zèngquàn** (赠 **zèng**: give as a gift;
'complimentary ticket' 券 **quàn**: ticket)
捐款 **juānkuǎn** 'donation' (捐 **juān**: donate; 款 **kuǎn**:
money, fund)
护照 **hùzhào** 'passport' (护 **hù**: protect; 照 **zhào**:
license, permit)
抽屉 **chōuti** 'draw' (抽 **chōu**: to draw; 屉 **tì**: drawer)
围裙 **wéiqún** 'apron' (围 **wéi**: wrap around; 裙 **qún**: skirt)
环境 **huánjìng** 'environment' (环 **huán**: surround; 境 **jìng**: situation)
现象 **xiànxiàng** 'phenomenon' (现 **xiàn**: appear; 象 **xiàng**: image)
骂名 **màmíng** 'bad name, infamy' (骂 **mà**: abuse, swear at;
名 **míng**: name)
配方 **pèifāng** 'prescription' (配 **pèi**: mix; 方 **fāng**: directions,
instructions)

where the modified is a verb:

零用 **língyòng** 'pocket money'　　(零 **líng**: sundry; 用 **yòng**: use)
广告 **guǎnggào** 'advertisement'　　(广 **guǎng**: extensive; 告 **gào**: tell)
邻居 **línjū** 'neighbour'　　(邻 **lín**: next door; 居 **jū**: reside, live)
电视 **diànshì** 'television'　　(电 **diàn**: electricity; 视 **shì**: look)
速写 **sùxiě** 'sketch'　　(速 **sù**: speedy; 写 **xiě**: write)
反馈 **fǎnkuì** 'feedback'　　(反 **fǎn**: counter, return;
　　　　　　　　　　　　　　馈 **kuì**: feed)

In trisyllables, two rhythmic subtypes[15] can be found: (1) XX + X or (2) X + XX

XX + X:

高跟鞋 **gāogēnxié** 'high-heeled shoes'　　(高 **gāo**: high; 跟 **gēn**: heel;
　　　　　　　　　　　　　　鞋 **xié**: shoe)

口香糖 **kǒuxiāngtáng** 'chewing-gum'　　(口 **kǒu**: mouth; 香 **xiāng**:
　　　　　　　　　　　　　　aromatic; 糖 **táng**: sweets)

日记本 **rìjìběn** 'diary'　　(日 **rì**: day; 记 **jì**: to record;
　　　　　　　　　　　　　　本 **běn**: mw for books)

孩子气 **háiziqì** childishness　　(孩子 **háizi**: child; 气 **qì**: style)
身份证 **shēnfenzhèng** 'identity card'　　(身份 **shēnfen**: status, identity;
　　　　　　　　　　　　　　证 **zhèng**: evidence)

猫眼石 **māoyǎnshí** 'cat's eye'　　(猫 **māo**: cat; 眼 **yǎn**: eye;
　　　　　　　　　　　　　　石 **shí**: stone)

螺丝刀 **luósīdāo** 'screwdriver'　　(螺丝 **luósī**: screw; 刀 **dāo**: knife)
橡皮圈 **xiàngpíquān** 'rubber band'　　(橡皮 **xiàngpí**: (vulcanised)
　　　　　　　　　　　　　　rubber; 圈 **quān**: circle, ring)

压力锅 **yālìguō** 'pressure cooker'　　(压力 **yālì**: pressure; 锅 **guō**:
　　　　　　　　　　　　　　pot, pan, boiler, cauldron)

工具箱 **gōngjùxiāng** 'tool kit'　　(工具 **gōngjù**: tool, implement;
　　　　　　　　　　　　　　箱 **xiāng**: box, case)

图书馆 **túshūguǎn** 'library'　　(图 **tú**: map, picture;
　　　　　　　　　　　　　　书 **shū**: book; 馆 **guǎn**: hall)

室内乐 **shìnèiyuè** 'chamber music'　　(室 **shì**: room; 内 **nèi**: inside;
　　　　　　　　　　　　　　乐 **yuè**: music)

终点站 **zhōngdiǎnzhàn** 'terminal'　　(终点 **zhōngdiǎn**: destination;
　　　　　　　　　　　　　　站 **zhàn**: station)

专利权 **zhuānlìquán** 'patent'　　(专利 **zhuānlì**: patent;
　　　　　　　　　　　　　　权 **quán**: power, authority)

囫囵觉 **húlunjiào**　　(囫囵 **húlún**: whole;
'a good night's sleep'　　　觉 **jiào**: sleep)

---

[15] Here the word 'rhythm' is used to define the boundary between the modifier and the modified. In actual speech, both subtypes are always said with a conventional XX-X rhythm ignoring even the word boundaries.

问题单 **wèntídān** 'questionnaire' (问题 **wèntí**: question;
单 **dān**: list, bill)

哑巴亏 **yǎbakuī** (哑巴 **yǎba**: a dumb person;
'an unutterable grievance' 亏 **kuī**: grievance)

The headword may often be a nominalised verb or adjective:

剖腹产 **pōufùchǎn** 'Caesarean birth' (剖 **pōu**: cut open; 腹 **fù**:
abdomen; 产 **chǎn**: give birth)

现世报 **xiànshìbào** (现世 **xiànshì**: this life;
'retribution in this life' 报 **bào**: requite)

睁眼瞎 **zhēngyǎnxiā** 'illiterate' (睁眼 **zhēngyǎn**: with eyes wide
open; 瞎 **xiā**: blind)

忘年交 **wàngniánjiāo** 'friendship (忘 **wàng**: forget; 年 **nián**: year;
despite great difference in age' 交 **jiāo**: make friends)

苹果绿 **píngguǒlǜ** 'apple green' (苹果 **píngguǒ**: apple; 绿 **lǜ** green)

鸭蛋青 **yādànqīng** 'pale blue' (鸭蛋 **yādàn**: duck's egg;
青 **qīng**: blue or green)

鱼肚白 **yúdùbái** 'grey dawn' (鱼肚 **yúdù**: fish's belly;
白 **bái**: white)

下马威 **xiàmǎwēi** 'severity shown by (下马 **xiàmǎ**: dismount; 威 **wēi**:
an official on assuming office' authority, might, power)

A verbal modifier is also fairly common in trisyllabic lexemes:

养老金 **yǎnglǎojīn** 'old age pension' (养老 **yǎnglǎo**: support old age;
金 **jīn**: money, fund)

说明书 **shuōmíngshū** 'manual' (说明 **shuōmíng**: explain;
书 **shū**: leaflet, document)

勘误表 **kānwùbiǎo** 'errata' (勘误 **kānwù**: correct errors;
表 **biǎo**: chart, list, table)

催眠曲 **cuīmiánqǔ** 'lullaby' (催眠 **cuīmián**: lull to sleep;
曲 **qǔ**: song, music)

保险箱 **bǎoxiǎnxiāng** 'a safe' (保险 **bǎoxiǎn**: secure, insure;
箱 **xiāng**: box)

旅差费 **lǚchāifèi** 'travel expenses' (旅 **lǚ**: travel; 差 **chāi**: errand;
费 **fèi**: fee)

望远镜 **wàngyuǎnjìng** 'telescope' (望 **wàng**: gaze; 远 **yuǎn**: far;
镜 **jìng**: mirror, lens)

摇钱树 **yáoqiánshù** 'money-spinner' (摇 **yáo**: shake; 钱 **qián**: money;
树 **shù**: tree)

落地窗 **luòdìchuāng** (落 **luò**: fall, drop; 地 **dì**:
'French window' ground; 窗 **chuāng**: window)

垫脚石 **diànjiǎoshí** 'stepping stone' (垫 **diàn**: to cushion;
脚 **jiǎo**: foot; 石 **shí**: stone)

寄生虫 **jìshēngchóng** 'parasite'   (寄生 **jìshēng**: parasitic;
虫 **chóng**: insect, worm)

人行道 **rénxíngdào**
'pavement'; 'sidewalk'   (人 **rén**: people; 行 **xíng**: walk;
道 **dào**: road, lane)

座谈会 **zuòtánhuì**
'forum'; 'symposium'   (座谈 **zuòtán**: have a discussion;
会 **huì**: meeting)

奠基礼 **diànjīlǐ** 'foundation stone
laying ceremony'   (奠基 **diànjī**: lay a cornerstone;
礼 **lǐ**: ceremony)

求知欲 **qiúzhīyù**
'thirst for knowledge'   (求 **qiú**: seek; 知 **zhī**: knowledge;
欲 **yù**: desire)

停车场 **tíngchēchǎng** 'car park'   (停车 **tíngchē**: park a car;
场 **chǎng**: a large place)

游乐园 **yóulèyuán** 'amusement park'   (游乐 **yóulè**: amuse oneself;
园 **yuán**: a park, garden)

洗手间 **xǐshǒujiān** 'toilet'; 'lavatory'   (洗手 **xǐshǒu**: wash the hand;
间 **jiān**: room)

任意球 **rènyìqiú** 'free kick'   (任意 **rènyì**: arbitrary; 球 **qiú**: ball)

选择题 **xuǎnzétí**
'multiple-choice question'   (选择 **xuǎnzé**: select, choose;
题 **tí** problem)

好奇心 **hàoqíxīn** 'curiosity'   (好奇 **hàoqí**: full of curiosity;
心 **xīn**: heart)

梦游症 **mèngyóuzhèng** 'sleepwalking'   (梦 **mèng**: dream; 游 **yóu**:
to tour; 症 **zhèng**: illness)

X + XX (where the modifier is usually an adjective):

高血压 **gāoxuèyā** 'hypertension'   (高 **gāo**: high; 血压 **xuèyā**:
blood pressure)

急刹车 **jíshāchē** 'emergency stop'   (急 **jí**: urgent; 刹车 **shāchē**:
put on the brakes)

空架子 **kōngjiàzi** 'mere skeleton'   (空 **kōng**: empty;
架子 **jiàzi**: frame)

私生活 **sīshēnghuó** 'private life'   (私 **sī**: private;
生活 **shēnghuó**: life)

死胡同 **sǐhútòng** 'blind alley';
'dead end'   (死 **sǐ**: dead; 胡同 **hútòng**: alley)

微血管 **wēixuèguǎn** 'blood capillary'   (微 **wēi**: tiny, minute;
血管 **xuèguǎn**: blood vessel)

真面目 **zhēnmiànmù** 'true colours'   (真 **zhēn**: true, real;
面目 **miànmù**: visage)

远距离 **yuǎnjùlí** 'remote';
'long distance'   (远 **yuǎn**: far; 距离 **jùlí**: distance)

酸牛奶 **suānniúnǎi** 'yoghurt'   (酸 **suān**: sour; 牛奶 **niúnǎi**: milk)

臭豆腐 **chòudòufu** 'smelly beancurd'   (臭 **chòu**: smelly;
豆腐 **dòufu**: beancurd)

晚礼服 **wǎnlǐfú** 'evening dress'   (晚 **wǎn**: evening; 礼服 **lǐfú**:
ceremonial robe or dress)

下意识 **xiàyìshí** 'subconsciousness'   (下 **xià**: under, underlying;
意识 **yìshí**: consciousness)

牛脾气 **niúpíqi** 'obstinacy'   (牛 **niú**: ox, cow; 脾气 **píqi**:
temperament, disposition)

手风琴 **shǒufēngqín** 'accordion'   (手 **shǒu**: hand; 风琴 **fēngqín**:
(music) organ)

Most trisyllabic constructions, if they are to be taken as established lexemes in the lexicon, have to be formed exactly according to the rhythmic plan we have just specified. Between the two, the XX + X rhythm is by far the most prevalent one for trisyllabic words. This conclusion is provable by looking into monosyllabic headwords like 场 **chǎng** 'a large place used for a particular purpose', 金 **jīn** 'money', 石 **shí** 'stone', etc. For example,

运动场 **yùndòngchǎng** 'sports ground'   (运动 **yùndòng**: sports)
体育场 **tǐyùchǎng** 'stadium'   (体育 **tǐyù**: physical culture)
屠宰场 **túzǎichǎng** 'slaughterhouse'   (屠宰 **túzǎi**: butcher, slaughter)

公积金 **gōngjījīn** 'public fund'   (公 **gōng**: public; 积 **jī**: accumulate)
抚恤金 **fǔxùjīn** 'pension for the   (抚恤 **fǔxù**: console, comfort)
family of the deceased'
奖学金 **jiǎngxuéjīn** 'scholarship'   (奖 **jiǎng**: reward, encourage;
学 **xué**: learning)

鹅卵石 **éluǎnshí** 'cobblestone'   (鹅 **é**: goose; 卵 **luǎn**: egg)
磨刀石 **módāoshí** 'whetstone';   (磨 **mó**: grind; 刀 **dāo**: knife)
'grindstone'
吸铁石 **xītiěshí** 'magnet'; 'lodestone'   (吸 **xī**: attract; 铁 **tiě**: iron)

In quadrisyllabic idioms, two formal subtypes can also be discerned: (1) and (2) with the classical particle 之 **zhī** (equivalent to modern 的 **de**); (3) a disyllabic modifier followed by a disyllabic modified. For example,

X + 之 **zhī** + XX
人之常情 **rén zhī chángqíng**   (人 **rén**: human; 常情 **chángqíng**:
'the way of the world'   normal sentiment)
天之骄子 **tiān zhī jiāozǐ**   (天 **tiān**: heaven; 骄子 **jiāozǐ**:
'God's favoured one – an   proud son)
unusually lucky person'

XX + 之 **zhī** + X
一孔之见 **yī kǒng zhī jiàn**   (一 **yī**: one; 孔 **kǒng**: hole;
'a narrow view'   见 **jiàn**: view)
两可之间 **liǎngkě zhījiān**   (两 **liǎng**: two; 可 **kě**: possible;
'either will do'   间 **jiān**: between)

害群之马 **hài qún zhī mǎ**　(害 **hài**: do harm to;
'black sheep'　　　　　群 **qún**: group, herd; 马 **mǎ**: horse)

患难之交 **huànnàn zhī jiāo**　(患难 **huànnàn**: trials and tribulations;
'friend in adversity'　　　交 **jiāo**: friendship)

弦外之音 **xián wài zhī yīn**　(弦 **xián**: string of a musical instrument;
'overtones'; 'implication'　　外 **wài**: outside; 音 **yīn**: sound)

XX + XX

十字路口 **shízì lùkǒu** 'crossroads'　(十字 **shízì**: a written character
　　　　　　　　　　　　　　　which looks like a cross;
　　　　　　　　　　　　　　　路口 **lùkǒu**: intersection)

空中楼阁 **kōngzhōng lóugé**　　(空中 **kōngzhōng**: in the air;
'castles in the air'　　　　　楼阁 **lóugé**: buildings and
　　　　　　　　　　　　　　pavilions)

Adjectives:

with a nominal headword:

少数 **shǎoshù** 'few'　　(少 **shǎo**: few, little; 数 **shù**: number)
长途 **chángtú** 'long-distance'　(长 **cháng**: long; 途 **tú**:
　　　　　　　　　　　　　distance, journey)
高级 **gāojí** 'high-quality'; 'senior'　(高 **gāo**: high; 级 **jí**: grade)
上等 **shàngděng** 'first-rate';　(上 **shàng**: above;
'superior'　　　　　　　等 **děng**: grade, class)
新式 **xīnshì** 'new style';　(新 **xīn**: new; 式 **shì**: type, pattern)
'latest type'
老牌 **lǎopái** 'old brand'　(老 **lǎo**: old; 牌 **pái**: brand)
廉价 **liánjià** 'low-priced'; 'cheap'　(廉 **lián**: inexpensive; 价 **jià**: price)
大量 **dàliàng** 'a large number'　(大 **dà**: big, large; 量 **liàng**: quantity)
全面 **quánmiàn** 'comprehensive'　(全 **quán**: complete; 面 **miàn**: aspect)
下流 **xiàliú** 'obscene'; 'mean'　(下 **xià**: low; 流 **liú**: class, grade)
黄色 **huángsè** 'pornographic';　(黄 **huáng**: yellow; 色 **sè**: colour)
'decadent'
热情 **rèqíng** 'enthusiastic';　(热 **rè**: hot, warm; 情 **qíng**: feeling)
'warmhearted'
博学 **bóxué** 'learned'; 'erudite'　(博 **bó**: abundant, erudite;
　　　　　　　　　　　　学 **xué**: learning)
厚道 **hòudao** 'honest and kind'　(厚 **hòu**: thick; 道 **dào**:
　　　　　　　　　　　　doctrine, principle)
客气 **kèqi** 'polite'; 'courteous'　(客 **kè**: guest; 气 **qì**: airs, manner)
正经 **zhèngjing** 'decent';　(正 **zhèng**: upright; 经 **jīng**:
'respectable'　　　　　canon, scripture)
细心 **xìxīn** 'careful'; 'attentive'　(细 **xì**: thin; 心 **xīn**: heart)
专制 **zhuānzhì** 'autocratic';　(专 **zhuān**: monopoly;
'despotic'　　　　　　制 **zhì**: system)

with a verbal headword:

罕见 **hǎnjiàn** 'rare'　　　　　　　(罕 **hǎn**: seldom, rarely; 见 **jiàn**: see)

万能 **wànnéng** 'omnipotent';　　　(万 **wàn**: ten thousand;
　'all-purpose'　　　　　　　　　　　能 **néng**: capable)

两用 **liǎngyòng** 'dual purpose'　　(两 **liǎng**: two; 用 **yòng**: use)

现成 **xiànchéng** 'ready-made'　　　(现 **xiàn**: present, current;
　　　　　　　　　　　　　　　　　　成 **chéng**: accomplish)

武断 **wǔduàn** 'arbitrary';　　　　(武 **wǔ**: military, aggressive;
　'subjective'　　　　　　　　　　　断 **duàn**: judge, decide)

私有 **sīyǒu** 'private';　　　　　　(私 **sī**: private; 有 **yǒu**: own, possess)
　'privately owned'

健谈 **jiàntán** 'be a good talker'　(健 **jiàn**: healthy, strong; 谈 **tán**: talk)

悲观 **bēiguān** 'pessimistic'　　　(悲 **bēi**: sad; 观 **guān**: observe)

暗藏 **àncáng** 'hidden'　　　　　　(暗 **àn**: secret, dark; 藏 **cáng**: hide)

平行 **píngxíng** 'parallel'　　　　(平 **píng**: even, parallel;
　　　　　　　　　　　　　　　　　　行 **xíng**: travel)

浓缩 **nóngsuō** 'condensed'　　　　(浓 **nóng**: thick; 缩 **suō**:
　　　　　　　　　　　　　　　　　　shrink, reduce)

紧张 **jǐnzhāng** 'tense'　　　　　　(紧 **jǐn**: tight; 张 **zhāng**: stretch)

外来 **wàilái** 'external'; 'foreign'　(外 **wài**: outside; 来 **lái**: come)

重叠 **chóngdié** 'overlapping'　　　(重 **chóng**: again; 叠 **dié**: pile up)

with an adjectival headword:

浅蓝 **qiǎnlán** 'light blue'　　　　(浅 **qiǎn**: shallow; 蓝 **lán**: blue)

深红 **shēn hóng** 'dark red'　　　　(深 **shēn**: deep; 红 **hóng**: red)

滚热 **gǔnrè** 'piping hot';　　　　(滚 **gǔn**: boil; 热 **rè**: hot)
　'boiling hot'

非凡 **fēifán** 'extraordinary';　　(非 **fēi**: not; 凡 **fán**: ordinary)
　'uncommon'

伪善 **wěishàn** 'hypocritical'　　　(伪 **wěi**: false, fake;
　　　　　　　　　　　　　　　　　　善 **shàn**: kind, nice)

Verbs:

generally with a verbal headword:

渴望 **kěwàng** 'thirst for'　　　　(渴 **kě**: thirstily;
　　　　　　　　　　　　　　　　　　望 **wàng**: gaze, hope)

深思 **shēnsī** 'ponderly deeply'　　(深 **shēn**: deeply; 思 **sī**: ponder)

反省 **fǎnxǐng** 'introspect'　　　　(反 **fǎn**: backwards;
　　　　　　　　　　　　　　　　　　省 **xǐng**: question oneself)

偏爱 **piān'ài** 'be partial to'　　　(偏 **piān**: onesidedly; 爱 **ài**: to love)

露宿 **lùsù** 'sleep in the open'　　(露 **lù**: outdoors; 宿 **sù**:
　　　　　　　　　　　　　　　　　　lodge for the night)

复习 **fùxí** 'revise one's lessons　(复 **fù**: repeatedly; 习 **xí**: practise)
　after class'

高举 **gāojǔ** 'hold high' （高 **gāo**: high; 举 **jǔ**: hold, lift)

前进 **qiánjìn** 'advance'; （前 **qián**: front; 进 **jìn**: go forward,
  'forge ahead'   advance)

后退 **hòutuì** 'draw back'; 'retreat' （后 **hòu**: behind; 退 **tuì**: retreat)

假设 **jiǎshè** 'assume'; 'hypothesise' （假 **jiǎ**: phoney, artificial;
  设 **shè**: set up)

回顾 **huígù** 'look back'; 'review' （回 **huí**: turn round, go back;
  顾 **gù**: attend to)

浑说 **húnshuō** 'talk nonsense'; （浑 **hún**: muddy, turbid;
  'drivel'   说 **shuō**: say, speak)

疾驶 **jíshǐ** (of vehicles) （疾 **jí**: fast, quick; 驶 **shǐ**: drive)
  'speed along'

始创 **shǐchuàng** 'initiate'; 'originate' （始 **shǐ**: beginning; 创 **chuàng**: create)

清算 **qīngsuàn** 'settle accounts' （清 **qīng**: clear up; 算 **suàn**: calculate)

A particular set of *adverbs* also occur with the modificational type: e.g.

非常 **fēicháng** 'extremely' （非 **fēi**: not; 常 **cháng**: ordinary)

不断 **bùduàn** 'continuously' （不 **bù**: not; 断 **duàn**: broken)

特意 **tèyì** 'specially' （特 **tè**: special; 意 **yì**: intention)

专程 **zhuānchéng** 'purposely' （专 **zhuān**: special; 程 **chéng**: trip)

直接 **zhíjiē** 'directly' （直 **zhí**: straight; 接 **jiē**: meet, receive)

亲身 **qīnshēn** 'in person' （亲 **qīn**: personal, intimate;
  身 **shēn**: body, oneself)

独自 **dúzì** 'on one's own' （独 **dú**: alone; 自 **zì**: self)

There are two further points to note about modificational lexemes. First, though a modificational lexeme usually has a prescribed word class assigned to it by convention despite the nature of its internal components, it is not impossible that in some cases, a particular lexeme may cross word-class boundaries. For example, a word like 零用 **língyòng** may be used as a noun, an adjective or a verb on different occasions. As a noun, it means 'pocket money', as an adjective, it means 'non-budgetary', and as a verb it means 'spend money on minor purchases'. The word 假设 **jiǎshè** means either 'hypothesis' or 'to hypothesise' and the word 热情 **rèqíng** means 'enthusiasm' as well as 'enthusiastic'.

Second, as a general rule, in the formation of a modificational lexeme, it is usually the modifer that changes to define a headword which remains constant, as we have seen from the above examples. However, it is not impossible to keep the modifier constant and change the headword to differentiate diversified components, purposes, activities, etc. or even different styles and registers. For example,

Nouns:

船舱 **chuáncāng** （船 **chuán**: ship, boat;
  'ship's hold'; 'cabin'   舱 **cāng**: cabin of a ship)

船身 **chuánshēn** 'hull (of a ship)' （身 **shēn**: body)

船首 **chuánshǒu** 'stem'; 'bow'; 'prow' (首 **shǒu**: head)
船尾 **chuánwěi** 'stern' (尾 **wěi**: tail, end)
船舷 **chuánxián** 'side (of a ship)' (舷 **xián**: the side of a ship or aircraft)

山顶 **shāndǐng** 'peak'; 'summit'; 'hilltop' (山 **shān**: hill, mountain; 顶 **dǐng**: top)
山脊 **shānjǐ** 'ridge (of a mountain or hill)' (脊 **jǐ**: ridge, spine)
山脚 **shānjiǎo** 'the foot of a hill' (脚 **jiǎo**: foot)
山谷 **shāngǔ** 'mountain valley'; 'ravine' (谷 **gǔ**: valley, gorge)
山坡 **shānpō** 'hillside'; 'mountain slope' (坡 **pō**: slope)
山腰 **shānyāo** 'halfway up the mountain' (腰 **yāo**: waist)
山崖 **shānyá** 'cliff' (崖 **yá**: cliff, precipice)

Verbs:

敬告 **jìnggào** 'beg to inform' (敬 **jìng**: respectfully; 告 **gào**: inform)
敬贺 **jìnghè** 'congratulate with respect' (贺 **hè**: congratulate)
敬候 **jìnghòu** 'await respectfully' (候 **hòu**: wait for)
敬请 **jìngqǐng** 'cordially invite' (请 **qǐng**: invite)
敬赠 **jìngzèng** 'send a gift with compliments' (赠 **zèng**: to present with)

瞎扯 **xiāchě** 'talk groundlessly' (瞎 **xiā**: blindly, groundlessly; 扯 **chě**: gossip)
瞎吹 **xiāchuī** 'boast in the most fantastic of terms' (吹 **chuī**: brag)
瞎聊 **xiāliáo** 'chat idly' (聊 **liáo**: chat)
瞎说 **xiāshuō** 'talk irresponsibly' (说 **shuō**: speak)
瞎诌 **xiāzhōu** (dialectal) 'tell cock-and-bull stories' (诌 **zhōu**: fabricate)
瞎掰 **xiābāi** (informal) 'talk nonsense' (掰 **bāi**: break off with one's fingers and thumb)

GOVERNMENTAL TYPE

Words of a governmental type follow the syntactic pattern of either 'verb + object' ('v + n') or 'preposition + object' ('p + n'). Both patterns seem to be extremely productive and compared with words of other types, words of this type are apparently the most numerous in the verb section of the lexicon. This is because even those verbs which are 'intransitive' when used independently, are not totally immune from being used transitively in the internal structure of a governmental type. For example,

走路 **zǒulù** 'walk' (走 **zǒu**: walk; 路 **lù**: road, way)
跑步 **pǎobù** 'run' (跑 **pǎo**: run; 步 **bù**: step)
睡觉 **shuìjiào** 'sleep' (睡 **shuì**: to sleep; 觉 **jiào**: a sleep)
坐车 **zuòchē** 'go by (坐 **zuò**: sit; 车 **chē**: vehicle)
car/bus/coach/train/etc.'

On the other hand, the noun n that is featured in a governmental verb may belong to any of the following major semantic categories. The great versatility in the intra-lexemic semantic relationship between v and n also accounts for the immense productivity of these governmental verbs.

Target

In this case the action contained in v is directed towards an object (indicated by n) which must be already in existence before the action takes place. The 把 **bǎ** structure test in Chinese syntax[16] may often be used to prove if the 'n' in a 'v + n' lexeme truly signifies a 'target':

念书 **niànshū** 'study' (念 **niàn**: read; 书 **shū**: book)
送礼 **sònglǐ** 'give presents' (送 **sòng**: send; 礼 **lǐ**: presents)
请客 **qǐngkè** 'invite to a meal' (请 **qǐng**: invite, entertain;
客 **kè**: guest)
开车 **kāichē** 'drive a car' (开 **kāi**: drive; 车 **chē**: vehicle)
照相 **zhàoxiàng** (照 **zhào**: shine; 相 **xiàng**:
'take pictures/photos' portrait, image)
泡茶 **pàochá** 'make tea' (泡 **pào**: brew, infuse, soak;
茶 **chá**: tea)
佐餐 **zuǒcān** 'go with rice or bread' (佐 **zuǒ**: assist; 餐 **cān**: meal)
举手 **jǔshǒu** 'put up one's hand' (举 **jǔ**: lift, raise; 手 **shǒu**: hand)
骂人 **màrén** 'swear'; 'abuse' (骂 **mà**: curse, swear;
人 **rén**: people)

Result

Contrary to the above, the object indicated by n comes into existence as a result of the action indicated by v, e.g.

---

[16] For example, with the word 念书 **niànshū** 'study' (lit. 'read books'), a 把 **bǎ** structure test means using n as the object of the co-verb 把 **bǎ**: 把书放好 **bǎ shū fàng hǎo** 'Put the book in a proper place.' If the resultant construction is a well-formed sentence, n is then semantically proved to be a true 'target'.

签字 **qiānzì** 'sign'; 'affix one's signature' （签 **qiān**: sign; 字 **zì**: Chinese character）

题词 **tící** 'write a few words of encouragement' （题 **tí**: inscribe; 词 **cí**: word, term）

写信 **xiěxìn** 'write a letter' （写 **xiě**: write; 信 **xìn**: letter）

捐款 **juānkuǎn** 'contribute money' （捐 **juān**: contribute, donate; 款 **kuǎn**: money）

讲课 **jiǎngkè** 'to lecture' （讲 **jiǎng**: talk, speak; 课 **kè**: lesson）

做饭 **zuòfàn** 'cook' （做 **zuò**: cook; 饭 **fàn**: rice）

画画儿 **huà huàr** 'paint or draw' （画 **huà**: draw; 画儿 **huàr**: picture）

作曲 **zuòqǔ** 'compose (music)' （作 **zuò**: compose; 曲 **qǔ**: music）

生火 **shēnghuǒ** 'make a fire' （生 **shēng**: start; 火 **huǒ**: fire）

发电 **fādiàn** 'generate electric power' （发 **fā**: issue; 电 **diàn**: electricity）

闯祸 **chuǎnghuò** 'get into trouble' （闯 **chuǎng**: rush, dash; 祸 **huò**: disaster）

做梦 **zuòmèng** 'have a dream' （做 **zuò**: make, create; 梦 **mèng**: dream）

作揖 **zuòyī** 'make a slight bow' （作 **zuò**: make; 揖 **yī**: a bow with hands clasped）

显能 **xiǎnnéng** 'show off one's talent' （显 **xiǎn**: reveal; 能 **néng**: ability）

摆阔 **bǎikuò** 'parade one's wealth' （摆 **bǎi**: put, display; 阔 **kuò**: wealth, riches）

行善 **xíngshàn** 'practise philanthropy' （行 **xíng**: practise, perform; 善 **shàn**: good, virtuous）

构思 **gòusī** 'work out the plot of a story' （构 **gòu**: construct; 思 **sī**: idea）

卖乖 **màiguāi** 'show off one's cleverness' （卖 **mài**: show off; 乖 **guāi**: clever, shrewd）

There are some verbs of this type that may be labelled 'cognate' verbs where the result in n is already contained in v:

说话 **shuōhuà** 'talk' （说 **shuō**: speak, say; 话 **huà**: word）

唱歌 **chànggē** 'sing' （唱 **chàng**: sing; 歌 **gē**: song）

跳舞 **tiàowǔ** 'dance' （跳 **tiào**: jump; 舞 **wǔ**: dance）

鞠躬 **jūgōng** 'bow' （鞠 **jū**: bend forward; 躬 **gōng**: bend, bow）

磕头 **kētóu** 'kowtow' （磕 **kē**: knock (against sth hard); 头 **tóu**: head）

摔跤 **shuāijiāo** 'tumble'; 'trip and fall' （摔 **shuāi**: tumble; 跤 **jiāo**: fall）

洗澡 **xǐzǎo** 'take a bath' （洗 **xǐ**: wash, bathe; 澡 **zǎo**: bath）

跑步 **pǎobù** 'run' （跑 **pǎo**: run; 步 **bù**: step）

游泳 **yóuyǒng** 'swim' （游 **yǒu**: swim; 泳 **yǒng**: swim）

睡觉 **shuìjiào** 'sleep' （睡 **shuì**: to sleep; 觉 **jiào**: a sleep）

欠债 **qiànzhài** 'go into debt' （欠 **qiàn**: owe; 债 **zhài**: debt）

A particular set concerns ways of human secretion: e.g.

叹气 **tànqì** 'to sigh' (叹 **tàn**: to sigh; 气 **qì**: breath)
吐痰 **tǔtán** 'spit'; 'expectorate' (吐 **tǔ**: spit; 痰 **tán**: phlegm)
流泪 **liúlèi** 'shed tears' (流 **liú**: flow; 泪 **lèi**: tears)
出汗 **chūhàn** 'to sweat'; 'perspire' (出 **chū**: emit; 汗 **hàn**: sweat)
拉屎 **lāshǐ** 'defecate'; 'shit' (拉 **lā**: empty the bowels;
　　　　　　　　　　　　　　　　　　屎 **shǐ**: excrement, faeces)
撒尿 **sāniào** 'piss'; 'pee' (撒 **sā**: cast, let out; 尿 **niào**: urine)
放屁 **fàngpì** 'break wind' (放 **fàng**: set free, release;
　　　　　　　　　　　　　　　　　　屁 **pì**: wind from bowels)

Another set concerns human verbal activities: e.g.

说情 **shuōqíng** 'plead for (说 **shuō**: say, speak;
　mercy for sb' 　情 **qíng**: feeling, mercy)
论理 **lùnlǐ** 'reason' (with sb) (论 **lùn**: discuss, talk about;
　　　　　　　　　　　　　　　　　　理 **lǐ**: reason, truth)

道歉 **dàoqiàn** 'apologise' (道 **dào**: say; 歉 **qiàn**: apology)
称谢 **chēngxiè** 'express one's thanks' (称 **chēng**: say, state; 谢 **xiè**: thanks)
谈心 **tánxīn** (谈 **tán**: talk; 心 **xīn**: heart)
　'have a heart-to-heart talk'
告辞 **gàocí** 'take leave (告 **gào**: tell; 辞 **cí**: leave)
　(of one's host)'
叙别 **xùbié** 'have a farewell talk' (叙 **xù**: talk, chat; 别 **bié**: leave, part)
话旧 **huàjiù** 'talk over old times' (话 **huà**: talk; 旧 **jiù**: old)
诉苦 **sùkǔ** 'vent one's grievances' (诉 **sù**: complain; 苦 **kǔ**: bitter)
讲和 **jiǎnghé** 'make peace' (讲 **jiǎng**: speak; 和 **hé**: peace)
宣誓 **xuānshì** 'take an oath' (宣 **xuān**: declare, proclaim;
　　　　　　　　　　　　　　　　　　誓 **shì**: pledge, vow)

赌咒 **dǔzhòu** 'take an oath'; 'swear' (赌 **dǔ**: bet, gamble; 咒 **zhòu**: curse)
报喜 **bàoxǐ** 'report success' (报 **bào**: announce; 喜 **xǐ**: good news)
提议 **tíyì** 'propose'; 'suggest' (提 **tí**: raise, put forward;
　　　　　　　　　　　　　　　　　　议 **yì**: suggestion)

献计 **xiànjì** 'offer advice' (献 **xiàn**: offer, present;
　　　　　　　　　　　　　　　　　　计 **jì**: idea, ruse, plan)

授命 **shòumìng** 'give orders' (授 **shòu**: vest, give;
　　　　　　　　　　　　　　　　　　命 **mìng**: order, command)

传教 **chuánjiào** 'do missionary (传 **chuán**: preach, teach;
　work' 　教 **jiào**: religion)
布道 **bùdào** 'preach the Gospel' (布 **bù**: spread; 道 **dào**:
　　　　　　　　　　　　　　　　　　doctrine, principle)

问安 **wèn'ān** 'wish sb good health' (问 **wèn**: ask about; 安 **ān**: safety)
祝福 **zhùfú** 'benediction'; 'blessing' (祝 **zhù**: wish, pray for;
　　　　　　　　　　　　　　　　　　福 **fú**: happiness)

致敬 **zhìjìng** 'pay one's respects to' (致 **zhì**: send, extend; 敬 **jìng**: respect)

赔罪 **péizuì** 'apologise' (赔 **péi**: compensate;
罪 **zuì**: crime, fault)

撒谎 **sāhuǎng** 'tell a lie' (撒 **sā**: let out, tell; 谎 **huǎng**: lie)

造谣 **zàoyáo** 'start a rumour' (造 **zào**: invent; 谣 **yáo**: rumour)

喝彩 **hècǎi** 'cheer' (喝 **hè**: shout; 彩 **cǎi**: bravo, excellent)

许愿 **xǔyuàn** 'promise a reward' (许 **xǔ**: promise; 愿 **yuàn**:
a wish to do something)

表态 **biǎotài** 'make known one's
position' (表 **biǎo**: express; 态 **tài**: attitude)

示意 **shìyì** 'signal'; 'hint'; 'motion' (示 **shì**: show, indicate;
意 **yì**: idea, meaning, desire)

聊天 **liáotiān** 'chat' (聊 **liáo**: chat; 天 **tiān**: heaven)

抬杠 **táigàng** 'bicker'; 'wrangle' (抬 **tái**: lift, raise;
杠 **gàng**: a thick stick, bar)

起哄 **qǐhòng** (of a crowd)
'create a disturbance' (起 **qǐ**: start; 哄 **hòng**: uproar)

A small number indicate psychological responses:

挟嫌 **xiéxián** 'bear a grudge' (挟 **xié**: hold sth under the arm;
嫌 **xián**: suspicion)

怀恨 **huáihèn** 'nurse hatred' (怀 **huái**: keep in mind, harbour;
恨 **hèn**: hatred)

记仇 **jìchóu** 'harbour bitter
resentment' (记 **jì**: remember; 仇 **chóu**: animosity)

埋怨 **mányuàn** 'blame'; 'complain' (埋 **mán**: blame; 怨 **yuàn**: resentment,
enmity)

携贰 **xié'èr** 'be disloyal' (携 **xié**: carry, take along;
贰 **èr**: defect)

蓄谋 **xùmóu** 'premeditate' (蓄 **xù**: store up, save up;
谋 **móu**: plan, scheme)

抱憾 **bàohàn** 'feel regret' (抱 **bào**: cherish, harbour;
憾 **hàn**: regret)

负疚 **fùjiù** 'feel guilty' (负 **fù**: carry; 疚 **jiù**: remorse)

In some cases, n is, on the contrary, brought into non-existence by v, which may indicate an action, deliberate or non deliberate: e.g.

消炎 **xiāoyán**
'diminish inflammation' (消 **xiāo**: eliminate;
炎 **yán**: inflammation)

止痛 **zhǐtòng** 'relieve pain' (止 **zhǐ**: stop; 痛 **tòng**: pain)

退热 **tuìrè** 'allay a fever' (退 **tuì**: remove; 热 **rè**: fever)

免费 **miǎnfèi** 'free of charge' (免 **miǎn**: exempt; 费 **fèi**: fee)

旷课 **kuàngkè** 'cut school' (旷 **kuàng**: absent without leave;
课 **kè**: class)

缺席 **quēxí** 'absent' (缺 **quē**: miss out; 席 **xí**: seat at a meeting, etc.)

卸妆 **xièzhuāng** 'remove make-up' (卸 **xiè**: take off; 妆 **zhuāng**: make-up)
去污 **qùwū** 'cleanse' (去 **qù**: remove; 污 **wū**: dirt)
跑味 **pǎowèi** 'lose flavour' (跑 **pǎo**: escape; 味 **wèi**: flavour)
走神 **zǒushén** 'be absent-minded' (走 **zǒu**: wander; 神 **shén**: spirit, concentration)

失眠 **shīmián** 'suffer from insomnia' (失 **shī**: lose; 眠 **mián**: sleep)
流血 **liúxuè** 'shed blood'; 'bleed' (流 **liú**: let flow; 血 **xuè**: blood)
脱毛 **tuōmáo** 'moult or shed' (脱 **tuō**: shed; 毛 **máo**: hair, feather)
褪色 **tuìshǎi** (of colour) 'fade ' (褪 **tuì**: shed; 色 **shǎi**: colour)
泄劲 **xièjìn** 'lose heart' (泄 **xiè**: lose; 劲 **jìn**: energy, zeal)
亏本 **kuīběn** 'lose money in business' (亏 **kuī**: lose (money, etc.); 本 **běn**: capital)
贬值 **biǎnzhí** 'devalue' (贬 **biǎn**: reduce; 值 **zhí**: value)
停战 **tíngzhàn** 'armistice'; 'truce' (停 **tíng**: stop, cease; 战 **zhàn**: war, battle, fight)

休业 **xiūyè** 'suspend business' (休 **xiū**: stop, cease; 业 **yè**: trade, line of business)

离职 **lízhí** 'leave one's job' (离 **lí**: leave, part from; 职 **zhí**: job, duty, post)

赖帐 **làizhàng** 'go back on one's word' (赖 **lài**: deny; 帐 **zhàng**: account)

Time

过年 **guònián** 'celebrate the Spring Festival' (过 **guò**: pass (time); 年 **nián**: New Year)
度假 **dùjià** 'spend one's holidays' (度 **dù**: spend, pass; 假 **jià**: holidays)
逾期 **yúqī** 'be overdue' (逾 **yú**: exceed, go beyond; 期 **qī**: deadline)
歇晌 **xiēshǎng** 'take a midday nap' (歇 **xiē**: have a rest; 晌 **shǎng**: noon)
适时 **shìshí** 'in good time'; 'timely' (适 **shì**: suit; 时 **shí**: times)
换季 **huànjì** 'change garments according to the season' (换 **huàn**: change; 季 **jì**: season)
改日 **gǎirì** 'some other day'; 'another day' (改 **gǎi**: change; 日 **rì**: day)
熬夜 **áoyè** 'stay up late or all night' (熬 **áo**: endure (hard times, etc.); 夜 **yè**: night)
考古 **kǎogǔ** 'engage in archaeological studies' (考 **kǎo**: investigate; 古 **gǔ**: ancient)
守岁 **shǒusuì** 'stay up late or all night on New Year's Eve' (守 **shǒu**: keep watch; 岁 **suì**: the year)

Location

逛街 **guàngjiē** 'go window-shopping' (逛 **guàng**: ramble, roam; 街 **jiē**: street)

跑堂 **pǎotáng** 'wait on restaurant diners' (跑 **pǎo**: run; 堂 **táng**: hall, court)

站岗 **zhàngǎng** 'stand guard'; 'be on sentry duty' (站 **zhàn**: stand; 岗 **gǎng**: sentry)

出席 **chūxí** 'be present (at a meeting, etc.)'; 'attend' (出 **chū**: come out; 席 **xí**: seat)

入座 **rùzuò** 'take one's seat (at a feast, etc.)' (入 **rù**: enter; 座 **zuò**: seat)

回家 **huíjiā** 'return home' (回 **huí**: return; 家 **jiā**: home)

跳水 **tiàoshuǐ** 'dive' (跳 **tiào**: jump; 水 **shuǐ**: water)

溜冰 **liūbīng** 'skate' (溜 **liū**: glide; 冰 **bīng**: ice)

滑雪 **huáxuě** 'ski' (滑 **huá**: slide; 雪 **xuě**: snow)

爬山 **páshān** 'go hill-walking/ mountain-climbing' (爬 **pá**: climb; 山 **shān**: hill/mountain)

越轨 **yuèguǐ** 'transgress' (越 **yuè**: exceed; 轨 **guǐ**: track, path)

出界 **chūjiè** 'outside'; 'out-of-bounds' (出 **chū**: go out; 界 **jiè**: boundary)

进场 **jìnchǎng** 'march into the arena' (进 **jìn**: enter; 场 **chǎng**: arena, place)

坐牢 **zuòláo** 'be imprisoned' (坐 **zuò**: sit; 牢 **láo**: prison)

住院 **zhùyuàn** 'be hospitalised' (住 **zhù**: live, stay; 院 **yuàn**: hospital)

落荒 **luòhuāng** 'take to the wilds'; 'take to flight' (落 **luò**: settle; 荒 **huāng**: wasteland)

退伍 **tuìwǔ** 'be demobilised' (退 **tuì**: retreat from; 伍 **wǔ**: army)

炸窝 **zhàwō** 'leave the nest when startled' (炸 **zhà**: explode, scamper; 窝 **wō**: nest)

煳锅 **húguō** (of food) 'get burnt in a pot' (煳 **hú**: get burnt; 锅 **guō**: pot, pan)

串门 **chuànmén** 'call at sb's home'; 'drop in' (串 **chuàn**: string together; 门 **mén**: door)

This is particularly true with the first verbs originally derived from direction:

上市 **shàngshì** 'go on the market' (上 **shàng**: come on to; 市 **shì**: market)

下楼 **xiàlóu** 'go downstairs' (下 **xià**: go down; 楼 **lóu**: stairs)

进口 **jìnkǒu** 'to import' (进 **jìn**: enter; 口 **kǒu**: opening)

出笼 **chūlóng** (derog.) 'come forth' (出 **chū**: come out; 笼 **lóng**: bamboo steamer)

回锅 **huíguō** 'cook again' (回 **huí**: return to; 锅 **guō**: pot, wok)

过境 **guòjìng** 'be in transit' (过 **guò**: to cross; 境 **jìng**: territory)

起床 **qǐchuáng** 'get up'; 'get out of bed' (起 **qǐ**: get up; 床 **chuáng**: bed)

The location implied in n may signify either the point of departure or the point of arrival, e.g.

跳楼 **tiàolóu**
'commit suicide by jumping *from* the upper storeys of a building'
   (跳 **tiào**: jump, leap; 楼 **lóu**: a storied building)
跳水 **tiàoshuǐ** 'dive' (lit. 'jump *into* water')
   (跳 **tiào**: jump, leap; 水 **shuǐ**: water)

And depending on the context, 出场 **chūchǎng** (出 **chū** 'come out'; 场 **chǎng** 'place') may mean either 'to appear on the scene' or 'to leave the scene'.

Instrument

In fact, object of instrument can be verified by the co-verb 用 **yòng** 'use'.[17]

打夯 **dǎhāng** 'to ram (the earth)'   (打 **dǎ**: to pound;
                                           夯 **hāng**: rammer)

放枪 **fàngqiāng** 'to shoot'   (放 **fàng**: release; 枪 **qiāng**: rifle)
  (lit. 'to fire a gun')

开刀 **kāidāo** 'operate or be operated on'   (开 **kāi**: open;
                                           刀 **dāo**: knife, scalpel)

打针 **dǎzhēn** 'give or have an injection'   (打 **dǎ**: give/have;
                                           针 **zhēn**: injection, needle)

吵嘴 **chǎozuǐ** 'bicker'; 'quarrel'   (吵 **chǎo**: make a noise, wrangle;
                                           嘴 **zuǐ**: mouth)

鼓掌 **gǔzhǎng** 'applaud';   (鼓 **gǔ**: strike, drum;
'clap one's hands'   掌 **zhǎng**: palm, hand)

猜拳 **cāiquán**   (猜 **cāi**: guess; 拳 **quán**: fist)
'play the finger-guessing game'

烤火 **kǎohuǒ** 'warm oneself by a fire'   (烤 **kǎo**: bake; 火 **huǒ**: fire)

Cause

缩水 **suōshuǐ** (of cloth) 'shrink'   (缩 **suō**: shrink; 水 **shuǐ**: water)
逃荒 **táohuāng** 'flee from famine'   (逃 **táo**: escape; 荒 **huāng**: famine)
避难 **bìnàn** 'take refuge'   (避 **bì**: evade; 难 **nàn**: disaster)
卧病 **wòbìng** 'be confined to bed';   (卧 **wò**: lie down; 病 **bìng**: illness)
  'be laid up'
殉道 **xùndào** 'die for a cause'   (殉 **xùn**: die; 道 **dào**: cause)
怯场 **qièchǎng** 'have stage fright'   (怯 **qiè**: be timid; 场 **chǎng**:
                                               audience, arena)

---

[17] This means that n in the lexeme can be used as the object of 用 **yòng** 'use', but it must also be pointed out that it might not be possible to retain v in a free syntactic construction. In such cases, a new verb must be found.

悔棋 **huǐqí** 'retract a false move in a chess game'   (悔 **huǐ**: regret; 棋 **qí**: chess)

谢幕 **xièmù** 'answer a curtain call'   (谢 **xiè**: thank; 幕 **mù**: curtain, screen)

吻别 **wěnbié** 'kiss sb goodbye'   (吻 **wěn**: kiss; 别 **bié**: goodbye)

拜寿 **bàishòu** 'congratulate an elderly person on his/her birthday'   (拜 **bài**: pay a courtesy call; 寿 **shòu**: longevity)

Incident

There is a particular set of 'v + n' in which n typifies an incident or event, pleasant or unpleasant, and v indicates that its potential grammatical subject is either a victim or a benefactor of the said incident or event: e.g.

遭殃 **zāoyāng** 'suffer disaster'   (遭 **zāo**: suffer; 殃 **yāng**: disaster)

受骗 **shòupiàn** 'be deceived'   (受 **shòu**: receive; 骗 **piàn**: deception, cheating)

上当 **shàngdàng** 'be duped'; 'be taken in'   (上 **shàng**: go to; 当 **dàng**: pawn shop)

失望 **shīwàng** 'be disappointed'   (失 **shī**: lose; 望 **wàng**: hope)

着凉 **zháoliáng** 'catch cold'   (着 **zháo**: catch; 凉 **liáng**: a chill)

罹难 **línàn** 'die in an accident'   (罹 **lí**: suffer from, meet with; 难 **nàn**: accident)

遇险 **yùxiǎn** 'be in distress'   (遇 **yù**: meet with; 险 **xiǎn**: danger, mishap)

害病 **hàibìng** 'fall ill'   (害 **hài**: suffer from; 病 **bìng**: illness)

吃苦 **chīkǔ** 'bear hardships'   (吃 **chī**: eat; 苦 **kǔ**: bitterness)

丁忧 **dīngyōu** 'be in mourning for a parent'   (丁 **dīng**: incur; 忧 **yōu**: sorrow)

挨打 **áidǎ** 'get a thrashing'   (挨 **ái**: endure, suffer; 打 **dǎ**: beating)

负伤 **fùshāng** 'be injured'; 'be wounded'   (负 **fù**: bear; 伤 **shāng**: injury)

中毒 **zhòngdú** 'be accidentally poisoned'   (中 **zhòng**: be hit by; 毒 **dú**: poison)

得胜 **déshèng** 'to triumph'   (得 **dé**: win, get; 胜 **shèng**: victory)

获救 **huòjiù** 'be rescued'   (获 **huò**: get, reap; 救 **jiù**: rescue)

享福 **xiǎngfú** 'live in ease and comfort'   (享 **xiǎng**: enjoy; 福 **fú**: happiness)

沾光 **zhānguāng** 'benefit from association with sb'   (沾 **zhān**: be stained with; 光 **guāng**: light)

Two most versatile verbs used for this purpose are obviously 受 **shòu** 'receive'; 'suffer' and 得 **dé** 'win'; 'obtain'; 'get':

受苦 **shòukǔ** 'have a rough time' (受 **shòu**: receive, suffer;
                                      苦 **kǔ**: bitterness)
受害 **shòuhài** 'fall victim' (害 **hài**: injury, harm)
受惊 **shòujīng** 'be startled' (惊 **jīng**: fright)
受伤 **shòushāng** 'be injured' (伤 **shāng**: wound, injury)
受罪 **shòuzuì** 'have a hard time' (罪 **zuì**: hardship)
得奖 **déjiǎng** 'win a prize' (得 **dé**: get, win; 奖 **jiǎng**: prize)
得势 **déshì** 'be in power' (势 **shì**: power)
得逞 **déchěng** (derog.) (逞 **chěng**: success in a scheme)
    'have one's way'
得益 **déyì** 'benefit from' (益 **yì**: benefit)
得法 **défǎ** 'get the knack' (法 **fǎ**: method, the proper way)

Purpose

请假 **qǐngjià** 'ask for leave' (请 **qǐng**: ask for; 假 **jià**: a leave)
候诊 **hòuzhěn** 'wait to see the doctor' (候 **hòu**: wait; 诊 **zhěn**: examine
                                      (a patient))
赴约 **fùyuē** 'keep an appointment' (赴 **fù**: go to; 约 **yuē**: appointment)
奔丧 **bēnsāng** 'hasten home for the (奔 **bēn**: hasten; 丧 **sāng**: funeral)
    funeral of a parent'
殉道 **xùndào** 'die for a cause' (殉 **xùn**: die for; 道 **dào**: belief)
看病 **kànbìng** 'consult a doctor' (看 **kàn**: see; 病 **bìng**: illness)
报考 **bàokǎo** 'enter for an (报 **bào**: submit, declare;
    examination'   考 **kǎo**: take a test)
防锈 **fángxiù** 'rustproof' (防 **fáng**: prevent; 锈 **xiù**: rust)
歇闲 **xiēxián** 'stop to rest' (歇 **xiē**: have a rest;
                                   闲 **xián**: not busy, idle)
躲懒 **duǒlǎn** 'shy away from work' (躲 **duǒ**: hide; 懒 **lǎn**: lazy)
求婚 **qiúhūn** (of marriage) 'propose' (求 **qiú**: beg, request;
                                   婚 **hūn**: wed, marry)
讨饶 **tǎoráo** 'beg for mercy' (讨 **tǎo**: beg for; 饶 **ráo**:
                                   have mercy on, let sb. off)
催眠 **cuīmián** 'lull (to sleep)'; (催 **cuī**: urge, hurry, press;
    'hypnotise'   眠 **mián**: sleep)

Agent/initiator

These words generally indicate common phenomena in nature and in society,
e.g.

刮风 **guāfēng** (of the wind) 'blow' (刮 **guā**: blow; 风 **fēng**: wind)
下雨 **xiàyǔ** 'to rain' (下 **xià**: come down; 雨 **yǔ**: rain)
打雷 **dǎléi** 'to thunder' (打 **dǎ**: hit, strike; 雷 **léi**: thunder)

闪电 **shǎndiàn** 'lightning'　　　(闪 **shǎn**: flash; 电 **diàn**: electricity)
起雾 **qǐwù** 'a fog rises'　　　　(起 **qǐ**: start, rise; 雾 **wù**: fog)
退潮 **tuìcháo** 'ebb'　　　　　　(退 **tuì**: move back, retreat;
　　　　　　　　　　　　　　　　　潮 **cháo**: tide)

开花 **kāihuā** 'blossom'; 'bloom'　(开 **kāi**: open, open out;
　　　　　　　　　　　　　　　　　花 **huā**: flower, blossom)
结果 **jiéguǒ** 'bear fruit'　　　　(结 **jié**: form, bear; 果 **guǒ**: fruit, result)
涨价 **zhǎngjià** (of price) 'rise';　(涨 **zhǎng**: rise, go up; 价 **jià**: price)
　'go up'
漏气 **lòuqì** (of gas) 'leak'　　　(漏 **lòu**: leak; 气 **qì**: air, gas)

Objective

A goal to be achieved by a v in a 'causative' sense. The formal object n is
brought into a particular state by v, e.g.

延期 **yánqī** 'postpone'　　　　　(延 **yán**: postpone; 期 **qī**: time, period)
降级 **jiàngjí** 'demote'　　　　　(降 **jiàng**: lower, drop; 级 **jí**: grade)
断交 **duànjiāo**　　　　　　　　(断 **duàn**: sever; 交 **jiāo**: relations)
　'sever diplomatic relations'
破例 **pòlì** 'make it an exception'　(破 **pò**: break; 例 **lì**: example)
住口 **zhùkǒu** 'shut up'　　　　　(住 **zhù**: stop; 口 **kǒu**: mouth)
抬头 **táitóu** 'raise one's head'　　(抬 **tái**: lift, raise; 头 **tóu**: head)
提神 **tíshén**　　　　　　　　　(提 **tí**: raise; 神 **shén**: spirit)
　'refresh oneself, perk up'
骋目 **chěngmù** 'look as far as　　(骋 **chěng**: gallop, give free rein to;
　the eye can see'　　　　　　　　目 **mù**: eye)
罢工 **bàgōng** 'go on strike'　　　(罢 **bà**: stop, cease;
　　　　　　　　　　　　　　　　　工 **gōng**: work, labour)

破案 **pò'àn** 'crack a criminal case'　(破 **pò**: lay bare; 案 **àn**: case)

A number of adjectives have been verbalised in this connection: e.g.

亮相 **liàngxiàng**　　　　　　　(亮 **liàng**: brighten;
　'appear on the scene'　　　　　　相 **xiàng**: appearance)
美言 **měiyán** 'put in a good word'　(美 **měi**: beautify;
　　　　　　　　　　　　　　　　　言 **yán**: speech, word)
壮胆 **zhuàngdǎn** 'embolden'　　　(壮 **zhuàng**: make strong;
　　　　　　　　　　　　　　　　　胆 **dǎn**: gallbladder)
宽心 **kuānxīn** 'feel relieved'　　　(宽 **kuān**: set at ease; 心 **xīn**: heart)
弯腰 **wānyāo** 'stoop'; 'bend over'　(弯 **wān**: bend; 腰 **yāo**: waist)
圆谎 **yuánhuǎng** 'patch up lies'　(圆 **yuán**: make round;
　　　　　　　　　　　　　　　　　谎 **huǎng**: lies, untruth)
松劲 **sōngjìn** 'slacken';　　　　　(松 **sōng**: slack; 劲 **jìn**: vigour)
　'relax one's efforts'

活血 **huóxuè** (Chinese med.)   (活 **huó**: liven; 血 **xuè**: blood)
'invigorate the circulation
of blood'
健胃 **jiànwèi** 'be good for the   (健 **jiàn**: make healthy;
stomach'   胃 **wèi**: stomach)
坏事 **huàishì** 'make things worse'   (坏 **huài**: spoil; 事 **shì**: matter, affair)
干杯 **gānbēi** 'drink a toast'   (干 **gān**: dry up; 杯 **bēi**: glass)
满月 **mǎnyuè** (of a baby)   (满 **mǎn**: fill up; 月 **yuè**: month)
'be one month old'

In one or two instances, even a noun has been verbalised to do the
'causative' job: e.g.

铁心 **tiěxīn** 'make up one's mind'   (铁 **tiě**: iron; 心 **xīn**: heart)
鼓嘴 **gǔzuǐ** 'pout'   (鼓 **gǔ**: drum; 嘴 **zuǐ**: mouth)

A 'monosyllabic v + disyllabic n' construction (i.e. one of an overriding
X + XX rhythm) seems to be the most favoured structure for a trisyllabic vernacular idiom. There are hundreds of this type in the lexicon. This
prolificacy is perhaps due to the fact that the monosyllabic verbal component is usually taken from the stock of everyday verbs, whose meaning
in the idiom is generally metaphorically stretched; and as there is no limit
to the figurative extension of a sense, such verbs are often used in more than
one idiom, e.g. 吃 **chī** 'eat' in

吃老本 **chī lǎoběn** 'rest on one's laurels'   (老本 **lǎoběn**: capital)
吃官司 **chī guānsī** 'be the object of a lawsuit'   (官司 **guānsī**: lawsuit)
吃豆腐 **chī dòufu** (dial.) 'flirt with a woman'   (豆腐 **dòufu**: beancurd)
吃鸭蛋 **chī yādàn** 'score nothing in a game   (鸭蛋 **yādàn**:
or get a zero in an exam'   a duck's egg)

The following examples will also demonstrate that the monosyllabic verb used
in such idioms is of an extremely colloquial nature:

吹冷风 **chuī lěngfēng**   (吹 **chuī**: blow; 冷风 **lěngfēng**:
'throw cold water on'   cold wind)
穿小鞋 **chuān xiǎoxié**   (穿 **chuān**: wear; 小鞋 **xiǎoxié**:
'make life hard for somebody'   small shoes)
出洋相 **chū yángxiàng**   (出 **chū**: emit; 洋相 **yángxiàng**:
'make an exhibition of oneself'   awkward show)
吊胃口 **diào wèikǒu** 'tantalise'   (吊 **diào**: suspend; 胃口 **wèikǒu**:
                           appetite)
凑热闹 **còu rènào** 'join in the fun'   (凑 **còu**: move close to; 热闹 **rènào**:
                           a scene of bustle and excitement)

If we compare some of these 'vernacular idioms' with their counterparts in
English, we shall find that, though they might use different imagery, they often
seem to be, in style as well as in register, casts from similar moulds: e.g.

Chinese	English
翘辫子 **qiào biànzi** (翘 **qiào**: turn upwards; 辫子 **biànzi**: plait; pigtail)	'turn up one's toes'
泼冷水 **pō lěngshuǐ** (泼 **pō**: splash; 冷水 **lěngshuǐ**: cold water)	'pour cold water on'
兜圈子 **dōu quānzi** (兜 **dōu**: go around; 圈子 **quānzi**: circle)	'beat about the bush'
露马脚 **lù mǎjiǎo** (露 **lù**: reveal; 马脚 **mǎjiǎo**: a horse's feet)	'let the cat out of the bag'

We call these trisyllabic verbal expressions 'vernacular idioms' because overall they have a dominant ring of coarseness about them. Most of them are metaphorical, as we can see from the above examples; but there are also more literal ones. Further examples include:

metaphorical:

擦屁股 **cā pìgu**
'clear up the mess left by sb else' (擦 **cā**: wipe; 屁股 **pìgu**: buttocks)

唱高调 **chàng gāodiào**
'mouth high-sounding words' (唱 **chàng**: sing; 高调 **gāodiào**: high tone)

咬耳朵 **yǎo ěrduo** 'whisper in sb's ear' (咬 **yǎo**: bite; 耳朵 **ěrduo**: ears)

嚼舌头 **jiáo shétou**
'wag one's tongue'; 'gossip' (嚼 **jiáo**: chew, munch; 舌头 **shétou**: tongue)

抱佛脚 **bào fójiǎo**
'make a hasty last-minute effort' (抱 **bào**: hug; 佛 **fó**: Buddha; 脚 **jiǎo**: feet)

踢皮球 **tī píqiú** 'pass the buck'; 'shift responsibility' (踢 **tī**: kick; 皮球 **píqiú**: rubber ball)

捞稻草 **lāo dàocǎo**
'take advantage of a situation' (捞 **lāo**: dredge up; 稻草 **dàocǎo**: rice straw)

走后门 **zǒu hòumén**
'get sth done through influence' (走 **zǒu**: go through; 后门 **hòumén**: back door)

挤牙膏 **jǐ yágāo** 'be forced to tell the truth bit by bit' (挤 **jǐ**: squeeze, press; 牙膏 **yágāo**: toothpaste)

打算盘 **dǎ suànpán** 'calculate'; 'scheme' (打 **dǎ**: move the beads; 算盘 **suànpán**: abacus)

挖墙脚 **wā qiángjiǎo**
'undermine the foundation' (挖 **wā**: dig; 墙脚 **qiángjiǎo**: the foot of a wall)

literal:

开玩笑 **kāi wánxiào** 'crack a joke'; 'make fun of' (开 **kāi**: start; 玩笑 **wánxiào**: play a prank on)

献殷勤 **xiàn yīnqín**
'do everything to please' (献 **xiàn**: offer, donate; 殷勤 **yīnqín**: attentive)

皱眉头 **zhòu méitóu**
'knit one's brows'; 'frown' (皱 **zhòu**: wrinkle, crease; 眉头 **méitóu**: brows)

丢眼色 **diū yǎnsè** 'tip sb the wink' (丢 **diū**: throw; 眼色 **yǎnsè**: a meaningful glance)

掏腰包 **tāo yāobāo** 'foot a bill'; 'pick sb's pocket' (掏 **tāo**: pull out; 腰包 **yāobāo**: purse)

顾面子 **gù miànzi** 'save face' (顾 **gù**: attend to; 面子 **miànzi**: face, reputation)

捉迷藏 **zhuō mícáng** 'play hide-and-seek' (捉 **zhuō**: catch, capture; 迷藏 **mícáng**: hide-and-seek)

赶时髦 **gǎn shímáo** 'follow the fashion' (赶 **gǎn**: catch up with; 时髦 **shímáo**: fashion, vogue)

够朋友 **gòu péngyou** 'deserve to be called a true friend' (够 **gòu**: sufficient; 朋友 **péngyou**: friend)

闹情绪 **nào qíngxù** 'be disgruntled' (闹 **nào**: give vent to; 情绪 **qíngxù**: moodiness, the sulks)

There are only a few trisyllabic vernacular idioms in the lexicon that do not conform to this 'monosyllabic verb + disyllabic object' pattern and adopt an 'adverb + verb + object' rhythm: e.g.

闲磕牙 **xiánkēyá** 'have an idle chat' (闲 **xián**: idle, unoccupied; 磕 **kē**: knock; 牙 **yá**: tooth)

活见鬼 **huójiànguǐ** 'sheer nonsense' (活 **huó**: alive; 见 **jiàn**: see; 鬼 **guǐ**: ghost)

质言之 **zhì yán zhī** 'frankly speaking' (质 **zhì**: plain, simple; 言 **yán**: speak of; 之 **zhī**: that)

乱弹琴 **luàntánqín** 'act or talk like a fool' (乱 **luàn**: in confusion; 弹 **tán**: play; 琴 **qín**: lute)

So far we have concentrated on governmental verbs. As a matter of fact, apart from verbs, the 'v + n' pattern also produces quite a number of *adjectives*: e.g.

露天 **lùtiān** 'outdoor' (露 **lù**: reveal; 天 **tiān**: the sky)
落后 **luòhòu** 'backward' (落 **luò**: fall; 后 **hòu**: behind)
吃香 **chīxiāng** (colloq.) 'to be popular' (吃 **chī**: eat; 香 **xiāng**: good smell)
认真 **rènzhēn** 'serious'; 'earnest' (认 **rèn**: recognise; 真 **zhēn**: true)
费解 **fèijiě** 'hard to understand' (费 **fèi**: require; 解 **jiě**: explanation)

讨厌 **tǎoyàn** 'disgusting'; 'repugnant' (讨 **tǎo**: invite, court; 厌 **yàn**: dislike)

透明 **tòumíng** 'transparent' (透 **tòu**: pass through; 明 **míng**: bright, light)

忘我 **wàngwǒ** 'oblivious of oneself'; 'selfless' (忘 **wàng**: forget; 我 **wǒ**: me, myself)

Many of these adjectives make use of an n which indicates a physical or psychological component of a human:[18]

动人 **dòngrén** 'touching' (动 **dòng**: move, stir; 人 **rén**: people)

出众 **chūzhòng** 'outstanding' (出 **chū**: exceed; 众 **zhòng**: multitude)

超群 **chāoqún** 'head and shoulders above others' (超 **chāo**: surpass; 群 **qún**: crowd)

开胃 **kāiwèi** 'appetising' (开 **kāi**: open; 胃 **wèi**: stomach)

醒目 **xǐngmù** 'eye-catching' (醒 **xǐng**: awaken; 目 **mù**: eye)

碍眼 **àiyǎn** 'unpleasant to look at' (碍 **ài**: offend; 眼 **yǎn**: eye)

悦耳 **yuè'ěr** 'pleasing to the ear' (悦 **yuè**: please, delight; 耳 **ěr**: ear)

拗口 **àokǒu** 'hard to pronounce' (拗 **ào**: twist, disobey; 口 **kǒu**: mouth)

绕嘴 **ràozuǐ** 'difficult to articulate' (绕 **rào**: coil, confuse; 嘴 **zuǐ**: mouth)

拿手 **náshǒu** 'adept'; 'good at' (拿 **ná**: hold, grasp; 手 **shǒu**: hand)

蹩脚 **biéjiǎo** 'inferior'; 'shoddy' (蹩 **bié**: lame; 脚 **jiǎo**: foot)

丢脸 **diūliǎn** 'shameful' (丢 **diū**: lose; 脸 **liǎn**: face)

裸体 **luǒtǐ** 'naked' (裸 **luǒ**: expose; 体 **tǐ**: body)

合身 **héshēn** 'fit' (合 **hé**: suit; 身 **shēn**: body)

挠头 **náotóu** 'difficult to tackle' (挠 **náo**: scratch; 头 **tóu**: head)

调皮 **tiáopí** 'naughty'; 'mischievous' (调 **tiáo**: tease; 皮 **pí**: skin)

露骨 **lùgǔ** 'undisguised' (露 **lù**: expose; 骨 **gǔ**: bone)

费劲 **fèijìn** 'tough'; 'arduous' (费 **fèi**: need, spend; 劲 **jìn**: effort)

吃力 **chīlì** 'strenuous' (吃 **chī**: eat, exhaust; 力 **lì**: strength)

匿名 **nìmíng** 'anonymous' (匿 **nì**: conceal; 名 **míng**: name)

致命 **zhìmìng** 'fatal' (致 **zhì**: incur; 命 **mìng**: life)

满意 **mǎnyì** 'satisfied'; 'pleased' (满 **mǎn**: fill; 意 **yì**: wish, desire)

伤心 **shāngxīn** 'sad' (伤 **shāng**: hurt; 心 **xīn**: heart)

淘神 **táoshén** (inf.) 'trying'; 'bothersome' (淘 **táo**: to tax; 神 **shén**: spirit)

缺德 **quēdé** 'wicked' (缺 **quē**: lack; 德 **dé**: virtue, morals)

担忧 **dānyōu** 'worried' (担 **dān**: carry; 忧 **yōu**: worry)

着急 **zháojí** 'anxious' (着 **zháo**: be affected by; 急 **jí**: anxiety)

纳闷 **nàmèn** (colloq.) 'be perplexed' (纳 **nà**: accept; 闷 **mèn**: puzzle)

吃惊 **chījīng** 'be shocked' (吃 **chī**: eat; 惊 **jīng**: surprise)

惹气 **rěqì** 'irritating' (惹 **rě**: provoke; 气 **qì**: anger)

耐烦 **nàifán** 'patient' (耐 **nài**: be able to bear; 烦 **fán**: trouble)

怕羞 **pàxiū** 'shy/bashful' (怕 **pà**: to fear; 羞 **xiū**: shame)

The most flexible of all in this group is the mononym 人 **rén** 'person', which may follow many verbs to form this type of adjective: e.g.

---

[18] It must be understood that we are only quoting one item from each category. In some instances, there can be dozens of established lexemes.

迷人 **mírén** 'of enchanting beauty'   (迷 **mí**: fascinate, enchant)
宜人 **yírén** 'pleasant'; 'delightful'   (宜 **yí**: to suit, be appropriate for)
喜人 **xǐrén** 'gratifying'   (喜 **xǐ**: to please, gratify)
恼人 **nǎorén** 'irritating'; 'annoying'   (恼 **nǎo**: irritate, annoy)
困人 **kùnrén** (of weather)   (困 **kùn**: press hard, surround)
　　'oppressive'; 'close'
羞人 **xiūrén** 'shameful'   (羞 **xiū**: shy, feel ashamed)
丢人 **diūrén** 'disgraceful'   (丢 **diū**: lose, throw)
累人 **lèirén** 'tiring'   (累 **lèi**: tire, wear out, strain)
逼人 **bīrén** 'pressing'; 'threatening'   (逼 **bī**: force, compel, press)
吓人 **xiàrén** 'frightening'   (吓 **xià**: frighten)
惊人 **jīngrén** 'astonishing'; 'amazing'   (惊 **jīng**: astonish, amaze)

A large number of adjectives of this governmental type can be retrieved from the existing lexicon or coined anew by using such verbs as 有 **yǒu** 'possess', 无 **wú** 'lack' or 发 **fā** 'become': e.g.

attributive/predicative adjectives:
有名 **yǒumíng** 'famous'   (有 **yǒu**: have, possess;
　　　　　　　　　　　　　　　　　　　　　　名 **míng**: name, fame)

有钱 **yǒuqián** 'rich'; 'wealthy'   (钱 **qián**: money)
有害 **yǒuhài** 'pernicious';   (害 **hài**: harm)
　　'detrimental'
有理 **yǒulǐ** 'reasonable'   (理 **lǐ**: reason)
有趣 **yǒuqù** 'interesting'   (趣 **qù**: interest)
有效 **yǒuxiào** 'effective'   (效 **xiào**: effect)
有用 **yǒuyòng** 'useful'   (用 **yòng**: use, usefulness)
有罪 **yǒuzuì** 'guilty'   (罪 **zuì**: guilt)

无耻 **wúchǐ** 'impudent'   (无 **wú**: have no; 耻 **chǐ**: shame)
无敌 **wúdí** 'invincible'   (敌 **dí**: enemy, foe)
无辜 **wúgū** 'innocent'   (辜 **gū**: guilt)
无能 **wúnéng** 'incompetent'   (能 **néng**: ability)
无情 **wúqíng** 'merciless'   (情 **qíng**: feeling)
无限 **wúxiàn** 'infinite'   (限 **xiàn**: limit)
无私 **wúsī** 'selfless'   (私 **sī**: self-interest, privacy)
无知 **wúzhī** 'ignorant'   (知 **zhī**: knowledge)

predicative adjectives only:
发霉 **fāméi** 'go mouldy';   (发 **fā**: to issue; 霉 **méi**: mildew)
　　'become mildewed'
发臭 **fāchòu** 'become smelly'   (臭 **chòu**: bad smell)
发酸 **fāsuān** 'turn sour'   (酸 **suān**: sour)
发愣 **fālèng** (colloq.) 'stare blankly'   (愣 **lèng**: in a daze)
发怒 **fānù** 'infuriate'; 'flare up'   (怒 **nù**: anger, angry)
发愁 **fāchóu** 'be anxious'   (愁 **chóu**: anxiety, grief)

发冷 **fālěng** 'feel cold/chilly'   (冷 **lěng**: cold)
发热 **fārè** 'have a fever'   (热 **rè**: heat, fever)
发疯 **fāfēng** 'crazy'   (疯 **fēng**: madness)

Governmental type of *nouns* are found in the following semantic areas:

sports and activities:

跳绳 **tiàoshéng** 'rope-skipping'   (跳 **tiào**: skip; 绳 **shéng**: rope)
游泳 **yóuyǒng** 'swimming'   (游 **yóu**: to swim; 泳 **yǒng**: a swim)
唱歌 **chànggē** 'singing'   (唱 **chàng**: sing; 歌 **gē**: song)
插曲 **chāqǔ** 'theatrical interlude'   (插 **chā**: insert; 曲 **qǔ**: melody)
画像 **huàxiàng** 'portrait';   (画 **huà**: draw; 像 **xiàng**: image)
  'portrayal'
作文 **zuòwén** 'composition'   (作 **zuò**: create, make; 文 **wén**: essay)
写生 **xiěshēng** 'sketch from   (写 **xiě**: write, describe;
  nature/life'   生 **shēng**: life)
传真 **chuánzhēn** 'fax'   (传 **chuán**: pass on; 真 **zhēn**: true, real)
剪纸 **jiǎnzhǐ** 'paper-cut'   (剪 **jiǎn**: cut; 纸 **zhǐ**: paper)

articles of clothing, etc.:

枕头 **zhěntou** 'pillow'   (枕 **zhěn**: to cushion; 头 **tóu**: head)
披肩 **pījiān** 'cape'; 'shawl'   (披 **pī**: drape; 肩 **jiān**: shoulder)
围嘴 **wéizuǐ** 'bib'   (围 **wéi**: surround; 嘴 **zuǐ**: mouth)
护膝 **hùxī** 'kneecap'; 'kneepad'   (护 **hù**: protect; 膝 **xī**: knee)
绑腿 **bǎngtuǐ** 'puttees'   (绑 **bǎng**: bind; 腿 **tuǐ**: leg)

specially cooked food:

烤肉 **kǎoròu** 'roast'; 'barbecue'   (烤 **kǎo**: roast; 肉 **ròu**: meat)
泡菜 **pàocài** 'pickled vegetables'   (泡 **pào**: pickle; 菜 **cài**: vegetable)
烤鸭 **kǎoyā** 'roast duck'   (烤 **kǎo**: roast; 鸭 **yā**: duck)
炼乳 **liànrǔ** 'condensed milk'   (炼 **liàn**: condense; 乳 **rǔ**: milk)
腌肉 **yānròu** 'bacon'   (腌 **yān**: to cure, to salt; 肉 **ròu**: meat)
卤蛋 **lǔdàn** 'stewed   (卤 **lǔ**: stew in soy sauce; 蛋 **dàn**: egg)
  hard-boiled eggs'
熏鱼 **xūnyú** 'smoked fish'   (熏 **xūn**: to smoke; 鱼 **yú**: fish)
醉虾 **zuìxiā**   (醉 **zuì**: to steep in wine;
  'wine-steeped prawn'   虾 **xiā**: prawn)
烧酒 **shāojiǔ** 'spirit distilled   (烧 **shāo**: burn; 酒 **jiǔ**: alcohol)
  from sorghum'
炒饭 **chǎofàn** 'fried rice'   (炒 **chǎo**: stir-fry; 饭 **fàn**: cooked rice)
烙饼 **làobǐng**   (烙 **lào**: bake; 饼 **bǐng**: pancake)
  'baked wheat pancake'

The above-quoted nouns should be distinguished from those which are superficially of a similar 'v + n' format but belong to the modificational type rather than to the governmental type: e.g.

舞女 **wǔnǚ** 'dancing girl';   (舞 **wǔ**: dance; 女 **nǚ**: girl)
  'taxi dancer'

喷泉 **pēnquán** 'fountain'   (喷 **pēn**: spurt; 泉 **quán**: spring water)

The difference lies in the semantic relationship between v and n in the construction. In a governmental lexeme, n is the object of v whereas in a modificational lexeme, the relationship is usually the other way round. In other words, the noun following the verb may be the agent that initiates the action indicated by the verb in question. For instance, in the above examples, it is the 'girl' who 'dances' and the 'spring water' that 'spurts'.

people who are in charge of various operations:

主席 **zhǔxí** 'chairperson'   (主 **zhǔ**: to head; 席 **xí**: a board)

司机 **sījī** 'driver'   (司 **sī**: control; 机 **jī**: engine)

导演 **dǎoyǎn**   (导 **dǎo**: to direct; 演 **yǎn**: performance)
  'director (of a play)'

掌柜 **zhǎngguì** 'shopkeeper';   (掌 **zhǎng**: control, grasp;
  'manager'   柜 **guì**: counter, cabinet)

监工 **jiāngōng** 'foreman';   (监 **jiān**: supervise, oversee;
  'overseer'   工 **gōng**: work)

管家 **guǎnjiā** 'housekeeper';   (管 **guǎn**: manage; 家 **jiā**: family, home)
  'steward'

领队 **lǐngduì**   (领 **lǐng**: lead; 队 **duì**: group)
  'group/team leader'

董事 **dǒngshì** '(board) director'   (董 **dǒng**: supervise; 事 **shì**: matters)

将军 **jiāngjūn** 'general'   (将 **jiāng**: lead; 军 **jūn**: army)

and others:

替身 **tìshēn** 'scapegoat'   (替 **tì**: replace; 身 **shēn**: body, oneself)

跟班 **gēnbān** 'attendant'   (跟 **gēn**: follow, join; 班 **bān**: shift)

知己 **zhījǐ** 'bosom friend'   (知 **zhī**: know; 己 **jǐ**: oneself)

跑街 **pǎojiē** 'employee   (跑 **pǎo**: run; 街 **jiē**: street)
  who runs errands'

miscellaneous:

屏风 **píngfēng** 'screen'   (屏 **píng**: shield off; 风 **fēng**: wind)

扶手 **fúshou** 'handrail';   (扶 **fú**: (of hand) find support;
  'banisters'   手 **shǒu**: hand)

顶针 **dǐngzhen** 'thimble'   (顶 **dǐng**: push from below;
                        针 **zhēn**: needle)

挂毯 **guàtǎn** 'tapestry'   (挂 **guà**: hang up; 毯 **tǎn**: carpet)

塑像 **sùxiàng** 'statue'   (塑 **sù**: mould; 像 **xiàng**: portrait)

插图 **chātú** 'book illustrations'   (插 **chā**: insert; 图 **tú**:
                        drawings, pictures)

提琴 **tíqín** 'violin'   (提 **tí**: raise, lift; 琴 **qín**: harp, etc.)

拖网 **tuōwǎng** 'trawl'   (拖 **tuō**: drag; 网 **wǎng**: net)

存款 **cúnkuǎn** 'bank saving' (存 **cún**: deposit; 款 **kuǎn**: money)
遗嘱 **yízhǔ** 'testament'; 'will' (遗 **yí**: leave behind; 嘱 **zhǔ**: enjoin)
结果 **jiéguǒ** 'result'; 'outcome' (结 **jié**: bear (fruit); 果 **guǒ**: fruit)
表情 **biǎoqíng** (表 **biǎo**: express;
   'facial expression'   情 **qíng**: feeling, sentiment)
化石 **huàshí** 'fossil' (化 **huà**: turn into; 石 **shí**: stone)

If we move on to 'p + n' constructions, we will find that words following a 'p + n'[19] pattern will generally result in adverbs. These adverbs usually indicate notions related to time, space, sequence, direction, opportunity, or extent. e.g.

time:

当面 **dāngmiàn** 'face to face' (当 **dāng**: in the presence of;
   面 **miàn**: face)

随时 **suíshí** 'whenever necessary' (随 **suí**: follow; 时 **shí**: time)
向来 **xiànglái** 'always'; 'all along' (向 **xiàng**: towards; 来 **lái**: come)
照常 **zhàocháng** 'as usual' (照 **zhào**: according to;
   常 **cháng**: normal)
依旧 **yījiù** 'as before'; 'as of old' (依 **yī**: in keeping with; 旧 **jiù**: past)
从新 **cóngxīn** 'again'; 'anew'; (从 **cóng**: from; 新 **xīn**: new, fresh)
   'afresh'
往后 **wǎnghòu** 'henceforth' (往 **wǎng**: towards;
   后 **hòu**: behind, after)

起先 **qǐxiān** 'at first' (起 **qǐ**: start; 先 **xiān**: first, before)
及早 **jízǎo** 'as early as possible' (及 **jí**: touch; 早 **zǎo**: early)
届时 **jièshí** 'on the occasion' (届 **jiè**: fall due; 时 **shí**: time)
按期 **ànqī** 'on schedule'; (按 **àn**: according to;
   'on time'   期 **qī**: period, time)
迄今 **qìjīn** 'up to now'; 'so far' (迄 **qì**: till; 今 **jīn**: today)
临终 **línzhōng** (临 **lín**: on the point of;
   'on one's deathbed'   终 **zhōng**: end)
连忙 **liánmáng** 'promptly' (连 **lián**: link, join; 忙 **máng**: busy)
赶快 **gǎnkuài** 'quickly' (赶 **gǎn**: try to catch;
   快 **kuài**: fast, quick)
凌晨 **língchén** 'before dawn' (凌 **líng**: approach;
   晨 **chén**: morning, dawn)
傍晚 **bàngwǎn** 'at dusk' (傍 **bàng**: close to (in time);
   晚 **wǎn**: evening)
薄暮 **bómù** (literary) 'twilight' (薄 **bó**: approach, near;
   暮 **mù**: nightfall)

---

[19] It should be remembered that the n in 'p + n' construction may also be a nominalised adjective or verb.

space:

就地 **jiùdì** 'on the spot'

(就 **jiù**: take advantage of;
地 **dì**: place, location)

当场 **dāngchǎng**
'then and there'

(当 **dāng**: in the presence of;
场 **chǎng**: place, area)

到处 **dàochù** 'everywhere'

(到 **dào**: arrive in/at; 处 **chù**: place)

沿途 **yántú** 'all the way'

(沿 **yán**: along; 途 **tú**: journey, way)

朝前 **cháoqián** 'ahead'

(朝 **cháo**: towards; 前 **qián**: front)

迎面 **yíngmiàn** 'head-on';
'in one's face'

(迎 **yíng**: move towards;
面 **miàn**: face)

劈头 **pītóu** 'at the very start'

(劈 **pī**: right against; 头 **tóu**: head)

sequence:

挨次 **āicì** 'one after another';
'in turn'

(挨 **āi**: follow; 次 **cì**: sequence, order)

循序 **xúnxù** 'in proper order
or sequence'

(循 **xún**: abide by; 序 **xù**: order)

opportunity:[20]

顺手 **shùnshǒu**
'without extra trouble'

(顺 **shùn**: in the same direction as;
手 **shǒu**: hand)

趁便 **chènbiàn**
'at one's convenience'

(趁 **chèn**: avail oneself of;
便 **biàn**: convenience)

乘机 **chéngjī**
'seize the opportunity'

(乘 **chéng**: take advantage of;
机 **jī**: opportunity)

随手 **suíshǒu**
'conveniently'

(随 **suí**: follow; 手 **shǒu**: hand)

赶紧 **gǎnjǐn**
'without losing time'

(赶 **gǎn**: rush for; 紧 **jǐn**: urgency)

碰巧 **pèngqiǎo** 'by chance'

(碰 **pèng**: chance upon;
巧 **qiǎo**: coincidence)

抽空 **chōukòng**
'manage to find time'

(抽 **chōu**: take out, obtain;
空 **kòng**: spare time)

偷闲 **tōuxián** 'snatch a
moment of leisure'

(偷 **tōu**: steal; 闲 **xián**: leisure)

extent:

到底 **dàodǐ** 'to the end'; 'finally'

(到 **dào**: reach; 底 **dǐ**: bottom)

究竟 **jiūjìng** 'after all'

(究 **jiū**: go into; 竟 **jìng**: the whole)

至少 **zhìshǎo** 'at least'

(至 **zhì**: reach; 少 **shǎo**: few, little)

起码 **qǐmǎ** 'minimum'; 'at least'

(起 **qǐ**: start; 码 **mǎ**:
number/measurement)

尽量 **jǐnliàng** 'to the best of
one's ability'

(尽 **jǐn**: to the greatest extent;
量 **liàng**: amount)

---

[20] Quite a number of items in this category use 'v + n' pattern rather than just 'p + n' pattern.

破格 **pògé** 'making an exception'   (破 **pò**: break; 格 **gé**: standard)
过度 **guòdù** 'excessively'   (过 **guò**: exceed; 度 **dù**: extent)
由衷 **yóuzhōng** 'from the   (由 **yóu**: from; 衷 **zhōng**:
  bottom of one's heart'   inner feelings)
索性 **suǒxìng** 'might as well';   (索 **suǒ**: follow; 性 **xìng**:
  'simply'   temperament)

basis:
  对号 **duìhào** 'check the number'   (对 **duì**: compare, check;
                        号 **hào**: number)

  凭票 **píngpiào** '(admission)   (凭 **píng**: base on; 票 **piào**: ticket)
    by ticket only'
  据说 **jùshuō** 'It is said . . .'   (据 **jù**: according to;
                        说 **shuō**: what is said)

  论理 **lùnlǐ** 'to reason with sb'   (论 **lùn**: discuss; 理 **lǐ**: reason)
  为何 **wèihé** 'for what reason'   (为 **wèi**: for; 何 **hé**: what reason)
  因此 **yīncǐ** 'therefore'   (因 **yīn**: because of; 此 **cǐ**: this)
  于是 **yúshì** 'thereupon'; 'hence'   (于 **yú**: with regard to; 是 **shì**: this)
  如实 **rúshí** 'strictly by the facts' (如 **rú**: in compliance with;
                        实 **shí**: fact)

  凭空 **píngkōng** 'groundless'   (凭 **píng**: relying on;
                        空 **kōng**: empty, void)
  仗势 **zhàngshì** 'take advantage   (仗 **zhàng**: take advantage of;
    of sb else's power'   势 **shì**: power)

Those adverbs indicating manner, however, will generally follow the 'v + n'
pattern (instead of 'p + n' in the foregoing cases) and the n in such a construction is usually related to human characteristics:

manner:
  并肩 **bìngjiān**   (并 **bìng**: combine;
    'shoulder to shoulder'   肩 **jiān**: shoulder)
  促膝 **cùxī** 'sitting side by side' (促 **cù**: urge, touch; 膝 **xī**: knee)
  接踵 **jiēzhǒng** '(written)   (接 **jiē**: to touch; 踵 **zhǒng**:
    on somebody's heels'   (written) heel)
  埋头 **máitóu** 'being engrossed in' (埋 **mái**: bury; 头 **tóu**: head)
  尽情 **jìnqíng** 'to one's   (尽 **jìn**: exhaust, use up;
    heart's content'   情 **qíng**: feeling)
  蓄意 **xùyì** 'premeditated';   (蓄 **xù**: store up; 意 **yì**: intention)
    'deliberate'
  决心 **juéxīn** 'be determined'   (决 **jué**: determine; 心 **xīn**: heart)
  努力 **nǔlì** 'exert oneself'   (努 **nǔ**: put forth, exert;
                        力 **lì**: strength)

Though 'p + n' structure usually produce adverbs, we cannot say for sure
that not a single verb will follow this pattern. Here are some examples,

照办 **zhàobàn**   (照 **zhào**: according to; 办 **bàn**: handle, tackle)
  'act accordingly'
对比 **duìbǐ** 'contrast'   (对 **duì**: against; 比 **bǐ**: compare)
在望 **zàiwàng** 'be in sight' (在 **zài**: at, in; 望 **wàng**: gaze into the distance)

However, these lexemes can perhaps be regarded as telescopic forms, which can be semantically analysed as a '(p + n) + v' structures, where the true object of the preposition is a formally suppressed noun in the underlying concept. For instance, 照办 **zhàobàn** means 'handling something in accordance with certain instructions', where in fact the noun 'instructions' should be the object of the preposition 照 **zhào**. Moreover, 'p + n' structure will certainly produce no nouns or adjectives.

Whilst a governmental type of verb with its internal 'v + o' structure does not generally take any more objects in larger syntactic constructions, there is, however, a limited number of such verbs, which, through usage, have been used more often with further objects:[21] e.g.

增产 **zēngchǎn** 'increase production'   (增 **zēng**: increase;
                          产 **chǎn**: produce, yield)
出土 **chūtǔ** 'be unearthed';   (出 **chū**: come out; 土 **tǔ**: earth)
  'be excavated'
进口 **jìnkǒu** 'to import'   (进 **jìn**: enter; 口 **kǒu**: mouth, port)
造福 **zàofú** 'bring benefit to';   (造 **zào**: make, create;
  'benefit'   福 **fú**: happiness)
献身 **xiànshēn** 'dedicate oneself to' (献 **xiàn**: offer, dedicate;
                          身 **shēn**: body)

关心 **guānxīn** 'show concern for'   (关 **guān**: involve; 心 **xīn**: heart)
注意 **zhùyì** 'pay attention to'   (注 **zhù**: pour; 意 **yì**: attention)
作客 **zuòkè** 'to visit';   (作 **zuò**: be; 客 **kè**: visitor, guest)
  'to go as a guest'
下榻 **xiàtà** 'stay   (下 **xià**: settle down;
  (at a place during a trip)'   榻 **tà**: bed, couch)
就职 **jiùzhí** 'assume office'   (就 **jiù**: undertake;
                          职 **zhí**: job, duty, post)

涉足 **shèzú** 'set foot in'   (涉 **shè**: wade, ford; 足 **zú**: foot)
列席 **lièxí** 'attend (a meeting)   (列 **liè**: enter in a list;
  as an observer'   席 **xí**: seat, place)
致函 **zhìhán** 'write (a letter) to'   (致 **zhì**: send, write to; 函 **hán**: letter)
讨好 **tǎohǎo** 'fawn on'   (讨 **tǎo**: invite, ask for;
                          好 **hǎo**: good, favour)
得罪 **dézuì** 'offend'; 'displease'   (得 **dé**: get, obtain;
                          罪 **zuì**: crime, guilt, fault)

---

[21] A fuller discussion of such verbs may be found in Rao, Changrong (饶长溶) 1984.

驰名 **chímíng** 'be known
   far and wide'
出版 **chūbǎn** 'come off the press';
   'publish'
劳驾 **láojià** '(polite) may
   I trouble you . . .'

(驰 **chí**: spread, gallop;
   名 **míng**: name)
(出 **chū**: come out;
   版 **bǎn**: printing plate)
(劳 **láo**: put sb to the trouble of;
   驾 **jià**: you)

PREDICATIONAL TYPE

Words of a predicational type are usually compounds in which the first element is a nominal indicating the subject and the second element a verbal/ adjectival forming its predicator. The resultant word may be a noun or a verb/adjective. For example,

noun: 雪崩 **xuěbēng** 'avalanche'   (雪 **xuě**: snow; 崩 **bēng**: collapse)
adjective: 胆小 **dǎnxiǎo** 'timid'   (胆 **dǎn**: gallbladder; 小 **xiǎo**: small)
verb: 神往 **shénwǎng**   (神 **shén**: spirit; 往 **wǎng**:
           'be carried away/rapt'   go towards)

Sometimes, of course, a predicational word may be used as either a noun or a verb:

舌战 **shézhàn** 'argue heatedly with';
   'a verbal battle'
意料 **yìliào** 'anticipate';
   'what one has anticipated'

(舌 **shé**: tongues; 战 **zhàn**: fight)

(意 **yì**: idea; 料 **liào**: expect)

In the following sections we will examine the behaviour of this structural type in different word classes.

Nouns

'Subject + predicator' type of nouns, except for a small hodgepodge of miscellanies, seem to fall neatly into two main semantic categories:

(1) Natural phenomena, particularly natural calamities or catastrophes:
   地震 **dìzhèn** 'earthquake'   (地 **dì**: land; 震 **zhèn**: shake)
   海啸 **hǎixiào** 'tsunami'   (海 **hǎi**: sea; 啸 **xiào**: roar)
   风蚀 **fēngshí** 'wind erosion'   (风 **fēng**: wind; 蚀 **shí**: erode)
   日照 **rìzhào** 'sunshine'   (日 **rì**: sun; 照 **zhào**: shine)
   月食 **yuèshí** 'lunar eclipse'   (月 **yuè**: the moon; 食 **shí**: eat)
   龙卷风 **lóngjuǎnfēng** 'tornado'   (龙 **lóng**: dragon; 卷 **juǎn**: roll up;
                                           风 **fēng**: wind)

In quadrisyllabic classical idioms, where the four syllables are of two such parallel 'subject + predicator' juxtapositions, this structure becomes all the more productive and encompasses a much wider scope of meaning in relation to nature. However, such structures often result in verbal or adjectival idioms rather than nominal ones. For example,

风调雨顺 **fēng tiáo yǔ shùn**　　(风 **fēng**: wind; 调 **tiáo**: suit well;
　'favourable weather'　　　　　　雨 **yǔ**: rain; 顺 **shùn**: agree with)
山明水秀 **shān míng shuǐ xiù**　　(山 **shān**: hills; 明 **míng**: bright;
　'picturesque scenery'　　　　　水 **shuǐ**: waters; 秀 **xiù**: beautiful)
日新月异 **rì xīn yuè yì**　　　　(日 **rì**: day; 新 **xīn**: new; 月 **yuè**: month;
　'change with each passing day'　异 **yì**: different)
海阔天空 **hǎi kuò tiān kōng**　　(海 **hǎi**: sea; 阔 **kuò**: broad; 天 **tiān**: sky;
　'boundless as the sea and sky'　空 **kōng**: empty)

(2) Human illnesses and discomforts. The 'subject' monomym in this case is, therefore, mostly part of the human body.

耳鸣 **ěrmíng** '(med.) tinnitus'　　(耳 **ěr**: ear; 鸣 **míng**: ring, sound)
牙疼 **yáténg** 'toothache'　　　　(牙 **yá**: tooth; 疼 **téng**: ache)
心跳 **xīntiào** 'palpitation'　　　(心 **xīn**: heart; 跳 **tiào**: beat)
头晕 **tóuyūn** 'dizziness'　　　　(头 **tóu**: head; 晕 **yūn**: dizzy)
胃痛 **wèitòng** 'stomach ache'　　(胃 **wèi**: stomach; 痛 **tòng**: ache)
腹泻 **fùxiè** 'diarrhoea'　　　　(腹 **fù**: abdomen;
　　　　　　　　　　　　　　　泻 **xiè**: have loose bowels)
痉挛 **jìngluán** 'convulsion';　　(痉 **jìng**: sinew; 挛 **luán**: twitch)
　'spasm'
肛裂 **gāngliè** (med.) 'anal fissure'　(肛 **gāng**: anus; 裂 **liè**: split)
阳痿 **yángwěi** 'impotence'　　　(阳 **yáng**: male genitals;
　　　　　　　　　　　　　　　痿 **wěi**: flaccid paralysis)
血亏 **xuèkuī** (Chinese med.)　　(血 **xuè**: blood; 亏 **kuī**: have a deficit)
　'anaemia'
便闭 **biànbì** (med.) 'constipation'　(便 **biàn**: urine or excrement;
　　　　　　　　　　　　　　　闭 **bì**: stop up)
食积 **shíjī** (Chinese med.)　　　(食 **shí**: food; 积 **jī**: amass, accumulate)
　'indigestion'
气喘 **qìchuǎn** 'asthma'　　　　(气 **qì**: breath; 喘 **chuǎn**: pant)
骨折 **gǔzhé** (med.) 'fracture'　　(骨 **gǔ**: bone; 折 **zhé**: break, snap)
痰厥 **tánjué** (Chinese med.)　　(痰 **tán**: phlegm; 厥 **jué**:
　'coma due to the blocking of　　lose consciousness)
　the respiratory system'

A few similar structures exceptionally do not indicate illnesses:

内疚 **nèijiù** 'compunction'　(内 **nèi**: inner feelings; 疚 **jiù**: remorse)
脉搏 **màibó** 'pulse'　　　　(脉 **mài**: arteries and veins; 搏 **bó**: beat, throb)

In some cases, the predicator can often be expanded when necessary into a disyllabic verb, e.g.

脑溢血 **nǎoyìxuè**　　　　（脑 **nǎo**: brain; 溢 **yì**: overflow; 血 **xuè**: blood)
　　'cerebral haemorrhage'
胃溃疡 **wèikuìyáng**　　　（胃 **wèi**: stomach; 溃 **kuì**: ulcerate; 疡 **yáng**: sore)
　　'gastric ulcer'
尿失禁 **niàoshījìn**　　　　（尿 **niào**: urine; 失禁 **shījìn**: lose control)
　　'urinary incontinence'
鬼剃头 **guǐtìtóu** (med.)　　（鬼 **guǐ**: ghost; 剃头 **tìtóu**: have a haircut)
　　'alopecia areata'

Apart from the two main semantic categories discussed above, there are miscellaneous lexemes which defy neat classification:

政治 **zhèngzhì** 'politics'　　　（政 **zhèng**: politics; 治 **zhì**: rule, govern)
事变 **shìbiàn** 'incident'　　　（事 **shì**: matter, affair; 变 **biàn**: change)
军需 **jūnxū** (military) 'supplies'　（军 **jūn**: armed forces; 需 **xū**: need)
病变 **bìngbiàn**
　　'pathological changes'　　　（病 **bìng**: illness; 变 **biàn**: change)
友爱 **yǒu'ài** 'friendly affection'　（友 **yǒu**: friend; 爱 **ài**: love)

Adjectives

Compared with nouns of similar structure, 'subject + predicator' adjectives are much greater in number. They are, with a few exceptions, almost exclusively 'humanly' oriented. The 'subject' mononyms are either (1) part or whole of the human body; or (2) the individual 'self'. For example,

(1) part or whole of the human body:
　　头昏 **tóuhūn** 'dizzy'; 'giddy'　　（头 **tóu**: head; 昏 **hūn**: dizz)
　　面善 **miànshàn** 'look familiar'　（面 **miàn**: face; 善 **shàn**: friendly)
　　脸嫩 **liǎnnèn** 'bashful'; 'shy'　　（脸 **liǎn**: face; 嫩 **nèn**: tender)
　　眼生 **yǎnshēng** 'look unfamiliar'　（眼 **yǎn**: eye; 生 **shēng**: raw,
　　　　　　　　　　　　　　　　　　　　　uncooked)
　　耳熟 **ěrshú** 'familiar to the ear'　（耳 **ěr**: ear; 熟 **shú**: ripe, cooked)
　　口渴 **kǒukě** 'thirsty'　　　　　　（口 **kǒu**: mouth; 渴 **kě**: thirsty)
　　嘴馋 **zuǐchán**　　　　　　　　　（嘴 **zuǐ**: mouth;
　　　　'fond of good food'　　　　　　　馋 **chán**: gluttonous)
　　肉麻 **ròumá** 'disgusting'　　　　（肉 **ròu**: flesh; 麻 **má**: tingle)
　　心焦 **xīnjiāo** 'anxious'; 'worried'　（心 **xīn**: heart; 焦 **jiāo**:
　　　　　　　　　　　　　　　　　　　　　burnt, scorched)
　　胆怯 **dǎnqiè** 'cowardly'　　　　（胆 **dǎn**: gallbladder;
　　　　　　　　　　　　　　　　　　　　怯 **qiè**: frightened)
　　性急 **xìngjí** 'short-tempered'　　（性 **xìng**: disposition;
　　　　　　　　　　　　　　　　　　　　急 **jí**: impatient)
　　手提 **shǒutí** 'portable'　　　　（手 **shǒu**: hand; 提 **tí**: carry in
　　　　　　　　　　　　　　　　　　　　one's hand with the arm down)

腿勤 **tuǐqín** 'tireless in running around'   (腿 **tuǐ**: leg; 勤 **qín**: diligent)

人为 **rénwéi** 'artificial'   (人 **rén**: man; 为 **wéi**: do)

年迈 **niánmài** 'old'; 'aged'   (年 **nián**: age; 迈 **mài**: advanced in years)

The versatility of such a construction is convincingly reflected in the established idioms of 嘴 **zuǐ** 'mouth':

嘴笨 **zuǐbèn** 'clumsy of speech'   (嘴 **zuǐ**: mouth; 笨 **bèn**: stupid)

嘴馋 **zuǐchán** 'fond of good food'   (馋 **chán**: gluttonous)

嘴尖 **zuǐjiān** 'sharp-tongued'   (尖 **jiān**: pointed)

嘴紧 **zuǐjǐn** 'tight-lipped'   (紧 **jǐn**: tight)

嘴快 **zuǐkuài** 'have a loose tongue'   (快 **kuài**: fast, quick)

嘴碎 **zuǐsuì** 'loquacious'   (碎 **suì**: fragmentary)

嘴甜 **zuǐtián** 'smooth-tongued'   (甜 **tián**: sweet, honeyed)

嘴稳 **zuǐwěn** 'able to keep a secret'   (稳 **wěn**: steady, firm)

嘴硬 **zuǐyìng** 'stubborn and reluctant to admit mistakes or defeats'   (硬 **yìng**: hard)

嘴乖 **zuǐguāi** (of children) 'pleasant when speaking to elders'   (乖 **guāi**: well-behaved)

嘴欠 **zuǐqiàn** (dial.) 'garrulous'   (欠 **qiàn**: (dial.) be fidgety)

(2) the individual represented by 'self': e.g.

自发 **zìfā** 'spontaneous'   (自 **zì**: self; 发 **fā**: start)

自满 **zìmǎn** 'complacent'   (满 **mǎn**: full)

自大 **zìdà** 'self-important'   (大 **dà**: big)

自动 **zìdòng** 'automatic'   (动 **dòng**: move)

自私 **zìsī** 'selfish'   (私 **sī**: private)

(3) miscellaneous subject mononyms:

机动 **jīdòng** 'power-driven'   (机 **jī**: machine; 动 **dòng**: move, propel)

天生 **tiānshēng** 'inborn'; 'innate'   (天 **tiān**: nature; 生 **shēng**: give birth to)

民办 **mínbàn** 'be run by the local people'   (民 **mín**: people; 办 **bàn**: run, manage)

With some adjectives, the subject mononyms are, semantically speaking, merely pseudo-subjects in relation to their predicators. What these subject mononyms do is actually to highlight a metaphorical resemblance: e.g.

冰冷 **bīnglěng** 'icy cold'   (冰 **bīng**: ice; 冷 **lěng**: cold)

火热 **huǒrè** 'burning hot'; 'fervent'   (火 **huǒ**: fire; 热 **rè**: hot)

风凉 **fēngliáng** 'cool'   (风 **fēng**: wind; 凉 **liáng**: cool)

水灵 **shuǐling** (dial.) 'radiant'   (水 **shuǐ**: water; 灵 **líng**: vivacious)

锋利 **fēnglì** 'sharp'; 'incisive' (锋 **fēng**: cutting edge; 利 **lì**: sharp)
肤浅 **fūqiǎn** 'superficial' (肤 **fū**: skin; 浅 **qiǎn**: shallow)
笔挺 **bǐtǐng** 'straight as a ramrod' (笔 **bǐ**: pen; 挺 **tǐng**: upright, straight, trim)
晶亮 **jīngliàng** 'glistening'; 'glittering' (晶 **jīng**: crystal; 亮 **liàng**: bright)
墨黑 **mòhēi** 'pitch-dark' (墨 **mò**: Chinese ink; 黑 **hēi**: black, dark)

A particular set concentrates on different shades of colours:

草绿 **cǎolǜ** 'grass green' (草 **cǎo**: grass; 绿 **lǜ**: green)
金黄 **jīnhuáng** 'golden' (金 **jīn**: gold; 黄 **huáng**: yellow)
天蓝 **tiānlán** 'azure' (天 **tiān**: sky; 蓝 **lán**: blue)
酱紫 **jiàngzǐ** 'dark reddish purple' (酱 **jiàng**: thick soy-bean sauce; 紫 **zǐ**: purple)
雪白 **xuěbái** 'snowy white' (雪 **xuě**: snow; 白 **bái**: white)
漆黑 **qīhēi** 'jet-black' (漆 **qī**: lacquer, paint; 黑 **hēi**: black)
银灰 **yínhuī** 'silver grey' (银 **yín**: silver; 灰 **huī**: grey)
血红 **xuèhóng** 'blood red' (血 **xuè**: blood; 红 **hóng**: red)
铁青 **tiěqīng** 'ashen'; 'livid' (铁 **tiě**: iron; 青 **qīng**: blue or green)

Verbs

Similar to adjectives, 'subject + predicator' type of verbs also have 'subject' mononyms which fall neatly into two broad categories, namely (1) human body parts; and (2) the individual 'self'. But in addition to those, the 'subject' mononyms can be (3) different animals whose characteristic features are here metaphorically projected onto human beings themselves.

(1) human body parts as 'subject' mononyms:

身受 **shēnshòu** 'experience (personally)' (身 **shēn**: body; 受 **shòu**: receive, suffer)
体察 **tǐchá** 'experience and observe' (体 **tǐ**: body; 察 **chá**: examine)
心寒 **xīnhán** 'be utterly disappointed' (心 **xīn**: heart; 寒 **hán**: cold)
脸红 **liǎnhóng** 'blush' (脸 **liǎn**: face; 红 **hóng**: red)
首肯 **shǒukěn** 'nod approval' (首 **shǒu**: head; 肯 **kěn**: consent)
鼻塞 **bísāi** 'have a stuffy nose' (鼻 **bí**: nose; 塞 **sāi**: fill in, stuff)
目睹 **mùdǔ** 'see with one's own eyes' (目 **mù**: eye; 睹 **dǔ**: see)
发指 **fàzhǐ** 'bristle with anger' (发 **fà**: hair; 指 **zhǐ**: point at)
口吃 **kǒuchī** 'stutter'; 'stammer' (口 **kǒu**: mouth; 吃 **chī**: eat)
齿冷 **chǐlěng** 'laugh sb to scorn' (齿 **chǐ**: tooth; 冷 **lěng**: cold)

手痒 **shǒuyǎng**
'have an itch to do sth'

(手 **shǒu**: hand; 痒 **yǎng**: itch)

掌握 **zhǎngwò** 'grasp'; 'master'

(掌 **zhǎng**: palm;
握 **wò**: hold, grasp)

肩负 **jiānfù** 'undertake'

(肩 **jiān**: shoulder; 负 **fù**: carry
on the back/shoulder)

神游 **shényóu**
'make a spiritual tour'

(神 **shén**: spirit;
游 **yóu**: travel, tour)

情愿 **qíngyuàn** 'be willing'

(情 **qíng**: feeling;
愿 **yuàn**: willing)

气馁 **qìněi** 'become dejected'

(气 **qì**: spirit, morale;
馁 **něi**: disheartened)

胆敢 **dǎngǎn**
'have the audacity to'

(胆 **dǎn**: gallbladder, courage;
敢 **gǎn**: dare)

意会 **yìhuì**
'perceive by intuition'

(意 **yì**: meaning; 会 **huì**:
comprehend, grasp)

言传 **yánchuán**
'explain in words'

(言 **yán**: words, language;
传 **chuán**: pass on)

声称 **shēngchēng**
'profess'; 'assert'

(声 **shēng**: voice; 称 **chēng**: claim)

语塞 **yǔsè**
'be unable to utter a word'

(语 **yǔ**: words, language;
塞 **sè**: blocked, stopped)

(2) the individual 'self': e.g.

自拔 **zìbá** 'free oneself
(from pain or evildoing)'

(自 **zì**: oneself; 拔 **bá**: pull out,
pull up)

自白 **zìbái** 'make clear one's
meaning or position'

(白 **bái**: explain)

自供 **zìgōng** 'confess'

(供 **gōng**: own up)

自绝 **zìjué** 'alienate oneself'

(绝 **jué**: cut off, sever)

(3) animals:

蚕食 **cánshí** 'nibble'

(蚕 **cán**: silkworm; 食 **shí**: eat)

蜂拥 **fēngyōng** 'swarm'

(蜂 **fēng**: bee; 拥 **yōng**: swarm)

蛊惑 **gǔhuò**
'poison and bewitch'

(蛊 **gǔ**: a legendary venomous
insect; 惑 **huò**: delude)

鼠窜 **shǔcuàn**
'scamper off like a rat'

(鼠 **shǔ**: mouse, rat;
窜 **cuàn**: flee, scurry)

鲸吞 **jīngtūn** 'annex (territory)'

(鲸 **jīng**: whale; 吞 **tūn**: swallow)

雀跃 **quèyuè** 'jump for joy'

(雀 **què**: sparrow; 跃 **yuè**: jump)

蛇行 **shéxíng** (written)
'move with the body on
the ground'; 'crawl'

(蛇 **shé**: snake; 行 **xíng**: travel)

龟缩 **guīsuō** 'withdraw into
passive defence'

(龟 **guī**: tortoise;
缩 **suō**: draw back)

狐媚 **húmèi**
'bewitch by cajolery'

(狐 **hú**: fox; 媚 **mèi**: fawn on)

兔脱 **tùtuō** 'escape'; 'flee'

(兔 **tù**: hare, rabbit;
脱 **tuō**: get out of)

鸟瞰 **niǎokàn**
'get a bird's-eye view'

(鸟 **niǎo**: bird; 瞰 **kàn**:
look down from a height)

蝉联 **chánlián**
'continue to hold a title'

(蝉 **chán**: cicada – its continuous
noise; 联 **lián**: join)

鹊起 **quèqǐ** (formal) 'act
according to circumstances'

(鹊 **què**: magpie; 起 **qǐ**: rise)

獭祭 **tǎjì** 'load one's writing
with fancy phrases'

(獭 **tǎ**: otter; 祭 **jì**:
display the caught fish)

牛饮 **niúyǐn** 'drink gallons'

(牛 **niú**: ox; 饮 **yǐn**: drink)

猱升 **náoshēng** (formal)
'climb a tree as nimbly as a
monkey'

(猱 **náo**: monkey; 升 **shēng**:
go up)

狼顾 **lánggù** 'be very nervous
or suspicious'

(狼 **láng**: wolf; 顾 **gù**: turn round
and look back)

猬集 **wèijí** '(of matters)
happen at the same time'

(猬 **wèi**: (spines of) hedgehog;
集 **jí**: collect)

Semantically speaking, these animals are not real subjects – the real subject is the human being in the underlying structure. When we say, for instance, 鸟瞰 **niǎokàn** 'get a bird's-eye view', there is no mistake that it is the human being who gets the view, but that he does it in the way a bird does. Therefore, these disyllabic lexemes should, strictly speaking, be regarded as a particular set of a modificational type of verbs despite their formal 'subject + predicator' structures.

Similarly, this is also true with words having miscellaneous nominal mononyms which occupy the subject position but are not real subjects. They actually indicate resemblance, instrument, etc.:

resemblance:

鬼混 **guǐhùn** 'fool around'

(鬼 **guǐ**: ghost; 混 **hùn**: muddle along)

杜撰 **dùzhuàn** 'fabricate';
'make up'

(杜 **dù**: a surname;
撰 **zhuàn**: compose)

局限 **júxiàn** 'limit'

(局 **jú**: state of affairs;
限 **xiàn**: set a limit)

沟通 **gōutōng** 'link up'

(沟 **gōu**: channel; 通 **tōng**: go through)

瓦解 **wǎjiě** 'disintegrate';
'crumble'

(瓦 **wǎ**: tiles on the roof;
解 **jiě**: disintegrate)

鼎峙 **dǐngzhì** 'tripartite
confrontation'

(鼎 **dǐng**: tripod; 峙 **zhì**: stand erect)

云集 **yúnjí** 'come together
in crowds'

(云 **yún**: cloud; 集 **jí**: gather)

星散 **xīngsàn** 'be scattered far and wide' （星 **xīng**: star; 散 **sàn**: disperse, scatter)

林立 **línlì** 'stand in great numbers' （林 **lín**: forest; 立 **lì**: stand)

蔓延 **mànyán** 'spread' （蔓 **màn**: trailing plant; 延 **yán**: extend)

丛生 **cóngshēng** (of plants) 'grow thickly' （丛 **cóng**: clump, thicket; 生 **shēng**: grow)

鳞比 **línbǐ** 'in tight rows'; 'row upon row' （鳞 **lín**: scale (of fish, etc.); 比 **bǐ**: close together)

泥醉 **nízuì** 'dead drunk' （泥 **ní**: mud, mire; 醉 **zuì**: drunk, intoxicated)

棋布 **qíbù** 'spread all over the place' （棋 **qí**: chess; 布 **bù**: spread, disseminate)

奴役 **núyì** 'enslave' （奴 **nú**: bondservant, slave; 役 **yì**: use as a servant)

脔割 **luángē** 'slice up'; 'carve up' （脔 **luán**: a small slice of meat; 割 **gē**: cut)

瓜分 **guāfēn** 'carve up'; 'divide up' （瓜 **guā**: melon; 分 **fēn**: divide)

囊括 **nángkuò** 'include'; 'embrace' （囊 **náng**: bag; 括 **kuò**: include)

辐射 **fúshè** 'radiate (from a central point)' （辐 **fú**: spoke of a wheel; 射 **shè**: radiate)

冰释 **bīngshì** (of misgivings) 'vanish' （冰 **bīng**: ice; 释 **shì**: dispel, clear up)

波及 **bōjí** 'involve'; 'affect' （波 **bō**: waves; 及 **jí**: spread to)

席卷 **xíjuǎn** 'sweep across'; 'engulf' （席 **xí**: mat; 卷 **juǎn**: roll up)

梭巡 **suōxún** 'to patrol' （梭 **suō**: shuttle; 巡 **xún**: patrol)

instrument:

海运 **hǎiyùn** 'transport by sea' （海 **hǎi**: sea; 运 **yùn**: transport)

盆栽 **pénzāi** 'cultivated in a pot'; 'potted' （盆 **pén**: pot; 栽 **zāi**: to plant)

碇泊 **dìngbó** 'anchor'; 'berth' （碇 **dìng**: killick; 泊 **bó**: to moor)

宴请 **yànqǐng** 'entertain (to dinner)' （宴 **yàn**: banquet; 请 **qǐng**: invite, entertain)

粉刷 **fěnshuā** 'whitewash' （粉 **fěn**: powder; 刷 **shuā**: brush)

机耕 **jīgēng** 'to tractor-plough' （机 **jī**: machine; 耕 **gēng**: plough)

渠灌 **qúguàn** 'canal irrigation' （渠 **qú**: irrigation ditch; 灌 **guàn**: irrigate, pour)

电焊 **diànhàn** 'to electric-weld' （电 **diàn**: electricity; 焊 **hàn**: weld)

火葬 **huǒzàng** 'cremate' （火 **huǒ**: fire; 葬 **zàng**: bury)

音译 **yīnyì** 'transliterate' （音 **yīn**: sound; 译 **yì**: translate)

谣传 **yáochuán**
'rumour has it that . . .'

(谣 **yáo**: rumour; 传 **chuán**: spread, pass on)

邮购 **yóugòu** 'order by mail'

(邮 **yóu**: post, mail; 购 **gòu**: purchase)

函授 **hánshòu** 'teach by correspondence'

(函 **hán**: letter, correspondence; 授 **shòu**: teach)

笔耕 **bǐgēng**
'make a living by writing'

(笔 **bǐ**: pen; 耕 **gēng**: plough)

伞投 **sǎntóu**
'drop by parachute'

(伞 **sǎn**: umbrella; 投 **tóu**: throw, drop, hurl)

鞭打 **biāndǎ** 'to whip'; 'flog'

(鞭 **biān**: a whip; 打 **dǎ**: beat, hit)

枪杀 **qiāngshā** 'shoot dead'

(枪 **qiāng**: gun, rifle; 杀 **shā**: kill, slaughter)

禳解 **rángjiě** 'avert disasters by prayers'

(禳 **ráng**: sacrificial ceremony; 解 **jiě**: resolve, avert)

窝藏 **wōcáng** 'harbour'; 'shelter'

(窝 **wō**: nest, lair; 藏 **cáng**: hide, conceal)

仓储 **cāngchǔ** 'keep grain, goods, etc. in a storehouse'

(仓 **cāng**: warehouse; 储 **chǔ**: store up)

针对 **zhēnduì** 'be directed against'; 'counter'

(针 **zhēn**: needle; 对 **duì**: to counter)

These notions of resemblance and instrument are not lacking in quadrisyllabic idioms:

instrument:

管窥蠡测 **guǎnkuī lícè** 'have a restricted view'
(lit. look at the sky through a bamboo tube and measure the sea with a calabash)
(管 **guǎn**: tube; 窥 **kuī**: look; 蠡 **lí**: calabash; 测 **cè**: to measure)

口诛笔伐 **kǒuzhū bǐfá** 'condemn both in speech and in writing'
(口 **kǒu**: mouth; 诛 **zhū**: punish; 笔 **bǐ**: pen or writing brush; 伐 **fá**: attack)

绳捆索绑 **shéng kǔn suǒ bǎng** 'truss up'; 'tie up'
(绳 **shéng**: rope, string; 捆 **kǔn**: bundle up; 索 **suǒ**: a large rope; 绑 **bǎng**: bind, tie)

resemblance:

土崩瓦解 **tǔbēng wǎjiě** 'distintegrate'; 'crumble'; 'fall apart'
(土 **tǔ**: earth, soil; 崩 **bēng**: collapse; 瓦 **wǎ**: tile; 解 **jiě**: separate, disintegrate)

烟消云散 **yānxiāo yúnsàn** 'vanish completely'
(烟 **yān**: smoke; 消 **xiāo**: vanish; 云 **yún**: cloud; 散 **sàn**: disperse)

龙飞凤舞 **lóngfēi fèngwǔ** 'a flamboyant style of calligraphy'
(龙 **lóng**: dragon; 飞 **fēi**: fly; 凤 **fèng**: phoenix; 舞 **wǔ**: dance)

狼吞虎咽 **lángtūn hǔyàn** 'wolf down'; 'gobble up'
(狼 **láng**: wolf; 吞 **tūn**: swallow; 虎 **hǔ**: tiger; 咽 **yàn**: swallow)

In trisyllabic idioms, the construction often appears as 'n + v + n', a mirrored expression. The resultant lexeme, in the majority of cases, is an adverb or an adjective. For example,

狗咬狗 **gǒu yǎo gǒu** 'dog-eat-dog'　　　(狗 **gǒu**: dog; 咬 **yǎo**: bite)
面对面 **miàn duì miàn** 'face-to-face'　　(面 **miàn**: face; 对 **duì**: opposite)
心连心 **xīn lián xīn**　　　　　　　　　(心 **xīn**: heart; 连 **lián**: connect)
　'heart linked to heart'
肩并肩 **jiān bìng jiān**　　　　　　　　(肩 **jiān**: shoulder;
　'shoulder to shoulder'　　　　　　　　　并 **bìng**: side by side)
手拉手 **shǒu lā shǒu**　　　　　　　　　(手 **shǒu**: hand; 拉 **lā**: pull)
　'hand in hand'
桥归桥, 路归路　　　　　　　　　　　　(桥 **qiáo**: bridge; 归 **guī**:
　qiáo guī qiáo | lù guī lù　　　　　　　be counted as, belong to;
　'distinguish different things'　　　　　　路 **lù**: path)

So long as it is a mirrored expression, in some cases adjectives are used instead, e.g.

实打实 **shí dǎ shí** 'most assuredly'　　　(实 **shí**: solid; 打 **dǎ**: hit)
硬碰硬 **yìng pèng yìng** 'confront　　　　(硬 **yìng**: hard; 碰 **pèng**: run into)
　the tough with toughness'

In quadrisyllabic idioms, such predicational constructions become all the more common and the structure is usually a symmetrical 'n + v'; the semantic categories of the subject also become more varied, and the resultant idioms are mostly adjectival or verbal instead of nominal in nature. For example,

complementary:
风和日丽 **fēng hé rì lì** (of weather) 'warm and sunny'
　(风 **fēng**: wind; 和 **hé**: gentle; 日 **rì**: sun; 丽 **lì**: beautiful, bright)
山清水秀 **shān qīng shuǐ xiù** 'picturesque scenery'
　(山 **shān**: mountain, hill; 清 **qīng**: clear, green; 水 **shuǐ**: water; 秀 **xiù**:
　elegant)
家喻户晓 **jiā yù hù xiǎo** 'widely known'
　(家 **jiā**: family; 喻 **yù**: understand; 户 **hù**: household; 晓 **xiǎo**: know)
街谈巷议 **jiē tán xiàng yì** 'the talk of the town'
　(街 **jiē**: street; 谈 **tán**: talk; 巷 **xiàng**: alley; 议 **yì**: discuss)
心满意足 **xīn mǎn yì zú** 'be perfectly content/satisfied'
　(心 **xīn**: heart; 满 **mǎn**: full; 意 **yì**: intention; 足 **zú**: sufficient)
情投意合 **qíng tóu yì hé** 'find each other congenial'
　(情 **qíng**: affection; 投 **tóu**: agree with; 意 **yì**: idea, thought; 合 **hé**: suit,
　match)
面红耳赤 **miàn hóng ěr chì** 'be red in the face'; 'be flushed'
　(面 **miàn**: face; 红 **hóng**: red; 耳 **ěr**: ear; 赤 **chì**: crimson)
眉飞色舞 **méi fēi sè wǔ** 'enraptured'; 'exultant'
　(眉 **méi**: eyebrow; 飞 **fēi**: fly; 色 **sè**: complexion; 舞 **wǔ**: dance)

兴高采烈 **xìng gāo cǎi liè** 'in high spirits'; 'jubilant'

(兴 **xìng**: mood; 高 **gāo**: high; 采 **cǎi**: spirit (of a person); 烈 **liè**: strong, intense)

手忙脚乱 **shǒu máng jiǎo luàn** 'in a rush'; 'in a flurry'

(手 **shǒu**: hand; 忙 **máng**: busy; 脚 **jiǎo**: foot; 乱 **luàn**: confused)

魂飞魄散 **hún fēi pò sàn**

'be scared out of one's wits'; 'be half dead with fright'

(魂 **hún**: soul; 飞 **fēi**: fly; 魄 **pò**: daring, boldness; 散 **sàn**: disperse, scatter)

腰酸背痛 **yāo suān bèi tòng** 'backache'

(腰 **yāo**: waist; 酸 **suān**: sour; 背 **bèi**: back; 痛 **tòng**: ache)

精疲力竭 **jīng pí lì jié** 'worn out'; 'spent'

(精 **jīng**: spirit; 疲 **pí**: tired out; 力 **lì**: energy; 竭 **jié**: exhausted)

contrastive:

貌合神离 **mào hé shén lí** 'seemingly in harmony but actually at variance'

(貌 **mào**: appearance; 合 **hé**: agree; 神 **shén**: spirit; 离 **lí**: separate)

亲痛仇快 **qīn tòng chóu kuài**

'sadden one's friends and gladden one's enemies'

(亲 **qīn**: next of kin; 痛 **tòng**: feel sad; 仇 **chóu**: enemy; 快 **kuài**: feel pleased)

事半功倍 **shì bàn gōng bèi** 'get twice the result with half the effort'

(事 **shì**: event, effort; 半 **bàn**: half; 功 **gōng**: success, result; 倍 **bèi**: doubled)

identical subject:

群策群力 **qún cè qún lì** 'pool the wisdom and efforts of everyone'

(群 **qún**: crowd; 策 **cè**: plan; 力 **lì**: make efforts)

自吹自擂 **zìchuī zìlèi** 'blow one's own trumpet'

(自 **zì**: self; 吹 **chuī**: blow; 擂 **lèi**: beat a drum)

This is not saying that continuous (instead of symmetrical) patterns, though comparatively fewer, are impossible: e.g.

XX subject + XX predicator:

良药苦口 **liángyào kǔ kǒu** 'good medicine tastes bitter'

(良药 **liángyào**: good medicine; 苦 **kǔ**: bitter; 口 **kǒu**: mouth)

漏洞百出 **lòudòng bǎi chū** 'full of loopholes'

(漏洞 **lòudòng**: loophole; 百 **bǎi**: hundred; 出 **chū**: appear)

门庭若市 **méntíng ruò shì** 'the courtyard is as crowded as a marketplace'

(门庭 **méntíng**: courtyard, house; 若 **ruò**: be like, similar to; 市 **shì**: marketplace)

愚公移山 **Yúgōng yí shān** 'with dogged perseverance'

(愚公 **Yúgōng**: the foolish Old Man; 移 **yí**: remove; 山 **shān**: mountain)

鱼目混珠 **yúmù hùn zhū** 'pass off sth sham as genuine'

(鱼目 **yúmù**: fish eye; 混 **hùn**: mix with, pass off as; 珠 **zhū**: pearl)

面面相觑 **miàn miàn xiāng qù** 'look at each other in blank dismay'
(面面 **miàn miàn**: faces; 相 **xiāng**: mutual; 觑 **qù**: look)
众目睽睽 **zhòng mù kuíkuí** 'with everybody watching'
(众 **zhòng**: public, the crowd; 目 **mù**: eye; 睽睽 **kuíkuí**: stare, gaze)
忠心耿耿 **zhōngxīn gěnggěng** 'loyal and devoted'
(忠 **zhōng**: loyal, faithful; 心 **xīn**: heart; 耿耿 **gěnggěng**: devoted)

X subject + XXX predicator:
自得其乐 **zì dé qí lè** 'be content with one's lot'; 'derive pleasure from sth'
(自 **zì**: oneself; 得 **dé**: get; 其 **qí**: his; 乐 **lè**: joy, pleasure)
名符其实 **míng fú qí shí** 'be worthy of the name'
(名 **míng**: name; 符 **fú**: to match; 其 **qí**: its; 实 **shí**: reality)
情不自禁 **qíng bù zì jìn** 'cannot refrain from/cannot help doing sth'
(情 **qíng**: feeling; 不 **bù**: not; 自 **zì**: itself; 禁 **jìn**: refrain)

COMPLEMENTAL TYPE

A 'verb + complement' disyllabic lexeme, theoretically speaking, may assume one of the following characteristic forms:

predicator	+	complement
v	+	v
v	+	a
a	+	v
a	+	a

But in actuality, we shall soon find that these structures are not equally productive. Before we involve ourselves with the specific analysis of each of these structures and its peculiarities, we might find it useful to have an overall look at the general orientation of this type of disyllabic lexemes. In fact, two most distinctive features should be noted: (1) it is almost exclusively confined to the verb class; (2) it is structurally the most constructive type of disyllabic verb in the lexicon.

The first point just made is factual and needs little verification. With a few exceptions like 跳高 **tiàogāo** (v + a) 'jump high' or 'high jump', 突出 **tūchū** (v + v) 'stand out' or 'outstanding', 坏透 **huài tòu** (a + v) 'downright bad'; 'rotten to the core', etc., which may either assume double word classes or come out as nouns or adjectives, the rest of such structures are exclusively verbs, including even most of the structures with adjectives as 'predicators' e.g. 累坏 **lèi huài** (a + a) 'be tired out'; 'be exhausted', 急死 **jí sǐ** (a + v) 'be worried to death'.

The second point about the constructiveness of the type, however, can be seen from the powerful combinatory relationship between the two constituent monosyms. First, almost no monosyllabic verbal or adjectival monosyms which can be used independently are possible with a complement. Second, the 'complement' mononym is available from three distinctive categories: (1) aspectual markers, e.g. 了 **le** (finished aspect), 着 **zhe** (unfinished or continuous aspect), and 过 **guo** (experiential aspect); (2) directional markers, e.g. 来 **lái** 'towards', 去 **qù** 'away from', 上 **shàng** 'upwards', 下 **xià** 'downwards', 过 **guò** 'across', 回 **huí** 'back', 出 **chū** 'out', 进 **jìn** 'into', 起 **qǐ** 'skyward', etc. plus a disyllabic set based on the combination of 来 **lái** and 去 **qù** with the others, e.g. 起来 **qǐlai**, 上去 **shàngqu**, etc.; (3) resultative markers, which comprise all the monosyllabic adjectives (plus some commonly used disyllabic adjectives) and a particular set of monosyllabic resultative verbs[22] in the lexicon.

Nevertheless, there is a different degree of 'complementability' among the three categories of 'complement' mononyms. The aspectual markers are used to complement all verbs and adjectives and can therefore be considered a purely syntactic device: they were themselves originally verbs which have been grammaticalised into such markers.

The directional markers (again, originally verbs) seem to be an in-between category enjoying greater lexical orientation. With some verbs, the idea of 'direction' can be incorporated literally, indicating movement 'towards', 'away from', etc. related to the position of the speaker (cf. English verbs 'bring' and 'take', where the notion of 'direction' is built into the lexemes themselves) and the directional markers are therefore broadly used as a syntactic device, e.g.

带来 **dàilai** 'bring'	(带 **dài**: carry; 来 **lái**: towards)
带去 **dàiqu** 'take'	(带 **dài**: carry; 去 **qù**: away from)
回来 **huílai** 'come back'	(回 **huí**: return; 来 **lái**: towards)
出去 **chūqu** 'go out'	(出 **chū**: exit; 去 **qù**: away from)

However, with other verbs, the idea of 'direction' may be transferred onto a figurative plane and the resulting notions defy neat categorisation. Here, of course, we will be more interested in the lexical potential of these directional markers, e.g.

看来 **kànlai** 'in one's opinion'	(看 **kàn**: see)
想来 **xiǎnglai** 'presumably'	(想 **xiǎng**: think)
看上去 **kàn shàngqu** 'look as if'	(看 **kàn**: see; 上去 **shàngqu**: go up)

As far as 'resultative markers' are concerned, there is no other criterion which may decide which monosyllabic verb or adjective can be complemented by which resultative marker other than that of meaning. In theory, as long as 'meaning' allows, any monosyllabic verb or adjective can take any monsyllabic (or disyllabic) adjective or any of the set of monosyllabic verbs as its resultative marker. In practice, however, adjectival 'predicators' have predictable complement markers while verbal 'predicators' do not.

---

[22] By resultative verbs we mean a set of verbs which have an inbuilt concept of result in them, e.g. 破 **pò** 'break', 满 **mǎn** 'fill', 死 **sǐ** 'die', etc.

Adjectival predicators seem to limit themselves to the following two kinds of 'resultative complement'. They are more of a syntactic nature. For example,

(1) of an extreme degree:

湿透 **shī tòu** 'wet through' (湿 **shī**: wet, damp, humid; 透 **tòu**: fully, thoroughly)

好极 **hǎo jí** 'extremely good' (好 **hǎo**: good; 极 **jí**: extremely, exceedingly)

亮多 **liàng duō** 'much (or far) brighter' (亮 **liàng**: bright; 多 **duō**: much more, far more)

羞煞 **xiū shà** 'exceedingly shameful' (羞 **xiū**: ashamed; 煞 **shà**: in the extreme, exceedingly)

乐死 **lè sǐ** 'overjoyed' (乐 **lè**: happy, cheerful, joyful; 死 **sǐ**: extremely, to death)

(2) into an undesirable state:

松掉 **sōng diào** 'become loose' (松 **sōng**: loose; 掉 **diào**: get into an undesirable state)

累坏 **lèi huài** 'be dog-tired' (累 **lèi**: tired, fatigued, weary; 坏 **huài**: badly, awfully)

With 'verb' predicators, however, we find an extremely 'kaleidoscopic' picture of possible combinations. On the one hand, we see that the action expressed by one and the same monosyllabic verb may incur different results; and on the other, the same resultative marker can be used to complement different verbs. For example,

(1) the same verb taking on different resultative markers:

打倒 **dǎdǎo** 'overthrow' (打 **dǎ**: strike, hit; 倒 **dǎo**: fall, topple)

打断 **dǎduàn** 'interrupt' (断 **duàn**: break)

打开 **dǎkāi** 'open'; 'unfold' (开 **kāi**: open, loose, away, etc.)

(2) the same resultative marker applied to different verbs:

解开 **jiěkāi** 'untie'; 'undo' (解 **jiě**: untie; 开 **kāi**: open, loose, away, etc.)

离开 **líkāi** 'part from' (离 **lí**: leave; 开 **kāi**: open, loose, away, etc.)

分开 **fēnkāi** 'separate'; 'part' (分 **fēn**: divide; 开 **kāi**: open, loose, away, etc.)

In view of the diverse possibilities of combination between the verb mononym and the resultative marker, we will in this discussion focus our attention on the resultative markers and their combinatory relationship with the verbal mononym in the structure, that is to say, on the two most constructive sub-types we have listed at the beginning of this discussion: (a) v + v; (b) v + a.

As we said earlier, any monosyllabic verb can take on any resultative marker as long as the outcome makes sense in real life or can be 'metaphorically' reinterpreted. It follows therefore that the list of possible 'verb + complement' structures always remains open. For instance, in addition to the ten established disyllabic items listed in *A Chinese–English Dictionary* (Commercial Press Peking 1980) concerning 打 **dǎ** 'hit', a far greater number of *ad hoc* combinations can be made up whenever the appropriate situation demands it. For example, you may think in terms of

'a bullet piercing some object':	打穿 **dǎ chuān**	(穿 **chuān**: pierce through, penetrate)
'winning a basketball match':	打赢 **dǎ yíng**	(赢 **yíng**: win, beat)
'shooting down aeroplanes':	打落 **dǎ luò**	(落 **luò**: fall, drop).

Actually, you can think in terms of any result which can be produced by 打 **dǎ** in any of its polysemous senses on any occasion.

On the other hand, if we keep the adjective monomym like 碎 **suì** 'smashed' constant, we can think in terms of the instrument used to produce this result: e.g.

剪碎 **jiǎn suì** 'cut into pieces (with scissors)'	(剪 **jiǎn**: cut with scissors; 碎 **suì**: into tiny pieces)
切碎 **qiē suì** 'cut into pieces (with a knife)'	(切 **qiē**: cut with a knife; 碎 **suì**: into tiny pieces)
捣碎 **dǎo suì** 'pound to pieces (with a pestle)'	(捣 **dǎo**: pound with a pestle; 碎 **suì**: mashed)
碾碎 **niǎn suì** 'pulverise (with a roller)'	(碾 **niǎn**: grind; 碎 **suì**: mashed)

Or we can also think in terms of the method employed: e.g.

敲碎 **qiāo suì** 'knock to pieces'	(敲 **qiāo**: knock, strike; 碎 **suì**: smashed)
压碎 **yā suì** 'crush to pieces'	(压 **yā**: press down; 碎 **suì**: smashed)
踩碎 **cǎi suì** 'trample to pieces'	(踩 **cǎi**: step on, trample; 碎 **suì**: smashed)

If this time we take a verbal monomym 醒 **xǐng** 'wake up' instead of an adjectival monomym as the resultative marker, we can think of different ways in which the 'waking up' can be brought about: e.g.

叫醒 **jiào xǐng** 'wake sb up (by calling)'	(叫 **jiào**: to shout; 醒 **xǐng**: wake up)
推醒 **tuī xǐng** 'wake sb up (by pushing)'	(推 **tuī**: push)
闹醒 **nào xǐng** 'wake sb up (by the alarm clock)'	(闹 **nào**: make a noise)
吵醒 **chǎo xǐng** 'wake sb up (by making a lot of noise)'	(吵 **chǎo**: make a noise)

So we see that '*meaning compatibility*' seems to be the sole criterion at work. If we do not say, for example, 吃醒 **chī xǐng** 'wake up by eating', it is not because the resultant disyllable is formally impossible but because it is incompatible with the meaning. In fact, we can find a most convincing example in the following pair: for 养 **yǎng** 'support, provide for', the expected result must be 活 **huó** 'alive'; 'living' (e.g. 养活 **yǎnghuo** 'feed somebody to keep him/her alive'); and for 杀 **shā** 'kill', the designed result must be 死 **sǐ** 'dead' (e.g. 杀死 **shā sǐ** 'put to death'), for one will never expect the outcome in either case to be the opposite.

But before we can explain for sure how the two monosyms of a 'verb + complement' structure are related, we must first of all be able to differentiate between the two monosyms. The verb monosyms, by definition, must be monosyllabic verbs. But the resultative markers on the other hand can be either adjectives or verbs. As we shall see, almost all adjectives can be 'complement' monosyms and this is fairly straightforward. The remaining problem will then be with monosyllabic verbs, which can be either the verb monosym or the 'complement' monosym in the structure. We may well ask if there is any line of demarcation between the two? Fortunately, the answer is a definite 'yes'.

To qualify for a resultative marker, a monosyllabic verb must (1) indicate not an action or a process but a result, which can therefore no longer associate with 着 **zhe** (the continuous aspect), e.g. 倒 **dǎo** 'fall, topple' as a resultative marker in 打倒 **dǎdǎo** 'overthrow' or 跌倒 **diēdǎo** 'trip and fall, tumble', etc. cannot produce 倒着 **dǎo zhe**; nor can 止 **zhǐ** 'stop' in 防止 **fángzhǐ** 'prevent', 禁止 **jìnzhǐ** 'prohibit', etc. have 止着 **zhǐ zhe**; and at the same time as a resultative marker it must (2) acquire a more diversified network of meaning than when it is used independently on its own, e.g. the verb 开 **kāi** 'open' as a resultative marker can mean:

(a) 'open'	in	撬开 **qiàokāi** 'prise open'
(b) 'aside'		撇开 **piēkāi** 'leave aside'; 'bypass'
(c) 'apart'		分开 **fēnkāi** 'separate'
(d) 'away'		走开 **zǒukāi** 'go away'
(e) 'begin'		说开(了) **shuōkāi le** 'begin to talk about something'
(f) 'broad-minded'		看开(些) **kànkāi (xiē)** 'not take something too much to heart'
(g) 'cause to function'		打开 **dǎkāi** 'switch on'
(h) 'expand'		泡开 **pàokāi** 'begin to expand when soaked in water'

As complements, resultative verbs, interestingly enough, can be sorted into several most distinctive categories indicating:

(a) stoppage/severance (i.e. bringing an end to something):
     推脱 **tuītuō** 'evade'; 'shirk'   (推 **tuī**: push, shove;
                                      脱 **tuō**: escape from)

拒绝 **jùjué** 'refuse' (拒 **jù**: reject; 绝 **jué**: cut off)

抵消 **dǐxiāo** 'offset'; (抵 **dǐ**: compensate for;
  'cancel out'   消 **xiāo**: eliminate)

磨灭 **mómiè** 'obliterate' (磨 **mó**: rub; 灭 **miè**: extinguish)

埋没 **máimò** 'neglect'; 'stifle' (埋 **mái**: bury; 没 **mò**: submerge)

制止 **zhìzhǐ** 'check curb' (制 **zhì**: restrict; 止 **zhǐ**: stop)

评定 **píngdìng** 'pass (评 **píng**: evaluate, assess;
  judgement on'   定 **dìng**: fixed, settled)

平息 **píngxī** 'suppress'; (平 **píng**: suppress; 息 **xī**: cease)
  'put down'

刹住 **shāzhù** 'stop'; 'brake' (刹 **shā**: put on the brake;
  住 **zhù**: stop)

改掉 **gǎidiào** 'give up' (改 **gǎi**: change, transform;
  掉 **diào**: come off)

割断 **gēduàn** 'sever'; 'cut off' (割 **gē**: cut; 断 **duàn**: break off)

摧毁 **cuīhuǐ** 'destroy' (摧 **cuī**: destroy; 毁 **huǐ**: ruin)

驳倒 **bódǎo** 'outargue' (驳 **bó**: refute; 倒 **dǎo**: fall, topple)

推翻 **tuīfān** 'overthrow'; (推 **tuī**: push; shove;
  'topple'   翻 **fān**: turn over (or up))

征服 **zhēngfú** 'conquer' (征 **zhēng**: go on an expedition/a
  campaign; 服 **fú**: obey)

睡着 **shuì zháo** 'fall asleep' (睡 **shuì**: go to bed;
  着 **zháo**: fall asleep)

离开 **líkāi** 'leave'; (离 **lí**: go away from;
  'deviate from'   开 **kāi**: separate)

关上 **guānshàng** (关 **guān**: shut; 上 **shàng**: closed)
  'close'; 'shut'

(b) completion (a notion akin to 'stoppage'):

做完 **zuòwán** 'finish' (做 **zuò**: do, make;
  完 **wán**: complete)

走遍 **zǒubiàn** 'travel the (走 **zǒu**: walk; 遍 **biàn**: everywhere)
  length and breadth of'

到齐 **dàoqí** (到 **dào**: arrive; 齐 **qí**: complete)
  'everybody is present'

使尽 **shǐjìn** 'do one's utmost' (使 **shǐ**: use; 尽 **jìn**: to the greatest
  extent)

开足 **kāizú** (开 **kāi**: drive (a car); 足 **zú**: fully)
  'as fast as one can drive'

(c) revelation:

揭穿 **jiēchuān** 'expose' (揭 **jiē**: bring to light;
  穿 **chuān**: penetrate)

揭晓 **jiēxiǎo** 'announce'; (揭 **jiē**: expose; 晓 **xiǎo**: know)
  'publish'

听懂 **tīng dǒng**   (听 **tīng**: listen; 懂 **dǒng**:
  'listen with understanding'   understand)

梦见 **mèngjiàn** 'see in a dream'   (梦 **mèng**: dream; 见 **jiàn**: see)

学会 **xuéhuì** 'learn'; 'master'   (学 **xué**: study, learn;
                                   会 **huì**: grasp)

突出 **tūchū**   (突 **tū**: stick out;
  'give prominence to'   出 **chū**: go or come out)

发现 **fāxiàn** 'discover'   (发 **fā**: open up; 现 **xiàn**: appear)

说明 **shuōmíng** 'explain';   (说 **shuō**: say; 明 **míng**: obvious)
  'illustrate'

弄清 **nòngqīng** 'clarify'   (弄 **nòng**: handle, manage;
                                   清 **qīng**: clear)

(d) attainment:

取得 **qǔdé** 'acquire'   (取 **qǔ**: get; 得 **dé**: obtain)

达到 **dádào** 'attain'   (达 **dá**: arrive; 到 **dào**: reach)

造就 **zàojiù** 'bring up'   (造 **zào**: create; 就 **jiù**: accomplish)

完成 **wánchéng**   (完 **wán**: to complete;
  'bring to fruition'   成 **chéng**: successfully)

猜中 **cāizhòng** 'guess right'   (猜 **cāi**: guess; 中 **zhòng**: right)

打赢 **dǎyíng** 'beat'; 'defeat'   (打 **dǎ**: hit, fight; 赢 **yíng**: win)

改善 **gǎishàn** 'improve';   (改 **gǎi**: transform;
  'ameliorate'   善 **shàn**: good, satisfactory)

So long as it is allowed by meaning, resultative verbs may easily combine with action verbs into disyllabic units indicating an undesirable state of affairs. These disyllabic forms may well become established if there is a frequent demand for them. In fact some of them have already become part of the existing lexicon: e.g.

result related to the grammatical object:

吹爆 **chuī bào**   (吹 **chuī**: blow, puff; 爆 **bào**: burst)
  'blow sth till it bursts'

记串 **jì chuàn** 'mix things   (记 **jì**: remember; 串 **chuàn**: mixed up)
  up in one's memory'

穿反 **chuān fǎn** 'wear one's   (穿 **chuān**: wear; 反 **fǎn**: inside out)
  clothes inside out'

搞混 **gǎo hùn** 'mix up'   (搞 **gǎo**: do, carry on;
                                混 **hùn**: mix, confuse)

抄落 **chāo là** 'drop a word   (抄 **chāo**: copy;
  or line whilst copying'   落 **là**: be left out, missing)

问愣 **wèn lèng** 'ask sb till   (问 **wèn**: ask; 愣 **lèng**:
  he/she is confused'   dazzed, dumbfounded)

晒裂 **shài liè**   (晒 **shài**: to sun; 裂 **liè**: to slit, crack)
  'sun sth till it cracks'

放乱 **fàng luàn** 'leave things around at random'   (放 **fàng**: put; 乱 **luàn**: in a mess)

弄散 **nòng sǎn** 'loosen'; 'spread out'   (弄 **nòng**: handle, play with; 散 **sǎn**: loose)

撞折 **zhuàng shé** 'snap sth by running into it'   (撞 **zhuàng**: run into; 折 **shé**: snap)

驱散 **qū sàn** 'disperse'   (驱 **qū**: drive, expel; 散 **sàn**: break up)

冲垮 **chōng kuǎ** 'burst'; 'shatter'   (冲 **chōng**: rush at; 垮 **kuǎ**: collapse)

打死 **dǎ sǐ** 'beat to death'   (打 **dǎ**: beat; 死 **sǐ**: dead)

result related to the grammatical subject:

说崩 **shuō bēng** (of talks) 'break down'   (说 **shuō**: talk; 崩 **bēng**: collapse)

饿瘪 **è biě** 'be famished'   (饿 **è**: go hungry; 瘪 **biě**: shrivelled, shrunken)

累病 **lèi bìng** 'work oneself to death'   (累 **lèi**: tired; 病 **bìng**: ill)

吓蒙 **xià mēng** 'be scared out of one's wits'   (吓 **xià**: frighten, scare; 蒙 **mēng**: senseless)

喝醉 **hē zuì** 'get drunk'   (喝 **hē**: drink; 醉 **zuì**: drunk)

Formally speaking, the 'verb + complement' type of disyllabic lexemes with a verbal complement are easily confused with the 'sequential juxtaposition' type because they are both of a 'v + v' structure. However, the fact is that the second verbal monynym in the former structure is of an entirely different nature from that in the latter, that is: the second verb monynym in a 'verb + complement' structure encodes a kind of result and therefore most of them cannot associate themselves with the 'unfinished or continuous' aspect marker 着 **zhe** as we have already pointed out; whereas there can be no such restrictions on the second verb monynyms in a 'sequential juxtaposition', where the notion of 'purpose' in the verb monynym is perhaps stronger than that of 'result'.

It might be of value to make a rough estimate of the number of the set of 'verbal' resultative markers we have so far been able to differentiate. The number is over fifty.[23] And it is these fifty and more verbal resultative markers in conjunction with all the mono- (or di-) syllabic adjectives in the lexicon that play a vitally important role in constructing all the established or *ad hoc* 'verb + complement' types of disyllabic (or sometimes trisyllabic) lexemes in the vocabulary of the language, as we can see particularly from the examples given as free collocations above.

[23] For an exhaustive list of potential adjectival/verbal resultative indicators in the language, cf. Wang, Yannong et al. (王砚农) 1987.

To conclude, we must not forget that the majority of Chinese lexemes are disyllabic and these disyllabic lexemes are mostly generated structurally in keeping with the syntactically oriented patterns discussed above; and quadrisyllabic or multisyllabic idioms and sayings are but extensions of these patterns. A true comprehension of these compounding rules, therefore, has extremely important implications: it not only provides the speaker of the language with insights into the internal construction of Chinese words but also enables him/her to coin readily acceptable words when occasions demand.

5 PHONAESTHETIC FEATURES OF THE CHINESE LEXICON

Phonaesthemes in the lexicon of a language have long been noted but have rarely been fully investigated. Ever since the 'bow-wow' theory of the origin of language and its like fell into disrepute, the 'arbitrariness' of the association between meaning and sound has often been emphasised. We cannot very well justify, for example, the statement that it is only natural for a language like Chinese to have 吃 **chī** 'eat' incorporate a 'dental' consonant and 喝 **hē** 'drink' a 'velar' because one eats with one's teeth and drinks through one's throat. For most people, that is perhaps stretching the imagination too far. Even with the most phonaesthetic of the phonaesthemes, that is, with onomatopoeic words, one cannot yet doggedly assert that Chinese ducks should automatically cry 嘎嘎 **gāgā** while English ducks cry 'quack-quack'. When a Chinese person feels a sudden pain, 哎哟 **āiyō** comes almost instinctively to him; yet however well-versed he is in English, the interjection 'ouch' in a similar situation seems to sound ever so awkward and unbecoming to his ear. He was brought up to cry 哎哟 **āiyō** when he feels a pain and was accustomed to hearing the ducks quack 嘎嘎 **gāgā**.

Despite the indisputable truth behind all this, arbitrariness or convention alone does not seem to tell the whole story.

Though it is most unlikely that a limited number of linguistic sounds in human speech could ever hope to imitate unlimited categories of sounds in nature, yet the motive behind the imitation can be clearly seen. It is not important that Chinese dogs should 汪汪 **wāngwāng** 'yap' and English dogs 'bow-wow' (after all, they are 'speaking' two different languages); what seems essential is that in both languages there is a veritable intention to imitate (and quite coincidentally, both come up with a bilabial w, one being more like a 'yap' and the other a 'growl').

What is more, there is virtually no limit as to how far linguistic sounds can and cannot go. If they can be made to imitate natural sounds with the aim of representing them, why can they not be made to represent the entities, qualities and events associated with these sounds? A cat does not only 咪咪 **mīmī** 'mew' in Chinese but is itself called 猫 **māo**; 知了 **zhīliǎo** 'cicada' in Chinese, whenever it makes that persistent noise, is supposed to be forever calling its own name.

Step by step and eventually, phonaesthemes forget their initial purposes of sound imitation; what they remember is their own sound images. And as soon as linguistic sounds turn upon themselves for inspiration, the result is not just onomatopoeia, but alliteration, rhyme, etc., and the ultimate *inspired arbitrariness.*[1] Linguistic sounds, in the process of encoding meaning, are thus seen to have traversed the whole journey from crude imitation to sound metaphor and to the final leg of complete, arbitrary representation.

In language, it can be seen that, on the one hand, lexemes like 嘎嘎 **gāgā** or 'quack-quack' are purely phonaesthetically motivated while, on the other hand, a particular lexeme seems to be drawing on the sound image of another in closely related areas of thought. For example, though we must not over-generalise, neither must we overlook, from a synchronic point of view, the striking inter-lexemic phonaesthetic similarities found in the following sets of words or mononyms: e.g.

细 **xì**	'thin'
小 **xiǎo**	'small'
稀 **xī**	'sparse'
鲜 **xiǎn**	'rare'
修 **xiū**	'tall and slender'
狭 **xiá**	'narrow'
纤 **xiān**	'fine'; 'minute'
限 **xiàn**	'limit'

And:

蒙 **méng**	'to cover'
濛 **méng**	'drizzly'; 'misty'
朦 **méng**	(of moonlight) 'dim'; 'hazy'
曚 **méng**	(of sunlight) 'dim'
矇 **méng**	'drowsy'; 'somnolent'
蒙 **mēng**	'baffled'; 'senseless'
懵 **měng**	'muddled'; 'ignorant'
梦 **mèng**	'dream'
冥 **míng**	'dark'; 'obscure'
盲 **máng**	'blind'
霾 **mái**	'haze'
埋 **mái**	'to cover up (with earth, etc.)'; 'bury'
没 **mò**	'sink'; 'submerge'; 'disappear'
灭 **miè**	'extinguish'; 'exterminate'
泯 **mǐn**	'vanish'; 'die out'
墓 **mù**	'grave'; 'tomb'
暮 **mù**	'dusk'; 'sunset'
幕 **mù**	'curtain'; 'screen'
幔 **màn**	'curtain'

---

[1] Cf. Bolinger and Sears 1981.

蒙 **mēng**	'dupe'; 'deceive'
谩 **mán**	'hoodwink'
瞒 **mán**	'hide the truth from'
颟 **mān**	'muddleheaded'
迷 **mí**	'confused'
谜 **mí**	'riddle'; 'conundrum'
秘 **mì**	'mysterious'
密 **mì**	'secret'

In fact, this 'muffled', 'muddled' and 'befuddled' state or condition develops into an associative meaning of boundlessness and pervasiveness:

渺 **miǎo**	(of an expanse of water) 'vast'
邈 **miǎo**	'faraway'; 'remote'
漠 **mò**	'vast and lonely'
绵 **mián**	'continuous'
弥 **mí**	'to cover'; 'fill'
漫 **màn**	'be all over the place'; 'be everywhere'
满 **mǎn**	'full'; 'filled'; 'packed'
茫 **máng**	'boundless and indistinct'
莽 **mǎng**	'huge'; 'vast'; 'boundless'

From these example, we can clearly see that it is at this inter-lexemic level that phonaesthemes become more amenable to meaningful analysis.

Phonaesthetic motivation, as we said, arises either from crude imitation or from sound association, which can be regarded respectively as (1) onomatopoeic; and (2) symbolic. Onomatopoeic motivation chiefly stems from imitation of human, animal or natural sounds in the extralinguistic world; whereas symbolic motivation has nothing whatsoever to do with 'acoustics' of the natural or human world but is purely intralinguistic, a kind of sound awareness in different correlations, which calls forth phonaesthetic imageries and connotations at once favourable and peculiar to the linguistic conventions of a particular language community. A third type called 'sound-translation' from foreign languages might also be regarded as arising from phonaesthetic motivation; but as it is only intended for copying foreign pronunciation and is limited to a small number of loan items, it does not belong to the phonaesthetic network of the language and is therefore of minor importance.[2]

Phonaesthetic categories in Chinese, whether onomatopoeic or symbolic, are found to use systematically such phonaesthetic devices as (1) sound imageries – onomatopoeia, alliteration, rhyme, reduplication, assonance, etc. and (2) tone imageries – tonal variation, tonal harmony, interjection, etc.

---

[2] This will be discussed in Chapter 10 on loanwords.

A table will make things clear:

phonaesthetic devices used	phonaesthetic categories discerned	
sound imageries	onomatopoeia	onomatopoeic
	alliteration rhyme reduplication assonance	onomatopoeic or symbolic
tone imageries	tonal variation tonal harmony interjection	symbolic
imitation of foreign pronunciation		sound-translation

SOUND IMAGERIES

(a) Onomatopoeia

Onomatopoeia is to be understood as linguistic sounds being used to copy sounds in nature or in the human world. As we said earlier, linguistic sounds cannot be expected to mould perfect replicas of the sounds of nature; and besides, human speakers seem to respond wilfully to quite different traits of the sounds they hear. Whatever they do, they are only in a position to recapture a noise-teeming nature in the limited set of linguistic sounds they are capable of and accustomed to.

Chinese onomatopoeic terms have specifically two distinctive characteristics of their own. Phonologically, they are all represented by a first (i.e. level) tone. Orthographically, they are all (except a few) marked by a 口 **kǒu** 'mouth' radical. These conventional features are generally adhered to not only in established items but also in fresh coinages.

Semantically, onomatopoeia is found to register acoustic imageries mainly in the following areas:

  (1) noise made by animals, birds and insects:

咪咪 **mīmī**	'mew'
汪汪[3] **wāngwāng**	'yap'; 'bark'
咩 **miē**	'baa'; 'bleat'
哞 **mōu**	'moo'
咴儿咴儿 **huīrhuīr**	'neigh'
喔喔 **wōwō**	'cock-a-doodle-doo', 'crow'
嘎嘎 **gāgā**	'quack'

[3] This is one of the few exceptions where the orthographical representation does not incorporate a 口 'mouth' radical.

咯咯 gēgē	'cackle'
咕咕 gūgū	'coo'
喳喳 zhāzhā	(magpie) 'chatter'
哑哑 yāyā	(crow) 'caw'
吱吱 zīzī	(mouse) 'squeak'
唧唧 jījī	(insect) 'chirp'
嗡嗡 wēngwēng	(bee) 'buzz'

As we know, 猫 **māo** 'cat' in Chinese, which has a first tone, is phonaesthetically motivated. We may likewise surmise that 鸭 **yā** 'duck', 鸡 **jī** 'chicken', 鸦 **yā** 'crow', and 鸽子 **gēzi** 'pigeon' too, might have a similar phonaesthetic motivation, judging from their first-tone representations.

(2) noise of objects coming together, falling apart, etc.:

   (a) friction:

咝 sī	(of bullets flying) 'whistle'
唰 shuā	'swish'
哧 chī	'rip off'
嚓 cā	'screech'
呀 yā	'creak'
噗 pū	'puff'
嗖 sōu	'whiz'
呼啦 hūlā	'flap'
唏嗦 xīsū	'rustle'
咯吱 gēzhī	'creak'
咕唧 gūjī	'squelch'

   (b) bumping/exploding:

乒 pāng	'bang'
砰 pēng	'bang'
哐 kuāng	'crash'
嘣 bēng	'thump'
噔 dēng	'thud'
吭 kēng	'clang'
啪 pā	'pop'

   (c) persistent sounds:

呜 wū	'toot'
嘟 dū	'hoot'
鼟 tēng	'roll of drums'
咕隆 gūlōng	'rumble'

   (d) consecutive sounds:

咯噔 gēdēng	'click'
咕噔 gūdēng	'flip'
噗通 pūtōng	'flop'

(3) speech or non-speech sounds made by human beings:

哇 **wā**	'burst out crying'
叽咕 **jīgu**	'talk in a low voice'
叽哩咕噜 **jīligūlū**	'indistinct gabble'
噗哧 **pūchī**	'titter'
哼哧 **hēngchī**	'puff hard'
呼哧 **hūchī**	'puff and blow'
咕嘟 **gūdu**	'gurgle'

This classification along semantic lines shows clearly that it is at the inter-lexemic level that phonaesthemes begin to acquire manifest semantic associations: (a) banging and bumping sounds, as we can see, are largely encoded in 'plosive' initials like p, b, t, d, k with ng finals, e.g. 乓 **pāng**, 蹦 **bēng**, 藤 **tēng**, 噔 **dēng**; rubbing and rustling sounds in 'fricatives or affricates' like s, sh, c, ch, z, zh, x, etc., 嗖 **sōu**, 唰 **shuā**, 嚓 **cā**, 哧 **chī**; rumbling sounds in 'liquids', e.g. 咕隆 **gūlōng** 'rattle', etc.; longish sounds in 'semi-vowels', e.g. 哇 **wā**, 呜 **wū**, etc.; (b) all onomatopoeic lexemes, as distinguished from more firmly established lexemes in alliteration, rhyme, etc., which incorporate all the four tones, are invariably encoded in the first (i.e. level) tone; (3) onomatopoeic lexemes are largely monosyllables, but they are never used monosyllabically. They follow a quadrisyllabic formula when denoting short and abrupt sounds: 'the monosyllabic onomatopoeic lexeme + the adjectival suffix 的 **de** + 一声 **yī shēng** (meaning: 'one instance of such a sound'), e.g. 乓的一声 **pāng de yī shēng**, 嚓的一声 **cā de yī shēng**, etc.; or in some cases, when the onomatopoeic lexeme is itself a disyllable or a reduplication of a monosyllabic mononym, the adjectival suffix 的 **de** is then omitted to keep to the quadrisyllabic rhythm of the expression, e.g. 噗通一声 **pūtōng yī shēng** (where 通 **tōng** fills in the required rhythm provided by 的 **de**); if a kind of repetitive sound is to be indicated, it follows either a trisyllabic formula: 'a reduplication of the monosyllabic onomatopoeic lexeme + adverbial suffix 地 **de**', e.g. 吱吱地 **zīzī de**, etc., or a pentasyllabic formula (in the case of disyllabic lexemes): 'reduplicated disyllabic onomatopoeic lexeme + adverbial suffix 地 **de**', e.g. 叭唧叭唧地 **bājī bājī de**, 咯噔咯噔地 **gēdēng gēdēng de**, etc.

(b) Alliteration and Rhyme

Disyllables with alliterated or rhymed elements in Chinese are words composed of two mononyms which are semantically dependent on each other. In these instances of alliteration and rhyme we find linguistic sounds turning inwards upon themselves. It is now their own resemblance to each other that matters: in the former case, the beginning consonant/semi-vowel; in the latter, the end vowel or 'vowel + consonant n/ng'. It is true that sometimes what alliteration does for 蜘蛛 **zhīzhū** 'spider' and rhyme for 蜻蜓 **qīngtíng** 'dragon-fly' seems no different from what onomatopoeia does for 知了 **zhīliǎo** 'cicada' (which is supposed to be the acoustic impression made by the noise of the insect on the ears of the ancient Chinese). But what distinguishes them is that once freed from ties to the extralinguistic world, alliteration and rhyme, quite differently from onomatopoeia, can give fuller play to their potentialities. Now, there is nothing that cannot be covered: from physical appearances 旖旎 **yǐnǐ** (liter.) 'charming'; 'enchanting', 苗条 **miáotiao** (of a woman) 'slim', etc. to psychological traits 犹豫 **yóuyù** 'irresolute', 糊涂 **hútu** 'muddled', etc., and even characteristic actions 流浪 **liúlàng** 'roam about', 徘徊 **páihuái** 'pace up and down', etc.

One outstanding orthographical feature of these disyllabic lexemes of alliteration and rhyme is that the two component mononyms often share the same meaningful radical, e.g. 崎岖 **qíqū** 'rugged' (with a 山 **shān** 'hill' radical), 褴褛 **lánlǚ** 'shabby' (with a 衣 **yī** 'clothing' radical), 蜿蜒 **wǎnyán** 'zigzag', 'meander' (with 虫 **chóng** 'snake' radical), 恍惚 **huǎnghū** 'absent-minded' (with a 忄 'heart' radical), etc.[4]

We will first take a look at how onomatopoeic features in disyllabic words are carried over from crude imitation into acoustic symbolism and become interwoven with alliterating and rhyming devices; and as onomatopoeia gradually gives way to purer alliteration and rhyme, other tones than the first (i.e. level) creep in:

(a) alliteration:

咿呀 **yīyā**	'creak' (of a violin, etc.)
叮当 **dīngdāng**	'ding-dong'
乒乓 **pīngpāng**	'rattle'
滴答 **dīdā**	'tick-tock'
噼啪 **pīpā**	(of hands) 'clap'
啁哳 **zhāozhā**	(formal) 'twitter'
哼儿哈儿 **hēng(r)hā(r)**	'hem and haw'
澎湃 **pēngpài**	'surge'
嘹亮 **liáoliàng**	'loud and clear'

(b) rhyme:

吧嗒 **bādā**	'click'
啪嗒 **pādā**	'patter'; 'clatter'; 'pitter-patter'
啪喳 **pāchā**	'sound of something clashing'
欻拉 **chuālā**	'sizzle'
嘎巴 **gābā**	'crack'; 'snap'
哐啷 **kuānglāng**	'crash'
咕嘟 **gūdū**	'bubble'

[4] Cf. Wang, Liaoyi (王了一) 1957. Alliterated and rhymed forms with identical radical representation are a norm. Such homologousness seems to be a prevailing tendency in writing an alliterated or rhymed form. However, form is only subordinate to sound. In a number of cases, for example, 褴褛 were originally written as 蓝缕 **lánlǚ** and 恍惚 as 恍忽 **huǎnghū**. They are still widely used by some as alternative forms.

咕噜 **gūlū**	'whisper'
哇啦 **wālā**	'hullabaloo'
淅沥 **xīlì**	'the patter of rain'
锒铛 **lángdāng**	'clanking or clanging sound'
汹涌 **xiōngyǒng**	'turbulent'

But alliteration and rhyme do not confine themselves to sound imitation. They have higher goals to attain. Their sound-symbolic qualities are seen to find expression in a set of verbs denoting 'lingering indecision':[5]

(a) alliteration:

缠绵 **chánmián**	(of an illness or emotion) 'be lingering'
踟蹰 **chíchú**	'hesitate'
彳亍 **chìchù**	(written) 'walk to and fro'
踌躇 **chóuchú**	'shilly-shally'
流连 **liúlián**	'linger on'
流浪 **liúlàng**	'roam about'
犹豫 **yóuyù**	'hesitate'; 'be irresolute'

(b) rhyme:

徘徊 **páihuái**	'pace up and down'
盘桓 **pánhuán**	(written) 'linger'
蹒跚 **pánshān**	'walk haltingly'
徜徉 **chángyáng**	(formal) 'wander about unhurriedly'
彷徨 **pánghuáng**	'walk back and forth, not knowing which way to go'
踉跄 **liàngqiàng**	'stagger'
逛荡 **guàngdang**	(derog.) 'loiter'; 'loaf about'
踱躞 **diéxiè**	(formal) 'pace about'
蹉跎 **cuōtuó**	'waste time'

Alliteration and rhyme are, of course, also found with verbs indicating other forms of human activity, physical as well as psychological:

(a) physical:
alliteration:

辨别 **biànbié**	'differentiate'; 'distinguish'
抽搐 **chōuchù**	'twitch'; 'tic'
到达 **dàodá**	'arrive'; 'reach'
抵挡 **dǐdǎng**	'keep out'; 'ward off'
颠倒 **diāndǎo**	'reverse'; 'invert'
对待 **duìdài**	'treat'; 'approach'
绘画 **huìhuà**	'draw'; 'paint'

---

[5] Some examples are from Ren, Xueliang (任学良) 1981.

料理 **liàolǐ**	'attend to'; 'take care of'
借鉴 **jièjiàn**	'draw lessons from'; 'draw on the experience of'
进击 **jìnjī**	'advance on (the enemy)'
救济 **jiùjì**	'extend relief to'; 'relieve the distress of'
笼络 **lǒngluò**	'win sb by any means'; 'draw over'
濡染 **rúrǎn**	'immerse'; 'imbue'
铺排 **pūpái**	'put in order'; 'arrange'
搜索 **sōusuǒ**	'search for'; 'hunt for'
违迕 **wéiwǔ**	'violate'; 'disobey'
消闲 **xiāoxián**	'fill one's spare time'; 'while away the time'
休息 **xiūxi**	'have (or take) a rest'
学习 **xuéxí**	'study'; 'learn'
寻衅 **xúnxìn**	'pick a quarrel'; 'provoke'
宴饮 **yànyǐn**	'wine and dine'
迎迓 **yíngyà**	'meet'; 'welcome'
夤缘 **yínyuán**	'make use of one's connections to climb up the social ladder'
诊治 **zhěnzhì**	'make a diagnosis and give treatment'
征召 **zhēngzhào**	'enlist'; 'conscript'
追逐 **zhuīzhú**	'pursue'; 'chase'

rhyme:

叛变 **pànbiàn**	'turn traitor'; 'turn renegade'
编纂 **biānzuǎn**	'compile'
锻炼 **duànliàn**	'have physical training'
团圆 **tuányuán**	(of family members) 'reunite'
装璜 **zhuānghuáng**	'mount' (a picture, etc.); 'decorate'
吵闹 **chǎonào**	'wrangle'; 'kick up a row'
祷告 **dǎogào**	'pray'; 'say one's prayers'
搅扰 **jiǎorǎo**	'disturb'; 'annoy'
犒劳 **kàoláo**	'reward with food and drink'
抛锚 **pāomáo**	'drop anchor'; 'cast anchor'
骚扰 **sāorǎo**	'harass'; 'molest'
讨好 **tǎohǎo**	'fawn on'; 'curry favour with'
效劳 **xiàoláo**	'work in the service of'; 'work for'
照料 **zhàoliào**	'take care of'; 'attend to'
砥砺 **dǐlì**	'temper'; 'encourage'
祭祀 **jìsì**	'offer sacrifices to gods or ancestors'
栖息 **qīxī**	'(of birds) perch'; 'rest'
袭击 **xíjī**	'make a surprise attack on'
治理 **zhìlǐ**	'administer'; 'govern'
经营 **jīngyíng**	'manage'; 'operate'; 'run'
透漏 **tòulòu**	'divulge'; 'leak'; 'reveal'

储蓄 **chǔxù**	'save'; 'deposit'
俘虏 **fúlǔ**	'capture'; 'take prisoner'
匍匐 **púfú**	'crawl'; 'creep'
屈服 **qūfú**	'subdue'; 'submit'; 'yield'
驱逐 **qūzhú**	'drive out'; 'expel'
侮辱 **wǔrǔ**	'insult'; 'humiliate'
畜牧 **xùmù**	'raise livestock'
摧毁 **cuīhuǐ**	'destroy'; 'smash'
荟萃 **huìcuì**	(of distinguished people or exquisite objects) 'gather together'

(b) psychological:

alliteration:

猜测 **cāicè**	'guess'; 'conjecture'; 'surmise'
掂掇 **diānduo**	'consider'; 'weigh up'
懂得 **dǒngde**	'understand'; 'know'; 'grasp'
洞达 **dòngdá**	'understand thoroughly'
恚恨 **huìhèn**	(formal) 'hate'
悔恨 **huǐhèn**	'regret deeply'
咀嚼 **jǔjué**	'ruminate'; 'mull over'
领略 **lǐngluè**	'understand'; 'appreciate'
冒昧 **màomèi**	'make bold'; 'venture'; 'take the liberty'
祈求 **qíqiú**	'earnestly hope'; 'pray for'
相信 **xiāngxìn**	'believe in'; 'trust'
愿意 **yuànyì**	'be willing'
斟酌 **zhēnzhuó**	'consider'; 'deliberate'

rhyme:

盘算 **pánsuan**	'calculate'; 'plan'
瘫痪 **tānhuàn**	'be paralysed'; 'break down'
眷恋 **juànliàn**	'be sentimentally attached to'
眷念 **juànniàn**	'think fondly of'
想象 **xiǎngxiàng**	'imagine'; 'fancy'; 'visualize'
向往 **xiàngwǎng**	'yearn for'; 'look forward to'
记忆 **jìyì**	'remember'; 'recall'
矢志 **shǐzhì**	'pledge one's devotion' (to a cause)
惕厉 **tìlì**	'watch out for'; 'be vigilant'
希冀 **xījì**	'hope for'; 'wish for'; 'aspire after'
绸缪 **chóumóu**	'be sentimentally attached'
觳觫 **húsù**	(formal) 'shiver out of fear'

Alliteration and rhyme are particularly prolific with descriptive terms in the lexicon, that is, adjectives indicating human physical appearances and various kinds of psychological states that have apparent outward manifestations:

(a) physical:

alliteration:

仓促 **cāngcù**	'hurried'
褴褛 **lánlǚ**	'shabby'
蹊跷 **qīqiāo**	'odd'; 'strange'; 'fishy'
妖冶 **yāoyě**	'seductive'; 'bewitching'
矫健 **jiǎojiàn**	'strong and vigorous'
袅娜 **niǎonuó**	(literary) (of female a figure) 'graceful'
威武 **wēiwǔ**	'mighty'; 'powerful'

rhyme:

腌臜 **āzā**	(dial.) 'filthy'; 'dirty'
肮脏 **āngzāng**	'dirty'
邋遢 **lātā**	(colloq.) 'slovenly'
龌龊 **wòchuò**	'filthy'
慌张 **huāngzhāng**	'flurried'; 'flustered'; 'confused'
郎当 **lángdāng**	(of clothes) 'loose-hanging'; 'untidy'
老耄 **lǎomào**	(formal) 'senile'; 'decrepit'
臃肿 **yōngzhǒng**	'too fat to move'
翩跹 **piānxiān**	'lightly'; 'trippingly'
昂藏 **ángcáng**	(formal) 'tall'; 'strapping'; 'manly'
窈窕 **yǎotiǎo**	(of a woman) 'gentle and graceful'
苗条 **miáotiao**	(of a woman) 'slender'
娉婷 **pīngtíng**	(of a woman) 'have a graceful demeanour'
轻盈 **qīngyíng**	'slim and graceful'; 'lithe'; 'lissom'
妖娆 **yāoráo**	'enchanting'; 'bewitching'

(b) psychological:

alliteration:

懊恼 **àonǎo**	'annoyed'
惆怅 **chóuchàng**	'melancholy'
怠惰 **dàiduò**	'lazy'; 'indolent'
尴尬 **gāngà**	'awkward'
骇怪 **hàiguài**	'astonished'; 'shocked'
恍惚 **huǎnghū**	'in a trance'
惶惑 **huánghuò**	'perplexed and alarmed'
激进 **jījìn**	'radical'
骄矜 **jiāojīn**	'self-important'; 'proud'; 'haughty'
狷急 **juànjí**	'impetuous'; 'rash'
劳累 **láolèi**	'tired'; 'run-down'; 'overworked'
恼怒 **nǎonù**	'angry'; 'indignant'
缭乱 **liáoluàn**	'confused'
蒙昧 **méngmèi**	'uncivilised'; 'uncultured'

扭捏 **niǔniè**	'bashful'
偏颇 **piānpō**	'biased'; 'partial'
荏弱 **rěnruò**	'weak'; 'feeble'
松散 **sōngsǎn**	'inattentive'
忐忑 **tǎntè**	'perturbed'
佻佻 **tiāotà**	(formal) 'frivolous'
颓唐 **tuítáng**	'dejected'; 'dispirited'
拖沓 **tuōtà**	'laggard'
风发 **fēngfā**	'energetic'
果敢 **guǒgǎn**	'courageous and resolute'
憨厚 **hānhòu**	'simple and honest'
坚决 **jiānjué**	'firm'; 'resolute'
洁净 **jiéjìng**	'clean'; 'spotless'
狷介 **juànjiè**	'upright'; 'incorruptible'
拘谨 **jūjǐn**	'over-cautious'; 'reserved'
慷慨 **kāngkǎi**	'generous'
倔强 **juéjiàng**	'stubborn'
老练 **lǎoliàn**	'seasoned'; 'experienced'
磊落 **lěiluò**	'open and upright'
伶俐 **línglì**	'clever'
亲切 **qīnqiè**	'cordial'; 'kind'
倜傥 **tìtǎng**	'free and easy'
悉心 **xīxīn**	'devote all one's attention'
虚心 **xūxīn**	'open-minded'; 'modest'
英勇 **yīngyǒng**	'heroic'; 'valiant'

rhyme:

懒散 **lǎnsǎn**	'sluggish'; 'negligent'; 'indolent'
颟顸 **mānhan**	'muddleheaded'
难堪 **nánkān**	'intolerable'; 'unbearable'
散漫 **sǎnmàn**	'undisciplined'; 'slack'
贪婪 **tānlán**	'avaricious'; 'greedy'
腼腆 **miǎntiǎn**	'shy'
仓惶 **cānghuáng**	'in panic'
猖狂 **chāngkuáng**	'savage'; 'furious'
怅惘 **chàngwǎng**	'distracted'; 'listless'
浪荡 **làngdàng**	'dissolute'
莽撞 **mǎngzhuàng**	'crude and impetuous'; rash'
慌张 **huāngzhāng**	'flurried'
暴躁 **bàozào**	'irascible'; 'irritable'
骄傲 **jiāo'ào**	'arrogant'; 'conceited'
潦倒 **liǎodǎo**	'frustrated'
愤懑 **fènmèn**	(formal) 'depressed and discontented'; 'resentful'

鄙俚 **bǐlǐ**	'vulgar'; 'philistine'
势利 **shìlì**	'snobbish'
殷勤 **yīnqín**	'eagerly attentive'; 'solicitous'
伶仃 **língdīng**	'lonely'
酩酊 **mǐngdǐng**	'dead drunk'
抠搜 **kōusou**	'(informal) stingy'
忧愁 **yōuchóu**	'worried'; 'depressed'
活络 **huóluò**	'non-committal'
落寞 **luòmò**	'lonely'; 'desolate'
懦弱 **nuòruò**	'cowardly'
粗疏 **cūshū**	'careless'; 'inattentive'
糊涂 **hútu**	'muddled'
迂腐 **yūfǔ**	'pedantic'
昂扬 **ángyáng**	'high-spirited'
恬淡 **tiándàn**	'indifferent to fame or gain'
逍遥 **xiāoyáo**	'free and unfettered'
深沉 **shēnchén**	'deep'; 'undemonstrative'
审慎 **shěnshèn**	'cautious'; 'careful'
振奋 **zhènfèn**	'rouse oneself'; 'be inspired with enthusiasm'
仔细 **zǐxì**	'careful'; 'attentive'
勤谨 **qínjin**	'diligent'; 'industrious'
辛勤 **xīnqín**	'industrious'; 'hardworking'
英明 **yīngmíng**	'wise'; 'brilliant'
从容 **cōngróng**	'calm and unhurried'
悃款 **kǔnkuǎn**	'sincere'
驯顺 **xùnshùn**	'tame and docile'
爽朗 **shuǎnglǎng**	'candid'
活泼 **huópo**	'lively'; 'vivacious'; 'vivid'
旖旎 **yǐnǐ**	(liter.) 'charming'; 'enchanting'

By comparison, terms that have a negative meaning about human psychological or physical conditions far exceed those that have a positive meaning.

Adjectives describing the natural environment, too, are seen to make ample use of alliteration and rhyme:

(a) alliteration:

参差 **cēncī**	'uneven'
葱翠 **cōngcuì**	'fresh green'; 'luxuriantly green'
璀璨 **cuǐcàn**	(written) 'resplendent'
芬芳 **fēnfāng**	'sweet-smelling'; 'fragrant'
浩瀚 **hàohàn**	(formal) 'vast'
坎坷 **kǎnkě**	'bumpy'
凛冽 **lǐnliè**	'piercingly cold'

淼茫 **miǎománg**	(of an expanse of water) 'stretching as far as the eye can see'
明媚 **míngmèi**	'bright and beautiful'
偏僻 **piānpì**	'remote'; 'out-of-the-way'
崎岖 **qíqū**	'rugged'
馨香 **xīnxiāng**	(of burning incense, etc.) 'pervasively fragrant'
遥远 **yáoyuǎn**	'distant'; 'remote'
隐约 **yǐnyuē**	'indistinct'; 'faint'
氤氲 **yīnyūn**	(literary) (of smoke or mist) 'dense, enshrouding'

(b) rhyme:

斑斓 **bānlán**	'multicoloured'
灿烂 **cànlàn**	'splendid'
潺湲 **chányuán**	(liter.) 'slow flowing'
烂漫 **lànmàn**	'brilliant'
蜿蜒 **wǎnyán**	'zigzag'
潋滟 **liànyàn**	(literary) 'rippling'
绚烂 **xuànlàn**	'gorgeous'
敞亮 **chǎngliàng**	'light and spacious'
莽苍 **mǎngcāng**	(of scenery) 'blurred'; 'misty'
荒凉 **huāngliáng**	'bleak and desolate'
圹埌 **kuànglàng**	(formal) (of open country) 'boundless'
料峭 **liàoqiào**	(literary) 'chilly'
飘渺 **piāomiǎo**	'dimly discernible'; 'misty'
萧条 **xiāotiáo**	'desolate'; 'bleak'
迟滞 **chízhì**	'sluggish'
绮丽 **qǐlì**	'gorgeous'
凄迷 **qīmí**	(of scenery) 'dreary and hazy'
迤逦 **yǐlǐ**	'winding'
邻近 **línjìn**	'nearby'
宁静 **níngjìng**	'quiet'; 'calm'
宁靖 **níngjìng**	'tranquil'; 'in peace'
葱茏 **cōnglóng**	'luxuriant'
茏葱 **lóngcōng**	'verdant'
馥郁 **fùyù**	(formal) 'sweet-scented'; 'sweet-smelling'
混沌 **hùndùn**	'chaos – the primeval state of the universe'

Directly related to the above-cited major categories, alliterated and rhymed adjectives also abound in areas where human beings can be seen to be making direct evaluations, particularly of their own mental capacity or organisation and physical well-being:

mental situation:

粗糙 **cūcāo**	'coarse'; 'rough'
琐碎 **suǒsuì**	'trifling'; 'trivial'
详细 **xiángxì**	'detailed'; 'minute'

优越 **yōuyuè**   'superior'; 'advantageous'
浮泛 **fúfàn**   'superficial'
间接 **jiànjiē**   'indirect'; 'secondhand'
简捷 **jiǎnjié**   'simple and direct'; 'forthright'
凶险 **xiōngxiǎn**   'dangerous'; 'perilous'
榔槺 **lángkāng**   'bulky'; 'cumbersome'
堂皇 **tánghuáng**   'grand'; 'stately'; 'magnificent'
细腻 **xìnì**   'fine and smooth'; 'exquisite'; 'minute'
笼统 **lǒngtǒng**   'general'; 'sweeping'
简便 **jiǎnbiàn**   'simple and convenient'; 'handy'
牢靠 **láokao**   'firm'; 'sturdy'; 'dependable'
潦草 **liáocǎo**   (of handwriting) 'hasty and careless'; 'sloppy'
高超 **gāochāo**   'superb'; 'excellent'
奥妙 **àomiào**   'profound and subtle'
空洞 **kōngdòng**   'empty'; 'hollow'; 'devoid of content'
完善 **wánshàn**   'perfect'; 'consummate'
荒唐 **huāngtáng**   'absurd'; 'preposterous'
糟糕 **zāogāo**   'how terrible'; 'too bad'
完全 **wánquán**   'complete'; 'whole'
均匀 **jūnyún**   'even'; 'well-distributed'

physical condition:

匆促 **cōngcù**   'hastily'; 'in a hurry'
和缓 **héhuǎn**   'gentle'; 'mild'
拮据 **jiéjū**   'in straitened circumstances'
困苦 **kùnkǔ**   'in privation'
丰富 **fēngfù**   'rich'; 'abundant'; 'plentiful'

悠游 **yōuyóu**   'leisurely and carefree'
舒服 **shūfu**   'comfortable'
美满 **měimǎn**   'happy'; 'perfectly satisfactory'
富庶 **fùshù**   'rich and populous'
富足 **fùzú**   'plentiful'; 'abundant'
艰难 **jiānnán**   'difficult'; 'hard'
惨淡 **cǎndàn**   'gloomy'; 'dismal'; 'dim'
奇异 **qíyì**   'unusual'; 'strange'; 'bizarre'

miscellaneous conditions:

凌乱 **língluàn**   'in disorder'; 'in a mess'
缭乱 **liáoluàn**   'in a turmoil'
纷繁 **fēnfán**   'numerous and complicated'
玲珑 **línglóng**   (of things) 'exquisite'
杂沓 **zátà**   'numerous and disorderly'
零星 **língxīng**   'fragmentary'; 'piecemeal'
肃穆 **sùmù**   'solemn and quiet'; 'solemn and respectful'
荏苒 **rěnrǎn**   (of time) 'elapse imperceptibly'; 'slip by'

永远 **yǒngyuǎn**	'always'; 'forever'	
新鲜 **xīnxiān**	'fresh'; 'new'; 'novel'	
荡漾 **dàngyàng**	'ripple'; 'undulate'	
飘摇 **piāoyáo**	'sway in the wind'	
缭绕 **liáorǎo**	'curl up'; 'wind around'	
古朴 **gǔpǔ**	(of art, architecture, etc.) 'of primitive simplicity'	
简单 **jiǎndān**	'simple'; 'uncomplicated'	
渺小 **miǎoxiǎo**	'tiny'; 'insignificant'; 'paltry'	

If onomatopoeia does little to represent human speech, alliteration and rhyme (together with reduplication) do a great deal:

(a) alliteration:

揶揄 **yéyú**	(written) 'ridicule'
怂恿 **sǒngyǒng**	'instigate'
吩咐 **fēnfù**	'instruct'
唏嘘 **xīxū**	(formal) 'sob or sigh'
呼唤 **hūhuàn**	'call'; 'shout to'
举荐 **jǔjiàn**	'recommend' (a person)
批评 **pīpíng**	'criticise'
诬枉 **wūwǎng**	'slander'; 'calumniate'
挑剔 **tiāoti**	'nitpick'; 'be fastidious'

含糊 **hánhu**	'ambiguous'
含混 **hánhùn**	'indistinct'
流利 **liúlì**	'fluent'
淋漓 **línlí**	(of writing or speech) 'free from inhibition'
喑哑 **yīnyǎ**	(formal) 'mute'; 'dumb'
戏谑 **xìxuè**	'banter'; 'crack jokes'

(b) rhyme:

唠叨 **láodao**	'chatter'
叨唠 **dāolao**	'talk on and on'
咕噜 **gūlu**	'murmur'
命令 **mìnglìng**	'order'; 'command'
宣传 **xuānchuán**	'conduct propaganda'
号召 **hàozhào**	'call'; 'appeal'
报告 **bàogào**	'report'; 'make known'
嘱咐 **zhǔfu**	'enjoin'; 'exhort'
叮咛 **dīngníng**	'urge again and again'; 'exhort'
指使 **zhǐshǐ**	'instigate'; 'incite'

罗嗦 **luōsuō**	'long-winded'
婉转 **wǎnzhuǎn**	'mild and indirect'
荒唐 **huāngtáng**	'absurd'
汗漫 **hànmàn**	'wide of the mark'; 'rambling'

Interestingly enough, not all the lexical items denoting insects, birds, animals
and plants are hyponymically organised; some of them, as we have seen, are
phonaesthetically motivated. The nearest guess we can make about such a
motivation is that these devices of alliteration and rhyme seem to serve to
knit the two constituent mononyms together into a single, unified form, denoting a single entity in the extralinguistic world. Here are some examples:

(a) alliteration:

蜘蛛 **zhīzhū**	'spider'
蟾蜍 **chánchú**	(written) 'toad'
孑孓 **jiéjué**	'wiggler'
蚰蜒 **yóuyán**	'slug'
枇杷 **pípá**	'loquat'

(b) rhyme:

蜻蜓 **qīngtíng**	'dragon-fly'
螟蛉 **mínglíng**	'corn earworm'
螳螂 **tángláng**	'praying mantis'
蛤蟆 **hámá**	'toad'
蜥蜴 **xīyì**	'lizard'
蟑螂 **zhāngláng**	'cockroach'
蜣蜋 **qiāngláng**	'dung beetle'
蚂蚱 **màzha**	(dialectal) 'locust'
蝤蛑 **yóumóu**	'swimming crab'
鹪鹩 **jiāoliáo**	'wren'
鸳鸯 **yuānyāng**	'mandarin duck'
骆驼 **luòtuo**	'camel'
葫芦 **húlu**	'calabash'
苜蓿 **mùxu**	'lucerne'; 'alfalfa'
蒺藜 **jíli**	'puncture vine'

Alliteration and rhyming may, of course, be sporadically found in all types
of words:

仿佛 **fǎngfú**	'seemingly'; 'as if'
饕餮 **tāotiè**	'glutton'; 'gourmand'
阴阳 **yīnyáng**	'(in Chinese thought) *yin* and *yang*, the two opposing principles in nature, the former feminine and negative, the latter masculine and positive'

Rhyme, in particular, is often found to be alternating in -i and -a/-u patterns
in onomatopoeic or symbolic quadrisyllabic expressions:

叽哩呱啦 **jīliguālā**	'talking loudly'
劈里啪啦 **pīlipālā**	'crackling and spluttering'
稀里哗啦 **xīlihuālā**	'sound of rain (falling down)'

滴里搭拉 **dīlidālā**	'hanging loose'
旯里旮旯儿 **jīligālār**	(dial.) 'every nook and cranny'
喊哩喀喳 **qīlikāchā**	'snappy and clear-cut in speaking and doing things'
丁零当郎 **dīnglingdānglāng**	'jingle-jangle'; 'cling-clang'
旯哩咕噜 **jīligūlū**	'talking indistinctly'
稀里呼噜 **xīlihūlū**	(inf.) 'sound of snoring'
嘀哩嘟噜 **dīlidūlū**	'mumbling'; 'muttering'
稀里糊涂 **xīlihútú**	'not knowing what one is doing'

Rhyme is also an outstanding feature of the 'recurrent' patterns of polysyllabic sayings, e.g. (a) recurrent pattern of hexasyllables (i.e. bi-trisyllables): XXX / XXX; (b) bi-quadrisyllables: XXXX / XXXX; (c) bi-pentasyllables: XXXXX / XXXXX; and (d) bi-heptasyllables: XXXXXX / XXXXXX.

Rhyme in such recurrent patterns, too, seems to serve as a 'cohesive' device, meshing the two parts phonaesthetically together:

(a) XXX / XXX:

墙头草/随风倒 **qiángtóu cǎo | suí fēng dǎo**	'grass on the top of a wall which sways with every wind – a fence-sitter' (墙头 **qiángtóu**: the top of a wall; 草 **cǎo**: grass; 随 **suí**: along with; 风 **fēng**: wind; 倒 **dǎo**: fall)
人心齐/泰山移 **rénxīn qí | tàishān yí**	'solidarity moves mountains – unity is almighty' (人心 **rénxīn**: public feeling; 齐 **qí**: together; 泰山 **Tàishān**: Mount Tai (in Shandong Province); 移 **yí**: remove)
灯要亮/火要旺 **dēng yào liàng | huǒ yào wàng**	'lamps must shine brightly and fires burn brightly – things are expected to serve their useful purposes' (灯 **dēng**: lamp; 要 **yào**: want; 亮 **liàng**: light; 火 **huǒ**: fire; 旺 **wàng**: flourishing, vigorous)
不怕难/只怕懒 **bù pà nán | zhǐ pà lǎn**	'it is not difficulty but laziness that is to be feared' (不 **bù**: not; 怕 **pà**: fear; 难 **nán**: difficulty; 只 **zhǐ**: just; 懒 **lǎn**: lazy)

(b) XXXX / XXXX:

一贵一贱/交情乃见
yī guì yī jiàn |
jiāoqíng nǎi jiàn

'true friendship will be revealed when one becomes a V.I.P. and the other remains a commoner'
(一 **yī**: one; 贵 **guì**: noble; 贱 **jiàn**: common 交情 **jiāoqíng**: friendship; 乃 **nǎi**: therefore; 见 **jiàn**: can be seen)

小孔不补/大孔叫苦
xiǎo kǒng bù bǔ |
dà kǒng jiào kǔ

'if one doesn't patch up the holes when they are small, one will feel miserable when the holes become big'
(小孔 **xiǎo kǒng**: small hole; 不 **bù**: not; 补 **bǔ**: mend; 大孔 **dà kǒng**: big hole; 叫苦 **jiào kǔ**: complain)

瓜无滚圆/人无十全
guā wú gǔnyuán |
rén wú shíquán

'there is no melon which is perfectly round nor a person perfect in everyway – nothing is perfect'
(瓜 **guā**: melon; 无 **wú**: cannot be; 滚圆 **gǔnyuán**: rollingly round; 人 **rén**: person; 十全 **shíquán**: perfect)

一顿吃伤/十顿吃汤
yī dùn chī shāng |
shí dùn chī tāng

'overeat in one meal and you will have to fast in ten afterwards'
(一 **yī**: one; 顿 **dùn**: meal; 吃 **chī**: eat; 伤 **shāng**: hurt; 十 **shí**: ten; 汤 **tāng**: soup)

(c) XXXXX / XXXXX:

一个碗不响/两个碗叮当
yī gè wǎn bù xiǎng |
liǎng gè wǎn dīngdāng

'a single bowl will not produce any sound; but when two are put together, they will go "clang, clang" – it takes two to make a quarrel'
(一 **yī**: one; 个 **gè**: measure word; 碗 **wǎn**: bowl; 不 **bù**: not; 响 **xiǎng**: make noise; 两 **liǎng**: two; 叮当 **dīngdāng**: clang)

三个臭皮匠/气死诸葛亮
**sān gè chòu píjiàng |
qìsǐ Zhūgé Liàng**

'three stinking leather-tanners will vex Zhuge Liang to death – three cobblers with their wits combined will be able to outwit Zhuge Liang, the master mind'
(三 **sān**: three; 臭 **chòu**: stinking; 皮匠 **píjiàng**: cobbler; 气死 **qìsǐ**: vex; 诸葛亮 **Zhūgé Liàng**: a historical figure)

工欲善其事/必先利其器
**gōng yù shàn qí shì |
bì xiān lì qí qì**

'a workman must first sharpen his tools if he is to do his work well'
(工 **gōng**: workman; 欲 **yù**: want to; 善 **shàn**: make better; 其 **qí**: his; 事 **shì**: work; 必 **bì**: must; 先 **xiān**: first; 利 **lì**: sharpen; 器 **qì**: tool)

只要功夫深/铁杵磨成针
**zhǐyào gōngfu shēn |
tiěchǔ mó chéng zhēn**

'if you work at it hard enough, you can grind an iron rod into a needle – perseverance spells success'
(只要 **zhǐyào**: only if; 功夫 **gōngfu**: effort; 深 **shēn**: deep; 铁杵 **tiěchǔ**: iron rod; 磨成 **mó chéng**: be ground into; 针 **zhēn**: needle)

(d) XXXXXXX / XXXXXXX:
一个篱笆三个桩/
一个好汉三个帮
**yī gè líba sān gè zhuāng |
yī gè hǎohàn sān gè bāng**

'one good fence needs three stakes to make it fast; one brave man needs three other men to help him – everybody needs help'
(一 **yī**: one; 个 **gè**: measure word; 篱笆 **líba**: hedge; 三 **sān**: three; 桩 **zhuāng**: stake; 好汉 **hǎohàn**: hero; 帮 **bāng**: help)

又要马儿快快跑/
又要马儿不吃草
**yòu yào mǎr kuàikuài pǎo |
yòu yào mǎr bù chī cǎo**

'one wishes that the horse would gallop fast without eating grass – getting without giving'
(又 **yòu**: also; 要 **yào**: want; 马儿 **mǎr**: horse; 快 **kuài**: fast; 跑 **pǎo**: run; 不 **bù**: not; 吃 **chī**: eat; 草 **cǎo**: grass)

It must be noted that in a disyllabic word, alliteration does not usually concur with rhyme as that will generally produce a reduplication, which will be the topic for discussion in the next section. However, there are a small number of disyllabic words in the lexicon which do adopt alliteration with rhyme, with or without tonal variation:[6]

alliteration with rhyme with tonal variation:

崴嵬 **wēiwéi**	(literary) 'towering'	
积极 **jījí**	'active'; 'enthusiastic'	
审慎 **shěnshèn**	'cautious'	
余裕 **yúyù**	'enough and to spare'	
想象 **xiǎngxiàng**	'imagination'; 'fancy'; 'visualise'	
宵小 **xiāoxiǎo**	'thieves or robbers who act under cover of night'	

alliteration with rhyme without tonal variation:

秘密 **mìmì**	'secretive'
和合 **héhé**	'harmonious'
逝世 **shìshì**	'pass away'
鞑靼 **dádá**	'Tartar'
蝇营狗苟 **yíngyíng gǒugǒu**	'shamelessly seek personal gain'

(c) Reduplication

Reduplications are words composed of two reiterated elements neither of which may exist independent of the other. Onomatopoeia and sound symbolism are both carried over into reduplication, particularly in depicting repetitive sounds:

嗒嗒 **dādā**	(of horses' hoofs) 'clatter'
啪啪 **pāpā**	'sound of gun or clapping'
铮铮 **zhēngzhēng**	'clang'
欻欻 **chuāchuā**	'tramp, tramp, tramp'
怦怦 **pēngpēng**	'go pit-a-pat'
霍霍 **huòhuò**	'the scrape of a sword being sharpened'
隆隆 **lónglóng**	(of thunder, gunfire, etc.) 'rumble'
磷磷 **línlín**	'rattle'
辘辘 **lùlù**	(of wheels) 'rumble'

This is especially true of noises made by the blowing wind and the flowing water:

呼呼 **hūhū**	(of wind) 'blowing'
嗖嗖 **sōusōu**	'rustle'

---

[6] This is only possible in a tonal and graphic language like Chinese. However, such lexemes are extremely rare in the lexicon.

啸啸 **xiāoxiāo**	(of the wind and rain) 'whistling and pattering'
瑟瑟 **sèsè**	(of the wind) 'rustle'
飒飒 **sàsà**	'sough'
簌簌 **sùsù**	'rustle'
习习 **xíxí**	(of the wind) 'blow gently'
涓涓 **juānjuān**	(written) 'trickling sluggishly'
潺潺 **chánchán**	'babble'
淙淙 **cóngcóng**	'gurgling'
涔涔 **céncén**	(written) 'dripping'
汩汩 **gǔgǔ**	'gurgle'

Human panting, shouting, laughing, talking, etc. are especially at home with reduplication, the notion of 'repetition' being perhaps the underlying motivating force:

咻咻 **xiùxiù**	'pant noisily'
絮絮 **xùxù**	'puff hard'
嚷嚷 **rāngrang**	(colloq.) 'yell'
吵吵 **chāochao**	'make a row'
嗷嗷 **āo'āo**	'crying out loud'
哈哈 **hāhā**	'laugh heartily'
呵呵 **hēhē**	'roar with laughter'
嗤嗤 **chīchī**	'titter'
叽叽嘎嘎 **jījigāgā**	'laughing'; 'cackling'
喳喳 **chācha**	'whisper'
嚷嚷 **nāngnang**	'speak in a low voice'
喊喊喳喳 **qīqīchāchā**	'jabber'; 'chatter'
叽叽喳喳 **jījizhāzhā**	'chattering away'
喃喃 **nánnán**	'mutter'
哝哝 **nóngnong**	'talk in undertones'
琅琅 **lángláng**	'the sound of reading'

This is a prolific device in quadrisyllabic idioms about 'talking'. Among a few dozens are the following:

侃侃而谈 **kǎnkǎn ér tán**	'speak with fervour and assurance'
念念有词 **niànniàn yǒu cí**	'mutter incantations'
切切私语 **qièqiè sīyǔ**	'talk in whispers'
娓娓不倦 **wěiwěi bùjuàn**	'talk tirelessly'

Reduplication seems also to have derived from the notion of 'repetition' and its related notions of 'plurality' and 'continuation', etc.:

事事 **shìshì**	'everything'
处处 **chùchù**	'everywhere'
层层 **céngcéng**	'layer upon layer'

框框 **kuāngkuang**	'restrictions'
累累 **léiléi**	'clusters of'
家家户户 **jiājiāhùhù**	'every household'
坛坛罐罐 **tántánguànguàn**	'pots and pans'

These underlying concepts of repetition and plurality (and therefore intensity) find their reflection in the formulation of some of the adverbs and adjectives in the language, e.g.

渐渐 **jiànjiàn**	'little by little'
每每 **měiměi**	'often'
迟迟 **chíchí**	'slowly'
久久 **jiǔjiǔ**	'for a long time'
源源 **yuányuán**	'in a steady stream'
悄悄 **qiāoqiāo**	'quietly'; 'on the quiet'
偷偷 **tōutōu**	'stealthily'; 'on the sly'

了了 **liǎoliǎo**	(formal) 'know clearly'
脉脉 **mòmò**	'affectionate'; 'loving'; 'amorous'
嚅嚅 **rúrú**	'hem and haw'
巍巍 **wēiwēi**	'towering'; 'lofty'
森森 **sēnsēn**	'dense'
莽莽 **mǎngmǎng**	'luxuriant'; 'rank'
茫茫 **mángmáng**	'vast and indistinct'

Some adverbs are seen to derive from monosyllabic adjectival lexemes through reduplication. The reiterated part either retains its original tone or changes to the first (i.e. level) tone when 'erised' (儿化 **érhuà**):

慢慢 **mànmàn** 'slow'	慢慢儿(的) **mànmānr(de)** 'slowly'
静静 **jìngjìng** 'quiet'	静静儿(的) **jìngjīngr(de)** 'quietly'
好好 **hǎohǎo** 'good'	好好儿(的) **hǎohāor(de)** 'well'

With disyllabic adjectival lexemes (AB), reduplication can take the form of either AABB or ABAB. There are, however, more reduplications of the first type than the second:[7]

(a) AABB:

恭敬 **gōngjìng** 'respectful'	恭恭敬敬 **gōnggōngjìngjìng**
冷清 **lěngqīng** 'desolate'	冷冷清清 **lěnglěngqīngqīng**
空洞 **kōngdòng** 'devoid of content'	空空洞洞 **kōngkōngdòngdòng**
干净 **gānjìng** 'neat and tidy'	干干净净 **gāngānjìngjìng**
快乐 **kuàilè** 'cheerful'	快快乐乐 **kuàikuàilèlè**
太平 **tàipíng** 'peaceful and tranquil'	太太平平 **tàitàipíngpíng**

---

[7] Cf. Lü, Shuxiang (吕叔湘) 1980.

With the AABB type, the BB either retains its original tone or changes to first (i.e. level) tone, e.g.

干干净净 **gānganjìngjìng**　　vs　　干干净净 **gānganjīngjīng**
空空洞洞 **kōngkongdòngdòng**　vs　　空空洞洞 **kōngkongdōngdōng**

A few of them even have alternative forms of A li AB, e.g.

古怪 **gǔguài** 'eccentric'　　　　古里古怪 **gǔligǔguài**
糊涂 **hútu** 'muddled'　　　　　糊里糊涂 **húlihútu**
罗嗦 **luōsuō** 'long-winded'　　　罗里罗嗦 **luōliluōsuō**

　(b)　ABAB:
　　　　滚烫 **gǔntàng** 'boiling hot'　　滚烫滚烫 **gǔntànggǔntàng**
　　　　通亮 **tōngliàng** 'brightly lit'　通亮通亮 **tōngliàngtōngliàng**
　　　　喷香 **pènxiāng** 'delicious'　　喷香喷香 **pènxiāngpènxiāng**

Reduplication is seen to be extremely productive. We find that the reduplicative elements in quadrisyllabic idioms may come first or last in the idiom or parallel with each other, e.g.

彬彬有礼 **bīnbīn yǒu lǐ**　　　'refined and courteous'
昏昏欲睡 **hūnhūn yù shuì**　　'drowsy'
欣欣向荣 **xīnxīn xiàng róng**　'flourishing'
津津乐道 **jīnjīn lè dào**　　　'take delight in talking about';
　　　　　　　　　　　　　　　'dwell upon with great relish'

衣冠楚楚 **yīguān chǔchǔ**　　'immaculately dressed'
神采奕奕 **shéncǎi yìyì**　　　'glowing with health and radiating
　　　　　　　　　　　　　　　vitality'
忧心忡忡 **yōuxīn chōngchōng**　'deeply worried'; 'care-laden';
　　　　　　　　　　　　　　　'weighed down with anxieties'
可怜巴巴 **kěliánbābā**　　　'pitiable'; 'pathetic'

熙熙攘攘 **xīxī rǎngrǎng**　　'bustling with activity'
兢兢业业 **jīngjīngyèyè**　　　'cautious and conscientious'
鬼鬼祟祟 **guǐguǐsuìsuì**　　　'sneaking'
轰轰烈烈 **hōnghōnglièliè**　　'on a grand and spectacular scale';
　　　　　　　　　　　　　　　'vigorous'; 'dynamic'

In trisyllabic adjectives and adverbs, phonaesthetic elements are also found to be attached to their meaningful stems. The presence of these phonaesthemes intensifies or heightens the emotion or atmosphere originally associated with these adjectives or adverbs, which largely belong to perceptive categories:[8]

---

[8] Cf. Lü, Shuxiang 1980: 642–53.

hearing:

乱哄哄 **luànhōnghōng**   'in a hubbub'; 'tumultuous'; 'in an uproar'

闹嚷嚷 **nàorāngrāng**   'boisterous'

冷清清 **lěngqīngqīng**   'cold and cheerless'

sight:

colour:

红彤彤 **hóngtōngtōng**   'bright red'

黑黝黝 **hēiyōuyōu**   'shiny black'

黄澄澄 **huángdēngdēng**   'glistening yellow'

蓝盈盈 **lányīngyīng**   'bright blue'

绿茸茸 **lǜrōngrōng**   'lush green'

白皑皑 **bái'ái'ái**   (of snow, frost, etc.) 'pure white'

灰蒙蒙 **huīméngméng**   'dusky'; 'overcast'

金灿灿 **jīncàncàn**   'glittering'

miscellaneous:

亮晶晶 **liàngjīngjīng**   'glittering'; 'sparkling'; 'glistening'

厚墩墩 **hòudūndūn**   'very thick'

直挺挺 **zhítǐngtǐng**   'bolt upright'

密匝匝 **mìzāzā**   'thick'; 'dense'

空荡荡 **kōngdàngdàng**   'empty'; 'deserted'

满登登 **mǎndēngdēng**   'full'

光秃秃 **guāngtūtū**   'bare'; 'bald'

稀溜溜 **xīliūliū**   (of porridge, soup, etc.) 'very thin'

水汪汪 **shuǐwāngwāng**   'full of water'; 'very wet'

油汪汪 **yóuwāngwāng**   'dripping with oil'; 'glossy'

清凌凌 **qīnglīnglīng**   (of water) 'clear and rippling'

appearances resulting from different physical or psychological conditions:

矮墩墩 **ǎidūndūn**   'pudgy'; 'dumpy'; 'stumpy'

胖乎乎 **pànghūhū**   (of children) 'plump'; 'chubby'; 'podgy'

慢悠悠 **mànyōuyōu**   'unhurried'; 'leisurely'

活生生 **huóshēngshēng**   'real'; 'living'

虚飘飘 **xūpiāopiāo**   'shaky'; 'unsteady'

傻呵呵 **shǎhēhē**   'simple-minded'; 'silly'

文绉绉 **wénzhōuzhōu**   'genteel'

空荡荡 **kōngdàngdàng**   'empty'; 'deserted'

孤零零 **gūlīnglīng**   'solitary'; 'lonely'

急巴巴 **jíbābā**   'anxious'; 'impatient'

眼睁睁 **yǎnzhēngzhēng**   'looking on helplessly or unfeelingly'

直勾勾 **zhígōugōu**   (stare) 'fixedly'

懒洋洋 **lǎnyāngyāng**   'languid'; 'listless'

醉醺醺 **zuìxūnxūn**   'sottish'; 'drunk'

赤裸裸 **chìluǒluǒ**   'stark naked'; 'undisguised'

怒冲冲 **nùchōngchōng**	'in a rage'
怯生生 **qièshēngshēng**	'in a timid manner'
羞答答 **xiūdādā**	'coy'; 'shy'; 'bashful'
娇滴滴 **jiāodīdī**	'affectedly sweet'
嗲溜溜 **diǎliūliū**	'coquettish'; 'flirtatious'
兴冲冲 **xìngchōngchōng**	'with joy and expedition'; 'excitedly'
乐陶陶 **lètáotáo**	'cheerful'; 'happy'; 'joyful'
笑眯眯 **xiàomīmī**	'smiling'; 'with a genial smile on one's face'
面团团 **miàntuántuán**	'chubby'; 'podgy'
汗津津 **hànjīnjīn**	'sweaty'; 'moist with sweat'
泪汪汪 **lèiwāngwāng**	(eyes) 'brimming with tears'
气咻咻 **qìxiūxiū**	'panting'; 'gasping for breath'

smell:

香喷喷 **xiāngpēnpēn**	'sweet-smelling'
臭烘烘 **chòuhōnghōng**	'stinking'; 'foul-smelling'; 'smelly'

taste:

甜丝丝 **tiánsīsī**	'pleasantly sweet'
辣乎乎 **làhūhū**	'peppery'; 'hot'
酸溜溜 **suānliūliū**	'sour'; 'pungent'; 'tingle'
咸津津 **xiánjīnjīn**	'with a nice saltish taste'

touch:

光溜溜 **guāngliūliū**	'smooth'
软绵绵 **ruǎnmiānmiān**	'soft'; 'weak'
冷飕飕 **lěngsōusōu**	(of wind) 'chilling'; 'chilly'
紧巴巴 **jǐnbābā**	'tight'
硬绷绷 **yìngbēngbēng**	'very hard'; 'very stiff'
沉甸甸 **chéndiàndiàn**	'heavy'
轻飘飘 **qīngpiāopiāo**	'light'; 'buoyant'
热烘烘 **rèhōnghōng**	'very warm'
凉丝丝 **liángsīsī**	'coolish'; 'rather cool'
火辣辣 **huǒlālā**	'burning'
暖洋洋 **nuǎnyángyáng**	'warm'
干巴巴 **gānbābā**	'dull and dry'; 'insipid'; 'dry-as-dust'
潮呼呼 **cháohūhū**	'damp'; 'dank'; 'clammy'
湿漉漉 **shīlūlū**	'moist'; 'damp'
滑溜溜 **huáliuliu**	'slippery'

metaphor:

响当当 **xiǎngdāngdāng**	(of a person) 'of resounding fame'; 'outstanding'
顶呱呱 **dǐngguāguā**	'tip-top'; 'first-rate'; 'excellent'

In many cases, more than one type of phonaestheme may be attached to an individual stem. Then the phonaesthemes may also become meaning differentiators:[9] e.g.

黑压压 **hēiyāyā**	used in association	'dense crowds of people'
黑黝黝 **hēiyǒuyōu**	with	'colour of skin tanned by sunshine'
黑漆漆 **hēiqīqī**		'a dark place'
黑黢黢 **hēiqūqū**		'a dark surrounding'
黑沉沉 **hēichēnchēn**		'colour of the sky'
黑洞洞 **hēidōngdōng**		'darkness in an enclosure'
黑糊糊 **hēihūhū**		'vague mass in the distance'
黑油油 **hēiyǒuyōu**		'blackness with a shiny surface'

Phonaesthemes in trisyllabic adjectives, while usually suffixed, are in a few instances prefixed:

蒙蒙亮 **mēngmēngliàng**	'first glimmer of dawn'; 'daybreak'
笔笔直 **bǐbǐzhí**	'perfectly straight'; 'straight as a ramrod'
喷喷香 **pènpènxiāng**	'fragrant'; 'delicious'
麻麻黑 **māmahēi**	(dial.) 'dusk'
团团转 **tuántuánzhuàn**	'round and round'

As a general rule, the meaningful reiterative phonaesthemes either retain their original tones or change uniformly to the first (i.e. level) tone when incorporated into the trisyllabic lexemes. So we see that in reduplication, there is often the distant echoing of the first tone in onomatopoeia and an awareness of tonal variation and harmony in sound symbolism.

It is interesting to find that kinship terms in their address forms are mostly reduplications. Perhaps they started off with the addresser's intention to draw emphatically the attention of the addressee:

爸爸 **bàba** 'dad'
妈妈 **māma** 'mum'
爷爷 **yéye** 'grandpa'
奶奶 **nǎinai** 'grandma'
哥哥 **gēge** '(elder) brother'
弟弟 **dìdi** '(younger) brother'
姐姐 **jiějie** '(elder) sister'
妹妹 **mèimei** '(younger) sister'

But reduplication as a phonaesthetic feature of lexical structures must be distinguished from reduplication as a syntactic device, which, in fact, is freely applicable to verbs, marking (a) brief duration, e.g. 看 **kàn** 'look' → 看看

---

[9] Cf. Yip Po-Ching & Zhang Xiaoming 1995: 44.

kànkan 'have a look', 介绍 **jièshào** 'introduce' → 介绍介绍 **jièshàojièshào** 'give a brief introduction'; or (b) augmentation, e.g. 谢谢 **xièxie** 'many thanks', etc.

Reduplication, however, is not the only way of phonaesthetic elongation of a lexical item for the sake of emphasis. An *echoing rhyme* with the help of an unstressed, meaningless syllable such as 不 *bu* in a quadrisyllabic form is also a familiar device with some adjectives indicating perceptions: e.g.

> 黑不溜秋 **hēibuliūqiū** (dial.) 'swarthy'
> 酸不溜丢 **suānbuliūdiū** (dial.) 'unpleasantly sour'
> 花不棱登 **huābulēngdēng** 'flashy'; 'gaudy'
> 滑不唧溜 **huábujīliū** (dial.) 'slippery'
> 灰不喇唧 **huībulājī** (dial.) 'dull grey'
> 凉不丝儿 **liángbusīr** (inf.) 'cool'
> 咸不唧儿 **xiánbujīr** (dial.) 'saltyish'
> 黑咕隆咚 **hēigulōngdōng** 'pitch-dark'
> 苦剌吧唧 **kǔlabājī** 'bitter'

(d) Telescopation

If reduplication or reiterated rhyme is the lengthening of a sound image for the sake of descriptive impressiveness, telescopation is then the very opposite of it, a shortening of a sound image through syllabic sandhi or assimilation for the sake of verbal brevity. Here are some examples:

不要 **bù yào**	→	别 **bié** 'don't'
不用 **bù yòng**	→	甭 **béng** 'needn't'
窟窿 **kūlong**	→	孔 **kǒng** 'hole'; 'opening'; 'aperture'
胡同 **hútòng**	→	巷 **xiàng** 'lane'; 'alley'[10]
(诉)之于 **(sù) zhī yú**	→	(诉)诸 **(sù) zhū** 'resort to'
(勉)之焉 **(miǎn) zhī yān**	→	(勉)旃 **(miǎn) zhān** 'encourage'; 'urge'

TONE IMAGERIES

(a) Tonal Conversion

Conversion is an economic way of word formation. It is achieved by making use of an identical word form (or monomym) for different word classes. In most cases in Chinese, only the verbal co-text can provide clues to the part of speech in which a word is used as there are usually no phonological or morphological changes involved. These conversions from one word class to another by means of providing a specific verbal or textual environment may be called *co-textual conversions*. For example,

---

[10] Cf. the pronunciation of 巷 in 巷道 **[hàngdào]** '(mining) tunnel'.

奶 **nǎi** (breast) 'milk'	→	奶 **nǎi** 'breast-feed'; 'suckle'
漆 **qī** 'paint'	→	漆 **qī** 'to paint'
弓 **gōng** 'a bow'	→	弓着背 **gōngzhe bèi** 'arch one's back'
梗 **gěng** 'a slender piece of wood	→	梗着脖子 **gěngzhe bózi** 'straighten up one's neck'
湾 **wān** 'river bend'; 'gulf'; 'bay'	→	湾 **wān** 'to cast anchor'; 'to moor'
岐视 **qíshì** 'discriminate'	→	岐视 **qíshì** 'discrimination against'
搭档 **dādàng** 'team up'	→	搭档 **dādàng** 'partner'
沿河 **yán hé** 'along the river'	→	河沿儿 **héyánr** 'riverside'

In a small number of cases, however, a tone change can be seen in the process of conversion. These conversions can therefore be labelled as *tonal conversions*. Tonal conversion, in fact, is no longer a productive means of word formation in Modern Standard Chinese. Here are a few examples:

钉子 **dīngzi** 'nail'	→	钉钉子 **dìng dīngzi** 'drive in a nail'
膏 **gāo** 'ointment'	→	膏车 **gào chē** 'lubricate the axle of a cart'
王 **wáng** 'monarch'	→	王天下 **wàng tiānxià** 'rule over the empire'
妻子 **qīzi** 'wife'	→	妻 **qì** (formal) 'marry a girl to a man'
泥 **ní** 'mud'	→	泥墙 **nì qiáng** 'cover the crevices in a wall with plaster'
瓦 **wǎ** 'tile'	→	瓦瓦 **wà wǎ** 'cover a roof with tiles'
语言 **yǔyán** 'language'	→	语人 **yù rén** '(written) inform people'

While co-textual conversions in Chinese take place between all parts of speech, tonal conversions occur mostly between nouns and verbs. It seems that the verb derived from the noun (whatever tone it originally had) was generally assigned a fourth (i.e. falling) tone as we can see from the above examples. However, if the original noun was already in a fourth tone, the verb was then given a first (i.e. level) tone: e.g.

扇子 **shànzi** 'fan'	→	扇扇子 **shān shànzi** 'fan oneself'; 'use a fan'
背 **bèi** '(of body) back'	→	背孩子 **bēi háizi** 'carry a baby on one's back'
担子 **dànzi** 'loads' (on a shoulder pole)	→	担水 **dān shuǐ** 'carry water' (with a shoulder pole)
秤 **chèng** 'steelyard'	→	称 **chēng** 'weigh' (something)[11]
教育 **jiàoyù** 'education'	→	教 **jiāo** 'teach'; 'instruct'

---

[11] Note that in the last example there is a slight modification in the written form: 秤, the noun versus 称, the verb.

If a fourth tone noun produces a fourth tone verb, it is to be regarded as a co-textual conversion rather than an exceptional case in tonal conversion:

手铐 **shǒukào** 'handcuffs'   →   铐起来 **kào qǐlái** 'put handcuffs on'
锉 **cuò** 'a file'   →   锉 **cuò** 'to file'
锯 **jù** 'a saw'   →   锯 **jù** 'to saw'

In fact all nouns indicating instruments or tools in the language (whichever tones they are in) are capable of such a co-textual conversion.

Where we find that the verb adopts a third (i.e. falling-rising) or a second (i.e. rising) tone with matching nouns in the fourth tones, these could very well be cases where the nouns are derivatives of the verbs (which were originally of various tones) instead of the other way round. For example,

扫帚 **sàozhou** 'broom'   ←   扫雪 **sǎo xuě** 'sweep away the snow'
簸箕 **bòji** 'winnowing fan'   ←   簸谷 **bǒ gǔ** 'winnow away the chaff'
数 **shù** 'number'; 'figure'   ←   数 **shǔ** 'count'
缝 **fèng** 'crack'; 'seam'   ←   缝 **féng** 'stitch'; 'sew'
量 **liàng** 'quantity'   ←   量 **liáng** 'measure'; 'estimate'
磨 **mò** 'millstones'   ←   磨 **mó** 'rub'; 'grind'
处所 **chùsuǒ** 'location'   ←   相处 **xiāngchǔ** 'get along (with one another)'

Semantically speaking, tonal conversions seem to favour derivations from nouns indicating instruments or materials to verbs indicating actions or activities employing these instruments or materials.

苫 **shān** 'straw mat'   →   苫 **shàn** 'cover with a straw mat, tarpaulin, etc.'
钢 **gāng** 'steel'   →   钢 **gàng** 'sharpen'; 'whet'; 'strop'
泥 **ní** 'mud'; 'plaster'   →   泥 **nì** 'daub with plaster, putty, etc.'
咽喉 **yānhóu** 'throat'   →   咽 **yàn** 'swallow'

There are a small number of tonal conversions from adjectives to verbs following a similar pattern:

凉 **liáng** 'cool'; 'cold'   →   凉 **liàng** 'let something cool off'
散 **sǎn** 'scattered'   →   散 **sàn** 'break up'; 'disperse'[12]
好 **hǎo** 'good'   →   好 **hào** 'like'

A tonal change (sometimes with a slight modification in the sounds as well) can encode cognate or related ideas. For instance,

(a) In some cases, a tonal change produces an antonym, synonym or cognate word:

[12] Note that 散 [**sǎn**] also has a co-textual conversion: 散 [**sǎn**] 'come loose'; 'fall apart'; 'not hold together'.

买 **mǎi** 'buy'   vs   卖 **mài** 'sell'
晃 **huǎng** 'flash past'   晃 **huàng** 'shake'; 'sway'
少 **shǎo** 'few'; 'little'; 'less'   少 **shào** 'young'
鲜 **xiān** 'fresh'   鲜 **xiǎn** 'rare'; 'little'[13]
横 **héng** 'horizontal'   横 **hèng** 'harsh'; 'perverse'
和 **hé** 'and'; 'gentle'; 'peace'   和 **hè** 'join in singing';
                                          'compose a poem in reply'
转身 **zhuǎnshēn** 'turn round'   转动 **zhuàndòng** 'revolve'; 'rotate'

(b) In other cases, a slight modification produces related ideas:

乐 **lè** 'happy'   vs   乐 **yuè** 'music'
传 **chuán** 'pass on'   传 **zhuàn** 'biography'
弹 **tán** 'shoot' (with a catapult, etc.)   弹 **dàn** 'pellet'; 'bullet'

In the second situation, a tonal conversion is often accompanied by a reduction in the aspiration of the initial consonant:[14]

长 **cháng** 'long'   vs   长 **zhǎng** 'grow'
重 **chóng** 'duplicate'   重 **zhòng** 'heavy'
藏 **cáng** 'hide'; 'conceal'   宝藏 **bǎozàng** 'treasure'
囤 **tún** 'store up'; 'hoard'   囤 **dùn** 'a grain bin'
驮 **tuó** (of animal)   驮子 **duòzi** 'load'
    'carry on the back'   (on a pack animal)
调 **tiáo** 'mix'; 'adjust'   调 **diào** 'transfer'; 'melody'

(b) Word Stress

Among disyllabic words, word stress is often used to distinguish meanings or word classes between homonyms or homophones. As a general rule, if the first syllable is stressed, the second syllable can be either unstressed or semi-stressed, whereas if the second syllable is stressed, the first syllable is usually semi-stressed.[15]

To indicate the three different levels of stress, we will use the notations: *s* for stressed syllables, *s* for semi-stressed syllables and *u* for unstressed syllables. There are, therefore, three possible stress constructions in all the disyllabic words of the lexicon:

s u   s s   s s

In Chinese, there are more '*s s*' stress constructions than '*s u*' and '*s s*' constructions taken together. Sometimes different stress patterns are:

---

[13] Note that the third tone 鲜 is found in 寡廉鲜耻 [**guǎ lián xiǎn chǐ**] 'lost to shame'; 'shameless'.
[14] According to Li, Baorui (李葆瑞) 1960: 29–31.
[15] Cf. Yan, Zuoyan (殷作炎) 1982; Shi, Dingguo (史定国) 1992.

(1) for differentiation of meaning:

s u / s s	vs	*s s*
人家 **rénjia** 'others'; 'other people'		**rénjiā** 'family'
地方 **dìfang** 'place'; 'space'		**dìfāng** 'local'; 'regional'
来往 **láiwang** 'social intercourse'		**láiwǎng** 'come and go'
不管 **bùguǎn** 'regardless of'		**bùguǎn** 'pay no heed to'
本事 **běnshi** 'skill'; 'ability'		**běnshì** 'this matter'
大意 **dàyi** 'careless'		**dàyì** 'gist'; 'general idea'
过去 **guòqu** 'to pass by'; 'go over'		**guòqù** 'in the past'; 'formerly'
冷战 **lěngzhan** 'shiver'		**lěngzhàn** 'cold war'
地道 **dìdao** 'typical'; 'genuine'; 'idiomatic'		**dìdào** 'tunnel'
等等 **děngdeng** 'wait a minute'		**děngděng** 'and so on'

(2) for differentiation of word class:

s u / s s	vs	*s s*
多少 **duōshao** pronoun: 'how many'		**duōshǎo** adjective: 'how many'
报告 **bàogao** verb: 'to report'		**bàogào** noun: 'a report'
练习 **liànxi** verb: 'to drill'		**liànxí** noun: 'drills'
记录 **jìlu** verb: 'to take minutes'		**jìlù** noun 'minutes'; 'records'
下场 **xiàchang** noun: 'bad consequence'		**xiàchǎng** verb: 'to go off the stage'
编辑 **biānjí** verb: 'to edit'; 'compile'		**biānjí** noun: 'editor'; 'compiler'
将军 **jiāngjūn** noun: 'a general'		**jiāngjūn** verb: 'to checkmate'

(3) a remedy against homophonic disyllabic words: e.g.

s u / s s	vs	*s s*
报酬 **bàochou** 'reward'		报仇 **bàochóu** 'to revenge'
主意 **zhǔyi** 'idea'; 'suggestion'		主义 **zhǔyì** '-ism'; 'principle'
敢情 **gǎnqing** 'of course'; 'indeed'		感情 **gǎnqíng** 'feeling'; 'emotion'
散布 **sànbù** 'disseminate'		散步 **sànbù** 'take a walk'

(c) Tonal Sequence, Variation and Harmony

In the majority of cases (80%), the preferred tonal sequence seems to be an internal requirement of lexical composition in the juxtapositional type of disyllabic lexemes.[16] The general rule is that, in cases where meaning does not over-rule, the tones normally follow the order of : first (level), second (rise),

---

[16] Chen, Ai-wen and Yu, Ping (陈爱文 于平) 1979.

third (fall–rise) and fourth (fall) tones, supposedly the easiest way of pronouncing these juxtapositions. So the tonal patterns of such a juxtapositional disyllabic lexeme can be:

1/1			
1/2	2/2		
1/3	2/3	3/3	
1/4	2/4	3/4	4/4
攻击 gōngjī			
'attack'			
光明 guāngmíng	疲乏 pífá		
'bright'	'weary'		
聪颖 cōngyǐng	烦恼 fánnǎo	侮辱 wǔrǔ	
'intelligent'	'vexed'	'insult'	
骄傲 jiāo'ào	惭愧 cánkuì	谨慎 jǐnshèn	盼望 pànwàng
'proud'	'ashamed'	'prudent'	'hope for'

This is borne out by the fact that when we look at a set of juxtapositional disyllabic lexemes with the same juxtaposer mononym, if it is a level tone, it generally becomes the first mononym in the concatenation (e.g. 悲惨, 悲愁, 悲伤, 悲痛, etc.), and if it is a falling tone, it is most likely to become the second mononym (e.g. 华丽, 美丽, 秀丽, etc.). But when the preferred tonal sequence is not followed, there are usually factors involving a semantic contrast, an inherent logic in meaning, or a lexical analogy, etc., e.g.

紧要 jǐnyào 'crucial'	要紧 yàojǐn 'essential'
欢喜 huānxǐ 'delighted'	喜欢 xǐhuan 'like'
兵士 bīngshì 'soldier'	士兵 shìbīng 'rank-and-file'
始终 shǐzhōng	3/1 (analogous to 始末 shǐmò, which is 3/4)
'from start to finish'	
恐慌 kǒnghuāng 'panic'	3/1 (analogous to 恐惧 kǒngjù, which is 3/4)
秀美 xiùměi 'graceful'	4/3 (analogous to 秀丽 xiùlì, which is 4/4)

In polysyllabic units, tonal variation and harmony are seen to follow a classical dichotomous contrast of level tones (which are first and second tones) and oblique tones (which are third and fourth tones).

In a quadrisyllabic idiom of ABCD, therefore, B and D must be either in tonal variation (i.e. level tones versus oblique tones) or in tonal harmony (i.e. level tones versus level tones or oblique tones versus oblique tones). As far as A and C are concerned, it is not important whether they are level or oblique tones if B and D are in tonal variation. However, it becomes im-portant that A and C or at least one of them, i.e. either A or C, should be in tonal contrast with B and D if the latter are in tonal harmony. That is to say, if B and D are two level tones, at least one oblique tone must be introduced in A or C; likewise, if B and D are two oblique tones, at least one level tone is necessary in A or C. This is to retain a tonal opposition in the idiom. In other words, there must be at least one opposing tone in an idiom. This gives us fourteen tonal possibilities in a quadrisyllabic idiom as L L L L and O O O O are ruled out:

L L L O   L L O O   L O O O   L O L O   L O O L
L L O L   L O L L   O O O L   O O L L   O L L L
O L O L   O L L O   O O L O   O L O O

In the following, one example is given for each:

L L L O	东拼西凑 **dōng pīn xī còu**	'scrape together'; 'knock together'
L L O O	劈头盖脸 **pītóu gàiliǎn**	'right in the face'
L O O O	食古不化 **shí gǔ bù huà**	'be half-baked pedant' (lit. swallow ancient learning without digesting it)
L O L O	黄道吉日 **huángdào jírì**	'propitious date'; 'lucky day'
L O O L	十室九空 **shí shì jiǔ kōng**	'a scene of desolation' (lit. nine houses out of ten are deserted)
L L O L	披沙拣金 **pī shā jiǎn jīn**	'get essentials from a large mass of material' (lit. sort out the fine gold from the sand)
L O L L	劳燕分飞 **láo yàn fēn fēi**	'separate or part company' (lit. like the shrike and the swallow who fly in different directions)
O O O L	乳臭未干 **rǔ chòu wèi gān**	'be wet behind the ears' (lit. still smell of one's mother's milk)
O O L L	各奔前程 **gè bèn qiánchéng**	'each pursues his own course'
O L L L	反戈一击 **fǎn gē yī jī**	turn against those one has wrongly associated with (lit. turn one's weapon around and strike)
O L O L	去粗取精 **qù cū qǔ jīng**	'discard the dross and select the essential'
O L L O	径情直遂 **jìng qíng zhí suì**	'as smoothly as one would wish'
O O L O	洞若观火 **dòng ruò guān huǒ**	'see something as clearly as a blazing fire'
O L O O	娇柔造作 **jiǎoróu zàozuò**	'affected'; 'artificial'

One might find an exception here and there that does not adhere to this tonal contrast. For example, 声东击西 **shēng dōng jī xī** 'make a feint to the east and attack the west' is an LLLL. But this is probably due to tonal changes of some of the words over the ages. 击 **jī** in this idiom might well be an 'entering tone' in classical Chinese, as it still is in present-day Cantonese.

In pentasyllabic or heptasyllabic idioms, definite patterns of tonal variation and harmony are found. Being a leftover from Tang poetics, such tonal alterations are but an acoustic flourish and not a universal requirement in these polysyllabic units, which have been in fact acquired through the ages from vernacular sources as well as classical ones and are not all taken from Tang poems.

Any bi-pentasyllable or bi-peptasyllable will be regarded as being in conformity with the tonal requirement if it follows patterns like:[17]

Standard		Variation		
OOLLO	or	LOLLO		
LLOOL				
LLLOO		OLLOO	or	LLOLO
OOLLL		LOOLL		

From this we see that the tone of the first mononym in the pentasyllable can be varied. In heptasyllables, we have the following tonal patterns:

Standard	Variation	
LL/OOLLO	OL/- - - -	
OO/LLOOL	LO/- - - -	
OO/LLLOO	LO/- - - -	etc.
LL/OOOLL	OL/- - - -	

We find that in heptasyllables the tonal patterns of the latter half, i.e. the five syllables counted from the end, are in exact correspondence with the tonal patterns of pentasyllables. The variation of heptasyllables therefore occurs in the first of the first two syllables. The fact that OLOOL or OO/OLOOL are impossible derives from a strict requirement of Tang poetics that in any one line of poem there should be no less than one instance in which two level tones occur in succession. Here are some examples:

妙在不言中 **miào zài bù yán zhōng** 'the charm lies in what is left unsaid'
O O O L L

贪多嚼不烂 **tān duō jiáo bù làn** 'bite off more than one can chew'
L L L O O

万丈高楼平地起 **wànzhàng gāolóu píngdì qǐ**
O O L L L O O
'great oaks from little acorns grow'

[17] Wang, Li (王力) 1977.

不是冤家不聚头 **bùshì yuānjia bù jùtóu**
O O L L O O L
'enemies and lovers are destined to meet'

In a synchronic analysis, however, because tones have changed over the ages, there is no absolute guarantee that all such sayings will conform to the required tonal contrasts.

INTERJECTIONS

Interjections are phonaesthetically oriented words which are spontaneous expressions of positive or negative feelings and attitudes of the utterer and which usually herald other more meaningful utterances. They are perhaps the best examples of the interplay between various tones in the language. Interjections in Chinese, except for a few disyllables, are generally monosyllabic.

In more emotional or lively contexts, only vowel sounds are heard:

啊 **ā**	admiration
啊 **á**	asking another speaker to repeat
啊 **ǎ**	suspicion
啊 **à**	agreement or promise
哎 **āi**	pleasant surprise
唉 **ái**	disappointment
嗳 **ǎi**	disagreement
嗳 **ài**	regret
喔 **ō**	sudden realisation
哦 **ó**	disbelief
嚄 **ǒ**	surprise
噢 **ò**	enlightenment

It is not surprising to find that the arbitrariness of tones seems to become less arbitrary in interjections. Generally speaking, level tones seem to be representative of more pleasant feelings: **ā** (admiration), **āi** (pleasant surprise), **ē** (greeting); rising tones, of questioning attitude: **á** (asking for repetition), **é** (disbelief); falling-rising tones, of contradiction: **ǎ** (suspicion), **ǎi** (disagreement), **ě** (contradiction); falling tones, of finality: **à** (agreement), **ài** (regret), **è** (promise), **ò** (enlightenment). It is perhaps also true to say that a change in the vowel does not seem to matter as much as a change in the tone on such occasions as they all express more or less identical or overlapping feelings.

When sometimes these pure vowels are modified, they are usually modified by the semi-vowels w or y or the velar fricative h:

哟 **yō**	expressing unexpectedness
咦 **yí**	bewilderment
喂 **wèi**	calling attention (= hello)
嘿 **hēi**	calling attention
嘿嘿 **hēihēi**	self-satisfaction
哈哈 **hāhā**	satisfaction

When a different consonant is introduced, something unusual can be expected, e.g.

呸 **pēi**	abormination or detest
嘘 **shī**	'hush, sh (be quiet)'
唏 **xī**	expressing contempt

In some cases, only consonant (usually nasal) sounds are heard:

嗯 **ńg**	asking for repetition or explanation
嗯 **ňg**	expressing surprise
嗯 **ǹg**	indicating agreement
呣 **ń**	'really?'; 'pardon?'
呣 **m̀**	'um-hum'; 'uh-huh'
哼 **hng**	'humph'

But whether vowels or consonants are used, it is their associated tones that reveal the linguistic functions (or the inner emotions) they intend to impart or convey.

THE PHONAESTHETIC NETWORK

Sound and tone imageries – that is, phonaesthemes – in a given lexicon are not merely a collection of words whose sounds or tones demonstrate some kind of aesthetic effect or have an associative bearing on their meaning. They constitute a unique phonaesthetic network of the language in question.

They are not to be confused with sound translation of foreign loanwords, which introduces into the enriched language a flavour of 'exoticism' and 'authenticity', but which is also as arbitrary as any other type of coinage falling outside the phonaesthetic network. For example,

咖啡 **kāfēi**	'coffee'
咖哩 **gālí**	'curry'
甲克 **jiǎkè**	'jacket'
袈裟 **jiāshā**	'kasaya' (a patchwork outer vestment worn by a Buddhist monk)
吗啡 **mǎfēi**	(medicine) 'morphine'
耶苏 **yēsū**	(religion) 'Jesus'

The native pronunciation is only a rough-and-ready imitation of the foreign. Even if sometimes meaning is taken into account in conjunction with the pronunciation in the loan translation, there is only an intra-lexemic correlation on individual and isolated occasions.

A phonaesthetic network, on the other hand, is significant in its interlexemic correlations. It is based on *sound analogy* or *sound affinity*. In other words, even if we cannot say very well that sounds (or sometimes tones) are co-terminous with meaning, we may nevertheless clearly see that related meanings often tend to be contaminated with similar sounds (or tones).

Onomatopoeic words in Chinese, as we have seen, are invariably couched in the first (i.e. level) tone. This is true not only of monosyllabic onomatopoeic terms indicating sounds or noises made by objects, animals or human beings, but also of onomatopoeic reduplications or rhymed quadrisyllables. This level-tone tendency is carried over to trisyllabic or quadrisyllabic descriptive terms, where a sound metaphor in terms of a *sense transfer* (i.e. vivifying a descriptive term derived from the experience of other senses through the perception of hearing) plays a major phonaesthetic role.

The associated phonaesthemes in a term either enhance the original perception: e.g.

干巴巴 **gānbābā**	'dull and dry'; 'dry-as-dust'
皱巴巴 **zhòubābā**	'wrinkled'; 'crumpled'
紧巴巴 **jǐnbābā**	'anxious'; 'impatient'
急巴巴 **jíbābā**	'tight'; 'hard up'

or help to conjure up different images: e.g.

湿答答 **shīdādā**	'dripping wet'
湿呼呼 **shīhūhū**	'damp'
湿津津 **shījīnjīn**	'moist with sweat'
湿淋淋 **shīlīnlīn**	'drenched'
湿漉漉 **shīlūlū**	'moist'
湿蒙蒙 **shīmēngmēng**	(of air) 'damp'

And with quadrisyllabic extensions, if 干干净净 **gāngānjìngjìng** 'spotlessly clean' sounds more emphatic than 干净 **gānjìng** 'clean', **gānganjīngjīng(r)** certainly sounds more lively and perhaps more metaphorical as well.

But more essentially, it is the consonantal sounds (rather than tones) that can more readily provide sound analogy or affinity in a phonaesthetic network. These sound analogies and affinities may be seen from different angles.

From the perspective of sound analogy, the following words or monyms, synchronically speaking, are obviously phonaesthetically related:

圈 **quān**	'circle'
拳 **quán**	'curl'; 'bend'; 'fist'
蜷 **quán**	'curl up'; 'huddle up'
鬈 **quán**	(of hair) 'curly'; 'wavy'
曲 **qū**	'bent'; 'curved'
屈 **qū**	'bend'; 'bow'; 'submit'

If we take into account sound affinity, we are able to retrieve more phonaesthetically related words or mononyms from the same set of palatal consonants – j/q/x/y:

卷 **juǎn**	'roll up'	
旋 **xuán**	'revolve'; 'spin'	
漩 **xuán**	'whirlpool'; 'eddy'	
圆 **yuán**	'round'; 'circular'; 'spherical'	

Diachronically, if sound change can be established between velars (g/k/h + w) and palatals, then the following words or mononyms may also be included as being phonaesthetically related to the above sets:

环 **huán**	'ring'; 'hoop'
缳 **huán**	'noose'
鬟 **huán**	(of hair) 'bun'
还 **huán**	'give back'; 'return'
回 **huí**	'go back'; 'to wind'; 'to circle'
归 **guī**	'go back'; 'give back'
箍 **gū**	'bind round'; 'hoop'
轱 **gū**	(inf.) 'wheel'
框 **kuāng**	'frame'; 'circle'
弯 **wān**	'curved'; 'crooked'
湾 **wān**	'a bend in a stream'; 'bay'
蜿 **wān**	'to wind'; 'zigzag'; 'meander'
绾 **wǎn**	'coil up' (e.g. one's hair)
围 **wéi**	'surround'; 'encircle'
涡 **wō**	'vortex flow'

As one semantic field fades into another, it is possible to go further and further afield till all the phonaesthetic ramifications are accounted for. But a minute phonaesthetic description of the entire lexicon is not our immediate task.

However, equipped with the notion of sound analogy and sound affinity, one does not have to look very far to be able to see phonaesthetic correlations in almost endless sets of words or mononyms in the lexicon, either from a diachronic or synchronic point of view.

Diachronically, the following pairs of words are related: e.g.

婚 **hūn** 'marriage'/昏 **hūn** 'twilight'; 'dusk'
(because people got married in the evening in the old days)
房 **fáng** 'room'/旁 **páng** 'side'
(because rooms are on the sides of a hall)
援 **yuán** 'climb'/猿 **yuán** 'ape'
(because apes are good at climbing)
责 **zé** 'responsibility'/债 **zhài** 'debt'
(责 **zé** with a 贝 radical indicating money, originally means 'debt' and later develops into the meaning of 'responsibility')

希 **xī** 'hope for'/稀 **xī** 'rare'

(希 **xī** originally means 'rare' as can still be seen in a juxtapositional word 希罕 **xīhan** 'rare', and because things are rare, people hope to obtain them, hence the meaning transfer)

掌 **zhǎng** 'palm'/张 **zhāng** 'extend'; 'spread out'

(掌 **zhǎng** 'palm' is related to 张 **zhāng** 'spread out' in the same way as 拳 **quán** 'fist' is to 卷 **juǎn** 'roll up')

乙 **yǐ** 'the second of the Ten Heavenly Stems'/燕 **yàn** 'swallow'

(both are developed from original pictographs depicting a swallow)

But our main concern is the synchronic semantic correlations between words or mononyms in terms of sound analogy and affinity. Apparently, similarly pronounced words or mononyms that share similar components are most likely to be phonaesthetically related:[18] e.g.

鱼/渔 **yú/yú**	'fish' / 'fishing'
住/驻 **zhù/zhù**	'live'; 'reside' / 'be stationed'
坐/座 **zuò/zuò**	'sit' / 'seat'; 'pedestal'
拦/栏 **lán/lán**	'block'; 'hold back' / 'fence'; 'railing'
披/被 **pī/bèi**	'wrap around' / 'cover (with)'
受/授 **shòu/shòu**	'receive'; 'accept' / 'award'; 'confer'
取/娶 **qǔ/qǔ**	'take'; 'get' / 'marry (a woman)'
家/嫁 **jiā/jià**	'family'; 'household' / '(of a woman) marry'
非/诽 **fēi/fěi**	'wrong' / 'slander'
低/底 **dī/dǐ**	'low' / 'bottom'
知/智 **zhī/zhì**	'know' / 'wisdom'; 'wit'
皱/绉 **zhòu/zhòu**	'wrinkle'; 'crease' / 'crape'; 'crepe'
裂/咧 **liè/liě**	'split'; 'crack' / 'draw back the corners of the mouth'
飘/漂 **piāo/piāo**	'float (in the air)' / 'float'; 'drift'
牙/芽 **yá/yá**	'tooth' / 'bud'; 'sprout'; 'shoot'
福/富 **fú/fù**	'good fortune'; 'happiness' / 'rich'; 'wealthy'; 'abundant'
朝/潮 **zhāo/cháo**	'early morning' / 'morning tide'
夕/汐 **xī/xī**	'sunset'; 'evening' / 'night-tide'
刷/涮 **shuā/shuàn**	'scrub with a brush' / 'rinse'
训/驯 **xùn/xùn**	'instruct'; 'admonish' / 'to tame'
散/撒 **sàn/sǎ**	'break up'; 'disperse' / 'scatter', 'sprinkle'
脱/蜕 **tuō/tuì**	'come off'; 'take off' / 'slough off'; 'moult'
道/导 **dào/dǎo**	'path'; 'way' / 'lead'; 'guide'
井/阱 **jǐng/jǐng**	'a well' / 'trap'; 'pit'
囱/窗 **cōng/chuāng**	'chimney' / 'window'
公/翁 **gōng/wēng**	'old man'; 'father-in-law' / 'old man'; 'father-in-law'

---

[18] To illustrate the point in question, we have only quoted pairs of words or mononyms. This does not mean that all phonaesthetic relations come symmetrically in pairs.

Otherwise, despite the fact that no similar component can be found in a pair of words or monoyms, a similar pronunciation (with unmistakable meaning correlation) leaves no doubt as to their phonaesthetic relationship: e.g.

看/瞰 **kàn/kàn**	'see'; 'look at' / 'peep'; 'spy'
拴/闩 **shuān/shuān**	'tie', 'fasten' / 'door bolt', 'latch'
碍/隘 **ài/ài**	'be in the way of' / 'a narrow pass'
董/督 **dǒng/dū**	'to direct'; 'supervise' / 'superintend and direct'
仓/藏 **cāng/cáng**	'warehouse' / 'to store'; 'lay by'
装/妆 **zhuāng/zhuāng**	'dress up', 'attire' / 'apply makeup'
叉/岔 **chā/chà**	'branching off' / 'forked'
怨/冤 **yuàn/yuān**	'complain' / 'wrong'; 'injustice'
盈/溢 **yíng/yì**	'be full of'; 'have a surplus of' / 'overflow'
促/速 **cù/sù**	'urge'; 'urgent' / 'fast'; 'speedy'
疆/界 **jiāng/jiè**	'boundary'; 'border' / 'boundary'; 'extent'
集/辑 **jí/jí**	'gather'; 'collect' / 'compile'
喂/胃 **wèi/wèi**	'feed' / 'stomach'

Precisely because of these tendencies in sound analogy or affinity, it is plausible to believe that meaning-related words, not only synonyms as quoted above but also antonyms or hyponyms, may sometimes be phonaesthetically related:

alliteration:	男女 **nánnǚ** 'male and female'
	好坏 **hǎohuài** 'benefit' (lit. good or bad)
rhyme:	老少 **lǎoshào** 'old and young'
	龃龉 **jǔyǔ** (formal) 'the upper and lower teeth not meeting properly – discord'
tonal variation:	买卖 **mǎimài** 'transaction'; 'business' (lit. buy and sell)
	夫妇 **fūfù** 'husband and wife'

In the field of 'honesty and hypocrisy', we may even find that the positive terms seem to favour the set of 'retroflex' consonants zh/ch/sh/r whereas the negative terms, the set of 'palatal' consonants j/q/x/y:[19]

positive terms	negative terms
诚实 **chéngshí** 'honest'	狡黠 **jiǎoxiá** 'dishonest'; 'sly'
真挚 **zhēnzhì** 'sincere'	奸邪 **jiānxié** 'crafty'; 'evil'
直率 **zhíshuài** 'straightforward'; 'above board'	虚假 **xūjiǎ** 'hypocritical'; 'false'
热忱 **rèchén** 'enthusiastic'; 'earnest'	阴险 **yīnxiǎn** 'insidious'; 'treacherous'

To stretch one's imagination a little, a fairly regular phonaesthetic pattern of vowel codification seems discernible with terms indicating outward shape, size, etc.: e.g.

[19] This, of course, is not to say that every single lexeme in the field will follow this phonaesthetic principle. Nor does this mean that other fields might not use these sets of consonants in an entirely different way.

positive terms favour a/e/o/u	negative terms favour i/ia
大 **dà** 'big'	小 **xiǎo** 'small'
高 **gāo** 'high'	低 **dī** 'low'
宽 **kuān** 'wide'	狭 **xiá** 'narrow'
深 **shēn** 'deep'	浅 **qiǎn** 'shallow'
厚 **hòu** 'thick'	扁 **biǎn** 'thin'
粗 **cū** 'thick all around'	细 **xì** 'thin all around'

In one particular instance, such sound analogy and affinity may even be seen to be related to the tactile movements of the specific parts of the oral and nasal cavities involved in the production of the terms: e.g. 吃 **chī** 'eat' with an alveolar (like 齿 **chǐ** 'tooth'), 喝 **hē** 'drink' with a velar (like 喉 **hóu** 'throat'),[20] 嚼 **jiáo** 'chew' and 咬 **yǎo** 'bite' with a palatal (like 牙 **yá** 'tooth'), 舔 **tiǎn** 'lap up liquid' with an alveolar using the tip of the tongue, 吻 **wěn** 'kiss' (which used to begin with m- as it still does in present-day Cantonese) with a bilabial, 吹 **chuī** 'blow' and 呼 **hū** 'exhale' both with a vowel that protrudes one's lips, and 吸 **xī** 'inhale' with a vowel which causes one's lips to spread; and 哼 **hēng** 'hum, croon', with a velar initial and nasal final as if one were humming. The sound analogy with oral and nasal tactile association behind all these Chinese words cannot be explained away by mere arbitrariness or coincidence.

The above examples are but illustrations of the tip of the phonaesthetic iceberg. A fuller exploration of the real potential and size of the iceberg will need painstaking research, which is beyond the scope of the present chapter. These examples have, however, revealed to us the diverse avenues through which phonaesthetic correlations may be tapped between meaningfully related lexemes. In other words, a phonaesthetic network should not just be an account of the sum total of the lexicon's existing phonaesthetic-oriented lexemes but an enlightening synchronic description of all the possible inter-lexemic manifestations in which phonaesthetic motivation can be clearly discerned in terms of the kind of semantic relations words or expressions contract with each other.

It is certainly not true to say that most of the words in the lexicon will neatly fall within the phonaesthetic network, for there are other linguistic motivations. But there is no doubt that as phonaesthemes are pervasive in identifiable areas of the lexicon, their regularities can be defined and their role can be ascertained.

---

[20] The word 饮 **yǐn** 'drink' in classical Chinese may also be related to 咽 **yān** 'pharynx'; 'throat' in classical Chinese.

6 RHETORICAL FEATURES OF THE CHINESE LEXICON

Rhetoric is traditionally understood as a mechanism for sentence or discourse manipulation; but in fact it is also a dynamic process of lexical composition. The Chinese lexicon, for example, is permeated not only with (1) *figures of speech* built into its diverse types of lexemes, but also with (2) *aesthetic forms of speech*, particularly in the formulation of the lexicon's polysyllabic units. Important features of the lexicon will certainly be missed if this lively rhetorical device is not closely studied and fully appreciated.

In 'figures of speech', we can discern two fairly consistent sets of figures: (1) *metaphorical comparison*, e.g. analogy, metonymy, synecdoche, personification, depersonalisation, allusion, etc.; and (2) *masquerading expression*, e.g. hyperbole, irony, pun, etc. In 'aesthetic forms of speech', we find polysyllabic lexical units codified on the conventional five- or seven-syllable verse line rhythms or on such symmetrical patterns as antithesis or unithesis, progression, partial reversal, loop, etc.

In the following sections we shall discuss the different rhetorical devices in turn.

METAPHORICAL COMPARISON

All metaphorical comparisons are built on the resemblance or similarity between two different images. First, if between two images A and B, which are being thus compared, there is not even a single point of resemblance or association, no metaphor can be established; second, if the two images A and B are too similar, say, if they are immediate co-hyponyms in a hyponymous paradigm, metaphorical comparison again becomes most unlikely. For instance, one does not usually compare 'rose' to 'tulip', or 'push' to 'pull'. So in a metaphorical comparison, it is not merely the fact that A is compared to B, but that A is compared to a non-co-hyponymous B. Comparison between co-hyponyms is, of course, perfectly legitimate and possible but that will not generally result in a metaphor.

As to which aspect of the images can be chosen as the focus of comparison, the choice seems to be infinitely open. For instance, in

大头针 **dàtóuzhēn** 'pin'　　　(大 **dà**: big; 头 **tóu**: head; 针 **zhēn**: needle)
螺丝钉 **luósīdīng** 'screw'　　(螺 **luó**: spiral shell; 丝 **sī**: silk thread;
　　　　　　　　　　　　　　　钉 **dīng**: nail)

the comparison can be easily pinned down to 'shape' and the comparison is 'transparent'; but in

粗心大意 **cūxīn dàyì** 'careless'   (粗 **cū**: thick; 心 **xīn**: heart; 大 **dà**: big;
                                          意 **yì**: idea)

it will be hard to imagine how 'heart' can be 'thick' or 'idea' be 'big'. The comparison is already a few steps removed from reality and has become less transparent, and in

粗枝大叶 **cū zhī dà yè**   (粗 **cū**: thick; 枝 **zhī**: branch; 大 **dà**: big;
 'slapdash'   叶 **yè**: leaf)

one has even greater difficulty, perhaps due to little knowledge about the origin of the idiom (which is about painting leaves and branches with crude brushstrokes), in telling what 'branch' or 'leaf' has to do with a person's way of doing things. The comparison is therefore 'opaque'.

Besides this 'transparent' and 'opaque' distinction,[1] metaphorical comparison in lexemes is seen to differ in yet another dimension. In some lexical units, where the two images being compared are both present, the metaphor can be said to be 'partial'; but if the unit only encodes the thing being compared to but leaves out the thing for which the comparison is intended, the metaphor is said to be 'complete'. A partial metaphor was traditionally known as a 'transferred epithet'; a 'complete' metaphor is metaphor *per se*.

Metaphorical comparisons, whether transparent or opaque, partial or complete, can be differentiated in keeping with the human and non-human dichotomy into the following subtypes: (a) if A, a human or non-human, is compared to B, one of its own kind (but certainly not co-hyponymous), it is *analogy*; (b) if A, a human or non-human, is compared to B, part of itself (e.g. its own attributes, functions, etc.), it is *metonymy*; or if A, a human or non-human class, is compared to B, a member of the class, it is *synecdoche*; (c) if A, a non-human, is compared to B, a human, it is *personification*; (d) if A, a human, is compared to B, a non-human, it is *depersonalisation*; (e) if A, a human or non-human, is compared to B, a human or non-human historical or legendary figure or object, it is *allusion*.

If any of the above comparisons between A and B is made in an implicit fashion, it is called *metaphor*; if made in an explicit fashion by a term like 如 **rú** 'as', 似 **sì** 'like', 若 **ruò** 'resemble', etc. in Chinese, it is called *simile*. A table will be able to sum up the differences clearly:

Overt	$\rightarrow$	*Comparisons*	$\leftarrow$	*Covert*
		analogy		
		metonymy		
Simile		synecdoche		Metaphor
		personification		
		depersonalisation		
		allusion		

[1] The labels 'transparent' and 'opaque' were borrowed from Ullmann 1962.

Either simile or metaphor can be partial or complete in a lexical unit or convey its comparison in a transparent or opaque way:

simile

partial/transparent:	宾至如归 **bīn zhì rú guī** 'a home from home' (lit. 'the guest arrives as if he had come home')
partial/opaque:	势如破竹 **shì rú pò zhú** 'with irresistible force' (lit. 'a momentum like splitting bamboo')
complete/transparent:	如鱼得水 **rú yú dé shuǐ** 'like a duck to water' (lit. 'like a stranded fish being put back to water')
complete/opaque:	趋之若鹜 **qū zhī ruò wù** 'scramble for sth' (lit. 'go after sth like a flock of ducks')

metaphor

partial/transparent:	怒发冲冠 **nù fà chōng guān** 'bristle with anger' (lit. 'angry hair pushes up the hat')
partial/opaque:	笑容可掬 **xiàoróng kě jū** 'radiant with smiles' (lit. 'smiles can be scooped up by the handful')
complete/transparent:	雪中送炭 **xuě zhōng sòng tàn** 'provide timely help' (lit. 'send charcoal in snowy weather')
complete/opaque:	四面楚歌 **sìmiàn chǔ gē** 'besieged on all sides' (lit. 'songs of Chu could be heard on all sides') (During the war between Han and Chu, the army of Chu under its commander Xiang Yu found itself besieged and hearing songs of Chu arising from all sides, he thought that all the land of Chu had fallen into the hands of Liu Bang, the commander of the Han army.)

Analogy

Analogy is certainly an inbuilt process of human cognition and is identifiably a motivating force behind the creation of all meaningful elements in a language's lexicon. Synchronically, however, most of the analogies originally intended are lost to a language's speakers and it will be too far-fetched to re-establish their diachronic comparison to any useful purpose. For example, for native speakers of Chinese, both 江 **jiāng** and 河 **hé** mean literally 'river' and no more. They are not aware (and quite rightly so) of the fact that the two words were actually once respective aural impressions of the roaring waters of the Yangtse and the Yellow River. The present-day generalisation is only a later analogy to the originally separate identifications that have long been forgotten. Similarly, a word like 影响 **yǐngxiǎng** means nothing more than the holistic notion of 'influence' to the average speakers. How are they supposed to know that diachronically the meaning of 'influence' is derived from an analogy to the invariable 'hold' of 影 **yǐng** 'shadow' or 响 **xiǎng** 'echo' on every object or sound?

What is of concern to us in our present study is not a diachronic recounting of these dead metaphors, but an intensive survey of the kind of analogy which is still very much alive in the public consciousness of the language's speakers, the kind of comparison whose metaphorical dynamism continues to chart and shape the future of the language.

Measure words in Chinese, for instance, are of metaphorical origin but their metaphorical force has long been spent through frequent use, e.g. 支 **zhī**, a common measure word for longish objects like pencil, toothpaste, rifle, etc., must have derived its meaning from something like the twig of a tree or a section of bamboo, but no speaker would ever re-trace the analogy when he is using the word a dozen times a day in association with something like pen, cigarette, match, etc. However, when measure words are used in connection with more abstract notions, sometimes the metaphorical impact still remains fairly strong, e.g. in

一线希望 **yī xiàn xīwàng** 'a gleam of hope'
  (一 **yī**: one; 线 **xiàn**: thread; 希望 **xīwàng**: hope)
一团漆黑 **yī tuán qīhēi** 'pitch-dark'; 'utterly hopeless'
  (一 **yī**: one; 团 **tuán**: roll; 漆黑 **qīhēi**: pitch-dark)

where 'slim hope' is measured in terms of 'thread' and 'complete darkness' in terms of 'roll'.

In many disyllabic lexemes, similar analogy can still be clearly felt. As we said earlier, it can be partial or complete. For example,

partial:
  汗珠 **hànzhū** 'beads of sweat' (汗 **hàn**: sweat; 珠 **zhū**: pearl)
  雪花 **xuěhuā** 'snowflakes' (雪 **xuě**: snow; 花 **huā**: flower)
  火舌 **huǒshé** 'tongues of fire' (火 **huǒ**: fire; 舌 **shé**: tongue)

where sweat is compared to beads, snow to flower petals and flame to tongues. Or in

渴望 **kěwàng** 'thirst for' (渴 **kě**: thirsty; 望 **wàng**: yearn for)
飞驰 **fēichí** 'speed along' (飞 **fēi**: to fly; 驰 **chí**: to speed along)

where hope or yearning is likened to thirst and speeding along the surface of the land is likened to flying in the air. Or in

火热 **huǒrè** 'burning hot' (火 **huǒ**: fire; 热 **rè**: hot)
泥醉 **nízuì** 'badly drunk' (泥 **ní**: mud; 醉 **zuì**: drunk)

where heat is compared to fire and drunkenness to mud.

But in all these cases, one of the mononyms in the lexeme, either the first or the second, keeps to its literal meaning, which then decides the sense of the resultant lexeme. In 雪花 **xuěhuā** 'snowflake', for instance, the first mononym meaning 'snow' remains literal; in 渴望 **kěwàng** 'thirst for', the second mononym meaning 'hope for' remains literal.

In the following lexemes, however, the analogy is complete and if the meaning is not learned together with the lexeme itself, one has no way of knowing what is being referred to.

complete:
包袱 **bāofu** 'mental burden' (包 **bāo**: a bundle wrapped in cloth; 袱 **fú**: cloth-wrapper)
  – A mental burden is compared to a bundle that weighs one down.
头角 **tóujiǎo** (of a young person) 'brilliance' (头 **tóu**: head; 角 **jiǎo**: horn)
  – The brilliance of a person is described as if he had sharp and prominent horns on his head.
嚆矢 **hāoshǐ** 'harbinger'; 'forerunner' (嚆 **hāo**: make a noise; 矢 **shǐ**: arrow)
  – A harbinger is compared to an arrow that announces its arrival with an unmistakable noise.
枝叶 **zhīyè** 'non-essentials'; 'minor details' (枝 **zhī**: branch, twig; 叶 **yè**: leaf)
  – Minor details (or non-essentials) are compared to twigs and leaves of a tree.
皮毛 **pímáo** 'superficial knowledge' (皮 **pí**: skin; 毛 **máo**: hair)
  – Superficial knowledge is compared to what is on the surface of a human body: skin and hair.
秕糠 **bǐkāng** 'worthless stuff' (秕 **bǐ**: blighted seeds; 糠 **kāng**: chaff)
  – Something which is worthless is compared to blighted seeds and chaff.
瓜葛 **guāgé** 'connection'; 'implication' (瓜 **guā**: melon, gourd; 葛 **gé**: kudzu vine)
  – Connection is compared to the clinging nature of a gourd or kudzu vine with its tendrils.
滥觞 **lànshāng** 'origin'; 'beginning' (滥 **làn**: overflow, flood; 觞 **shāng**: drinking vessel)
  – The origin of something is compared to setting afloat a drinking vessel at a river source.

问鼎 **wèndǐng** 'compete for a championship' (问 **wèn**: enquire about; 鼎 **dǐng**: tripod)
  – Competing for the first prize is likened to aspiring after the tripod, an emblem of the throne.

携贰 **xié'èr** 'be disloyal' (携 **xié**: carry, take along; 贰 **èr**: two, second, halfheartedness)
  – Disloyalty is compared to one's entertaining in one's mind second thoughts.

择席 **zháixí** 'be unable to sleep well in a new place' (择 **zhái**: select; 席 **xí**: mat)
  – Not sleeping well in a new place is likened to being particular about the mat one sleeps on.

顶牛 **dǐngniú** 'be at loggerheads' (顶 **dǐng**: gore, butt; 牛 **niú**: bull)
  – Being at loggerheads is compared to two bulls locking their horns in a fight to prevail.

定弦 **dìngxián** 'make up one's mind' (定 **dìng**: to tune; 弦 **xián**: the string of a musical instrument)
  – Making up one's mind is likened to tuning up the string of a musical instrument.

撑腰 **chēngyāo** 'support'; 'back up' (撑 **chēng**: prop up; 腰 **yāo**: waist)
  – Backing somebody up is likened to propping up his waist.

穿凿 **chuānzáo** 'give a far-fetched interpretation' (穿 **chuān**: pierce; 凿 **záo**: to chisel)
  – Giving a far-fetched interpretation is likened to a painstaking process of chiselling or piercing.

吃醋 **chīcù** (usually of a rival in love) 'be jealous' (吃 **chī**: eat; 醋 **cù**: vinegar)
  – Being jealous is compared to drinking vinegar and tasting the sourness of it.

兑现 **duìxiàn** 'honour a commitment' (兑 **duì**: convert into; 现 **xiàn**: cash)
  – Honouring a commitment is compared to cashing a cheque.

刻板 **kèbǎn** 'mechanical'; 'inflexible' (刻 **kè**: engrave, cut; 板 **bǎn**: wooden board)
  – Being inflexible is likened to printing blocks that have been cut and cannot be changed.

棘手 **jíshǒu** (of a problem) 'thorny'; 'knotty' (棘 **jí**: brambles; 手 **shǒu**: hand)
  – A problem which is thorny is likened to something that pricks the hand that deals with it.

焦灼 **jiāozhuó** (formal) 'deeply worried'; 'very anxious' (焦 **jiāo**: burn, char; 灼 **zhuó**: scorch)
  – Worry or anxiety is compared to one's heart being charred and scorched.

咋舌 **zhàshé** 'speechless with wonder' (咋 **zhà**: bite; 舌 **shé**: tongue)
  – One being left speechless with wonder is likened to one biting one's tongue.

In trisyllabic words or quadrisyllabic expressions, analogy abounds, e.g.

transparent:

鹤嘴锄 **hèzuǐchú** 'pickaxe' (鹤 **hè**: crane; 嘴 **zuǐ**: beak; 锄 **chú**: hoe)

鹅卵石 **éluǎnshí** 'cobblestone' (鹅 **é**: goose; 卵 **luǎn**: egg; 石 **shí**: stone)

蝴蝶结 **húdiéjié** 'bow (tie)' (蝴蝶 **húdié**: butterfly; 结 **jié**: knot)

金字塔 **jīnzìtǎ** 'pyramid' (金 **jīn**: shape of the character 金; 字 **zì**: Chinese script; 塔 **tǎ**: tower)

蛤蟆夯 **hámahāng** 'rammer' (蛤蟆 **háma**: frog, toad; 夯 **hāng**: rammer)

老虎钳 **lǎohǔqián** 'vice'; 'pincer pliers' (老虎 **lǎohǔ**: tiger; 钳 **qián**: pincers, pliers, tongs)

雪花膏 **xuěhuāgāo** 'vanishing cream' (雪花 **xuěhuā**: snowflake; 膏 **gāo**: paste, cream, ointment)

万花筒 **wànhuātǒng** 'kaleidoscope' (万花 **wànhuā**: ten thousand flowers; 筒 **tǒng**: cylinder)

瓜葛亲 **guāgéqīn** 'distant relatives' (瓜葛 **guāgé**: gourd and kudzu vine; 亲 **qīn**: next of kin)

With these partially metaphoric trisyllables, it is usually the last mononym in the structure that keeps to its literal meaning, e.g. 鹤嘴锄 **hèzuǐchú** is a kind of 锄 **chú** 'hoe' and 鹅卵石 **éluǎnshí** is a kind of 石 **shí** 'stone'. Sometimes, the literal meaning of such a headword mononym is, however, derived from a more generic term chosen from the same hyponymous field, which is therefore only partially synonymous with that of the resultant lexeme, e.g. 'bow (tie)' is regarded as a kind of 'knot' and 'pyramid' a kind of 'tower'.

opaque:

耳边风 **ěrbiānfēng** 'unheeded advice' (耳边 **ěrbiān**: by the ear; 风 **fēng**: wind)

绊脚石 **bànjiǎoshí** 'stumbling block' (绊 **bàn**: to trip; 脚 **jiǎo**: foot; 石 **shí**: stone)

敲门砖 **qiāoménzhuān** 'stepping-stone' (敲门 **qiāomén**: knock on the door; 砖 **zhuān**: brick)

回头路 **huítóulù** 'the road of retrogression' (回头 **huítóu**: turn round; 路 **lù**: road)

保护伞 **bǎohùsǎn** 'umbrella' (i.e. a protecting power) (保护 **bǎohù**: protect; 伞 **sǎn**: umbrella)

斧凿痕 **fǔzáohén** 'traces of conscious artistry' (斧 **fǔ**: axe; 凿 **záo**: chisel; 痕 **hén**: traces)

方便之门 **fāngbiàn zhī mén** 'give the green light to' (方便 **fāngbiàn**: convenient; 之 **zhī**: grammatical particle; 门 **mén**: door)

如意算盘 **rúyì suànpan** 'smug calculations'; 'wishful thinking' (如意 **rúyì**: as one wishes, be gratified; 算盘 **suànpán**: abacus, calculation)

世外桃源 **shìwài táoyuán** 'a haven of peace' (世外 **shìwài**: beyond the world; 桃源 **táoyuán**: the land of peach blossoms)

糖衣炮弹 **tángyī pàodàn** 'something that lures but hurts in the end' (lit. 'sugar-coated bullet') (糖衣 **tángyī**: sugarcoating; 炮弹 **pàodàn**: cannon ball)

In these less transparent examples we can see that 'unheeded advice' is compared to 'a gust of wind which passes by somebody's ear and vanishes completely'; a 'stumbling stock', to 'a piece of stone left there purposely to trip people and make them fall'; 'giving the green light to someone', to 'opening the so-called convenient door for somebody to enter or pass through'; and 'something that tastes sweet at the beginning but turns out to be bitter at the end', to 'sugar-coated cannon balls'.

There is a particular set of trisyllabic vernacular idioms in the lexicon which usually adopt the structure: 'monosyllabic verb + disyllabic noun or noun phrase'. These idioms are mostly 'complete' analogies, e.g.

> 捞稻草 **lāo dàocǎo** 'take advantage of sth'
> (捞 **lāo**: fish for; 稻草 **dàocǎo**: hay, straw)
> 穿小鞋 **chuān xiǎoxié** 'make it hot for sb'
> (穿 **chuān**: wear; 小 **xiǎo**: small; 鞋 **xié**: shoes)
> 揪辫子 **jiū biànzi** 'capitalise on sb's vulnerable point'
> (揪 **jiū**: seize; 辫子 **biànzi**: pigtail)
> 连锅端 **lián guō duān** 'get rid of the whole lot'
> (连 **lián**: together with; 锅 **guō**: pot; 端 **duān**: carry)
> 喝墨水 **hē mòshuǐ** 'go to school' (喝 **hē**: drink; 墨水 **mòshuǐ**: ink)

In these trisyllabic vernacular idioms, 'taking advantage of something' is compared to 'fishing for straw'; 'making it hot for somebody', to 'making him or her wear very tight shoes'; 'capitalising on someone's vulnerable point', to 'seizing his or her pigtail'; 'getting rid of the whole lot', to 'doing away not only with what is in the pot but also with the pot itself'; and 'going to school to acquire learning', to 'drinking sufficient ink'.

With quadrisyllabic classical idioms, the analogy may be again partial or complete. As partial analogy in a quadrisyllabic classical idiom of ABCD, if it is a recurrent pattern, it is usually B and D that become metaphorical:

> 枪林弹雨 **qiāng lín dàn yǔ** 'a hail of bullets'
> (枪 **qiāng**: gun; 林 **lín**: forest; 弹 **dàn**: rifle; 雨 **yǔ**: rain)
> 唇枪舌剑 **chún qiāng shé jiàn** 'a battle of words'
> (唇 **chún**: lip; 枪 **qiāng**: spear; 舌 **shé**: tongue; 剑 **jiàn**: sword)

If it is a continuous pattern, either AB or CD might become metaphorical or remain literal:

> 铁石心肠 **tiě shí xīncháng** 'a heart of stone'
> (铁 **tiě**: iron; 石 **shí**: stone; 心肠 **xīncháng**: heart)
> 小道消息 **xiǎodào xiāoxi** 'hearsay'
> (小道 **xiǎodào**: footpath; 消息 **xiāoxi**: news)
> 救命稻草 **jiùmìng dàocǎo** 'a straw to clutch at'
> (救命 **jiùmìng**: life-saving; 稻草 **dàocǎo**: straw)
> 小家碧玉 **xiǎojiā bìyù** 'a pretty girl of humble birth'
> (小家 **xiǎojiā**: lowly family; 碧玉 **bìyù**: jade)

A particular type which incorporates 之 **zhī** (i.e. a classical equivalent of the adjectival marker 的 **de** in Modern Standard Chinese) in the third mononym consists largely of partial analogies. In such a structure, the last mononym in the combination suggests the literal meaning while the attribute encoded in the form of 之 is metaphorical. There are a large number of such idioms in the lexicon, e.g.

燃眉之急 **rán méi zhī jí** 'a matter of extreme urgency'
  (燃 **rán**: burn; 眉 **méi**: eyebrows; 急 **jí**: urgent)
肺腑之言 **fèifǔ zhī yán** 'words from the bottom of one's heart'
  (肺 **fèi**: lung; 腑 **fǔ**: internal organs; 言 **yán**: speech)

Sometimes, if the last mononym is also used in a metaphorical sense, then the analogy is complete, e.g.

无米之炊 **wú mǐ zhī chuī** 'make bricks without straw'
  (无 **wú**: without; 米 **mǐ**: rice; 炊 **chuī**: cooking)
弦外之音 **xián wài zhī yīn** 'implication'
  (弦 **xián**: the string of a musical instrument; 外 **wài**: outside; 音 **yīn**: sound)

And, of course, other types of quadrisyllabic classical idioms, whether recurrent or continuous, may also be complete analogies: e.g.

天罗地网 **tiān luó dì wǎng** 'tight encirclement'
  (天 **tiān**: heaven; 罗 **luó**: trap; 地 **dì**: earth; 网 **wǎng**: net)
破釜沉舟 **pò fǔ chén zhōu** 'burn one's boats'; 'cut off all means of retreat'
  (破 **pò**: break; 釜 **fǔ**: cauldron; 沉 **chén**: sink; 舟 **zhōu**: boat)
木已成舟 **mù yǐ chéng zhōu** 'the die is cast'
  (木 **mù**: wood; 已 **yǐ**: already; 成 **chéng**: become, be made into; 舟 **zhōu**: boat)
铁树开花 **tiěshù kāi huā** 'sth seldom seen or hardly possible'
  (铁树 **tiěshù**: iron tree, i.e. sago cycas; 开花 **kāi huā**: burst into blossoms)

In polysyllabic sayings:

partial:
  休管他人瓦上霜 **xiū guǎn tārén wǎ shang shuāng**
  'don't poke your nose into others' business'
  (休 **xiū**: don't; 管 **guǎn**: bother about; 他人 **tārén**: other people; 瓦上 **wǎ shang**: on the roof; 霜 **shuāng**: frost)
  有钱能使鬼推磨 **yǒu qián néng shǐ guǐ tuī mò**
  'money makes the mare go'
  (有 **yǒu**: have; 钱 **qián**: money; 能 **néng**: can; 使 **shǐ**: to cause; 鬼 **guǐ**: ghost; 推 **tuī**: push; 磨 **mò**: mill)
  新官上任三把火 **xīn guān shàngrèn sān bǎ huǒ** 'a new broom sweeps clean'
  (新官 **xīn guān**: new official; 上任 **shàngrèn**: come into office; 三 **sān**: three; 把 **bǎ**: measure word; 火 **huǒ**: fire)

In these septisyllabic idioms, the last three monomyns are metaphorical, e.g. 瓦上霜 **wǎshang shuāng** 'frost on roof-tiles' is to be metaphorically interpreted as 'other people's business', 鬼推磨 **guǐ tuī mò** 'ghost pushing the mill' as 'nothing is impossible when even ghosts can be made to push the mill for one', and 三把火 **sān bǎ huǒ** 'three successive fires' as 'drastic measures'.

In symmetrically balanced polysyllabic sayings, it is a general rule to make half of the idiom metaphorical and keep the other half literal, e.g.

人要脸, 树要皮 **rén yào liǎn | shù yào pí**
'every person has his or her dignity'
　　(人 **rén**: person; 要 **yào**: want, need; 脸 **liǎn**: face, dignity; 树 **shù**: tree; 皮 **pí**: skin, bark)

人不知, 鬼不觉 **rén bù zhī | guǐ bù jué**
'without anybody knowing anything about it'
　　(人 **rén**: person; 不 **bù**: not; 知 **zhī**: know; 鬼 **guǐ**: ghost; 觉 **jué**: be aware)

人要衣装, 佛要金装 **rén yào yī zhuāng | fú yào jīn zhuāng**
'clothes make the man'
　　(人 **rén**: people; 要 **yào**: want; 衣 **yī**: clothes; 装 **zhuāng**: dress up; 佛 **fú**: Buddha; 金 **jīn**: gold)

路遥知马力, 日久见人心 **lù yáo zhī mǎ lì | rì jiǔ jiàn rénxīn**
'time will tell what kind of man one is'
　　(路 **lù**: way; 遥 **yáo**: far; 知 **zhī**: know, tell; 马力 **mǎ lì**: horse's strength; 日 **rì**: day; 久 **jiǔ**: long; 见 **jiàn**: see; 人心 **rénxīn**: a person's heart)

水至清则无鱼, 人至察则无徒 **shuǐ zhì qīng zé wú yú | rén zhì chá zé wú tú**
'he who is too critical has few friends'
　　(水 **shuǐ**: water; 至 **zhì**: most; 清 **qīng**: clear; 则 **zé**: therefore; 无 **wú**: no; 鱼 **yú**: fish; 察 **chá**: critical; 徒 **tú**: disciple)

As we can see from the examples, the literal half is often adequate enough on its own to recover the meaning of the whole idiom. The other dispensable half is simply there to serve as a metaphorical flourish to bring the meaning of the whole idiom more forcibly home.

There are, of course, continuous idioms, in which the metaphor is built into the whole saying. The analogy may be partial or complete, transparent or opaque, and the sayings may or may not retain their symmetrical form: e.g.

continuous:
　　本地姜不辣 **běndì jiāng bù là** 'distant fields are always greener'
　　　　(本地 **běndì**: local; 姜 **jiāng**: ginger; 不 **bù**: not; 辣 **là**: peppery, spicy)
　　无风不起浪 **wú fēng bù qǐ làng** 'there's no smoke without fire'
　　　　(无 **wú**: without; 风 **fēng**: wind; 不 **bù**: not; 起 **qǐ**: start, rise; 浪 **làng**: wave)
　　脚踏两只船 **jiǎo tà liǎngzhī chuán** 'have a foot in either camp'
　　　　(脚 **jiǎo**: foot; 踏 **tà**: step on, straddle; 两 **liǎng**: two; 只 **zhī**: mw; 船 **chuán**: boat)
　　有奶便是娘 **yǒu nǎi biàn shì niáng** 'whoever suckles me is my mother'
　　　　(有 **yǒu**: have; 奶 **nǎi**: milk; 便 **biàn**: then; 是 **shì**: be; 娘 **niáng**: mother)

磨刀不误砍柴工 **mó dāo bù wù kǎncháigōng**
'sharpening the axe won't inferfere with the cutting of firewood'
(磨 **mó**: rub, grind; 刀 **dāo**: sword; 不 **bù**: not; 误 **wù**: miss; 砍 **kǎn**: chop;
柴 **chái**: firewood; 工 **gōng**: time spent in doing sth)

胜败乃兵家常事 **shèngbài nǎi bīngjiā chángshì**
'for a military commander, winning or losing a battle is a common
occurrence'
(胜败 **shèngbài**: victory or defeat; 乃 **nǎi**: be; 兵家 **bīngjiā**: military
circles; 常事 **chángshì**: routine)

一言既出，驷马难追 **yī yán jì chū | sì mǎ nán zhuī**
'what is spoken cannot be retrieved'
(一 **yī**: one; 言 **yán**: word; 既 **jì**: already; 出 **chū**: go out; 驷马 **sì mǎ**:
a team of four horses; 难 **nán**: difficult; 追 **zhuī**: chase)

recurrent:
干打雷，不下雨 **gān dǎ léi | bù xià yǔ** 'much bruit, little fruit'
(干 **gān**: dry; 打雷 **dǎ léi**: to thunder; 不 **bù**: not; 下雨 **xià yǔ**: to rain)
水有源，树有根 **shuǐ yǒu yuán | shù yǒu gēn** 'everything has its origin'
(水 **shuǐ**: river; 有 **yǒu**: have; 源 **yuán**: source; 树 **shù**: tree; 根 **gēn**: root)

三天打鱼，两天晒网 **sān tiān dǎyú | liǎng tiān shài wǎng**
'work by fits and starts'
(三 **sān**: three; 天 **tiān**: day; 打鱼 **dǎyú**: catch fish; 两 **liǎng**: two; 晒 **shài**:
to dry; 网 **wǎng**: fish-net)

一朝被蛇咬，十年怕井绳 **yī zhāo bèi shé yǎo | shí nián pà jǐngshéng**
'once bitten, twice shy'
(一朝 **yī zhāo**: once; 被 **bèi**: passive indicator 'by'; 蛇 **shé**: snake; 咬 **yǎo**:
bite; 十 **shí**: ten; 年 **nián**: year; 怕 **pà**: be afraid of; 井绳 **jǐngshéng**: rope
for fetching water from the well)

There is another type of polysyllabic idiom called a two-part allegorical saying which behaves more or less in the same way. That is, the first part invariably encodes the analogy when the second part gives the literal explanation
– often in the form of a pithy saying or a polysemic or homonymic pun.[2]
For instance,

千里送鹅毛 – 礼轻情义重 **qiānlǐ sòng émáo | lǐ qīng qíngyì zhòng**
'a goose feather sent from a thousand miles away – the gift is trifling but
the feeling is profound'
(千里 **qiānlǐ**: a thousand miles; 送 **sòng**: send; 鹅毛 **émáo**: goose feather;
礼 **lǐ**: gift; 轻 **qīng**: light, not heavy; 情意 **qíngyì**: friendly feeling; 重 **zhòng**:
heavy)

---

[2] For examples of polysemic or homonymic puns, see the section on puns in this chapter.

七个西瓜分两份 – 不三不四 **qī gè xīguā fēn liǎng fèn | bù sān bù sì**
'seven water melons to be divided into two equal shares – neither three nor four'

    (七 **qī**: seven; 个 **gè**: measure word; 西瓜 **xīguā**: water melon; 分 **fēn**: divide between; 两 **liǎng**: two; 份 **fèn**: portion; 不 **bù**: not; 三 **sān**: three; 四 **sì**: four; 不三不四 is also an idiom meaning: neither one thing nor another)

瞎子点灯 – 白费蜡 **xiāzi diǎn dēng | bái fèi là**
'a sheer waste' (lit. 'lighting a candle for a blind person – a sheer waste of wax')

    (瞎子 **xiāzi**: a blind person; 点 **diǎn**: to light; 灯 **dēng**: lamp; 白 **bái**: in vain; 费 **fèi**: to waste; 蜡 **là**: wax)

哑巴吃黄连 – 有苦说不清 **yǎba chī huánglián | yǒu kǔ shuōbuqīng**
'be forced to suffer in silence' (lit. 'a dumb person tasting bitter herbs – be unable to express one's discomfort')

    (哑巴 **yǎba**: a dumb person; 吃 **chī**: eat, consume; 黄连 **huánglián**: the rhizome of Chinese goldthread; 有 **yǒu**: have; 苦 **kǔ**: bitterness; 说不清 **shuōbuqīng**: cannot explain clearly)

An interesting point to note is that, as a popular idiom on everybody's lips in everyday conversation, sometimes the same two-part allegorical saying (especially a frequently quoted one) goes through a variety of forms, that is, as long as the second part (where the literal explanation is) remains constant, the first part where the analogy is can be varied. For example, a saying like the following may have three alternative versions:

兔子尾巴 – 长不了 **tùzi wěiba – chángbuliǎo**
'a rabbit's tail – can't be long → can't last long'

    (兔子 **tùzi**: rabbit; 尾巴 **wěiba**: tail; 长不了 **chángbuliǎo**: can't grow to a great length)

草稍上的露水 – 长不了 **cǎoshāo shang de lùshui – chángbuliǎo**
'dewdrops on grasstips – can't remain long'

    (草稍上 **cǎoshāo shang**: on grasstips; 的 **de**: particle; 露水 **lùshui**: dew; 长不了 **chángbuliǎo**: cannot remain long)

剃头的扁担 – 长不了 **tìtóu de biǎndan – chángbuliǎo**
'the carrying-pole of a travelling barber – can't get longer'

    (剃头的 **tìtóu de**: barber; 扁担 **biǎndan**: carrying pole)

Sometimes such an allegorical saying may have as many different versions as the analogy made in the first part can be partially or completely reworded, e.g.

肉包子打狗 – 有去无回 **ròu bāozi dǎ gǒu – yǒu qù wú huí**
'hitting a dog with a meat dumpling – one can't expect to have it back'

    (肉 **ròu**: meat; 包子 **bāozi**: dumplings; 打 **dǎ**: hit; 狗 **gǒu**: dog; 有 **yǒu**: have; 去 **qù**: go; 无 **wú**: not; 回 **huí**: return)

肉馒头打狗 – 有去无回 **ròu mántou dǎ gǒu – yǒu qù wú huí**
'hitting a dog with a meat pie – one can't expect to have it back'
    (肉 **ròu**: meat; 馒头 **mántou**: bun; 打 **dǎ**: hit; 狗 **gǒu**: dog)

肉骨头打狗 – 有去无回 **ròu gǔtou dǎ gǒu – yǒu qù wú huí**
'hitting a dog with a bone – one can't expect to have it back'
    (肉 **ròu**: meat; 骨头 **gǔtou**: bones)

黄鼠狼拖小鸡 – 有去无回 **huángshǔláng tuō xiǎojī – yǒu qù wú huí**
'a weasel snatching away a chick – one can't expect to have it back'
    (黄鼠狼 **huángshǔláng**: weasel; 拖 **tuō**: pull, drag; 小鸡 **xiǎojī**: chicken)

大雾天放鸽子 – 有去无回 **dà wùtiān fàng gēzi – yǒu qù wú huí**
'freeing a pigeon on a foggy day – one can't expect to have it back'
    (大雾天 **dà wùtiān**: foggy day; 放 **fàng**: release; 鸽子 **gēzi**: pigeons)

泥牛入海 – 有去无回 **níniú rù hǎi – yǒu qù wú huí**
'a clay bull going into the sea – one can't expect to have it back'
    (泥牛 **níniú**: clay bull; 入 **rù**: enter; 海 **hǎi**: sea)

Metonymy

Most of the measure words in Chinese can be used metonymically, that is, the measure for the thing measured, the container for the thing contained, and so on. For example, in 喝一杯 **hē yī bēi** (lit. 'drink a cup'), 杯 **bēi** does not mean literally 'cup' or 'glass' but metonymically 'a cup of tea' or 'a glass of wine'. Here are some other examples:

有两手 **yǒu liǎng shǒu** 'really know one's stuff'
    (有 **yǒu**: have; 两 **liǎng**: two; 手 **shǒu**: hand)
买一本 **mǎi yī běn** 'buy one copy'
    (买 **mǎi**: buy; 一 **yī**: one; 本 **běn**: mw for books)
唱三首 **chàng sān shǒu** 'sing three songs'
    (唱 **chàng**: sing; 三 **sān**: three; 首 **shǒu**: mw for songs)

Where 手 **shǒu** 'hand', 本 **běn** 'copy', 首 **shǒu** 'measure word for songs' are used metonymically to stand for the kind of thing they respectively represent: 'good skill', 'book', and 'song'.

    Again, metonymy in a lexical unit can be partial or complete. In the disyllabic and trisyllabic lexemes quoted below the metonymy is complete; while the metonymy in the four quadrisyllabic idioms is partial. On the whole, metonymy, unlike analogy, is usually quite transparent.

白宫 **Bái Gōng** 'the White House' (白 **bái**: white; 宫 **gōng**: palace)
    ('the house' in which the president works stands for the government)
茅台 **máo tái** 'Maotai (spirit)' (茅台 is a small town in Renhuai County of Guizhou Province)
    ('the town' where the spirit is made stands for the spirit)

铁窗 **tiěchuāng** 'prison' (铁 **tiě**: iron; 窗 **chuāng**: window)
   ('iron-barred windows' stands for the whole prison)
手足 **shǒuzú** 'brothers' (手 **shǒu**: hand; 足 **zú**: foot)
   ('hands and feet' are part of the same parent body)
学问 **xuéwèn** 'knowledge' (学 **xué**: learn; 问 **wèn**: ask)
   ('learning' and 'asking' are supposedly part of the process in which knowledge is acquired)
铜臭 **tóngchòu** 'the stink of money' (铜 **tóng**: copper; 臭 **chòu**: stink)
   ('copper' of which money is made stands for money, whilst 'the smell
   of money' stands for profit-seeking mentality)
碎嘴子 **suìzuǐzi** 'a garrulous person'; 'a chatterbox' (碎 **suì**: fragmentary;
嘴子 **zuǐzi**: mouth)
   ('the gossipy mouth' stands for the gossiper)
白费唇舌 **báifèi chúnshé** 'waste one's breath' (白费 **báifèi**: waste; 唇 **chún**:
lip; 舌 **shé**: tongue)
   ('lips and tongues' stands for words uttered)
单枪匹马 **dān qiāng pǐ mǎ** 'single-handed' (单 **dān**: single; 枪 **qiāng**: rifle;
匹 **pǐ**: mw; 马 **mǎ**: horse)
   ('a single rifle and horse' stands for fighting a battle all alone)
另请高明 **lìng qǐng gāomíng** 'find someone better qualified (than myself)'
   (另 **lìng**: separately; 请 **qǐng**: invite; 高明 **gāomíng**: high and bright)
   ('high and bright' stands for someone who is able and wise)
瞒上欺下 **mán shàng qī xià** 'deceive one's superiors and bully one's subordinates' (瞒 **mán**: deceive; 上 **shàng**: above; 欺 **qī**: bully; 下 **xià**: below)
   ('above and below' stands for one's superiors and subordinates)

There is an interesting, though not really important, distinction between
metonymy and synecdoche, the former being part for the whole (including
the attributes, accessories, etc., e.g. 薄脆 **bócuì** 'crisp fritter': literally, 'thin
and crispy') and the latter being member(s) for a whole group (i.e. co-hyponyms
for the superordinate term). Examples of synecdoche are:

儿女 **érnǚ** 'children' (儿 **ér**: son; 女 **nǚ**: daughter)
父母 **fùmǔ** 'parents' (父 **fù**: father; 母 **mǔ**: mother)
眉眼 **méiyǎn** 'appearance'; 'looks' (眉 **méi**: eyebrows; 眼 **yǎn**: eyes)
岁月 **suìyuè** 'years' (岁 **suì**: year; 月 **yuè**: month)
薪水 **xīnshuǐ** 'salary' (薪 **xīn**: firewood and 水 **shuǐ**: water – two important
   things in old times)
之乎者也 **zhī hū zhě yě** 'pedantic terms' (之 **zhī**, 乎 **hū**, 者 **zhě**, 也 **yě**: four
   grammatical words used in classical Chinese)
柴米油盐 **chái mǐ yóu yán** 'chief daily necessities' (柴 **chái**: firewood; 米 **mǐ**:
   rice; 油 **yóu**: oil; 盐 **yán**: salt)
拘守绳墨 **jūshǒu shéngmò** 'stick to rules and regulations' (拘守 **jūshǒu**:
   adhere to; 绳墨 **shéngmò**: string and ink, i.e. a carpenter's line-marking
   tool)

Sometimes, as we can see, metonymy is itself to be understood on a metaphorical plane, which therefore becomes opaque. For example, in 手足 **shǒuzú** 'brothers' and 学问 **xuéwèn** 'knowledge', we find the juxtaposition of 手 **shǒu** 'hand' and 足 **zú** 'foot' to stand for the intimate and inseparable relation of brotherhood and that of 学 **xué** 'learn' and 问 **wèn** 'inquire', the very means through which knowledge is acquired, to stand for learning itself.

In some everyday words, very often the metonymy originally associated with them has been lost to their speakers if attention is not drawn to it. For example,

What a person does for what he or she is:

经理 **jīnglǐ** 'manager'; 'director' (经 **jīng**: manage, deal in; 理 **lǐ**: manage, run)

代办 **dàibàn** (diplomacy) 'chargé d'affaires' (代 **dài**: on behalf of; 办 **bàn**: handle, attend to)

参谋 **cānmóu** (mil.) 'staff officer' (参 **cān**: join; take part in; 谋 **móu**: to plan, scheme)

顾问 **gùwèn** 'adviser'; 'consultant' (顾 **gù**: attend to, take into consideration; 问 **wèn**: ask)

会计 **kuàijì** 'bookkeeper'; 'accountant' (会 **kuài**: calculate annually; 计 **jì**: count, calculate)

出纳 **chūnà** 'cashier' (出 **chū**: pay out; 纳 **nà**: receive)

传达 **chuándá** 'janitor' (传 **chuán**: pass on; 达 **dá**: reach)

看守 **kānshǒu** 'warder'; 'guard' (看 **kān**: look after; 守 **shǒu**: guard, defend)

跑堂 **pǎotáng** 'waiter' (in a restaurant, etc.) (跑 **pǎo**: run about doing sth; 堂 **táng**: hall)

导演 **dǎoyǎn** 'director' (of a film or play) (导 **dǎo**: guide, conduct; 演 **yǎn**: perform, performance)

指挥 **zhǐhuī** 'conductor' (of an orchestra) (指 **zhǐ**: point at; 挥 **huī**: wave, wield)

编辑 **biānjí** 'editor'; 'compiler' (编 **biān**: edit, compile; 辑 **jí**: edit, compile, collect)

翻译 **fānyì** 'translator'; 'interpreter' (翻 **fān**: translate, interpret; 译 **yì**: translate, interpret)

裁缝 **cáifeng** 'tailor' (裁 **cái**: cut cloth with scissors; 缝 **féng**: sew with needle and thread)

领队 **lǐngduì** 'the leader of a group, sports team etc.' (领 **lǐng**: lead; 队 **duì**: team, group)

司仪 **sīyí** 'master of ceremony' (司 **sī**: be in charge; 仪 **yí**: ceremony)

助手 **zhùshǒu** 'assistant'; 'aide' (助 **zhù**: help, assist, aid; 手 **shǒu**: hand)

对手 **duìshǒu** 'opponent'; 'adversary' (对 **duì**: oppose, counter; 手 **shǒu**: hand)

扒手 **páshǒu** 'pickpocket' (扒 **pá**: dig out; 手 **shǒu**: hand)

A person's physical or mental characteristic for what a person is:

麻脸 **máliǎn** 'pockmarked person' (麻 **má**: pocked, pockmarked; 脸 **liǎn**: face)

兔唇 **tùchún** 'harelipped person' (兔 **tù**: hare; 唇 **chún**: lips)

瘸腿 **quétuǐ** 'cripple' (瘸 **qué**: be lame, limp; 腿 **tuǐ**: leg)

驼背 **tuóbèi** 'hunchback'; 'humpback' (驼 **tuó**: hunchbacked, humpbacked; 背 **bèi**: back)

痢痢头 **làlìtóu** 'person with favus on the scalp' (痢痢 **làlì**: favus of the scalp; 头 **tóu**: head)

神经病 **shénjīngbìng** 'neurotic person' (神经 **shénjīng**: nerve; 病 **bìng**: illness)

油嘴 **yóuzuǐ** 'a glib talker' (油 **yóu**: oil, oily; 嘴 **zuǐ**: mouth)

A person's make-up, dress or association for what a person is:

丫鬟 **yāhuan** 'servant girl' (丫 **yā**: bifurcation; 鬟 **huán**: (of hair) bun)

便衣 **biànyī** 'plainclothesman' (便 **biàn**: plain, ordinary; 衣 **yī**: clothes)

花脸 **huāliǎn** 'role in Beijing opera with an elaborately painted face' (花 **huā**: flowery; 脸 **liǎn**: face)

青衣 **qīngyī** 'a female role in Beijing opera portraying a good woman' (青 **qīng**: blue; 衣 **yī**: robe)

老衲 **lǎonà** (formal) 'old monk' (老 **lǎo**: old; 衲 **nà**: patchwork vestment worn by a Buddhist monk)

泥水匠 **níshuǐjiàng** 'bricklayer'; 'plasterer' (泥 **ní**: mud; 水 **shuǐ**: water; 匠 **jiàng**: artisan)

A thing's function or component for what a thing is:

绑腿 **bǎngtuǐ** 'puttees' (绑 **bǎng**: wrap, bind; 腿 **tuǐ**: leg)

调羹 **tiáogēng** 'spoon' (调 **tiáo**: stir, adjust; 羹 **gēng**: soup)

护封 **hùfēng** 'book jacket' (护 **hù**: protect; 封 **fēng**: book cover)

套袖 **tàoxiù** 'oversleeve' (套 **tào**: slip over; 袖 **xiù**: sleeve)

兵燹 **bīngxiǎn** 'ravages of war' (兵 **bīng**: soldier; 燹 **xiǎn**: wild fires)

知识 **zhīshi** 'knowledge' (知 **zhī**: know; 识 **shí**: recognise)

买卖 **mǎimài** 'business'; 'transaction' (买 **mǎi**: buy; 卖 **mài**: sell)

行止 **xíngzhǐ** 'whereabouts' (行 **xíng**: walk; 止 **zhǐ**: stop)

招呼 **zhāohu** 'greet' (招 **zhāo**: beckon; 呼 **hū**: call)

谈吐 **tántǔ** 'style of conversation' (谈 **tán**: talk; 吐 **tǔ**: tell)

Depersonalisation

In 'depersonalisation', the human being is often compared either to (1) animals or to (2) inanimate things.

In the lexicon there is a particular set of juxtapositions of two different animals to refer to individuals who possess characteristics similar to these animals (i.e. depersonalisation realised in terms of synecdoche).

禽兽 **qínshòu** 'a beast in human clothing' (禽 **qín**: fowls; 兽 **shòu**: beasts)

豺狼 **cháiláng** 'cruel and evil people' (豺 **chái**: jackal; 狼 **láng**: wolf)

牛马 **niúmǎ** 'people who work like beasts of burden' (牛 **niú**: ox; 马 **mǎ**: horse)

鹰犬 **yīngquǎn** 'hired thugs' (鹰 **yīng**: falcon; 犬 **quǎn**: dog)

鸳鸯 **yuānyāng** 'affectionate couple' (鸳 **yuān**: mandarin drake; 鸯 **yāng**: mandarin duck)

Depersonalisation is found in a number of trisyllabic words and polysyllabic expressions:

落水狗 **luòshuǐgǒu** 'bad people who are down' (落 **luò**: fall into; 水 **shuǐ**: water; 狗 **gǒu**: dog)

落汤鸡 **luòtāngjī** 'a drowned rat' (落 **luò**: fall into; 汤 **tāng**: broth; 鸡 **jī**: chicken)

替罪羊 **tìzuìyáng** 'scapegoat' (替 **tì**: in place of; 罪 **zuì**: crime, punishment; 羊 **yáng**: goat)

地头蛇 **dìtóushé** 'local bully' (地头 **dìtóu**: locality, place; 蛇 **shé**: snake)

可怜虫 **kěliánchóng** 'wretch' (可怜 **kělián**: pitiful, pitiable; 虫 **chóng**: insect or worm)

狗崽子 **gǒuzǎizi** 'son of a bitch' (狗 **gǒu**: dog; 崽子 **zǎizi**: whelp, bastard)

秋后的蚂蚱 **qiū hòu de màzha**
'on one's last legs' (lit. 'like a grasshopper at the end of autumn')
(秋 **qiū**: autumn; 后 **hòu**: at the end of; 的 **de**: attributive marker; 蚂蚱 **màzha**: grasshopper)

热锅上的蚂蚁 **rè guō shang de mǎyǐ** 'restless' (lit. 'ants in a hot pan')
(热 **rè**: hot; 锅 **guō**: pan; 上 **shang**: on; 的 **de**: attributive marker; 蚂蚁 **mǎyǐ**: ant)

Also in polysyllabic vernacular idioms:

枪打出头鸟 **qiāng dǎ chūtóu niǎo**
'one who takes the lead is liable to be fired at'
(枪 **qiāng**: rifle; 打 **dǎ**: shoot; 出头 **chūtóu**: come forward, appear in public; 鸟 **niǎo**: bird)

老虎屁股摸不得 **lǎohǔ pìgu mōbude** 'not to be provoked'
(老虎 **lǎohǔ**: tiger; 屁股 **pìgu**: bottom; 摸不得 **mōbude**: no one dares to touch)

驴唇不对马嘴 **lǘchún bù duì mǎzuǐ** 'incongruous'; 'irrelevant'
(驴唇 **lǘchún**: donkey's lips; 不对 **bù duì**: don't match; 马嘴 **mǎzuǐ**: horses' jaw)

兔子不吃窝边草 **tùzi bù chī wōbiān cǎo**
'a villain doesn't harm his next-door neighbours'
(兔子 **tùzi**: rabbit; 不 **bù**: not; 吃 **chī**: eat; 窝边 **wōbiān**: beside its warren; 草 **cǎo**: grass)

狗嘴里吐不出象牙 **gǒuzuǐli tǔbuchū xiàngyá**
'what you can expect from a dog but a bark'
(狗嘴里 **gǒuzuǐli**: in a dog's mouth; 吐不出 **tǔbuchū**: can't issue forth; 象牙 **xiàngyá**: ivory)

癩蛤蟆想吃天鹅肉 **làihámá xiǎng chī tiān'é ròu**
'aspiring after something one is not worthy of'
    (癩蛤蟆 **làihámá**: toad; 想 **xiǎng**: want; 吃 **chī**: eat; 天鹅 **tiān'é**: swan;
肉 **ròu**: meat, flesh)

One set of disyllabic words which transfers animal action onto human beings:

雀跃 **quèyuè** 'jump for joy' (雀 **què**: sparrow; 跃 **yuè**: jump)
鸟瞰 **niǎokàn** 'get a bird's-eye view' (鸟 **niǎo**: bird; 瞰 **kàn**: gaze)
蜂拥 **fēngyǒng** 'swarm' (to a place) (蜂 **fēng**: bee; 拥 **yǒng**: to swarm)[3]

Depersonalisation is particularly common with quadrisyllabic idioms, in which
there is almost no animal a human has not been compared to, e.g.

过街老鼠 **guò jiē lǎoshǔ**
'a person who arouses public anger' (lit. 'a rat crossing the street')
    (过 **guò**: cross; 街 **jiē**: street; 老鼠 **lǎoshǔ**: rat)
初生之犊 **chū shēng zhī dú**
'young people who are dauntless' (lit. 'newborn calves who have no fear
for tigers')
    (初生 **chū shēng**: newborn; 之 **zhī**: grammatical particle; 犊 **dú**: calf)
网中之鱼 **wǎng zhōng zhī yú** 'a captive' (lit. 'a fish in the net')
    (网中 **wǎng zhōng**: in the net; 鱼 **yú**: fish)
瓮中之鳖 **wèng zhōng zhī biē** 'bottled up or trapped' (lit. 'like a turtle in a jar')
    (瓮中 **wèng zhōng**: in the urn; 鳖 **biē**: turtle)
一丘之貉 **yī qiū zhī hé** 'birds of a feather' (lit. 'jackals from the same lair')
    (一 **yī**: one, same; 丘 **qiū**: knoll, hill; 之 **zhī**: grammatical particle; 貉 **hé**:
racoon dog)
惊弓之鸟 **jīng gōng zhī niǎo**
'a badly startled person' (lit. 'a bird that starts at the twang of a bow')
    (惊 **jīng**: start at, fear; 弓 **gōng**: a bow; 鸟 **niǎo**: bird)
噤若寒蝉 **jìn ruò hánchán**
'keep quiet out of fear' (lit. 'as silent as the cicada in cold weather')
    (噤 **jìn**: quiet; 若 **ruò**: like, as; 寒蝉 **hánchán**: cicada in the cold)
鹤立鸡群 **hè lì jī qún**
'head and shoulders above others' (lit. 'a crane standing among chickens')
    (鹤 **hè**: crane; 立 **lì**: stand; 鸡 **jī**: chicken; 群 **qún**: flock)
鸦雀无声 **yā què wú shēng**
'not a breath stirring' (lit. 'not a crow or sparrow is heard')
    (鸦 **yā**: crow; 雀 **què**: sparrow; 无 **wú**: no; 声 **shēng**: sound)
如鱼得水 **rú yú dé shuǐ** 'in one's element' (lit. 'like fish in water')
    (如 **rú**: like; 鱼 **yú**: fish; 得 **dé**: get, take to; 水 **shuǐ**: water)
打草惊蛇 **dǎ cǎo jīng shé**
'act rashly and alert the enemy' (lit. 'beat the grass and startle the snake')
    (打 **dǎ**: beat; 草 **cǎo**: grass; 惊 **jīng**: frighten; 蛇 **shé**: snake)

---

[3] For more examples, see predicational juxtaposition in Chapter 4.

对牛弹琴 **duì niú tán qín**
'address the wrong audience' (lit. 'play the lute to a cow')
  (对 **duì**: to; 牛 **niú**: ox; 弹 **tán**: pluck; 琴 **qín**: lute)
金蝉脱壳 **jīnchán tuō qiào** 'escape by cunning manoeuvring'
(lit. 'slip out of a predicament like a cicada sloughing its skin')
  (金蝉 **jīnchán**: cicada; 脱 **tuō**: slough; 壳 **qiào**: skin)
狼吞虎咽 **láng tūn hǔ yàn** 'wolf down (one's food)'
  (狼 **láng**: wolf; 吞 **tūn**: swallow; 虎 **hǔ**: tiger; 咽 **yàn**: swallow)
鸡鸣狗盗 **jī míng gǒu dào** 'resort to petty tricks'
(lit. 'have the ability to crow like a rooster and snatch like a dog')
  (鸡 **jī**: rooster; 鸣 **míng**: to crow; 狗 **gǒu**: dog; 盗 **dào**: rob)

Depersonalisation into animals is also a peculiar feature of the metaphorical part of two-part allegorical sayings. Among dozens of them are:

老鼠上称钩 – 自称自 **lǎoshǔ shàng chènggōu | zì chēng zì**
'sing praises of oneself' (lit. 'a mouse climbs onto the hook of a steelyard to weigh itself')
  (老鼠 **lǎoshǔ**: mouse; 上 **shàng**: climb onto; 称钩 **chènggōu**: hook of a steelyard; 自 **zì**: self; 称 **chēng**: weigh, which is homophonic with 称 **chēng** in 称赞 **chēngzàn** 'praise')

八个麻雀抬轿 – 担当不起 **bā gè máquè tái jiào | dān dāng bù qǐ**
'cannot assume the responsibility' (lit. 'eight sparrows trying to carry a sedan chair')
  (八 **bā**: eight; 个 **gè**: measure word; 麻雀 **máquè**: sparrow; 抬 **tái**: carry; 轿 **jiào**: sedan chair; 担当 **dāndāng** is polysemous, meaning 'hold up' and 'understake'; 不起 **bù qǐ**: not able)

飞蛾扑火 – 自取灭亡 **fēi'é pū huǒ | zì qǔ mièwáng**
'seeking one's own destruction' (lit. 'a moth darts into a flame')
  (飞蛾 **fēi'é**: a flying moth; 扑 **pū**: throw oneself at; 火 **huǒ**: fire; 自 **zì**: self; 取 **qǔ**: to court; 灭亡 **mièwáng**: destruction)

狗逮老鼠 – 多管闲事 **gǒu dǎi lǎoshǔ | duō guǎn xiánshì**
'poking one's nose into others' business' (lit. 'dogs catching mice')
  (狗 **gǒu**: dog; 逮 **dǎi**: catch; 老鼠 **lǎoshǔ**: mouse; 多 **duō**: more; 管 **guǎn**: in charge of; 闲事 **xiánshì**: not one's own business)

黄鼠狼给鸡拜年 – 没安好心 **huángshǔláng gěi jī bàinián | méi ān hǎoxīn**
'not the best of intentions' (lit. 'the weasel wishing the chicken "Happy New Year"')
  (黄鼠狼 **huángshǔláng**: weasel; 给 **gěi**: to; 鸡 **jī**: chicken; 拜年 **bàinián**: go to sb's place to wish him a Happy New Year; 没 **méi**: not; 安 **ān**: have; 好心 **hǎoxīn**: good intentions)

鸡抱鸭子 – 白操心 **jī bào yāzi | bái cāoxīn**
'worrying in vain' (lit. 'chicken trying to nurse ducklings')
  (鸡 **jī**: chicken; 抱 **bào**: embrace; 鸭子 **yāzi**: duck; 白 **bái**: in vain; 操心 **cāoxīn**: worry about)

猫哭老鼠 – 假慈悲 **māo kū lǎoshǔ | jiǎ cíbēi**
'shed crocodile tears' (lit. 'the cat weeping over the dead mouse')
(猫 **māo**: cat; 哭 **kū**: weep over; 老鼠 **lǎoshǔ**: mouse; 假 **jiǎ**: false; 慈悲 **cíbēi**: merciful)

麻雀落在糠堆上 – 空欢喜 **máquè luò zài kāngduī shang | kōng huānxǐ**
'rejoice too soon' (lit. 'sparrows landing on a pile of chaff')
(麻雀 **máquè**: sparrow; 落 **luò**: to land; 在 **zài**: at; 糠堆 **kàngduī**: pile of chaff; 上 **shang**: on; 空 **kōng**: empty, in vain; 欢喜 **huānxǐ**: feel happy)

螃蟹过门槛 – 七手八脚 **pángxiè guò ménkǎn | qī shǒu bā jiǎo**
'with everybody lending a hand' (lit. 'crabs crossing the threshold – hands and legs all into action')
(螃蟹 **pángxiè**: crab; 过 **guò**: cross; 门槛 **ménkǎn**: threshold; 七 **qī**: seven; 手 **shǒu**: hand; 八 **bā**: eight; 脚 **jiǎo**: leg)

乌鸦笑猪黑 – 不晓得自己 **wūyā xiào zhū hēi | bù xiǎode zìjǐ**
'not knowing what itself is like' (lit. 'the crow calling the pig black')
(乌鸦 **wūyā**: crow; 笑 **xiào**: laugh at; 猪 **zhū**: pig; 黑 **hēi**: black; 不 **bù**: not; 晓得 **xiǎode**: know; 自己 **zìjǐ**: oneself)

煮熟的鸭子 – 逃不了 **zhǔ shú de yāzi | táobuliǎo**
'a cooked duck – can't escape'
(煮 **zhǔ**: to cook; 熟 **shú**: cooked; 的 **de**: attributive marker; 鸭子 **yāzi**: duck; 逃不了 **táobuliǎo**: cannot escape)

Depersonalisation into inanimate objects is equally common in various types of words and idioms:

靠山 **kàoshān** 'backer'; 'patron' (靠 **kào**: lean against, rely on; 山 **shān**: mountain, hill)

后台 **hòutái** 'backstage supporter'; 'behind-the-scenes backer' (后 **hòu**: back, rear; 台 **tái**: stage)

支柱 **zhīzhù** 'pillar'; 'mainstay' (支 **zhī**: prop up; support; 柱 **zhù**: pillar, column)

裙钗 **qúnchāi** 'women' (裙 **qún**: skirt; 钗 **chāi**: hairpin formerly worn by women for adornment)

须眉 **xūméi** 'man' (须 **xū**: beard, moustache; 眉 **méi**: eyebrows)

桃李 **táolǐ** 'one's pupils or disciples' (桃 **táo**: peaches; 李 **lǐ**: plums)

祸根 **huògēn** 'the root of the trouble' (祸 **huò**: misfortune, disaster; 根 **gēn**: root)

饭桶 **fàntǒng** 'fathead' (饭 **fàn**: rice; 桶 **tǒng**: bucket)

草包 **cǎobāo** 'blockhead' (草 **cǎo**: straw; 包 **bāo**: sack)

炮灰 **pàohuī** 'cannon fodder' (炮 **pào**: cannon; 灰 **huī**: ash)

鱼肉 **yúròu** 'at somebody's mercy' (鱼 **yú**: fish; 肉 **ròu**: meat)

眼中钉 **yǎnzhōngdīng** 'a thorn in one's side' (眼中 **yǎn zhōng**: in one's eyes; 钉 **dīng**: nail)

肉中刺 **ròuzhōngcì** 'a thorn in one's flesh' (肉中 **ròu zhōng**: in one's flesh; 刺 **cì**: thorn)

牺牲品 **xīshēngpǐn** 'victim'; 'prey' (牺牲 **xīshēng**: a beast slaughtered for sacrifice; 品 **pǐn**: product)

垫脚石 **diànjiǎoshí** 'stepping-stone' (垫脚 **diànjiǎo**: to pad, to cushion; 石 **shí**: stone)

出气筒 **chūqìtǒng** (fig.) 'punching bag' (出气 **chūqì**: vent one's spleen; 筒 **tǒng**: cylinder)

受气包 **shòuqìbāo** 'one who always takes the rap' (受气 **shòuqì**: be bullied; 包 **bāo**: bundle)

半瓶醋 **bànpíngcù** 'dabbler' (半 **bàn**: half; 瓶 **píng**: bottle; 醋 **cù**: vinegar)

王八蛋 **wángbadàn** 'bastard' (王八 **wángba**: tortoise; 蛋 **dàn**: egg)

掌上明珠 **zhǎng shang míngzhū** 'a beloved daughter'
　(掌 **zhǎng**: palm; 上 **shang**: on; 明珠 **míngzhū**: pearl)

众矢之的 **zhòng shǐ zhī dì** 'a target of public criticism (or censure)'
　(众矢 **zhòng shǐ**: everybody's arrow; 之 **zhī**: grammatical particle; 的 **dì**: target, bull's eye)

寻花问柳 **xúnhuā wènliǔ** 'visit prostitutes'
　(寻 **xún**: look for; 花 **huā**: flowers; 问 **wèn**: ask for; 柳 **liǔ**: willow)

酒囊饭袋 **jiǔnáng fàndài** 'a good-for-nothing'
　(酒 **jiǔ**: wine; 囊 **náng**: pocket; 饭 **fàn**: rice; 袋 **dài**: bag)

青梅竹马 **qīngméi zhúmǎ** 'a girl and a boy playing innocently together'
　(青梅 **qīngméi**: green plum; 竹马 **zhúmǎ**: bamboo horse)

Also in polysyllabic sayings:

有眼不识泰山 **yǒu yǎn bù shí tàishān**
'not knowing that one is dealing with a VIP' (lit. 'have eyes but fail to see Taishan Mountain')
　(有 **yǒu**: have; 眼 **yǎn**: eye; 不 **bù**: not; 识 **shí**: know, recognise; 泰山 **tàishān**: Mount Tai)

茶壶里煮饺子 – 有货倒不出来 **cháhúli zhǔ jiǎozi | yǒu huò dàobuchūlai**
'a learned person who is incapable of imparting his knowledge to others'
(lit. 'dumplings cooked in a teapot can't be poured out')
　(茶壶 **cháhú**: teapot; 里 **li**: in; 煮 **zhǔ**: cook; 饺子 **jiǎozi**: dumpling; 有 **yǒu**: have; 货 **huò**: goods, substance; 倒 **dào**: pour out; 不 **bu**: not; 出来 **chūlai**: out)

大树底下好乘凉 **dàshù dǐxia hǎo chéngliáng**
'one finds protection from somebody in a high position' (lit. 'one can enjoy the cool in the shade of a big tree')
　(大树 **dàshù**: big tree; 底下 **dǐxia**: under; 好 **hǎo**: good for; 乘凉 **chéngliáng**: enjoy the cool)

一朵鲜花插在牛粪上 **yī duǒ xiānhuā chā zài niúfèn shang**
'a beautiful girl married to an ugly or unworthy man' (lit. 'a beautiful flower stuck in cow dung')

(一 **yī**: one; 朵 **duǒ**: mw; 鲜花 **xiānhuā**: fresh flowers; 插在 **chā zài**: stick in; 牛粪 **niúfèn**: cow dung; 上 **shang**: on)

Depersonalisation is largely derogatory in sense.

Personification

Personification in the lexical structure seems to be found only in the form of 'transferred epithet'.

死水 **sǐshuǐ** 'stagnant water' (死 **sǐ**: dead; 水 **shuǐ**: water)
瘦煤 **shòuméi** 'lean coal' (瘦 **shòu**: lean; 煤 **méi**: coal)
秃笔 **tūbǐ** 'poor writing ability' (秃 **tū**: bald; 笔 **bǐ**: writing brush)
坐劲 **zuòjìn** (of a rifle) 'recoil' (坐 **zuò**: sit; 劲 **jìn**: energy)
活火山 **huó huǒshān** 'active volcano' (活 **huó**: live, active; 火山 **huǒshān**: volcano)

One common practice of personification in Chinese is the transposition of human body parts onto inanimate objects, e.g.

车头 **chētóu** 'the front of a vehicle' (车 **chē**: car; 头 **tóu**: head)
机身 **jīshēn** 'fuselage' (机 **jī**: aeroplane; 身 **shēn**: body)
椅背 **yǐbèi** 'the back of a chair' (椅 **yǐ**: chair; 背 **bèi**: back)
屋脊 **wūjǐ** 'ridge' (of a roof) (屋 **wū**: house; 脊 **jǐ**: spine, backbone)
山脚 **shānjiǎo** 'the foot of a hill' (山 **shān**: mountain, hill; 脚 **jiǎo**: foot)
峰顶 **fēngdǐng** 'top of the peak; summit' (峰 **fēng**: peak; 顶 **dǐng**: top)
炉膛 **lútáng** 'the chamber of a stove or furnace' (炉 **lú**: stove, oven, furnace; 膛 **táng**: chest)
针眼 **zhēnyǎn** 'the eye of a needle' (针 **zhēn**: needle; 眼 **yǎn**: eye)
瓶颈 **píngjǐng** 'neck of the bottle' (瓶 **píng**: bottle, vase, jar; 颈 **jǐng**: neck)
靶心 **bǎxīn** 'bull's eye' (靶 **bǎ**: target; 心 **xīn**: heart)
球胆 **qiúdǎn** 'bladder (of a ball)' (球 **qiú**: ball; 胆 **dǎn**: gallbladder)
路口 **lùkǒu** 'crossing'; 'intersection' (路 **lù**: road; 口 **kǒu**: mouth)
壶嘴 **húzuǐ** 'mouth of the pot or kettle' (壶 **hú**: kettle, pot; 嘴 **zuǐ**: mouth)
裤腰 **kùyāo** 'waist of trousers' (裤 **kù**: trousers; 腰 **yāo**: waist)
烟屁股 **yānpìgu** 'cigarette end' (烟 **yān**: cigarette; 屁股 **pìgu**: buttocks, bottom)
门脸儿 **ménliǎnr** (dial.) 'the facade of a shop'; 'shop front' (门 **mén**: door; 脸儿 **liǎnr**: face)
桌子腿 **zhuōzituǐ** 'legs of a table' (桌子 **zhuōzi**: table; 腿 **tuǐ**: leg)

Allusion

Allusion is a distinctive feature especially of polysyllabic (particularly quadrisyllabic) idioms, many of which have their origin in historical incidents or folk legends, e.g.

毛遂自荐 **Máo Suì zì jiàn**
'volunteers one's services' (lit. 'offer one's services as Mao Sui of the Warring State Period did')
    (毛遂 **Máo Suì**: name of a person; 自 **zì**: oneself; 荐 **jiàn**: recommend)

名落孙山 **míng luò Sūn Shān**
'fail a competitive exam' (lit. 'fall behind Sun Shan, the last on the list of successful candidates')
    (名 **míng**: name; 落 **luò**: fall behind; 孙山 **Sūn Shān**: name of a person)

Sometimes, without quoting proper names in the idiom, the allusion remains opaque and has to be studied to be properly understood, e.g.

紧箍咒 **jǐngūzhòu**
'inhibition' (lit. 'the Incantation of the Golden Hoop')
    (紧 **jǐn**: tight; 箍 **gū**: hoop, bind round; 咒 **zhòu**: curse, damn)

负荆请罪 **fù jīng qǐng zuì**
'offer a humble apology' (lit. 'as Lian Po did to Lin Xiangru during the Warring State Period')
    (负 **fù**: carry on one's back; 荆 **jīng**: chaste-tree twig; 请 **qǐng**: ask for; 罪 **zuì**: punishment)

图穷匕首见 **tú qióng bǐshǒu xiàn**
'hidden intentions are revealed in the end' (lit. 'when the map was unrolled, the dagger was revealed')
    (图 **tú**: map; 穷 **qióng**: come to an end when unrolled; 匕 **bǐshǒu**: dagger; 见 **xiàn**: appear)

If the legendary or historical event behind the idiom is not known it will be difficult to understand what connections there are between an incantation and inhibition, between hiding a dagger in a rolled-up map and someone's hidden intentions, and between carrying a chaste-tree twig on one's back and a humble apology.

The first allusion actually refers to the Golden Hoop worn by the Monkey King in the novel 西游记 **xīyóujì** *Pilgrimage to the West*. To keep the Monkey King under control, his master the Monk (唐僧 **tángsēng**) would recite the incantation and the Golden Hoop on the Monkey King's head would get smaller to cause a devastating headache.

The second allusion refers to two high officials in the State of Zhao during the Warring State Period. One of them called Lian Po was jealous of the quick promotion conferred on his colleague Lin Xiangru and waited for a chance to humiliate the latter. However, when Lin realised Lian's intentions, he conceded in every way to avoid such a conflict for the benefit of the state. When Lian learned of this, he felt so ashamed of himself that he stripped himself to the waist and, carrying a chaste-tree twig on his back, went to see Lin to ask for a flogging.

The third allusion refers to an incident in the Period of Warring States. An assassin named **Jīng Kē** (荆柯) was sent by the crown prince of the State of Yan with a map to the emperor of the state of Qin as if he were going to present his majesty with territory on a map for annexation, but there was in fact a dagger hidden in the map as it was rolled up. So when the map was gradually unrolled before the emperor, the hidden dagger would be revealed, which the assassin could then use to kill the emperor. In the end, however, the assassin was not successful and his intentions being exposed, he met his tragic death.

Simile

Simile can be said to be all kinds of metaphorical comparisons made 'transparent' by overt markers such as 如 **rú**, 似 **sì**, 若 **ruò**, etc., all meaning 'similar to, resemble': e.g.

> 归心似箭 **guīxīn sì jiàn** 'anxious to return'
> (归心 **guīxīn**: a heart that wishes to return; 似 **sì**: resemble; 箭 **jiàn**: arrow)
> 口若悬河 **kǒu ruò xuán hé** 'speak volubly'
> (口 **kǒu**: mouth; 若 **ruò**: be similar to; 悬 **xuán**: hanging; 河 **hé**: river)
> 守口如瓶 **shǒu kǒu rú píng** 'be tight-mouthed'
> (守 **shǒu**: guard; 口 **kǒu**: mouth; 如 **rú**: as if; 瓶 **píng**: bottle)

Here the heart for speeding home is compared to 箭 **jiàn** 'a flying arrow', a person's eloquence is compared to 悬河 **xuánhé** 'a river cascading unceasingly from a height', and not breathing a word about something is thought of as if someone were guarding his mouth like a 瓶 **píng** 'bottle', which was carefully stopped up in order not to let out the secret.

This is also true of other polysyllabic sayings: e.g.

> 百闻不如一见 **bǎi wén bùrú yī jiàn**
> 'seeing is believing' (lit. 'hearing it a hundred times is not as good as seeing it once')
> (百 **bǎi**: one hundred; 闻 **wén**: hear; 不如 **bùrú**: not as good as; 一 **yī**: one;
> 见 **jiàn**: see)

The type of hexasyllabic idiom quoted above can be found in dozens in the established lexicon. The overwhelming features of these hexasyllables are: (a) the overt marker 如 **rú** is more often used than its synonymous cousins 似 **sì** or 若 **ruò**; (b) the comparison is often rendered in the negative; (c) the structure is extremely productive, that is to say, an extemporaneous hexasyllabic idiom can always be coined in keeping with the pattern XX / 不如 **bùrú** / XX to carry the comparison forcibly home. Here are some other examples,

百治不如一防 **bǎi zhì bùrú yī fáng**
'prevention is better than cure' (lit. 'a hundred cures are no better than one prevention')

> (百 **bǎi**: one hundred; 治 **zhì**: treat (a disease); 不如 **bùrú**: not as good as; 一 **yī**: one; 防 **fáng**: prevent from)

好头不如好尾 **hǎo tóu bùrú hǎo wěi**
'a good beginning will need a good ending' (lit. 'a good beginning is no better without a good ending')

> (好 **hǎo**: good; 头 **tóu**: beginning; 尾 **wěi**: end)

求人不如求己 **qiú rén bùrú qiú jǐ**
'self-help is better than help from others'; 'God helps those that help themselves'

> (求人 **qiúrén**: ask sb for help; 不如 **bùrú**: not as good as; 求己 **qiújǐ**: ask oneself)

In fact, with 不如 **bùrú** serving as a pivot, any balanced structure e.g. X 不如 **bùrú** X, or XXX 不如 **bùrú** XXX can be achieved:

多一事不如少一事 **duō yī shì bùrú shǎo yī shì**
'don't meet trouble half-way' (lit. 'one thing more to deal with is not as good as one thing less')

> (多 **duō**: many; 一 **yī**: one; 事 **shì**: thing, matter; 少 **shǎo**: less)

Sometimes in quadrisyllables, 如 **rú**, 似 **sì**, 若 **ruò**, etc. are used twice (in a staggered way) in the same idiom if the thing for which the comparison is intended is left unsaid:

如火如荼 **rú huǒ rú tú** 'like a raging fire'
> (如 **rú**: like, as if; 火 **huǒ**: fire; 荼 **tú**: a bitter edible plant)

若即若离 **ruò jí ruò lí**
'keep somebody at arm's length' (lit. 'be neither close nor distant')
> (若 **ruò**: as if; 即 **jí**: be near, approach; 离 **lí**: leave)

如饥似渴 **rú jī sì kě** 'eager' (lit. 'as if thirsting or hungering for something')
> (如 **rú**: like, as if; 饥 **jī**: hungry; 似 **sì**: like, seem; 渴 **kě**: thirsty)

The position of these overt markers can be varied: e.g. (i) 如 XXX; (ii) X 如 XX; (iii) XX 如 X.

似水流年 **sì shuǐ liúnián** 'youth slips away like flowing water'
> (似 **sì**: like, seem; 水 **shuǐ**: water; 流年 **liúnián**: fleeting time)

多如牛毛 **duō rú niúmáo** 'innumerable' (lit. 'as many as the hairs on an ox')
> (多 **duō**: many, much; 如 **rú**: like, as if; 牛毛 **niúmáo**: ox hair)

受宠若惊 **shòu chǒng ruò jīng** 'be overwhelmed by an unexpected favour'
> (受 **shòu**: receive; 宠 **chǒng**: bestow favour on; 若 **ruò**: as if; 惊 **jīng**: frightened)

There is a particular set of adjectives, of which the second adjectival monomym is qualified by a noun in the first monomym, which usually denotes the object to which the kind of quality in the second adjectival monomym can be attributed. The second monomym always carries the literal part of the meaning, which usually falls within the area of colour or physical properties, e.g.

血红 **xuèhóng**	'blood red' (血 **xuè**: blood; 红 **hóng**: red)
雪白 **xuěbái**	'snow white' (雪 **xuě**: snow; 白 **bái**: white)
天蓝 **tiānlán**	'sky blue' (天 **tiān**: sky; 蓝 **lán**: blue)
碧绿 **bìlǜ**	'dark green' (碧 **bì**: jade; 绿 **lǜ**: green)
墨黑 **mòhēi**	'pitch-dark' (墨 **mò**: ink-slab; 黑 **hēi**: black)
橙黄 **chénghuáng**	'orange' (colour) (橙 **chéng**: oranges; 黄 **huáng**: yellow)
滚圆 **gǔnyuán**	'round as a ball' (滚 **gǔn**: rolling; 圆 **yuán**: round)
笔直 **bǐzhí**	'straight as a ramrod' (笔 **bǐ**: pen; 直 **zhí**: straight)
油滑 **yóuhuá**	'slippery' (油 **yóu**: oil; 滑 **huá**: slippery)
毛糙 **máocao**	'coarse' (毛 **máo**: hair; 糙 **cāo**: rough)
冰冷 **bīnglěng**	'ice-cold' (冰 **bīng**: ice; 冷 **lěng**: cold)
火热 **huǒrè**	'burning hot' (火 **huǒ**: fire; 热 **rè**: hot)
滚烫 **gǔntàng**	'boiling hot' (滚 **gǔn**: boiling; 烫 **tàng**: scald, burn)
瓷实 **císhi**	'solid' (瓷 **cí**: porcelain; 实 **shí**: solid)
锋利 **fēnglì**	'sharp' (锋 **fēng**: the sharp point or cutting edge of a sword; 利 **lì**: sharp)

The simile contained in the lexeme is realised without an explicit simile marker (e.g. 如 **rú** etc.) and the disyllabic word could be understood as a short cut to a potentially longer expression, e.g. 雪白 **xuěbái** 'snow white' or 冰冷 **bīnglěng** 'ice-cold' could be respectively interpreted as 'as white as snow' or 'as cold as ice'.

MASQUERADING EXPRESSION

A masquerading expression, like a metaphorical comparison, is a lexical device, by which meaning is encoded beyond the spoken word. In *hyperbole*, the over- or under-statement is not to be taken literally, the speaker's intention is rather to achieve emphasis in either direction; in *euphemism*, the unpleasant meaning is camouflaged behind more pleasant words; in *irony* the surface value of the expression is to be perceived as contrary to the true meaning intended; and in *pun*, the meaning of the expression presented only serves to call forth an entirely different alternative meaning of the same word or even of a totally unrelated homophone in the lexicon.

Hyperbole

Hyperbole is found in lexical units of all types, especially in quadrisyllabic idioms. Hyperbolic units in the lexicon are licensed exaggeration for the sake of emphasis.

参天 **cāntiān** 'reaching to the sky' (参 **cān**: join, enter; 天 **tiān**: sky)

无比 **wúbǐ** 'unparalleled' (无 **wú**: without; 比 **bǐ**: compare)

一眨眼 **yī zhǎyǎn** 'in the twinkling of an eye' (一 **yī**: one; 眨 **zhǎ**: blink, wink; 眼 **yǎn**: eye)

沧海一粟 **cānghǎi yī sù** 'a drop in the ocean' (沧海 **cānghǎi**: sea; 一 **yī**: one; 粟 **sù**: millet)

摩天大楼 **mótiān dálóu** 'skyscraper' (摩天 **mótiān**: skyscraping; 大楼 **dàlóu**: building)

天壤之别 **tiānrǎng zhī bié** 'a world of difference' (天壤 **tiānrǎng**: heaven and earth; 之 **zhī**: grammatical particle; 别 **bié**: difference)

垂涎三尺 **chuíxián sān chǐ** 'drool with envy' (lit. 'spittle three feet long') (垂涎 **chuíxián**: drool, slaver; 三 **sān**: three; 尺 **chǐ**: a traditional unit of length)

寸步难行 **cùn bù nán xíng** 'be unable to do anything' (lit. 'unable to move even the step of an inch') (寸 **cùn**: an inch; 步 **bù**: a step; 难 **nán**: difficult; 行 **xíng**: to walk)

一日千里 **yī rì qiān lǐ** 'with giant strides' (lit. 'a thousand miles in a day') (一 **yī**: one; 日 **rì**: day; 千 **qiān**: thousand; 里 **lǐ**: a traditional unit of length)

俯拾即是 **fǔ shí jí shì** 'be found everywhere' (lit. 'you only have to bend to pick it up') (俯 **fǔ**: bow (one's head); 拾 **shí**: pick up (from the ground); 即 **jí**: be, mean; 是 **shì**: yes)

千头万绪 **qiāntóu wànxù** 'a multitude of things to deal with' (lit. 'thousands of loose ends') (千 **qiān**: thousand; 头 **tóu**: thread ends; 万 **wàn**: ten thousand; 绪 **xù**: remnants)

挥汗如雨 **huī hàn rúyǔ** 'dripping with sweat' (挥 **huī**: wipe off; 汗 **hàn**: sweat; 如 **rú**: like, as if; 雨 **yǔ**: rain)

三头六臂 **sān tóu liù bì** 'superhuman powers' (lit. 'with three heads and six arms') (三 **sān**: three; 头 **tóu**: head; 六 **liù**: six; 臂 **bì**: arm)

九牛二虎之力 **jiǔ niú èr hǔ zhī lì** 'tremendous effort' (lit. 'the strength of nine bulls and two tigers') (九 **jiǔ**: nine; 牛 **niú**: ox; 二 **èr**: two; 虎 **hǔ**: tiger; 之 **zhī**: grammatical particle; 力 **lì**: strength)

跳到黄河洗不清 **tiào dào huánghé xǐbuqīng** 'find it hard to clear oneself of a charge' (lit. 'be unable to cleanse oneself even if one plunges into the Yellow River') (跳到 **tiào dào**: jump into; 黄河 **huánghé**: the Yellow River; 洗不清 **xǐbuqīng**: cannot wash oneself clean)

Euphemism

Euphemism, as we said, is used to camouflage unpleasant associations or taboo references by the use of pleasanter or non-taboo terms.

后事 **hòushì**	'funeral affairs'	(后 **hòu**: after; 事 **shì**: business)
解手 **jiěshǒu**	'relieve oneself'	(解 **jiě**: untie; 手 **shǒu**: hand)
有喜 **yǒuxǐ**	'pregnant'	(有 **yǒu**: have; 喜 **xǐ**: happy event)

行房 **xíngfáng**	(of a married couple) 'make love'	(行 **xíng**: act, do; 房 **fáng**: room)
例假 **lìjià**	'menstrual period'	(例 **lì**: regular; 假 **jià**: holiday)
婚外恋 **hūnwàiliàn**	'adultery'	(婚外 **hūnwài**: outside marriage; 恋 **liàn**: love)
第三者 **dì sān zhě**	'an illicit lover'	(第三者 **dì sān zhě**: the third party)

There are a lot of terms to avoid referring to death:

百年 **bǎinián**	'a hundred years' (百 **bǎi**: hundred; 年 **nián**: year)
去世 **qùshì**	'depart from the world' (去 **qù**: leave; 世 **shì**: lifetime)
逝世 **shìshì**	'take leave of the world' (逝 **shì**: pass; 世 **shì**: lifetime)
归天 **guītiān**	'return to heaven' (归 **guī**: return, go back to; 天 **tiān**: sky)
病故 **bìnggù**	'taken away by illness' (病 **bìng**: illness; 故 **gù**: die)
长眠 **chángmián**	'take a long sleep' (长 **cháng**: long; 眠 **mián**: sleep)
永别 **yǒngbié**	'goodbye forever' (永 **yǒng**: perpetual; 别 **bié**: part with, say goodbye to)
羽化 **yǔhuà**	'(sprout wings and) become an immortal' (羽 **yǔ**: wings; 化 **huà**: change into)

Irony and Sarcasm

In irony, the meaning is contrary to the spoken word:

宝贝 **bǎobèi** 'good-for-nothing' (宝贝 **bǎobèi**: treasure, treasured object)

尊容 **zūnróng** 'what a face' (尊 **zūn**: distinguished, respectable; 容 **róng**: face, complexion)

好容易 **hǎoróngyì** 'with great difficulty' (好 **hǎo**: very; 容易 **róngyì**: easy)

In sarcasm, the meaning conveyed is meant to ridicule:

掩耳盗铃 **yǎn ěr dào líng** 'bury one's head in the sand'
    (掩 **yǎn**: cover, plug; 耳 **ěr**: ear; 盗 **dào**: steal; 铃 **líng**: bell)

螳臂当车 **táng bì dāng chē**
'overrate oneself in the face of an overwhelmingly superior force'
    (螳 **táng**: mantis; 臂 **bì**: arm; 当 **dāng**: obstruct; 车 **chē**: car)

Pun

In a two-part allegorical saying, as we have already touched upon in discussing metaphorical analogy, the first part of the saying must necessarily be a metaphor, the second part (which can sometimes be left out: hence the name 歇后语 **xiēhòuyǔ**) is a literal explanation of the analogy made in the first part.[4]

---

[4] Cf. Ma, Guofan and Gao (马国凡等) 1979.

The explanation, as we shall see, can be (a) plain and straightforward; or (b) a pun, which exploits the double sense of the word or the sense of any of its homophonic counterparts in the lexicon. For instance,

straightforward explanation:

泥菩萨过河 – 自身难保 **nípúsà guò hé | zìshēng nán bǎo**
'like a clay idol fording a river – hardly able to save oneself (let alone anyone else)'

(泥 **ní**: mud, mire; 菩萨 **púsà**: Bodhisattva; 过 **guò**: cross; 河 **hé**: river; 自身 **zìshēn**: self, oneself; 难 **nán**: difficult; 保 **bǎo**: protect)

泼出去的水 – 收不回来 **pō chūqù de shuǐ | shōubuhuílai**
'what's been done cannot be undone' (lit. 'water that has been spilt cannot be retrieved')

(泼 **pō**: spill, splash; 出去 **chūqu**: out; 的 **de**: attributive marker; 水 **shuǐ**: water; 收不回来 **shōubuhuílai**: cannot be retrieved)

double-sense pun:

擀面杖吹火 – 一窍不通 **gǎnmiànzhàng chuī huǒ | yī qiào bù tōng**
'there is no knack to help one through' (lit. 'try to blow the fire with a rolling pin – there is no hole for the air to go through')

(擀面杖 **gǎnmiànzhàng**: rolling pin; 吹 **chuī**: blow; 火 **huǒ**: fire; 一 **yī**: one; 窍 **qiào**: aperture, knack; 不 **bù**: not; 通 **tōng**: go through)
(The pun lies in the double sense of the word 窍 **qiào**.)

耗子进风箱 – 两头儿受气 **hàozi jìn fēngxiāng | liǎngtóur shòuqì**
'be blamed by both parties' (lit. 'a mouse gets into the bellows, where air comes from both ends')

(耗子 **hàozi**: mouse; 进 **jìn**: enter; 风箱 **fēngxiāng**: bellows; 两头儿 **liǎngtóur**: two sides, both ends; 受气 **shòuqì**: get air, be blamed or criticised)
(The pun lies in the double sense of the word 气 **qì**.)

洗脸盆儿里扎猛子 – 不知深浅 **xǐliǎnpénr li zhā mèngzi | bùzhī shēnqiǎn**
'have an exaggerated opinion of one's abilities' (lit. 'dive in a wash-basin, not knowing how deep it actually is')

(洗脸盆儿 **xǐliǎnpénr**: wash-basin; 里 **li**: in; 扎猛子 **zhā mèngzi**: dive; 不知 **bùzhī**: not know; 深浅 **shēnqiǎn**: depth, proper limits for one's action)
(The pun lies in the double sense of the word 深浅 **shēnqiǎn**.)

homophonic pun:

外甥打灯笼 – 照舅 **wàishēng dǎ dēnglóng | zhàojiù**
'as of old' (lit. 'the nephew holds the lantern – to light the way for the uncle')

(外甥 **wàishēng**: nephew; 打 **dǎ**: hold; 灯笼 **dēnglóng**: lantern; 照 **zhào**: light up; 舅 **jiù**: mother's brother, uncle)
(The pun lies in the homophonic nature of the two expressions 照舅 **zhào jiù** 'light the way for one's uncle' and 照旧 **zhàojiù** 'as of old'.)

和尚打伞 – 无发无天 **héshang dǎsǎn | wú fà wú tiān**
'be absolutely lawless'; 'run wild' (lit. 'like a Buddhist monk holding an umbrella, i.e. somebody without hair and now being unable to see heaven')
　　(和尚 **héshang**: Buddhist monk; 打伞 **dǎsǎn**: hold up an umbrella; 无 **wú**: without; 发 **fà**: hair; 天 **tiān**: heaven)
　　(The pun lies in the near-homophonic nature of the two expressions 无发 **wú fà** 'having no hair – as a Buddhist monk keeps a shaven head' and 无法 **wú fǎ** 'not obeying laws'.)

绱鞋不使锥子 – 针好 **shàngxié bù shǐ zhuīzi | zhēn hǎo**
'Great!'; 'Fantastic!' (lit. 'sole a shoe without having to use an awl because the needle is really good')
　　(绱鞋 **shàngxié**: sole a shoe; 不 **bù**: not; 使 **shǐ**: use; 锥子 **zhuīzi**: awl; 针 **zhēn**: needle; 好 **hǎo**: good)
　　(The pun lies in the homophonic nature of the two expressions 针好 **zhēn hǎo** 'the needle is good' and 真好 **zhēn hǎo** 'really good'.)

老虎拉车 – 谁赶 **lǎohǔ lā chē | shuí gǎn**
'Who dares (to do anything like that)' (lit. 'when a tiger is drawing the cart, who dares to drive it')
　　(老虎 **lǎohǔ**: tiger; 拉 **lā**: pull; 车 **chē**: cart; 谁 **shuí**: who; 赶 **gǎn**: to drive)
　　(The pun lies in the homophonic nature of the two expressions 谁赶 **shuí gǎn** 'who is going to drive (the cart)' and 谁敢 **shuí gǎn** 'who dares (to do a thing like that)'.)

蛤蟆跳井 – 扑通 **háma tiào jǐng | pūtōng**
'I don't understand' (lit. 'the toad jumps into the well – splash')
　　(蛤蟆 **háma**: toad; 跳 **tiào**: jump; 井 **jǐng**: well; 扑通 **pūtōng**: flop, splash)
　　(The pun exploits the near homophony between the two expressions 扑通 **pūtōng** 'flop'; 'splash' and 不懂 **bù dǒng** 'don't understand'.)

打破沙锅问到底 **dǎpò shāguō wèn dàodǐ**
'insist on getting to the bottom of the matter' (lit. 'when the clay pot breaks, the crack goes from the top to the bottom')
　　(打破 **dǎpò**: break; 沙锅 **shāguō**: clay pot; 问 **wèn**: ask; 到底 **dàodǐ**: reach the bottom)
　　(The pun exploits the homophony between 问 **wèn** 'ask' and 璺 **wèn** 'crack'.)

不蒸馒头争口气 **bù zhēng mántou zhēng kǒuqì**
'show to people how good one is' (lit. 'even if one does not steam buns, at least one should strive to show one's worth')
　　(不 **bù**: not; 蒸 **zhēng**: to steam; 馒头 **mántou**: steamed bun; 争口气 **zhēng kǒu qì**: try to make a good showing, try to win credit)
　　(The pun exploits the homophony between 蒸 **zhēng** 'to steam' and 争 **zhēng** 'strive for' in the idiom 争口气 **zhēng kǒu qì** 'strive to show how good one is'.)

AESTHETIC FORMS OF SPEECH

Aesthetic forms of speech are based either on conventional five- or seven-syllable verse-line rhythms or on linguistic symmetry. Generally speaking, these symmetrical forms seek the same number of syllables on either side of a rhythmic pause or a linguistic pivot (e.g. 不如 **bùrú** 'unlike', etc.). They may be collectively called parallelism. Antithesis, progression, loop, partial inversion, etc. are all specific types of parallelism.

This can perhaps be made clearer in a table like the following:

Conventional Verse Lines	*Parallelism*
five-syllable verse line e.g.	antithesis e.g. ABCD/ABCD
XX/XXX	progression e.g. ABCD / DBCE
seven-syllable verse line e.g.	loop e.g. ABCD / DBCA
XXXX/XXX	partial inversion e.g. ABCD / ABDC

Conventional Verse Lines

Native speakers of Chinese, because of their education in traditional Chinese poetry, respond to five- or seven-syllable lines as the most acceptable aesthetic forms of speech: e.g.

five-syllable lines with a rhythm of XX/XXX:

万事开头难 **wànshì kāitóu nán** 'everything's hard in the beginning'
(万事 **wànshì**: everything; 开头 **kāitóu**: begin, start; 难 **nán**: difficult)

隔行如隔山 **géháng rú gé shān**
'different trades are separated as if by mountains'
(隔 **gé**: separate; 行 **háng**: different trades or professions; 如 **rú**: as if; 山 **shān**: mountains)

功到自然成 **gōng dào zìrán chéng** 'constant effort yields sure success'
(功 **gōng**: effort; 到 **dào**: reach a point; 自然 **zìrán**: naturally; 成 **chéng**: successful)

贪多嚼不烂 **tānduō jiáo bù làn** 'bite off more than one can chew'
(贪 **tān**: covet; 多 **duō**: too much; 嚼 **jiáo**: chew, munch; 不 **bù**: not; 烂 **làn**: mashed)

seven-syllable lines with a rhythm of XXXX/XXX:

不到黄河心不死 **bù dào Huánghé xīn bù sǐ**
'refuse to give up until all hope is gone' (lit. 'not stop until one reaches the Huanghe River')
(不 **bù**: not; 到 **dào**: reach; 黄河 **Huánghé**: The Yellow River; 心 **xīn**: heart; 死 **sǐ**: die)

车到山前必有路 **chē dào shānqián bì yǒu lù**
'things will sort themselves out' (lit. 'the cart will find its way round the hill when it gets there')
(车 **chē**: cart; 到 **dào**: reach; 山前 **shānqián**: in front of the hill; 必 **bì**: definitely; 有 **yǒu**: have; 路 **lù**: a way out)

此地无银三百两 **cǐdì wú yín sān bǎi liǎng**
'a clumsy denial resulting in self-exposure' (lit. 'there are no 300 taels of silver buried here')
　　(此地 **cǐdì**: here; 无 **wú**: no; 银 **yín**: silver; 三百两 **sān bǎi liǎng**: 300 taels)

聪明反被聪明误 **cōngming fǎn bèi cōngming wù**
'cleverness may overreach itself' (lit. 'clever people may be victims of their own cleverness')
　　(聪明 **cōngming**: clever; 反 **fǎn**: on the contrary; 被 **bèi**: by; 误 **wù**: suffer, hinder)

上山容易下山难 **shàngshān róngyì xiàshān nán**
'the end crowns all'; 'things get more difficult at the finishing stages' (lit. 'it is easy to climb up the hill but more difficult to come down as it is more difficult to balance oneself when one gets tired')
　　(上山 **shàngshān**: go up a hill; 容易 **róngyì**: easy; 下山 **xiàshān**: come down a hill; 难 **nán**: difficult)

Antithesis and Unithesis

So long as either side of the rhymthic pause of a recurrent pattern is similar in structure or correlated in meaning, it is a form of parallelism. If the meaning is contrastive, it is an antithesis; if the meaning is additive, it may be called a unithesis, a term which we have coined specifically for the purpose. Both antithesis and unithesis are a most prominent feature of the 'staggered' pattern of quadrisyllabic idioms:

antithesis:
逆来顺受 **nì lái shùn shòu**
'meekly submit to oppression'; 'resign oneself to adversity'
　　(逆 **nì**: adversity; 来 **lái**: come, arrive; 顺 **shùn**: submissively; 受 **shòu**: accept)

深入浅出 **shēn rù qiǎn chū** 'explain the profound in simple terms'
　　(深入 **shēn rù**: penetrate deep; 浅 **qiǎn**: shallow; 出 **chū**: come out)

同床异梦 **tóng chuáng yì mèng**
'be strange bedfellows' (lit. 'share the same bed but dream different dreams')
　　(同床 **tóngchuáng**: share the same bed; 异 **yì**: different; 梦 **mèng**: dream)

一箭双雕 **yī jiàn shuāng diāo**
'kill two birds with one stone' (lit. 'kill two hawks with one arrow')
　　(一箭 **yī jiàn**: one arrow; 双 **shuāng**: two; 雕 **diāo**: vulture)

价廉物美 **jià lián wù měi**
(of a commodity) 'cheap but good'
　　(价 **jià**: price; 廉 **lián**: cheap; 物 **wù**: goods; 美 **měi**: nice)

貌合神离 **mào hé shén lí**
(of two persons or parties) 'be seemingly in harmony but actually at variance'
 (貌 **mào**: appearance; 合 **hé**: suit; 神 **shén**: spirit, mind; 离 **lí**: part from)

unithesis:
灯红酒绿 **dēng hóng jiǔ lǜ**
'feasting and revelry' (lit. 'lanterns are red and wine is green')
 (灯 **dēng**: lamp; 红 **hóng**: red; 酒 **jiǔ**: wine; 绿 **lǜ**: green)

心甘情愿 **xīn gān qíng yuàn** 'be most willing to'
 (心 **xīn**: heart; 甘 **gān**: of one's own accord; 情 **qíng**: feeling; 愿 **yuàn**: willing)

低声下气 **dī shēng xià qì**
'meek and subservient' (lit. 'speak under one's breath')
 (低 **dī**: low; 声 **shēng**: voice; 下 **xià**: downward; 气 **qì**: breath)

赤手空拳 **chìshǒu kōngquán** 'bare-handed'; 'unarmed'
 (赤手 **chìshǒu**: bare-handed; 空拳 **kōngquán**: mere fist)

七拼八凑 **qīpīn bācòu** 'piece together'; 'knock together'
 (七 **qī**: seven; 拼 **pīn**: piece together; 八 **bā**: eight; 凑 **còu**: gather together)

胡言乱语 **húyán luànyǔ** 'talk nonsense'; 'rave'
 (胡言 **húyán**: nonsense; 乱语 **luànyǔ**: ravings)

Taken together, there is far more unithesis than antithesis in quadrisyllabic idioms.

Antithesis and unithesis also occur in all other types of polysyllabic units:

antithesis:
穿新鞋, 走老路 **chuān xīnxié | zǒu lǎolù**
'make no real change' (lit. 'tread the old path in new shoes')
 (穿 **chuān**: wear; 新鞋 **xīnxié**: new shoes; 走 **zǒu**: walk; 老路 **lǎolù**: old path)

当面是人, 背后是鬼 **dāngmiàn shì rén | bèihòu shì guǐ**
'double-faced'; 'double dealing'
 (当面 **dāngmiàn**: to sb's face; 是 **shì**: be; 人 **rén**: person; 背后 **bèihòu**: at the back; 鬼 **guǐ**: ghost)

病来如山倒, 病去如抽丝 **bìng lái rú shān dǎo | bìng qù rú chōu sī**
'agues come on horseback, but go away on foot' (lit. 'illness strikes like a landslide, recovery is as slow as reeling silk')
 (病 **bìng**: sickness; 来 **lái**: come; 如 **rú**: as if; 山 **shān**: mountain, hill; 倒 **dǎo**: collapse; 去 **qù**: go; 抽丝 **chōusī**: reel off raw silk from cocoons)

好事不出门, 坏事传千里 **hǎoshì bù chūmén | huàishì chuán qiānlǐ**
'good news never goes beyond the gate, while bad news spreads far and wide'

> (好事 **hǎoshì**: good things; 不 **bù**: not; 出门 **chūmén**: go out; 坏事 **huàishì**: bad things; 传 **chuán**: spread; 千里 **qiānlǐ**: a thousand li – a long distance or a vast expanse)

踏破铁鞋无觅处, 得来全不费功夫
tà pò tiěxié wú mìchu | délai quán bù fèi gōngfu
'fancy finding by sheer luck what one has searched for far and wide' (lit. 'you can wear out iron shoes in fruitless searching, and yet by a lucky chance you may find the lost thing without even looking for it')

> (踏 **tà**: tread; 破 **pò**: broken; 铁鞋 **tiěxié**: iron shoes; 无 **wú**: without; 觅 **mì**: hunt for; 处 **chù**: place; 得来 **délai**: get sth; 全 **quán**: complete; 不 **bù**: not; 费 **fèi**: spend; 功夫 **gōngfu**: time, effort)

unithesis:

扇阴风, 点鬼火 **shān yīnfēng | diǎn guǐhuǒ**
'foment trouble' (lit. 'fan the winds of evil and spread the fires of turmoil')

> (扇 **shān**: to fan; 阴风 **yīnfēng**: an ill wind; 点 **diǎn**: to light; 鬼火 **guǐhuǒ**: will-o'-the-wisp)

人一走, 茶就凉 **rén yī zǒu | chá jiù liáng**
'out of sight, out of mind' (lit. 'when the guest leaves, the tea will be cold')

> (人 **rén**: person; 一 **yī**: as soon as; 走 **zǒu**: go away; 茶 **chá**: tea; 就 **jiù**: soon; 凉 **liáng**: cool)

看菜吃饭, 量体裁衣 **kàn cài chīfàn | liáng tǐ cáiyī**
'act according to actual circumstances' (lit. 'fit the appetite to the dishes and the dress to the figure')

> (看 **kàn**: look at; 菜 **cài**: dishes; 吃 **chī**: eat; 饭 **fàn**: rice; 量 **liáng**: measure; 体 **tǐ**: body; 裁 **cái**: cut; 衣 **yī**: cloth)

一朝被蛇咬, 十年怕井绳 **yīzhāo bèi shé yǎo | shí nián pà jǐngshéng**
'once bitten, twice shy' (lit. 'once bitten by a snake, for ten years one shies at a rope')

> (一朝 **yīzhāo**: once; 被 **bèi**: by; 蛇 **shé**: snake; 咬 **yǎo**: bite; 十 **shí**: ten; 年 **nián**: year; 怕 **pà**: fear; 井绳 **jǐngshéng**: a rope tied to a bucket for drawing water from a well)

Sometimes, with a recurrent pattern (whether it is an antithesis or a unithesis), some elements in the idiom are repeated:

不痛不痒 **bù tòng bù yǎng** 'superficial' (lit. 'neither ache nor itch')

> (不 **bù**: not; 痛 **tòng**: ache, pain; 痒 **yǎng**: itch, tickle)

半信半疑 **bàn xìn bàn yí**
'not quite convinced' (lit. 'half-believing, half-doubting')

> (半 **bàn**: half; 信 **xìn**: trust; 疑 **yí**: doubt, suspect)

出尔反尔 **chū ěr fǎn ěr** 'go back on one's words'
(lit. 'it originates from you and it contradicts you')
    (出 **chū**: originate from; 尔 **ěr**: you; 反 **fǎn**: oppose)
得过且过 **dé guò qiě guò** 'get by however one can'
    (得 **dé**: manage; 过 **guò**: muddle along; 且 **qiě**: for the time being)

活到老, 学到老 **huó dào lǎo | xué dào lǎo** 'one is never too old to learn'
    (活 **huó**: live; 到 **dào**: to; 老 **lǎo**: old age; 学 **xué**: learn)

善有善报, 恶有恶报 **shàn yǒu shàn bào | è yǒu è bào**
'good is rewarded with good; evil with evil'
    (善 **shàn**: good, virtuous; 有 **yǒu**: have; 报 **bào**: requite; 恶 **è**: evil, vice, wicked)

嫁鸡随鸡, 嫁狗随狗 **jià jī suí jī | jià gǒu suí gǒu**
'follow the man you marry, be he fowl or cur'
    (嫁 **jià**: marry; 鸡 **jī**: rooster; 随 **suí**: follow; 狗 **gǒu**: dog)

有福同享, 有难同当 **yǒu fú tóng xiǎng | yǒu nàn tóng dāng**
'share joys and sorrows'; 'share weal and woe'
    (有 **yǒu**: have; 福 **fú**: happiness; 同 **tóng**: together; 享 **xiǎng**: share; 难 **nàn**: trouble; 当 **dāng**: bear, endure)

公说公有理, 婆说婆有理 **gōng shuō gōng yǒulǐ | pó shuō pó yǒulǐ**
'each says he is right'
    (公 **gōng**: husband; 说 **shuō**: say; 有理 **yǒulǐ**: in the right; 婆 **pó**: wife)

有理走遍天下, 无理寸步难行 **yǒulǐ zǒu biàn tiānxià | wúlǐ cùnbù nán xíng**
'with justice on your side, you can go anywhere; without it, you can't take a step'
    (有理 **yǒulǐ**: reasonable, in the right; 走遍 **zǒu biàn**: travel (all over a place); 天下 **tiānxià**: land under heaven – the world or China; 无理 **wúlǐ**: unreasonable; 寸步 **cùnbù**: a single step; 难行 **nán xíng**: difficult to walk)

你走你的阳关道, 我走我的独木桥
nǐ zǒu nǐde yángguāndào | wǒ zǒu wǒde dúmùqiáo
'you take the open road, I'll cross the log bridge – you go your way, I'll go mine'
    (你 **nǐ**: you; 走 **zǒu**: walk; 你的 **nǐde**: your; 阳关道 **yángguāndào**: broad highway; 我 **wǒ**: I; 我的 **wǒde**: my; 独木桥 **dúmùqiáo**: single-plank or single-log bridge)

Symmetry is often achieved by using the negator 不 **bù** 'not' in the third syllable of such a polysyllabic saying:

中看不中吃 **zhōngkàn bù zhōngchī** 'look nice but taste nasty'
    (中看 **zhōngkàn**: nice to look at; 不 **bù**: not; 中吃 **zhōngchī**: nice to eat)

八九不离十 **bā jiǔ bù lí shí** 'about right'; 'pretty close'
  (八 **bā**: eight; 九 **jiǔ**: nine; 不 **bù**: not; 离 **lí**: far from; 十 **shí**: ten)

不打不相识 **bù dǎ bù xiāngshí**
'no discord, no concord' (lit. 'out of blows friendship grows')
  (不 **bù**: not; 打 **dǎ**: fight; 相识 **xiāngshí**: know each other)

赶早不赶晚 **gǎnzǎo bù gǎnwǎn** 'better early than late'
  (赶早 **gǎnzǎo**: do sth as early as possible; 不 **bù**: not; 赶晚 **gǎnwǎn**: do sth late)

水火不相容 **shuǐhuǒ bù xiāngróng** 'be incompatible as fire and water'
  (水火 **shuǐhuǒ**: fire and water; 不 **bù**: not; 相 **xiāng**: each other; 容 **róng**: tolerate)

井水不犯河水 **jǐngshuǐ bù fàn héshuǐ**
'I'll mind my own business, you mind yours' (lit. 'well water does not intrude into river water')
  (井水 **jǐngshuǐ**: well water; 不 **bù**: not; 犯 **fàn**: invade; 河水 **héshuǐ**: river water)

远水不解近渴 **yuǎn shuǐ bù jiě jìn kě**
'distant water can't quench present thirst'
  (远 **yuǎn**: distant; 水 **shuǐ**: water; 不 **bù**: not; 解 **jiě**: quench; 近 **jìn**: nearby; 渴 **kě**: thirst)

真金不怕火炼 **zhēnjīn bù pà huǒ liàn**
'a person of integrity can stand severest tests' (lit. 'true gold fears no fire')
  (真金 **zhēnjīn**: true gold; 不怕 **bù pà**: have no fear for; 火 **huǒ**: fire; 炼 **liàn**: smelt)

家丑不可外扬 **jiāchǒu bùkě wàiyáng**
'don't wash your dirty linen in public' (lit. 'a family scandal should never be spread abroad')
  (家丑 **jiāchǒu**: family scandal; 不可 **bùkě**: should not; 外扬 **wàiyáng**: spread abroad)

脚正不怕鞋歪 **jiǎo zhèng bù pà xié wāi**
'an upright man fears no gossip' (lit. 'a straight foot is not afraid of a crooked shoe')
  (脚 **jiǎo**: foot; 正 **zhèng**: straight; 不怕 **bù pà**: have no fear for; 鞋 **xié**: shoe; 歪 **wāi**: crooked)

身正不怕影儿斜 **shēn zhèng bù pà yǐngr xié**
'an upright man fears no gossip' (lit. 'a man standing straight has no worry for his shadow slanting')
  (身 **shēn**: body; 正 **zhèng**: straight; 不怕 **bù pà**: have no fear for; 影儿 **yǐngr**: shadow; 斜 **xié**: slanting)

好汉不吃眼前亏 **hǎohàn bù chī yǎnqiánkuī**
'a wise man doesn't fight against impossible odds'
    (好汉 **hǎohàn**: wise man; 不 **bù**: not; 吃 **chī**: eat, suffer from; 眼前亏 **yǎnqiánkuī**: trouble right before the eyes)

小车不倒尽管推 **xiǎochē bù dǎo jǐnguǎn tuī**
'one does one's best as long as one lives'
    (小车 **xiǎochē**: handcart; 不 **bù**: not; 倒 **dǎo**: fall; 尽管 **jǐnguǎn**: feel free to; 推 **tuī**: push)

Sometimes, symmetry is achieved by the sheer contrast of the ideas. Under such circumstances, the linguistic pivot incorporating the negator 不 **bù** may appear anywhere in the polysyllabic idiom: e.g.

远水救不了近火 **yuǎn shuǐ jiùbuliǎo jìn huǒ**
'a slow remedy cannot meet an emergency'
    (远 **yuǎn**: distant; 水 **shuǐ**: water; 救不了 **jiùbuliǎo**: cannot save; 近 **jìn**: near; 火 **huǒ**: fire)

跑了和尚跑不了庙 **pǎole héshang pǎobuliǎo miào**
'the monk may run away, but the temple can't run with him'
    (跑了 **pǎole**: escape; 和尚 **héshang**: monk; 跑不了 **pǎobuliǎo**: can't escape; 庙 **miào**: temple)

真人面前不说假话 **zhēnrén miànqián bù shuō jiǎhuà**
'one doesn't cheat a gentleman'
    (真人 **zhēnrén**: true man; 面前 **miànqián**: before (sb); 不 **bù**: not; 说 **shuō**: speak; 假话 **jiǎhuà**: lie, falsehood)

Progression

In progression, the end of the first part is carried over as the beginning of the second part of the parallel structure; and some of the monosyms in the lexeme are usually repeated, e.g.

知无不言, 言无不尽 **zhī wú bù yán | yán wú bù jìn**
'I'll tell you if I know it and I'll tell all that I know'
    (知 **zhī**: know; 无 **wú**: without; 不 **bù**: not; 言 **yán**: talk about; 尽 **jìn**: thorough)

大事化小, 小事化无 **dàshì huà xiǎo | xiǎoshì huà wú**
'reduce something of a major serious nature to the status of a minor matter'
    (大事 **dàshì**: sth major; 化 **huà**: reduce; 小 **xiǎo**: small; 小事 **xiǎoshì**: sth minor; 无 **wú**: nothing)

木匠怕漆匠, 漆匠怕光匠 **mùjiang pà qījiang | qījiang pà guāngjiang**
'the carpenter's work is shown up by the lacquerer and the lacquerer's by light'
    (木匠 **mùjiang**: carpenter; 怕 **pà**: fear; 漆匠 **qījiang**: lacquerer; 光匠 **guāngjiang**: light)

是福不是祸，是祸躲不过 **shì fú bù shì huò | shì huò duǒbuguò**
'there's no escape from misfortune' (lit. 'it's all right if it isn't misfortune;
if it is, it is unavoidable')

> (是 **shì**: be; 福 **fú**: happiness; 不是 **bù shì**: be not; 祸 **huò**: misfortune;
> 躲不过 **duǒbuguò**: there's no dodging from)

大鱼吃小鱼，小鱼吃虾米 **dàyú chī xiǎoyú | xiǎoyú chī xiāmǐ**
'the most powerful wins in the end'

> (大鱼 **dàyú**: big fish; 吃 **chī**: eat; 小鱼 **xiǎoyú**: small fish; 虾米 **xiāmǐ**:
> shrimps)

Loop

In loop, the parallelism is achieved by the realignment of the same composing
monomyns in a circular fashion, e.g.

来者不善，善者不来 **láizhě bù shàn | shànzhě bù lái**
'he who has come is surely strong or he'd never have come along'
> (来者 **láizhě**: comer; 不 **bù**: not; 善 **shàn**: be kind; 善者 **shànzhě**: kind
> person; 来 **lái**: come)

水深不响，水响不深 **shuǐ shēn bù xiǎng | shuǐ xiǎng bù shēn**
'water that runs deep does not make a noise and water that makes a noise
does not run deep'
> (水 **shuǐ**: water; 深 **shēn**: deep; 不 **bù**: not; 响 **xiǎng**: make a noise)

会者不难，难者不会 **huìzhě bù nán | nánzhě bù huì**
'easy for those who know; difficult for those who don't'
> (会者 **huìzhě**: those who know how to do sth; 不 **bù**: not; 难 **nán**: difficult;
> 难者 **nánzhě**: those who find it difficult to do sth; 会 **huì**: cannot do sth)

成人不自在，自在不成人 **chéng rén bù zìzài | zìzài bù chéng rén**
'if one wishes to become somebody, one cannot indulge in a free and easy
life; if one indulges in a free and easy life, one will not be able to become
somebody'
> (成人 **chéng rén**: be somebody; 不 **bù**: not; 自在 **zìzài**: feel free)

真的假不了，假的真不了 **zhēnde jiǎ bù liǎo | jiǎde zhēn bù liǎo**
'what is true cannot be false; what is false cannot be true'
> (真的 **zhēnde**: what is real or true; 假的 **jiǎde**: what is false; 不了 **bùliǎo**:
> cannot be)

好事儿不背人，背人没好事儿 **hǎoshìr bù bèi rén | bèi rén méi hǎoshìr**
'what is good does not go behind one's back; what goes behind one's back
cannot be good'
> (好事儿 **hǎoshìr**: a good thing; 不 **bù**: not; 背 **bèi**: go behind sb's back;
> 人 **rén**: person; 没 **méi**: there is no)

便宜没好货, 好货不便宜 **piányi méi hǎohuò | hǎohuò bù piányi**
'what is good cannot be cheap; what is cheap cannot be good'
    (便宜 **piányi**: cheap; 没 **méi**: there is no; 好货 **hǎohuò**: sth good; 不 **bù**: not)

Partial Inversion

In partial inversion, the parallelism is achieved by using the same mononyms in either part of the parallel structure but reversing the order of some of them in the second part, e.g.

不怕一万, 就怕万一 **bù pà yī wàn | jiù pà wànyī**
'just in case; if by any chance' (lit. 'fear not ten thousand cases which present no problem but one in ten thousand that causes the accident')
    (不怕 **bù pà**: fear not; 一万 **yī wàn**: ten thousand; 就怕 **jiù pà**: just fear; 万一 **wànyī**: in case)

有枣三竿子, 无枣竿子三 **yǒu zǎo sān gānzi | wú zǎo gānzi sān**
'do something indiscriminately despite the changed situation' (lit. 'hit the tree three times with one's pole when there are dates on it; and do the same with one's pole when there are none')
    (有 **yǒu**: have; 枣 **zǎo**: (biol.) dates; 三 **sān**: three; 竿子 **gānzi**: bamboo pole; 无 **wú**: no)

祸兮福所倚, 福兮祸所伏 **huò xī fú suǒ yǐ | fú xī huò suǒ fú**
'good fortune lieth with bad, bad fortune lurketh within good'
    (祸 **huò**: misfortune; 兮 **xī**: exclamatory particle; 福 **fú**: fortune; 所 **suǒ**: functional particle; 倚 **yǐ**: rely on; 伏 **fú**: lurk within)

THE RHETORICAL SCHEME OF THE LEXICON

If any generalisation can be made concerning the rhetorical scheme of the Chinese lexicon, three features seem to stand out more prominently than others. First, abstract notions have a greater tendency for metaphorical representation whereby they become tangible and acquire specific imageries. Second, negative concepts, for some reason, are more inclined than positive ones to find metaphorical substitutions in the Chinese lexicon. Third, a conscious effort for rhythmic parallelism has become more than a rhetorical means of originating aesthetic forms of speech: it is also a regulatory device for engendering lexical acceptability. In other words, rhythm has a dual role to play: institutional as well as rhetorical.

We shall now briefly illustrate the statements we have just made with specific examples.

(a) Abstract Notions

In every area of abstraction, some kind of concrete imagery is introduced in the form of quadrisyllabic (or polysyllabic) idioms as an alternative representation of the more commonly used (abstract) disyllabic words. If we take human psyche as an example, we find the following very frequently quoted metaphors:

高兴 **gāoxìng** 'happy'; 'cheerful'
　心花怒放 **xīn huā nùfàng** 'wild with joy'
　　(心 **xīn**: heart; 花 **huā**: flower; 怒放 **nùfàng**: in full bloom)
　眉飞色舞 **méi fēi sè wǔ** 'enraptured'
　　(眉 **méi**: eyebrow; 飞 **fēi**: fly; 色 **sè**: complexion; 舞 **wǔ**: dance)

悲伤 **bēishāng** 'grieved'; 'sorrowful'
　心如刀割 **xīn rú dāo gē** 'feel as if a knife were piercing one's heart'
　　(心 **xīn**: heart; 如 **rú**: as if; 刀 **dāo**: knife; 割 **gē**: cut)

忧愁 **yōuchóu** 'worried'; 'depressed'
　愁眉苦脸 **chóuméi kǔliǎn** 'wear a worried look'
　　(愁眉 **chóuméi**: knitted brows; 苦脸 **kǔliǎn**: worried look)

愤怒 **fènnù** 'indignant'; 'angry'
　脸红脖子粗 **liǎn hóng bózi cū** 'flush with agitation'
　　(脸 **liǎn**: face; 红 **hóng**: red; 脖子 **bózi**: neck; 粗 **cū**: wide)

得意 **déyì** 'pleased with oneself'; 'complacent'
　摇头晃脑 **yáotóu huàngnǎo**
　'assume an air of self-approbation or self-satisfaction'
　　(摇头 **yáotóu**: wag one's head; 晃脑 **huàngnǎo**: sway one's head)

灰心 **huīxīn** 'lose heart'; 'be discouraged'
　垂头丧气 **chuítóu sàngqì** 'be crestfallen'; 'be dejected'
　　(垂头 **chuítóu**: hang one's head; 丧气 **sàngqì**: feel disheartened)

自慰 **zìwèi** 'console oneself'
　望梅止渴 **wàng méi zhǐkě** 'feed on fancies'
　　(望 **wàng**: look at; 梅 **méi**: plums; 止渴 **zhǐkě**: quench one's thirst)
　画饼充饥 **huà bǐng chōngjī** 'feed on illusions'
　　(画 **huà**: draw; 饼 **bǐng**: cakes; 充饥 **chōngjī**: allay or appease one's hunger)

不安 **bù'ān** 'unpeaceful'; 'unstable'
　如坐针毡 **rú zuò zhēnzhān** 'be on pins and needles'; 'be on tenterhooks'
　　(如 **rú**: as if; 坐 **zuò**: sit; 针毡 **zhēnzhān**: a blanket of needles)
　芒刺在背 **mángcì zài bèi**
　'feel prickles down one's back – feel nervous and uneasy'
　　(芒 **máng**: awn; 刺 **cì**: thorn, splinter; 在 **zài**: on; 背 **bèi**: back)

惭愧 **cánkuì** 'be ashamed'
无地自容 **wú dì zì róng** 'can find no place to hide oneself for shame'
(无 **wú**: not have; 地 **dì**: place; 自 **zì**: oneself; 容 **róng**: hold)

镇静 **zhènjìng** 'calm'; 'composed'; 'unruffled'
面不改色 **miàn bù gǎisè**
'without turning a hair'; 'without batting an eyelid'
(面 **miàn**: face; 不 **bù**: not; 改 **gǎi**: change; 色 **sè**: colour)

慌张 **huāngzhāng** 'flurried'; 'flustered'
心惊肉跳 **xīnjīng ròutiào** 'have the jitters'
(心 **xīn**: heart; 惊 **jīng**: start, be frightened; 肉 **ròu**: flesh, muscle; 跳 **tiào**: leap)

急切 **jíqiè** 'eager'; 'impatient'
如饥似渴 **rú jī sì kě** 'with great eagerness'
(如 **rú**: as if; 饥 **jī**: hungry; 似 **sì**: as if; 渴 **kě**: thirsty)

犹豫 **yóuyù** 'hesitate'; 'be irresolute'
举棋不定 **jǔ qí bù dìng** 'be unable to make up one's mind'
(举 **jǔ**: hold up; 棋 **qí**: chessman; 不定 **bù dìng**: unable to decide)

无法 **wúfǎ** 'unable'; 'incapable'
心有余而力不足 **xīn yǒuyú ér lì bùzú**
'one's ability falls short of one's wishes'
(心 **xīn**: heart; 有余 **yǒuyú**: have enough and to spare; 而 **ér**: yet; 力 **lì**: ability; 不足 **bùzú**: insufficient)
望洋兴叹 **wàng yáng xīngtàn**
'bemoan one's inadequacy in the face of a great task'
(望 **wàng**: gaze at; 洋 **yáng**: ocean; 兴叹 **xīngtàn**: heave a sigh)

麻痹 **mábì** 'lower one's guard'; 'slacken one's vigilance'
高枕无忧 **gāo zhěn wú yōu** 'sit back and relax'
(高 **gāo**: high; 枕 **zhěn**: pillow; 无 **wú**: without; 忧 **yōu**: worry)

专心 **zhuānxīn** 'be absorbed'
聚精会神 **jùjīng huìshén** 'be all attention'
(聚精 **jùjīng**: concentrate one's attention; 会神 **huìshén**: collect one's wits)

分心 **fēnxīn** 'divert (or distract) one's attention'
心猿意马 **xīn yuán yì mǎ** 'restless'; 'perturbed'
(心 **xīn**: heart; 猿 **yuán**: (capering) ape; 意 **yì**: mind; 马 **mǎ**: (galloping) horse)

迷惑 **míhuo** 'perplex'; 'baffle'
一叶障目, 不见泰山 **yī yè zhàng mù | bù jiàn Tàishān**
'the important overshadowed by the trivial'
(一 **yī**: one; 叶 **yè**: leaf; 障 **zhàng**: obstruct; 目 **mù**: eye; 不 **bù**: not; 见 **jiàn**: see; 泰山 **Tàishān**: Mount Tai)

醒悟 **xǐngwù** 'come to realise (or see) the truth'; 'wake up to reality'
大梦初醒 **dà mèng chū xǐng** 'wake up from one's dream'
   (大 **dà**: big; 梦 **mèng**: dream; 初 **chū**: just beginning; 醒 **xǐng**: wake up)

害怕 **hàipà** 'be afraid'; 'be scared'
提心吊胆 **tíxīn diàodǎn**
'have one's heart in one's mouth'; 'be on tenterhooks'
   (提心 **tíxīn**: worry, feel anxious; 吊 **diào**: hang, suspend; 胆 **dǎn**: gallbladder)
草木皆兵 **cǎo mù jiē bīng** 'a state of extreme suspicion and fear'
   (草木 **cǎo mù**: grass and trees; 皆 **jiē**: each and every; 兵 **bīng**: soldier)
前怕狼，后怕虎 **qián pà láng | hòu pà hǔ**
'fear wolves ahead and tigers behind – be full of fears'
   (前 **qián**: in front; 怕 **pà**: fear; 狼 **láng**: wolves; 后 **hòu**: at the rear; 虎 **hǔ**: tiger)

激动 **jīdòng** 'be excited'; 'be agitated'
心潮澎湃 **xīncháo péngpài** 'feel an upsurge of emotion'
   (心潮 **xīncháo**: surging thoughts and emotions; 澎湃 **péngpài**: surge)

感激 **gǎnjī** 'feel grateful'; 'be thankful'
谢天谢地 **xiè tiān xiè dì** 'thank goodness'
   (谢 **xiè**: thank; 天 **tiān**: heaven; 地 **dì**: earth)

(b) Negative Terms

In the human psyche, negative factors, perhaps because they are more alarming, always seem to stand out more prominently than positive factors. Human weaknesses, rather than human strengths, find analogies in almost every conceivable image: e.g.

compared to inanimate objects:
脓包 **nóngbāo** 'a worthless fellow' (脓 **nóng**: pus; 包 **bāo**: swelling, lump)
乏货 **fáhuò** (dial.) 'ne'er-do-well' (乏 **fá**: dull, insipid; 货 **huò**: (offens.) goods, guy)
朽木 **xiǔmù** 'hopeless case' (朽 **xiǔ**: rotten, decayed; 木 **mù**: wood)
爪牙 **zhǎoyá** 'lackeys'; 'underlings' (爪 **zhǎo**: claw, talon; 牙 **yá**: teeth)
花瓶 **huāpíng** 'a woman who only knows how to make herself up and does no useful work' (花瓶 **huāpíng**: flower vase)

老油条 **lǎoyóutiáo** 'wily old bird' (老 **lǎo**: old; 油条 **yóutiáo**: deep-fried twisted dough sticks)
老古董 **lǎogǔdǒng** 'old fogey'; 'fuddy-duddy' (老 **lǎo**: old; 古董 **gǔdǒng**: antique, curio)
炮筒子 **pàotǒngzi** 'one who shoots his mouth off' (炮筒 **pàotǒng**: (of big gun) barrel; 子 **zi**: suffix)

话匣子 **huàxiázi** 'chatterbox' (话 **huà**: words; 匣子 **xiázi**: small box)

窝囊废 **wōnangfèi** 'good-for-nothing' (窝囊 **wōnang**: hopelessly stupid; 废 **fèi**: disabled, maimed)

万金油 **wànjīnyóu** 'jack of all trades' (万金 **wànjīn**: good for ten thousand illnesses; 油 **yóu**: ointment)

三只手 **sānzhīshǒu** 'pickpocket' (三 **sān**: three; 只 **zhī**: mw; 手 **shǒu**: hand)

势利眼 **shìliyǎn** 'snob' (势利 **shìli**: snobbish; 眼 **yǎn**: eye)

摇钱树 **yáoqiánshù** 'a woman who is a man's ready source of money' (摇 **yáo**: shake down; 钱 **qián**: money; 树 **shù**: tree)

传声筒 **chuánshēngtǒng** 'one who parrots another' (传 **chuán**: pass on; 声 **shēng**: voice; 筒 **tǒng**: tube)

compared to animals:

狗熊 **gǒuxióng** 'coward' (狗熊 **gǒuxióng**: black bear)

懒虫 **lǎnchóng** 'lazybones' (懒 **lǎn**: lazy, indolent; 虫 **chóng**: insect, worm)

鼠辈 **shǔbèi** 'mean creatures'; 'scoundrels' (鼠 **shǔ**: mouse; 辈 **bèi**: the like)

走狗 **zǒugǒu** 'lackey'; 'flunkey'; 'stooge' (走 **zǒu**: walk; 狗 **gǒu**: dog)

野鸡 **yějī** 'streetwalker'; 'unlicensed prostitute' (野鸡 **yějī**: pheasant)

乌龟 **wūguī** 'cuckold' (乌龟 **wūguī**: tortoise)

豺狼 **cháiláng** 'cruel and evil people' (豺 **chái**: jackal; 狼 **láng**: wolf)

蛇蝎 **shéxiē** 'vicious people' (蛇 **shé**: snake; 蝎 **xiē**: scorpion)

老狐狸 **lǎohúli** 'crafty scoundrel' (老 **lǎo**: old; 狐狸 **húli**: fox)

铁公鸡 **tiěgōngjī** 'a stingy person' (铁 **tiě**: iron; 公鸡 **gōngjī**: rooster)

馋猫子 **chánmāozi** 'a gluttonous person' (馋 **chán**: gluttonous; 猫子 **māozi**: cat)

变色龙 **biànsèlóng** 'a fickle person' (esp. in politics) (变色龙 **biànsèlóng**: chameleon)

应声虫 **yìngshēngchóng** 'yes-man' (应声 **yìngshēng**: to echo; 虫 **chóng**: insect, worm)

井底蛙 **jǐngdǐwā** 'a person with a limited outlook' (井底 **jǐngdǐ**: the bottom of a well; 蛙 **wā**: frog)

癞皮狗 **làipígǒu** 'loathsome creature' (癞皮狗 **làipígǒu**: mangy dog)

害群之马 **hài qún zhī mǎ** 'a black sheep' (害 **hài**: to harm; 群 **qún**: herd; 之 **zhī**: part.; 马 **mǎ**: horse)

衣冠禽兽 **yīguān qínshòu** 'a brute' (衣冠 **yīguān**: hat and clothes; 禽兽 **qínshòu**: birds and beasts)

Most interesting is the fact that the word 骨头 **gǔtou** 'bones' is picked out for labelling particular traits in a person. Amongst five such established tri-syllabic expressions, only one is positive in tone; all the others depict some kind of undesirable human characteristics:

硬骨头 **yìnggǔtou** 'a dauntless person' (硬 **yìng**: hard)

老骨头 **lǎogǔtou** 'an old person' (disrespectfully or jocularly) (老 **lǎo**: old; 骨头 **gǔtou**: bones)

贱骨头 **jiàngǔtou** 'miserable wretch' (贱 **jiàn**: cheap, despicable)
轻骨头 **qīnggǔtou** 'contemptible wretch' (轻 **qīng**: of little weight, light)
软骨头 **ruǎngǔtou** 'a weak-kneed person'; 'a coward' (软 **ruǎn**: soft)

This metaphorical tendency to embody negative concepts is only too obvious when it is considered from the perspective of the whole lexicon. Despite the fact that the Chinese people are an optimistic race (with a stock of 150 lexemes for 'beautiful' and only 20 for 'ugly', with 140 terms indicating 'good' and only 50 indicating 'bad'), their metaphorical creations cannot but reflect the historical realities of the country, where plight and predicament seem to have always overwhelmed favourable circumstances. As soon as one goes from optimistic generalisations to actual specifications, negative terms begin to dominate: e.g. there are only 14 terms about 'cleanliness' in the language's vocabulary whilst there are 20 about 'dirtiness'; 16 about 'comfort' as opposed to 37 about 'hardship'; 14 about 'safety' as opposed to 50 about 'danger'; and 22 about 'modesty' as opposed to 66 about 'haughtiness'.[5]

(c) Rhythmic Parallelism

Rhythmic parallelism seems to be an essential requirement in the combination of monoyms into lexical units. Let us look at the following pairs which indicate words and non-words: e.g.

words	vs	non-words
父亲 **fùqin** 'father'		* 父 **fù**
杯子 **bēizi** 'cup'; 'glass'		* 杯 **bēi**
头发 **tóufa** 'hair' (on the human head)		* 发 **fā**
衣服 **yīfu** 'clothes'		* 衣 **yī** or * 服 **fú**
身体 **shēntǐ** 'body'		* 身 **shēn** or * 体 **tǐ**
牙齿 **yáchǐ** 'tooth'		* 牙 **yá** or * 齿 **chǐ**

However, in the formation of further acceptable lexical units using these words as components, the situation is reversed, that is, the non-word or truncated form will now become the accepted form in the concatenation. Disyllabicity being the norm, it is therefore not unusual for only one of the monoyms from the original word most appropriate for the intended meaning to be chosen to combine with another monoym to form a new disyllabic lexeme:

non-words	vs	words
* 继父亲 **jì fùqin**		继父 **jìfù** 'stepfather'
* 茶杯子 **chá bēizi**		茶杯 **chábēi** 'teacup'
+ 金头发 **jīn tóufa**		金发 **jīnfa** 'golden locks'

---

[5] The statistics presented above were obtained by counting the items listed in Mei, Jiaju et al. (梅家驹等) (eds) 1983.

* 衣服架 **yīfu jià**	衣架 **yījià** 'coat hanger'
* 礼衣服 **lǐ yīfu**	礼服 **lǐfú** 'formal attire'
* 上身体 **shàng shēntǐ**	上身 **shàngshēn** 'the upper part of the body'
* 身体重 **shēntǐ zhòng**	体重 **tǐzhòng** '(body) weight'
+ 假牙齿 **jiǎ yáchǐ**	假牙 **jiǎyá** 'false tooth'; 'denture'
* 牙齿龈 **yáchǐ yín**	齿龈 **chǐyín** 'gums'

The principle behind this lexical formulation practice is clearly the matching up of the rhythm of the constituent elements: a monosyllable with a monosyllable in this case.

We shall now examine another set of words:

words	vs	non-words
明星 **míngxīng** '(film, sports) star'		* 星 **xīng**
电影 **diànyǐng** 'film'; 'movie'		* 影 **yǐng**
假期 **jiàqī** 'holiday'		* 假 **jià**
展览 **zhǎnlǎn** 'exhibition'; 'show'		* 展 **zhǎn**

How do they combine with each other or other mononyms or words to form new lexemes?

non-words	vs	words
* 电影星 **diànyǐng xīng**		影星 **yǐngxīng** 'movie star'
* 影明星 **yǐng míngxīng**		电影明星 **diànyǐng míngxīng** 'movie star'
* 足球星 **zúqiú xīng**		足球明星 **zúqiú míngxīng** 'football star'
* 病假期 **bìng jiàqī**		病假 **bìngjià** 'sick leave'
* 公众假 **gōngzhòng jià**		公众假期 **gōngzhòng jiàqī** 'public holiday'
* 图画展 **túhuà zhǎn**		画展 **huàzhǎn** 'exhibition of paintings'
* 服装展 **fúzhuāng zhǎn**		服装展览 **fúzhuāng zhǎnlǎn** 'fashion show'

It is obvious that monosyllables have to match up with monosyllables and disyllables with disyllables, the resultant lexemes being either a disyllabic word or a quadrisyllabic expression.

It is only when a pseudo-suffix mononym[6] (e.g. -界 **jiè** 'circles (of professionals)', -节 **jié** 'festival', -坛 **tán** 'circles'; 'world', 迷 **mí** 'enthusiast'; 'fan', etc.) is used in the combination can the new lexeme take various alternative forms as allowed by the suffix-like mononym: e.g.

界 **jiè** and 节 **jié** are more prone to trisyllables than disyllables:
> 电影界 **diànyǐngjiè** 'film (or movie) circles'
> 足球界 **zúqiújiè** 'football circles'
> 学术界 **xuéshùjiè** 'academic circles'
> 政界 **zhèngjiè** 'political circles'; 'government circles'

---

[6] See Chapter 3 on morphological features of the Chinese lexicon.

电影节 **diànyǐngjié** 'film festival'
宰牲节 **zǎishēngjié** (Islam) 'Corban'
春节 **Chūnjié** 'the Spring Festival'

坛 **tán**, on the other hand, only allows disyllabic combinations:
球坛 **qiútán** 'the ball-playing world'
文坛 **wéntán** 'the literary world'; 'the world of letters'
影坛 **yǐngtán** 'film (or movie) circles'

迷 **mí**, for one, is equally happy and versatile with di- or trisyllabic lexemes:
影迷 **yǐngmí** 'film (or movie) fan'
电影迷 **diànyǐngmí** 'film fan'
球迷 **qiúmí** '(ball game) fan'
足球迷 **zúqiúmí** 'football fan'

It is probably true to say that few languages pay more attention to the aesthetic form of parallelism in the formation of acceptable lexical units in the lexicon than does Chinese.

7 SENSE RELATIONS IN THE CHINESE LEXICON

Though different languages have their own specific ways of organising meaning in their lexicons, the basic semantic relations amongst the individual senses of the items in the lexicon (or these items themselves for that matter) seem to remain the same.

Such relations as hyponymy, polysemy, antonymy and perhaps synonymy are fundamental to the semantic structure of all natural languages. It is difficult to imagine that a language deprived of all these basic semantic relations would be able to function adequately in communication.

However, one point must be made clear at the very outset that analysing a lexicon using similar semantic principles does not mean that we may expect specific structures of meaning to correlate very much across languages. It largely remains unknown why one language considers some kind of semantic difference significant while another does not. Here is a comparison between Chinese and English:

thick: 粗 **cū** 厚 **hòu** 稠 **chóu**   thin: 细 **xì** 薄 **bó** 稀 **xī**
多 **duō**: many, much   少 **shǎo**: few, little

In Chinese 粗 **cū** and 细 **xì** take into consideration the circumference of the thing being described and 厚 **hòu** and 薄 **bó** only thickness in a vertical sense, and 稠 **chóu** and 稀 **xī** are limited to 'liquids' whereas the English 'thick' and 'thin' serve all these purposes. On the other hand, the English pairs 'many'; 'few' and 'much'; 'little' take into account whether the thing being considered is countable or uncountable, whereas 多 **duō** and 少 **shǎo** in Chinese do not at all make the distinction.

In the following sections we shall look at these semantic relations in turn with reference to their intra-lexemic as well as inter-lexemic characteristics in the formation of the Chinese lexicon.

HYPONYMY

Hyponymy seems to be by far the most important notion in the structure of meaning. It can perhaps be compared to a *'semantic pyramid'*, where a unique beginner forms the apex and from which stem two or more hyponyms, each of which in turn serves as the superordinate term of a new set of hyponyms it dominates. This goes on until the base of the 'pyramid' is reached. The items that form the base are in a sense 'terminal' sets of hyponyms because from there no further established items in the lexicon can be found as hyponyms of a lower rank.[1] For example,

---

生物 shēngwù *'organisms'*				
动物 **dòngwù** 'animal'	微生物 **wēishēngwù** 'bacteria'	植物 zhíwù 'plants'		
		花 **huā** 'flower'		草 **cǎo** 'grass' etc.
	玫瑰 **méigui** 'rose'	郁金香 **yùjīnxiāng** 'tulip'	菊花 **júhuā** 'chrysanthemum' etc.	

Here we see two kinds of relationship in a hyponymous pyramid: the relationship between the *superordinate term* (or *hypernym*) and its *hyponyms* and that between the hyponyms themselves (or co-hyponyms, as they are generally called).

The relationship between the superordinate term and its hyponyms might be regarded as '*bi-directional inclusion*'. Extensionally speaking, the superordinate term includes the hyponyms, e.g. flowers include roses, tulips, chrysanthemums, etc., but one cannot possibly say that roses or tulips or chrysanthemums include flowers; whereas intensionally speaking, 'roses', 'tulips' or 'chrysanthemums' etc. cover all the meanings contained in 'flowers' and some more, and that is why one can say 'roses, etc. are flowers' but not vice versa. Therefore, an item lower in the 'pyramid' is more specific or more pregnant with meaning than one higher in the hierarchy, which has a more generic meaning. This 'bi-directional inclusion' is also 'transitive' in the sense that each item in the hyponymous structure is related in the same way to each other far above or below the adjacent rung along the same nodal path. That is to say, if plants include flowers and flowers include roses, it is also plausible to say that plants include roses; and if 'roses' are 'flowers' and 'flowers' are 'plants', it is also legitimate to say that 'roses are plants'.

The relationship between co-hyponyms is that of 'incompatibility'. Each co-hyponym shares the same superordinate term, which gives it a *semantic denominator*, but each at the same time differs from another in the additional meaning it has. Semantically, they are therefore immediately related but also mutually exclusive: roses, tulips, etc. are all flowers; yet roses are roses and cannot be tulips. However, this difference should not be regarded as the same as that between 'cow' and 'chair' because in the latter case the two items

---

[1] Kay 1971: 870. The terminal sets of hyponyms in the average lexicon may not be the same as those in a specialist's lexicon, where finer and finer distinctions are being made. This distinction is one between a lexicon and an encyclopaedia.

concerned do not at all belong to the same hyponymous system and the question of 'incompatibility' simply does not arise.

It might also be worth mentioning at this point that hyponymous structures in natural languages cannot be expected to be complete, flawless systems: there might well be gaps and asymmetries. For instance, for the set of co-hyponymous mononyms in the quadrisyllabic idiom 鳏寡孤独 **guān guǎ gū dú** (widowers, widows, orphans and the childless) in Chinese, there is no super-ordinate term like 'the bereaved' (and in fact, juxtaposing these co-hyponyms to form a quadrisyllabic unit is just to serve the purpose of filling this gap); but when rendered into disyllabic lexemes in colloquial speech, only corres-pondences for the first three – 鳏夫 **guānfū**, 寡妇 **guǎfu**, 孤儿 **gū'ér** – are found but no correspondence for the fourth. The system is asymmetrical.[2]

Hyponym with a 'referential' nature is seen to be of two major types: (i) genus-differentia type; and (ii) part-whole type (or *'partonymy'*[3]).The genus-differentia type registers (through the prescriptive lens of individual languages, of course) the qualitative or functional differences in natural or artificial cat-egories; whereas the part-whole type registers largely quantitative or spatial dif-ferences. This shows that hyponymy, as an innate schema of human cognition, is itself a hierarchical structure.

From a linguistic point of view, however, hyponymy can perhaps be seen as a kind of 'progressive lexical differentiation' of a more general notion into more and more refined notions, e.g. plant → flower → rose, tulip, etc. If taken to logical conclusions, this refining process could go on forever. But no lan-guage for its average speakers ever goes to such uneconomic lengths. What usually happens is that where lexicalisation ends, syntactic configuration takes over; and when one's subjective lexicon recalls no ready lexical unit, one's syntactic competence can come in to rescue the situation. As a general rule, 'attribution or modification' is the syntactic device corresponding to this process of 'hyponymous' lexicalisation. In other words, an extemporaneous syntactic construction can always be coined to fill in a 'hyponymous' gap in terms of a 'modifier + headword' structure, where the headword should be a more general term nearer to the apex than the immediate gap. That dictionary definitions and explanatory remarks are possible is a convincing proof of the mutual convertibility of these linguistic devices: a lexicalised item expanded into a free syntactic structure or a well-established syntactic combination turned into an institutionalised compound in the lexicon. This kind of semantic conversion can be expressed in a formula like:

lexicalisation	↔	*syntactic construction*
hyponym	↔	modifier + superordinate term

where ↔ means 'mutually (and potentially) convertible into each other'.

---

[2] Cf. Palmer 1981: 85–7.
[3] The term is borrowed from Miller and Johnson-Laird 1976.

In Chinese, as we have seen in Chapter 4, the kind of 'syntactic combination' discussed here is actually the main lexicalisation device of deriving specific co-hyponyms from a more generic term. For example, from the more general notion of 译 **yì** 'translation' can be derived the more refined notions of 口译 **kǒuyì** '(oral) interpreting', 笔译 **bǐyì** '(written) translation', etc. The manifest 'progressive' nature of this kind of lexical differentiation in Chinese can perhaps be best illustrated by the following examples:

车 **chē**	'vehicle'
汽车 **qìchē**	'automobile' (lit. 'gas vehicle')
长途汽车 **chángtú qìchē**	'coach' (lit. 'long-distance gas vehicle')
镜 **jìng**	'lens'
显微镜 **xiǎnwēijìng**	'microscope' (lit. 'reveal-minutia lens')
电子显微镜 **diànzǐxiǎnwēijìng**	'electron microscope' (lit. 'electronic reveal-minutia lens')

It is also one of the major organisational principles in a large number of lexemes in the lexicon, particularly disyllables. Here, the relationship between the component monomyms is seen to follow strictly the formula set out in the first section. For example,

(i) genus-differentia type:
  树 **shù** 'tree'
  松树 **sōngshù** 'pine' 柏树 **bǎishù** 'cypress' 杨树 **yángshù** 'poplar' 樟树 **zhāngshù** 'camphor tree' etc.

  车 **chē** 'vehicle'
  火车 **huǒchē** 'train' 汽车 **qìchē** 'automobile' 电车 **diànchē** 'tram' 缆车 **lǎnchē** 'cable car' etc.

(ii) part-whole type:
  树 **shù** 'tree'
  树皮 **shùpí** 'bark' 树枝 **shùzhī** 'branch' 树梢 **shùshāo** 'treetop' 树干 **shùgàn** 'trunk' etc.

  车 **chē** 'vehicle'
  车把 **chēbǎ** 'handlebar' 车架 **chējià** 'frame' 车轮 **chēlún** 'wheel' 车轴 **chēzhóu** 'axletree' etc.

The structural difference between the genus-differentia and the part-whole type is that the former has the generic term in the second monomym (i.e. the headword) whereas the latter has it in the first monomym (i.e. the modifier).

Despite the examples given, part-whole hyponymy is to be understood in its broader sense. That is to say, part-whole relationship is not confined to spatial *continuity* but is also applied to spatial *contiguity*. In lexemes like 树墩 **shùdūn** 'stump' and 树胶 **shùjiāo** 'gum (of a tree)', the stump and the gum can be understood as part of the tree; but in lexemes like 树鸲 **shùqú** 'tree shrew' and 树蛙 **shùwā** 'tree frog', the shrew and the frog are found to have a spatial connection with the tree but are not necessarily part of it.

Hyponymous structure in the lexeme, as we have already seen, is also applicable to non-nominal monyms. Here we find a taxonomic structure becoming more linguistically oriented; in other words, we are now more concerned with 'sense' categorisation or organisation in the language than with 'referential' classification of natural or artificial objects into a taxonomy or their dissection into parts.

In Chinese, for example, 'shake', 'swing' 'vibrate' etc. may all be viewed as different categories of 'movement':[4]

动 **dòng** 'move'
摇动 **yáodòng** 'shake' 摆动 **bǎidòng** 'swing' 振动 **zhèndòng** 'vibrate'
波动 **bōdòng** 'fluctuate' etc.

And 'pink', 'scarlet', 'crimson', etc. may be viewed as different categories of 'redness':

红 **hóng** 'red'
粉红 **fěnhóng** 'pink' 鲜红 **xiānhóng** 'scarlet' 绯红 **fēihóng** 'crimson'
紫红 **zǐhóng** 'purplish red' etc.

In these hierarchies, a verbal monynym like 动 **dòng** 'move' or an adjectival monynym like 红 **hóng** 'red' becomes the 'superordinate unifier' of meaning.

Even in sound translations from foreign languages, this hyponymous concept is often incorporated into a lexeme to make the meaning more explicit, e.g.

啤酒 **píjiǔ** 'beer' (where 啤 **pí** transliterates 'beer' while 酒 **jiǔ** 'liquor'[5] registers the category)
烧酒 **shāojiǔ** 'spirit usually distilled from sorghum or maize' (烧 **shāo**: burn; 酒 **jiǔ**: wine)
米酒 **mǐjiǔ** 'rice wine' (米 **mǐ**: rice; 酒 **jiǔ**: wine)
葡萄酒 **pútáojiǔ** '(grape) wine' (葡萄 **pútáo**: grape; 酒 **jiǔ**: wine)

So far we have been looking at the way lexemes were formed working from top to bottom in the hyponymous structure. We get to a hyponym by taking a superordinate term and narrowing it down with a modifier. But interestingly enough in Chinese, this procedure can be somewhat reversed. We can actually get to a superordinate term by juxtaposing two or more co-hyponyms. This juxtaposition will then suggest the superordinate term concerned, either metonymically or metaphorically: e.g.

---

[4] Cf. Chapter 4 on modificational type.
[5] In Chinese, no distinction between 'wine' and 'liquor' is made; they are both 酒 **jiǔ**.

metonymic:

眉眼 **méiyǎn** 'appearance'; 'looks' (眉 **méi**: eyebrow; 眼 **yǎn**: eye)

穿戴 **chuāndài** 'dress' (穿 **chuān**: wear clothes; 戴 **dài**: wear hat)

跋涉 **báshè** 'trudge' (跋 **bá**: cross mountains; 涉 **shè**: ford streams)

衣食住行 **yī shí zhù xíng** 'basic necessities of life' (lit. 'food, clothing, shelter and transportation')

metaphorical:

负担 **fùdān** 'burden'

(负 **fù**: carry on the back; 担 **dān**: carry on the shoulder)

冷淡 **lěngdàn** 'indifferent' (冷 **lěng**: cold; 淡 **dàn**: insipid.)

青红皂白 **qīng hóng zào bái** 'right or wrong'

(青 **qīng**: green; 红 **hóng**: red; 皂 **zào**: black; 白 **bái**: white. Together they suggest the superordinate notion of 'colour' and when used in a negative clause beginning with 不分 **bù fēn** 'do not distinguish', they mean 'lack of discrimination'.)

酸甜苦辣 **suān tián kǔ là** 'joys and sorrows of life'

(酸 **suān**: sour; 甜 **tián**: sweet; 苦 **kǔ**: bitter; 辣 **là**: spicy. Together they suggest all sorts of experience in life.)

So we see that in the Chinese lexicon, hyponymy is one of the major features of lexical composition, which can be summarised in a schema like the following:

superordinate → *hyponym*	*hyponym* → *superordinate*
genus-differentia or part-whole	disyllabic or quadrisyllabic
modifier + headword	juxtaposition of co-hyponyms

One important thing to note is that not every 'modifier + headword' structure will necessarily form a hyponym in a hyponymous structure. This is analogous to 'restrictive' and 'non-restrictive' distinctions. Restrictive modifiers are indispensable information to the 'modified' term in question; whereas non-restrictive modifiers only strengthen (or make more transparent) information already contained implicitly or potentially in the headword. 鲤鱼 **lǐyú** 'carp' belongs to a hyponymous structure because 鲤 **lǐ** 'carp' supplies indispensable information to 鱼 **yú** 'fish'; but 公演 **gōngyǎn** 'give a public performance' does not because 公 **gōng** 'public' only reinforces the idea already contained in 演 **yǎn** 'perform': when one performs, one generally does it for the public, for an audience.

What is more, we must not forget that, inter-lexically, we are not sure if the members of the class (or hyponyms of the same superordinate term) will all have overt lexical connections. For example, in 啄木鸟 **zhuómùniǎo** 'woodpecker', 相思鸟 **xiāngsīniǎo** 'red-billed leiothrix', 知更鸟 **zhīgēngniǎo** 'robin', etc. we still have the 'superordinate unifier' 鸟 **niǎo** 'bird', but in

老鹰 **lǎoyīng** 'eagle'   麻雀 **máquè** 'sparrow'   喜鹊 **xǐque** 'magpie' the 'superordinate unifier' is gone, though a meaning element (e.g. 鸟 'long-tailed bird' and 隹 'short-tailed bird') can still be found in the structure of one of the written mononyms in the combination. However, in

燕子 **yànzi** 'swallow'   画眉 **huàméi** 'thrush'   八哥儿 **bāger** 'mina'

we have lost the 'superordinate unifier' or the meaning element altogether, despite the fact that there might be etymological clues in some of the written mononyms or their combinations, which are definitely not the concern of ordinary speakers of the language.

On other occasions, the opposite might be the case: the overtly incorporated 'superordinate unifier' in the lexemic or mononymic structure may even be misleading. For instance, 鳄鱼 **èyú** 'crocodile' is certainly not a fish (though 鱼 **yú** 'fish' is embedded both in the lexeme and in the written mononyms) nor is 田鸡 **tiánjī** (a common name for frog) a chicken.

A further point to be made is whether there is any criterion for setting up an inter-lexemic hyponymy. It seems that the organisation of terms relating to 'entities' depends heavily on their 'referential' correspondences in the real world. Even so, when it comes to how a hyponymy should be constructed, which superordinate terms should be chosen, etc., it becomes very much a question of the demarcation that needs to be drawn or the similarities and differences that need to be highlighted.

With nominal items, where 'references' to the real world can often be found, a taxonomy will not be too difficult to establish by reference to pragmatic experience. However, with terms denoting actions, events, qualities or relations associated with these entities, a hyponymous structure can perhaps only be set up with reference to these entities. Such hyponymies, as we can very well imagine, can rarely be constructed as neatly. Generally speaking, only those terms basic to the language form a co-hyponymous paradigm while their related 'superordinates' or 'subordinates' either simply do not exist or merely belong to more technical or literary domains.

Tentatively, we have classified together the following verbs with the 'super-ordinate' notion of 'the function of human lower limbs' (excuse the awkward phrasing for lack of an adequate superordinate term in the language):

(1) 走 **zǒu** 'walk'   跑 **pǎo** 'run'   跳 **tiào** 'jump'
(2) 踢 **tī** 'kick'   踩 **cǎi** 'trample'   跨 **kuā** 'stride'
(3) 蹲 **dūn** 'squat'   坐 **zuò** 'sit'   站 **zhàn** 'stand'

The first set might be regarded as 'move with both feet' but, if the direction of the movement is taken into account, 走 **zǒu** 'walk' and 跑 **pǎo** 'run' involve 'horizontal' movement while 跳 **tiào** 'jump' mainly involves 'vertical' movement. The second set might be regarded as 'move with one foot while keeping the other foot still' but, if 'contact' is taken into account, 踢 **tī** 'kick' and 踩 **cǎi** 'trample' both involve 'immediate contact' while 跨 **kuā** 'step over' avoids 'contact'. The third set might be regarded as 'keep the feet in a certain state' but, if the movement prior to the desired posture is taken into account, 蹲 **dūn** 'squat' and 坐 **zuò** 'sit' both involve 'downward' movement while 站 **zhàn** 'stand' involves 'upward' movement. No matter how one constructs such hyponymies, there will always be the 'odd man out'.

POLYSEMY

Polysemy is a natural semantic growth of individual lexemes being used in different syntagmatic cotexts (or mononyms, in different lexical combinations); it seems also an inherent design of all natural languages in terms of linguistic economy. To put it the other way round, it is an inhibitive device to curb any unnecessary proliferation of linguistic symbols while allowing the natural multiplication of meaning in every conceivable context. One linguistic form in the language is thus made to stand for more than one unit of meaning.

How is polysemy made possible? Is there a kind of 'semantic cohesion' among the different senses which is strong enough to hold them together under the same polysemous word and not to let them fall apart as homonyms or separate lexemes?

If we look at the syntagmatic behaviour of a mononym like 清 **qīng** (also an independent lexeme), we might want to differentiate its meaning into the following six senses:

(1)	pure	from	清水 **qīngshuǐ**	'clear water'
(2)	unmixed		清汤 **qīngtāng**	'vegetable soup'
(3)	clarified		分清 **fēnqīng**	'make a clear distinction'
(4)	quiet		清夜 **qīngyè**	'small hours of the night'
(5)	honest		清官 **qīngguān**	'incorruptible official'
(6)	complete		清单 **qīngdān**	'complete list'

We wonder if the six senses which we have thus differentiated by 'syntagmatic' means can be reduced to a common 'semantic denominator':

(1)	pure:	without impurities
(2)	unmixed:	without extra ingredients
(3)	clarified:	without vagueness
(4)	quiet:	without noise
(5)	honest:	without corruption
(6)	complete:	without remnant

If we go a step further, we might find that we can extract the meaning 'something undesirable' from 'impurities', 'vagueness', 'noise', 'corruption' and 'remnant'. 'Extra ingredients' alone can be neutral in meaning, depending on one's likes and dislikes. So we get 'without (something unpleasant or neutral)' as the semantic denominator and the 'impurities' etc. as semantic numerators. The relationship can perhaps be expressed diagrammatically in a meaning complex fraction like this:

neutral	→	extra ingredients
undesirable	→	impurities; noise; corruption; remnant

without

With a mononym 老 **lǎo** (also a lexeme), we can do the same:

(1) old:	e.g. 老人 **lǎorén**	'old man'
(2) familiar:	老朋友 **lǎo péngyou**	'old friend'
(3) dated:	老机器 **lǎo jīqì**	'old machines'
(4) overgrown:	老菜 **lǎocài**	'overgrown vegetables'
(5) overcooked:	牛肉太老了 **niúròu tài lǎo le**	'the beef is overcooked'
(6) skilful:	老手 **lǎoshǒu**	'old hand'
(7) original:	老地方 **lǎo dìfang**	'old place'

A meaning complex fraction will give:

without change	→	place; looks; temper; etc.
with change	→	age; acquaintance; fashion; greens; dish; skill

long time passed

Here we find that the relationship of the 'semantic denominator' with each of the 'semantic numerators' is a shift in the 'sphere of application'.

This might be termed '*analogous extension*' of meaning. In the second example, we see how the time notion in 'old age' is analogously extended to 'fashion' to produce the concept of 'being dated', and to 'acquaintance or friend' to produce 'familiarity'. 'Analogous extension' is particularly common among adjectival mononyms or lexemes (e.g. 'transferred epithet').

In some polysemous mononyms or lexemes, however, 'semantic cohesion' is not based on a common 'semantic denominator', but on the very 'basic' (or 'central') sense of the lexeme itself. This basic sense is often taken as the point of departure and the other senses are derived directly from that. For instance,

眼 **yǎn** 'eye'	(1) organ → eye	e.g. 眼睛 **yǎnjing** 'eye'
	(2) function → glance	看了一眼 **kàn le yī yǎn** 'have a look'
	(3) resemblance → aperture	扎个眼 **zhā ge yǎn** 'pierce a hole'
	(4) importance → key point	节骨眼 **jiēguyǎn** 'critical juncture'
画 **huà** 'draw'	(1) action → draw or paint	画图 **huà tú** 'draw a picture/map'
	(2) product → drawing or painting	画儿 **huàr** 'picture, drawing'
	(3) function → decorated with paintings	画廊 **huàláng** 'painted corridor'

A mononym like 角 **jiǎo** 'horn' will start from this basic sense:

organ   →   牛角 **niújiǎo** 'horn of an ox'

and develop into:

shape of   →   (a) musical instrument: 号角 **hàojiǎo** 'bugle'
                    (b) corner: 墙角 **qiángjiǎo** 'corner'
                    (c) figure: 三角形 **sānjiǎoxíng** 'triangle'
                    (d) penisula: 好望角 **hǎowàngjiǎo** 'Cape of Good Hope'

In such cases, the different senses are, in a way, 'metonymically' evolved from the basic (or nuclear) sense of the lexeme. In other words, the derived senses can all be considered as being 'in close connection with' the original central sense (e.g. in attribute, shape, function, product, etc.). This might be termed *'metonymic extension'* of meaning. It may often be realised by a change of word class in the original monym or lexeme.

In yet other monoyms or lexemes, the derived senses seem sometimes too far removed from the original to be aptly regarded as either 'analogous' or 'metonymic' extensions. For example, 走狗 **zǒugǒu** 'lackey, stooge' originally meant 'a dog that runs'. That is why when it was once translated into English as 'running dog', it provoked quite a bit of good-natured criticism from native speakers of the language, who could not make head or tail of what it really means. But why can the meaning of 'running dog' be transferred to 'lackey'? The comparison is perhaps not only in the 'running' but also in the 'servile nature' (if not understood as 'loyalty') of dogs.

This might be termed as a kind of *'metaphorical extension'*, where however far-fetched, a point of similarity is being sought; but that goes far beyond the kind of 'analogous extension' we have mentioned. Here is an example for illustration:

客 **kè**	客人 **kèren** 'guest'	one who visits the host
	旅客 **lǚkè** 'traveller'	one who visits a place to see sights
	乘客 **chéngkè** 'passenger'	one who visits a place using public transport
	顾客 **gùkè** 'customer'	one who visits a shop to look for commodities or service
	刺客 **cìkè** 'assassin'	one who visits a person with murderous intentions
	客观 **kèguān** 'objective'	(lit. 'observe like an outsider')

The senses above the line are 'analogous extensions' since they all share a common semantic denominator: one who visits a person or a place with a particular intention in mind; but the one sense below the line is 'metaphorical extension' since it goes beyond the literal part of the original meaning and borrows the idea of being 'a visitor' → not being one of the family → not being involved in any kind of emotion → being able to observe with cool-headed reason.

Therefore, at least three different types of sense relations can be discerned in a polysemous mononym or lexeme, namely (i) 'analogous extension'; (ii) 'metonymic extension'; and (iii) 'metaphorical extension'. And more often, these different devices join forces to attain polysemy.

Sometimes, the reconstruction of the relations of those major senses in a polysemous lexeme might reveal interesting facts about a culture. For example,

土 **tǔ** 'soil' → 'land or country' → 'local' or 'native' → 'unrefined'
(as compared with advanced foreign technology)

The metaphorical extension of 'local or native' into 'unrefined' is only 'psychologically' possible in a culture which deems itself technologically less advanced.

Whatever the ways in which the different senses in a polysemous mononym or lexeme are related, that these different senses, close or remote, can be united under the same mononym or lexeme lies in the fact that they can all be traced back to a common source of meaning. This shared source might be called their *'joint semantic base'*. And the very underlying aim common to all these different methods of sense extension is to procure, in a most economic and convenient way, a shift in the 'sphere of application' without losing sight of their 'joint semantic base'.

An additional point to note is that amongst mononyms or lexemes with certain semantic relations, one can always predict a similar kind of sense extension. If 推 **tuī** 'push' goes from the spatial plane to the temporal plane to mean 'postpone', so does its antonym 拖 **tuō** 'drag' or 拉 **lā** 'pull' in 拖拉 **tuōlā** 'dilatory'; if 甜 **tián** 'sweet' can be transferred from taste to feeling in 甜丝丝 **tiánsīsī** 'gratified', we can expect similar applications in such co-hyponymous terms as 酸 **suān** 'sour' in 酸溜溜 **suānliūliū** 'envious', 辣 **là** 'peppery' in 毒辣 **dúlà** 'sinister' or 苦 **kǔ** 'bitter' in 痛苦 **tòngkǔ** 'agony'. If the meaning of 眼 **yǎn** 'eye' can be metonymically extended, so can perhaps other terms indicating human body parts, e.g.

眼 **yǎn** 'eye' → 'hole'	as in	针眼 **zhēnyǎn** (eye of a needle)
耳 **ěr** 'ear' → 'ear-like thing'		木耳 **mùěr** (fungus)
口 **kǒu** 'mouth' → 'shape of a cut'		伤口 **shāngkǒu** (wound)
手 **shǒu** 'hand' → 'hand-like thing'		佛手 **fóshǒu** (fingered citron)
头 **tóu** 'head' → 'head-like thing'		蒜头 **suàntóu** (bulb of garlic)

Traditionally, linguists tend to regard polysemy as the result of 'sense development' in terms of the 'broadening' or 'narrowing' of meaning or the 'transference' from concrete to abstract or from commendatory to derogatory or vice versa. For instance,

(1) broadening of meaning:

江 **jiāng** used to mean 'the Yangtse River' and 河 **hé** 'river' used to mean 'the Yellow River'. But nowadays, both 江 **jiāng** and 河 **hé** are used to indicate 'rivers' in general.

匠 **jiàng** 'artisan'; 'craftsman' used to mean 'carpenter' only, but is now applicable to all trades, e.g. 铁匠 **tiějiang** 'blacksmith', 石匠 **shíjiang** 'stonemason', 鞋匠 **xiéjiang** 'shoemaker', etc.

(2) narrowing of meaning:

臭 **chòu/xiù** used to mean 'all kinds of odour, good or bad', as can still be found in a common expression in chemistry: 无色无臭 **wú sè wú xiù** 'colourless and odourless' (note: **xiù** is an alternative reading of **chòu**, preferred in nouns and verbs); but today, when used independently, it is confined to 'bad smells' only. ˙

坟 **fén** used to mean 'high ground near the riverside', but nowadays it is limited to 'tomb' only.

(3) transference of meaning:

(a) between concrete and abstract:

道 **dào** in 道路 **dàolù** 'road' changes into 'way or device' in 养生之道 **yǎngshēng zhī dào** 'the way to keep in good health'
把 **bǎ** 'handle' → 把 **bǎ** 'grasp' → 把 **bǎ** 'the grammatical particle which shifts the object to a pre-verb position'

(b) from derogatory to commendatory or vice versa:

左 **zuǒ** 'left' was at first neutral in meaning, was later found to become derogatory as in the classical idiom 左道旁门 **zuǒdào pángmén** 'heresy', and was then found to become commendatory as in 左派 **zuǒpài** 'the left wing' (supposed to be 'inclined towards the revolution').

(c) from one sense to another:

闻 **wén** 'hear or smell' used to denote 'hear' alone as we can see from the meaning element 耳 **ěr** 'ear' incorporated in its written mononym; but now it is used more often with the meaning of 'smell' rather than that of 'hear'.

Though we have not been able to completely avoid using terms and symbols with a 'diachronic' implication in our discussion (e.g. extension, evolve, →, etc.), yet diachronic approaches such as these have no relevance for our present synchronic analysis of polysemy.

SYNONYMY

Linguists generally distinguish between two types of synonyms: (i) perfect synonyms, which are interchangeable in all contexts; and (ii) partial synonyms, which are synonymous in certain contexts but not in others.

Perfect synonyms are not a necessary design feature of language and are therefore comparatively rare. They are mostly the result of enrichment coming from various dialects. Partial synonyms, on the other hand, seem to be a natural growth of languages in their need to attain greater and greater precision, expressiveness and discreteness in communication.

In the analysis of polysemous lexemes, we have noted that the sharing of a joint base of meaning can be the semantic tie among the different senses of a single mononym or lexeme and these different senses are not supposed to be synonymous to one another in any sense. On the other hand, different mononyms or lexemes (obviously, in terms of a particular sense in one or another) may come together as synonyms. The following diagram might illustrate the point just made:

	lexeme A		lexeme B	
	sense 1		sense 1	
	sense 2	synonymous	← sense 2	
polysemous	sense 3 →	relations	sense 3	polysemous
relations	sense 4		sense 4	relations
	sense n		sense n	

For example,

打败 **dǎbài** 'to defeat' synonymous with 赢 **yíng** 'win', 'gain'
   antonymous with   antonymous with
打败 **dǎbài** 'suffer defeat' synonymous with 输 **shū** 'lose', 'be beaten'

The lexeme 打败 **dǎbài** can therefore be said to be synonymous with 赢 **yíng** 'win' in one sense and with 输 **shū** 'lose' in the other.

In fact, if the difference in the 'sphere of application' constitutes the basis for polysemy, it is the similarity in the 'sphere of application' that constitutes the basis for synonymy: e.g.

高 **gāo** high
        tall
        of a high level/degree
        loud →   synonymous with ← loud   响 **xiǎng**
        expensive → synonymous with ← costly 贵 **guì**

Since most synonyms are partial, conditional or context-dependent, there are bound to be differences between them; these differences can only be told from the specific 'syntagmatic co-texts' they associate themselves with in usage. To refer back to our previous examples, 响 **xiǎng** and 贵 **guì** with 'loud' and 'expensive' as their primary senses collocate with anything (e.g. a radio) that can be 'loud' and anything (e.g. a book) that can be 'expensive'; but 高 **gāo** with 'loud' or 'expensive' as its transferred or secondary sense has a much narrower collocability: without the overt presence of a specific 'syntagmatic context' like 'voice which can be high' (e.g. 高声 **gāoshēng**) or 'price which can be high' (e.g. 高价 **gāojià**), the meaning of 'loud' or 'expensive' in 高 **gāo** (with its primary sense of 'high') cannot be evoked.

The relationship between polysemy and synonymy can therefore be recapitulated as:

synonymy	versus	polysemy
specific syntagmatic co-text	versus	sphere of application
shared sphere of application		joint semantic base

What is below the line may be regarded as the shared point of departure and what is above the line as the factor for mutual differentiation.

We can put this formulation to a further test. If we choose 'age' as the sphere of application and obtain as many collocations as we can, we call forth the synonymous senses in the following monyms or lexemes:

words indicating 'age'	the meaning of 老 **lǎo** 'old' is being applied	conditional synonyms obtained
年 – **nián**	年迈 **niánmài** 'aged'	迈 **mài** 'advanced'
年纪 – **niánjì**	年纪大 **niánjì dà** 'old'	大 **dà** 'big'
– 年岁 **niánsuì**	上了年岁 **shàng le niánsuì** 'getting old in years'	上 **shàng** 'gone up'
– 龄 **líng**	高龄 **gāolíng** 'venerable age'	高 **gāo** 'high'
– 寿 **shòu**	长寿 **chángshòu** 'longevity'	长 **cháng** 'long'

Once again we are led to believe that what we have concluded is true. First, as 老 **lǎo** has 'old' as its primary sense, it is freely applicable to any person or animate being to mean 'old'; and 'age', being part of its meaning, does not have to be explicitly expressed. But with the other terms, a specific syntagmatic context in the sphere of 'age' must be given if their respective sense of 'old' is to be evoked. Second, if we look at the primary senses of these conditional synonyms, we find that they are not unrelated with their secondary sense of 'old'. They all share with 老 **lǎo** 'old' a joint semantic base, which is measurement of some kind of position in a scale. What usually differentiates them is their different spheres of application: 大 **dà** 'big' in size, 高 **gāo** 'high' in height, 长 **cháng** 'long' in length, 上了 **shàngle** 'gone up' similar to 高 **gāo** and 迈 **mài** 'advanced' similar to 长 **cháng**.

However, it is a common misunderstanding among many people that a shared meaning component is the 'patent' basis for synonyms. It is true, of course, that synonyms do have shared meaning components; but it is definitely incorrect to say that every lexical unit with shared meaning components will be a synonym and it will undoubtedly be futile to try to recruit synonyms by relying on shared meaning components alone. The following diagram shows the multiple possibilities that shared meaning components can produce:

shared meaning components   →   different senses of a polysemous lexeme
                                         →   synonyms
                                         →   antonyms
                                         →   co-hyponyms
                                         →   paronyms (i.e. a root lexeme and its derivatives)

where → means 'can produce'.

Intra-lexically, synonymy in the Chinese lexicon (as we have seen in Chapter 4) is a most important structural design of disyllabic lexemes of the juxtapositional type, which can be found in nouns, verbs, adjectives and many lexemes of other word classes.

If we look more closely into such combinations, we find that one of the monyms in the juxtaposition rather than the other has often established itself in the lexicon as a more active combiner with a whole paradigm of lexemes behind it. This is what we have called the 'juxtaposer' in comparison with the other less active member in the combination, which we have called the 'juxtaposed'. Generally speaking, the 'juxtaposer' determines the sphere of application and the 'juxtaposed' determines the specific syntagmatic co-text in usage. It is perfectly natural for a monym to be a 'juxtaposer' in one set of combinations and a 'juxtaposed' in another.

Distribution in sets of lexemes of similar construction often provides the clue as to which is the 'juxtaposer' or the 'juxtaposed' monym in the given structure. For example, in

美丽 **měilì**	'beautiful'
秀丽 **xiùlì**	'pretty'
艳丽 **yànlì**	'brightly coloured and beautiful'
明丽 **mínglì**	'bright and beautiful'
绮丽 **qǐlì**	'gorgeous'
华丽 **huálì**	'resplendent'
壮丽 **zhuànglì**	'majestic'
瑰丽 **guīlì**	'surpassingly beautiful'

there is little doubt that the second monym (of the set) 丽 **lì** 'beautiful' (a bound morpheme) is the 'juxtaposer', which determines that the sphere of application for the whole set should be 'some person or object of beauty'; the first monyms 美 **měi** 'beautiful', 秀 **xiù** 'graceful', 艳 **yàn** 'brightly coloured', 明 **míng** 'bright', 绮 **qǐ** 'gorgeous', 华 **huá** 'splendid'; 'magnificent', 壮 **zhuàng** 'grand', 瑰 **guī** 'rare'; 'marvellous' are all 'juxtaposed' monyms, which determine the specific syntagmatic co-texts of application for each: e.g. 'beautiful girl' in the first two instances, 'beautiful dresses' in the third, 'beautiful scenery' in the fourth, fifth, seventh and eighth, and 'beautiful palace' in the sixth. Incidentally, as 美丽 **měilì** is also the most general term of the set, it seems to be applicable to most contexts.

The 'juxtaposer' can, of course, also come first in the combination; but the analysis will remain the same, e.g.

贫穷 **pínqióng**	'poor'
贫苦 **pínkǔ**	'poverty-stricken'
贫困 **pínkùn**	'in straitened circumstances'
贫寒 **pínhán**	'impoverished'
贫贱 **pínjiàn**	'in straitened and humble circumstances'
贫瘠 **pínjí**	'infertile'
贫乏 **pínfá**	'lacking'

As the 'juxtaposer' often seems to be more generic and the 'juxtaposed' more specific in sense in the given set of combinations, it is not totally unfeasible to view these juxtapositions as being 'hyponymically' organised:

美 **měi**	'beautiful'
秀 **xiù**	'gracefully beautiful'
艳 **yàn**	'colourfully beautiful'
明 **míng** – 丽 **lì** 'beautiful'	'brightly beautiful'
绮 **qǐ**	'gorgeously beautiful'
华 **huá**	'resplendently beautiful'
壮 **zhuàng**	'majestically beautiful'
瑰 **guī**	'surpassingly beautiful'

This is to look at the meaning of the 'juxtaposer' as being the 'constant' (= hypernym or superordinate term) and the meanings of the synonymous 'juxtaposed' monosyms as 'variables' (= co-hyponyms). From this point of view, synonymy is closely akin to hyponymy.[6]

With this kind of structural design, that is, a lexeme being composed of partially synonymous monosyms, it is inevitable that these disyllabic juxtapositions sometimes become interestingly 'circular' (to allow versatility in speech or writing?), e.g.

poor:	贫苦 **pínkǔ**	贫穷 **pínqióng**	穷苦 **qióngkǔ**	i.e.	AB AC CB
beautiful:	美丽 **měilì**	秀丽 **xiùlì**	秀美 **xiùměi**		AB CB CA
help:	援助 **yuánzhù**	救助 **jiùzhù**	援救 **yuánjiù**		AB CB AC
blame:	责骂 **zémà**	斥骂 **chìmà**	斥责 **chìzé**		AB CB CA

---

[6] Cf. Lyons 1968. Synonymy is 'symmetrical or bilateral' hyponymy.

or increasingly 'removed' from the starting-point (to allow diversity?), e.g.

正直 **zhèngzhí**	'upright'
直爽 **zhíshuǎng**	'straightforward'
爽快 **shuǎngkuài**	'brisk'
快乐 **kuàilè**	'happy'
愉快 **yúkuài**	'cheerful'
欢愉 **huānyú**	'joyous'
喜欢 **xǐhuan**	'pleased'
欢畅 **huānchàng**	'delighted'
畅怀 **chànghuái**	'to one's heart's content'

In trisyllabic lexemes we find a unique type of juxtaposition, in which the 'juxtaposer' is followed by a pair of 'meaningful phonaesthemes' as the 'juxtaposed' mononyms,[7] e.g.

乱纷纷 **luànfēnfēn**	'tumultuous'	'crowd'
乱哄哄 **luànhōnghōng**	'in a hubbub'	'argument'
乱蓬蓬 **luànpēngpēng**	'dishevelled'	'hair'
乱腾腾 **luàntēngtēng**	'confused'	'mind'
乱糟糟 **luànzāozāo**	'chaotic'	'room'

乱 **luàn** 'in disorder' is the 'juxtaposer' which determines the sphere of application and the pairs of meaningful phonaesthemes, e.g. 纷纷 **fēnfēn**, 哄哄 **hōnghōng**, etc. are the 'juxtaposed' mononyms, which determine that the specific syntagmatic co-texts of application should be 人群 **rénqún** 'crowd' in the first instance, 议论 **yìlùn** 'argument' in the second, and so on.

In quadrisyllabic 'classical' idioms, we find interestingly diversified forms of synonymous juxtaposition as discussed in Chapter 4.

Inter-lexemic synonymy, as we shall see, is a particularly prominent feature of the adjectival lexicon. The proliferation and thinning out of synonyms in the lexicon might be compared to the 'ebb and flow' of the contemporaneous cultural tide.

However, we must hasten to add that areas where synonyms abound are usually areas of perennial interest to the linguistic community. They echo the linguistic temperament of the nation. One should not be surprised to learn that in Chinese there are six times as many synonyms for 'beautiful' as for 'ugly'. A nation, like an individual, tends to think more of something she dreams of having.[8] And once these synonyms have been born and accepted, they die hard, particularly in literature.

According to tradition, eight types of inter-lexemic synonymous relations can be discerned.[9] They are:

---

[7] Cf. Chapter 5 on phonaesthetic features of the Chinese lexicon.
[8] Cf. Chapter 6 on rhetorical features of the Chinese lexicon.
[9] Cf. Gao, Qingci (高庆赐) 1957; Palmer 1981: 88–93.

(1) classical Chinese versus modern Chinese:

classical	*modern*
诞辰 **dànchén** 'birthday'	生日 **shēngrì** 'birthday'
逝世 **shìshì** 'pass away'	死 **sǐ** 'die'

(2) standard versus dialectal:

standard	*dialectal*
路费 **lùfèi** 'travelling expenses'	盘缠 **pánchán** 'money for the journey'
玉米 **yùmǐ** 'maize'	包谷 **bāogǔ** 'Indian corn'

(3) general versus technical:

general	*technical*
天河 **tiānhé** 'the Milky Way'	银河 **yínhé** 'the Galaxy'
石灰 **shíhuī** 'lime'	氧化钙 **yǎnghuàgài** 'Calcium dioxide'

(4) vulgar versus euphemistic:

vulgar	*euphemistic*
拉屎 **lāshǐ** 'shit'	大便 **dàbiàn** 'big convenience'
拉尿 **lāliào** 'make water'	小便 **xiǎobiàn** 'small convenience'

(5) native versus translation of foreign terms:

indigenous	*foreign*
诙谐 **huīxié** 'jocular'	幽默 **yōumò** 'humorous' (transliterating 'humour')
时髦 **shímáo** 'in vogue'	摩登 **módēng** 'fashionable' (translating 'modern')

(6) colloquial versus written:

colloquial	*written*
迎接 **yíngjiē** 'meet'	迎迓 **yíngyà** 'welcome'
边境 **biānjìng** 'border'	边陲 **biānchuí** 'frontier'

(7) full form versus abbreviation:

full form	*abbreviation*
科学研究 **kēxué yánjiū** 'scientific research'	科研 **kēyán** 'scientific research'
劳动模范 **láodòng mófàn** 'model worker'	劳模 **láomó** 'model worker'

(8) root-creation or compounding:

    (a) *reordering:*

        商洽 **shāngqià** 'arrange with somebody'/洽商 **qiàshāng** 'talk over with'

        一发千钧 **yī fà qiān jūn**/千钧一发 **qiān jūn yī fà** 'in imminent peril'

(b) *substitution:*

立足点 **lìzúdiǎn**/立脚点 **lìjiǎodiǎn** 'foothold', 'footing'

助桀为虐 **zhù jié wéi nuè**/助纣为虐 **zhù zhòu wéi nuè** 'aid King Jie/Zhou in his tyrannical rule – help a tyrant to do evil'

(c) *coinage:*

词组 **cízǔ**/短语 **duǎnyǔ** 'phrase'

谨慎 **jǐnshèn** 'prudent'/小心 **xiǎoxīn** 'cautious'

(d) *introducing changes in one of the mononyms in a disyllabic lexeme:*

时间 **shíjiān** 'duration of time'/时期 **shíqī** 'period'

理想 **lǐxiǎng** 'ideal'/梦想 **mèngxiǎng** 'fond dream'

(e) *sense-intersection as a result of contextual polysemy:*

贵 **guì** 'expensive'/高(价) **gāo jià** 'high' (price)

响 **xiǎng** 'loud'/大(声) **dà shēng** 'loud noise'

The demarcation line between synonyms of the first seven types is self-explanatory – always a difference in style: a classical, written or technical lexeme will naturally sound more formal than a modern, colloquial or more general one; and a vulgar, dialectal or abbreviated form will be far more informal than its euphemistic, standard or full form; and so on. It is in the last category of root-creation and compounding that we are truly confronted with the giant reservoir of synonyms that are differentiable by virtue of meaning.

Whatever linguistic devices are employed to create these synonyms for the convenience of communication and expression, the overall formula applies: the sphere of application will be the joint starting-point and the specific syntagmatic co-text will be the criterion of differentiation. If any semantic differentiation may be made about these synonyms, they can generally be seen to differ in the following respects:

(a) scope:

天气 **tiānqì** 'weather' (narrower)/气候 **qìhòu** 'climate' (broader)

(b) individual or collective:

书 **shū** 'book' (individual)/书本 **shūběn** 'books' (collective)

(c) degree of emphasis:

后悔 **hòuhuǐ** 'regret' (weak)/悔恨 **huǐhèn** 'regret deeply' (strong)

(d) commendatory or derogatory:

后果 **hòuguǒ** 'consequence' (bad)/成果 **chéngguǒ** 'achievement' (good)

(e) degree of emotional colouring:

父母 **fùmǔ** 'parents' (less emotional)/双亲 **shuāngqīn** 'father and mother' (more emotional)

(f) difference in goal or objective:

招募 **zhāomù** 'recruit'

招聘 **zhāopìn** 'invite applications for a job'

招徕 **zhāolái** 'solicit (customers)'

But the list must remain open.

What we see in the composition of these synonyms is the sharing of a particular mononym. This seems to be overwhelmingly the favoured device of the Chinese lexicon to construct synonymous items with minute differences in application or nuance.

ANTONYMY

It has long been a standing practice in lexicography to list antonyms side by side with synonyms. The respect for antonymy is not unfounded but seems largely intuitive. The term antonymy has often been loosely used to mean 'oppositeness' or 'contradictoriness', just like the term synonymy, which has often been vaguely used to mean 'sameness' or 'equivalence'. However, when analysed closely, antonymy resolves itself, as many linguists suggest, into three different types: (i) incompatible terms; (ii) gradable terms; and (iii) convertible terms.[10]

If two terms A and B are incompatible with each other, the affirmation of one will mean the denial of the other or vice versa. For example, if something is a 'rose', it cannot be a 'tulip', a 'chrysanthemum', etc.; if it is 'red', it cannot be 'yellow', or 'blue' or any other colour again. So 'rose' and 'tulip' or 'red' and 'yellow' are incompatible terms (= co-hyponyms). But this happens in a multiple-item set. If the set consists of only two items, 'incompatibility' turns into 'complementarity'[11] – a question of 'either-or'. For example, the affirmation or denial of 'female' will necessarily be the corresponding denial or affirmation of 'male'.

If two terms A and B are gradable antonyms, though the affirmation of one implies the denial of the other, the denial of one does not necessarily imply the affirmation of the other. For instance, if something is 'not big', it does not mean that it must be 'small'; if someone is not a 天才 **tiāncái** 'genius', he is not necessarily a 蠢材 **chǔncái** 'idiot': there are intermediate points or categories to consider. So, with gradable antonyms, we are actually dealing with two points at or near either extreme of a scale with a lot of middle ground in between. As they are largely adjectives, gradable antonyms display two interesting features: (1) being attributes to certain things, they are implicitly norm-based, that is to say, any 'bigness' or 'smallness' is relative to the thing

---

[10] Palmer 1981: 94–100. Palmer calls the last category 'relational opposites'.

[11] Cf. Lyons 1968.

being described, e.g. the 'biggest' fly can probably be a hundred thousand times smaller than the 'smallest' elephant; (2) being just two representative points on a scale, one (often the positive term) is selected to represent not only positive but also neutral ideas, e.g. 'how large is the room?' does not in the least presume that the room must necessarily be large: it leaves the answer open to any possibilities; while on the other hand, 'how small is the room?' presupposes from the start the 'smallness' of the room on the part of the questioner. The former is therefore generally thought of as being 'unmarked' and the latter as being 'marked'. Chinese and English seem to differentiate and use these marked and unmarked terms in a similar way.

If two terms A and B are convertible into each other, the conversion naturally involves the reversal of places for (usually) the two parties X and Y related or associated with them. For instance, if X buys from Y, then Y sells to X; if X is Y's husband, then Y is X's wife; if X 娶 **qǔ** 'marry (a woman)' Y, then Y 嫁 **jià** 'marry (a man)' X. So we say 'buy' and 'sell' or 'husband' and 'wife' or 嫁 **jià** and 娶 **qǔ** are convertible antonyms. But, sometimes, the two parties concerned might involve more than one individual on either side; then the conversion, though still tenable, will have multiple choices: e.g. if X is Y's father, Y can be either X's son or his daughter; if X is Y's son, Y can be either X's father or his mother. Sometimes, if the two parties involved are on a completely equal footing, the conversion becomes reciprocal, e.g. if X is Y's partner, Y is also X's partner; if X is Y's friend, Y is also X's friend. This is where convertible antonyms become synonymous themselves.

But with whatever meticulous care we might delimit our categories, the system of a natural language defies such rigid differentiation. For example, when one says no to 单人床 **dānrénchuáng** 'single bed', one will be taken to mean 双人床 **shuāngrénchuáng** 'double bed' and not other quite impossible possibilities: 三 **sān** 'triple-', 四 **sì** 'quadruple-' etc. When one says 半生不死 **bàn shēng bù sǐ** lit. 'half-alive and not-dead', one does not really mean that 'dead' and 'alive' are both gradable. If X 教 **jiāo** 'teach' Y, one cannot say for sure that Y will definitely 学 **xué** 'learn from' X. Y might refuse to learn.

However, one consolation is that no matter how capriciously antonyms sometimes behave, there must be some underlying factor that unites them together into these patterned relationships. Apparently, 'rose' and 'chair' do not form incompatible pairs; nor do 'large' and 'hot' contract a gradable antonymous relationship with each other; and certainly we cannot say that 'buy' and 'love' are convertible terms. The fact that one term can be said to be antonymous with another lies in a shared 'superordinate notion' (not necessarily an available term in a language) to which they are respectively hyponymous. Without the categorial notion of flower behind 'rose' and 'tulip', they cannot form incompatible pairs; without the unifying notion of temperature, 'hot' and 'cold' are not gradable antonyms; without the underlying idea of transaction in terms of money and goods, 'buy' and 'sell' cannot come together as convertible terms.

This should become very clear if we vary the unifying notion. In the context of, say, a watering-can, 'rose' is incompatible with 'lid', etc. and not with 'tulip'; in the context of a host's attitude towards his guests, 'cold' is not opposed to 'hot' but to 'warm'; and if one is told that X (a person) was 'sold', Y (another person) certainly did not 'buy' him: he 'deceived' him. From this we can perhaps deduce the fact that antonymy is in a broader sense co-hyponymy, comparable yet incompatible notions under a shared superordinate notion. Antonymy equates with 'incompatibility'. In our present analysis, however, we would like to adhere to the traditional term 'antonymy', but use it in a narrower sense: antonymy equates to 'symmetric incompatibility' or 'complementarity'. In other words, if 'hot', 'cold', 'warm', 'cool', 'lukewarm' are all taken to be 'incompatible' terms under a norm-based superordinate notion of 'temperature', intuition seems to affirm that 'hot' and 'cold' or 'warm' and 'cool' form better antonymous pairs, supported by an underlying sense of symmetry.

This intuition matches the time-honoured practice of two different kinds of 对联 **duìlián** 'antithetical coupling' in Chinese poetics, in which either specific terms are opposed, for instance, 'rose' to 'tulip', 'red' to 'blue', 'buy' to 'sell', 'before' to 'after', etc. (traditionally called 'detailed coupling') or more general syntactic categories are opposed, for instance, noun to noun, adjective to adjective, verb to verb, preposition to preposition, etc. (traditionally called 'broad coupling'). Matching syntactic categories (such as those of 'thingness', 'quality', 'action', etc.), as we can see, exemplify 'complementarity' in its broadest sense.

So we see that antonymy is integrally related to hyponymy and synonymy. It differs from hyponymy in its symmetrical nature. If hyponymy usually consists of mutiple contrasts under a superordinate hypernym, antonymy comprises only a dichotomy set up to account for one particular contrast; and it differs from synonymy in choosing rather than avoiding the same syntagmatic co-texts. In other words, if different syntagmatic co-texts are essential for setting up a set of synonyms, the very sameness of the syntagmatic co-text is required to establish a pair of antonyms. For example,

粥很稠 **zhōu hěn chóu**	vs	粥很稀 **zhōu hěn xī**
'the porridge is thick'		'the porridge is thin'
人口稠密 **rénkǒu chóumì**	vs	人口稀少 **rénkǒu xīshǎo**
'densely populated'		'sparsely populated'
头发浓密 **tóufa nóngmì**	vs	头发稀疏 **tóufa xīshū**
'thick/dense hair'		'thin/sparse hair'

Clearly, it is the sameness of the syntagmatic co-text that brings together 稠 **chóu** and 稀 **xī** (in the context of porridge), 稠密 **chóumì** and 稀少 **xīshǎo** (in the context of population), 浓密 **nóngmì** and 稀疏 **xīshū** (in the context of hair) as pairs of antonyms. Formulaically,

synonymy	specific syntagmatic co-text	hyponymy	multiple-entry hierarchy
antonymy	similar syntagmatic co-text	antonymy	specific dichotomy

We shall now look at the intra-lexemic behaviour of antonyms.

Like the juxtaposition of two co-hyponyms, the juxtaposition of two antonyms, as we have seen, may also call forth a 'superordinate' notion,[12] e.g.

大小 **dàxiǎo** 'size'   (大 **dà**: big; 小 **xiǎo**: small)
长短 **chángduǎn** 'length'   (长 **cháng**: long; 短 **duǎn**: short)
高矮 **gāo'ǎi** 'height'   (高 **gāo**: tall; 矮 **ǎi**: short)
深浅 **shēnqiǎn** 'depth'   (深 **shēn**: deep; 浅 **qiǎn**: shallow)
疏密 **shūmì** 'density'   (疏 **shū**: sparse; 密 **mì**: dense)
冷暖 **lěngnuǎn** (of temperature)   (冷 **lěng**: cold; 暖 **nuǎn**: warm)
    'changes'
浓淡 **nóngdàn** (of colour) 'shade';   (浓 **nóng**: strong; 淡 **dàn**: weak)
    (of taste) 'strength'
买卖 **mǎimài** 'business'; 'transaction'   (买 **mǎi**: buy; 卖 **mài**: sell)
酬酢 **chóuzuò** 'social intercourse'   (酬 **chóu**: host proposes a toast to guest; 酢 **zuò**: guest proposes a toast to host)

Here we see that gradable antonyms indicating two points nearer to the extreme are listed to cover 'the whole range'. This can be seen in a set of adverbs:

反正 **fǎnzhèng** 'in any case'   (反 **fǎn**: the reverse side; 正 **zhèng**: the obverse side)
横竖 **héngshu** 'in any case'   (横 **héng**: horizontal; 竖 **shù**: vertical)
好歹 **hǎodǎi** 'in any case'   (好 **hǎo**: good; 歹 **dǎi**: bad)
迟早 **chízǎo** 'sooner or later'   (迟 **chí**: late; 早 **zǎo**: early)
高低 **gāodī** 'on any account'   (高 **gāo**: high; 低 **dī**: low)

Sometimes, however, only one idea in the juxtaposition is emphasised:

安危 **ānwēi** 'danger'   (安 **ān**: safe; 危 **wēi**: dangerous)
巨细 **jùxì** 'small matters'   (巨 **jù**: big; 细 **xì**: small)

With the juxtaposition of antonymous verbs, there is often the integrated notion of:

direction: e.g.
    收支 **shōuzhī** 'income and expenses'
    进退 **jìntuì** 'advance and retreat'
    吞吐 **tūntǔ** (of a harbour) 'take in and send out goods in large quantities'
    往返 **wǎngfǎn** 'travel to and fro'

[12] Cf. Chapter 4.

attitude: e.g.

赏罚 **shǎngfá** 'rewards and punishments'
褒贬 **bāobiǎn** 'appraise' (lit. 'praise and censure')
取舍 **qǔshě** 'accept or reject'
离合 **líhé** 'separation and reunion'

Convertible or complementary antonyms, on the other hand, will generally retain the additive meaning of the two component monyms when thus juxtaposed:

宾主 **bīnzhǔ** 'host and guest' (宾 **bīn**: host; 主 **zhǔ**: guest)
夫妇 **fūfù** 'husband and wife' (夫 **fū**: husband; 妇 **fù**: wife)
敌友 **díyǒu** 'enemy and friends' (敌 **dí**: enemy; 友 **yǒu**: friends)
先后 **xiānhòu** 'those who come early and those who come late'
      (先 **xiān**: early; 后 **hòu**: late)

In quadrisyllabic idioms antonyms appear in either adjacent or staggered positions: e.g.

adjacent:[13]

内外夹攻 **nèiwài jiāgōng** 'attack from both within and without'
      (内 **nèi**: within; 外 **wài**: without; 夹攻 **jiāgōng**: attack from both sides)
不知好歹 **bù zhī hǎodǎi** 'unable to tell what's good or bad for one'
      (不 **bù**: not; 知 **zhī**: know; 好歹 **hǎodǎi**: good or bad)

staggered:

以寡敌众 **yǐ guǎ dí zhòng** 'pit the few against the many'
      (以 **yǐ**: use; 敌 **dí**: against; 寡 **guǎ**: few; 众 **zhòng**: many)
转危为安 **zhuǎn wēi wéi ān** 'take a turn for better'
      (转 **zhuǎn**: change; 为 **wéi**: become; 危 **wēi**: danger; 安 **ān**: safety)
因小失大 **yīn xiǎo shī dà** 'try to save a little only to lose a lot'
      (因 **yīn**: because; 失 **shī**: lose; 小 **xiǎo**: small; 大 **dà**: big)
口是心非 **kǒushì xīnfēi** 'say one thing and mean another'
      (口 **kǒu**: mouth; 心 **xīn**: heart; 是 **shì**: yes; 非 **fēi**: no)
你死我活 **nǐsǐ wǒhuó** 'life-and-death'
      (你 **nǐ**: you; 我 **wǒ**: me; 死 **sǐ**: dead; 活 **huó**: alive)
阳奉阴违 **yángfèng yīnwéi** 'overtly agree but covertly oppose'
      (阳 **yáng**: overt; 阴 **yīn**: covert; 奉 **fèng**: obey; 违 **wéi**: do something contradictory)

In a polysyllabic saying, the contrasted ideas come on either side of a linguistic pivot (which is either a rhythmic pause shown in the following quotations by a vertical slash or a word or expression shown between two vertical slashes) if the saying is continuous, or in the first or second part of the saying if it is a recurrent pattern:

[13] Cf. Chapter 4 on antonymous juxtaposition.

continuous:

驴唇 | 不对 | 马嘴 **lǘchún bù duì mǎzuǐ** 'far off the mark'
(驴唇 **lǘchún**: lips of a donkey; 不对 **bù duì**: don't match; 马嘴 **mǎzuǐ**: mouth of a horse)

好了疮疤 | 忘了痛 **hǎo le chuāngbā wàng le tòng**
'the pain is forgotten as soon as the scar is healed'
(好了 **hǎo le**: healed; 疮疤 **chuāngbā**: scar; 忘了 **wàng le**: forgotten; 痛 **tòng**: pain)

只敬衣衫 | 不敬人 **zhǐ jìng yīshān bù jìng rén**
'respect the dress the person wears but not the person himself'
(只 **zhǐ**: only; 敬 **jìng**: respect; 衣衫 **yīshān**: dress; 不 **bù**: not; 人 **rén**: person)

饱汉 | 不知 | 饿汉饥 **bǎohàn bù zhī èhàn jī**
'he whose belly is full does not know the feeling of him who is hungry'
(饱汉 **bǎohàn**: man who has eaten his fill; 不 **bù**: not; 知 **zhī**: know; 饿汉 **èhàn**: a hungry man; 饥 **jī**: starving)

心有余 | 而 | 力不足 **xīn yǒu yú ér lì bùzú**
'the heart is willing but the flesh is weak'
(心 **xīn**: heart; 有 **yǒu**: have; 余 **yú**: more than enough; 而 **ér**: yet; 力 **lì**: strength; 不足 **bùzú**: insufficient)

有百利 | 而 | 无一害 **yǒu bǎi lì ér wú yī hài**
'it is profitable from every angle and entirely without harm'
(有 **yǒu**: have; 百 **bǎi**: a hundred; 利 **lì**: advantage; 而 **ér**: yet; 无 **wú**: have not; 一 **yī**: one; 害 **hài**: disadvantage)

生米 | 煮成了 | 熟饭 **shēng mǐ zhú chéng le shú fàn**
'what's done can't be undone'
(生 **shēng**: uncooked; 米 **mǐ**: rice; 煮 **zhǔ**: cook; 成 **chéng**: become; 了 **le**: particle of perfect aspect; 熟 **shú**: cooked; 饭 **fàn**: cooked rice)

recurrent:

干打雷, 不下雨 **gān dǎléi | bù xiàyǔ** 'much ado about nothing'
(干 **gān**: only; 打雷 **dǎléi**: thunder; 不 **bù**: not; 下雨 **xiàyǔ**: rain)

挂羊头, 卖狗肉 **guà yángtóu | mài gǒuròu**
'cry up wine and sell vinegar'
(挂 **guà**: hang up; 羊头 **yángtóu**: head of a sheep; 卖 **mài**: sell; 狗肉 **gǒuròu**: dog's meat)

前人栽树, 后人乘凉 **qiánrén zāi shù | hòurén chéngliáng**
'one soweth and another reapeth'
(前人 **qiánrén**: ancestors; 栽 **zāi**: to plant; 树 **shù**: tree; 后人 **hòurén**: later generations; 乘凉 **chéngliáng**: cool oneself in the shade)

明察秋毫, 不见舆薪 **míng chá qiūháo | bù jiàn yúxīn**
'none so blind as those who will not see'
(明 **míng**: clearly; 察 **chá**: observe; 秋毫 **qiūháo**: fine down on birds in autumn; 不 **bù**: not; 见 **jiàn**: see; 舆薪 **yúxīn**: cartload of firewood)

宁可信其有, 不可信其无 **nìngkě xìn qí yǒu | bùkě xìn qí wú**
'hope for the best and prepare for the worst'
    (宁可 **nìngkě**: rather; 信 **xìn**: believe; 其 **qí**: it; 有 **yǒu**: exist; 不可 **bùkě**: must not; 无 **wú**: does not exist)

满瓶子不响, 半瓶子晃荡 **mǎn píngzi bù xiǎng | bàn píngzi huàngdang**
'empty vessels make the most sound'
    (满 **mǎn**: full; 瓶子 **píngzi**: bottle; 不 **bù**: not; 响 **xiǎng**: make a sound; 半 **bàn**: half; 晃荡 **huàngdang**: splash about)

Inter-lexically, Chinese, like English, has a prolific supply of negative prefixes in the lexicon, which are a ready source of antonyms.

不 **bù** 'not'	否 **fǒu** 'not'	没 **méi** 'without'	未 **wèi** 'not yet'
被 **bèi** 'passive'	非 **fēi** 'non-'		无 **wú** 'have not'
	反 **fǎn** 'counter-'		
	防 **fáng** 'anti-'		

It is not known why there should be so many of these negative particles (most of them function both as prefixes and as independent lexemes) in the lexicon; but the fascinating thing about them is that they seem to be derived from one and the same archi-mononym, for the regularity in their 'labial' consonantal variation tells at least part of the story:

    b   (p)   m   f   w

In the formation of a pair of corresponding antonyms, an existing lexeme is either prefixed or has one of its components replaced by these negators: e.g.

existing lexemes	*prefixed or partially replaced*
平衡 **pínghéng** 'balanced'	不平衡 **bù pínghéng** 'imbalanced'
乘数 **chéngshù** 'multiplier'	被乘数 **bèichéngshù** 'multiplicand'
肯定 **kěndìng** 'confirm'	否定 **fǒudìng** 'deny'
正式 **zhèngshì** 'formal'	非正式 **fēizhèngshì** 'informal'
批评 **pīpíng** 'criticism'	反批评 **fǎnpīpíng** 'counter-criticism'
腐蚀剂 **fǔshíjì** 'corrodent'	防腐剂 **fángfǔjì** 'antiseptic'
有脸 **yǒuliǎn** 'have the face to'	没脸 **méiliǎn** 'feel ashamed'
成年 **chéngnián** 'come of age'	未成年 **wèichéngnián** 'under age'
有机 **yǒujī** 'organic'	无机 **wújī** 'inorganic'

A few more examples to show the versatility of this group of negators in creating antonymy:

承认 **chéngrèn** 'confess'	→	否认 **fǒurèn** 'deny'
决定 **juédìng** 'decide'		否决 **fǒujué** 'veto'
平凡 **píngfán** 'ordinary'		非凡 **fēifán** 'extraordinary'
合法 **héfǎ** 'legal'		非法 **fēifǎ** 'illegal'
正面 **zhèngmiàn** 'obverse side'		反面 **fǎnmiàn** 'reverse side'
赞成 **zànchéng** 'support'; 'agree'		反对 **fǎnduì** 'oppose'

已婚 **yǐhūn** 'married'   未婚 **wèihūn** 'unmarried'
已知 **yǐzhī** 'known'   未知 **wèizhī** 'unknown'
有关 **yǒuguān** 'have sth to   无关 **wúguān** 'have nothing to
do with'   do with'
有限 **yǒuxiàn** 'limited'   无限 **wúxiàn** 'unlimited'
主动 **zhǔdòng** 'initiative'   被动 **bèidòng** 'passive'
原告 **yuángào** 'the plaintiff'   被告 **bèigào** 'the accused'

This correlates with the general way of obtaining antonymous dichotomies
by varying one of the corresponding constituent mononyms:

直接 **zhíjiē** 'direct'   间接 **jiànjiē** 'indirect'
高级 **gāojí** 'advanced'   低级 **dījí** 'elementary'
上级 **shàngjí** 'superiors'   下级 **xiàjí** 'subordinates'
生理 **shēnglǐ** 'physical'   心理 **xīnlǐ** 'psychological'
优点 **yōudiǎn** 'merit'; 'virtue'   缺点 **quēdiǎn** 'shortcoming'; 'drawback'
益处 **yìchu** 'benefit'   害处 **hàichu** 'harm'
特性 **tèxìng** 'specific property'   共性 **gòngxìng** 'general character'
质量 **zhìliàng** 'quality'   数量 **shùliàng** 'quantity'
悦耳 **yuè'ěr**   刺耳 **cì'ěr** 'grating on the ear'
'pleasing to the ear'
年老 **niánlǎo** 'old'   年轻 **niánqīng** 'young'
洋气 **yángqì** 'foreign flavour';   土气 **tǔqì** 'rustic style'; 'uncouth'
'Western style'
全面 **quánmiàn**   片面 **piànmiàn** 'unilateral'; 'one-sided'
'comprehensive'; 'all-round'
主要 **zhǔyào** 'main'; 'primary'   次要 **cìyào** 'less important';
'secondary'
可爱 **kě'ài** 'lovable'; 'lovely'   可恨 **kěhèn** 'detestable'
公立 **gōnglì** 'maintained by   私立 **sīlì** 'privately run'
the government'
乐观 **lèguān** 'optimistic'   悲观 **bēiguān** 'pessimistic'
积极 **jījí** 'positive'   消极 **xiāojí** 'negative'
升级 **shēngjí** 'promote'   降级 **jiàngjí** 'demote'
入选 **rùxuǎn** 'be selected';   落选 **luòxuǎn** 'fail to be chosen'
'be chosen'
丰收 **fēngshōu**   歉收 **qiànshōu** 'crop failure';
'bumper harvest'   'poor harvest'
享受 **xiǎngshòu** 'enjoy'   遭受 **zāoshòu** 'suffer'
食肉动物 **shíròudòngwù**   食草动物 **shícǎodòngwù**
'carnivore'   'herbivore'

However, due to the polysemic nature of mononyms, it is perfectly possible
that one mononym will have different 'opposites' in different antonymous
pairs, e.g.

好处 **hǎochu** 'advantage'　　坏处 **huàichu** 'disadvantage'
好感 **hǎogǎn** 'favourable impression'　　恶感 **ègǎn** 'ill feeling', 'malice'
好看 **hǎokàn** 'good-looking'　　难看 **nánkàn** 'unsightly'

Sometimes, both of the component mononyms are changed to their 'opposites':

下降 **xiàjiàng** 'descend'　　上升 **shàngshēng** 'ascend'
前进 **qiánjìn** 'advance'　　后退 **hòutuì** 'retreat'
过去 **guòqù** 'past'　　未来 **wèilái** 'future'

Generally speaking, however, antonymy, based on sameness of syntagmatic co-text as it is, does not have to have an explicitly shared form:

好转 **hǎozhuǎn** 'improve'　　恶化 **èhuà** 'deteriorate'
歌颂 **gēsòng** 'eulogise'　　耻笑 **chǐxiào** 'sneer at'; 'mock'
遵守 **zūnshǒu** 'abide by'　　违反 **wéifǎn** 'violate'
奖励 **jiǎnglì** 'award'; 'reward'　　惩罚 **chéngfá** 'punish'; 'penalise'
高兴 **gāoxìng** 'happy'　　悲伤 **bēishāng** 'sad'
勤奋 **qínfèn** 'diligent'; 'industrious'　　懒惰 **lǎnduò** 'lazy'

Though the notion of antonymy is omnipresent, it does not follow that every positive term will necessarily have a negative term to match. Language does not need to lexicalise every negative notion because it can be easily obtained by means of an impromptu syntactic construction. For example, 读 **dú** 'read (a book)': if one does not 'read', one just does not do it, one does not necessarily have to 'un-read' or 'de-read'.

MEANING STRUTURE IN THE MONONYMS

In the above sections, we devoted our discussion exclusively to intra- and inter-lexical meaning organisations. In this section, we shall look specifically at the meaning structure in the written mononyms, a peculiarity of the Chinese language.

In fact, hyponymy is the inherent structural design of over 90 per cent of existing written mononyms in the Chinese lexicon.[14] For instance, under a 'semantic categoriser' (traditionally known as 'radicals') like 艹 'grass', we have words or mononyms such as the following:

草 **cǎo**　　　　'grass'
花 **huā**　　　　'flowers'
茶 **chá**　　　　'tea'
萍 **píng**　　　　'duckweed'

[14] Cf. Chapter 2.

药 **yào**	'(herbal) medicine'
荷花 **héhuā**	'lotus'
菊花 **júhuā**	'chrysanthemum'
茉莉 **mòli**	'jasmine'
蔬菜 **shūcài**	'vegetables'
蘑菇 **mógu**	'mushroom'
葡萄 **pútao**	'grape'
芦苇 **lúwěi**	'reed'
苔藓 **táixiǎn**	'moss'

葩 **pā**	(formal) 'flower'
芽 **yá**	'sprout'; 'shoot'
苗 **miáo**	'seedling'; 'sapling'
蒂 **dì**	'the base of a fruit'
茎 **jīng**	'stem'; 'stalk'
茵 **yīn**	'a carpet of green grass'
荫 **yìn**	'shade under a tree'
茬 **chá**	'stubble'; 'crop'
蓓蕾 **bèilěi**	'bud'
芬芳 **fēnfāng**	'fragrant'
葱茏 **cōnglóng**	'verdant'
荒芜 **huāngwú**	'lie waste'; 'go out of cultivation'

落 **luò**	'fall'
蔫 **niān**	'wither'; 'shrivel up'; 'droop'
莳 **shì**	'cultivate'; 'transplant (rice seedlings)'
葬 **zàng**	'bury'
墓 **mù**	'tomb'

As can be clearly seen, all the mononyms and words listed here have something to do with 'grass': categories like flowers, algae, reeds, vegetables, fruit, tea, herbal medicine, etc. and their parts and attributes like bud, sprout, stem, seedling, shade, fragrance, luxuriance, wither, fall, etc., and even actions carried out with grass or on grass or entities associated with it, e.g. transplant, bury and tomb.

The very fact that these different concepts can be organised under the same radical means that this semantic categoriser too may develop polysemy: e.g. from 花 **huā** 'flower' to its parts 蓓蕾 **bèilěi** 'bud', to its attributes 芬芳 **fēnfāng** 'fragrant' and 蔫 **niān** 'wither'; 'shrivel up'; 'droop' and to what happens to it in the end 落 **luò** 'fall'.

It is also a well-known practice in the orthographical tradition to unify the mononyms in disyllabic lexemes with the same 'semantic categoriser'. This phenomenon can be clearly seen with the kind of agglutinated juxtapositions discussed in Chapter 4, e.g.

俊俏 **jùnqiào** (inf.) 'pretty and charming'	(亻 'person')
峻峭 **jùnqiào** 'high and steep'	(山 'mountain')
纤细 **xiānxì** 'slender'; 'tenuous'	(纟 'silk')
热烈 **rèliè** 'enthusiastic'; 'animated'	(灬 'fire')
评议 **píngyì** 'appraise'	(讠 'speech')

Even a word like 家具 **jiājù** 'furniture' has, without rhyme or reason, been changed into 傢俱 (with 亻 'person' as the 'semantic categoriser').

More interesting still is perhaps the fact that these same 'semantic categorisers' should be able to unify antonyms under them, e.g.

明 **míng** 'bright'/暗 **àn** 'dark'	with the meaning element 日 **rì** 'sun'
清 **qīng** 'clear'/浊 **zhuó** 'muddy'	with the meaning element 氵 'water'
远 **yuǎn** 'far'/近 **jìn** 'near'	with the meaning element 辶 'walk'

It is not difficult to see how these meaning unifiers are able to hold antonymous notions together. For example, in

祸 **huò** 'misfortune'	福 **fú** 'good fortune'
嫁 **jià** (of a woman) 'marry'	娶 **qǔ** (of a man) 'marry'
醉 **zuì** 'drunk'	醒 **xǐng** 'wake up'; 'sober up'

'misfortune' and 'good fortune' both come under the meaning element of 'god or altar', which possibly means that in the old times people prayed and made sacrifices before the god or altar not only to avoid 'misfortune' but also to ask for 'good fortune'; despite the fact that in Chinese 'a woman marries a man' is a different word from 'a man marries a woman' but with the 'bride' playing a central role, both are unified under the same meaning element 女 **nǚ** 'female'; as 'get drunk' is associated with the meaning element 酉 **yǒu** 'wine jug', so its antonym becomes 'sober up'; 'wake up'.

We can perhaps quote a few more examples to show that no matter what original association with the meaning element the monosyms might have, the notion of antonymous correlation must have been there when the words were coined or later developed into their present form:

强 **qiáng** 'strong'	弱 **ruò** 'weak'	both under 弓 **gōng** 'bow'
快 **kuài** 'fast'	慢 **màn** 'slow'	both under 忄 'heart'
轻 **qīng** 'light'	重 **zhòng** 'heavy'	both under 车 **chē** 'cart'
进 **jìn** 'advance'	退 **tuì** 'retreat'	both under 辶 'walk'
忆 **yì** 'recall'	忘 **wàng** 'forget'	both under 忄 or 心 'heart'
燃烧 **ránshāo** 'burn'	熄灭 **xīmiè** (fire) 'go out'	both under 火 'fire'
贵 **guì** 'expensive'	贱 **jiàn** 'cheap'	both under 贝 'shell = money'
早 **zǎo** 'early'	晚 **wǎn** 'late'	both under 日 'sun'
吞 **tūn** 'swallow'	吐 **tǔ** 'spit'	both under 口 'mouth'
雌 **cí** 'female'	雄 **xióng** 'male'	both under 隹 'short-tailed bird'
左 **zuǒ** 'left'	右 **yòu** 'right'	both under 𠂇 'left'

Not only can antonymous notions be unified under the same 'semantic categoriser', they can also be contained in one and the same lexeme. As we have already seen, 打败 **dǎbài** 'to defeat' and 打胜 **dǎshèng** 'to win' are synonymous, but 打败 **dǎbài** can also mean 'suffer defeat', which is then antonymous with 打胜 **dǎshèng**. Two antonymous senses are thus encapsulated within the same polysemous word. Similar instances may be found in words like 借 **jiè** 'borrow'; 'lend', 租 **zū** 'hire or rent'; 'let or rent out', etc. Only the context or co-text will be able to resolve which of the antonymous meanings in the lexeme is to be invoked.

8 CULTURAL AND SOCIO-POLITICAL FEATURES OF THE CHINESE LEXICON

The lexicon of a language is always the part which is most susceptible to any change in society, whether political, technological, ethical or otherwise. It functions like a linguistic barometer, keeping records of every change in the social or cultural climate, however ephemeral. From these records we can see that 'words may come and words may go, but change goes on forever'. And by looking closely into these records we can also experience in our imagination the epic journey made by the speakers of the language down their road to civilisation: their ethics, their culture, their achievements, their knowledge of the world and their philosophy of life.

Interesting as such an investigation many seem, it poses an almost impossible task within our limited space to review a nation's entire culture or philosophy through its lexicon. Here we have therefore adopted a reasonably comprehensive yet manageable scheme of analysis by concentrating on five major areas: (1) the part of the lexicon that evidences the nation's historical past; (2) the part of the lexicon that indicates the nation's views of the world; (3) the part of the lexicon that embodies the nation's specific way of life; (4) the part of the lexicon that reveals the nation's dominant fields of cultural and scientific interest; and finally, (5) the neologisms in the lexicon that reflect their speakers' changing philosophy and attitudes.

In the following sections we shall deal with each of these in turn.

CHINA'S HISTORICAL PAST

Proliferation or shortage in certain specialised areas of a language's lexicon has often been regarded as a reflection of the cultural foci or emphases of its speakers. Eskimos' multifarious expressions for snow and the Hopi's lack of a precise term to refer to 'aircraft' are classic examples of such a proliferation or shortage. Incidentally, as it does not usually snow in winter in the southern part of China, the southerners in the old days had difficulty in distinguishing between ice and snow and frost. Interestingly therefore, though ice-lolly is called 冰棍儿 **bīnggùnr** 'ice lolly' in Beijing, it is called 雪条 **xuětiáo** 'snow lolly' in Guangzhou and 霜条 **shuāngtiáo** 'frost lolly' in Xiamen.

A close examination of the once prolific areas of the Chinese lexicon will soon convince one of the different stages of Chinese societal development – a transition from a pastoral to an agricultural society, or to be more specific, from fishing and hunting to sericulture, animal husbandry and agriculture. The kind of linguistic distinction made in the vocabulary of those days has been well preserved in older dictionaries and may be studied as linguistic fossils of the nation's cultural past. If the ancient Chinese had not been expert fishermen or hunters, the word 网 **wǎng** 'net' in the present-day lexicon would not have had at one stage so many verbal counterparts referring to nets of different sizes, structures and functions to indicate whether they were used to catch fish, birds, hares or wild boars. For example,

	big	small	with a bag	for fish	for birds	for hares	for boars
net:	罛 **gū**	麗 **lù**	罭 **yù**	罾 **zēng**	罗 **luó**	罘 **fú**	矕 **luán**

all with " ", i.e. 网, category unifier or radical on top.[1]

Actually the first transaction must have been carried out in terms of the exchange between " " (i.e. 网) 'net' (i.e. a tool for earning a livelihood) and 貝 (simplified as 贝) **bèi** 'shell', which was the currency of the time, for the word 買 **mǎi** (simplified as 买) 'to buy' in Chinese is exactly a combination of 'net' and 'shell'. The opposite process 賣 (simplified as 卖) **mài** 'to sell', as we can see, was coined in a similar way: with a 出 **chū** 'to go out' corrupted into the form of 士 above 買 to mean that the transaction was reversed.

The most conclusive proof of this nomadic or pastoral stage, however, may be found in the two words meaning 'to learn' and 'to teach', both of which have incorporated the component 'net' to indicate the tradition of children learning or being taught the skills of weaving a net as part of their education or upbringing:

學 (simplified as 学) **xué** 'to learn' – the top component clearly indicates two hands on the sides with two crosses signifying 'net' in the middle as the skills to be learned; the middle part signifies the roof of the school and the lower part is 子 **zǐ** the 'child (learner)'.

教 **jiāo** 'to teach' – the top left-hand component is actually a stylised form of two crosses signifying 'net' as part of the school syllabus; the lower left-hand part is again 子 **zǐ** the 'child (learner)'; the right-hand component signifies a hand (perhaps that of a teacher) holding a stick to enforce the learning process.

Two important place names in the north and north-west of China may also testify to this:

哈尔滨 **hā'ěrbīn** 'Harbin' – means 'drying ground for nets' in Manchu dialect
乌鲁木齐 **wūlǔmùqí** 'Urumqi' – means 'beautiful pasture' in Mongolian

---

[1] There are other characters (or words) in the language which originally meant 'net' for catching animals or birds, e.g. 畢 **bì** and 率 **shuài**, but whose meanings have changed since.

Hunting like fishing was definitely a specific concern of a pastoral society, hence the general word 打猎 **dǎliè** used today to mean 'hunting' had at one stage four synonymous terms differentiated according to different seasons of the year as if hunting, like agriculture, had something important to do with the weather:

	in spring	in summer	in autumn	in winter
hunting:	蒐 **sōu**	苗 **miáo**	狝 **xiǎn**	狩 **shòu**

As the society progressed and nomads settled down as farmers, animal husbandry and sericulture became people's primary concern. Then dozens and dozens of names were coined to identify domestic animals, particularly horses, cattle and sheep, in accordance with their colour, size, age, function and even their intrinsic qualities;[2] and also many words were similarly invented which not only referred to various kinds of silk but also added to the colour terms of the vocabulary by comparison with the dyeing process of silk. For example,

red	*crimson*	*green*	*purple*	*yellow*	*blue*	*orange*	*pink*
红 **hóng**	绛 **jiàng**	绿 **lǜ**	紫 **zǐ**	緗 **xiāng**	绀 **gàn**	缇 **tí**	纁 **xūn**
white	*black*
素 **sù**	缁 **zī**

which are equivalent to present-day colloquial terms like the following:

红	深红	绿	紫	黄	蓝	橙	粉红	白	黑
hóng	**shēnhóng**	**lǜ**	**zǐ**	**huáng**	**lán**	**chéng**	**fěnhóng**	**bái**	**hēi**

No wonder the English word 'silk' is borrowed from Chinese 丝 **sī** 'silk' and as silk became the main export of the country following the opening up of the 丝绸之路 **sīchóu zhī lù** 'Silk Route', and the Chinese themselves became known as Seres 'the silk people' in ancient Europe.

Animal husbandry and organised farming gradually became part of the settlers' lives. The word 家 **jiā** 'family' clearly indicates a 豕 **shǐ** 'pig' under the 宀 'roof' of the house, where, pigs were commonly kept in those days as part of the family's livestock. The word 牢 **láo** originally meaning 'byre'; 'cowshed', where 牛 **niú** 'oxen' were kept, however, later acquired the meaning of 'prison'.

田 **tián** is a clear pictographic indication of 'cultivated fields' and the character 農 **nóng** 'agriculture' (now simplified as 农 **nóng**) is obviously composed of 曲 **qǔ** at the top and 辰 **chén** at the bottom. In fact, 曲 **qǔ** is a corruption of 田 **tián** and 辰 **chén** indicates the shell of a big clam, which was used as a farming tool in early antiquity. This may be easily proved because 辰 **chén** 'a clam-shell farm tool' is also found in 耨 **nòu** 'to weed', which further

---

[2] As these words are no longer in use today, we will not list them here.

incorporates 耒 **lěi** of 耒耜 **lěisì** 'a plough-like farm implement used in the old days' and 寸 **cùn**, which represents a human hand. A similar character 耕 **gēng** 'to plough or cultivate' is represented by the combination of 耒 **lěi** and 井 **jǐng** 'well', where water might be obtained for irrigation.

As farmwork was laborious and needed 力 **lì** 'strength' (a sinewy representation of a human arm), men became the dominant labourers. That is why 男 **nán** 'male' draws its inspiration from 田 **tián** 'cultivated fields' and 力 **lì** 'strength', and the notion of 好 **hǎo** 'good' is derived from the very assumption that a 女 **nǚ** 'woman' is able to give birth to a 子 **zǐ** 'baby boy' – a male descendant. This psyche has ruled China thenceforth till the present day.

The growth of agriculture made it necessary to register the seasons and their accompanying climatic conditions to facilitate all stages of farmwork. The Chinese have therefore developed a system of 节气 **jiéqi** 'solar terms' with reference to the position of the sun on the ecliptic which falls every month on the sixth and the twenty-first from January to June and then on the eighth and twenty-third from July to December, dividing each month into two equal climatic periods. These solar terms are:

solar calendar month	solar terms	English translations
January	小寒 **xiǎohán**	'Lesser Cold'
	大寒 **dàhán**	'Great Cold'
February	立春 **lìchūn**	'Beginning of Spring'
	雨水 **yǔshuǐ**	'Rain Water'
March	惊蛰 **jīngzhé**	'the Waking of Insects'
	春分 **chūnfēn**	'the Spring Equinox'
April	清明 **qīngmíng**	'Pure Brightness'
	谷雨 **gǔyǔ**	'Grain Rain'
May	立夏 **lìxià**	'the Beginning of Summer'
	小满 **xiǎomǎn**	'Lesser Fullness of Grain'
June	芒种 **mángzhòng**	'Grain in Beard'
	夏至 **xiàzhì**	'the Summer Solstice'
July	小暑 **xiǎoshǔ**	'Lesser Heat'
	大暑 **dàshǔ**	'Great Heat'
August	立秋 **lìqiū**	'the Beginning of Autumn'
	处暑 **chǔshǔ**	'the End of Heat'
September	白露 **báilù**	'White Dew'
	秋分 **qiūfēn**	'the Autumn Equinox'
October	寒露 **hánlù**	'Cold Dew'
	霜降 **shuāngjiàng**	'Frost's Descent'
November	立冬 **lìdōng**	'the Beginning of Winter'
	小雪 **xiǎoxuě**	'Lesser Snow'
December	大雪 **dàxuě**	'Greater Snow'
	冬至 **dōngzhì**	'Winter Solstice'

From the word 年 **nián** 'year', a stylised picto-synthetic character integrating two pictographs 禾 **hé** 'grain' and 人 **rén** 'person' and signifying a person carrying a grain stalk on his back, we may easily see that the time notion of a year in an agricultural society revolves around its yearly harvest.

CHINESE VIEWS OF THE WORLD

The ancient Chinese used to be a most superstitious people. They believed that their destiny was controlled by 'heaven'. When embarking on a course of action, they wanted to make sure beforehand that it was the right course for them to follow. So they took to divination by roasting tortoise shells or ox shoulder blades to foretell their future by examining the patterns of cracks these scorched oracle shells or bones yielded.

The word 卜 **bǔ** 'to divine' in Chinese is a pictographic representation of the shape of such a crack.[3] The word 占 **zhān**, which also means 'to divine', with a 口 **kǒu** 'mouth' beneath 卜 **bǔ** 'the crack', indicates an oral interpretation of the oracular message, which was then inscribed onto the shells or bones used for the purpose and kept as records. Fortunately, thousands of such oracular shells or bones were later discovered and unearthed. They have, since their discovery, provided invaluable evidence and insight into the very formation of the Chinese script.[4]

The nation's past beliefs in 'heaven' may be summed up in a most prevailing popular saying: 天人合一 **tiān rén hé yī** 'the heaven and the humans are one'. The word 'heaven' itself was indicated by a horizontal line 一 above the head of a person standing with outstretched arms 大 **dà**, thus 天 **tiān**. The emperor was regarded as 天子 **tiānzǐ** 'the son of the heaven'. His rule over his subjects was believed to be a mandate from heaven. If he abused his power and ruled badly, people would arise and withdraw the mandate from him on heaven's behalf. As a matter of historical fact, all peasant uprisings and changes of dynasties were staged and carried out in the name of the will of heaven. It therefore transpires that 天命 **tiānmìng** means 'destiny, i.e. orders or instructions from heaven' and 革命 **gémìng** 'revolution' in Chinese means transferring the orders or instructions from heaven, that is, taking the mandate from one ruler to give it to another.

The ancient Chinese believed that intervention from heaven in terms of the heavenly mandate might take various forms. If heaven was angry, there could be floods, droughts and other natural disasters which would immediately affect the livelihood of an agricultural society. A supernatural being was believed to be behind all these doings and undoings. From the

[3] The word 'omen' in the language is written as 兆 **zhào**, which is also a pictographic representation of the cracks that appear on oracular shells in the process of divination.
[4] It is generally said that 4,600 characters have been discovered on these oracle shells and bones and 1,700 of them have been identified.

inspiration of the streaky and snaky forms of lightning and flowing rivers, an imaginary animal giant was born by the name of 龙 **lóng** 'dragon' which combined all the remarkable features of those animals known to the ancients: the body of a snake, the head of a pig, the antlers of a deer, the ears of an ox, the beards of a goat, the claws of an eagle and the scales of fish.[5] Spurting fire or water, it could fly in the air or dive in the sea. Being a totem of almightiness, it also became the symbol of authority and power, the symbol of an emperor. The clothes an emperor wore were therefore called 龙袍 **lóngpáo**, the bed he slept on was called 龙床 **lóngchuáng**, etc. And the Chinese called themselves 龙的传人 **lóng de chuánrén** 'the descendants of the dragon'. 舞龙灯 **wǔ lóngdēng** 'dragon lantern dance' became an essential part of festivities.

It cannot therefore be coincidental that words like 風 **fēng** 'wind' and 虹 **hóng** 'rainbow', apart from their respective phonetic indicators 凡 **fán** and 工 **gōng** should have shared a meaning indicator 虫 **chóng** 'insect'; 'animal' to imply that the enormous force and arch in heaven must have been caused by a gigantic animal like the dragon.[6]

The ancient Chinese also believed that all the events in the natural world were the result of the conflict between two opposing forces 阴 **yīn** 'female' and 阳 **yáng** 'male', which was pictorially represented by a 太极 **tàijí** 'the Supreme Ultimate' circle:

And 八卦 **bāguà**, i.e. the Eight Trigrams (as specified in 易经 **yìjīng** 'the Book of Changes') present a divinatory picture of the conflict of these two forces, which are represented in writing as 爻 **yáo**. 阳爻 **yáng yáo** is represented by a horizontal unbroken line: — and 阴爻 **yīn yáo**, by a horizontal broken line: --. 爻 **yáo** will then combine in threes to form 卦 **guà** 'divinatory symbols'. A set of three unbroken lines, one above the other, represents 乾 **qián** 'heaven' (☰) and a set of three broken lines one above another represents 坤 **kūn** 'earth' (☷). Arranged from top to bottom, two broken lines with an unbroken line in between represent 坎 **kǎn** 'water' (☵); two unbroken lines with a broken line in between represent 离 **lí** 'fire' (☲); two broken lines above an unbroken one represent 震 **zhèn** 'thunder' (☳); one unbroken line above two broken ones represents 艮 **gèn** 'mountain' (☶); two unbroken lines

---

[5] Cf. Han, Jiantang (韩鉴堂) 1994.

[6] It is inevitable that tracing the origin of the words will have a conjectural element. There are actually different interpretations of these characters.

above a broken one represent 巽 **xùn** 'wind' (☴); and one broken line above two unbroken ones represents 兌 **duì** 'swamp' (☱). The above-mentioned eight trigrams will then combine in twos to form a total of 64 divinatory sets which are set out in the *Book of Changes* with related arguments and notes claiming to explain the diverse potential fortunes and misfortunes of mankind.

The **yīn** and **yáng** dichotomy finds its most eloquent expression in the distinction between life and death. The world inhabited by live human beings is called 阳间 **yángjiān** whereas the nether world, which houses the dead, is supposed to be 阴间 **yīnjiān**. From this distinction naturally stems the notion of ancestor worship. The people in this world will have to seek protection not only from gods in heaven but also from their ancestors down in the earth. The practices of offering sacrifices to gods and ancestors have therefore become an important part of Chinese life since time immemorial. By analysing the words 祭神 **jìshén** 'to offer sacrifices to gods' and 祭祖 **jìzǔ** 'to offer sacrifices to ancestors', we find that the character 祭 **jì** 'to offer sacrifices' comprises three parts: in the top left-hand corner there is 'meat' in the shape of ⺼, and next to it in the right-hand corner is a 'hand' in the form of ⺄, and at the bottom is the 'altar' in the form of 示 **shì**. 神 **shén** 'god' is indicated by integrating 'altar' (a radicalised 礻) with 申 'lightning', which was supposed to represent god; and 祖 **zǔ** 'ancestor' is likewise indicated by inegrating a radicalised altar 礻 with 且 **qiě** 'ancestral tablet'.[7]

The **yīn** and **yáng** dichotomy also finds its way into the explanation of sets of everyday opposites: e.g.

yīn	**yáng**
female	male
inside	outside
abdomen	back
cold	heat
spirit	form

Apart from the belief in the two opposing forces which regulate nature, it was also believed that the whole universe was spiritually as well as materially composed of and governed by five elements known as 五行 **wǔxíng**, namely: 金 **jīn** 'metal', 木 **mù** 'wood', 水 **shuǐ** 'water', 火 **huǒ** 'fire', and 土 **tǔ** 'earth'. The word 行 **xíng** conjures up the notion of 'movement and change'. These five cosmic elements are supposedly in a perpetual cycle of 相生相克 **xiāng shēng xiāng kè** 'mutual promotion and restraint', keeping the world and everything it contains in dynamic equilibrium. A **tàijí** circle may now be filled out in detail as follows:[8]

---

[7] Some scholars argue that 且 represents the male sex organ 'penis' as a sign of the ancients' worship of reproduction.

[8] The diagram is borrowed from Han, Jiantang (韩鉴堂) 1994: 374.

In the diagram, a solid arrow means 'promotion' whilst a hollow one means 'restraint'.

This overriding belief in the constant conflict between **yīn** and **yáng** and the perpetual promotion and restraint between the five elements naturally produced a dialectic perspective of the mechanism of the universe and found expression, for example, in the Taoist philosophy: 道 **dào** 'the way (of the world)', a law supposedly universally applicable to every entity under the sun, known as 器 **qì**.

Despite the inherent dialectic nature of **yīn** and **yáng**, the mathematical notion of a dichotomy and five elements nevertheless led to a metaphysical system explaining natural phenomena in terms of numbers and the number five became its favourite. This idealistic and counter-empirical approach soon turned into a scholarly vogue. The designation of a numbered schema offered as a superficially elegant explanation to any natural or social phenomenon results in many a specification like the following:[9]

colour:	五彩 **wǔcǎi**	'five colours: blue, yellow, red, white, black'
sound:	五音 **wǔyīn**	'pentatonic notes: 1, 2, 3, 5, 6'
taste:	五味 **wǔwèi**	'five flavours: sweet, sour, bitter, peppery, salty'
smell:	五香 **wǔxiāng**	'five spices: prickly ash, star aniseed, cinnamon, clove, fennel'
direction:	五方 **wǔfāng**	'all directions: north, south, east, west, centre'
sense organ:	五官 **wǔguān**	'five sense organs: ears, eyes, lips, nose, tongue'
internal organ:	五脏 **wǔzàng**	'five viscera: heart, liver, spleen, lungs, kidney'

[9] Only natural or social phenomena catalogued by five are partially listed here for illustration. Other examples may include: 三好 **sānhǎo** 'three goods: ethics, academic performance, health'; 四害 **sìhài** 'four pests: rat, bedbug, fly, mosquito'; 六畜 **liùchù** 'the six domestic animals: pig, ox, goat, horse, fowl, dog'; 七情 **qīqíng** 'seven emotions: joy, anger, sorrow, fear, worry, grief, fright'; etc.

cereal:	五谷 **wǔgǔ**	'five cereals: rice, maize, millet, wheat, beans'
metal:	五金 **wǔjīn**	'five metals: gold, silver, copper, iron, tin'
relationship:	五伦 **wǔlún**	'the five cardinal Confucian relationships: emperor–subjects; father–son; brothers; husband–wife; friends'
virtue:	五常 **wǔcháng**	'the five constant Confucian virtues: benevolence, uprightness, propriety, knowledge, good faith'

CHINESE WAYS OF LIFE

Life, for the Chinese, is a journey between birth and death. 生 **shēng** 'to be born'; 'to give birth to' is clearly a pictorial depiction of a plant coming out of the earth signifying the beginning of a life; and 死 **sǐ** 'to die'; 'to be dead' is a curled up man 匕 **bǐ** against his broken bones 歹 **dǎi**. Then comes the burial, which features the dead, once again returning to the earth: 葬 **zàng** 'to bury' – with 死 **sǐ** between grass on top and at the bottom 廾. So, Longfellow's line: 'from dust thou comest and to dust thou returnest' seems to find matching inspiration in the creation of the two Chinese words 生 **shēng** 'to give birth to' and 葬 **zàng** 'to bury'.

The traditional concept of an ideal life for a Chinese person may be summed up in a four-character phrase: 福禄寿喜 **fú lù shòu xǐ** 'happiness, official position, longevity and immense delight'.

福 **fú** 'happiness' undoubtedly means being rich and well-fed. A combination of a radicalised 'altar' 礻, and 畐 the picture of a wine vessel, the word clearly suggests the bestowing of wine by heaven (if wine is in plenty, other foods cannot be lacking). Wine is also unmistakably a symbol of riches, for the word 富 **fù** 'rich', which rhymes with 福 **fú**, also incorporates a wine vessel under a roof 宀, indicating a well-to-do household. 有福气 **yǒu fúqì** (lit.) 'to enjoy good fortune' is always a good thing to say to older people to wish them well when they have nice children and a happy, contented life.

禄 **lù** 'official rank and salary' may again be seen as being bestowed by heaven from its 'altar' radical. The right-hand component indicates the sound but also suggests through folk etymology the idea of being successful in an official examination (录取 **lùqǔ** 'enrolled') and being therefore entitled to promotion to officialdom (录用 **lùyòng** 'employed').

寿 **shòu** 'longevity' has always been the preoccupation of the whole Chinese nation, from emperors to subjects, since time immemorial. The traditional couplet 福如东海, 寿比南山 **fú rú dōnghǎi, shòu bǐ nánshān** 'May your happiness be as vast as the east sea, and may you live as long as the southern mountains' is invariably used as a greeting to old people during their birthday celebrations. 万岁 **wànsuì** (lit.) 'ten thousand years old', on the other hand, used to be a pseudonym of the emperor and was later used in slogans to mean 'Long live . . .'. Its more elaborate equivalent, the phrase 万寿无疆 **wànshòu wú jiāng** (lit.) 'a life without limit' officially became a well-wisher slogan used solely in connection with Mao Zedong during the Cultural Revolution (1966–76). It was written on walls, sung in songs and chanted by everyone in front of Mao's portrait each morning after getting out of bed and before starting a meal.

喜 **xǐ** 'immense delight' usually refers to happy occasions such as weddings or giving birth to a child. The set expressions 办喜事 **bàn xǐshì** 'to organise a wedding' and 有喜 **yǒuxǐ** 'to be pregnant' testify to these associations. However, every piece of good news may be regarded as 喜事 **xǐshì** (lit.) 'a happy event'. Wherever any of these happy celebrations takes place, the word may be seen written on a wall as a big, double 囍 **xǐ**, which was said to be coined by a scholar who later became a high-ranking government official to commemorate his successful passing of his examination and being accepted by a good family to marry their daughter – two happy events in quick succession, hence the 'double happiness'.[10] Congratulations on any happy occasion are always rendered as 恭喜恭喜 **gōngxǐ gōngxǐ**.

This outlook on life has made the Chinese nation an extremely status-conscious nation. The most convincing proof comes from a quadrisyllabic idiom:

门当户对 **méndāng hùduì** 'be well-matched in social and economic status (for marriage)'
> (门 **mén**: door; 当 **dāng**: equal; 户 **hù**: door, household, family; 对 **duì**: right, correct)

That is, in an arranged marriage in the old days, the parents of the families would make sure that their son or daughter was married to the right person. 门 **mén** (a simplified form of 門, signifying a rich family, the big door of whose house opens in the middle) should be matched with 门 **mén**, a family of equal status, and 户 **hù** (signifying a poor family, the small door of whose house opens only to one side) should thus be matched with 户 **hù**.

This status-consciousness is directly related to relationship-consciousness. This may be seen from the elaborate system of kinship terms whether in reference or address forms. They are defined in accordance not only with directness of descent, age (i.e. generation) and sex, but also with patriarchal or matriarchal linearity. For example,

---

[10] The scholar is said to be 王安石 **Wáng Anshí**, the prime minister of the Song dynasty between AD 1070 and 1078.

	direct descent			
	male		female	
	reference form	address form	reference form	address form
generation 3	曾祖父 **zēngzǔfù** 'great-grandfather'	太爷 **tàiyé** 'great-grandfather'	曾祖母 **zēngzǔmǔ** 'great-grandmother'	太婆 **tàipó** 'great-grandmother'
generation 2	祖父 **zǔfù** 'grandfather'	爷爷 **yéye** 'grandfather'	祖母 **zǔmǔ** 'grandmother'	奶奶 **nǎinai** 'grandmother'
generation 1	父亲 **fùqin** 'father'	爸爸 **bàba** 'father'	母亲 **mǔqin** 'mother'	妈妈 **māma** 'mother'
older:	哥哥 **gēge** 'elder brother'	哥哥 **gēge**	姐姐 **jiějie** 'elder sister'	姐姐 **jiějie**
generation 0		ONESELF		
younger:	弟弟 **dìdi** 'younger brother'		妹妹 **mèimei** 'younger sister'	
generation −1	儿子 **érzi** 'son'		女儿 **nǚ'ér** 'daughter'	
	son's	daughter's	son's	daughter's
generation −2	孙子 **sūnzi** 'grandson'	外孙 **wàisūn**	孙女 **sūnnǚ** 'granddaughter'	外孙女 **wàisūnnǚ**
generation −3	曾孙 **zēngsūn** 'great-grandson'	外曾孙 **wàizēngsūn**	曾孙女 **zēngsūnnǚ** 'great-granddaughter'	外曾孙女 **wàizēngsūnnǚ**

Moreover, it is customary in the family to use proper address forms when greeting older generation members. But when dealing with members in the family younger than oneself, first names (particularly pre-school names within the family) are often used instead.

When it comes to relatives, they are differently referred to or addressed depending on whether they are related to father or mother:

	relations			
	patriarchal		matriarchal	
	male	female	male	female
	reference/address	reference/address	reference/address	reference/address
generation 2	伯公 **bógōng** 'paternal great-uncle'	伯婆 **bópó** 'paternal great-aunt'	舅公 **jiùgōng** 'maternal great-uncle'	舅婆 **jiùpó** 'maternal great-aunt'
older than parents:	伯父/伯伯 **bófù/bóbo** 'paternal uncle'	姑妈/姑姑 **gūmā/gūgu** 'paternal aunt'	舅父/舅舅 **jiùfù/jiùjiu** 'maternal uncle'	姨母/姨妈 **yímǔ/yímā** 'maternal aunt'
generation 1 younger than parents:	叔父/叔叔 **shūfù/shūshu** 'paternal uncle'	姑姐/姑姐 **gūjiě/gūjiě** 'paternal aunt'	小舅子/舅舅 **xiǎojiùzi/jiùjiu** 'maternal uncle'	小姨子/阿姨 **xiǎoyízi/āyí** 'maternal aunt'

	relations			
	patriarchal		*matriarchal*	
	male	*female*	*male*	*female*
	reference/address	*reference/address*	*reference/address*	*reference/address*
older: generation 0 younger:	堂兄 **tángxiōng** 'cousin' 堂弟 **tángdì** 'cousin'	堂姐 **tángjiě** 'cousin' ONESELF 堂妹 **tángmèi** 'cousin'	表兄 **biǎoxiōng** 'cousin' 表弟 **biǎodì** 'cousin'	表姐 **biǎojiě** 'cousin' 表妹 **biǎomèi** 'cousin'
generation –1	侄儿 **zhí'ér** 'nephew'	侄女儿 **zhínǚ'ér** 'niece'	外甥 **wàisheng** 'nephew'	外甥女 **wàishēngnǚ** 'niece'
generation –2	侄孙 **zhísūn** 'grand-nephew'	侄孙女 **zhísūnnǚ** 'grand-niece'		

If we go into spouse relationships, we find an even more intricate picture of reference forms, e.g.

father-in-law:	岳父 **yuèfù** or 岳丈 **yuèzhàng**	'wife's father'
	公公 **gōnggong**	'husband's father'
mother-in-law:	岳母 **yuèmǔ**	'wife's mother'
	婆婆 **pópo**	'husband's mother'
uncle (-in-law):	姑丈 **gūzhàng**	'husband of father's sister'
	姨丈 **yízhàng**	'husband of mother's sister'
aunt (-in-law):	大妈 **dàmā**	'wife of father's elder brother'
	婶母 **shěnmǔ**	'wife of father's younger brother'
	舅母 **jiùmǔ**	'wife of mother's brother'
brother-in-law:	姐夫 **jiěfu**	'elder sister's husband'
	妹夫 **mèifu**	'younger sister's husband'
	内兄 **nèixiōng**	'wife's elder brother'
	内弟 **nèidì**	'wife's younger brother'
	大伯子 **dàbǎizi**	'husband's elder brother'
	小叔子 **xiǎoshūzi**	'husband's younger brother'
sister-in-law:	大姑子 **dàgūzi**	'husband's elder sister'
	小姑子 **xiǎogūzi**	'husband's younger sister'
	嫂子 **sǎozi**	'elder brother's wife'
	弟妇 **dìfù**	'younger brother's wife'
	姨姐 **yíjiě**	'wife's elder sister'
	姨妹 **yímèi**	'wife's younger sister'
	舅嫂 **jiùsǎo**	'wife of wife's brother'
	小婶子 **xiǎoshěnzi**	'wife of husband's younger brother'
son-in-law:	女婿 **nǚxu**	'daughter's husband'
daughter-in-law:	媳妇 **xífù**	'son's wife'

Chinese consciousness of status is also reflected in the address form one adopts when encountering one's superiors or friends. As far as one's superior is concerned, address is never made in terms of first names. If one is to be polite, the address should always be couched in the formula of 'the addressee's surname + his/her professional title'. For example,

addressee's surname		title		address form
张 zhāng	+	minister	=	张部长 zhāng bùzhǎng
李 lǐ	+	headmaster	=	李校长 lǐ xiàozhǎng
姚 yáo	+	director	=	姚主任 yáo zhǔrèn
陈 chén	+	professor	=	陈教授 chén jiàoshòu

Among circles of intimate friends or colleagues, the general rule is to prefix either 老 lǎo 'old' or 小 xiǎo 'young' to the addressee's surname:

if the addressee is older than oneself	if the addressee is younger than oneself
老张 lǎo zhāng, etc.	小张 xiǎo zhāng, etc.

First-name addresses are usually confined to couples or young fellow students and if the addressee's first name consists of only one syllable it should always be used in conjunction with his/her surname.

Degree of politeness is always proportionate to the degree of intimacy between the addresser and the addressee or more often the degree of superiority of the addressee to the addresser. The greater the distance or the greater the superiority in status on the part of the addressee, the politer the term should be. Politeness is not only reflected in raising the status of one's addressee but also in humbling oneself. This is particularly so in formal communication or correspondence. This practice has over time produced an abundance of established polite dichotomies.

(a) raising the status of the addressee:

贵姓 guìxìng	'May I ask your name?'	(贵 guì: honourable; 姓 xìng: surname)
府上 fǔshang	'your family'	(府 fǔ: residence; 上 shang: above)
高见 gāojiàn	'your opinion'	(高 gāo: high; 见 jiàn: idea)
尊命 zūnmìng	'your instructions'	(尊 zūn: respectful; 命 mìng: instructions)
雅意 yǎyì	'your kind offer'	(雅 yǎ: elegant, kindly; 意 yì: thoughts)
玉体 yùtǐ	'your health'	(玉 yù: jade, fair; 体 tǐ: body)
宝眷 bǎojuàn	'your family'	(宝 bǎo: treasured; 眷 juàn: wife and children)
华翰 huáhàn	'your esteemed letter'	(华 huá: splendid; 翰 hàn: letter)

大作 **dàzuò**	'your writing'	(大 **dà**: big; 作 **zuò**: composition)
劳驾 **láojià**	'sorry for troubling you'	(劳 **láo**: work; 驾 **jià**: your good self)
光临 **guānglín**	'your presence'	(光 **guāng**: light; 临 **lín**: arrive)
惠存 **huìcún**	'please keep this as a souvenir'	(惠 **huì**: kindly; 存 **cún**: keep)
台鉴 **táijiàn**	(of letters) 'for your inspection'	(台 **tái**: (honor.) you; 鉴 **jiàn**: inspect)
钧启 **jūnqǐ**	(of letters) 'for you to open'	(钧 **jūn**: (honor.) you; 启 **qǐ**: open)
俯允 **fǔyǔn**	'condescend to give permission'	(俯 **fǔ**: stoop; 允 **yǔn**: permit)
垂念 **chuíniàn**	'show kind concern for (me)'	(垂 **chuí**: condescend; 念 **niàn**: think of)
久仰 **jiǔyǎng**	'I've long heard about you'	(久 **jiǔ**: for a long time; 仰 **yǎng**: admire)
赐教 **cìjiào**	'grant instruction'	(赐 **cì**: bestow; 教 **jiào**: teach, instruct)
赏脸 **shǎngliǎn**	'honour me with your presence'	(赏 **shǎng**: grant, award; 脸 **liǎn**: face)
托福 **tuōfú**	'thanks to you'	(托 **tuō**: owe to; 福 **fú**: good fortune)
借光 **jièguāng**	'excuse me'	(借 **jiè**: borrow; 光 **guāng**: honour, glory)
屈就 **qūjiù**	'condescend to take a post'	(屈 **qū**: to bend; 就 **jiù**: accommodate oneself to)

(b) humbling oneself:

鄙人 **bǐrén**	'your humble servant'; 'me'	(鄙 **bǐ**: lowly; 人 **rén**: person)
舍下 **shèxià**	'my humble abode'	(舍 **shè**: house; 下 **xià**: below)
敝处 **bìchù**	'my humble place'	(敝 **bì**: shabby; 处 **chù**: place)
拙见 **zhuójiàn**	'my humble opinion'	(拙 **zhuó**: clumsy; 见 **jiàn**: opinion)
愚意 **yúyì**	'my humble opinion'	(愚 **yú**: foolish; 意 **yì**: idea)
贱躯 **jiànqū**	'my health'	(贱 **jiàn**: cheap; 躯 **qū**: body)
过奖 **guò jiǎng**	'you flatter me'	(过 **guò**: exceed; 奖 **jiǎng**: praise)

岂敢 **qǐgǎn**	'you flatter me'	(岂 **qǐ**: how can (I);
		敢 **gǎn**: dare)
失陪 **shīpéi**	'excuse me, but	(失 **shī**: neglect;
	I must leave now'	陪 **péi**: keep sb company)
少礼 **shǎolǐ**	'excuse me for my	(少 **shǎo**: lack;
	lack of manners'	礼 **lǐ**: courtesy, etiquette)
捧读 **pěngdú**	'have the pleasure	(捧 **pěng**: hold in both
	of reading . . .'	hands; 读 **dú**: read)
恭请 **gōngqǐng**	'invite respectfully'	(恭 **gōng**: respectfully;
		请 **qǐng**: request, ask)
敬祝 **jìngzhù**	(used at the end of a	(敬 **jìng**: respectfully;
	letter) 'I wish you'	祝 **zhù**: wish)

Such status-consciousness also finds expression in male dominance. Quite a large number of words in the lexicon indicating low status or base human instincts are associated with 女 **nǚ** 'femininity' as a meaning category:

女 **nǚ** 'female' is itself a pictograph derived from the prostrate figure of a woman.

Discrimination against the feminine can be clearly seen in expressions concerned with the birth of a son or a daughter into a family. As we know, 玉 **yù** 'jade' was by far the most common precious stone for jewellery or art objects in ancient China. It was also a symbol of status or preference. The word 弄 **nòng** 'to play with' in the language is signified in writing by two hands (廾) holding up a piece of jade (玉). When a son was born to a family, he was called 弄璋 **nòngzhāng** 'the one who is given a kind of jadeware to play with'; but when a baby daughter was born, she was only called 弄瓦 **nòngwǎ** 'the one who is allowed to play with a spindle (rather than a piece of jade)'. This shows that Chinese families have always preferred male descendants.

Sex discrimination is unmistakably evident in the formation of many words in the language. Human failings or weaknesses, for example, are ascribed to women, as can be seen from the radical used:

奴婢 **núbì**	'slaves and maids'
奸佞 **jiānnìng**	'crafty and fawning'
贪婪 **tānlán**	'avaricious'
狂妄 **kuángwàng**	'arrogant'
妖妄 **yāowàng**	'absurd'
嫉妒 **jídù**	'be jealous'

Even when a man swears, he invariably utters the three-character set expression: 他妈的 **tā māde** 'his mother's', which, being an abbreviation, may sometimes be rendered in full: 他妈的屄 **tā māde bī**, where 屄 **bī** means 'cunt'. In a swear word, it is the female again that falls victim to the male-dominated conventions in the language.

Apart from male dominance, there is also a Han dominance attitude which is reflected in the derogatory names given to non-Han nationals in the old days. In the eye of the Hans, these non-Han people were contemptible savages and barbarians.

The Huns:	匈奴 **xiōngnú**	(匈 **xiōng**: transliteration, connoting 'fierce'; 奴 **nú**: slave)
Japanese pirates:	倭寇 **wōkòu**	(倭 **wō**: connoting 'short'; 寇 **kòu**: enemy)
All foreigners:	洋鬼子 **yángguǐzi**	(洋 **yáng**: across the ocean; 鬼子 **guǐzi**: ghost)

Some of the names given to non-Han peoples even had an animal or insect radical 犭 (i.e. originally derived from 犬 **quǎn** 'dog') or 虫 **chóng** to indicate the Hans' contempt for them: e.g.

猃狁 **xiǎnyǔn** 'a tribe in the north in ancient China'
北狄 **běidí** 'an ancient name for the tribes in the north'
南蛮 **nánmán** 'an ancient name for the tribes in the south'

From popular allegorical sayings, we may also find many an expression putting up physically or mentally handicapped people to ridicule simply to drive home a point in an argument. This practice of belittling those who are less fortunate than or inferior to oneself poses a stark contrast to the flattering of those who are one's superiors, demonstrating the status-conscious attitude of the whole society. For example,

长子看戏, 矮子吃屁 **zhǎngzi kàn xì | ǎizi chī pì**
'tall people watch the opera while short people catch wind from their behind'
瘸子打围 – 坐着喊 **quézi dǎwéi | zuòzhe hǎn**
'a cripple goes a-hunting, sitting there shouting'
(implying 'plenty of words but no actions')
瞎子上轿 – 摸不着门儿 **xiāzi shàng jiào | mō bù zháo ménr**
'a blind person trying to get into a sedan chair, not knowing where the door is'
(**ménr** is polysemous: it means 'knack'; 'the way' as well as 'door')
哑巴见面 – 没说的 **yǎba jiànmiàn | méi shuōde**
'when two dumb people meet, they have nothing to say to each other'
(**méi shuōde** is polysemous: it implies 'nothing to say against sth' as well as 'nothing to say')
聋子的耳朵 – 摆设儿 **lóngzi de ěrduo | bǎisher**
'the ears of the deaf – decorations (which are not for actual use)'
秃子头上的虱子 – 明摆着 **tūzi tóushang de shīzi | míng bǎizhe**
'a flea on a bald man's head – clear for everybody to see'

傻子洗泥巴 – 闲着没事干 **shǎzi xǐ níbā | xiánzhe méi shì gàn**
'a fool washing mud, having too much leisure to do anything useful'
(implying that it is only fool who would think that mud itself can ever
be washed clean)

The society is also extremely taboo-conscious. As the language is loaded with
homophones, on particular occasions, such as festivals or New Year, birth-
days or celebrations, homophones of words that have derogatory meanings
are invariably avoided. 'Pair or couple' is the best notion: hence the idiom
好事成双 **hǎo shì chéng shuāng** 'every good thing comes in pairs'. 八 **bā** 'eight'
is much sought after because it rhymes with 发 **fā** 'prosper' and 四 **sì** 'four'
is often evaded because it sounds like 死 **sǐ** 'die'.

Throughout history, people have been extremely colour-conscious, which
is, in fact, a metonymic replica of this status-consciousness. Colour became
the symbol of status. It was only the emperor who could wear 'yellow'; other
officials were allowed to wear only the colour which befitted their positions.
From the Tang dynasty, even the colour of clothing people were supposed to
wear became institutionalised in terms of their official rank. For example,

	emperor	officials above rank 3	ranks 4 and 5	ranks 6 and 7	ranks 8 and 9
colour:	yellow	purple	red	green	blue
	黄 **huáng**	紫 **zǐ**	绯 **fēi**	绿 **lù**	青 **qīng**

When it came to soldiers or men in the street, i.e. ordinary folk, they were
allowed only white or black:

	soldiers	ordinary citizens
colour:	black	white
	皂 **zào**	白 **bái**

Up to this day, there is still a common saying in the language: 不分青红皂白
bù fēn qīng hóng zào bái (lit.) 'not to distinguish between blue, red, black and
white' accusing people of not telling what is right from what is wrong, an
indelible piece of linguistic evidence with reference to the nation's colour-
consciousness. After 1949, red became the symbol of revolution, and white
that of reaction. Black was used to describe what was of counter-revolutionary
origin, and yellow what was pornographic. Red became supreme; only yellow
was downgraded, the status of the other colours remaining virtually the same.

DOMINANT FIELDS OF CULTURAL AND SCIENTIFIC INTEREST

The early birth of the Chinese script prompted the invention of 造纸 **zàozhǐ**
'paper-making' and 活字印刷 **huózì yìnshuā** 'printing techniques'; the pursuit

of longevity prompted the accidental invention of 火药 **huǒyào** 'gunpowder' in the process of alchemy; the necessity of travelling around in a vast land like China prompted the invention of 指南针 **zhǐnánzhēn** 'the compass'; the ingenuity shown in the making of beautiful 瓷器 **cíqì** 'porcelain' earned for itself a universally acclaimed name: 'china'; and the abundant export of 丝绸 **sīchóu** 'silk' and 茶叶 **cháyè** 'tea' owing to the nation's early development of sericulture and agriculture made its imprint in the vocabularies of other languages. If all this has demonstrated the wisdom and creativeness of the nation, then the metaphysical way of thinking advocated by traditional Confucian and other schools of thought must have hindered further progress in the empirical science of an otherwise remarkably ingenious people, whose immense wisdom and energy were now diverted towards and suffocated by symmetry, balance, parallelism, dichotomy and schematisation in all areas: e.g. in architecture, garden construction, martial arts, medicine, painting, literature, drama and cuisine. Wherever one looks, one finds descriptive or prescriptive lists of items categorising, generalising and summing up the rules of any particular field of endeavour by correlating them with a particular number.

We shall now go into some of the major fields by looking at the most commonly used terms and phrases related to those fields.

Architecture

The breath-taking beauty of Chinese architecture may be seen up and down the country from the following types of buildings:

宫殿 **gōngdiàn**	'palaces'
寺庙 **sìmiào**	'temples'
塔 **tǎ**	'pagodas'
民舍 **mínshè**	'residential houses'

The unique features of Chinese architecture find ready expression in the diverse shapes of roofs, in the symmetrical layout of a building, in its internal supporting structure and in the colourful tiling used. The indigenous terms associated with Chinese architecture are:

斗拱 **dǒugǒng** 'wooden brackets used between crossbeams and columns', where dovetailing does the work and no nails are ever needed

琉璃瓦 **liúliwǎ** 'glazed tiles' with their resplendent colours

四合院 **sìhéyuàn** 'quadrangular compound with houses built around a central courtyard (天井 **tiānjǐng**)' found essentially in the north.

The greatest architectural feat of China is 长城 **chángchéng** known as the Great Wall (or 万里长城 **wàn lǐ chángchéng** (lit.) 'a long wall of ten thousand miles'), part of which is to the north of Beijing. Associated with the Great Wall, there is a popular saying in the language which goes like this:

不到长城非好汉 **bù dào chángchéng fēi hǎohàn** (lit.) 'one cannot be counted as a hero if one has never been to the Great Wall' – an expression of one's determination to attain one's goal.

Garden Construction

Chinese classical gardens are an impressive element of Chinese civil engineering. The best examples may be found in the city of Suzhou (苏州 **sūzhōu**). Chinese gardens differ from Western gardens in that nature is not just preserved or controlled but literally remade and redeployed:

山 **shān** 'hills' assume the form of rockeries
水 **shuǐ** 'waters' find their embodiment in artificial lakes or pools
花 **huā** 'flowers' and 木 **mù** 'trees' of diverse shapes, sizes and colours are grown where most appropriate for effect

And, in the midst of all these rockeries, pools, flowers and trees, that is, amidst this re-created natural environment, stand a colourful variety of architectural individuals:

亭 **tíng**	'pavilion'
台 **tái**	'terrace'
楼 **lóu**	'storied building'
阁 **gé**	'bower'
廊 **láng**	'open corridor'
桥 **qiáo**	'bridge'
塔 **tǎ**	'pagoda'

Attached to these varied buildings are:

匾牌 **biǎn pái**	'horizontal and vertical inscribed plaques'
对联 **duìlián**	'antithetical couplets written on scrolls or inscribed on boards'
诗词 **shī cí**	'poems of equal or varied line-lengths'
绘画 **huìhuà**	'paintings'

to add intellectual as well as aesthetic inspiration to architectural beauty, which in turn blends in a most harmonious way with the surrounding beauty of man-made nature. Confucius says:

仁者乐山, 智者乐水 **rénzhě lè shān | zhìzhě lè shuǐ** 'the benevolent appreciate the mountains while the wise appreciate the waters'

This sums up the motif behind all Chinese gardens and, presumably, Chinese landscape paintings as well.

Martial Arts

Chinese martial arts, known as 武术 **wǔshù** or 功夫 **gōngfū**, may be divided into two broad categories: using bare hands or weapons.

With bare-fisted boxing, there is a popular saying amongst the martial arts circle itself:

南拳北腿 **nán quán běi tuǐ** (lit.) 'south-fist, north-leg'

That is to say, the kind of bare-handed boxing developed in the south of the country only uses hands in a fight whereas the kind of boxing developed in the north also uses legs for kicking.

The most popular type of boxing is called the 太极拳 **tàijí quán** 'taichi', because of its circular hand movement in the shape of the *taichi* diagram. A *taichi* boxer believes that his strength originates from and resides in *taichi*, that is, the human abdomen in this case. So when he practises *taichi*, the watchword is 守 **shǒu** 'abide by (the abdomen)'.

In other words, the most important thing for him to remember is to 意守丹田 **yì shǒu dāntián** (lit.) 'concentrate one's mind on and not let it wander from the abdomen'.

It is believed that his movement will then spread from his abdomen to the rest of his body and he will become

静 **jìng**	'totally exempted from worries'
松 **sōng**	'completely relaxed'
灵 **líng**	'extremely sensitive'
活 **huó**	'wonderfully agile'

Talking of the use of weaponry, people referred to a person skilful in martial arts in the old days by saying that he or she possessed:

十八般武艺 **shí bā bān wǔyì** (lit.) 'eighteen kinds of martial skills'.[11]

What this actually means is that the person knew how to use the eighteen different kinds of weapons available in those days, such as

枪 **qiāng**	'spear'
棍 **gùn**	'stick'
大刀 **dàdāo**	'broadsword'
剑 **jiàn**	'sword'
钩 **gōu**	'hook'
九节鞭 **jiǔjiébiān**	'nine-section whip'
三节棍 **sānjiégùn**	'three-section cudgel'
流星锤 **liúxīngchuí**	'two iron balls on a long iron chain'

Chinese Medicine

In Chinese medicine, the doctor generally follows four methods of diagnosis:

---

[11] The saying can now be used metaphorically to refer to a very skilled worker in any field of endeavour.

望 **wàng**	'looking at the patient's complexion'
闻 **wén**	'listening to the patient's voice'
问 **wèn**	'asking the patient about his or her conditions'
切 **qiè**	'feeling the patient's pulse'

Once the illness is known, the doctor may prescribe any of the following methods of cure:

草药 **cǎoyào**	'herbal medicine'
针灸 **zhēnjiǔ**	'acupuncture or moxibustion'
按摩 **ànmó**	'massage'
气功 **qìgōng**	'doing breathing exercises'

with the overall aim of restoring the **yīn** and **yáng** balance within the human body.

A good doctor is often commended as

扁鹊再世 **biǎn què zài shì** 'Bian Que reborn'

or   华佗再现 **huà tuó zài xiàn** 'Hua Tuo re-appears'.

Bian Que is actually a pseudonym given to a very famous physician named Qin Yueren at the time of the Warring States (fifth century BC) by his contemporaries and Hua Tuo is remembered as the most skilful surgeon, who lived sometime during the Eastern Han dynasty and died in the year AD 208.

Beijing Opera

Beijing opera came into vogue during the Qing dynasty about 200 years ago. It is an opera which combines singing, dancing, recitation, music and martial arts. The opera actor or actress are expected to be skilful in the four areas of:

唱 **chàng**	'singing'
念 **niàn**	'reciting'
做 **zuò**	'acting'
打 **dǎ**	'acrobatic fighting'

唱 **chàng** will generally be either in the high, sonorous tune of 西皮 **xīpí** or in the low and unaffected tune of 二黄 **èrhuáng**.

念 **niàn** will require melodious recitation in either 韵白 **yùnbái** 'Hubei accent' or 京白 **jīngbái** 'Beijing accent'.

做 **zuò** will involve facial expression, gesture, posture and steps, where the actor or actress will 虚拟 **xūnǐ**, that is, reproduce fictitious actions as if they were real, e.g. opening a door when there is no door to open, riding a horse when there is no horse to ride, etc.

打 **dǎ**, in fact, means that the actor or actress should be able to integrate martial arts with dancing skills when acrobatic fighting is to be performed on stage.

The roles that appear in a Beijing opera may be divided into four major categories:

生 **shēng**   'male roles'
旦 **dàn**   'female roles'
净 **jìng**   'painted face roles (usually depicting people of bold and
      unconstrained personality)'
丑 **chǒu**   'comedian roles'

Two make-up devices are usually employed:

贴片子 **tiēpiànzi** 'wig slices', which go on the side of the cheeks to produce
  the necessary face contour for the female role
脸谱 **liǎnpǔ** 'painted face variations', which highlight, change or stereotype
  the eyes, eyebrows, nose, mouth and forehead of the aforesaid painted
  face roles.

Singing is usually accompanied by music from 二胡 **èrhú** 'two-stringed fiddles' and movements by such percussion instruments as 鼓 **gǔ** 'drums', 锣 **luó** 'gongs' and 钹 **bó** 'cymbals'.

Chinese Painting

Chinese painting is different from Western painting in that it adopts a kind of dispersed perspective, making the overall effect less three-dimensional. It may usually be divided into three major categories:

工笔 **gōngbǐ**, a method of painting which pays attention to meticulous details
  and executes them with precision
写意 **xiěyì**, a method which intends to highlight only the spirit or contour
  of the thing being painted employing freehand brushwork
半工半写 **bàn gōng bàn xiě**, 'half detailed and half free', i.e. a compromise
  between the two above-mentioned methods

The theme of the paintings is generally:

人物 **rénwù**   'portraits'
山水 **shānshuǐ**   'landscapes'
花鸟 **huāniǎo**   'flowers and birds'

The instruments used nowadays are:

毛笔 **máobǐ**   'writing brush'
墨 **mò**   'inkslab'
宣纸 **xuānzhǐ**   'a kind of paper (thin and slightly rough) produced in
      the city of Xuan'
砚台 **yàntái**   'inkstone'

They are commonly known as 文房四宝 **wénfáng sìbǎo**, (lit.) 'the four treasures in a study'.

A good painter excels in lively brushwork and good use of 墨色 **mòsè** 'the varying degree of blackness of ink'. Different colours may also be introduced.

A painting invariably incorporates:

书法 **shūfǎ** 'calligraphy' in the form of a few lines of poetry
诗文 **shīwén** 'poetry or poetic lines' quoted from well-known poets or made up by the painter himself related to the theme of the painting
印章 **yìnzhāng** 'the red imprint of the painter's seal', following the signature of the artist, usually squarish or elongated, which recapitulates his or her name in a more artistic fashion.

The finished painting has to be 装裱 **zhuāngbiǎo** 'mounted' before it can be hung up for decoration or exhibition.

Chinese Literature

The best part of Chinese literature is Chinese poetry. Over the ages, the country has produced more poets than any other type of scholar. As people vied to excel in 对仗 **duìzhàng** 'antithesis' and 押韵 **yāyùn** 'rhyming' and preoccupied themselves with poetry-writing, they could not possibly have time for scientific research. Countless gems of good poetry were created at the expense of progress in the area of empirical science and the whole nation became ruled by their feelings rather than their brains. The first collection of poems is called:

诗经 **shījīng**   'Book of Songs'

followed by:

楚辞 **chǔcí**   'Songs of Chu by Qu Yuan (屈原)'
乐府 **yuèfǔ**   'Han Dynasty folk ballads and poems'
唐诗 **tángshī**   'Tang poetry with five- or seven-syllable lines'
宋词 **sòngcí**   'Song poetry with lines of varied lengths'
元曲 **yuánqǔ**   'Yuan poetry'

all shining with unfading inspiration, and lines taken from these poems have immensely enriched the language. Apart from poetry, there are books on history, philosophy, etc. written in prose.

At one stage, prose also tried to adopt a suffocated antithetical style known as 骈俪文 **piánlìwén**, which was later abandoned and changed to a much more refreshing and varied style known as 散文 **sǎnwén**.

Other types of literature include:

戏剧 **xìjù**	'drama'
寓言 **yùyán**	'fables and parables'
小说 **xiǎoshuō**	'fiction'[12]
相声 **xiàngshēng**	'comic dialogue'
对联 **duìlián**	'antithetical couplets'
灯谜 **dēngmí**	'riddles on lanterns'

the last two being unique to Chinese.

Chinese Cuisine

A nation with fairly frequent experience of famine will perhaps think more than most in terms of food and cooking. Chinese cuisine has developed to an excellence which has been accepted all over the world. To redeem scarcity in one particular type of food, one has to become more venturesome in one's eating habits and look for all possible sources of food: the Chinese, particularly people in the south of the country, eat 狗 **gǒu** 'dog', 猫 **māo** 'cat', 蛇 **shé** 'snake', etc., and up and down the country people regard the following:

木耳 **mù'ěr**	'lichen'
燕窝 **yànwō**	'bird's nest' (lit. 'swallow's nest')
海参 **hǎishēn**	'sea cucumber'
鱼翅 **yúcì**	'shark's fin'
干贝 **gānbèi**	'dried scallop'

as delicacies and call them 山珍海味 **shānzhēn hǎiwèi** (lit.) 'exotic delicacies from the mountains and the seas'.

To fight unpleasant tastes and enhance good ones, people use profusely varied condiments including:

盐 **yán**	'salt'
糖 **táng**	'sugar'
酱油 **jiàngyóu**	'soy sauce'
醋 **cù**	'vinegar'
味精 **wèijīng**	'gourmet powder'

and such spices as:

辣椒 **làjiāo**	'chili'
葱 **cōng**	'spring onion'
姜 **jiāng**	'ginger'
蒜 **suàn**	'garlic'

---

[12] The most well-known novels are: 水浒传 **shuǐhǔzhuàn** *Water Margin*, 西游记 **xīyóujì** *Journey to the West*, 红楼梦 **hónglóumèng** *The Red Chamber Dream*, 三国演义 **sānguóyǎnyì** *The Story of the Three Kingdoms*, etc.

In a banquet, dishes are presented with the appropriate

色 **sè**	'colour'
香 **xiāng**	'smell'
味 **wèi**	'taste'
形 **xíng**	'shape'

so as to make them appear more appetising.

Food may be cooked in one of the following dozens of ways:

炒 **chǎo**	'stir-fry'
煎 **jiān**	'fry in shallow oil without stirring'
炸 **zhá**	'fry in deep oil'
爆 **bào**	'quick-fry'
烩 **huì**	'braise'
煮 **zhǔ**	'boil'
蒸 **zhēng**	'steam'
烧 **shāo**	'stew after frying or fry after stewing'
烤 **kǎo**	'bake'; 'roast'
熘(溜) **liū**	'sauté (with thick gravy)'
炖 **dùn**	'stew till thoroughly cooked'
焖 **mèn**	'boil in a covered pot over a slow fire'
煨 **wēi**	'simmer'
涮 **shuàn**	'scald thin slices of meat in boiling water'; 'instant-boil'[13]

Besides paying attention to methods of cooking, experienced cooks often want, in very many cases, to adopt very fanciful names for their dishes: e.g. a dish with snake, cat and chicken cooked together may be called 龙虎凤 **lóng hǔ fèng** 'dragon, tiger and phoenix'.

Chinese Festivities

Chinese festivals may be divided into two types: traditional festivals and modern official holidays. Traditional festivals include:

Chinese New Year called 春节 **chūn jié** 'Spring Festival' (which usually falls in February in the Georgian calendar), when members of a family 团圆 **tuányuán** 'reunite' and friends and relatives 拜年 **bàinián** 'pay New Year visits to each other'. People put on their new clothes and the front door is flanked with 春联 **chūnlián** 'New Year couplets'. During the period, one is supposed to make only felicitous remarks. The best foods are cooked for New Year family feasts and ancestors are remembered and ceremoniously worshipped with food. Two particular foods stand out in popularity: one is 饺子 **jiǎozi** 'dumpling', eaten on New Year's Eve, which derives its now well-known name from the fact that the midnight

[13] Cf. Zheng, Yefu (郑也夫) 1993.

hours, traditionally called 子时 **zǐshí**, are now linking the old and the new years together, hence 交子 **jiāo zǐ** 'interconnecting the *zi* hours'.[14] The other is 年糕 **niángāo** 'New Year cake', which is generally made of mixed flour of glutinous and ordinary rice. As the word 糕 **gāo** 'cake' is a homophone of 高 **gāo** 'high', the eating of New Year cake therefore means going higher and higher in the social ladder or getting more and more prosperous.

元宵节 **yuánxiāo jié**, which falls on the fifteen of the first month, is celebrated with lantern parades or by eating roundish glutinous dumplings called 汤圆 **tāngyuán** (also called 元宵 **yuánxiāo**, of course).

清明节 **qīngmíng jié** on the fourth or fifth of the fourth month is the day for later generations to 扫墓 **sǎomù** 'visit their ancestors' graves' whilst taking advantage of the good weather to 野餐 **yěcān** 'have a picnic in the outskirts'.

端午节 **duānwǔ jié** on the fifth of the fifth month was originally marked to remember 屈原 Qū Yuán, an ancient patriotic poet who drowned himself for his country. It later developed into a festival where 龙舟比赛 **lóngzhōu bǐsài** 'dragon boat races' are organised and 粽子 **zòngzi** 'pyramid-shaped dumplings wrapped in reed leaves', which were originally supposed to be thrown into the river to feed Qu Yuan, are eaten.

中秋节 **zhōngqiū jié** is the so-called Mid-Autumn Festival on the fifteenth of the eighth month, when the moon is seen to be at its brightest and roundest. On the night of that day, families gather together to 赏月 **shǎng yuè** 'enjoy the moon' and eat 月饼 **yuèbǐng** 'mooncakes'.

重阳节 **chóngyáng jié** on the ninth of the ninth month is the day when people will climb hills as a token of their aspirations and a wish to avoid any possible misfortunes.

The traditional festivals, apart from the Chinese New Year, are celebrated without public holidays. On the other hand, the government marks:

元旦 **yuándàn** 'New Year's Day', that is, 1 January

劳动节 **láodòng jié** 'May Day', i.e. 1 May, the international Labour Day

国庆节 **guóqìng jié** 'National Day', which is 1 October for the mainland and 10 October Taiwan, which is known as 双十节 **shuāngshí jié** 'festival of the double ten'.

Chinese Artefacts

By Chinese artefacts we mean all specific objects which are Chinese inventions or uniquely Chinese realisations. They may include, for example, objects, articles of clothing, food, etc.[15]

---

[14] Cf. Han, Jiantang (韩鉴堂) 1994.
[15] Cf. Mei, Lichong (梅立崇) 1993.

鼎 **dǐng**	'an ancient cooking vessel with two loop handles and three or four legs'
筝 **zhēng**	'a 21- or 25-stringed plucked instrument in some ways similar to the zither'
算盘 **suànpán**	'abacus'
筷子 **kuàizi**	'chopsticks'
景泰蓝 **jǐngtàilán**	'cloisonné'
旗袍 **qípáo**	'cheongsam'; 'mandarin gown'
中山装 **zhōngshānzhuāng**	'Chinese tunic suit (named after Dr Sun Yatsen)'
馄饨 **húntun**	'won ton'; 'irregularly-shaped dumpling'
油条 **yóutiáo**	'deep-fried twisted dough sticks'
馒头 **mántou**	'steamed bun'
豆腐 **dòufu**	'bean curd'
象棋 **xiàngqí**	'Chinese chess'
麻将 **májiàng**	'mahjong tiles'

NEOLOGISMS

Neologisms of particular periods in history may very well reflect the dominant interest of the time. After 1949, owing to endless political movements and particularly the Cultural Revolution, new words and expressions emerged dramatically and in large numbers. Some appeared only very briefly and soon fell out of use while others were embedded into the nation's vocabulary and are there to stay. For example, as the whole nation changed its political orientation under the rule of the Chinese Communist Party after 1949, its political vocabulary also drastically changed. A great many terms reflecting political movements and ideological values made their appearance:

三反 **Sānfǎn** 'movement to oppose the three evils' (i.e. corruption, waste and bureaucracy within the Party, government, army and mass organizations)

五反 **Wǔfǎn** 'movement to oppose the five evils' (bribery, tax evasion, theft of state property, cheating on government contracts and stealing of economic information, as practised by owners of private industrial and commercial enterprises)

整风 **zhěngfēng**	'rectification of incorrect styles of work or thinking'
反右 **fǎnyòu**	'the Anti-Rightist Campaign' (1957)
大跃进 **Dàyuèjìn**	'the Great Leap Forward' (1958)
人民公社 **rénmín gōngshè**	'the movement to establish the people's communes'
右派分子 **yòupài fènzǐ**	'the right wing'; 'Rightist'
反革命 **fǎngémìng**	'counter-revolutionary'

只专不红 **zhǐ zhuān bù hóng**   'a specialist who is politically unsound'
平反 **píngfǎn**   'redress (a mishandled political case)';
   'rehabilitate'

During the so-called Cultural Revolution (文化大革命 **wénhuà dà gémìng**), there was an officially sanctioned advocacy of hereditary determinism, most eloquently reflected in a popular saying of the time:

龙生龙，凤生凤，老鼠儿子会打洞。
lóng shēng lóng | fèng shēng fèng | lǎoshǔ érzi huì dǎ dòng
'dragons beget dragons, phoenixes beget phoenixes – each after its own kind'
   (龙 **lóng**: dragon; 生 **shēng**: give birth to; 凤 **fèng**: phoenix; 老鼠 **lǎoshǔ**: rat; 儿子 **érzi**: son; 会 **huì**: can; 打 **dǎ**: dig; 洞 **dòng**: hole)

For a time, abusive terms targeted at people with bad family connections appeared one after another in newspapers and big-character posters all over the country:

狗崽子 **gǒuzǎizi** 'son of a bitch' (狗 **gǒu**: dog; 崽子 **zǎizi**: whelp, bastard)
砸烂狗头 **zálàn gǒutóu** (fig.) 'smash sb's head' (砸 **zá**: break, smash; 烂 **làn**: mashed; 狗头 **gǒutóu**: head of a dog)

Following the example of newspapers and broadcasts, people also indulged in absolutes and hyperlatives, e.g.

极端反动 **jíduān fǎndòng**   'reactionary in the extreme'
无限忠诚 **wúxiàn zhōngchéng**   'infinitely loyal'
彻底革命 **chèdǐ gémìng**   'thorough revolution'
最最最 **zuì zuì zuì**   'the most, the most, the most'

and the word 红 **hóng** 'red' became a 'linguistic upstart'.[16] Everything 'revolutionary' was supposed to be 'red': e.g.

红卫兵 **Hóngwèibīng**   'the Red Guards'
红海洋 **hónghǎiyáng**   'a sea of red (flags, posters, etc.)'
红宝书 **hóngbǎoshū**   'the little red book of Mao's quotations'
   (lit. 'red, treasured book')

and overnight 'red' worked its way into millions of young people's fashionable names. Mao himself was lauded as

最红最红的红太阳 **zuì hóng zuì hóng de hóng tàiyáng** 'the reddest, reddest, red sun' in people's hearts.

As 'red' was the sign of revolution, 黑 **hēi** 'black' became its opposite:

黑帮 **hēibāng**   'reactionary gang'
黑手 **hēishǒu**   'a vicious person manipulating sb or sth from behind the scenes'

[16] Borrowed from Zheng, Yefu (郑也夫) 1993.

黑七类 **hēiqīlèi**　'the seven black categories of counter-revolutionaries'
黑秀才 **hēi xiùcái**　'the black, i.e. counter-revolutionary, scholar who wields his pen'

A country-wide madness soon found a temporary unbridled release of its pent-up fury not only in a ransacking rampage but also in verbal extremism. Words became weapons and those who happened to be politically stigmatised as 牛鬼蛇神 **niúguǐ shéshén** 'monsters and demons' had to submit to this merciless linguistic barrage.

Present-day neologisms are the best proof of the nation's changing attitude and philosophy as the country strides forward into an entirely new stage of its development and 一国两制 **yī guó liǎng zhì** 'one state with two systems' has become a 'buzz expression'.

As commercial undertakings are no longer considered a decadent feature of capitalism but a rightful way to rid the country of its enduring poverty, neologisms in this area have soon appeared to reflect this new ideological orientation:[17]

特区 **tèqū**	'special zone – where joint or private enterprises are first allowed to set up and operate'
脱贫 **tuōpín**	'rid one of poverty'
展销 **zhǎnxiāo**	'exhibit in order to sell'
联营 **liányíng**	'joint management (of a business)'
行情 **hángqíng**	'(knowledge) of market prices'
调价 **tiáojià**	'regulate prices'
市场化 **shìchǎnghuà**	'marketise'
合资企业 **hézī qǐyè**	'joint enterprises'
商品经济 **shāngpǐn jīngjì**	'commodity economy'

Words which have disappeared since 1949 because of their so-called capitalistic nuance are also coming back into everyday use:

股票 **gǔpiào**	'share certificate'
债券 **zhàiquàn**	'bond'; 'debenture'
合同 **hétong**	'contract'
股份 **gǔfèn**	'share'; 'stock'
保险 **bǎoxiǎn**	'insurance'
拍卖 **pāimài**	'auction'
专利 **zhuānlì**	'patent'
承包 **chéngbāo**	'contract (to do a job)'
竞争 **jìngzhēng**	'compete'

---

[17] Cf. Xiao, Yan (萧雁) 1991; Yao, Hanming (姚汉铭) 1990.

The state used to be the sole employer in a so-called socialist economy and jobs were therefore assigned to individuals rather than chosen by them. As the country moves away from monolithism, people can now opt out of state assignments and take up their own preferences with private or joint enterprises. As a result, the following terms are enjoying a new lease of life:

聘任 **pìnrèn**	'engage sb as'; 'appoint sb to a position'
辞职 **cízhí**	'resign'; 'hand in one's resignation'
名片 **míngpiàn**	'visiting card'; 'namecard'

Following the opening up of the country and more frequent contacts with the outside world, people are also beginning to acquire a proclivity for neologisms of a foreign flavour, e.g.

hairdresser:	发廊 **fàláng**	vs the original	理发店 **lǐfàdiàn**
dialogue:	对话 **duìhuà**		交谈 **jiāotán**
taxi:	的士 **dīshì**		出租汽车 **chūzū qìchē**
goodbye:	拜拜 **bàibai**		再见 **zàijiàn**
electric rice cooker:	电饭煲 **diànfànbāo**		电饭锅 **diànfànguō**

And there are many more based on loan translations:

窗口 **chuāngkǒu**	'window – through which information can be communicated'
反馈 **fǎnkuì**	'feedback'
反思 **fǎnsī**	'to rethink'; 'introspection'
构想 **gòuxiǎng**	'to conceptualise'; 'proposition'
汉语热 **hànyǔrè**	'the Chinese language craze'
知识爆炸 **zhīshi bàozhà**	'knowledge explosion'
精神污染 **jīngshén wūrǎn**	'spiritual pollution'
绿色革命 **lǜsè gémìng**	'green revolution'
人才开发 **réncái kāifā**	'discovery and cultivation of talented people'

With greater political tolerance and freedom, new social phenomena are emerging which demand new coinages:

倒爷 **dǎoyé** 'profiteer'

公关 **gōngguān** 'public relations' (abbreviation of 公共关系 **gōnggòng guānxì**)

离休 **líxiū** (of veteran cadres) 'retire' (离 **lí**: leave; 休 **xiū**: rest)

回归 **huíguī** 'reversion' (with specific reference to Hong Kong)

菜篮子 **càilánzi** (lit.) 'the food basket – one's daily sustenance'

大呼窿 **dà hūlong** 'involving a lot of people only for show and not for efficiency'

关系户 **guānxihù** 'one who has connections with the authorities'

透明度 **tòumíngdù** (lit.) 'degree of transparency – a demand for governmental policies to become more accessible to the masses and to be couched in more explicit terms'

踢皮球 **tī píqiú** (lit.) 'kick the rubber ball to sb else', i.e. 'pass the buck – to shirk one's responsibility'

单亲家庭 **dānqīn jiātíng** 'single-parent family'

人口老化 **rénkǒu lǎohuà** 'ageing of the population'

表面文章 **biǎomiàn wénzhāng** 'only for show – behaviour not aiming at providing real solutions' (表面 **biǎomiàn**: superficial; 文章 **wénzhāng**: composition, essay)

牛郎织女 **Niúláng Zhīnǚ** 'husband and wife not yet been transferred to work in the same area' (lit. 牛郎 **Niúláng**: cowherd; 织女 **Zhīnǚ**: weaving-girl, a legendary couple in heaven, who were only allowed by the God of Heaven to meet once a year over a magpie bridge)

玻璃小鞋 **bōli xiǎoxié** (lit.) 'small glass shoes – creating difficulties for or taking revenge on people using one's power without being easily noticed' (based on the original idiom 穿小鞋 **chuān xiǎoxié** 'make life hard for someone by abusing one's power')

As we maintained at the beginning of the chapter, social and cultural changes are bound to affect in a most dramatic way the vocabulary of a language. Because of the momentous changes in the political and economic climate of the country in the last fifty years, there has been a correspondingly dramatic change in the lexicon of the language. At the centre of this linguistic drama, a thousand million speakers have unwittingly played the role of creating a host of fleeting neologisms and revamping lost expressions from yesteryear.

9 LOANWORDS IN THE CHINESE LEXICON

Loanwords in Chinese are, strictly speaking, loan translations. Except for a few direct borrowings in the original form of the source language (e.g. BBC, DNA, etc.), the rest are to be regarded as translations. The fact that Chinese, a language so different from European or other phonetically oriented languages, has managed to integrate, over history, a vast number of alien words into its lexicon is chiefly due to the inherent meaningfulness and mouldability of the language's phonetic and graphic elements, which enable translators to adopt diverse strategies in the production of optimally acceptable forms.

Before we go into detailed analyses of different translation strategies of these borrowed forms, we will try to recall here, only very briefly, the various historical events which appear to have prompted the need for borrowing from other languages. It seems more than obvious that all linguistic exchanges stem from and are co-terminous with contacts between peoples for various reasons: economic, political, cultural or even military.

A BRIEF HISTORY OF BORROWING

The first borrowings into the Chinese language are from the so-called Western Regions (西域 **xīyù**), which, according to the Chinese themselves, included present-day Xinjiang (新疆 **xīnjiāng**), west of Yumenguan (玉门关 **yùménguān**) and Central Asia (中亚 **zhōngyà**), following Zhang Qian's (张骞 **zhāng qiān**) diplomatic expedition to the area in 139 BC and the opening up of the Silk Road (丝绸之路 **sīchóu zhī lù**) as China began to trade with the outside world at about the same time. Western Regions is therefore a cover term used to refer to an area encompassing all those ancient nomadic tribes in or to the north(-west) of China and countries reaching as far as the Mediterranean Sea.

Here are some examples of such borrowings. Without accurate references from history, the indication of the country or people from which the said item was supposed to have been borrowed serves only as a very rough and often conjectural guide to its possible source:

borrowed from:	*items borrowed:*	*meaning:*
匈奴 **xiōngnú** the Huns	骆驼 **luòtuo**	'camel'
	琵琶 **pípá**	'lute-like string instrument'
	胭脂 **yānzhi**	'rouge'
	单于 **chányú**	'chief of the Huns'

北狄 **běidí** northern Chinese tribes	猩猩 **xīngxing**	'orang-utan'
大宛 **dàyuān** Fergana Valley	狮子 **shīzi**	'lion'
	苜蓿 **mùxu**	'lucerne'; 'alfalfa'
	葡萄 **pútáo**	'grape'
突厥 **tūjué** Attay Mountains	箜篌 **kōnghóu**	'ancient harp'
	觱篥 **bìlì**	'Tartar pipe'
	琥珀 **hǔpò**	'amber'
女真 **nǔzhēn** Manchu	西瓜 **xīguā**	'water melon'
	哈叭狗 **hǎbagǒu**	'Pekingese dog'
	萨其马 **sàqímǎ**	'a kind of Manchu candied fritter'
蒙古 **ménggǔ** Mongolia	站 **zhàn**	'station'
	胡同 **hútòng**	'lane'; 'alley'
	可汗 **kèhán**	'khan'
	蘑菇 **mógu**	'mushroom'
	歹 **dǎi**	'bad'; 'evil'; 'vicious'
西藏 **xìzàng** Tibet	喇嘛 **lǎma**	'lama'
	哈达 **hǎdá**	'khatagh'
波斯 **bōsī** Persia	石榴 **shíliu**	'pomegranate'
	唢呐 **suǒnà**	'trumpet-like wind instrument'
阿拉伯 **ālābó** Arabia	没药 **mòyào**	'myrrh'
	八哥 **bāge**	'myna bird'
	祖母绿 **zǔmǔlù**	'emerald'
印度 **yìndù** India	玻璃 **bōli**	'glass'
	琉璃 **liúli**	'coloured glaze'
	苹果 **píngguǒ**	'apple'
	菠萝 **bōluó**	'pineapple'
	茉莉 **mòlì**	'jasmine'
	檀香(旃檀) **tánxiāng**	(bot.) 'white sandalwood'
马来亚 **mǎláiyà** Malaya	槟榔 **bīnglang**	'areca'; 'betel palm'
尼伯尔 **níbó'ěr** Nepal	菠菜 **bōcài**	'spinach'
澳亚地区 **àoyà dìqū** Austroasiatic	狗 **gǒu**	'dog'
	虎 **hǔ**	'tiger'
	牙 **yá**	'tooth'; 'tusk'

The above trickle of loanwords over a long period of time are mostly transliterations, as one may find that in most cases the second syllable of the word is not stressed in Chinese and the borrowings, except for a few political, musical and architectural terms, are essentially confined to the flora and fauna of the country where the word was borrowed.

The first upsurge of borrowing in the linguistic history of Chinese, however, started with the translation of Buddhist scriptures from Sanskrit during the Han and Tang dynasties. Amongst the many Buddhist translators, Kumārajīva 鸠摩罗什 **jiūmóluóshí** (AD 344–413), Paramartha 真谛 **zhēndì** (AD 499–569) and Xuanzang 玄奘 **xuánzàng** (AD 602–4) are the most dedicated and resourceful exponents. Their translations have not only enriched the Chinese language but also set examples for later generations of translators to follow. Apart from a few terms purely related to Buddhism, e.g. 佛 **fó** 'Buddha', 禅 **chán** 'Zen (Buddhism)', 瑜珈 **yújiā** 'yoga', 菩提 **pútí** 'bodhi (enlightenment)', 和尚 **héshang** 'Buddhist monk', 涅槃 **nièpán** 'nirvana', etc., few native speakers of the language will know or realise that such native-like words as the following are actually loan translations from Buddhist scriptures: e.g.

塔 **tǎ**	'pagoda'; 'stupa'	世界 **shìjiè**	'world'
真理 **zhēnlǐ**	'truth'	理论 **lǐlùn**	'theory'
唯心 **wéixīn**	'idealistic'	悲观 **bēiguān**	'pessimistic'
智慧 **zhìhuì**	'wisdom'; 'intelligence'	觉悟 **juéwù**	'awareness'
		现在 **xiànzài**	'at present'
过去 **guòqù**	'in the past'	须臾 **xūyú**	'moment'; 'instant'
未来 **wèilái**	'future'		
平等 **píngděng**	'equal'; 'equality'	庄严 **zhuāngyán**	'solemn'; 'dignified'

In addition to words like the above there are also many quadrisyllabic idioms like the following:

空中楼阁 **kōngzhōng lóugé**	'castles in the air'
想入非非 **xiǎngrùfēifēi**	'indulge in fantasy'; 'allow one's fancy to run wild'
现身说法 **xiàn shēn shuō fǎ**	'advise sb or explain sth by citing one's own experience'
邪门歪道 **xiémén wāidào**	'underhand means'; 'dishonest practices or methods'
惟(唯)我独尊 **wéi wǒ dú zūn**	'overweening'; 'extremely conceited'
盲人摸象 **mángrén mō xiàng**	'a group of blind men trying to size up an elephant, each mistaking the part he touches for the whole animal – take a part for the whole'
一尘不染 **yī chén bù rǎn**	'spotless'; 'incorruptible'; 'not soiled by a speck of dust' (lit. 'not contaminated with one speck of dust')

三生有幸 **sānshēng yǒu xìng**	'lucky indeed'; 'consider oneself most fortunate' (to make sb's acquaintance, etc.) (lit. 'have luck even when one has three lives to live')
五体投地 **wǔ tǐ tóu dì**	'deeply admire'; 'prostrate oneself before sb' (lit. 'four limbs and the head touching the ground')
拖泥带水 **tuōní dàishuǐ**	'slovenly'; 'messy'; 'sloppy' (lit. 'drag along with mud and water')
隔靴搔痒 **gé xuē sāoyǎng**	'scratch an itch from outside one's boot – fail to get to the root of the matter'; 'fail to strike home'; 'take totally ineffective measures'; 'attempt an ineffective solution' (lit. 'scratch an itch from outside the boots')

It would not be an overstatement to say that without the massive translation of Buddhist scriptures, the Chinese language would not have been so rich and versatile in its vocabulary as it is today.

Though less dramatic than the Buddhist scriptural undertakings, the influx of borrowings continued with the arrival of Western scholars, merchants and missionaries like Marco Polo (马可波罗 **mǎkěbōluó** 1254–1324), Matteo Ricci (利玛窦 **lìmǎdòu** 1552–1610), and others. They, in conjunction with local scholars like 徐光启 Xu Guangqi (**xú guāngqǐ** 1562–1633), were the first to introduce into the Chinese language an enlightening batch of religious terms connected with Christianity and technical terms from Western empirical science. However, the second upsurge did not come until China was defeated in the Opium Wars (1840–2) and was determined to learn from the West by following Japan's successful example of political and economic reform. Setting his sights on the scientific literature of the West, Yan Fu (严复 **yán fù**) was one of those pioneer translators.

During this period, official translation agencies were set up in large cities like Beijing, Shanghai and Tianjin, for example, 北京同文馆 (**běijīng tóngwénguǎn** 1862–1902), 上海江南制造局附设翻译馆 (**shànghǎi jiāngnán zhìzàojú fùshè fānyìguǎn** 1870–1907), etc. and the Chinese scholars and translators who had been to Japan for further studies also borrowed profusely from the Japanese language in view of the fact that Japanese translations from Western literature using *kanji* (汉字 **hànzì**) and conforming to principles of word-formation in Chinese could be readily transplanted into the Chinese language without any modification at all. They even looked totally indigenous in script, though the Japanese transliterations had to be naturally sinicised in pronunciation: e.g.

瓦斯 **wǎsī**	'gas'	(Jap. g → Chi. w)
文化 **wénhuà**	'culture'	(Jap. b → Chi. w)
混凝土 **hùnníngtǔ**	'concrete'	(Jap. k → Chi. h)
俱乐部 **jùlèbù**	'club'	(Jap. k → Chi. j)
系统 **xìtǒng**	'system'	(Jap. k → Chi. x)

Generally, direct loans from Japanese translations were virtually indistinguishable from native Chinese words. Moreover, the borrowings cover all conceivable areas of human endeavour and the number is so huge that some scholars think that it comprises approximately half of the neologisms used in Modern Standard Chinese and has become an integral part of the language. Few native speakers of present-day Chinese would believe that such extremely commonly used words and expressions as those quoted below (and in fact hundreds more) were actually borrowings from Japanese. It seems immaterial to argue whether they were authentic loanwords or merely home-coming Chinese terms which had been borrowed (and in some cases, reworded) by the Japanese from classical Chinese into their own language at an earlier stage: e.g.

民族 **mínzú**	'nation'; 'ethnic group'
社会 **shèhuì**	'society'
历史 **lìshǐ**	'history'
科学 **kēxué**	'science'
代表 **dàibiǎo**	'delegate'; 'representative'
警察 **jǐngchá**	'police'; 'policeman'
阶级 **jiējí**	'(social) class'
活动 **huódòng**	'activity'; 'manoeuvre'
计划 **jìhuà**	'plan'; 'programme'
报告 **bàogào**	'report'
目的 **mùdì**	'purpose'; 'goal'; 'objective'
抽象 **chōuxiàng**	'abstract'
具体 **jùtǐ**	'concrete'; 'specific'
分析 **fēnxi**	'analyse'
服务 **fúwù**	'give service to'; 'serve'
改善 **gǎishàn**	'improve'; 'ameliorate'
图书馆 **túshūguǎn**	'library'
运动场 **yùndòngchǎng**	'sports (or athletic) ground'; 'stadium'
关节炎 **guānjiéyán**	'arthritis'
生产力 **shēngchǎnlì**	'productive forces'
可能性 **kěnéngxìng**	'possibility'
重工业 **zhònggōngyè**	'heavy industry'
土木工程 **tǔmù gōngchéng**	'civil engineering'
意识形态 **yìshí xíngtài**	'ideology'
资本主义 **zīběnzhǔyì**	'capitalism'

Contemporary history has witnessed the nation's temporary severance from the West under its communist rule for about twenty years between 1949 and early 1970s. Meanwhile, the language turned to borrow from the Russians, e.g.

苏维埃 **sūwéi'āi**	'soviet'
共产主义 **gòngchǎnzhǔyì**	'communism'
集体农庄 **jítǐ nóngzhuāng**	'collective farm'
习明纳尔 **xímíngnà'ěr**	'seminar'
布拉吉 **bùlājí**	another name for 连衣裙 **liányīqún** 'a dress' (a transliteration of Russian *platye*)

We are now in the very midst of the third upsurge, which started in the late 1970s when China, after its traumatic experience of the so-called Cultural Revolution (1966–76), decided to 'open its door' and looked to the West again for inspiration. This recent influx of loanwords reflects not only the country's effort to keep pace with the fast-developing science and ideology of today's world but also the voguish preference among the young generation of Chinese for everything foreign, including language. For example,

'gene'	基因 **jīyīn**
'quark'	夸克 **kuākè**
'generation gap'	代沟 **dàigōu**
'shampoo'	香波 **xiāngbō**
'taxi'	的士 **dīshì**
'bye-bye'	拜拜 **bàibai**
'yuppies'	雅皮士 **yǎpíshì**
'miniskirt'	迷你裙 **mínǐqún**
'stream of consciousness'	意识流 **yìshíliú**
'credit card'	信用卡 **xìnyòngkǎ**
'Disney'	迪斯尼 **dísīní**
'bikini'	比基尼 **bǐjīní**
'hamburger'	汉堡包 **hànbǎobāo**
'buffet'	自助餐 **zìzhùcān**
'euthanasia'	安乐死 **ānlèsǐ**
'karaoke'	卡拉 OK **kālā ōukēi**

In these new translation loans, we find, once again, a greater tendency for sound translations, as if the language has decided to go full circle back to its original strategies when it first started borrowing from other languages. Japanese offers no direct input any more because it, too, has opted for transliteration from other languages using *kana* instead of *kanji*.

This summary account certainly will not do justice to centuries of continual application on the part of the whole nation to absorb whatever other languages can offer and what the Chinese language needs desperately to fill all its linguistic gaps whilst trying to keep abreast with the times and the progressing world. It sounds almost beyond belief that half of the language's lexicon could have been loan translations from other languages in one way or another. Nevertheless even a very brief look at these linguistic upheavals during different periods in history will reveal the true nature of the language's vocabulary and will enable one to work out the diverse strategies the language has employed to achieve its present respectable repository of loanwords.

DIVERSE STRATEGIES OF BORROWING

Pure Phonetic Translation

The reason that a pure phonetic translation may succeed is because the succinctness of the phonetic translation in some cases may compete favourably with an otherwise potentially more clumsy semantic or explanatory rendition, e.g.

'aids' 艾滋病 **àizībìng**   vs   获得性免疫缺损综合症
                                  huódé xìngmiǎnyì quēsǔn zōnghézhèng

'TOEFL' 托福 **tuōfú**   vs   英语作为外国语的考试
                                  yīngyǔ zuòwéi wàiguóyǔ de kǎoshì

Other examples include:

'coffee' 咖啡 **kāfēi**   'pudding' 布丁 **bùdīng**
'cigar' 雪茄 **xuějiā**   'sofa' 沙发 **shāfā**
'disco' 迪斯科 **dísīkē**   'quark' 夸克 **kuākè**
'hertz' 赫兹 **hèzī**   'yo-yo' 游游 **yóuyóu**

A phonetic translation, due to its very nature, may assume various possible forms, and it is usually the simplest rendition that survives its competitors, e.g.

'chocolate' 巧克力 **qiǎokèlì**, survives 朱古律 **zhūgǔlù**, 巧格力 **qiǎogélì**, etc.

Generally speaking, unwieldy phonetic translations are no match for their less cumbersome and more meaningful semantic counterparts:

'democracy' 民主 **mínzhǔ**   supersedes   德谟克拉西 **démòkèlāxī**
'proletariat' 无产阶级   普罗列塔利亚 **pǔluóliètǎliyà**
wúchǎn jiējí
'ultimatum' 最后通牒   哀的美敦书 **āidíměidūnshū**
zuìhòu tōngdié
'stick' 手杖 **shǒuzhàng**   司的克 **sīdíkè**
'telephone' 电话 **diànhuà**   德律风 **délùfēng**
'cement' 水泥 **shuǐní**   水门汀/士敏土
                                               shuǐméntīng/shìmǐntǔ
'violin' 小提琴 **xiǎotíqín**   梵哑铃 **fànyǎlíng**
'piano' 钢琴 **gāngqín**   披阿娜 **pī'āná**

With proper names, however, sound translations seem to be the rule rather than the exception:

'London' 伦敦 **lúndūn**	'Paris' 巴黎 **bālí**
'Luxembourg' 卢森堡 **lúsēnbǎo**	'Mary' 玛丽 **mǎlì**
'rouble' 卢布 **lúbù**	'franc' 法郎 **fǎláng**

Semantic translations in such cases are exceptions arising out of the intrinsic meaningfulness of the original names:

'Oxford'	牛津 **niújīn**
'Mediterranean Sea'	地中海 **dìzhōnghǎi**
'Pearl Harbor'	珍珠港 **zhēnzhūgǎng**
'Cape of Good Hope'	好望角 **hǎowàngjiǎo**

Note that not all proper names are translated from English and therefore different transliterations might mean different source languages or that some kind of differentiation is to be made between alternative versions:

'John/Johann'	约翰 **yuēhàn**
'Jesus'	耶稣 **yēsū**
'German/Deutsche'	日耳曼 **rì'ěrmàn** for the race;
	德意志 **déyìzhì** for the country
'Zeus/Jupiter'	宙斯 **zhòusī** 朱庇特 **zhūpìtè**
'Cambridge'	剑桥 **jiànqiáo** (where Cambridge University is)
	坎布里奇 **kǎnbùlǐqí** (where Harvard University is)

Phonetic Translation plus Semantic Connotation

Phonetic translation with semantic connotation is actually quite a favoured strategy with many translators. This is possible because the Chinese language is replete with homophones which are thus open to choices in terms of whatever meaningful connotations may be established in relation to the term being translated. In this regard an intrinsically negative feature of the language is being put to positive use.

'station' (from	站 **zhàn**	'logic'	逻辑 **luójí**
Mongolian: *jam*)		'shock'	休克 **xiūkè**
'sonar'	声纳 **shēngnà**	'totem'	图腾 **túténg**
'bandage'	绷带 **bēngdài**	'champagne'	香槟 **xiāngbīn**
'opium'	鸦片 **yāpiàn**	'romantic'	浪漫 **làngmàn**
'radar'	雷达 **léidá**	'utopia'	乌托邦 **wūtuōbāng**
'punk'	朋客 **péngkè**	'hysteria'	歇斯底里 **xiēsīdǐlǐ**
'model'	模特儿 **mótèr**		

The acme of such attainment may be found in the loan translation from English coolie 苦力 **kǔlì** with the connotation of 'hard labour'. Without etymological investigation one might suspect that the original word was Chinese and the borrowing was the other way round.

Apart from seeking vague, suggestive connotations for this type of translation, the principle of 'maximal pleasant association' is often seen to be at work, e.g.

'TOEFL' 托福 **tuōfú** 'Coca Cola' 可口可乐 **kěkǒukělè**
'Benz' 奔驰 **bēnchí** 'Sprite' 雪碧 **xuěbì**

The official shift of the translation of Mozambique from 莫三鼻给 **mòsānbígěi** to 莫桑比克 **mòsāngbǐkè** is an eloquent illustration of this underlying principle.

Humorous versions not for serious purposes, which probably had their mnemonic roots in 洋泾浜 **yángjīngbīn** 'pidgin English',[1] are also found in this type of translation, e.g.

'gentlemen' 尖头鳗 **jiāntóumán** (lit. sharp-headed eel)
'ladies' 累得死 **lèidesǐ** (lit. tired to death)
'husband' 黑漆板凳 **hēiqī bǎndèng**
  (lit. wooden stool painted black)
'thank you very much' 生发油抹来抹去 **shēngfāyóu mò lái mò qù**
  (lit. hair oil being applied back and forth)

Phonetic Translation plus Semantic Annotation

Phonetic translation with semantic annotation operates by adding a meaning category to a sound translation to suggest which category of objects the translated term refers to. The indication of the relevant category may come at the end (as in **a**) or at the beginning (as in **b**). In other cases the meaningful annotation may be attached at the end working hand in hand with a meaningful connotation (as in **c**) or a related term may be added to complete the reference (as in **d**).

(a) Phonetic translation with a category annotation at the end

'beer' 啤酒 **píjiǔ** 'shirt' 恤衫 **xùshān**
'Tsar' 沙皇 **shāhuáng** 'card' 卡片 **kǎpiàn**
'pizza' 比萨饼 **bǐsàbǐng** 'sonnet' 商籁体 **shānglàitǐ**
'poker' 扑克牌 **pūkèpái** 'ballet' 芭蕾舞 **bālěiwǔ**
'aids' 艾滋病 **àizībìng** 'lymph' 淋巴腺 **línbāxiàn**
'jeep' 吉普车 **jípǔchē** 'sardine' 沙丁鱼 **shādīngyú**
'sauna' 桑拿浴 **sāngnáyù** 'Koran' 古兰经 **gǔlánjīng**
'golf' 高尔夫球 **gāo'ěrfūqiú** 'dahlia' 大丽花 **dàlìhuā**
'Islam' 伊斯兰教 **yīsīlánjiào** 'Gypsy' 吉卜赛人 **jíbǔsàirén**

---

[1] Cf. Zhang, Dexin (张德鑫) 1996c.

(b) Phonetic translation with a category annotation at the beginning

'bar' 酒吧 **jiǔbā**   'tyre' 车胎 **chētāi**
'index' 索引 **suǒyǐn**   '(egg) custard' 蛋挞 **dàntà**

(c) Phonetic translation with both semantic connotation and category annotation

'bowling'   保龄球 **bǎolíngqiú** (reducing ageing + ball)
'break'   霹雳舞 **pīlìwǔ** (thunderclap + dance)
'toffee'   太妃糖 **tàifēitáng** (princess + sweets)
'jazz'   爵士音乐 **juéshì yīnyuè** (duke + music)

(d) Phonetic translation to be used in conjunction with a related term

'show' 秀 **xiù** e.g.   脱口秀 **tuōkǒuxiù** 'talk show'
'park' 泊 **bó** e.g.   泊车 **bóchē** 'park one's car'

Other examples in history include, for example, 'repent' 忏悔 **chànhuǐ**, where the first syllable is a transliteration from Sanskrit, and the word can only be used with the supplement of the second syllable, which is a Chinese word that annotates the meaning. Again, in 'honey'; 'mead' 蜜 **mì**, the loan translation is more often than not used with a further annotation at the beginning or at the end as: 蜂蜜 **fēngmì** (lit. bee honey) or 蜜糖 **mìtáng** (lit. honey sugar).

Geographical names may also be transliterated and annotated by a topographical feature to indicate whether they are mountains, rivers, deserts, or whatever, e.g.

'the Alps'   阿尔卑斯山 **a'ěrbēisīshān** (山 **shān**: mountain)
'the Nile'   尼罗河 **níluóhé** (河 **hé**: river)
'Sahara'   撒哈拉沙漠 **sāhālāshāmò** (沙漠 **shāmò**: desert)
'Niagara'   尼亚加拉瀑布 **níyàjiālāpùbù** (瀑布 **pùbù**: waterfall)

Semi-Phonetic and Semi-Semantic Translation

Half of the term in question is translated by sound and the other half by meaning. This is a most useful and effective practice. Even proper names may, where possible, be translated thus, e.g.

'New Zealand'   新西兰 **xīnxīlán** (new: 新 **xīn**)
'Cambridge'   剑桥 **jiànqiáo** (bridge: 桥 **qiáo**)

The ordering, i.e. whether sound or meaning related component should come first, may vary depending on the nature of the term being translated.

(a) First element phonetic and second element semantic

'topology'	拓扑学 **tuòpūxué**	'X-ray'	爱克斯光 **àikèsīguāng**
'hula-hoop'	呼拉圈 **hūlāquān**	'motorbike'	摩托车 **mótuōchē**
'dengue fever'	登革热 **dēnggérè**	'Uncle Sam'	山姆大叔 **shānmǔ dàshū**

(b) First element semantic and second element phonetic

'ice-cream'	冰激淋 **bīngjilíng**	'credit card'	信用卡 **xìnyòngkǎ**

(c) First element phonetic with semantic connotation and second element purely semantic

'miniskirt'	迷你裙 **mínǐqún**	'neon lights'	霓虹灯 **níhóngdēng**
'Cinderella'	灰姑娘 **Huīgūniang**	'world wide web'	万维网 **wànwéiwǎng**

Literal Translation

These translations are called 仿词 **fǎngcí** in Chinese, meaning 'the exact copying of the translated word'.

(a) Pure literal translation

'superman'	超人 **chāorén**	'hard disk'	硬盘 **yìngpán**
'football'	足球 **zúqiú**	'honeymoon'	蜜月 **mìyuè**
'horse power'	马力 **mǎlì**	'black market'	黑市 **hēishì**
'blueprint'	蓝图 **lántú**	'hot spot'	热点 **rèdiǎn**
'hot dog'	热狗 **règǒu**	'gold medal'	金牌 **jīnpái**
'show one's cards'	摊牌 **tānpái**	'black box'	黑匣子 **hēixiázi**
'soft landing'	软着陆 **ruǎnzhuólù**	'data bank'	资料库/数据库 **zīliàokù/shùjùkù**
'soft drinks'	软饮料 **ruǎnyǐnliào**	'pulsar'	脉冲(动)星 **màichōng(dòng)xīng**
'break the record'	打破记录 **dǎpò jìlù**	'ivory tower'	象牙之塔 **xiàngyá zhī tǎ**
'test-tube baby'	试管婴儿 **shìguǎn yīng'ér**	'artificial intelligence'	人工智能 **réngōng zhìnéng**

Sometimes a literal translation may be further annotated or modified.

(b) Literal translation with category annotation

'rock and roll'	摇滚乐 (乐 **yuè** = music)
'cocktail'	鸡尾酒 (酒 **jiǔ** = alcoholic drinks)
'questionnaire'	问题单 (单 **dān** = list)

(c) Pseudo-literal translation

'television' 电视 **diànshì** where 'tele-' is not translated as 远 **yuǎn** 'far' but as 电 **diàn** 'electricity'

Semantic Translation

Translation carried out purely by resorting to meaning, e.g.

'inspiration'	灵感 **línggǎn**	'democracy'	民主 **mínzhǔ**
'science'	科学 **kēxué**	'laser'	激光 **jīguāng**
'veto'	否决 **fǒujué**	'penicillin'	青霉素 **qīngméisù**
'bionics'	仿生学 **fǎngshēngxué**	'gay'	同性恋 **tóngxìngliàn**
'memorandum'	备忘录 **bèiwànglù**	'take-away'	外卖店 **wàimàidiàn**
'scapegoat'	替罪羊 **tìzuìyáng**	'life jacket'	救生衣 **jiùshēngyī**

Semantic translation may also be supplemented at the beginning (particularly for the purpose of forming di- or tri-syllabic words) or annotated at the end:

(a) Supplemented at the beginning

'screen'	银幕 **yínmù**	(lit. silver screen)
'star'	明星 **míngxīng**	(lit. bright star)

(b) Annotated at the end

'earth'	地球 **dìqiú**	(lit. earthern globe)
'submarine'	潜(水)艇 **qián(shuǐ)tǐng**	(lit. diving boat)
'lyric'	抒情诗 **shūqíngshī**	(lit. express-feeling poetry)

Quadrisyllabic constructions are borderline cases. They may be words or expressions or even idioms depending on the internal cohesion of the concatenation, e.g.

'intelligentsia'	知识分子 **zhīshifènzǐ**
'multinational'	多国公司 **duōguó gōngsī**
'Murphy's Law'	墨菲定律 **mòfēi dìnglǜ**
'email'	电子邮件 **diànzǐ yóujiàn**

Semantic translation normally follows existing patterns. For example, from

'landscape'	风景 **fēngjǐng**

the language encodes further, e.g.

'streetscape'	街景 **jiējǐng**

When disyllabic words cannot cope with the situation, quadrisyllabic synonymous expressions are sought. For example,

'cityscape'	城市景象	chéngshì jǐngxiàng
'skyscape'	天空景象	tiānkōng jǐngxiàng
'moonscape'	月面景色	yuèmiàn jǐngsè

Explanatory Translation

A Chinese word, as we have seen, tends to confine itself to the usual length of one to three syllables. Constructions longer than three syllables are *ipso facto* suspect. A multisyllabic construction will certainly sound like an explanation, e.g.

'the pill'	口服避孕丸	kǒufú bìyùnwán
'sexism'	性歧视主义	xìngqíshì zhǔyì
'skydive'	缓张伞跳伞	huǎnzhāngsǎn tiàosǎn
'male chauvinist'	大男子主义者	dànánzǐ zhǔyìzhě
'Women's Lib'	妇女解放运动	fùnǚ jiěfàng yùndòng
'scuba'	配套水下呼吸器	pèitào shuǐxià hūxīqì
'time trial'	各别计时赛	gèbié jìshí sài

These explanatory expressions, however, may still be regarded as stylised constructions and used as self-contained lexical idioms. They are different from dictionary definitions, which are only *ad hoc* syntactic constructions for the purpose of explaining the meaning. They cannot therefore be used as lexical units, e.g.

'skydive' (a) 缓张伞跳伞 huǎnzhāngsǎn tiàosǎn   vs

    (b) (跳伞运动员在降落伞张开前)做空中造型动作
    (tiàosǎn yùndòngyuán zài jiàngluòsǎn zhāngkāi qián) zuò kōngzhōng
    zàoxíng dòngzuò 'parachutists, before opening their parachutes, display a particular shape or formation in mid-air'

'lollipop' (a) 棒糖 bàngtáng   vs

    (b) (上学和放学时帮助孩子穿越马路的纠察手中所持的)车辆暂停示意牌
    (shàngxué hé fàngxué shí bāngzhù háizi chuānyuè mǎlù de jiūchá
    shǒu zhōng suǒ chí de) chēliàng zàntíng shìyì pái 'a placard signalling
    vehicles to stop (held up by a picket who helps children to cross the road before or after school)

Here are some more examples:

'flotsam'	(遇难船只的)飘浮的残骸(或其他货物)
	(yùnàn chuánzhī de) piāofú de cánhái (huò qítā huòwù)
'circumstantial'	有关而非主要的 yǒuguān ér fēi zhǔyào de
'locate'	确定...的地点(范围) quèdìng ... de dìdiǎn (fànwéi)
'pro-am'	职业和业余运动员一起参加的比赛
	zhíyè hé yèyú yùndòngyuán yīqǐ cānjiā de bǐsài

Figurative Translation

Figurative translation has the versatility of rendering an alien term on a metaphorical plane when either semantic or explanatory translation fail to do the trick. For example,

'kaleidoscope'	万花筒 **wànhuātǒng** (lit. ten thousand flower tube)
'vampire'	吸血鬼 **xīxuèguǐ** (lit. bloodsucking ghost)
'distorting mirror'	哈哈镜 **hāhājìng** (lit. 'onomatopoeic: sound-of-laughter' mirror)
'hula-hula'	草裙舞 **cǎoqúnwǔ** (lit. metonymy: grass-skirt dance)
'pistachio'	开心果 **kāixīnguǒ** (lit. pun: burst-open-from-the-middle nuts/make-one-happy nuts)

Figurative translation, in fact, is more often used for translating source language idioms than words. Good figurative translations nourish and enrich the target language in a most amazing way. In some cases, native speakers of the target language accept these translations as if they were part of their own language and never suspect that they could be translations, e.g.

'lead by the nose'	牵着鼻子走 **qiān zhe bízi zǒu**
'cannot see the wood for the trees'	见树不见林 **jiàn shù bù jiàn lín**

Graphetic Translation

The shape of the Chinese script is in this case exploited for its resemblance to the referent of the term being translated. The second syllable is always the word 字 **zì** 'written character', e.g.

'pyramid'	金字塔 **jīnzìtǎ**	'cross'	十字架 **shízìjià**
'square'	丁字尺 **dīngzìchǐ**	'zigzag'	之字形 **zhīzìxíng**
'herringbone'	人字呢(衣服) **rénzìní (yīfu)**		

Here we should mention a similar type of what we might call 'referential translation', which does not translate the meaning or form of the linguistic term, but that of the physical characteristics of the referent itself: e.g.

'bikini'	三点式 **sāndiǎnshì** (lit. three-point style)
'macaroni'	通心粉 **tōngxīnfěn** (lit. hollow rice-noodle)
'roundabout'	环形路口 **huánxíng lùkǒu** (lit. ring-shaped road junction)
'potato'	马铃薯 **mǎlíngshǔ** (lit. bells-on-horses yam)

Innovative Graphetic Translation

While graphetic translation makes use of existing script, innovative graphetic translation sets out to coin a new script for the purpose in hand. The majority of these script innovations follow the principle of a phonetic element indicating the pronunciation coupled with a semantic annotation to indicate the meaning. This may occur over two syllables or characters. It may also be condensed into a monosyllabic character with a meaning element and sound element as in 形声 **xíngshēng** 'shape + sound' characters in the lexicon, e.g.

| 'uranium' | 铀 **yóu** |
| 'shark' | 鲨鱼 **shāyú** |

Almost all the chemical elements in the language are translated by such monographetic coinages, with a semantic categoriser and a phonetic indicator, e.g.

'tritium'	氚 **dāo**
'helium'	氦 **hài**
'argon'	氩 **yǎ**
'iodine'	碘 **diǎn**
'arsenic'	砷 **shēn**
'calcium'	钙 **gài**
'radium'	镭 **léi**
'magnesium'	镁 **měi**

(a) Identical meaning element in both forms

In a disyllabic word, the assignation of an identical meaningful element to both syllables (or characters) indicates the category being referred to:

'kasaya'	袈裟 **jiāshā** (衣: clothes)
(palaeontol.) 'mammoth'	猛犸 **měngmǎ** (犭: animals)
'agate'	玛瑙 **mǎnǎo** (王: jade, a precious stone)
'jasmine'	茉莉 **mòli** (艹: grass)
'lemon'	柠檬 **níngméng** (木: wood)
'curry'	咖哩 **gālí** (口: mouth and sound translation)
woollen fabric produced in Tibet	氆氇 **pǔlu** (毛: wool)

(b) Differentiating meaning element in a set

Phonetically, Chinese third-person pronouns are all pronounced alike as **tā**. However, the written form may be differentiated by their genders through radicals. This was first invented by a Chinese writer called Liu Bannong (刘半农 **liúbànnóng**) in the 1930s:

'he'	他 **tā**
'she'	她 **tā**
'it'	它 **tā**

Similarly, the two different components 石 **shí** 'stone' and 金 **jīn** 'gold' were brought into service to differentiate pound 磅 **bàng** (in weight) from pound 镑 **bàng** (in monetary terms). And the 'gathering of eminent people' in 'salon' 沙龙 **shālóng** may be distinguished from the 'Malay or Javanese garment' sarong 莎笼 **shālóng** with the addition of meaning elements on the top of the characters.

Again, for example, *mara* from Sanskrit was originally transliterated as 磨 **mó** 'grind' using an existing character in the lexicon. Later, in order to signify the underlying meaning more explicitly, the 石 **shí** 'stone' component in the character was replaced by the 鬼 **guǐ** 'ghost' component, thus a new character was invented:

魔 **mó**   'evil spirit'; 'demon'

(c) Sound element with meaning connotation

Sometimes both of the composing elements may be meaningful with one of them concurrently indicating the pronunciation: e.g. in the case of oxygen 氧 **yǎng** and hydrogen 氢 **qīng**, the component on top indicates that these elements are gases, whereas the lower components 羊 **yáng** (meant to be a curtailed form of 养 **yǎng** 'sustain'; 'raise') and 圣 (meant to be a curtailed form of 轻 **qīng** 'not heavy'; 'light') not only indicate the relevant pronunciations but also annotate their meanings: one to sustain life and the other very light.

To translate 'entropy' a new character 熵 **shāng** was created by a similar principle, where the left component 火 **huǒ** 'fire' indicates that the term has something to do with thermal energy and the right-hand component 商 **shāng** 'quotient' indicates not only how the measurement of entropy is mathematically obtained but also the pronunciation of the resultant character.[2] The translation of 'pump' as 泵 **bèng** is a remarkable illustration of the versatility of Chinese script in signifying sound and meaning. In this case, the pronunciation of the word is realised by the onomatopoeic element implied in the composition of the word as the 石 **shí** 'stone' falls into the 水 **shuǐ** 'water'.

Japanese coinages were also readily borrowed:

'cancer'   癌 **ái**   as in   胃癌 **wèi'ái**
'gland'   腺 **xiàn**   as in   甲状腺 **jiǎzhuàngxiàn**

We have seen from the above that diverse translation strategies are employed to make maximal use of the language's phonetic, semantic and graphetic resources. Apart from what is available as intrinsic properties of Chinese, other linguistic strategies are also fully exploited to facilitate the borrowing process. They are:

---

[2] Cf. Zhang, Dexin (张德鑫) 1996c.

Abbreviation

Disyllabicity is the predominant characteristic of the language's words. All transliterations which introduce more than two syllables tend to be abbreviated to a disyllabic form, e.g.

'Boddhisattva' 菩萨 **púsà**   ← 菩提萨埵 **pútísàduǒ**
'arahat' 罗汉 **luóhàn**   ← 阿罗汉 **āluóhàn**
'geometry' 几何 **jǐhé**   ← 几何米突 **jǐhémǐtū**
'ammonia' 氨 **ān**   ← 阿摩尼亚 **āmóníyà**
'pagoda' 塔 **tǎ**   ← 塔婆 **tǎpó**
'train' 火车 **huǒchē**   ← 火轮车 **huǒlúnchē**
'ship' 轮船 **lúnchuán**   ← 火轮船 **huǒlúnchuán**

Measure words in Chinese tend to become monosyllabic, e.g.

'yard' 码 **mǎ**
'ton' 吨 **dūn**
'gramme' 克 **kè**   ← 克兰姆 **kèlánmǔ**
'metre' 米 **mǐ**   ← 米突 **mǐtū**
'dozen' 打 **dá**   ← 打臣 **dáchén**

Sometimes even phonetically disyllabic words are written in a monographetic form:

'inch' 吋 **cùn**   ← 英寸 **yīngcùn**
'foot' 呎 **chǐ**   ← 英尺 **yīngchǐ**
'mile' 哩 **lǐ**   ← 英里 **yīnglǐ**
'nautical mile' 浬 **lǐ**   ← 海里 **hǎilǐ**
'kilowatt' 瓩 **qiānwǎ**   ← 千瓦 **qiānwǎ**

Back Loan

Back loan is not a common phenomenon in language.

'typhoon' (from English)   台风 **táifēng**   ← original Chinese:
                                           大风 **dàfēng** 'strong wind'
'past master'   把势 **bǎshì**   ← original Chinese:
   (from Mongolian)   博士 **bóshì** 'skilled personnel'
'lady' (from Manchurian)   福晋 **fújìn**   ← original Chinese
   (obsolete)   夫人 **fūrén** 'wife'
'tycoon' (from English)   大款 **dàkuǎn**   ← original Chinese 太公 **tàigōng**
                                           'great-grandfather'

The exceptional case is that quite a number of borrowings into Modern Standard Chinese are ready-made Japanese translations from Western literature in the form of *kanji*. They are actually original classical Chinese terms borrowed by the Japanese language at an earlier stage:

'economy'	经济 **jīngjì**	'way to govern' in classical Chinese
'organisation'	组织 **zǔzhī**	'spinning and weaving'; 'textile' in classical Chinese
'humanitarianism'	人道 **réndào**	'sex life between husband and wife'
'magazine'	杂志 **zázhì**	'reading notes' in classical Chinese
'metaphysics'	形而上学 **xíng'érshàngxué**	from Yi-jing (易经 **yìjīng** *Book of Changes*)

Alienation

Natural produce or artefacts from exotic lands are often referred to with terms prefixed with words indicating this foreignness using 胡 **hú**, 洋 **yáng**, 西 **xī**, 番 **fān**, etc., e.g.

'pepper'	胡椒 **hújiāo**	'onion'	洋葱 **yángcōng**
'sweet potato'	番薯 **fānshǔ**	'suit'	西装 **xīzhuāng**
'peep show'	西洋景 **xīyángjǐng**	'mange tout'	荷兰豆 **hélándòu**

Derivation

Taking as a model a morphological language like English with plenty of derivational suffixes and borrowing similar strategies from Japanese translations, Chinese also adopts a number of mono- and disyllabic forms with very general meaning and grammatical categorial properties as pseudo-suffixes. The following seems to be among the most common ones:[3]

学 **xué**	化学 **huàxué** 'chemistry'
	哲学 **zhéxué** 'philosophy'
	心理学 **xīnlǐxué** 'psychology'
化 **huà**	大众化 **dàzhònghuà** 'popularise'
	现代化 **xiàndàihuà** 'modernise'
	自动化 **zìdònghuà** 'automate'
力 **lì**	生产力 **shēngchǎnlì** 'productive forces'
	记忆力 **jìyìlì** 'the faculty of memory'
	想象力 **xiǎngxiànglì** 'the power of imagination'
性 **xìng**	可能性 **kěnéngxìng** 'possibility'
	必要性 **bìyàoxìng** 'necessity'
	偶然性 **ǒuránxìng** 'contingency'; 'fortuity'
界 **jiè**	文学界 **wénxué jiè** 'literary circles'
	艺术界 **yìshù jiè** 'art circles'
	教育界 **jiàoyù jiè** 'education circles'

[3] Cf. Chapter 3 on pseudo-suffixes.

感 **gǎn**	好感 **hǎogǎn** 'favourable impression'
	美感 **měigǎn** 'aesthetic perception'
	幽默感 **yōumògǎn** 'a sense of humour'
点 **diǎn**	重点 **zhòngdiǎn** 'emphasis'
	焦点 **jiāodiǎn** 'focus'
	出发点 **chūfādiǎn** 'the starting-point'
	(in a discussion, argument, etc.)
观 **guān**	主观 **zhǔguān** 'subjective'
	客观 **kèguān** 'objective'
	世界观 **shìjièguān** 'world outlook'
法 **fǎ**	看法 **kànfǎ** 'view'
	想法 **xiǎngfǎ** 'idea'; 'opinion'
	辩证法 **biànzhèngfǎ** 'dialectics'
主义 **zhǔyì**	浪漫主义 **làngmànzhǔyì** 'romanticism'
	资本主义 **zīběnzhǔyì** 'capitalism'
	个人主义 **gèrénzhǔyì** 'individualism'
问题 **wèntí**	人口问题 **rénkǒu wèntí** 'population problem'
	原则问题 **yuánzé wèntí** 'a matter of principle'
	作风问题 **zuòfeng wèntí** 'style of work'

Compounding

Once a transliteration has been accepted into the language, it begins a life of its own and proliferates in accordance with the same word-formation rules as other elements of the indigenous lexicon, e.g.

打的 **dǎdī** 'go by taxi'; 'take a taxi' (打 **dǎ**: use; 的 **dī**: taxi)
小巴 **xiǎobā** 'minibus' (小 **xiǎo**: small; 巴 **bā**: bus)
名模 **míngmó** 'famous model' (名 **míng**: famous; 模 **mó**: model)
鲜啤 **xiānpí** 'fresh beer' (鲜 **xiān**: fresh; 啤 **pí**: beer)
膜拜 **móbài** 'worship' (膜 **mó**: transliteration abbreviated from 南无 **nāmó**, a transliteration from Sanskrit *namas* which indicates respect for Buddha; 拜 **bài**: do obeisance)

Direct Transplantation

As the Chinese people become more and more receptive to foreign ideas, their language also becomes more and more receptive to foreign, particularly English, script. This has made direct transplantation possible, e.g.

(a) Direct transplantation

BBC	as BBC
DDT	as DDT
DNA	as DNA

(b) Partial transplantation and partial transliteration

'T-shirt' T恤 (恤 **xù**: transliteration) 'karaoke' 卡拉 (卡拉 **kālā**: transliteration) OK

Duplicate Translation

A term may be translated differently for different contexts or connotations.

'modern'	现代 **xiàndài**	摩登 **módēng**
'information'	信息 **xìnxī**	情报 **qíngbào**
'hysteria'	癔病 **yìbìng**	歇斯底里 **xiēsīdǐlǐ**
'dictatorship'	专政 **zhuānzhèng**	独裁 **dúcái**
'Internationale'	国际歌 **guójìgē** (the song itself)	英特那雄耐尔 **yīngtènàxióngnài'ěr** (a line in the song)

CONCLUDING REMARKS

As far as loanwords (or loan translations) are concerned, the Chinese language, with an escalating proclivity for lexis and structures originally alien to it, is in the very paradoxical process of naturalising and metamorphosing into what is foreign at the same time. Time will tell, for example, which of the following competing terms will, through their users' day-to-day linguistic referendum, finally gain the upper hand:

(a) Competition between connotative phonetic and merely semantic translations

	phonetic	*semantic*
'vitamin'	维他命 **wéitāmìng**	维生素 **wéishēngsù**
'UFO'	幽浮 **yōufú**	飞碟 **fēidié**
'miniskirt'	迷你裙 **mínǐqún**	超短裙 **chāoduǎnqún**
'laser'	镭射 **léishè**	激光 **jīguāng**
'waltz'	华尔兹 **huá'ěrzī**	圆舞曲 **yuánwǔqǔ**
'microphone'	麦克风 **màikèfēng**	扩音器 **kuòyīnqì**
'combine harvester'	康拜因 **kāngbàiyīn**	联合收割机 **liánhé shōugējī**
'cartoon'	卡通 **kǎtōng**	动画片 **dònghuàpiàn**
'hormone'	荷尔蒙 **hé'ěrméng**	激素 **jīsù**
'film'	菲林 **fēilín**	胶卷 **jiāojuǎn**
'myth'	迷思 **mísī**	神话 **shénhuà**
'DNA'	DNA	脱氧核糖核酸 **tuōyǎnghétánghésuān**
'Sierra Leone'	塞拉利昂 **sàilālì'áng**	狮子山国 **shīzishānguó**

(b) Competition between different semantic translations, largely due to differences between translations from Chinese-speaking communities in different parts of the world, particularly between mainland China, Taiwan, Hong Kong and Singapore:

'computer'	电子计算机 diànzǐjìsuànjī	电脑 diànnǎo
'software'	软件 ruǎnjiàn	软体 ruǎntǐ
'jet plane'	喷气机 pēnqìjī	喷射机 pēnshèjī
'space shuttle'	航天飞机 hángtiān fēijī	太空梭 tàikōngsuō
'spaceman'	宇航员 yǔhángyuán	太空人 tàikōngrén
'stereo'	立体声 lìtǐshēng	身历声 shēnlìshēng
'newspaper'	报纸 bàozhǐ	新闻纸 xīnwénzhǐ
'kindergarten'	幼儿园 yòu'éryuán	幼稚园 yòuzhìyuán
'epicentre'	震中 zhènzhōng	震央 zhènyāng
'status quo'	现状 xiànzhuàng	现况 xiànkuàng
'colour TV'	彩电 cǎidiàn	彩视 cǎishì
'chewing gum'	口香糖 kǒuxiāngtáng	香口胶 xiāngkǒujiāo
'vector'	向量 xiàngliàng	矢量 shǐliàng
'resonance'	共振 gòngzhèn	谐振 xiézhèn

The revival of a greater tendency for sound translation also brings with it the problem of standardisation in script representation, e.g.

'AIDS'	艾滋病 àizībìng	爱兹病 àizībìng
'sauna'	桑那浴 sāngnàyù	桑拿浴 sāngnáyù
'sandwich'	三明治 sānmíngzhì	三文治 sānwénzhì
'ice cream'	冰激淋 bīngjilín	冰淇淋 bīngqílín
'Mrs Thatcher'	撒切尔夫人 sāqiè'ěr fūren	佘契尔夫人 shéqī'ěr fūren
'Clinton'	克林顿 kèlíndùn	柯林顿 kēlíndùn
'Gabon'	加蓬 jiāpéng	加彭 jiāpéng

Loaded with an ever-increasing repertoire of borrowings, the language will, in time, as it has done before, find ways to absorb these alien newcomers while maintaining its linguistic integrity.

APPENDIX
INTRA- AND INTER-LEXICAL
STRATEGIES OF THE CHINESE
AND ENGLISH LEXICONS

PHONETIC[1]

(1) Homophone

Coincidence of sound with a different meaning, not an intentional design feature of the lexicon of a language, but an inevitable outcome of a limited number of pronounceable syllables coping with innumerable units of meaning:

> threw/through; practice/practise[2]
> 陪 **péi**[3] 'keep sb company'/赔 **péi** 'compensate'
> 发言 **fāyán** 'make a statement'/发炎 **fāyán** 'inflammation'
> 猎狗 **lièɡǒu** 'hound'/鬣狗 **lièɡǒu** 'hyena'
> 引证 **yǐnzhèng** 'cite as evidence'/印证 **yìnzhèng** 'confirm'; 'verify'[4]
> 拙见 **zhuōjiàn** 'my (humble) opinion'/卓见 **zhuójiàn** '(your) brilliant idea'/
>   灼见 **zhuójiàn** 'profound view'
> 单向 **dānxiàng** 'one-way'/单项 **dānxiàng** (sports) 'individual event'/单相
>   **dānxiàng** 'single-phase'
> 真实 **zhēnshí** 'true'; 'authentic'/诊视 **zhěnshì** 'cherish'; 'treasure'/诊室 **zhěnshì**
>   'consulting room'/阵势 **zhènshì** (mil.) 'disposition of troops'

(2) Regular Assimilation

Contextual sound shift:

> convert → conversion; decide → decision
> 似乎 **sìhū** 'as if'/似的 **shìde** 'a compound particle to indicate similarity after
>   nouns, etc.'

---

[1] The purpose of demarcation into broad categories such as these is to highlight the dominant motivation behind the formation of the lexical item in question. In some cases, a word might be dually or perhaps multiply motivated: e.g. for 'smog' or 'brunch' the motivation might be phonetic as well as morphological.
[2] The slash / indicates where comparison is being made.
[3] *Pinyin* is used throughout the book in conjunction with characters to indicate Chinese lexical items. The phonological system of the language is fully discussed in Chapter 1.
[4] In Chinese, homophones may be heterotonic.

(3) Tonal Variation

Regular tone shift for varied purposes:

I ↘ thought it would ↗ rain. (I was right.)/I → thought it would ↘ rain.
(I was wrong.)

辣 **là** 'peppery'; 'spicy' → 热辣辣 **rèlālā** 'scorching'; 'burning hot'

淋 **lín** 'drench' → 汗淋淋 **hànlīnlīn** 'dripping with sweat'

漉 **lù** 'seep through' → 湿漉漉 **shīlūlū** 'moist'; 'damp'

鼓 **gǔ** 'bulge'; 'swell' → 气鼓鼓 **qìgǔgǔ** 'fuming with rage' →
  气鼓鼓儿 **qìgūgūr**

沉 **chén** 'sink' → 闷沉沉 **mènchénchén** → 闷沉沉儿 **mènchēnchēnr**

冠 **guān** 'hat'/冠 **guàn** 'first place'; 'the best'

买 **mǎi** 'buy'/卖 **mài** 'sell'

(4) Syllabic Fusion[5]

A rough-and-ready combination of consonant and vowel from two or more separate syllables or words into one with a view to linguistic economy:

gonna/going to; won't/will not; Howdy?/How do you do?

别 **bié** 'don't' (不 **bù** 'not' + 要 **yào** 'want'; 'should')

甭 **béng** 'don't'; 'needn't' (不 **bù** 'not' + 用 **yòng** 'use'; 'need')

(5) Phonic Variation

Pronunciation difference of the same word owing to different speech habits or contexts:

grant: [grɑnt]/[grænt]; often: [ɔfn]/[ɔftn]

maintain: [men'tein]/[mein'tein]; finance: [fin'æns]/['fainæns]

往南 **wǎngnán/wàngnán** 'heading south'

尽量 **jǐnliàng** 'to the best one's ability'/尽力 **jìnlì** 'try one's best'

牲畜 **shēngchù** 'livestock'/畜牧 **xùmù** 'to raise or rear livestock'

恐吓 **kǒnghè** 'threaten'; 'blackmail'/吓唬 **xiàhu** (inf.) 'frighten'; 'scare'

颈 **jǐng** 'neck'/脖颈儿 **bógěngr** 'back of the neck'; 'nape'

请帖 **qǐngtiě** 'invitation card'/字帖 **zìtiè** 'copybook' (for calligraphy)

(6) Stress Variation

Change of stress pattern owing to different speech habits, for different grammatical categories, or for a different meaning:

---

[5] For 'sound fusion' of the archiphonemic exclamatory particle 啊 **ā**, see the section on *eri*sation and sound assimilation in Chapter 1.

necessarily: [ˈnɛsisərili]/[nɛsiˈsɛrili]
torment [ˈtɔːmənt] n./[tɔːˈmɛnt] v.
妻子 **qīzǐ** 'wife and children'/妻子 **qīzi** 'wife'
地道 **dìdào** 'tunnel'/地道 **dìdao** 'typical'; 'idiomatic'
对头 **duìtóu** 'correct'; 'on the right track'/对头 **duìtou** 'opponent'; 'adversary'
琢磨 **zhuómó** 'polish'; 'refine'/琢磨 **zuómo** 'think over'; 'ponder'

(7) **er**-isation or **zi**-risation[6]

Addition of the suffix *er* or *zi* for different denotations or connotations:

媳妇 **xífù** 'daughter-in-law'/媳妇儿 **xífur** (dial.) 'wife'
老头儿 **lǎotóur** (intimately) 'old chap'/老头子 **lǎotóuzi** (with contempt) 'old fogey'

PHONAESTHETIC

(8) Rhyme

Identity of sound between the endings of words or syllables:

hotshot; mumbo-jumbo; nitty-gritty; cocky-leaky; huff and puff
helter-skelter; hustle/bustle; stalactite/stalagmite
旖旎 **yǐnǐ** 'exquisite'
迤逦 **yǐlǐ** 'winding'; 'tortuous'
浩淼 **hàomiǎo** 'vast' (of watery expanse)
蜻蜓 **qīngtíng** 'dragonfly'
谈判 **tánpàn** 'negotiate'; 'negotiations'
怂恿 **sǒngyǒng** 'instigate'
谑而不虐 **xuè ér bù nüè** (formal) 'tease without embarrassing the one being teased'
要言不烦 **yào yán bù fán** 'pithy'; 'succinct'

(9) Alliteration

Identity of sound at the beginning of syllables, words or set expressions:

lilac; funfair; cash and carry; spick and span
咀嚼 **jǔjué** 'chew'; 'ruminate'
隙罅 **xìxià** 'crack'; 'fissure'
闲暇 **xiánxiá** 'leisure'
堆叠 **duīdié** 'pile up'; 'heap up'
明媚 **míngmèi** 'bright and beautiful'

---

[6] The suffixing of an unstressed **r** or **zi** to the lexical item in question.

(10) Alliteration Accompanied by Rhyme or Near Rhyme

On purpose or coincidental:

gobbledegook
嘀哩嘟噜 **dīlidūlū** 'mumbling'; 'muttering'
劈里啪啦 **pīlipālā** 'the successive sounds of cracking' (e.g. firecrackers)
秘密 **mìmì** 'secret'
逝世 **shìshì** 'pass away'
尿尿 **niàoniào** 'piss'; 'pass water'

(11) Consonance

Vowel or tonal variation within identical sound patterns in a word or expression:

flip/flop; drip/drop; tit for tat; tiptop; tick-tock; zig-zag; wishy-washy
叮当 **dīngdāng** 'jingle'; 丁冬 **dīngdōng** 'tinkle'
审慎 **shěnshèn** 'cautious'; 'circumspect'
先贤 **xiānxián** 'ancient sage'

(12) Echo

Sound analogy for related form or meaning:

sing, sang, sung/ring, rang, rung
burst/bust; splash/splotch; wiggle/wriggle
锤 **chuí** 'hammer'/捶 **chuí** 'beat' (with a stick or fist)
踟蹰 **chíchú** 'irresolute'/踯躅 **zhízhú** 'loiter'
一齐 **yīqí** 'in unison'; 'simultaneously'/一起 **yīqǐ** 'together'
叽哩咕噜 **jīligūlū** 'talking indistinctly'/叽哩呱啦 **jīliguālā** 'talking loudly'
明 **míng** 'bright'/暝 **míng** 'dusk'
渊薮 **yuānsǒu** 'den'; 'haunt' (lit. a gathering place of fish or beasts)
    (渊 **yuān** vs 鱼 **yú** 'fish'; 薮 **sǒu** vs 兽 **shòu** 'beast')

(13) Onomatopoeia

Linguistic representation of natural sounds:

mew; bang; cuckoo; sizzle; cock-a-doodle-doo
咪咪 **mīmī** 'mew'
怦怦 **pēngpēng** 'pit-a-pat'
哗啦啦 **huālālā** (of stream) 'gurgling'; (of rain) 'pouring'; (of leaves)
    'rustling'; (of flags) 'fluttering'; etc.
嘻嘻哈哈 **xīxīhāhā** 'laughing merrily'
蛐蛐儿 **qūqur** 'cricket' (an insect)

(14) Interjection

Linguistic outbursts of inner feelings:

    oh; ouch; phew; whoops
    唉 **ài** 'a sigh of sadness or regret'
    呸 **pēi** 'pah'; 'pooh'; 'an expression of disdain'
    哎呀 **āiyā** 'an expression of surprise or amazement'

(15) Shared Phonaestheme

Suggestion of meaning through comparable sound elements:

    slur/slow/sluggish
    细 **xì** 'slender'/小 **xiǎo** 'small'/稀 **xī** 'scarce'/狭 **xiá** 'narrow'
    凉丝丝 **liángsīsī** 'coolish'/甜丝丝 **tiánsīsī** 'pleasantly sweet'; 'happy'
    兴冲冲 **xìngchōngchōng** 'animatedly'/怒冲冲 **nùchōngchōng** 'furiously'

(16) Sound Translation

Transliteration into a different language:

    kowtow; wok
    咖啡 **kāfēi** 'coffee'; 巧克力 **qiǎokèlì** 'chocolate'

(17) Sub-Morphemic Correlation

Sharing of a non-meaningful or faintly meaningful linguistic pattern:

    retain/detain/contain
    领子 **lǐngzi** 'collar'/袖子 **xiùzi** 'sleeve'/里子 **lǐzi** 'lining'
    梗 **gěng** 'a slender piece of wood or metal'/鲠 **gěng** 'fishbone'/哽 **gěng** 'choke'
    辉 **huī** 'brightness'; 'splendour'/晖 **huī** 'sunshine'
    回 **huí** 'to circle'; to wind'; 'to return'/洄 **huí** (formal) 'whirl'
    迢迢 **tiáotiáo** 'remote'; 'far away'/岧岧 **tiáotiáo** (of mountain) 'high'
    规避 **guībì** 'evade'; 'avoid'/回避 **huíbì** 'dodge'; 'avoid meeting sb'

(18) Reduplication

Reiteration of a particular linguistic form:

    bye-bye; goody-goody
    妈妈 **māma** 'mum'; 'mother'; 爸爸 **bàba** 'dad'; 'father'
    喳喳 **chācha** 'whisper'
    喳喳派 **zhāzhāpài** 'yes-men'
    觑觑眼 **qūqūyǎn** (dial.) 'short-sightedness'

顶呱呱 **dǐngguāguā** 'tip-top'
忙忙叨叨 **mángmangdāodāo** 'busy and flustered'

MORPHOLOGICAL

(19) Inflection

Addition of regular or less regular suffixes to word stems for grammatical meaning:

book/books; child/children
孩子 **háizi** 'child'/孩子们 **háizimen** '*the* children'
姑娘 **gūniang** 'girl'/姑娘家 **gūniangjia** 'those who are girls'

(20) Derivation

Coinage of related meaningful forms through attaching affixes to existing word stems:

speak/speaker; dine/dinner; love/lovely
学 **xué** 'study'; 'learn'/学者 **xuézhě** 'scholar'
中间 **zhōngjiān** 'middle'; 'centre'/中间人 **zhōngjiānrén** 'go-between'
爱 **ài** 'love'/可爱 **kě'ài** 'lovely'

(21) Back Formation

Formation of a word from its seeming derivation, which is in fact originally an independent creation:

edit ← editor; laze ← lazy; sightsee ← sightseeing

(22) Stump Term

A clipped form of an originally longer word or idiom:

examination → exam; mathematics → maths; influenza → flu
有时候 **yǒu shíhou** → 有时 **yǒushí** 'sometimes'
吹牛皮 **chuī niúpí** → 吹牛 **chuīniú** 'boast'; 'brag'
耍滑头 **shuǎ huátóu** → 耍滑 **shuǎhuá** 'act in a slick way'
阿罗汉 **āluóhàn** → 罗汉 **luóhàn** 'arahat'

(23) Contextual Stump

A curtailed form which is context-dependent:

跳舞 *tiàowǔ* → 跳 **tiào** 'dance'; 游泳 *yóuyǒng* → 游 **yóu** 'swim'

(24) Abbreviation

A lengthy expression shortened to a disyllabic word:

人大 **rén dà** 'National People's Congress'; 'People's University' ←
人民代表大会 **rénmín dàibiǎo dàhuì**; 人民大学 **rénmín dàxué**
人流 **rénliú** 'induced abortion' ← 人工流产 **réngōng liúchǎn**
尖刻 **jiānkè** 'acrimonious'; 'biting' ← 尖酸刻薄 **jiānsuān kèbó**
向慕 **xiàngmù** 'admire' ← 向往爱慕 **xiàngwǎng àimù**
荧屏 **yíngpíng** 'telescreen'; 'luminescent screen' ← 荧光屏 **yíngguāngpíng**
影视 **yǐngshì** 'film and television' ← 电影电视 **diànyǐng diànshì**
菩萨 **púsà** 'Bodhisattva' ← 菩提萨埵 **pútísàduǒ**
阎罗 **yánluó** 'King of Hell' ← 阎魔罗阇 **yánmóluóshé**
耍赖 **shuǎlài** 'act shamelessly' ← 耍无赖 **shuǎ wúlài**
殊勋 **shūxūn** 'outstanding merit' ← 特殊的功勋 **tèshū de gōngxūn**

(25) Nonce Word

An impromptu word coinage for a specific situation:

illiterate[7] – people who do not care about litter
bagonise[8] – wait anxiously for one's suitcase to appear on the baggage
    carousel
丰奢 **fēngshē** 'plenty and extravagant'

(26) Portmanteau Word[9]

A telescopic blend of two words for a coalition of meaning:

smog; brunch; motel; Oxbridge; Amerindian
(Carroll's) chortle; (Joyce's) beehivour
大小便 **dàxiǎobiàn** 'defecate and urinate' ← 大便、小便 **dàbiàn xiǎobiàn**
中小学 **zhōngxiǎoxué** 'secondary and primary schools' ← 中学、小学
    zhōngxué xiǎoxué

(27) Root Creation

An independent coinage:

googol
铌 **ní** 'niobium'; 氕 **piē** 'protium'; 氚 **dāo** 'tritium'; 碘 **diǎn** 'iodine'; 汞 **gǒng**
    'mercury'

---

[7] Quoted from Crystal 1995: 133.
[8] Ibid.
[9] Ullmann 1962: 29.

(28) Folk Etymology

Formation arising from a mistaken identity:

> spit and image → spitting image
> an ewt → a newt
> (Middle English) than anes → nonce
> 裕 **yù** 'rich'; 'plenty' as in 富裕 **fùyù** 'well-off' (y- in 衣 **yī** 'clothes' + -u in 谷 **gǔ** 'grain')

(29) Humorous Infix[10]

A word or set expression interrupted by another linguistic element for meaning or emphasis:

> abso-posi-lutely ← absolutely
> fan-damn-tastic ← fantastic
> 滚蛋 **gǔndàn** 'beat it'; 'scram'; 'piss off' → 滚你妈的蛋 **gǔn nǐ māde dàn** 'get lost'
> 喝醉 **hē zuì** 'get drunk' → 喝他一个醉 **hē tā yī gè zuì** (intentionally) 'have a drinking spree'
> 将军 **jiāngjūn** 'put sb on the spot'; 'embarrass' 将他一军 **jiāng tā yī jūn** 'put him on the spot'

SYNTACTIC

(30) Conversion[11]

A shift from one grammatical category to another sometimes with stress, tone or sound modification:

> man (n.)/man (v.); surmise (n.)/surmise (v.)
> 钉 **dīng** 'a nail'/钉 **dìng** 'to nail'; 量 **liàng** 'quantity'/量 **liáng** 'to measure'
> 夹 **jiá** (adj.) 'double-layered'; 'lined'/夹 **jiā** (v.) 'place in between'; 'grip with a pair of tongs', etc.
> 福 **fú** 'happiness'/福了一福 **fú le yī fú** 'make a curtsy'
> 网 **wǎng** 'net'/网鱼 **wǎng yú** 'to net fish'
> 关心 **guānxīn** (n.) 'concern'/(v.) 'be concerned about'
> 搭档 **dádàng** (n.) 'partner'/(v.) 'team up'
>
> 长 **cháng** 'long'/长 **zhǎng** 'grow'
> 重 **chóng** 'duplicate'/重 **zhòng** 'heavy'
> 囤 **tún** 'store up'; 'hoard'/囤 **dùn** 'a grain bin'
> 驮 **tuó** (of animal) 'carry on the back'/驮子 **duòzi** 'load' (on a pack animal)

---

[10] Bolinger and Sears 1981: 29.
[11] Ullmann 1962: 52–3.

(31) Compounds[12]

Combination of two originally independent words into one:

blackboard; overdo; killjoy
菜单 **càidān** 'menu'; 下雨 **xiàyǔ** 'to rain'; 乞求 **qǐqiú** 'beg for'; 'implore'

(32) Phrasal Compounds[13]

Combination of dependent and independent elements into a set expression:

build up; give rise to
想起 **xiǎngqǐ** 'remember'; 'think of'; 走开 **zǒukāi** 'get away'; 'clear off'

(33) Frozen Patterns[14]

Set phrases inviting little change in use:

as far as I know; if I were you; further to my letter of . . .
如上所述 **rú shàng suǒ shù** 'as mentioned above'
众所周知 **zhòng suǒ zhōu zhī** 'as everyone knows'
一般说来 **yībān shuō lái**/一般来说 **yībān lái shuō** 'generally speaking'

(34) Humorous Syntactic Imitation

Lexical analogy attended by humour:

路透社 **lùtòushè** 'Reuter's News Agency; Reuters'/路边社消息 **lùbiānshè xiāoxi** 'grapevine news' (路边 **lùbiān** 'wayside'; 社 **shè** 'news agency'; 消息 **xiāoxi** 'news')
促进 **cùjìn** 'promote'; 'advance'/促退 **cùtuì** 'help to retrogress'
大我 **dàwǒ** 'the big self – the collective'/小我 **xiǎowǒ** 'the individual'; 'the self'
大哥大 **dàgēdà** (popular) 'mobile phone'/大姐大 **dàjiědà** (inf.) 'woman with power'

(35) Reversion

Change in the order of the elements within a word for meaning or mere style:

气力 **qìlì** 'effort'; 'energy'/力气 **lìqi** 'physical strength'
直率 **zhíshuài** 'frank'; 'candid'/率直 **shuàizhí** 'straightforward'; 'blunt'

---

[12] The majority of words in the Chinese lexicon may be regarded as compounds.
[13] Cf. Adams 1973: 9.
[14] Cf. Carter 1987: 76 on polywords and deictic locutions.

空闲 **kòngxián** 'idle'; 'free'/闲空 **xiánkòng** 'spare time'; 'leisure'
妒忌 **dùjì**/忌妒 **jìdu** 'be jealous or envious of'
海拔 **hǎibá**/拔海 **báhǎi** 'above sea level'
喉结 **hóujié**/结喉 **jiéhóu** 'Adam's apple'
俭省 **jiǎnshěng** 'economical'; 'thrifty'/省俭 **shěngjiǎn** (dial.)
篱笆 **líba** 'bamboo or twig fence'/笆篱 **bālí** (dial.)
钟乳石 **zhōngrǔshí**/石钟乳 **shízhōngrǔ** 'stalactite'
绘声绘影 **huìshēng huìyǐng**/绘影绘声 **huìyǐng huìshēng** 'vivid'; 'lively'
  (description)

SEMANTIC

(36) Synonym

Words or elements in a word with similar meanings:

big/large; drawing pin (BE)/thumbtack (AE)
图钉 **túdīng** 'drawing pin'/揿钉 **qìndīng** (dial.)
南瓜 **nánguā** 'pumpkin'/北瓜 **běigua** (dial.)/老倭瓜 **lǎowōgua** (dial.)
甘薯 **gānshǔ** 'sweet potato'/
  colloquial terms: 红薯 **hóngshǔ**/白薯 **báishǔ**
  dialectal terms: 番薯 **fānshǔ**/山芋 **shānyù**/地瓜 **dìguā**/红苕 **hóngsháo**
拔腿 **bátuǐ**/拔脚 **bájiǎo** (lit.) 'lift one's foot' ('to run')
跌价 **diējià**/掉价 **diàojià** 'fall or drop in price'
美丽 **měilì** 'beautiful' (美 **měi** 'beautiful'/丽 **lì** 'beautiful')
愤怒 **fènnù** 'indignant' (愤 **fèn** 'indignant'/怒 **nù** 'angry')

(37) Antonym

Words or elements in a word with opposite meanings:

big/small
大 **dà** 'big'/小 **xiǎo** 'small'
大小 **dàxiǎo** 'size'
迟早 **chízǎo** 'sooner or later' (迟 **chí** 'late'/早 **zǎo** 'early')
先后 **xiānhòu** 'one after another' (先 **xiān** 'before'/后 **hòu** 'after')
出入 **chūrù** 'discrepancy' (出 **chū** 'go out'/入 **rù** 'come in')
翕张 **xīzhāng** 'furl and unfurl'; 'open and shut'
盈亏 **yíngkuī** 'profit and loss'
旺季 **wàngjì** 'busy season'/淡季 **dànjì** 'slack season'
微观 **wēiguān** 'microcosmic'/宏观 **hóngguān** 'macroscopic'
得宠 **déchǒng** (derog.) 'be in sb's good graces'/失宠 **shīchǒng** (derog.)
  'be out of favour'

(38) Converse Term

Two words or elements in a word related in such a way that the mention of one presupposes the other:

buy/sell; employer/employee; husband/wife; above/below
夫妇 **fūfù** 'husband and wife'
宾主 **bīnzhǔ** 'host and guest'
买卖 **mǎimài** 'business deal'; 'transaction'
收支 **shōuzhī** 'income and expenditure'

(39) Complementary Term

Two words or elements in a word, the assertion of one implies the denial of the other:

single/married; male/female; boy/girl
兄弟 **xiōngdì** 'brothers' (兄 **xiōng** 'elder brother'/弟 **dì** 'younger brother')
男女老少 **nán nǚ lǎo shào** 'men and women, old and young'

(40) Hyponym

Words or elements of a word with a taxonomic meaning relationship between them:

花儿 **huār** 'flowers'/玫瑰 **méigui** 'rose'; 郁金香 **yùjīnxiāng** 'tulip'; etc.
岁月 **suìyuè** 'time'; 'years' (岁 **suì** 'year'; 月 **yuè** 'month')
宇宙 **yǔzhòu** 'universe'; 'cosmos' (宇 **yǔ** 'space'; 宙 **zhòu** 'time')

(41) Meronym[15]

Words or elements of a word with a part-whole meaning relationship between them:

tree/trunk, branch, root, leaf, etc.
树 **shù** 'tree'/树干 **shùgàn** 'tree trunk'; 树枝 **shùzhī** 'branch'; 'twig'; 树根 **shùgēn** 'root'; 树叶 **shùyè** 'leaf'; 树皮 **shùpí** 'bark'; etc.

(42) Consecutives

Words belonging to a hierarchy or series:

星期一 **xīngqī yī** 'Monday', 星期二 **xīngqī èr** 'Tuesday', etc.
一月 **yīyuè** 'January', 二月 **èryuè** 'February', etc.
班 **bān** 'squad', 排 **pái** 'platoon', 连 **lián** 'company', 营 **yíng** 'battalion', etc.

---

[15] Carter 1987: 21.

(43) Polyseme

A word with more than one related meaning:

human leg/leg of a journey
脚 **jiǎo** 'foot'/墙脚 **qiángjiǎo** 'foot of a wall'
功夫 **gōngfu** 'time'/'effort'/'skill'

(44) Homonym

Words identical in form but totally different in meaning:

bank (= financial institution)/bank (of a river)
杜鹃 **dùjuān** (zool.) 'cuckoo'/(bot.) 'azalea'

(45) Periphrasis

The same idea expressed in different derivatives or clusters of words:

happier/more happy; works/does work
好容易 **hǎo róngyi**/好不容易 **hǎo bù róngyi** 'not at all easy'; 'with great
   difficulty'
不得了 **bùdéliǎo**/了不得 **liǎobude** (as a complement) 'extremely'; 'exceedingly'
不禁 **bùjīn**/禁不住 **jīnbuzhù** 'can't help (doing)'

(46) Pun

A word or utterance ambiguous by virtue of sound or syntax:

flying aeroplanes can be dangerous
I am finished.
我完了。**wǒ wán le** 'I'm finished.'
隐君子 **yǐnjūnzǐ** 'a retired scholar/a drug addict'
   (a pun on 隐 **yǐn** 'retired' and 瘾 **yǐn** 'addicted')
外甥打灯笼 – 照舅(旧)。**wàisheng dǎ dēnglong | zhàojiù**
'as before' (lit. 'the nephew carries the lantern – to light the way for his uncle')
   (a pun on 照舅 **zhàojiù** 'light the way for one's uncle' and 照旧 **zhàojiù**
   'as before')

下雨天留客，天留我不留。**xiàyǔ tiān liú kè | tiān liú wǒ bù liú**
'The rainy day invites the guest to stay – the rain does, but I (as the host)
don't.'
下雨天，留客天。留我不? 留! **xiàyǔ tiān | liú kè tiān | liú wǒ bù | liú**
'A rainy day is the day for the guest to stay. Are you going to ask me to
stay then? Yes, I am.'
   (a pun exploiting the potential pauses in a discourse)

(47) Omnibus Term[16]

A cover term with a hazy and general meaning:

> thing; thingummy/something whose name has been forgotten
> 什么 **shénme** 'everything'; 'anything'
> 哪儿 **nǎr** 'everywhere'; 'anywhere'

(48) Commonised Term

An original proper name developed into a common noun:

> watt; hoover
> 红娘 **hóngniáng** 'matchmaker' (name of the maid in 西厢记 *Western Chamber*)
> 阿斗 **ādǒu** 'a failure or fool' (last emperor of 蜀汉 Shu Han between AD 221 and 263)
> 阿Q **ākiū** 'one who interprets defeats as moral victories' (a character in 鲁迅 Lu Xun's fiction)

GRAPHETIC

(49) Homograph

Words sharing the same written form yet having a different meaning and sometimes a different pronunciation:

> bank of river/bank for money
> slough [slau] 'swamp'/slough [slʌf] 'cast off skin'
> 吐 **tǔ** 'spit' (voluntarily)/吐 **tù** 'vomit' (involuntarily)
> 扛 **káng** 'carry on the shoulder'/扛 **gāng** (dial.) (of two or more people) 'carry together'
> 雪茄 **xuějiā** 'cigar'/番茄 **fānqié** 'tomato'
> 供养 **gōngyǎng** 'provide for parents'/供养 **gòngyǎng** 'make offerings to ancestors'
> 便宜 **biànyí** 'convenient'/便宜 **piányi** 'cheap'
> 澄清 **chéngqīng** 'clarify'/澄清 **dèngqīng** (of a liquid) 'settle'
> 埋 **mái** 'bury'/埋怨 **mányuàn** 'complain'
> 熨 **yùn** 'to iron (clothes)'/熨贴 **yùtiē** (of wording) 'apt'; 'appropriate'
> 罢了 **bàle** 'that's all'; 'nothing else'/罢了 **bàliǎo** 'forget it'
> 空心 **kōngxīn** 'hollow inside'/空心 **kòngxīn** 'on an empty stomach'

---

[16] Ullmann 1962: 230.

(50) Heterograph

The same word or element of a word written or/and pronounced differently:

harbour/harbor; woke/waked; formulae/formulas; disc/disk; balk/baulk
茄克 **jiākè**/甲克 **jiǎkè** 'jacket'
茨菰/慈姑 **cígu** (bot.) 'arrowhead'
倒霉/倒楣 **dǎoméi** 'down on one's luck'
模仿/摹仿 **mófǎng** 'imitate'; 'copy'
莫名其妙/莫明其妙 **mò míng qí miào** 'be baffled'; 'inexplicable'
得意洋洋/得意扬扬 **déyì yángyáng** 'be immensely proud'
当当/铛铛/璫璫 **dāngdāng** (onom.) 'clank'; 'clang'
惊慌 **jīnghuāng**/惊惶 **jīnghuáng** 'panic-stricken'
报道 **bàodào**/报导 **bàodǎo** 'report or cover (news)'
倒塌 **dǎotā**/倒坍 **dǎotān** 'collapse'; 'topple down'
男小囡/囝 **nán xiǎonān** 'a little boy'/女小囡/囝 **nǚ xiǎonān** 'a little girl'

(51) Initialism

Initial letters of a set expression lumped together to form an abbreviation:

VIP; MP; BBC

(52) Acronym

Initial letters of a set expression lumped together to form a pronounceable word:

laser; scuba; AIDS; ROM; DOS

(53) Initialism plus Acronym[17]

CDROM

(54) Inversion

Two mirror-image graphetic forms combined to form a word or expression:

乒乓 **pīngpāng** 'table tennis'
孑孓 **jiéjué** 'wiggler'; 'wriggler'
凹凸 **āotū** 'concave-convex'
上下 **shàngxià** 'above and below'

---

[17] Crystal 1995: 120.

(55) Division

A word or expression formed from one or two halves of an existing word:

彳亍 **chìchù** 'walk slowly'; 'loiter' ← 行 **xíng** 'walk'
丘八 **qiūbā** (slang) 'soldier' ← 兵 **bīng** 'soldier'
爿 **pán** 'slit bamboo or chopped wood'; 'classifier' ← 半 **bàn** 'half'

(56) Conflation

Two forms combined into one form to represent one meaning:

卡 **qiǎ** 'get stuck'; 'wedge' ← 上 **shàng** 'above' and 下 **xià** 'below'
粜 **tiào** 'sell grain' ← 出 **chū** 'out' and 米 **mǐ** 'grain'; 'rice'
汆 **tǔn** 'deep-fry' ← 入 **rù** 'enter' and 水 **shuǐ** 'water'; 'liquid'
孥 **nú** 'sons and daughters' ← 子 **zǐ** 'son' and 女 **nǚ** 'daughter'
吋 'inch' ← 英寸 **yīngcùn**
浬 'nautical mile' ← 海里 **hǎilǐ**
圕 'library' ← 图书馆 **túshūguǎn**

(57) Graphetic Resemblance

A graphetic form to represent the form of a real-life object:

丫 **yā** in 丫杈 **yāchà** 'fork' (of a tree)
串 **chuàn** 'to string together'
金字塔 **jīnzìtǎ** 'pyramid'
十字路口 **shízì lùkǒu** 'crossroad'

(58) Graphetic Metaphor

A graphetic form to be appreciated metaphorically:

扒手 **páshǒu** 'pickpocket'
大众 **dàzhòng** 'the masses'
炎热 **yánrè** (of weather) 'scorching'; 'blazing'
浩淼 **hàomiǎo** (of water) 'vast expanse'

(59) Shared Element

A shared graphetic form for meaning-related words:

强弱 **qiáng ruò** 'the strong and the weak' (弓)
公私 **gōng sī** 'public and private' (厶)
阴阳 **yīn yáng** '*yin* and *yang* opposites' (阝)
湿 (unsimplified: 濕) **shī** 'wet'/隰 **xí** 'low marshy land'; 'swamp'/曝 **qī** (of
    wet things) 'getting dry' (㬎)

(60) Uni-Radicalization

A shared graphetic element for separate forms within the same word:

烂漫 → 烂熳 **lànmàn** 'bright-coloured' (radical: 火 'fire')
罗嗦 → 啰嗦 **luōsuo** 'long-winded' (radical: 口 'mouth')
嘹亮 → 嘹喨 **liáoliàng** 'resonant'; 'loud and clear' (radical: 口 'mouth')
逗留 → 逗遛 **dòuliú** 'stay'; 'linger' (radical: 辶 'travel')
愣怔 **lèngzheng** 'dazed'; 'dumbstruck' (radical: 忄 'heart') = 睖睁 **lèngzheng** (radical: 目 'eye')

COLLOCATIONAL

(61) Selectional Restriction

Sequences of words which often belong together:

blond hair; black tea
金发 **jīn fà** 'blond hair' (金 **jīn** 'gold'; 'golden'; 发 **fà** 'hair')
红茶 **hóng chá** (红 **hóng** 'red'; 茶 **chá** 'tea')
冒险 **màoxiǎn** 'take risks' (冒 **mào** 'to brave'; 险 **xiǎn** 'danger')
交换意见 **jiāohuàn yìjiàn** 'exchange views'/交流经验 **jiāoliú jīngyàn** 'compare notes'

(62) Idiom[18]

Peculiar word combinations with a meaning different from their constituent elements:

kick the bucket; spill the beans
翘尾巴 **qiào wěiba** 'get cocky' (翘 **qiào** 'stick up'; 尾巴 **wěiba** 'tail')
自讨没趣 **zì tǎo méiqù** 'court a rebuff' (自 **zì** 'self'; 讨 **tǎo** 'ask for'; 没趣 **méiqù** 'snub')

(63) Formulaic Sentence

Situation-dependent linguistic formulae:

how are you?; nice to meet you; are you sure?; God bless you
你好 **nǐ hǎo** 'how are you'; 'how do you do' (lit. 'you good')
谢谢 **xièxie** 'thanks'
再见 **zàijiàn** 'goodbye' (lit. 'again see')
恭喜 **gōngxǐ** 'congratulations'
一路平安 **yī lù píng'ān** 'a safe journey' (lit. 'safe all the way')

[18] Makkai 1972: 42.

(64) Binominal or Coordinate Pair[19]

Two words or elements always linked together to form a word, a set expression or a set format:

kith and kin; back and forth; either . . . or; neither . . . nor
亲友 **qīnyǒu** 'friends and relatives'
父母 **fùmǔ** 'parents'
不但 **bùdàn** . . . 而且 **érqiě** 'not only . . . but also'

(65) Paradigmatic Semantic Association

Meaning correlation which directly reflects real-life connections:

sweet/sugar; sour/vinegar
咸 **xián** 'salty'/盐 **yán** 'salt'; 苦 **kǔ** 'bitter'/药 **yào** 'medicine'

(66) Anomalous Collocation

A violation to lexical cohesion or an incongruity or discrepancy between a word and its usual concomitants:[20]

colourless green ideas

STYLISTIC

(67) Register (formal/inf.)

Words or expressions with different degrees of formality:

罗嗦 **luōsuo** (neut.)/噜苏 **lūsū** (dial.) 'long-winded'
棘手 **jíshǒu** (neut.)/辣手 **làshǒu** (inf.) 'thorny'; 'troublesome'
下雨 **xiàyǔ** (neut.)/掉点儿 **diàodiǎnr** (inf.) 'raining'
调情 **tiáoqíng** (neut.)/吊膀子 **diàobàngzi** (dial.) 'flirt'
龋齿 **qǔchǐ** (tech.) 'dental caries'/蛀齿 **zhùchǐ** (neut.)/虫牙 **chóngyá** (colloq.) 'decayed tooth'
愆期 **qiānqī** (very formal)/逾期 **yúqī** (formal)/过期 **guòqī** (colloq.) 'exceed the deadline'
诸位 **zhūwèi** 'ladies and gentlemen' (very formal)/各位 **gè wèi** 'everybody' (formal)/大家 **dàjiā** 'everyone' (inf.)
说不定 **shuōbudìng** (colloq.)/备不住 **bèibuzhù** (dial.) 'cannot say for sure'
搬家 **bānjiā** (neut.)/挪窝儿 **nuówōr** (dial.) 'move (house)'

[19] Adams 1973; Makkai 1972; Evans et al. 1980: 220.
[20] Cf. Carter 1987: 106–7, 174.

口讷 **kǒunè** (written)/嘴笨 **zuǐbèn** (colloq.) 'inarticulate'; 'clumsy of speech'

拨冗 **bōrǒng** (polite)/抽时间 **chōu shíjiān** (colloq.) 'find time'

逝世 **shìshì** (formal) 'pass away'/死 **sǐ** (colloq.) 'die'/蹬腿 **dēngtuǐ** (inf. humor.) 'kick the bucket'

受挫 **shòucuò** (formal) 'suffer a setback'/失败 **shībài** (neut.) 'fail'/吹了 **chuī le** (colloq.)/黄了 **huáng le** (inf.)/砸锅 **záguō** (dial.)/漂了 **piào le** (slangy) 'fall through'

(68) Provenance (religious/political/technical/etc.)

Words from specific area of study:

佛 **fó** 'Buddha' (religion)

弹劾 **tánhé** 'impeach (an official)' (politics)

折衷主义 **zhézhōng zhǔyì** 'eclecticism' (philosophy)

势能 **shìnéng** 'potential energy' (physics)

加速度 **jiāsùdù** 'acceleration' (mechanics)

氧化 **yǎnghuà** 'oxidise'; 'oxidate' (chemistry)

程序 **chéngxù** 'programme' (for computers) (automation)

法人 **fǎrén** 'legal person' (law)

贻贝 **yíbèi** (zool.)/淡菜 **dàncài** (food) 'mussel'

沥青 **lìqīng** (tech.)/柏油 **bǎiyóu** (pop.) 'asphalt'; 'bitumen'

(69) Idiolect (established/coined)

Words reflecting idiosyncratic use of language:

美丽 **měilì** 'beautiful' (established)

亮丽 **liànglì** 'bright and beautiful' (e.g. scenery) (coined)

流丽 **liúlì** 'fluent and beautiful' (e.g. art) (coined)

(70) Chronological Feature (classical/contemporary)

Historical linguistic residue or contemporary linguistic innovation:

醯 **xī** (classic)/醋 **cù** (contem.) 'vinegar'

冠 **guān** (classic)/帽子 **màozi** (contem.) 'hat'

庠序 **xiángxù** (classic)/学校 **xuéxiào** (contem.) 'school'

界说 **jièshuō** (classic)/定义 **dìngyì** (contem.) 'definition'

赧颜 **nǎnyán** (classic)/脸红 **liǎnhóng** (contem.) 'red in the face'

搦管 **nuòguǎn** (classic)/执笔 **zhíbǐ** (contem.) 'take up the pen'

颔首 **hànshǒu** (classic)/点头 **diǎntóu** (contem.) 'nod'

振翮高飞 **zhèn hé gāo fēi** (classic)/振翅高飞 **zhèn chì gāo fēi** (contem.) 'fly high'

(71) Connotative Distinction (neutral/metaphorical)

Additional meaning association:

drink/imbibe
武器 **wǔqì** (neut.)/刀枪 **dāoqiāng** (meta.) 'weapons'
  (刀 **dāo** 'broadsword'; 枪 **qiāng** 'spear'; 'gun')
武术 **wǔshù** (neut.)/拳棒 **quánbàng** 'martial arts' (meta.)
  (拳 **quán** 'fist'; 棒 **bàng** 'stick'; 'club')
贫嘴 **pínzuǐ** 'loquacious' (meta.)/饶舌 **ráoshé** 'garrulous' (meta.)/
  唠叨 **láodao** 'chatter interminably' (neut.)/
  磨牙 **móyá** 'argue pointlessly' (meta.; dial.)

(72) Literary Type (prosaic/poetic)

Degree of creativeness:

人世 **rénshì** (prosaic)/尘寰 **chénhuán** (poetic) 'this world'
月亮 **yuèliang** (prosaic)/婵娟 **chánjuān** (poetic) 'the moon'
酒 **jiǔ** (prosaic)/杜康 **dùkāng** (liter.) 'wine'; 'spirit'; 'alcohol'
眼帘 **yǎnlián** (literary)/眼睑 **yǎnjiǎn** (prosaic)/眼皮 **yǎnpí** (colloq.) 'eyelid'

(73) Locality Flavour (standard/dialectal or native/foreign)

Geographical associations:

蛞蝓 **kuòyú** (zoological)/鼻涕虫 **bítìchóng** (popular)/蜒蚰 **yányóu** (dial.) 'slug'
引擎 **yǐnqíng** (foreign)/发动机 **fādòngjī** (native) 'engine'
马达 **mǎdá** (foreign; colloq.)/电动机 **diàndòngjī** (native; neut.) 'motor'
温室 **wēnshì** (neut.)/暖房 **nuǎnfáng** (dial.) 'greenhouse'
麦克风 **màikèfēng** (foreign)/话筒 **huàtǒng** (native) 'microphone'
星相 **xīngxiàng** (foreign) 'horoscope'/生肖 **shēngxiào** (native) '12 symbolic
  animals associated with a person's year of birth'

CULTURAL

(74) Taboo

Blasphemous, profane and abusive terms:

fuck; shit
他妈的 **tā māde** – a swear word; an abusive term
王八蛋 **wángbadàn** 'bastard'; 'son of a bitch'

(75) Euphemism

Pleasant words representing unpleasant ideas:

pass away = die
去世 **qùshì** 'pass away' (lit. 'leave the world') = 死 **sǐ** 'die'
有了 **yǒu le** 'pregnant' (lit. 'have got it') = 怀孕 **huáiyùn** 'pregnant'
房事 **fángshì** 'sex between husband and wife'
　　= 性交 **xìngjiāo** 'sexual intercourse'
抱娃娃 **bàowáwa** 'give birth to a child' (lit. 'hold babies in one's arms')
　　= 生孩子 **shēng háizi** 'give birth to a child'

(76) Cliché

Established proverbial sayings for all occasions:

a friend in need is a friend indeed; no pains, no gains
开绿灯 **kāi lǜdēng** 'give the go-ahead'
两面三刀 **liǎngmiàn sāndāo** 'double-dealing' (lit. 'two faces and three knives')
礼多人不怪 **lǐ duō rén bù guài** 'nobody will blame you for being too polite'
人要脸, 树要皮 **rén yào liǎn | shù yào pí** 'face is as important to man as the bark is to the tree'
好汉不吃眼前亏 **hǎohàn bù chī yǎnqiánkuī** 'a wise man will not fight when the odds are against him'
天下无不散的宴席 **tiānxià wú bù sàn de yànxí** 'all good things must come to an end' (lit. 'there never was a feast but the guests had to depart')
千里之行, 始于足下 **qiān lǐ zhī xíng | shǐ yú zú xià** 'a thousand-mile journey begins with the first step'
天下无难事, 只怕有心人 **tiānxià wú nánshì | zhǐpà yǒuxīnrén** 'nothing is impossible to a willing mind' (lit. 'nothing under heaven is too difficult so long as there are people who have the heart to do it')

(77) Slogan

Public notices and so on:

safety first; trespassers will be prosecuted; private
安全第一 **ānquán dìyī** 'safety first'
闲人莫进 **xiánrén mò jìn** 'no admission'; 'private' (lit. 'no entrance for outsiders')
此路不通 **cǐ lù bù tōng** 'no thoroughfare'

(78) Neologisms

Catch phrases or vogue words:

> virtual reality; cyberspace; genetic engineering; quark; buzz word
> 筛选 **shāixuǎn** 'screening'; 'sieving'
> 弱智 **ruòzhì** 'mentally deficient'; 'retarded'
> 涉外 **shèwài** 'concerning foreign affairs or foreign nationals'
> 下岗 **xiàgǎng** 'be made redundant'
> 下海 **xiàhǎi** (inf.) 'engage in trade'; 'become a businessman'

BIBLIOGRAPHY

Adams, V. (1973). *An Introduction to Modern English Word-Formation*. Longman.

Anderson, O. B. (1981). *The 'Radicals' of the Chinese Script*. Curzon Press. London.

Aronoff, M. (1979). *Word Formation in Generative Grammar*. MIT Press. Cambridge, MA.

Austin, J. L. (1962). *How To Do Things With Words*. Oxford University Press. Oxford.

Bai, Ping (白平). (1989). '汉语词汇三题' in 山西大学学报 4.

Baxter, William H. and Sagart Laurent (1998). 'Word Formation in Old Chinese', in Jerome L. Packard (ed.), *New Approaches to Chinese Word Formation*. Mouton de Gruyter. Berlin.

Beijing Daxue Zhongguo Yuyanwenxuexi Yuyanxue Jiaoyanshi (北京大学中国语言文学系 语音学教育室) (1964). 汉语方言词汇. 文字改革出版社.

Beijing Waiguoyu Daxue Yingyuxi Hanying Cidian Zu (北京外国语大学英语系《汉英词典》组 (ed.) (1995). 汉英词典(修订版). 外语教学与研究出版社. 北京.

Beijing Yuyan Xueyuan (北京语言学院 语言教学研究所) (1985). 汉语词汇的统计与分析. 外语教学与研究出版社.

Black, M. (1972). *The Labyrinth of Language*, Penguin. Harmondsworth.

Bodde, Derk. (1975). *Festivals in Classical China*. Princeton University Press. Princeton.

Bodde, Derk. (1981). *Essays on Chinese Civilization*. Princeton University Press. Princeton.

Bolinger, D. (1980). *Language – The Loaded Weapon*. Longman.

Bolinger, Dwight and Sears, Donald A. (1981). *Aspects of Language* (3rd Edition), Harcourt Brace Jovanovich, Inc. New York.

Cao, Congsun (曹聪孙). (1992). '汉语隐语说略' in 中国语文 1.

Cao, Xianzhuo (曹先擢). (1979). '并列式同素异序同义词' in 中国语文 6.

Carter, Ronald. (1987). *Vocabulary – Applied Linguistic Perspectives*. Allen and Unwin. London.

Cen, Qixiang (岑麒祥). (1956). '关于汉语构词法的几个问题' in 中国语文 12.

Chang, Jingyu (常敬宇). (1985). '同素词简论' in 语言教学与研究 2.

Chang, Xuan and Quan, Ji (昌煊全基). (1958). '论成语' in 中国语文 10.

Chao, Yuen-ren (1968). *A Grammar of Spoken Chinese*. University of California Press. Berkeley and Los Angeles.

Chen, Ai-wen and Yu, Ping. (陈爱文 于平). (1979). '并列双音词的字序' in 中国语文 2.

Chen, Bingtiao (陈炳迢). (1985). 辞书概要. 福建人民出版社. 福州.

Chen, Caijun (陈才俊). (1991). '语言与文化透视' in 暨南学报: 哲社版 1.

Chen, Guanglei (陈光磊). (1994). 汉语词法论. 学林出版社. 上海.

Chen, Guanglei (陈光磊). (1997). '改革开放中汉语词汇的变动' in 语言教学与研究 2.

Chen, Jianmin (陈建民). (1984). 汉语口语. 北京出版社.

Chen, Jianmin (陈建民). (1996). '改革开放以来中国大陆的词汇变异' in 语言文字应用 1.

Chen, Liu (陈榴). (1990). '汉语外来语与汉民族文化心理' in 辽宁师范大学学报: 社科版 5.

Chen, Ping. (1999). *Modern Chinese – History and Sociolinguistics*. Cambridge University Press. Cambridge.

Chen, Ruiheng (陈瑞衡). (1989). '当今"联绵字": 传统名称的"挪用"' in 中国语文 4.

Chen, Shujing (陈淑静). (1991). '北方话词汇的内部差异与规范' in 河北大学学报: 哲社版 3.

Chen, Wangdao (陈望道). (1954). 修辞发凡. 新文艺出版社. 上海.

Chen, Weiwu (陈伟武). (1992). '骂詈行为与汉语詈词探论' in 中山大学学报: 社科版 4.

Chen, Weiwu (陈伟武). (1996). '甲骨文反义词研究' in 中山大学学报: 社科版 3.

Chen, Yueming (陈月明). (1995). '汉语词汇的思维特征管窥' in 宁波大学学报: 人文科学版 2.

Chen, Zeping (陈泽平). (1993). '关于现代汉语带有后缀"然"的复合词的划界问题' in 河北师专学报: 文科版 1.

Chen, Zhanghan (陈章太). (1996). '普通话词汇规范问题' in 中国语文 3.

Cheng, Jiashu and Zhang, Yunhui (程家枢 张云徽). (1989). '并列式双音复合名词的字序规律新探' in 云南教育学院学报: 社科版 1.

Chou, Fa-kao. (1986). *Papers in Chinese Linguistics and Epigraphy*. The Chinese University Press. Hong Kong.

Cihai Bianji Weiyuanhui (辞海编辑委员会) (ed.) (1980). 辞海. 上海辞书出版社.

Crystal, D. (1980). *A First Dictionary of Linguistics and Phonetics*. Cambridge University Press. Cambridge.

Crystal, D. (1988). *The Cambridge Encyclopedia of Language*. Guild Publishing. London.

Crystal, D. (1995). *The Cambridge Encyclopedia of the English Language*. Cambridge University Press. Cambridge.

Culler, J. (1976). *Saussure*. Fontana. London.

Dai, Kuiben (戴惠本). (1993). '对立词的构成及其它' in 中国对外汉语教学学会第四次学术讨论会论文选. 北京语言学院出版社.

Dawson, Raymond. (1978). *The Chinese Experience*. Weidenfeld and Nicolson. London.

DeFrancis, J. (1984). *The Chinese Langage – Fact and Fantasy*. University of Hawaii Press. Honolulu.

DeFrancis, J. (1997). *ABC Chinese-English Dictionary*. Curzon. Richmond.

Department of East Asian Languages and Cultures (1979). 'Productive Affixes in Modern Chinese Morphology' in *WORD* 30.3.

Dong, Shifu and Liu, Yongfa (董世福 刘永发). (1995). '试论体态成语' in 蒲峪学刊 2.

Dong, Weiguang (董为光). (1992). '汉语词汇双音代换管窥' in 语言研究 2.

Evans M. W. et al. (1980). *Lexical-Semantic Relations: A Comparative Survey*. Linguistic Research, Inc. Canada.

Fan, Xingan (范新干). (1993). '汉语复合词的词义构成' in 华中师范大学学报: 哲社版 专辑.

Fei, Jinchang (费锦昌). (1996). 现代汉语部件探究. 语言文字应用 2.

Fillmore, C. J. (1969). 'Types of Lexical Information' in Kiefer, F. (ed.) *Studies in Syntax and Semantics*. Foundations of Language (Supplementary Series) Vol. 10. Reidel. Dordrecht.

Firth, J. R. (1968). 'A Synopsis of Linguistic Theory, 1930–1955' in *Studies in Linguistic Analysis*. Blackwell. Oxford.

Fodor, J. D. (1977). *Semantics: Theories of Meaning in Generative Grammar*. The Harvester Press. Hassocks.

Forrest, R. A. D. (1965). *The Chinese Language*. Faber and Faber. London.

Fromkin, V. and Rodman, R. (1983). *An Introduction to Language* (3rd Edition). Hold-Saunders International Editions.

Fu, Donghua (傅东华). (1957). 汉字. 新知识出版社.

Fu, Hao (符浩). (1990). '词义演变过程中的离析与综合现象' in 广西师范大学学报: 哲社版 3.

Fu, Huaiqing (符淮青). (1985). 现代汉语词汇. 北京大学出版社.

Fu, Xingling and Chen, Zhanghuan (傅兴岭 陈章焕) (eds). (1982). 常用构词字典. 中国人民大学出版社.

Gao, Gengsheng et al. (高更生等) (eds). (1983). 现代汉语资料分题选编 (上册). 山东教育出版社. 济南.

Gao, Gengsheng et al. (高更生). (1984). 现代汉语. 山东教育出版社.

Gao, Mingkai (高名凯). (1957). '关于"社会习惯语"或"社会方言"的讨论' in 中国语文 5.

Gao, Qingci (高庆赐). (1957). 同义词和反义词. 新知识出版社. 上海.

Gao, Shougang (高守纲). (1981). '汉语中的词义转化兼类词' in 语言学论丛 7. 商务印书馆. 北京.

Gao, Zengliang (高增良). (1994). '语言借贷与文化交流' in 中国文化研究冬之卷.

Ge, Benyi and Yang, Zhenlan (葛本仪 杨振兰). (1990). '词义演变规律述略' in 文史哲 6.

Gleason, H. A. (1975). 'The Relation of Lexicon and Grammar' in F. W. Householder and S. Saporta (eds). *Problems in Lexicography*. Indiana University Press. Bloomington.

Grice, H. P. (1975). 'Logic and Conversation' in P. Cole and J. L. Morgan (eds) *Syntax and Semantics*. Academic Press. New York.

Gu, Jiazu et al. (顾嘉祖等) (eds). (1990). 语言与文化. 上海外语教育出版社.

Guo, Jinfu (郭锦桴). (1990). '语义网络初探' in 汉语学习 6.

Guo, Jinfu (郭锦桴). (1993). 汉语与中国传统文化. 中国人民大学出版社.

Guo, Liangfu (郭良夫). (1982). '论缩略' in 中国语文 2.

Guo, Liangfu (郭良夫). (1983). '现代汉语的前缀和后缀' in 中国语文 4.

Guo, Liangfu (郭良夫). (1990). 词汇与词典. 商务印书馆. 北京.

Hai, Yang (海阳). (1992). '论词义系统的构成及其功能' in 湘潭大学学报: 社科版 3.

Han, Jiantang (韩鉴堂). (1994). 中国文化. 国际文化出版公司. 北京.

Hanyu Pinyin Cihui Bianxiezu (汉语拼音词汇编写组) (ed.) (1991). 汉语拼音词汇 (1989 年重编本). 语文出版社. 北京.

He, Deyang (贺德扬). (1991). '论汉字的词根音谐声' in 聊城师范学院学报: 哲社版 3.

He, Jiuying and Jiang, Shaoyu (何九盈 蒋绍愚). (1980). 古汉语词汇讲话. 北京出版社.

He, Zhongjie (何鍾杰). (1953). '解决有音无字的问题' in 中国语文 7.

Henne, Henry et al. (1977). *A Handbook on Chinese Language Structure*. Universitetsforlaget. Oslo.

Hong, Chengyu (洪成玉). (1996). '词的义层' in 首都师范大学学报: 社科版 1.

Hou, Zhanhu (侯占虎). (1990). '利用谐声偏旁系联同源词探讨' in 古籍整理研究学刊 5.

Hu, Bingzhong (胡炳忠). (1978). '北京语音表在教学上的使用' in 语言教学与研究 3. 北京语言学院.

Hu, Shiyun (胡士云). (1989). '大陆与港台言语交际中的词汇问题' in 丹东师专学报: 哲社版 1.

Hu, Yushu et al. (胡裕树). (1981). 现代汉语. 上海教育出版社.

Huang, Changzhu (黄长著). (1994). '从某些外语专名的汉译看海峡两岸语言使用的同与异' in 中国语文 6.

Huang, Yuezhou (黄岳洲). (1980). '成语中数词所表示的抽象义' in 中国语文 6.

Huang, Zheng (黄征). (1992). '汉语俗语词研究的几个理论问题' in 杭州大学学报: 哲社版 2.

Huang, Zhiqiang and Yang, Jianqiao (黄志强 杨剑桥). (1990). '论汉语词汇双音节化的原因' in 复旦学报: 社科版 1.

Jerome L. Packard (ed.) (1998). *New Approaches to Chinese Word Formation*. Mouton de Gruyter. Berlin.

Jia, Yande (贾彦德). (1995). '汉语语义场的演变' in 中国语言学报 5.

Jiang, Shaoyu (蒋绍愚). (1989). '关于汉语词汇系统及其发展变化的几点想法' in 中国语文 1.

Jiang, Wenqin and Chen, Aiwen (蒋文钦 陈爱文). (1982). '关于并列结构固定词语的内部次序' in 中国语文 4.

Jin, Ximo (金锡谟). (1984). '合成词中的双音离合动词' in 语言论集 2. 中国人民大学出版社. 北京.

Karlgren, Bernhard (1923). *Sound & Symbol in Chinese*. Oxford University Press. London.

Karlgren, Bernhard (1926). *Philology & Ancient China*. H. Aschehong & Co. (W. Nygaard). Olso.

Karlgren, Bernhard (1949). *The Chinese Language*. The Ronald Press Company. New York.

Katz, J. J. and Fodor, J. A. (1963). 'The Structure of a Semantic Theory', *Language* 39.2.

Kay, P. (1971). 'Taxonomy and Semantic Contrast', *Language* 47.

Kempson, R. M. (1977). *Semantic Theory*. Cambridge University Press. Cambridge.

Kratochvil, P. (1968). *The Chinese Language Today, Features of Emerging Standard*. Hutchinson University Library. London.

Kurath, H. (1963). 'The Semantic Patterning of Words' in M. Zarechnak (ed.) *Monograph Series on Languages & Linguistics*. No. 14. Georgetown University Press. Washington.

Langacker, R. W. (1968). *Language and its Structure, Some Fundamental Linguistic Concepts*. Harcourt, Brace & World, Inc. New York.

Leech, G. (1981). *Semantics, The Study of Meaning*. Penguin. Harmondsworth.

Lehmann, Winfred P. (ed.) (1975). *Language & Linguistics in the People's Republic of China*. University of Texas Press. Austin.

Lehrer, A. (1974). *Semantic Fields and Lexical Structure*. North-Holland Publishing Company. Amsterdam.

Lei, Tao (雷涛). (1991). '骚语初探' in 天津教育学院学报: 社科版 2.

Li, Baorui (李葆瑞). (1960). '送气和不送气是不是音变造词的方法?' in 中国语文 1.

Li, Daren et al. (李达仁等) (eds). (1993). 汉语新词语词典. 商务印书馆. 北京.

Li, Gengjun (李赓钧). (1992). '三语素合成词说略' in 中国语文 2.

Li, Gengyang (李赓扬). (1998). '从早期的汉译佛经看汉语如何吸收外来词及相关的问题' in Wenqing Xie and Hui Sun (谢文庆 孙晖) (eds). 汉语文化研究 6. 天津人民出版社.

Li, Guoying (李国英). (1996). '论汉字形声字的义符系统' in 中国社会科学 3.

Li, Leyi (李乐毅). (1990). '现代汉语外来词的统一问题' in 语文建设 2.

Li, Miandong (李勉东). (1991). '语义结构中的结果范畴浅论' in 东北师大学报: 哲社版 3.

Li, Ming (李明). (1996). 'AB式双音节形容词重叠式的读音考察' in 教学与研究 1.

Li, Qianju (黎千驹). (1992). '浅谈系联同源字的标准' in 古汉语研究 1.

Li, Qiwen (李启文). (1990). '从成语特点看汉语词义的人文性' in 广东民族学院学报: 社科版 3.

Li, Renxiao (李仁孝). (1990). '论词的形象表现' in 内蒙古大学学报: 哲社版 3.

Li, Rong (李荣). (1953). '字汇和词汇' in 中国语文 5.

Li, Rongsong (李荣嵩). (1985). '谈外来词的汉化' in 天津师范大学学报 2.

Li, Shuxin (李树新). (1990). '汉语传统称谓与中国传统文化' in 内蒙古大学学报: 哲社版 3.

Li, Wanchun (李万春). (1992). 汉字与民俗. 云南教育出版社. 云南.

Li, Xiangeng (李先耕). (1990). '汉语同源反义动词试论' in 学术交流 8.

Li, Xiangzhen (李向真). (1953). '关于汉语的基本词汇' in 中国语文 4.

Li, Xinkui (李新魁). (1991). '汉语各方言的关系和特点' in 学术研究 2.

Li, Yunhan and Cheng, Daming (黎运汉 程达明). (1958). '大跃进中汉语词汇的新发展' in 中国语文 11.

Li, Ziyun (李子云). (1990). '补语的表述对象问题' in 中国语文 5.

Li, Zuonan (李作南). (1956). '从字的组合谈基本词汇' in 中国语文 12.

Liang, Bing (梁兵). (1991). '词义的演变与社会变异' in 新疆师范大学学报: 哲社版 1.

Liang, Donghan (梁东汉). (1959). 汉字的结构及其流变. 上海教育出版社.

Liang, Xiaohong (梁晓虹). (1991). '佛经用词特色杂议' in 浙江师大学报 社科版 (金华) 4.

Liang, Xiaohong (梁晓虹). (1993). '从佛教成语看佛教文化在中国的发展' in 语言与 文化多学科研究. 陈建民 and 谭志明 (eds). 北京语言学院出版社.

Liang, Xiaohong (梁晓虹). (1994). '论佛教词语对汉语词汇宝库的扩充' in 杭州大学 学报 哲社版 4.

Lin, Kexin (林克辛). (1989). '新词新义与社会文化' in 上海市语文学会 (ed.) 语文 论文集. 百家出版社.

Lin, Tao (林焘). (1954). '汉语基本词汇中的几个问题' in 中国语文 7.

Lin, Wenjin (林文金). (1992). '台湾汉语变异漫谈' in 修辞学习 3.

Lin, Xiangmei (林祥楣). (1991). 现代汉语. 语文出版社. 北京.

Lin, Yushan (林玉山). (1992). 中国辞书编纂史略, 中州古籍出版社, 北京.

Ling, Yun (凌云). (1995). '汉语义素运动造词' in 语言教学与研究 4.

Lipka, L. (1972). *Semantic Structure and Word-Formation*. Wilhelm Fink Verlag. Munich.

Liu, Eric Shan. (1973). *Frequency Dictionary of Chinese*. Mouton. The Hague.

Liu, Guifang (刘桂芳). (1996). '义素分析之我见' in 教学与研究 1.

Liu, Jiansan (刘剑三). (1994). '汉语单音成义在新时期的运用' in 语言文字应用 2.

Liu, Junjie (刘钧杰). (1985). '颜色词的构成' in 语言教学与研究 2.

Liu, Ningsheng (刘宁生). (1990). '论字符的同音替代及其意义' in 南京师大学报: 社科版 4.

Liu, Shuxin (刘叔新). (1980). '词语的形象色彩及其功能' in 中国语文 2.

Liu, Shuxin (刘叔新). (1985). '汉语复合词内部形式的特点与类别' in 中国语文 3.

Liu, Shuxin (刘叔新). (1991). '词语对比的聚合及其与反义聚合的比较' in 语文研究 3.

Liu, Shuxin (刘叔新). (1995). 汉语描写词汇学. 商务印书馆. 北京.

Liu, Yeqiu (刘叶秋). (1992). 中国字典史略. 中华书局. 北京.

Liu, Yinglin and Song, Shaozhou (刘英林 宋绍周). (1992). '汉语常用字词的统计与 分级' in 中国语文 3.

Liu, Youxin (刘又辛). (1982). '"右文说"说' in 语言研究 1.

Liu, Zexian (刘泽先). (1957). '汉语不能容纳外来语吗?' in 中国语文 5.

Lu, Danci (卢丹慈). (1990). '汉语多义词词义派生类型的重新划分' in 赣南师范学院学报 5.

Lu, Jiawen (卢甲文). (1981). '单音节反义词的分类及运用' in 语言学论丛 8.

Lu, Zhiwei (陆志韦). (1956). '构词学的对象和手续' in 中国语文 12.

Lu, Zhiwei et al. (陆志韦等). (1957). 汉语的构词法. 科学出版社. 北京.

Lu, Zongda (陆宗达). (1985). '因声求义论' in 中国语文研究 7. 香港中文大学中国文化研究所 吴多泰中国语文研究中心.

Lü Shuxiang (吕叔湘). (1963). '现代汉语单双音节问题初探' in 中国语文 1.

Lü Shuxiang (吕叔湘). (1979). '汉语语法分析问题'. 商务印书馆. 北京.

Lü, Shuxiang (吕叔湘) (ed.). (1980). 现代汉语八百词. 商务印书馆. 北京.

Luo, Changpei (罗常培). (1989). 语言与文化. 语文出版社. 北京.

Luo, Si (罗斯). (1980). '英语新词的产生与构成' in 读书 6. 北京.

Lyons, John (1968). *Introduction to Theoretical Linguistics*. Cambridge University Press. Cambridge.

Ma, Guofan (马国凡). (1958). '成语的定型和规范化' in 中国语文 10.

Ma, Guofan (马国凡). (1978). 成语. 内蒙古人民出版社. 呼和浩特.

Ma, Guofan (马国凡). (1989). '四字格结构的模糊性' in 内蒙古师大学报: 哲社版 3.

Ma, Guofan (马国凡). (1992). '汉语词源中的汉字沉积' in 内蒙古师大学报: 哲社版 3.

Ma, Guofan and Gao, Gedong (马国凡 高歌东). (1979). 歇后语. 内蒙古人民出版社. 呼和浩特.

Ma, Sizhou (马思周). (1956). '单字在词里出现的频率' in 中国语文 12.

Makkai, A. (1972). *Idiom Structure in English*. Mouton. The Hague.

Malinowski, B. (1923). 'The Problem of Meaning in Primitive Languages'. Supplement to C. K. Ogden and I. A. Richards. *The Meaning of Meaning*. K. Paul, Trench, Trubner. London.

Marchand, H. (1969). *The Categories and Types of Present-Day English Word-Formation*. Beck. Munich.

Markel, N. (1963). 'Connotative Meaning of Several Initial Consonant Clusters in English' in M. Zarechnak (ed). *Monograph Series on Languages & Linguistics*. No. 14. Georgetown University Press. Washington.

Masini, Federico (1993). *The Formation of Modern Chinese Lexicon and its Evolution toward a National Language: The Period from 1840 to 1898*. Monograph Series Number 6 of *Journal of Chinese Linguistics*. U.S.A.

Matthews, P. H. (1974). *Morphology: An Introduction to the Theory of Word-Structure*. Cambridge University Press. Cambridge.

Mei, Jiaju et al. (梅家驹等) (eds). (1983). 同义词词林. 上海辞书出版社.

Mei, Lichong (梅立崇). (1993). '汉语国俗词语刍议' in 世界汉语教学 1.

Meng, Pengsheng (孟蓬生). (1994). '汉语同源词刍议' in 河北学刊 4.

Midoux, M. (1971). *Vocabulaire usuel du chinois moderne* (Première Partie). Langues et Civilisations. Paris.

Miller, G. A. and Johnson-Laird, P. N. (1976). *Language and Perception*. Cambridge University Press. Cambridge.

Mu, Jinghu and Liu, Xingguo (木镜湖 刘兴国). (1993). '汉文化心理与汉文字的稳定性' in 思想战线 4.

Needham, Joseph. (1969). *Within the Four Seas*. George Allen & Unwin Ltd. London.

Ni, Haishu (倪海曙) (ed.). (1975). 现代汉字形声字字汇. 文字改革出版社.

Nida, E. A. (1958). 'Analysis of Meaning and Dictionary Making', *International Journal of American Linguistics* 24.

Nida, E. A. (1975a). *Componential Analysis of Meaning*. Mouton. The Hague.

Nida, E. A. (1975b). *Exploring Semantic Structure*. Fink. Müchen.

Nie, Yanzhi (聂言之). (1992). '通用成语与异体成语'. 江西师范大学学报: 哲社版 2.

Norman, Jerry. (1988). *Chinese*. Cambridge University Press. Cambridge.

Ohman, S. (1953). 'Theories of the Linguistic Field' in *WORD* 9.2.

Osgood, C. E. and Tannenbaum, P. H. (1957). *The Measurement of Meaning*. University of Illinois Press. Urbana.

Palmer, F. R. (1981). *Semantics* (2nd Edition). Cambridge University Press. Cambridge.

Pan, Wenguo (潘文国). (1990). '汉英构词法对比研究' in 汉语论丛. 华东师范大学出版社.

Pan, Wenguo et al. (潘文国 叶步青 韩洋). (1993). 汉语的构词法研究. 台湾学生书局.

Pan, Yunzhong (潘允中). (1957). '鸦片战争以前汉语中的借词' in 中山大学学报 3.

Pan, Ziyou (潘自由). (1987). 汉字部首浅析. 光明日报出版社. 北京.

Pulleyblank, E. G. (1983). *Middle Chinese: A Study in Historical Phonology*. University of British Columbia Press. Vancouver.

Qi, Yucun (戚雨村). (1992). '语言对比和文化对比' in 外国语 5.

Qiu, Xigui (裘锡圭). (1990). 文字学概要. 商务印书馆. 北京.

Qu, Da (曲烜). (1992). '现代汉语词义的派生方式新论' in 河池师专学报 2.

Ramsey, S. Robert. (1987). *The Languages of China*. Princeton University Press. Princeton.

Rao, Changrong (饶长溶). (1981). '试论非谓形容词' in 中国语文 2.

Rao, Changrong (饶长溶). (1984). '动宾组合带宾语' in 中国语文 6.

Rao, Shangkuan (饶尚宽). (1994). '先秦单音反义词简论'. 新疆师范大学学报: 哲社版 3.

Ren, Chongfen (任崇芬). (1994). '从正反同义聚合中看汉语的超逸灵活' in 修辞学习 5.

Ren, Jifang (任继昉). (1992). 汉语语源学. 重庆出版社.

Ren, Xueliang (任学良). (1981). 汉语构词法. 中国社会科学出版社. 北京.

Robins, R. H. (1964). *General Linguistics: An Introductory Survey*. Longman. London.

Rose, J. H. (1978). 'Types of Idioms', *Linguistics* 203.

Saussure, F. (1916). *Course in General Linguistics* (translated by W. Baskin 1959). McGraw-Hill. New York.

Selkirk, O. Elisabeth (1982). *The Syntax of Words*. The MIT Press.

Seybolt, Peter J. and Chiang, Gregory Kuei-ke (eds). (1979). *Language Reform in China – Documents and Commentary*. M. E. Sharpe, Inc. White Plains, NY.

Shao, Wenli (邵文利). (1989). '试论同源字' in 内蒙古民族学院学报 2.

Shen, Ming (沈明). (1994). '现代隐语的社会语言学的考察' in 民俗研究 3.

Shen, Xiaolong (申小龙). (1994). '汉字构形的主体思维及其人文精神' in 学术月刊 11.

Shen, Yang (沈阳). (1997). '现代汉语复合词的动态类型' in 语言教学与研究 2.

Shi, Dingguo (史定国). (1992). '普通话中必读的轻声词' in 语文建设 6.

Shi, Dingguo (石定果). (1993). '会意汉字内部结构的复合程序' in 第四届国际汉语教学讨论会论文. 北京语言学院出版社.

Shi, Youwei (史有为). (1983). '关于"动+有"'. 中国语言学会第二届年会. 合肥.

Shi, Youwei (史有为). (1992). '汉语文化语音学虚实谈' in 世界汉语教学 4.

Shi, Youwei (史有为). (1996). '外来词对接诸问题' in 语言文字应用 1. 语文出版社.

Shi, Yuzhi (石毓智). (1992). '同义词和反义词的区别和联系' in 汉语学习 1.

Smith, M. K., Pollio, H. R. and Pitts, M. K. (1981). 'Metaphor as Intellectual History: Conceptual Categories Underlying Figurative Usage in American English from 1675 to 1975', *Linguistics* 19-7/8.

Song, Yongpei (宋永培). (1992). '《说文》对反义同义同源关系的表述与探讨' in 河北大学学报: 社科版 4.

Su, Jinzhi (苏金智). (1994). '台港和大陆词语差异的原因、模式及其对策' in 语言文字应用 4.

Su, Peicheng (苏培成). (1994). '现代汉字的构字法' in 语言文字应用 3.

Su, Xinchun (苏新春). (1990). '汉语双音词化的根据和动因' in 广州师院学报: 社科版 4.

Su, Xinchun (苏新春). (1993). '同源词的同源线是形象义' in 古汉语研究 1.

Sun, C. C. (1981). *As the Saying Goes*. University of Queensland Press. Brisbane.

Sun, Changxu (孙常叙). (1956). 汉语词汇. 吉林人民出版社. 长春.

Sun, Manjun (孙曼均). (1996). '城市流行词语及其社会文化分析' in 语言文字应用 2.

Sun, Weizhang (孙维张). (1989). '文化流向与语言的扩散' in 吉林大学社会科学学报 1.

Sun, Yongchang (孙雍长). (1985). '古汉语的词义渗透' in 中国语文 3.

Tan, Daren (谭达人). (1989). '略论反义相成词' in 语文研究 1.

Tan, Daxian (谭达先). (1985). '歇后语试论' in 中国语文研究 7. 香港中文大学中国文化研究所 吴多泰中国语文研究中心.

Tan, Qixue (谭其学). (1991). '汉语动+形的结构及其语义关系辨析' in 暨南大学 研究生学报 1.

Tan, Yuliang (谭玉良). (1989). '关于声训问题的几点思考' in 四川师范大学学报: 社科版 4.

Tang, Chaoqun (唐朝群). (1990). '动宾式合成 词研究' in 华中师范大学学报: 哲社版 2.

Tang, Ting-chi (汤廷池). (1988). 汉语词法句法论集. 学生书局. 台湾.

Tang, Zhixiang (汤志祥). (1995). '中国大陆、台湾、香港、新加坡汉语词汇方面若干差异举例' in 徐州师范学院学报: 哲社版 1.

Tao, Huizhang (陶汇章). (1994). '谚语群初探' in 民间文学论坛 2.

Tao, Jian (陶健). (1988). '试论汉人思维方式对汉字的影响' in 郑州大学学报: 哲社版 6.

Tian, Huigang (田惠刚). (1993). '汉语方言区划分概说'. in 学术界. 3.

Tian, Ye (田野). (1988). '同义词的性质' in 盐城师专学报: 社科版 4.

Traugott, E. C. and Pratt, M. L. (1980). *Linguistics for Students of Literature*. Harcourt Brace Jovanovich, Inc. New York.

Ullmann, Stephen (1962). *Semantics – An Introduction to the Science of Meaning*. Basil Blackwell. Oxford.

Verschueren, Jef. (1981). 'Problems of Lexical Semantics', *Lingua* 53.

Wan, Shixiong (万世雄). (1992). '词的音义比较关系和词族' in 湖北师范学院学报: 哲社版 4.

Wang, Dechun (王德春). (1983). 词汇学研究. 山东教育出版社. 济南.

Wang, Guo'an (王国安). (1996). '论汉语文化词和文化意义' in 中国对外汉语教学学会第五次学术讨论会论文选. 北京语言学院出版社. 北京.

Wang, Hongjun (王洪君). (1994a). '从字和字组看词和短语' in 中国语文 2.

Wang, Hongjun (王洪君). (1994b). '汉语常用的两种语音构词法' in 语言研究 1.

Wang, Hongyuan (王宏源). (1993). 汉字字源入门. Sinolingua. 北京.

Wang, Li (王力). (1964). 汉语浅谈. 北京出版社.

Wang, Li (王力). (1977). 诗词格律. 中华书局. 北京.

Wang, Li (王力). (1980). '汉语滋生词的语法分析' in 语言学论丛 6.

Wang, Li (王力). (1982). 同源字典. 商务印书馆. 北京.

Wang, Liaoyi (王了一). (1957). 中国文字及其音读的类化法 in Zhong Shu (叔重) (ed.) (1957). 中国语文研究参考资料选辑, 中华书局.

Wang, Lida (王立达). (1958). '现代汉语中从日语借来的词汇' in 中国语文 2.

Wang, Ning (王宁). (1989). '论形训与声训' in 北京师范大学学报: 社科版 4

Wang, Qin (王勤). (1990). '俗语的性质和范围' in 湘潭大学学报: 社科版 4.

Wang, Sen (王森). (1992). '新词语的容量和寿命' in 兰州大学学报: 社科版 2.

Wang, Tiekun (王铁昆). (1993). '汉语新外来语的文化心理透视' in 汉语学习 1.

Wang, Yannong et al. (王砚农) (eds). (1987). 汉语动词-结果补语搭配词典. 北京语言学院出版社. 北京.

Wang, Zhenghong (王政红). (1992). '名形语素构词格分析' in 南京师大学报: 社科版 4.

Wang, Zhenkun (王振昆). (1998). '仿造词的形式及其规范化' in Wenqing Xie and Hui Sun (谢文庆 孙晖) (eds). 汉语文化研究 6. 天津人民出版社.

Wang, Zhongwen (王仲闻). (1953). '统一译名的迫切需要' in 中国语文 8.

Wang, Zuoxin (王作新). (1995a). '汉语复音词结构特征的文化透视' in 汉字文化 2.

Wang, Zuoxin (王作新). (1995b). '类义系统的文化关照' in 华中师范大学学报: 哲社版 5.

Watters, T. (1889). *Essays on The Chinese Language*. Presbyterian Mission Press. Shanghai.

Wei, Dongya (危东亚) (ed.) (1955). *A Chinese–English Dictionary* (Revised edition). Foreign Language Teaching and Research Press.

Wei, S. S. (韦少成). (1978). *A Practical Dictionary of Chinese Idioms, English Idioms, English Synonyms*. The Practical English Press. Hong Kong.

Wen, Duanzheng (温端政). (1981). '歇后语的语义' in 中国语文 6.

Wen, Duanzheng (温端政). (1984). '谚语的语义' in 中国语文 4.

Wen, Duanzheng et al. (温端政等) (eds). (1984). 歇后语词典. 北京出版社.

Wu, Hongkui (吴鸿逵). (1991). '论同义复词的类型及其作用' in 徐州师范学院学报: 哲社版 1.

Wu, Liquan (吴礼权). (1994). '汉语外来词音译的特点及其文化心态探究' in 复旦学报: 社科版 3.

Wu, Yan (吴艳). (1989). '"软":一个新起的类前缀' in 江西师范大学学报: 哲社版 2.

Wu, Zhankun (伍占坤) and Wang, Qin (王勤). (1983). 现代汉语词汇概要. 内蒙古人民出版社.

Xi, Boxian (奚博先). (1979). '从另一角度看声旁的表音功能' in 中国语文 5.

Xiang, Guangzhong (向光忠). (1989). '论成语蕴涵的时代因素' in 南开学报: 哲社版 5.

Xiao, Yan (萧雁). (1991). '新时期汉语新词的出现与新时期 社会心态' in 徐州教育学院学报. 1991.

Xin, Xiang (欣向). (1958). '成语的特性' in 中国语文 10.

Xiong, Wenhua (熊文华). (1979). '汉英名词的对译' in 语言教学与研究 1. 北京语言学院出版社.

Xiong, Wenhua (熊文华). (1993). '颜色词所体现的文化反差' in 第四届国际汉语教学讨论会论文. 北京语言学院出版社.

Xiong, Wenhua (熊文华). (1996). '汉语和英语中的借词' in 语言教学与研究 2. 北京语言学院出版社.

Xu, Dejiang (徐德江). (1990). '词结构新探' in 汉字文化 1.

Xu, Guanglie (许光烈). (1994). '汉语词的理据及其基本类型' in 内蒙古民族师院学报: 哲社版 1.

Xu, Jingqian (徐静茜). (1991). '禁忌语、委婉语和吉祥语' in 湖州师专学报 3.

Xu, Liu (徐流). (1990). '论同义复词' in 重庆师院学报: 哲社版 4.

Xu, Shenghuan (徐盛桓). (1992). '论词的语用意义' in 华南师范大学学报: 社科版 1.

Xu, Shenghuan (徐盛桓). (1993). '论词义的包含关系' in 华南师范大学学报: 社科版 3.

Xu, Tongqiang (徐通锵). (1994). '"字"和汉语研究的方法论' in 世界汉语教学 3.

Xu, Tongqiang (徐通锵). (1997). 语言论－语义型语言的结构原理和研究方法. 东北师范大学出版社.

Xun, Jingqian (徐静茜). (1992). '汉民族若干文化心理素质在汉语语词中的表现' in 湖州师专学报: 哲社版 2.

Yan, Fengqiang (严奉强). (1992). '台湾国语词汇与大陆普通话词汇的比较' in 暨南学报: 哲社版 2.

Yan, Ronggeng (严戎庚). (1990). '共时历时学说与现代汉语词汇研究'. 新疆大学学报: 哲社版 2.

Yan, Tingde (严廷德). (1989). '同源词管窥' in 四川大学学报: 哲社版 1.

Yan, Zuoyan (殷作炎). (1982). '关于普通话双音常用词轻重音的初步考察' in 中国语文 10.

Yang, Honghua (杨红华). (1993). '汉语构词法分类标准质疑' in 广西大学学报: 哲社版 4.

Yang, Hua and Jiang, Kexin (杨华 蒋可心). (1995). '浅谈新外来词及其规范问题' in 语言文字应用 1.

Yang, Xipeng (杨锡彭). (1992). '粘宾动词初探' in 南京大学学报: 哲学、人文、社科版 4.

Yao, Hanming (姚汉铭). (1990). '论新词语的文化分布、产生途径及成因' in 曲靖师专学报: 社科版 4.

Yi, Xiwu (易熙吾). (1954). '汉语中的双音词(上)&(下)' in 中国语文 10 and 11.

Yin, Binyong (尹斌庸). (1984). '汉语语素的定量研究'. in 中国语文 5.

Yin, Binyong (尹斌庸) and Johns, Rohsenow (1994). 现代汉字. Sinolingua. 北京.

Yin, Jiming (殷寄明). (1992). '论形声字的一种重要构成方式' in 南京师大学报: 社科版 2.

Yin, Menglun (殷孟伦). (1985). '从《尔雅》看古汉语词汇研究' in 子云乡人类稿. 齐鲁书社. 济南.

Yin, Zuoyan (殷作炎). (1982). '关于普通话双音常用词轻重音的初步考察' in 中国语文 3.

Ying, Yutian (应雨田). (1993). '比喻型词语的类型及释义' in 中国语文 4.

Yip, Po-Ching and Zhang, Xiaoming (叶步青 张小明). (1995). 'Consecutive Reduplication in Chinese' in *Journal of the Chinese Language Teachers' Association* 30.

You, Rujie (游汝杰). (1993). 中国文化语言学引论. 高等教育出版社. 北京.

Yu, Genyuan (于根元). (1987). '动宾式短语的类化作用' in 中国社会科学院 语言研究所 现代汉语研究室 (ed.). 句型和动词. 语文出版社. 北京.

Yu, Min (俞敏). (1954). '汉语的爱称和憎称的来源和区别' in 中国语文 2.

Yu, Min (俞敏). (1984). '化石语素' in 中国语文 1.

Yu, Yang (俞扬). (1992). '对偏义复词的再认识' in 宁波师院学报: 社科版 2.

Yu, Zhihong (余志鸿). (1994). '汉字文化与对外汉语教学' in 上海大学学报: 社科版 6.

Yuan, Hanqing (袁翰青). (1953). '从化学物质的命名看方块字的缺点' in 中国语文 4.

Yuan, Hongren (袁鸿仁). (1990). '汉语词义对词汇演变的推动作用' in 社科纵横 4.

Yuan, Yulin (袁毓林). (1995). '词类范畴的家族相似性' in 中国社会科学 1.

Zgusta, L. (1967). 'Multiword Lexical Units' in *WORD* 23.

Zhan, Renfeng. (詹人凤). (1987). '试论现代汉语中的"于"' in 叶长荫 詹人凤 赵锐 (ed.) 汉语论文集. 黑龙江人民出版社.

Zhan, Renfeng (詹人凤). (1989). '动结式短语的表述问题' in 中国语文 2.

Zhan, Xuzuo and Zhu, Liangzhi (詹绪左 朱良志). (1994). '汉字的文化功能' in 天津师大学报: 社科版 1.

Zhan, Yinxin (詹鄞鑫). (1990). '关于本义的两个问题' in 汉语论丛. 华东师范大学出版社.

Zhang, Bo (张博). (1991). '同源词 同族词 词族' in 固原师专学报 3.

Zhang, Dexin (张德鑫). (1993). '第三次浪潮 – 外来词引进和规范刍议' in 语言文字应用 3. 语文出版社.

Zhang, Dexin (张德鑫). (1994). '汉译取字用词漫品' in 语言教学与研究 2. 北京语言学院出版社.

Zhang, Dexin (张德鑫). (1995). '貌合神离 似是而非 – 汉英对应喻词中的"陷井"' in 语言文字应用 4.

Zhang, Dexin (张德鑫). (1996a). '汉英词语文化上的不对应' in 中国对外汉语教学学会秘书处 (ed.) 中国对外汉语教学学会成立十周年纪念论文选. 北京语言学院出版社.

Zhang, Dexin (张德鑫). (1996b). '谈颠倒词' in 中国对外汉语教学学会第五次学术讨论会论文选. 北京语言学院出版社. 北京.

Zhang, Dexin (张德鑫). (1996c). 中外语言文化漫议. Sinolingua. 北京..

Zhang, Hesheng (张和生). (1996). '汉语贬义词与汉民族观念文化' in 中国对外汉语教学学会秘书处 (ed.) 中国对外汉语教学学会成立十周年纪念论文选. 北京语言学院出版社.

Zhang, Jieming (张介明). (1995). '在外来文化的影响中 – 汉语现代书面语演变的历史和现状' in 宁波大学学报 人文科学版 1.

Zhang, Jingxian (张静贤). (1992). 现代汉字教程. 现代出版社. 北京.

Zhang, Kai (张凯). (1997). '汉语构词基本字的统计分析' in 语言教学与研究 1.

Zhang, Kaixin (张开信). (1996). '汉语成语、谚语的翻译与比较' in 语言教学与研究 2. 北京语言学院出版社.

Zhang, Qingchang (张清常). (1991). '一种误解被借的词原义的现象 – 兼论"胡同"蒙语水井的关系' in 语言教学与研究 4.

Zhang, Renli (张仁立). (1993). '试析词义演变中的相似现象' in 山西师大学报: 社科版 2.

Zhang, Shilu (张世禄). (1957). 普通话词汇. 新知识出版社. 上海.

Zhang, Shilu (张世禄). (1984a). '汉语同源词的孳乳' in 张世禄语言学论文集. 学林出版社. 上海.

Zhang, Shilu (张世禄). (1984b). '词义和字义' in 张世禄语言学论文集. 学林出版社. 上海.

Zhang, Suying (张素英). (1991). '对词是否成体系问题的刍议' in 锦州师院学报: 哲社版 3.

Zhang, Yinde (张应德). (1958). '现代汉语中能有这么多的日语借词吗?' in 中国语文 6.

Zhang, Yongyan (张永言). (1989). '汉语外来词杂谈' in 语言教学与研究 2.

Zhao, Shuhua and Zhang, Baolin (赵淑华 张宝林). (1996). '离合词的确定与离合词的性质' in 语言教学与研究 1.

Zhao, Yongxin (赵永新). (1997). '析ABAC式四字语' in 语言教学与研究 3.

Zheng, Baoqian (郑宝倩). (1992). '人名结构与社会历史文化的关系' in 语文研究 1.

Zheng, Dian (郑奠). (1958). '谈现代汉语中的"日语词汇"' in 中国语文 2.

Zheng, Huaide (郑怀德). (1987). '带结式动词和不带结式动词' in 中国社会科学院语言研究所 现代汉语研究室 (ed.) 句型和动词. 语文出版社. 北京.

Zheng, Linxi (郑林曦). (1992). '从同音词、同音字的最新统计看文字拼音化' in 北京市语言学会 (ed.) 语言研究与应用. 商务印书馆. 北京.

Zheng, Qiwu (郑启五). (1989). '海峡两岸用语差异初探' in 台湾研究集刊 1.

Zheng, Yefu (郑也夫). (1993). 礼语 咒语 官腔 黑话. 光明日报出版社. 北京.

Zhong, Jinghua (钟敬华). (1989). '同源字判定的语音标准问题' in 复旦学报: 社科版 1.

Zhong, Qin (钟梫). (1978). '关于汉语语音的若干问题' in 语言教学与研究 3. 北京语言学院.

Zhong, Ruxiong (钟如雄). (1991). '偏义复词成因初探'. 西南民族学院学报: 哲社版 5.

Zhong, Zhaohu (鍾兆琥). (1953). '外来学术名词应在什么原则上统一起来' in 中国语文 8.

Zhongguo Shehui Kexueyuan Yuyan Yanjiusuo Cidian Bianjishi (中国社会科学院语言研究所词典编辑室) (ed.) (1985). 现代汉语词典. 商务印书馆. 北京.

Zhonghua Shuju (中华书局). (1979). 现代汉字形声字字汇. 中华书局香港分局.

Zhou, Dafu (周达甫). (1957). '怎样研究梵汉翻译和对音' in 中国语文 4.

Zhou, Hongbo (周洪波). (1994). '修辞现象的词汇化' in 语言文字应用 1.

Zhou, Hongbo (周洪波). (1995). '外来词译音成分的语素化' in 语言文字应用 4.

Zhou, Huanqin (周换琴). (1996). '数词成语探' in 中国对外汉语教学学会秘书处 (ed.) 中国对外汉语教学学会成立十周年纪念论文选. 北京语言学院出版社.

Zhou, Jian (周荐). (1993). '比喻词语和词语的比喻义' in 语言教学与研究 4.

Zhou, Jian (周荐). (1994). '熟语的经典性和非经典性' in 语文研究 3.

Zhou, Lanxing (周兰星). (1994). '隐语黑话的演变及当代隐语黑话的特点' in 中国人民警官大学学报: 哲社版 1.

Zhou, Xiaobing (周小兵). (1993). '广州话地区近期流行的英语音译词' in 语言与文化多学科研究. 陈建民 and 谭志明 (eds). 北京语言学院出版社.

Zhou, Yimin (周一民). (1992). 北京俏皮话词典. 北京燕山出版社.

Zhou, Yimin and Zhu, Jiansong (周一民 朱建颂). (1994). '关于北京话中的满语词 (一)(二)' in 中国语文 3.

Zhou, Youguang (周有光). (1979). '现代汉字中的多音字问题' in 中国语文 6.

Zhou, Youguang (周有光). (1980). 汉字声旁读音便查. 吉林人民出版社.

Zhou, Youguang (周有光). (1992). '整理多音字的尝试' in 北京市语言学会 (ed.) 语言研究与应用. 商务印书馆. 北京.

Zhou, Zumo (周祖谟). (1983). '汉字与汉语的关系' in Gao, Gengsheng et al. (高更生等) (eds): 现代汉语资料分题选编(上册). 山东教育出版社. 济南.

Zhu, Dexi (朱德熙). (1990). '关于先秦汉语名词和动词的区分的一则札记' in 汉语论丛. 华东师范大学出版社.

Zhu, Guangqi (朱广祈). (1992). '港台词语研究与大汉语词汇研究' in 山东大学学报: 哲社版 2.

Zhu, Jianmang (朱剑芒). (1955). '成语的基本形式及其组织规律的特点' in 中国语文 2.

Zhu, Wenjun (朱文俊). (1996a). '声音的象征意念' in 世界汉语教学 1.

Zhu, Wenjun (朱文俊). (1996b). '译事杂谈: 理解与对应' in 语言教学与研究 1. 北京语言学院出版社.

INDEX